DATE DUE	RETURNED
NOV 3 0 2009	
JAN 2 1 2013	
FEB 0 1 2013	FEB 0 1 2013

Fundamentals of Television Production

Fundamentals of Television Production

second edition

Ralph R. Donald
Southern Illinois University, Edwardsville

Riley Maynard
Southern Illinois University, Edwardsville

Thomas Spann
University of Nebraska, Lincoln

PEARSON

Boston   New York   San Francisco
Mexico City   Montreal   Toronto   London   Madrid   Munich   Paris
Hong Kong   Singapore   Tokyo   Cape Town   Sydney

Editor-in-Chief: Karon Bowers
Acquisitions Editor: Jeanne Zalesky
Series Editorial Assistant: Brian Mickelson
Marketing Manager: Suzan Czajkowski
Production Editor: Karen Mason
Editorial Production Service: Black Dot Group/NK Graphics
Composition Buyer: Linda Cox
Manufacturing Buyer: JoAnne Sweeney
Electronic Composition: Black Dot Group/NK Graphics
Interior Design: Black Dot Group/NK Graphics
Cover Administrator: Elena Sidorova
Illustrations by Marlene DenHouter, Southern Illinois University Edwardsville, Department of Art

For related titles and support materials, visit our online catalog at www.ablongman.com.

Between the time website information is gathered and then published, it is not unusual for some sites to have closed. Also, the transcription of URLs can result in typographical errors. The publisher would appreciate notification where these errors occur so that they may be corrected in subsequent editions.

ISBN-13: 978-0-205-46232-2
ISBN-10: 0-205-46232-4

Library of Congress Cataloging-in-Publication Data
Donald, Ralph.
    Fundamentals of television production / Ralph R. Donald, Riley Maynard, Thomas Spann.
        p. cm.
    Includes bibliographical references and index.
    ISBN 0-205-46232-4 (alk. paper)
    1. Television—Production and direction.   I. Maynard, Riley.   II. Spann, Thomas.   III. Title.
PN1992.75.D66 2008
791.4502'32—dc22   2007026241

Printed in the United States of America

10 9 8 7 6 5 4 3 2 1   11 10 09 08 07

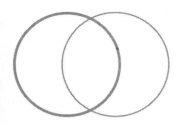

Brief Contents

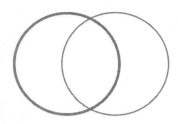

Contents

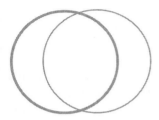

An Introduction to the Second Edition

One of the authors' former colleagues scoffed at the notion of using a text in a TV production course. A veteran of many productions, he believed the only way to teach production was to have people produce. We don't necessarily disagree with his basic premise.

It's only through repeated opportunities to apply your skills in the studio or field, to experience both successes and failures and to learn from them, that you make meaningful progress. Our combined nine-plus decades of experience teaching television production have taught us this, if nothing else.

However, our teaching experiences suggest that a good text can help us do many things we don't otherwise have time to do in the typical production course. Class time is best spent in hands-on, practical activities. Students who are serious about learning television production as a career need somewhere to turn for answers to those many questions that may arise outside of class, and some practical how-to instructions. In writing this book, we've tried to stress those things. We've adopted the philosophy that a text should underscore, amplify and go into more detail on what's presented by the instructor and, perhaps more important, expand the student's view of the production process beyond what's possible to replicate in the typical college environment.

The Big Picture

In spite of having watched many thousands of hours of TV programming growing up, most college students still have, at best, only a vague idea of the actual production process. Accordingly, we begin the text with an overview chapter that walks students through three productions. We believe that exposing students to the entire process of production as it might occur in different situations will help them start to understand and appreciate the more detailed information they will encounter later in the course.

It's our experience that students tend to assume that production begins only when they start handling the hardware. While we understand the fascination with the equipment and strongly support learning from hands-on experience, we stress the importance of preproduction planning throughout the text, noting that most productions should only involve the execution of plans formed well in advance. That's also why we include a chapter on the basics of writing for television. There would be no way to start preproduction without a script. Of course, we also stress the need to be flexible during production, to be prepared to solve unexpected problems quickly. But the text reflects our experience-informed belief that too many students give the preproduction process insufficient attention.

Talking the Talk

We assume that one of the major objectives of an introductory production course is to acquaint students with the terms and jargon of the field. Accordingly, we've included a wide range of terms and concepts dealing with almost all phases of television production. They are italicized in the text as they are introduced, and at the end of each chapter we provide definitions of these terms. We, and many other instructors, often quiz students over production vocabulary, because a part of being a professional is knowing—and using—the language of the profession.

Technology and Technophobia

Many of our students are uncomfortable with technical or theoretical information. Discussions with academic colleagues have convinced us that our experience is typical. Yet television production is deeply rooted in technology, and as we write this, sophisticated TV technology continues to expand exponentially. Indeed, many production techniques, and certainly production capabilities, are driven—and limited—by the technology and how skilled the producer is in exploiting it. Although a camera operator need not know how to build or repair the camera he or she uses, a basic knowledge of its operation provides a context for using the camera to its maximum potential. If students understand the physical laws governing the operation of lenses, they can better use a lens to maximize—or minimize—depth of field, to use selective focus to produce an aesthetically pleasing image or, equally important, avoid a displeasing one. A producer who understands the concept of lens speed and exposure is more likely to anticipate the need for auxiliary lighting on a remote shoot. An understanding of how gain works will help a camera operator decide whether to use more gain or increase the illumination on the scene, although either approach may produce a "usable" image.

In many chapters, while we show how to exploit, or work within the limits of, the technological capabilities of the equipment, we also warn against using technological capabilities simply because the hardware (or software) makes something possible. Just because a lens has a 40:1 zoom ratio, or a character generator can display dozens of fonts in hundreds of colors, does not mean one should constantly stretch these tools to their limits. As technology advances, there is increasing temptation to use every one of the available bells and whistles. But sometimes simple communication is best, and students must be challenged to explain how their planned exploitation of technology contributes to the communication of meaning, rather than just show off their mastery of a certain "cool" effect or process.

To make discussions of technology more palatable to technophobic students, the text explains how the technical information helps them achieve a desired communication goal. We believe that students accept technical or theoretical information more readily if they can see how it applies pragmatically to the tasks and challenges they will face during production. Even so, we're sensitive to the concerns instructors have about excessively technical information and, in many cases, we've segregated technical discussions in "Tech Manuals" that instructors can assign or skip as they please.

Pragmatism and Aesthetics

Balancing basic "how-to" and "hardware" information against discussions of aesthetics is a tricky business in a single-volume, introductory text. We believe most instructors want the text to deal effectively with pragmatic issues, but they want students to be more than camera pointers and button pushers. It's our experience, unfortunately, that the time limitations of the introductory production course typically result in instructors giving inadequate attention to aesthetic considerations. Instructors usually depend heavily on the assigned text and other outside reading to fill the gaps dealing with aesthetics. Accordingly, the role of aesthetic considerations in communicating mood and meaning are constant themes throughout the text, and especially in the chapters dealing with composition, lighting, scenic design and directing. Without apology we draw heavily on the techniques and traditions of theatre and the cinema for our examples, as well as citing examples from popular television fare.

As with technology, we also relate discussions of aesthetics to the pragmatic tasks students face in production. Just as we encourage students to apply their understanding of technology to the solution of practical production problems, we also urge them to look at each shot, each scene, with the eye of a visual artist. Although for clarity we sometimes treat them in isolation, we do not see clear distinctions among technical, pragmatic and aesthetic considerations. It is our experience that in actual practice, the three merge almost automatically in the mind of the professional, and this is the message we convey to the students.

The Wider Horizon

Finally, the text expands the horizons of the students by exposing them to equipment and production genres they are unlikely to experience directly in class. Few of us in college/university teaching have access to sophisticated production equipment such as helicopter camera mounts, perambulator booms and the latest digital camcorders. Seldom can students do a live remote broadcast of a major sporting event as a class exercise. Yet we want our students to be aware of cutting-edge production gear and have a basic understanding of how major remote and electronic field productions are conducted.

Production equipment technology advances at a dizzying pace, the speed of which increases constantly. No text can keep up with it, this one included. We know that the day after we ship the final draft of this text to the publisher, something covered in the book will be replaced by something new. But we have included many examples of sophisticated gear and discussed, to the best of our ability, the new digital technologies as they existed at the time of publication. We urge instructors and students to supplement their knowledge of evolving production hardware and software by reading professional trade publications and visiting production equipment exhibits at major industry conventions. Maintaining close contact with commercial and educational TV stations and production houses in your local TV market is also extremely helpful.

Acknowledgments

There are only three names on the cover of this book, but it's actually the product of the minds and experiences of many people we have leaned on for help during the years of preparation that went into writing it. We were blessed to have the cooperation of scores of students, former students, academic and professional colleagues both past and present, as well as helpful representatives of many equipment manufacturers.

We especially want to thank those persons and companies who allowed us to use their photographs for the many figures and exhibits in this text. Sometimes we needed repeated takes and, invariably, they were willing to give us a second (or third) chance. A special note of thanks is due the staff and management of Nebraska Educational Telecommunications, particularly the late staff photographer Larry Sheffield for his excellent photos, and General Manager Rod Bates who cleared the photos for publication. In addition to allowing us to use their images in many of the figures, the staff of Nebraska Educational Telecommunications answered dozens of technical questions and offered many suggestions that, we think, significantly improved our work. We also thank television stations KOLN-KGIN and their staff for help with many of the photos included.

Chief Engineer John Kautzer and Engineer Gus Wills of Southern Illinois University at Edwardsville have contributed much to this effort with great answers to difficult technical questions, as well as many hours of skillful production assistance during the time we were shooting graphics and photographs. Patrick Murphy, chair of the Department of Mass Communications, and Barb Randle, Mass Communications Department secretary, lent us great support. Also key players in getting the manuscript and the attendant paperwork to Allyn and Bacon were Abby Roetheli and Allison Stoner. Many thanks for all your hard work. "The other Patrick Murphy," as we refer to him at SIU Edwardsville, Vice President for Production at KETC-TV, St. Louis, provided us with valuable advice for the producing chapter. Emmy-winning sitcom director and author Mary Lou Belli gave us invaluable help with updating the "Overview and Tour" chapter for this second edition. Also, many thanks to Jay Johnson of Charter Cable in St. Louis.

Our academic colleagues displayed remarkable patience, and even enthusiasm, for our efforts over a number of years. Richard Alloway, Laurie Lee, Peter Mayeux, Jerry Renaud and Larry Walklin of the University of Nebraska and Hubert Brown of Syracuse University did much to keep Tom Spann on track during the process. Ralph Donald wishes to thank Rustin Greene of James Madison University, and Ralph Donald and Riley Maynard wish to thank SIU Edwardsville colleagues Brian Ledford (also of KPLR-TV-11, St. Louis) and Otis Sweazy, Valerie Goldson and Debra Brown-Thompson from SIU Edwardsville's Department of Theater and Dance for their help. Also, many, many thanks to Doug Hastings of Technisonic Studios in St. Louis, and ace videographer Bill McCormack of KMOV-TV-4, St. Louis. We would like to thank the reviewers for their insightful comments: Afif Arabi, Prairie View A&M University; Raymond Berry, College of the Siskiyous; Edward J. Carlin, Shippensburg University; Richard R. Heppner, Orange County Community College; John G. Hodgson, Oklahoma State University; Mary Beth Holmes, Marywood University; Frances L. Kendall, Salisbury University; and Kristine Trever, Wayne State University.

SIU Edwardsville Art Department's Marlene DenHouter is the talented artist responsible for the book's many illustrations. They added considerably to both editions, and we're sure readers of this new edition will find them invaluable. Also many thanks to the good folks at Black Dot Group, especially editors Katrina Ostler and Erin Tremouilhac, for keeping the three of us on the straight and narrow.

Last but certainly not least, all of our families also deserve recognition, and probably the Purple Heart for the wounds inflicted. We owe them many lost weekends, holidays and nights spent at the computer, writing and rewriting text or shooting and editing illustrations. We hope they find the product worthy of their sacrifice and we thankfully express our appreciation for their forbearance.

Fundamentals of Television Production

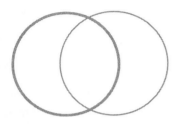

An Overview and Tour

Until recently, television production required the combined efforts of dozens of trained professionals, using extremely expensive and difficult-to-maintain equipment. Network-level TV programs still require many hands to produce a single show, but technological advances now allow virtually anyone with a digital *camcorder* and an $8 blank cassette to create a "video."

Video production today is truly no longer limited to "TV people," as evidenced by the growing number of amateur video enthusiasts. This textbook, however, concerns itself with the fundamental technical skills and aesthetic knowledge required of those who wish to earn their living in one of the many television production career fields.

At one end of the professional spectrum is the producer–writer–director–camera operator–editor who videotapes weddings, bar mitzvahs, high school plays and legal depositions. At the other end is the Hollywood-based executive producer commanding armies of artists and technicians engaged in network-level TV, producing America's most popular entertainment in a multimillion-dollar facility. Regardless of the size of a program's budget or intended audience, there are three production phases that all professional productions share. These phases are *preproduction, production* and *postproduction.*

Preproduction

The goal of this first phase is to assemble and efficiently organize the elements necessary for a successful production. Television professionals attest to its importance. At the network level, poor preparation during preproduction can add millions to the cost of producing a television series, which can mean the difference between profitability and ruin.

During preproduction, the program idea itself is created and the script is commissioned and written. Preproduction also is the time when personnel, who range from the highest-priced Hollywood talent to the lowliest production assistant, are hired. During this phase, sets are designed and built; locations found; props, costumes and production equipment selected, created, purchased or rented; and a complete production schedule established (see Figure O-1). Finally, as preproduction draws to a close, sets and props are moved into place on the studio floor or at the location site; lighting instruments are set, aimed and focused; and talent (performers) and production personnel complete their rehearsals.

Figure O-1. *Set building in progress.*

Production

This is the most visible phase to the viewing public and thus is best understood. However, most viewers are unaware that the production phase is only the tip of the iceberg, the result of days, weeks, months or even years of preparation. Production is the operational phase, when all the planning, writing, budgeting, worrying and dreaming that go into preproduction finally pay off: Program elements are efficiently orchestrated and recorded onto tape or some other form of digital media, or broadcast live, making reality out of a producer's dream.

Famous Swedish film director Ingmar Bergman once characterized the production phase as the "artistically devastating atmosphere of the studio." What Bergman meant was that the commotion and confusion of production draws the artist's mind away from the art, confounding one's creative attempts with mundane concerns. That's why it's essential that producers make most creative decisions in the more thoughtful, less hurried preproduction phase. The great film director Alfred Hitchcock told chronicler François Truffaut that the creative aspect of directing was finished when "Hitch"

completed his shooting script and storyboards. On the set, the great director simply executed the creative designs he had made in the relative quiet of his office.

When the production phase is finally over and the raw footage of the show is *in the can*, there is still more work ahead.

Postproduction

During postproduction (also called the *post*, *posting* or simply *post*), the best recorded video chosen by the director and the producer (the chief creative personnel of the production company) is edited electronically, and the program's audio (including music, sound effects and even audience reactions) is enhanced and augmented (see Figure O-2). Sophisticated computerized equipment can generate new pictures and sound for creative blending with video shot during production. Posting is complete when the producer presents a master tape to the client, syndicator or network for distribution (see Figure O-3).

So, three phases—preproduction, production and postproduction—contribute to the show's success or failure in specific ways. Now let's take a closer look at the organization of personnel and work in each of these phases.

Figure O-2. *A video-editing suite.*

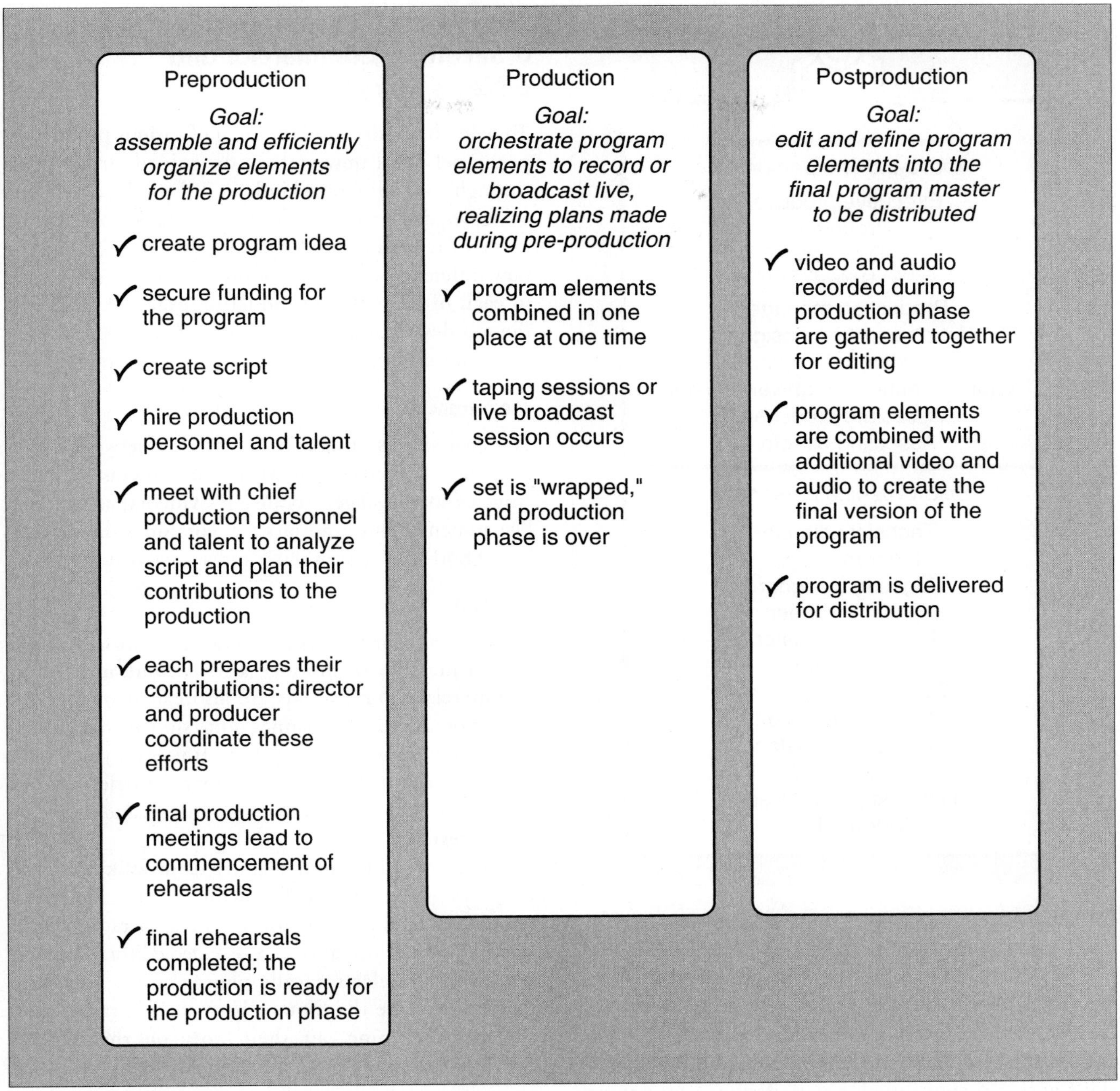

Preproduction	Production	Postproduction
Goal: *assemble and efficiently organize elements for the production*	*Goal:* *orchestrate program elements to record or broadcast live, realizing plans made during pre-production*	*Goal:* *edit and refine program elements into the final program master to be distributed*
✓ create program idea	✓ program elements combined in one place at one time	✓ video and audio recorded during production phase are gathered together for editing
✓ secure funding for the program	✓ taping sessions or live broadcast session occurs	✓ program elements are combined with additional video and audio to create the final version of the program
✓ create script	✓ set is "wrapped," and production phase is over	✓ program is delivered for distribution
✓ hire production personnel and talent		
✓ meet with chief production personnel and talent to analyze script and plan their contributions to the production		
✓ each prepares their contributions: director and producer coordinate these efforts		
✓ final production meetings lead to commencement of rehearsals		
✓ final rehearsals completed; the production is ready for the production phase		

Figure O-3. *The three phases of production.*

"Committee Art"

As noted, network-level television production is the product of the combined efforts of many individuals. A system designed for efficient division of labor and responsibility is a key factor contributing to a TV program's evolution from a collection of diverse parts into a functional, organic product.

Television production personnel divide into two general groups: those who bear the creative responsibility and those whose jobs are more technical in nature (see Figure O-4). For budgeting purposes, producers refer to the people in creative positions as *above-the-line* personnel. They include the producers themselves, directors, writers, talent (either announcers, newscasters or actors), musical composers and art directors. *Below-the-line* production personnel are mostly those who execute the instructions given them by the creative staff. This does not mean that below-the-line workers are not

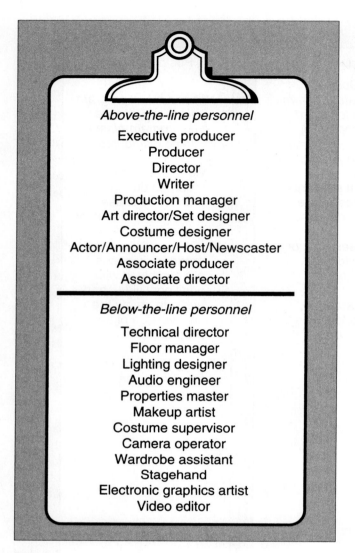

Above-the-line personnel

Executive producer
Producer
Director
Writer
Production manager
Art director/Set designer
Costume designer
Actor/Announcer/Host/Newscaster
Associate producer
Associate director

Below-the-line personnel

Technical director
Floor manager
Lighting designer
Audio engineer
Properties master
Makeup artist
Costume supervisor
Camera operator
Wardrobe assistant
Stagehand
Electronic graphics artist
Video editor

Figure O-4. *Television production personnel.*

creative. Actually, most of these individuals are "secondary creators," who practice their artistic and technical skills within a conceptual matrix designed by one or more above-the-line personnel. Below-the-line personnel include video technicians, camera and lighting people, unit production managers, sound recording specialists, video and audio editors, lighting technicians, set builders, stagehands (called *grips* in location TV and film production), prop and costume people, graphic artists, electronic graphic artists and production assistants. In this chapter, we discuss most of these above- and below-the-line personnel within the context of more than one type and budgetary level of television production.

"Tag Along" Virtual Tours Through a Sitcom, a Commercial and a News Story

To help you understand the roles of various production personnel, we'll now embark on guided virtual tours through three different kinds of TV productions. The examples chosen do not begin to exhaust the growing range of television product types, but they do suggest how differently the phases of production are conducted in each of these three production examples and how the job descriptions of the personnel involved in their creation vary from show to show.

The Sitcom

Our first stop is on the set of a weekly network *sitcom* (situation comedy) shot with four cameras on a Los Angeles sound stage. Because it's videotaped before a live audience, this kind of show combines the producing of both a television show and a stage play.

The Spot

Our second tour follows a production company shooting on location to produce a 30-second automobile commercial (commercials are also called *spots*). This spot is produced in a manner quite similar to commercials shot on motion picture film: It uses only one camera and occasionally requires many *takes* (tries) of each shot before the director judges it a success and moves on to the next one.

The third guided tour requires us to walk briskly to keep up, since we are following a television news reporter and her collaborator, a camera operator who, at this TV station, will also serve as video editor. They will report on and electronically photograph news as it is happening, take the footage back to the station and, that same evening, air their story on the station's evening newscast.

The Sitcom: Preproduction Phase

Long before the particular Thursday in early fall when we join the production company of this established network sitcom, writers have been hard at work creating the current week's script. (Sometimes only one writer is responsible for the first draft of the script, but often the production company's producers heavily revise the script before it's produced.)

Thursday is the first day of the production week for this company. It's the day they begin production on a new episode, the 18th of the 23 the network ordered this season. In seven days, the company must complete the preproduction and production phases. Posting begins for episode 18 next Thursday, while episode 19's production week is just beginning. This simultaneous episode development occurs with little confusion because the production company, in addition to employing a *line producer* for episode 18, also has a *postproduction supervisor*. A line producer is the person directly responsible for a particular episode, the boss of the show to whom even the director reports. The postproduction supervisor follows the course of production for two or more overlapping episodes, then takes up where the line producer leaves off, overseeing all aspects of postproduction, so the producer and director can focus attention on preproduction of the next program. Our sitcom also has an *executive producer*, who in this case also happens to be the program's creator, the ultimate boss of the show.

In this company, because this particular director is a talented, seasoned veteran (and is also available and willing), the executive producer plans to use him for as many successive shows as possible. So the director will direct shows 18 through 21 without a week off. Although this director is the guiding creative force during much of the production of show 18, neither he nor the line producer will have time to sit in the editing room and follow it through the process of posting. The director will provide the editor with notes on how he would like the show put together. He is also guaranteed by the rules of the Director's Guild that he will get to see the first assembly of the show and provide the editor with notes. The editor, with oversight by the postproduction supervisor, then creates the *director's cut* of show 18, which, when completed, will be turned over to the producer. After delivery of the director's cut, the producer can change anything she wishes. But these particular individuals have worked well together for many years, and it is rare when the finished product needs much fixing.

Each Thursday, the line producer, the director, the show's cast and certain key department supervisors gather around a large table for the first *read-through* of show 18. Although this is an informal gathering designed to familiarize everyone with this week's script, beneath the veneer of good fellowship and laughs, it's all business.

Later the same day, the show's *casting director* consults talent agency books and makes phone calls to schedule Friday's selections and interviews for the few guest speaking roles in this script. Also, six extras are needed for this week's script. The *assistant director* (or AD) will call central casting to arrange for the hiring of these individuals, giving the descriptions of the kind of persons required. By late Friday afternoon, extras (or their photos) will be available for the director's approval.

Costuming, makeup and hairstyling specialists consult their notes about the demands this script makes on their departments. It's an easy week for the costume supervisor: Unlike other weeks, episode 18 occurs in only two hours' *story time* (the actual time in the story, from beginning to end, during which the action takes place), and all but one of the actors appear in the same clothes, makeup and hairstyles throughout the show. This is quite unusual, because most episodes take place over a longer passage of time, and costume changes require much preparation. Sometimes, if major costume changes must occur during a show—such as the inclusion of a scene that flashes back to when the characters were much younger, requiring major costume, hairstyle and makeup changes—it may be shot and edited in advance and shown to the audience during the show's taping. On occasion, costumes are made by the network studio's costume shop and added to the sitcom's bill for the week, which includes studio and equipment rental and many other expenses. But since this is a contemporary sitcom, many costumes are "street clothes" bought off the rack at stores. Other specialty costumes and props, such as policemen's uniforms or a gorilla suit, etc., may be rented in Hollywood from companies such as Western Costume. Often this is cheaper than creating them from scratch.

For the director and actors, Friday is *blocking* day. Although blocking virtually always occurs on the show's sets on stage, part of this week the studio is using their stage to produce a special. So for a few days, in a rehearsal room with the measurements of the show's sets outlined with masking tape on the floor and with scripts in hand, the actors listen to the director's instructions as he explains the *business* for each scene (see Figure O-5). "Business" is a term referring to the actors' physical movement. After lunch, this group does a "run-through" of the show—just actors doing business and using a few hand props—no cameras yet. Blocking reveals rough spots in the show that need more work, and the production team makes minor script changes that work better.

Over the weekend, actors finish memorizing their lines and their blocking cues. Because this week's episode requires a fairly complicated new set, the

Figure O-5. *In a rehearsal room, with set dimensions outlined in masking tape on the floor, the director works with actors to block their movements.*

art director and the set construction crew must work on Saturday to assure that everything will be ready.

By Monday, actors are now *off-book* (that is, they have memorized all of their lines) and able to concentrate on fine-tuning their performances. The line producer was in and out during Friday's blocking rehearsals, but this is her first opportunity to sit in on an entire run-through of the episode. Although it is the director's show, the line producer's working relationship with him allows her the freedom to suggest changes in any scene.

Tuesday morning is the first time the director works with the camera, sound and control room crews. In what stage productions call a "tech rehearsal," the director takes the actors slowly through each scene, stopping often to explain to the camera operators, control room staff and audio personnel (via intercom headset) what he wants them to do, and when to do it (see Figure O-6). So in each scene, camera operators practice getting their assigned shots as dictated by the actors' business and lines in the script. A bank of TV sets called *monitors* on the studio floor display all four camera shots. Using these monitors, the director views his shots, explains them

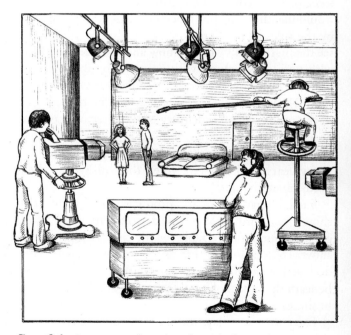

Figure O-6. *Directors usually work on the studio floor, rather than from the control room, to set camera shots during the tech rehearsal.*

when necessary to the cast and crew and makes changes he deems necessary. The operators of two huge microphone booms also rehearse their actions. They position the booms located on either side of the set and place the mikes above and in front of the actors, out of view of the cameras. The trick is to maneuver the mikes as close as they can to the actors without allowing either boom shadows or the mikes themselves to enter a camera's view.

Besides controlling the sound from these boom mikes and all the standard prerecorded sound used each week, the audio technician is responsible for three special (nonrecurring each week) sound effects (called *SFX*) for this week's show. There is the beeping of a personal computer, a loud clatter from off stage and some unusual street noises outside. When these SFX cues come up in the script, the audio technician inserts them into the program (see Figure O-7).

There are really two shows being prepared for recording. One is strictly for a feed to the overhead monitors that the studio audience will view during the taping, and the other is the all-important recording of the video from the four studio cameras and the program's audio to be blended together in the editing room into the final version of the show. Videotaped shows of the past were taped live before the audience, not just once, but twice in one day. The first performance was a taped *dress rehearsal,* and the second was the final performance. Each of these performances was videotaped before different audiences. Occasionally, a scene that worked better in the dress rehearsal was even edited into the final version of the episode. But with the advent of easier, more flexible ways to edit video and the expense and difficulty of scaring up two live audiences in the same day, the taping of rehearsals and live, real-time editing during the final performance have become less prevalent.

After the technical rehearsal and a lunch break, the *technical director* (or TD, who may also be simply called the *switcher* in some operations) spends most of Tuesday's remaining work time in the control room, surrounded by many monitors, including those displaying the four camera shots. Following the director's shooting script, the TD will switch the show live (between camera views) during the taping to provide the audience with an approximation of what the show will look like when all four of the camera shots are edited together. Even when the audience is present, the director will do his job (call the shots) from the studio floor.

For the TD in the control room, another monitor (the *preview monitor*) shows him the camera next in line to be selected, and the *line monitor*, also called the *program monitor*, displays the camera currently on the air (see Figure O-8).

Down on the floor with the director are the line producer and the *script supervisor*. Unlike many other crewpersons, the script supervisor has no official set of initials and is never called the "SS." In earlier days, the script supervisor usually was a woman, sometimes referred to simply as the "script girl." Both men and women now serve as script supervisors, and as always, efficient script supervision is vital to assuring pictorial continuity and script organization.

Figure O-7. *An audio technician readies the next audio cue.*

Figure O-8. *The AD, TD and assistants iron out problems and work the show from the control room.*

In the control room, the AD is busy helping "shape up" camera shots about to be switched onto preview and then onto line, keeping track of when to insert commercial breaks and monitoring the show's running time. The TD sits at an imposing piece of gear with an array of lighted buttons and levers called the *video switcher* (see Figure O-9).

From the control room, production staff communicate with the director, cast and crew down on the studio floor in four ways: (1) by intercom headsets that crew members wear; (2) through the *talkback* loudspeaker system in the studio; (3) indirectly via the *stage manager*, who relays commands and cues from the director and, in this case, from the control room to cast and crew

Figure O-9. *The TD sits at the video switcher.*

(it should be noted that in many other kinds of television shows, especially non-network-level productions, this position is essentially the same but is called the *floor manager*); and (4) by simply walking downstairs for a personal chat.

By Tuesday night, all is in readiness, and the cast and crew's preproduction work on episode 18 is nearly completed.

The end of the preproduction phase, the *final run-through*, what theatre people call the final dress rehearsal, occurs early on Wednesday. Afterward, the director gives the company his final notes and last-minute instructions to help fine-tune the timing of certain gags, cuts out a doubtful bit of business that's still not working, makes a few jokes and praises and encourages this troupe of nervous artists. After a meal, last-minute preparations are made for the performance in front of a live audience later that day.

The Sitcom: Production Phase

In this company, since the executive producer once did stand-up comedy and enjoys working a crowd, he and one of the show's writers do the audience *warm-up*, a short, informal interaction with the audience to get them into a jovial, receptive mood.

Minutes later, with the warm-up over, the house lights dimmed and the audience primed for comedy, the first scene begins. Four individual video recorders roll, recording the entire show from the points of view of each of the four cameras. This is the footage that will be later edited into the final version of the program. Each shot in the script has an identifying number, and each of the four camera operators has a list of his or her camera's shots clipped to their cameras. Up in the booth, to provide the audience with an approximate version of the show that will be edited together in the coming days, the AD calls the shots and the TD punches the appropriate camera's buttons on the switcher. For example, when the AD says, "Ready shot 15 on camera four," everyone knows what to do, especially that camera's operator, whose assignment is shot 15. After this *preparatory command*, at the exact moment he wants camera four's shot switched on line, the AD gives the *execution command*: In this case, he says, "Take four" (see Figure O-10). Other directors may just say, "Take it," or "On four," or simply snap a finger. The idiosyncrasies of the director are among the more intangible lessons the crew learns during the course of preproduction rehearsals. In other kinds of TV programs in which the director calls the shots from the control room, the AD may give the preparatory

Figure O-10. *The director calls shots live during the taping.*

commands, and then the director gives all execution commands.

Unlike a newscast, which is shot and aired live in the same 30 minutes, the taping of a half-hour sitcom may take as much as an hour or longer. This is because, as in a stage play, there are breaks in the action between scenes, while sets, costumes, makeup, hair and lighting are changed or adjusted. Another reason that a sitcom taping takes longer than real time is because errors occur, requiring a momentary halt in the taping. Missed lines and cues, defective or mishandled props, bungled entrances and missing or misplaced furniture most often cause these delays.

Some production companies also record the version of the show that the AD and TD switch to line for the audience to watch on the studio monitors. This version, a handy backup copy, is called a *line cut*. Although the director prefers not to do *retakes* (redoing a scene) during the final taping, he decides that one scene requires reshooting. Still not pleased with the retake, but unwilling to subject his studio audience to further delays, he tells the producer that tomorrow they can edit in a few *coverage* shots from the line cut to fix the troublesome scene. In multi-camera video production, the term "coverage" is defined as video footage inserted into a scene during postproduction editing to make a show's pictorial continuity flow smoother. In single-camera film production, "coverage" has a somewhat different meaning. During posting on Thursday, the editor will insert a long shot and one closeup from the line cut into this scene.

At taping's end, "thank-yous" are passed all around, sets are struck and the actors and most below-the-line

crew depart. The director, postproduction supervisor, AD and line producer meet briefly to discuss notes for episode 18's posting the next day.

The Sitcom: Postproduction Phase

In this episode, there are a few problems that will require fixing in postproduction. On Thursday morning, the director meets with the editor and provides notes to accompany the script. These will be the editor's guide in assembling the show the way the director has planned it. The editor may assemble the show in an editing suite filled with monitors, a switcher, videotape editing equipment, an audio mixer, banks of videotape recorders and other equipment. Or, more likely these days, the editing suite looks a lot like a computer lab with TV monitors, and the show is edited on a *nonlinear digital editing system*. In this digital environment, the taped digital footage is recorded onto the editing system's media storage disks. Music, additional sound effects and electronically generated graphics will also be imported into this digital editing system for use in the finished program. The editor then can meld together the various video and audio elements, adjust audio and video levels and create a wide range of special effects. Working in a nonlinear digital environment allows the editor to move or modify any program element located anywhere in the show with just a few keystrokes.

As in the preproduction and production phases, posting proceeds from a predetermined plan. The editor uses the director's specific instructions for editing the show. Meanwhile, the director has already moved on and this morning is conducting the first read-through of episode 19.

When the troublesome scene in episode 18 comes up, the editor uses coverage from the line cut, and as the director predicted, this combination of shots does the trick.

Audio "sweetening," such as boosting the volume of an actor's punch line or the audience's laughter at certain points, is also part of the postproduction process. Also, recognizable theme music that helps transition from scene to scene is added. The final master tape includes the standard beginning and this episode's end credits. The credits use only the left third of the video frame because the network plans to use the rest of the screen to promote its next program. The editor also adds the series' theme music to accompany these visuals and leaves the right two thirds of the screen black for the network to add the promotional information.

Later, after approving the director's cut, the line producer and executive producer meet to view the finished product. All are satisfied with the show, and they make a few backup copies from the master, just in case this valuable tape is lost or destroyed. The next day the network receives their copy. Episode 18 will air two weeks later. The attention of the company now turns toward the preproduction activities surrounding episode 19.

The Commercial, or Spot: Preproduction Phase

In contrast to the first phase of preproduction on the sitcom, preproduction activities at the commercial production company do not begin with scriptwriting. Usually the production company bids (often by invitation) on commercials already written and *storyboarded* by an advertising agency (see Figure O-11). In this example, the ad agency extended bid requests to three production companies they thought would do the best job for their client. Our company's bid was successful, and we begin our tour at the point after the contract is awarded.

The spot is being produced for a regional association of automobile dealers. The production company's director assigned to this project calls a meeting. Attending are some of his organization's staff people, the *business manager*, who is responsible for finances, and the *unit production manager*, or UPM, who is responsible for most of the logistics on a commercial production. However, the title of *producer* on this spot doesn't go to an employee of the production company; instead it goes to the ad agency's representative on this commercial.

Figures O-11. *A commercial storyboard is a graphic illustration of how the script would be realized. It is used to communicate what the commercial will look like to clients who might have difficulty visualizing it from just a script. It is also used by the commercial's producer and director to communicate to other crewpersons and talent what the spot is about.*

In her capacity, she acts as a creative and decision-making liaison between her ad agency and the production company.

This first meeting has the unwieldy title of pre-preproduction meeting. Unlike the read-through, the sitcom's first production meeting, everyone at this gathering received storyboard copies weeks ago and is now prepared to discuss their individual responsibilities. If anyone wants minor changes in the storyboards, the director and/or the producer decide on them during this pre-preproduction meeting. The next meeting, the preproduction meeting, will include the account executive (the ad agency's top liaison with the client) and two car dealership owners representing the dealers' association. The director knows that the ad agency looks better to the clients if he can work out changes to the storyboards before this gathering, so the pre-preproduction meeting is the time to suggest changes. The director's thoughtful attitude toward how the ad agency looks in front of the client will be remembered the next time the agency must decide which production company gets a bid.

It's at the pre-preproduction meeting that the UPM passes out a roster and audition schedule for a dozen preselected actors and actresses who will audition for the two nonspeaking roles in the spot. As with many other creative choices, the *ad agency producer* must approve the director's casting choices on behalf of her agency and their client. The UPM also distributes snapshots of prospective locations that he and the director have discovered and photographed and obtains the producer's approval for their use.

Having previously consulted the director and the business manager, the UPM distributes a proposed production schedule: In their bid to produce this spot, the UPM scheduled two days' location shooting and two days' postproduction time. After much discussion about this and other concerns (wardrobe, props, makeup, etc.), the pre-preproduction meeting adjourns.

Casting is the next step. Talent agencies contacted by the production company for this casting call send a dozen men and women to audition before the director, producer and UPM. Although actors all bring resumes and photos to this session, the UPM still takes pictures. There often is considerable difference between an actor's current appearance and his/her resume portraits. The director puts each actor through some simple drills to see how each responds to his direction. Notes are taken and all are thanked as they leave.

The most promising choices for talent return the next day for *callbacks* (a second round of auditions).

Finally, the decision about which actors to cast is made, their agents are notified and contracts are sent.

This spot also requires the services of a *voice-over announcer* and some jazzy music composition. A *voice-over* (VO) is the narration audio you hear in any production while you view the video. The production company does not bother auditioning these artists. Rather, they call a local radio announcer they've used before for similar voice-overs. Also, they decide to once again employ a talented local musician who specializes in writing, performing and recording commercial jingles. The ad agency producer knows them both, has worked with them before and mentions that the tone of the prospective announcer's voice and his vocal delivery are perfect for this spot.

Next they select below-the-line crew members, independent production personnel hired by the day. These include a *videographer* (director of video photography), who also operates the camera, and a camera/video assistant who doubles as sound recordist. The only on-location audio required for this particular spot is a 30-second loop of nonsynchronized ambient sound recorded on location, because this spot has no dialog. Ambient sound, such as wind, chirping birds and so on, is the background audio that exists "underneath" dialog and sound effects on a sound track. Production people call this ambient sound *room tone*, even though this particular spot is shot outdoors. *Taking tone* is the act of recording such ambient sound.

The production company also hires a specialist in location lighting and electricity, called a *gaffer*. This is an outdoors shoot, and all that's needed are two large reflectors to soften unwanted shadows in closeup shots, plus two small battery-powered lights to supplement the natural illumination in car interior shots. Rounding out the crew are a hairdresser/makeup artist and two *production assistants* (PAs) to run errands, fetch and carry and act as general "go-fors."

Finally, the director and UPM attend the final meeting of all concerned parties, called the preproduction meeting, held at the ad agency. They distribute their revised storyboards along with photos of the actors they've cast. This is to help prevent any surprised looks on the clients' faces during the screening of the final product.

Now all that remains are last-minute details, such as costuming, confirming transportation, motel reservations and on-location food catering. The company still must rent and check out video equipment, purchase videotape of the required format, inspect it for defects and so on.

The Spot: Production Phase

The production company's car caravan arrives at the location town on schedule, quickly checks into the motel and sets out for their first location, a quaint roadside cafe nearby. With the help of the owner of the cafe, the UPM has arranged for the parking lot to be empty, as required by the storyboards, and for its regular patrons to be absent. The first day's shooting calls for establishing shots (long shots, or shots taken from far away) of two cars, approaching the front of the cafe, arriving from different directions. The actors stop their cars, neatly facing each other, get out of their cars and approach each other. Then the director shoots coverage shots (in this instance, coverage means closeups of each actor and wider shots of each of them in their cars). Most of these shots are "in the can" (successfully completed) when he decides that they've "lost the light" for today. This means too little daylight remains to shoot additional shots that would have color saturation and shadowing that match video recorded earlier. But the producer and director feel the first day's shoot went well.

Day two's schedule calls for shooting both cars in action, cornering around rustic farmland roads, each supposedly on its way to the cafe. They shoot the shots on the storyboard out of order to exploit locations and crew setups most economically. But finally, they need to go back and pick up the coverage shots at the cafe that were postponed when they lost the light yesterday.

By mid day's lunch break, all but one of the six driving shots are in the can. One tricky shot remains. It features a shot of a driver, captured by the camera mounted inside the car, complete with battery-powered artificial lighting to equalize the light level inside the car with the light outside.

After lunch they record this remaining driving shot, although it takes three takes to get it right. Well before dusk this time, the director tapes the final coverage shots at the cafe and announces, "That's a wrap!" The production phase of this project is nearly over, and all that remains is packing up equipment, followed by the long drive home.

The Spot: Postproduction Phase

Unlike the sitcom, this spot requires more meticulous posting. During production the director recorded practically every shot twice and some required many retakes. Each camera move, every actor's physical nuance and even the positions of the clouds in the background were considered, permitting the storyboard to come to life with maximum persuasive effect. Now editing (often called *cutting* by production people who began their careers in film) begins, based on the detailed notes for each shot logged by one of the production assistants.

Present in the editing suite are the director, UPM, ad agency producer and one client representative. The goal is to assemble a master-edit videotape from the location footage in a manner nearly identical to the sitcom posting. The director won't stay at this posting session long: He has another commercial to work on for the production company, and today he has casting auditions for a number of important speaking roles.

The edit goes smoothly, as the producer and the UPM follow their notes and the storyboard, instructing the editor to call up certain shots for viewing and possible use. The director instructs the editor to play the tape, pausing or stopping it when needed. When the director finds the exact spot in the shot that looks best when joined to the end of the previous shot, he tells the editor to make a computerized note of its location. Then the editor previews this proposed edit, allowing everyone in the suite to see how it looks before making the edit. Once viewed and approved, the editor enters the edit in the videotape editor's computer memory. Should the director later change his mind, he can have the editor make adjustments in the final-edit tape by punching a few buttons and changing the record of edits in the computer, which is called the *edit decision list*, or EDL. This EDL keeps track of all the edits by noting the *time code* on the videotapes. Time code is an identifying number assigned to each frame of video and audio in a production to assist in editing. Finally, all the visual elements are in place, but the audio remains unfinished.

The next morning, the announcer is called in for the audio recording session. Rather than use the editing facility to record the announcer's voice-over, our company uses the music composer's own audio/video studio. The announcer's microphone is set up in the studio near a large TV monitor, on which a copy of the final master-edit videotape is displayed. This allows the announcer to precisely adjust the pace and synchronization of his voice-over to the images on the videotape. The producer explains to the announcer the mood and tone of voice required, and then the recording begins. The announcer, a seasoned commercial veteran, does the job quickly and efficiently.

Next, it's the composer's turn. Using his digital recording system, he builds an entire orchestral background for the commercial, one instrument (or section of instruments) at a time. Like the announcer, he views the spot

Figure O-12. *A music recording session. Synthesizers and computers now take the place of the bands and orchestras that were once required to produce the score for a production.*

on a monitor, enabling him to synchronize his performance to the all-important visuals (see Figure O-12). The composer creates a master piano track and then lays down additional tracks consisting of rhythm, strings, horns and wind instruments. All these sounds are created with an electronic synthesizer. Next, the composer *mixes down* (combines) all these tracks, plus the announcer's voice-over track and the loop of ambient sound recorded on location, onto a time-coded master audio tape.

The producer, UPM and director then attend a final editing session at the video editing facility to merge the audio and video onto a final, composite master videotape. This takes little time, because all they must do is check the synchronization of the audio and video tracks and combine them onto the master videotape. At this point the ad agency producer officially approves the commercial. This is an important financial step for the production company, because most standard contracts between agencies and outside producers stipulate that the production company's responsibility for changes ends when the producer "signs off" on a spot. From here on, revisions in the commercial requested by the agency or the client are outside the contract and subject to additional billing.

The producer, director and the client reps meet the next day. The two car dealers are pleased, especially with the lush music track. They commend the production company for securing such an "exquisite orchestra." This spot is now complete, ready for duplication and ad agency distribution to the regional TV stations chosen by the ad agency to air the client's commercial.

The News Story: Preproduction Phase

The news story's preproduction phase is brief. Unlike the sitcom and the spot, which began with complete script or storyboards, the final script for the news story won't exist until the postproduction phase. After postproduction of a taped story, the news anchor or the newscast's producer might change the anchor introduction (called an *intro*) to the story written by the reporter. Sometimes the reporter or the anchor also writes a *tag*, which is text read by the anchor immediately after the taped news story ends. A tag is usually some additional information not included in the taped story. For example, in the case of a taped story on the death of a well-known person, the anchor's tag might be something like, "The funeral is scheduled for Tuesday at the community church." Also, the director of the live newscast superimposes additional words and graphics over the video at certain points in the story as it plays on the air.

The story begins when the news department's assignment editor decides to cover a city councilman's announcement of his candidacy for mayor. There is to be a news conference on the front steps of city hall. Using the news department's computer network, a listing of all footage of the candidate found in the station's tape library is available to the reporter before she leaves for the press conference.

The news camera operator/videotape editor (often called a *photog*) checks all *electronic newsgathering* (ENG) equipment needed for the shoot while the reporter glances over a few research notes and grabs a spiral notebook and pens. Then the reporter and her photog pile the gear into one of the station's news vehicles and depart for city hall.

The News Story: Production Phase

Through some city hall mix-up, only a few reporters appear for the news conference. This allows our reporter to get close to the candidate, who ignores the podium prepared for him and stands surrounded by the small band of journalists. The candidate reads a short prepared speech to the cozy group and answers questions.

In this production format, the reporter is the de facto director, telling the photog what shots she needs. But having worked two years with this particular photog, and having started in TV news as a photog herself, the reporter knows that certain things are automatic between them. Usually, she just listens to the speech and asks questions, relying on the photog to shoot the needed coverage. The photog shoots two or three different-sized shots of the candidate and a few shots of the reporters and looks for other "targets of opportunity." Then, while a newspaper reporter asks a question, our reporter gives the photog a signal, which he recognizes as his cue to make a move.

Quickly, with the camera still running, he crosses to one side of the candidate so both his reporter and the candidate are in the same shot. Seeing her photog in position, the reporter chooses this moment to ask the candidate a question, and then a follow-up question.

Soon the news conference ends. The reporter checks with the photog to see how much and what kind of footage was shot. She asks for a few more *cutaways*, such as a long shot of the city hall's distinctive front arch and the Mayor's Office sign inside. Such shots may help later in the editing room. Then they shoot her *stand-up*, in this case a waist-up shot of the reporter on the steps of city hall, as she summarizes the story (see Figure O-13). All visual elements except electronic graphics are now in the can, so we can say that the production phase of this news story is over.

The News Story: Postproduction Phase

In TV news production, the reporter wears many hats: director, writer, on-camera talent and voice-over narrator. When the duo returns to the station, the reporter goes to her desk, while the photog heads for a video editing bay. A much simpler facility than the postproduction suites used by the sitcom and spot producers, it contains two videotape machines, an edit controller,

Figure O-13. *The news photog shoots the reporter's stand-up.*

Figure O-14. *An editor at work in a typical editing bay used for TV news.*

two color monitors, a small audio mixer and a disc-based audio playback machine (see Figure O-14).

After examining the station's file footage of the candidate, the reporter doesn't think that any of this footage is necessary, so she builds her story entirely on video they shot today. After examining the footage with the photog/editor, she writes an editing script to guide him in assembling this story. This script is saved to the newsroom server, so any news staffer, including the photog/editor and the newscast producer, can access it. This server can store text as well as video. The portion of the newsroom server system storing video is often referred to as a *video file server*. Next, the reporter enters a soundproof audio booth. There she records her narration voice-overs directly onto the newsroom server. At this point, the reporter's responsibility diminishes: She is assigned another story, which she will cover live during the evening's newscast. The photog finishes editing this story alone. He saves the finished piece onto the newsroom server and informs the news program producer. Accessing the reporter's edit script on the server, the producer can copy and paste the anchor intro and tag copy into the master newscast script. During the newscast, the program's director superimposes lettering created by a character generator at certain points in the story, identifying the city in which the story takes place, the candidate's name, the title of city councilman and the reporter's name along with the newscast's distinctive logo. Finally, postproduction of this two-minute program element is completed.

Conclusion

Our virtual tours through the three phases of production of a network situation comedy, an automobile commercial and a local news story are over. You should now have a better basic understanding of the three-phase process by which programs are created and recognize the job titles of key individuals who produce them. Also, remember that these examples are only three types of video productions. There are dozens of others, and each is produced a little differently, aimed toward different audiences, using different delivery systems. Even the ways our three types of program material—the sitcom, the commercial and the news story—are produced vary in different-sized markets and production companies.

Now we'll begin the process of introducing the fundamentals you would need to function as a below-the-line crew member within these and many other production settings. But our goal is not to teach you to become a technician or an engineer: That would be another textbook on electronic engineering for video production. Instead, we hope to help you understand and use the basic tools of television production. Then, once you understand these tools, you'll learn about the arts and crafts practiced by above-the-line creators of television productions.

A centerpiece of television is the video camera. Because the camera also is one of the first items of production gear you're likely to encounter in a TV production course, it is the topic of Chapter 1.

Important Vocabulary Terms

Above-the-line: Used to describe production personnel responsible for original creative input into a production, including producers, directors, writers, talent, etc.

Ad agency producer: An employee of the ad agency who acts as producer of a spot. This person acts as the liaison between the ad agency and the production company and is empowered to make decisions for the agency and its client.

Art director: The person responsible for the "look" of the production, in charge of set design, props and costume supervision.

Assistant director (AD): The person second in command to the director, responsible for "shaping up" camera shots and for timing the show, as well as a host of other responsibilities delegated by the director.

Below-the-line: Used to describe personnel—chiefly in the more technical areas—responsible for carrying out the creative ideas of above-the-line personnel.

Blocking: A process during which the director explains and rehearses the talents' physical movements (often called business) required by the script.

Business: An acting/directing term referring to actors' physical movement on the stage/set.

Business manager: The person responsible for finances at a production company.

Callbacks: Second-day auditions for talent who were not eliminated during the first-day auditions.

Camcorder: A TV camera/videotape recorder in one unit.

Casting director: The person responsible for making preliminary decisions about which actors may be right for certain parts.

Coverage: Video footage employed during postproduction editing to make a live-on-tape show's pictorial continuity flow smoother.

Cutaway: In a TV news story, typically a shot inserted into the story that shows a picture related to what the interviewee or the reporter is talking about on the audio track.

Cutting: Another term for editing, borrowed from the film industry.

Director's cut: The first edited version of a production. The director has the opportunity to complete his/her version, as guaranteed by the Director's Guild, and then the show is given over to the producer. The producer can then accept this version of the show, or choose to make changes.

Dress rehearsal: A final rehearsal of a show, performed with all the production values (costumes, makeup, props, sets, etc.) nearly exactly as the show will be during the actual performance. In a sitcom, this last rehearsal of the show used to be taped as if it were the actual performance—complete with a live audience—because footage from a dress rehearsal was sometimes edited into the final program version.

Edit decision list (EDL): A record of the beginning and end of edits in a production, referring to both the time code on footage tapes and the nature of the transition (cut, dissolve, etc.) performed at each edit point.

Electronic news gathering (ENG): A system of news reporting that involves the use of portable TV cameras to record video and sound, sometimes including the transmission of a signal to the TV station for immediate broadcast.

Execution command: A director's command that instructs crewmembers to perform a specified action, such as, "Take camera three, open mike and cue talent."

Executive producer: In a production company, the individual who supervises the entire operation, including the activities of subordinate line producers.

Final run-through: The last rehearsal before the dress rehearsal.

Floor manager: The person who relays commands and cues from the control room to the cast and crew on the studio floor. In network-level productions, this position is often called "stage manager."

Gaffer: A specialist in lighting and electricity.

Grip: The term used in location television and film productions to refer to a multipurpose stagehand, a "jack of all trades."

In the can: A phrase indicating that a program element (such as a shot or scene) or an entire program has been successfully completed and safely recorded onto tape or some other digital storage medium. The expression originated in the moviemaking industry in the 1930s, when recorded film was literally stored in a can or canister.

Intro: In a television newscast, an intro is the copy read by the anchor as an introduction to a taped story or some other program element, such as a live remote.

Line cut: A backup copy of a sitcom taping, recorded from the version of the show that the AD and TD switch to the line monitor for the benefit of the studio audience.

Line monitor: The monitor that shows the director the video that is currently on the air. Also called the program monitor.

Line producer: In a production company shooting a TV series, a person responsible for one particular episode. A line producer (or producing team) works on one episode, while another prepares the following week's episode.

Mix down: Combine multiple audio tracks into one composite track.

Monitors: TV sets displaying camera shots for the director and other crewmembers.

Nonlinear digital editing system: A computer-based editing system in which all source video and audio can be accessed directly rather than having to scroll through film or tape to reach a particular point. Such editing utilizes digital rather than tape-based storage devices and does not require physically cutting or otherwise damaging original footage.

Off-book: The stage of rehearsal at which the actors have committed their lines to memory.

Photog: TV news jargon for an ENG videographer.

Post/posting: Another term for postproduction.

Postproduction: The phase in which program audio and video is corrected, augmented and edited into its final form for airing or distribution. Also called "the post" or "posting" or simply "post."

Postproduction supervisor: A person responsible for overseeing all posting of a production company's shows.

Preparatory command: A director's command alerting crewmembers to an upcoming action, such as the switching from one camera to another.

Preproduction: The phase of production in which elements necessary for a successful production are organized, prepared and rehearsed.

Preview monitor: The monitor showing the director the next shot ready to go on line.

Producer: The general supervisor of a production, usually in charge of managing financial, administrative and even the creative aspects of the project.

Production: The actual shooting (recording or live broadcast) phase of the show, executing the plans made during preproduction.

Production Assistant (PA): Below-the-line production helper who runs errands, fetches and carries.

Program monitor: Another term for the line monitor, which shows the director the video that is currently on the air.

Read-through: A rehearsal in which all talent read and discuss their parts with the director and other creative staff. Discussion of plot, character and action ensues as the director explains his/her vision of the show concept.

Retakes: Repeated recordings of a scene, shot because the director feels that the original may be faulty in some way.

Room tone: Ambient sound recorded on location that later, during editing, serves as a background sound track.

Script supervisor: A person who takes notes during production, allowing the director to keep his/her eyes on the scene rather than on the script. This person has responsibility for helping to ensure script continuity, plus other duties.

SFX: An abbreviation for sound effects.

Sitcom: The television term for a situation comedy.

Spot: The television term for a commercial.

Stage manager: The person who relays commands and cues from the control room to the cast and crew on the studio floor. Also called the floor manager in non-network-level productions.

Stand-up: A shot during an ENG news report in which the reporter talks directly into the camera, either to narrate action we see in the shot or to provide more facts for the story.

Story time: The actual time in the story, from beginning to end, during which the action is supposed to have taken place.

Storyboard: A shot-by-shot graphic illustration of a script.

Switcher: This can either be a shortened name for the technical director or the name of a piece of control room video equipment used for visual transitions and special effects. A switcher may also be called a special effects generator or SEG.

Tag: In a television news story, it is the copy read by the anchor immediately following the airing of a taped news story. A tag usually adds some additional information not included in the taped story.

Take: As a noun, a take is one individual attempt to successfully tape a scene. As a verb, it is the command a director uses in a multiple-camera TV show to order a camera shot to be instantaneously switched from preview to line.

Taking tone: Recording room tone (ambient sound) during a location shoot.

Talkback: The use of a loudspeaker allowing the director to speak from the control room to all personnel on the studio floor.

Technical director (TD): The supervisor of the technical staff, he/she also operates the video switcher during the taping or broadcast.

Time code: An identifying number assigned to each frame of video in a production. It is used to assist in the editing process.

Unit production manager (UPM): The person responsible for logistics of a production company's shoot.

Video file server: Usually a multiple-disc-based recording system, sometimes referred to as a RAID (redundant array of independent discs), providing random access to nonsequential video files and allowing playback in real time.

Video switcher: Video equipment used to select which camera is on line. It is also capable of introducing special effects into the program and is sometimes referred to as a special effects generator (SEG) or simply as the switcher.

Videographer: The director of video photography.

Voice-over (VO): Narration audio you may hear in any production while you view the video.

Voice-over announcer: An announcer whose voice is heard explaining or narrating a scene but whose picture is not seen on camera.

Warm-up: A short, jovial chat with a studio audience prior to taping the show.

## chapter 1

The TV Camera

During the television industry's five decades of existence, the camera has undergone a number of important changes. In contrast to the film camera, the television camera captures pictures electronically. While film camera technology has improved at a relative snail's pace over the last half century, advances in electronics have spurred an exponentially-accelerating evolution in television camera technology.

Another major change is upon us as broadcasters have been charged by the *Federal Communications Commission* (FCC) to convert every phase of their operations, from initial TV picture acquisition to transmission, from the old *analog* standard to *digital*. To understand the difference between analog and digital, you first need to think about the way electronic recording of pictures and sound works. When a picture or sound is recorded, the recording device captures it and turns it into a kind of *code* that a recording device can store. Then, in playback, a recorder or a playback device *decodes* this information and converts it back into light energy (a picture) or sound waves.

In analog recording and playback, the video or audio signal coding consists of continually varying voltages that imitate (or represent) the original sound or picture. The result is an electronic representation called a *waveform.* You could say that an analog signal is an electronic "analogy" of the original picture and sound.

In contrast, coding of a digital video or audio signal can best be described as streams of numbers that describe the picture or sound. These coding numbers are based on a binary (two-digit) numbering system using only the digits zero and one. Because there are only zeroes and ones to decipher, a digital signal is much less susceptible to distortion during transmission compared to an analog signal. A digital signal is also easy to manipulate using modern computers, another significant advantage of digitally coded signals over analog signals. We discuss the impact of the transition from analog to digital transmission on camera technology later in this chapter. Read the story of the first TV cameras for a look back at how TV cameras evolved.

Today, professionals and consumers use dozens of types, sizes and models of color cameras. These vary in size from large studio cameras to studio/field production models not much larger than a shoe box to amazingly tiny devices so small that doctors can insert them into the human body to aid in testing and exploratory surgery.

Now professionals can also use a single basic camera, which, with accessories, can work in a broad range of applications. Until recently, cameras were often classified according to whether they met broadcast or non-broadcast standards. The term *broadcast-quality* simply meant that the camera's video output met the Federal Communications Commission's (FCC) technical standards for transmission by a television station; that of a non-broadcast-quality "industrial" or "consumer" camera didn't. Today, thanks to advancements in video-processing technology, video shot with inexpensive consumer camcorders is of high enough quality to be used on network news and reality shows.

Professional Camera Applications

Although it's possible to broadcast video coded by almost any camera, those designed for professional applications produce *higher-resolution* (sharper) pictures and provide

The First TV Cameras

A half-century ago, there was essentially only one kind of color television camera: a massive, heavy device with three huge image-sensing tubes. One of these image-sensing tubes alone was larger than many broadcast television cameras today. To mount one of these huge three-tube cameras onto a studio pedestal usually required the services of two or three strong technicians, who gripped it by two hefty handles mounted on each side of the camera (see Figures 1-1 and 1-2).

Figure 1-1. *Technological advances dramatically reduced the size of color tube-type cameras during the 1970s and 1980s. Now TV cameras, no longer restricted by tubes, exist that are only the size of a vitamin capsule and can be swallowed by patients undergoing gastrointestinal tests.*

Figure 1-2. *Broadcast equipment collector Chuck Pharis stands beside a massive RCA model TK-41 three-tube color camera, which used Image Orthicon (I-O) tubes as image-sensing devices. Pharis, now retired after almost 40 years in television, was senior video engineer for ABC TV Network, Hollywood, CA. His vintage TK-41 was perhaps the most popular color studio camera from the birth of color TV broadcasting in the mid-1950s, finally giving way in the early 1970s to the much less bulky, solid state RCA model TK-44 camera, which used much smaller, more efficient Plumbicon tubes as image-sensing devices. Here, behind Pharis and his TK-41, are three older black-and-white I-O cameras.*

Photo courtesy of Chuck Pharis. For a delightful and educational journey back into the history of early TV equipment, visit Mr. Pharis' website at http://www.pharis-video.com/index.htm.

greater creative control over the image than do cameras designed for casual consumer use. Even among cameras designed for professional applications, however, there is considerable variation in picture quality and operational features. With the understanding that application categories continue to merge, and that the same basic camera may be used in multiple applications, professionals often group cameras into three broad, descriptive categories, which may capture video in either standard or high definition:

1. *electronic news gathering* (ENG) and *electronic field production* (EFP) cameras;
2. studio production cameras; and
3. special high-definition *digital cinematography cameras* (DCC), now often used as replacements for the traditional 35 mm film camera used in theatrical Hollywood productions.

There is no generally accepted industry acronym for cameras specially designed for studio work: They're just called studio cameras. The arbitrary nature of these distinctions becomes apparent when stations and networks take studio cameras for use in covering football games, parades and other multiple-camera field productions. The distinction between television studio cameras and high-definition DCCs will continue to blur after all TV stations complete their conversion from analog to digital TV in 2008 and move relentlessly toward all-high-definition TV transmission.

Major Camera Components

All cameras have three major parts:

1. the camera head, containing the camera's image sensors and all related electronic circuits;
2. the lens, which transmits light into the camera body and forms the image on the camera's image sensors; and
3. the viewfinder, which allows the operator to compose the elements making up a shot and often also provides a visual interface with the camera's various controls.

ENG cameras also include a portable, externally mounted power source. Except for lenses and camera imaging systems, this chapter provides an overview of these components (see Figure 1-3). Lenses and imaging systems merit separate treatment and are discussed in Chapter 2.

As noted, the first cameras designed for the controlled environment of a TV production studio were

Figure 1-3. *A portable Panasonic AJ-HDX 400 High Definition color camera configured for ENG or documentary work. Two wireless microphone antennae are mounted on the back.*

Photo courtesy of Panasonic.

large and heavy. Small, lightweight and easier-to-use portable video cameras designed for news, documentary and other kinds of field production came later. These smaller cameras initially sacrificed picture quality for portability. Today this limitation is less acute as technology continues to improve the pictures produced by portable cameras. Production professionals appreciate the increased capabilities of these smaller cameras, and manufacturers offer most of their portable models as "convertibles," cameras easily configured for many different uses in a manner of minutes. Portable models are also increasingly used in studio applications.

The Self-Contained Camera

Cameras designed for portable use are self-contained. The camera itself contains all necessary controls, many of them adjusted automatically by sophisticated microprocessors. Cameras designed solely for studio production use a separate set of controls housed in a *camera control unit* (CCU) located in the production facility/TV station's production (or master) control room (see Figure 1-4).

The ENG Camera

The ENG Camera Viewfinder

The viewfinder is the critical interface between the camera and its operator. Except for some digital cameras that also feature small, flat, fold-out *liquid crystal displays*

Figure 1-4. *A camera and its assigned camera control unit. During studio productions, a video technician sits at a bank of CCUs, manually shading (adjusting) camera controls to attain the very best pictures they can deliver. Portable, highly mobile cameras trade off perfectly adjusted "studio-quality" pictures for the versatility and quick response required for field videography (motion photography using a video camera).*

Photo courtesy of Sony Corporation.

(LCDs), the camera viewfinder is found inside the ENG camera's eyepiece. The operator frames shots through the viewfinder's small (usually 1.5-inch) TV screen. In addition to showing what the camera lens is "seeing," the viewfinder provides displays alerting the operator to important camera functions (see Figure 1-5). Among the function indicators typically displayed in an ENG camera's viewfinder are the following:

- Battery level: the amount of power remaining in the battery (or batteries) that provides direct current (DC) to the camera and recorder
- Color balance information: whether or not the camera is adjusted properly for the color of the light falling on the subject
- Filter information: what color-correction or light-reducing filter is currently placed between the lens and the image-sensing device
- End-of-tape indicator: warns you when only a few minutes of recording time remain
- Record/standby: whether or not the video recorder is running
- Iris control: whether the amount of light entering the camera is being adjusted automatically or must be set manually by you
- Low-light warning: tells you that there's not enough light in the scene to produce technically acceptable video

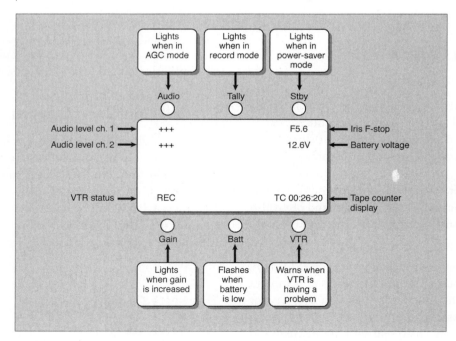

Figure 1-5. *A typical ENG camera viewfinder showing common indicators. Each brand and model of camera has different display arrays. Check the operator's manual for the camera you are using to learn which indicators are provided.*

The Evolution of the ENG Camera

Until the mid-1970s, TV journalists used 16 mm film cameras almost exclusively to gather news in the field (see Figure 1-5). Although shooting news on film required television stations to maintain large, expensive developing laboratories, the size, weight and power consumption of early television cameras made film the only medium capable of covering a breaking news story or shooting a field documentary. In the 1970s, advances in transistor technology and smaller video image-sensing tubes made possible much smaller, portable video cameras. Use of film cameras for day-to-day TV station production ended once U-Matic videocassettes containing 3/4-inch tape became available for portable video recording.

Originally, ENG cameras and their companion video recorders came in two separate units. The videographer typically rested the camera on the right shoulder and carried the relatively heavy recorder by a strap slung over the left shoulder. After a busy day lugging this kind of weight around, even the strongest videographers were exhausted. By the late 1980s, advancing technology allowed the merging of cameras and recorders into single units called *camcorders*. These were smaller, lighter cameras with high-quality video recorders on board. They replaced bulky 3/4-inch U-Matic videocassettes with half-inch and smaller cassettes (see Figure 1-6).

Today's top ENG cameras produce pictures technically comparable to those made by the best studio cameras of the recent past. These cameras can use high-quality lenses, and their image-sensing devices (discussed in Chapter 2) provide excellent video performance.

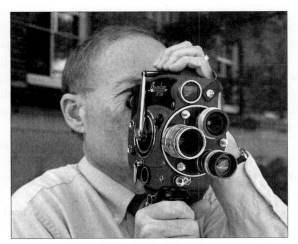

Figure 1-6. *Often spring-powered 16 mm film cameras with three lenses on a rotating turret were used for gathering TV news on location. Later more sophisticated, quieter 16 mm cameras, capable of recording synchronized sound right onto the film stock, were used. The use of film for news gathering was set aside after the development of small, relatively portable video cameras and recorders in the 1970s.*

Figure 1-7. *ENG photographers cheered the introduction of the camcorder. Compared to the heavy camera, the bulky, sometimes awkward connecting cable and the portable recorder slung over the opposite shoulder (right), the one-piece camcorder was a delight to operate and carry. Now, with smaller digital recording media, including discs and chips, top-quality camcorders can be even lighter and more compact.*

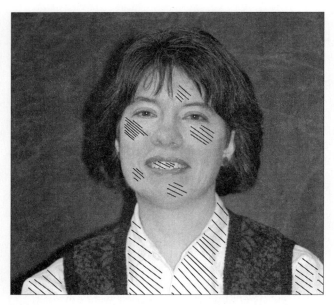

Figure 1-8. *This photo illustrates the appearance of a person seen through a viewfinder of a camera using an exposure indicator commonly called a "zebra." This is because of the diagonal lines or "zebra stripes" on portions of the image that exceed a certain pre-set brightness level. The zebra stripes appear only in the viewfinder to guide the operator in adjusting the camera for proper exposure, not in the image seen by viewers. Unlike this illustration, the "stripes" a camera operator sees actually appear to vibrate rather than remain static.*

- Possibly a *zebra pattern* (diagonal stripes) automatically imposed on the brightest areas within the viewfinder's picture (see Figure 1-8). This assists the camera operator in adjusting the amount of light the camera requires for proper exposure and the best possible picture. The zebra pattern and other in-viewfinder exposure indicators are discussed in depth in Tech Manual 1-3, found at the end of this chapter.

The number of displays continues to increase as portable camera technology tries to approximate the fine control capabilities of the studio camera. Thankfully, not all the displays operate simultaneously. Like the multiple displays provided by digital watches, operators may select individual displays as needed. Some indicators, such as end of tape, low light and low battery, appear automatically to warn the operator of a problem.

Adjusting the ENG Viewfinder   Camera operators principally use viewfinders to frame shots and compose visual elements within the frame. Viewfinders also may provide general information about image quality in terms of exposure, but only if the viewfinder is adjusted properly. Most viewfinders have controls allowing operators to adjust image brightness and contrast. Remember that these adjustments affect only the image in the viewfinder, not the video signal leaving the camera! Inexperienced operators typically adjust viewfinder brightness and contrast to suit their preferences, mistakenly assuming if the image looks properly exposed in the viewfinder that the video signal is also correct. Instead, the viewfinder's brightness and contrast should be set to most closely match the actual brightness and contrast of the video the camera has captured, so that the camera operator can better decide if any adjustments need to be made.

Proper viewfinder adjustment begins when you turn on the camera's internal *color bar generator.* Then you adjust the contrast control to render the bars most distinctly. Next, adjust the brightness control so that the darkest bar is about as dark as the edge of the viewfinder. With the brightness and contrast set using the color bars as a reference, the viewfinder provides a good relative indicator of the video being recorded or transmitted. The in-viewfinder exposure indicators discussed in Tech Manual 1-3 allow more precise monitoring of exposure and should be used for this purpose if your camera is so equipped.

ENG Power Supply

Most modern cameras operate on 12 volts DC, (direct current) and for ENG, one or more batteries supply this power. The battery may be housed inside the camera, but many are attached to the outside, or even in a battery belt strapped around the waist of the operator (see Figure 1-9). When it is practical, videographers power their cameras with an *AC adapter,* saving battery power. This adapter converts common household AC current to 12-volt DC power. The *power select switch* allows the camera operator to change the setting between AC and DC power. Some AC adapters are the size of a small shoe box, but many aren't much larger than the batteries they replace. Some are even designed to fit into a camera's battery compartment. Although AC adapters save on batteries, they limit your mobility to the length of the extension cord to the wall outlet.

ENG cameras can use several types of rechargeable batteries. The most popular type is one of the oldest, the *nickel-cadmium battery,* often called a nicad (or sometimes a NiCd). They are relatively inexpensive and recharge in a short time. Nicads can be charged more than 1,000 times if carefully maintained. But nicads are

1.

2.

Figure 1-9. *Shot 1 is an array of Anton Bauer batteries. These are all attached on the outside of various makes and models of ENG cameras and camcorders. Also pictured, under the second battery from the right, is a battery recharge unit. Shot 2 shows batteries for older, less expensive cameras. Batteries on the far left and right are inserted into the body of certain camcorders. Second from left is an externally mounted battery for an older ENG camera that requires a separate portable recorder. Third from the left is an AC adapter.*

Photo courtesy of the Anton Bauer Company.

a "use it or lose it" kind of battery, requiring frequent "exercising" (discharging and recharging) or they will gradually lose their ability to hold a full charge. Also, nicads are heavier than some other types of batteries. A relative of the nicad, the *nickel metal hydride* (NiMH) battery offers about 40 percent more power and doesn't require as much exercising as nicads, but can be recharged only about a third as many times before wearing out. The NiMH is about four times as expensive as a nicad, because of its power capacity. If size, weight and a relatively slow recharge rate are not critical factors, a *sealed lead acid* (SLA), or "gel cell," battery works well. Lead acid needs less exercising than either nicad or NiMH batteries, but can handle only half as many recharge cycles before exhaustion as nicad.

The *lithium ion* (Li-Ion) battery uses newer technology that puts a lot of energy into a small package. It has a recharge rate faster than SLA batteries but a little slower than nicad or NiMH types. A Li-Ion battery can be charged about the same number of times as a NiMH. Also, unlike other types, Li-Ion batteries hold their charge best in cold temperatures, an important factor in chilly climates. But Li-Ion batteries require built-in circuitry to protect the individual cells from abusive charging and discharging conditions. Li-Ion batteries are about six times more expensive than nicads.

Finally, the battery of the future: As Detroit experiments with ways to make the use of hydrogen cells to power automobiles more practical, a television-production application for hydrogen may be about to arrive. A new generation of power cells capable of

powering an ENG camera for over 100 hours could soon be in use in the industry. Such a cell could liberate the camera battery from spending hours on a recharger. When a hydrogen battery is discharged, one would fill it up again from a standard commercial hydrogen cylinder, which, in turn, could be replenished in the same way that your gas barbecue's propane tank is refilled at a local hardware store.

Battery Belts   A *battery belt* is a device containing several batteries connected together to provide enhanced power capacity. Although 12-volt battery belts may be used with cameras, they most often provide power for power-hungry, portable, camera-mounted lights. Most battery belts have built-in chargers, allowing recharging by simply plugging them into a common 115-volt wall AC outlet for 4 to 12 hours (see Figures 1-10 and 1-11).

Battery failure in the field is common, and professionals are careful to check that their batteries are fully charged before leaving on an ENG shoot. Most carry one or more fully charged spares as additional insurance against catastrophe. Make it your rule to take twice as many hours of battery power with you than you think you could possibly use.

ENG Camera Controls

All operating controls are built into the ENG camera head. The increasing use of microprocessors handling many camera functions has reduced the number of controls an operator must manipulate to record acceptable

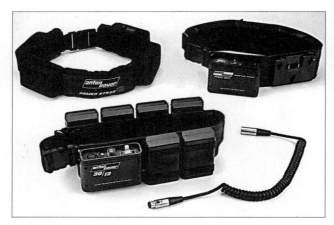

Figure 1-10. *These battery belts, worn around the waist or slung over the legs of a camera tripod, provide power to cameras, portable recorders or the small DC-powered lights that are often attached to the top of ENG cameras.*

Photo courtesy of the Anton Bauer Company.

video. But unlike consumer camcorders where simple, automatic operation is most important, professional cameras provide many controls the operator may wish to use to achieve a particular creative effect or deal with an unusual situation. Because the controls on modern ENG cameras vary greatly depending on the manufacturer and model, we suggest you consult the operator's manual for

Figure 1-11. *An example of an ENG camera light discussed in Figure 1-10's caption.*

Photo courtesy of the Anton Bauer Company.

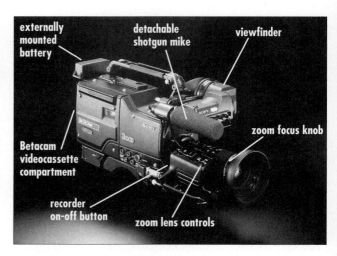

Figure 1-12. *A Sony BetacamSP® camcorder.*

Photo courtesy of Sony Corp.

your particular camera for a description of its controls and their operation. Figure 1-12 explains the controls for one popular ENG camera used by professionals.

ENG Camera Setup

One of the modern ENG camera's endearing features is that it automatically does so many things that previously required the services of a video technician. But most ENG cameras still need some simple initial setup involving *white balancing* and, in some instances, *black balancing.*

White balancing is a procedure that must be repeated frequently during an ENG or EFP production, because scenes recorded in the field may be illuminated by different color light. A blue jacket under a red light will not look the same when illuminated by a yellow light. The human eye and brain automatically adjust our sense of color so the jacket is perceived as blue in each case, but cameras must be "told" to render each scene as if it were illuminated by a pure white light even when it isn't. Failure to tell the camera what kind of light it's looking at can result in green or purple faces and yellow casts throughout. Exact procedures vary depending on the camera, but Tech Manual 1-1, found at the end of this chapter, explains white balancing in fundamental terms.

Black balance adjusts the camera's black sensitivity to a preset, standard level. Most ENG cameras feature completely automatic black balance controls. If not, the operator may have to put the lens cap on the camera and press a black balance switch. Minor errors in black balance are not as apparent as are white balance mistakes. Unlike the need to constantly check white balance, there is no need to perform a black balance each time the camera is moved to a new location or the illumination of the scene changes.

The Studio Camera

Studio cameras produce the finest, sharpest pictures available using existing technology. While ENG cameras are designed to operate in stand-alone configuration, studio cameras are designed for use cooperatively by more than one individual. During a typical studio production, the camera operator focuses exclusively on aesthetic concerns while a video technician at the CCU closely monitors and adjusts the camera's technical performance. Additionally, studio cameras use carefully counterbalanced mounting pedestals and other devices to provide smooth, jitter-free movement. The studio camera's zoom and focus controls are located on handles attached to the mounts, allowing operators to adjust these controls from behind the camera while watching the image in the camera's viewfinder. Studio cameras often share space on camera pedestals with *teleprompters* (prompter) and other accessories. Figure 1-13 shows both large and small studio-configured cameras with teleprompters.

Studio cameras typically have design features that make production easier or more efficient within the studio environment, such as a *call button* to silently signal the CCU technician that the operator needs assistance.

The Studio Camera Viewfinder

Modern studio camera viewfinders are attached externally to the camera, allowing them to tilt to accommodate operators of different heights and, if necessary, to rotate 360 degrees. This feature is especially helpful to technicians doing camera maintenance. Viewfinders on the very largest studio cameras can be as large as seven inches, providing a sharp image viewable at a distance of several feet. Studio cameras also usually have a *return video* button, which an operator can push to view either the program video or a shot from another camera. This is helpful when trying to compose a *split-screen* shot, which contains picture information from two video sources. Also, when a camera is operated in a remote field production, return video fed from the station to the remote truck and then on to the camera's return video is one way to cue the camera operator that the shot is now on the air (see Figure 1-14).

While viewfinder indicators designed for portable cameras provide mostly technical information regarding camera functions, those used on studio cameras assist the camera operator in composing shots aesthetically (see Figure 1-15). The usual indicators in a studio camera viewfinder include the following:

- The *zoom indicator*: tells the operator how far the lens is zoomed in or out
- The *center screen marker*: a small cross indicating the exact center of the screen

1.   2.

Figure 1-13. *Shot 1, left, is a large studio camera on a heavy pedestal with a teleprompter. The prompter, as they are sometimes called, consists of a monitor mounted either above or below a specially designed, slanted mirror. This mirror, made of partially-silvered glass, reflects what's on the face of the monitor, allowing talent to read the script while appearing to gaze directly into the camera's lens. The lens, focused farther out on the talent, can't see the script scrolling down. Shot 2, right, features a crewperson operating a much smaller studio/EFP camera on a heavy pedestal.*

1.

2.

3.

Figure 1-14. *This series demonstrates the components of a typical box shot, a composite of two shots, in which a newscaster is typically shown on one side of the screen, and a boxed graphic of some kind is electronically inserted over the picture on the other side of the screen. In shot 1, talent is positioned slightly left in the camera viewfinder to allow room for insertion of a graphic on the right side of the frame. In shot 2, the video, an electronically created graphic that has been digitally squeezed from a full frame to its present size, is positioned camera right. In shot 3, we see the original camera shot with the graphic image inserted to form the box composite that would be seen by viewers.*

- The *box cursor*: an adjustable box superimposed on a point on the screen, used for setting up the camera portion of a newscast box shot
- The essential area, also known as the *safe title area*: indicates how tight a shot of a *graphic card* (a poster card with lettering, a photo or other graphic material) can be framed so that none of the important information will be lost during recording and transmission

Video cameras are designed with a variety of viewfinder indicators. Always check the manual provided by the manufacturer to learn about the indicators found on your camera's viewfinder.

Studio camera operators must be careful to shield the viewfinder from external light that can wash out the image entirely. This is seldom a problem with portable cameras employing eye-piece viewfinders, but it can be extremely distracting when using studio cameras with their larger viewfinders or portable cameras configured for EFP. Viewfinders designed for studio and EFP applications usually have hoods to block light from hitting the screen. Sometimes it is necessary to tape an improvised extension (often a piece of cardboard) to the hood to eliminate the problem. This technique can also be used in field productions in which glare makes viewfinders hard to see. Studio camera operators are free to adjust the viewfinder brightness and contrast controls to suit their personal preferences, since camera exposure is controlled by a technician at the CCU.

While discussing viewfinder adjustments, we should mention that monitors located on the studio floor also require proper adjustment. Production personnel seem to bounce portable studio monitors around mercilessly,

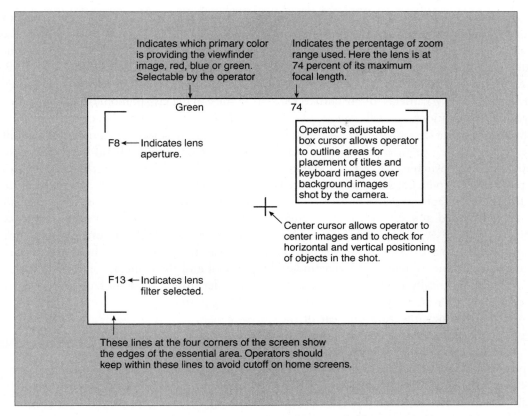

Indicates which primary color is providing the viewfinder image, red, blue or green. Selectable by the operator

Indicates the percentage of zoom range used. Here the lens is at 74 percent of its maximum focal length.

Green   74

F8 ← Indicates lens aperture.

Operator's adjustable box cursor allows operator to outline areas for placement of titles and keyboard images over background images shot by the camera.

Center cursor allows operator to center images and to check for horizontal and vertical positioning of objects in the shot.

F13 ← Indicates lens filter selected.

These lines at the four corners of the screen show the edges of the essential area. Operators should keep within these lines to avoid cutoff on home screens.

Figure 1-15. *A studio camera viewfinder display. The indicators are typical of those provided by a studio camera to help the operator compose shots and monitor camera operations. Different brands and models provide different indicators, many of them selectable or adjustable by the camera operator as needed during production.*

jarring internal adjustments. These monitors are often the most-poorly maintained and least-carefully calibrated pieces of gear in the entire production facility. Various crew members may also adjust the monitor's controls to suit their individual preferences, often without reference to a standard test signal. Additionally, light falling on the face of the studio monitor introduces errors. Using a portable studio monitor on the production floor to judge the picture quality delivered by your camera is a poor practice. Subjective aesthetic judgments regarding picture quality should be made while viewing a properly adjusted monitor in a room with indirect lighting.

Studio Camera Setup

Setting up studio cameras was once an almost mystic ritual performed exclusively by video technicians. Early studio cameras required adjustment of many individual circuits in an exact sequence before production began to ensure top-quality video. These cameras often required constant manual tweaking during production, because the setup adjustments drifted as electrical components changed temperature. Today technicians still perform setups for studio productions, but modern technology makes setup much less complicated. Initial setup by a technician usually involves use of a *waveform monitor* (WFM), covered in Tech Manual 1-2, found at the end of this chapter, and a vectorscope, discussed in Chapter 9. During production, the technician typically makes small adjustments based on subjective judgments about picture quality while watching the show on a high-resolution video monitor, while keeping an eye on the waveform monitor.

Although today's cameras are more stable and use microprocessors to automatically compensate for drift, the best pictures often result from subtle adjustments made by a technician with a "good eye."

The EFP Camera

Depending on the application, the demands on a camera used for EFP have much in common with both ENG and studio productions. EFP often involves multiple cameras connected to a video switcher and associated production equipment to produce studio-style productions outside the studio. A network football EFP may feature 7 to 12 to as many as 36 studio cameras (for a Super Bowl, for example) fitted with special lenses feeding pictures to a control center housed in two or more huge trailers. Specially configured ENG cameras often suffice for smaller-budget EFP applications. A small cable television EFP, for example, might feature two or three inexpensive ENG/EFP cameras feeding pictures into a small van equipped with basic video switching, recording and transmitting equipment. EFP productions may be transmitted live or recorded as live-on-tape programs, or each camera can be separately recorded and the video later edited extensively before airing.

The major configuration differences between EFP and ENG involve the cameras' lenses and viewfinders (see Figure 1-16). EFP typically requires better-quality lenses and externally mounted, studio-style, 5-inch viewfinders that permit viewing from the rear of the camera. Like a studio production, most EFP applications require cameras mounted on tripods, with zoom and focus operated by controls attached to the tripod's panhandles extending behind the camera. Not all EFP involves multiple cameras. A common single-camera EFP is a "live shot" during newscasts. In this situation, a single camera connects directly to a video truck that transmits the camera's live picture back to the station via a microwave hookup. Both single- and multiple-camera EFP productions usually require intercom headsets allowing camera operators to hear commands from the director.

A *remote control unit* (RCU), very similar to a CCU, is a redundant set of controls that duplicate those found on the camera. An RCU typically controls the ENG/EFP camera's technical functions during an EFP production. Just as during a studio production, assigning a technician in the van the task of monitoring and controlling camera functions frees operators to concentrate on the aesthetics and physical aspects of camera work. Multiple-camera EFPs may include hand-held cameras to provide increased mobility. The technical camera functions of handheld cameras may be controlled automatically by on-board microprocessors, or the cameras may be connected by cable to RCUs in the remote van, where an engineer controls them during production. Automatic control is appropriate when maximum mobility is needed and the camera is equipped with an on-board recorder storing shots on tape or disc for later insertion during postproduction editing.

Cameras for Digital TV Production

Digital processors began appearing in cameras 20 years ago, but these processors only helped improve the analog video signal. At this writing, the American broadcast industry is completing a conversion to digitally encoded signal transmission. This transition has its roots in three decades of efforts to develop a better quality TV image. TV's future is now in digital and *high-definition television* (HDTV). HDTV features a sharper picture and an *aspect ratio* (the width of an image relative to its height) of 16:9, compared to traditional TV's

1.

2.

Figure 1-16. *Shot 1 is a camera configured with an eyepiece viewfinder for ENG. To the right, in shot 2, is the same camera, configured for studio use or for EFP. The ENG eyepiece viewfinder has been replaced with a studio model.*

standard-definition 4:3 aspect ratio. Currently some TV is transmitted in digital form but is not up to HDTV quality. To the eye, it doesn't look much different than traditional TV, its aspect ratio is 4:3, but it's digitally encoded and decoded. In Chapter 2, there will be additional discussion of HDTV. Chapter 4, "Fundamentals of Composition," explains in more detail how to use TV's aspect ratio.

Many years ago, anticipating a time when TV and home video would change over to a wide-screen format, major motion picture and TV series producers used both DCC and wide-screen feature film cameras to capture wide-screen images. Initially recording TV series and motion picture footage in a wide-screen format permitted producers to create a more valuable, lasting product and to more easily create elaborate digital video effects. When movie producers used DCC to create release prints for theaters, a laser-transfer process, which converts digital images back from video to film for distribution, was used. This method saves much time and money, especially when creating visual effects, and the final footage looks virtually indistinguishable from what might have been shot originally on 35 mm film. Eventually, motion picture projection at neighborhood theaters will be done with digital video, and the 35 mm theater film projector, like the silent movie projector before it, will be relegated to a glass case in a movie museum.

The Future of TV Cameras

As technology advances, differences among television cameras in terms of their electrical and image-producing characteristics will be less apparent. Advances in electronic technology permit ever smaller, lighter and less costly equipment to produce quality pictures, blurring the distinctions between all classes and use categories of television cameras.

It is likely, however, that cameras designed principally for studio production will continue to be somewhat larger and heavier than those intended for ENG and EFP, but not because the studio camera requires a larger box to produce superior pictures. Rather, a heavier, larger studio camera provides more smoothness for panning, tilting and movement, plus it balances better on a camera pedestal when it's equipped with bulky teleprompting devices. If anything is clear, it is that all cameras will continue to shrink. On the other hand, although there have been huge reductions in the size of high-quality television cameras in the last two decades, there is only so much optical engineers can do to

shrink a lens before beginning to compromise either functionality or quality, or both.

Although less easy to predict, the transition to digital TV transmission probably will have a more dramatic effect on the broadcast industry than did conversion to color during the mid-1950s to 1960s. The wider screen and greater sharpness provided by high-definition television are factors video producers must consider increasingly as the conversion moves forward.

Camera Care and Basic Maintenance

We conclude this chapter on the color camera by touching on some basic points applicable to all types of cameras. In a quickly evolving field such as television production, basic camera care remains a constant concern and responsibility.

Technicians say more than half the problems they encounter with electronic equipment involve cables and connectors. Experienced videographers know cables and connectors are the weakest links in any system, meriting special consideration and care. Cameras used for ENG and EFP receive the greatest abuse because they are used in harsh environments, but studio cameras also require attention to avoid damage to their cables through carelessness. Although seldom appreciated, one of the camcorder's greatest advantages is the improved reliability resulting from elimination of external cables required to link the camera and recorder.

Major cable-damage can occur as a result of the following errors:

- Pulling on the cables rather than grasping the connector body itself, which can cause serious damage because most connectors are of the locking variety
- Forcing a plug into its receptacle, because most plugs and receptacles are keyed so that they work only when lined up properly
- Pinching the cables, either by closing doors on them or by stepping on them

There is seldom any need for an operator to disconnect the cable from a studio camera. Care must be exercised, however, not to strain the cable or its connector by stepping on it, pulling the camera by its cable or catching the cable on studio sets or props.

On either an outboard recorder or a camcorder, an audio cable is used to connect any external microphones. Although consumer camcorders typically feature a mike of doubtful quality permanently attached

Figure 1-17. *A directional mike is often attached externally to the ENG camera head to record the voices of interviewees or to collect ambient sound.*

Figure 1-18. *A handheld mike close to the interviewee almost always provides better audio quality than a camera-mounted microphone. A clip-on mike attached to the interviewee's clothing often provides even better audio quality than a handheld mike but may not be practical for fast-paced ENG shooting.*

to the camera body, using a higher quality external mike is almost always preferable. Professional ENG cameras have a clamp or accessory shoe on the camera permitting attachment of a high-quality external mike (see Figures 1-17 and 1-18).

Technicians cringe when they find nontechnical production personnel tinkering with cameras, and veterans in the production industry agree that most maintenance is best left to the organization's technical staff. However, there are certain things users can do to keep the camera operating at maximum efficiency. Keeping the lens clean when working under field conditions is difficult; Tech Manual 1-4, found at the end of this chapter, introduces a few techniques (and precautions) associated with this

chore. But we urge you to check with a technician to see what user maintenance is permitted, if any, and then attempt only procedures you know you can perform properly.

In the next chapter, we will introduce the rest of the TV camera: the lens and the imaging system.

tech manual 1-1   *White Balance*

To perform a white balance, a camera operator first selects the correct filter from the camera's filter wheel (see Figure 1-19). Some filter wheels are coded for daylight, fluorescent light or *quartz light* (the kind of white light produced by many portable TV and film lighting instruments). Others are coded with numbers corresponding to the *color temperature* of the dominant light source in a scene, such as 3,200 degrees, or 5,600 degrees. Color temperature is a light source's relative position along the spectrum of visible light, measured in degrees on the Kelvin scale (this will be discussed further in Chapter 5, "Lighting"). With the correct filter selected, the operator zooms in on a white object in the scene until the white

object either fills the viewfinder, or, in some cameras, the center of the screen. Then the operator presses the automatic white balance switch. Circuits within the camera adjust the image so the white object looks white, even if it is illuminated by a light with a blue or orange tint. The camera balances the colors by electronically removing any color imparted to objects in the scene by the source of illumination. White balancing would not be necessary if pure white light illuminated every scene. A display tells the operator if white balance was achieved. You must white balance each time you move to a new location, or if there is a change in the light source illuminating the scene you're shooting. Sometimes, when shooting outside, it's

1.

2.

Figure 1-19. *In shot 1, an assistant holds a white card at sufficient distance in front of the camera lens so that the white card will reflect the color temperature of light that will reflect off the subject to be photographed. In shot 2, with camera focused on the white card, the videographer depresses the automatic white balance button.*

necessary to repeat the white balance because the sun goes behind a cloud, which would cause a change in color temperature. The color of sunlight also changes quickly and significantly in the late afternoon. It's a good idea to white balance often during this time of day. Also, some cameras don't have the memory to hold white balance accurately if their power sources are temporarily disconnected. It's a good idea to white balance after restoring power to most cameras.

Many sophisticated professional cameras have *scene store circuits* that hold camera operating settings in memory for several particular shooting locations. Once settings for a given location are determined and stored, they can be instantly recalled later. This means that you don't have to perform a white balance each time you set up the camera in this location; you need only select the proper filter. It is assumed, of course, that the lighting has not changed since the settings were last stored in memory. If it has, your stored scene settings are useless, and you must perform another white balance and store the new operating parameters.

tech manual **1-2** *The Waveform Monitor*

The waveform monitor (WFM) is a vertically, rather than horizontally, oriented meter used essentially to measure the brightness, known as the *luminance*, of the picture. The WFM takes electrical signals making up the video image produced by the camera and converts them into waves visible on a vertical scale from 0 to 100. Figure 1-20 shows a typical studio shot as it looks on a picture monitor and as the same image appears on a WFM. Set for the usual display, a WFM shows both an odd and an even *field* of video for each *frame*. (A frame is a single, complete video picture.) Later you'll learn more about fields and frames, but for now, suffice it to say that two fields make up a full frame of interlaced analog video, and

cameras shoot 30 frames—60 fields—per second. WFMs tell us mostly about the luminance of the image. Concerning color, it indicates if *chrominance* (the part of a video signal conveying information related to an image's color) values are present, but not much more. Converting color information into a form that can be objectively evaluated is the job of the vectorscope (see Chapter 9 for more detail about this). Both waveform monitors and vectorscopes are found in control rooms, or can be powered by AC or batteries for use in EFP work.

The WFM shows you the relative brightness of objects in the picture and displays information about the video signal in a number of ways, depending on the settings of

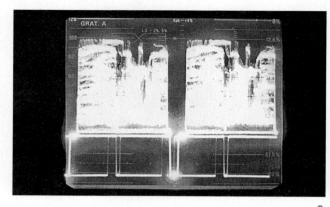

1.

2.

Figure 1-20. *Shot 1 is a frame of a newscaster. Shot 2 is what shot 1 looks like on a typical waveform monitor's two-field display. Looking at just the field on the right, the lightest areas, such as the news desk, rise to the top of the display (100 IRE unit mark), while the darker areas of the picture, such as the newscaster's jacket, show up much lower on the scale—almost down to black (the 7.5 IRE unit mark).*

its controls. During camera setup, the technician blocks all light passing through the lens and adjusts the camera's video output to register 7.5 on the WFM's brightness intensity scale. The WFM's scale is divided into video units as defined by the Institute of Radio Engineers (IRE). So 7.5 IRE units of video is defined as "TV black," the darkest image broadcast. The lens is uncovered and its iris set to a pre-scribed opening. A chart with known reflectance levels is placed before the lens and illuminated to a standard level of intensity. The camera's video controls are adjusted so the object on the chart representing "TV white" produces 100 IRE units of video as indicated on the WFM. The camera is now adjusted to standard values of video representing TV white and TV black (see Figure 1-20).

tech manual **1-3** *Camera Exposure*

Exposure Indicators

It is important to have read Tech Manual 1-2 explaining the WFM before continuing on to this section, because terms introduced there are used in this exhibit.

The human eye accommodates a wide range of light intensities, from a bright beach to a dim bedroom, adjusting as necessary to provide a usable image. Consumer camcorders also adjust exposure (the amount of light reaching the imaging device) automatically and provide amazingly good pictures regardless of the light intensity illuminating the scene. Consumer camcorders usually flash a "low light" message in the viewfinder when there is insufficient light, warning the operator to stop recording. Unless the camera flashes this warning, the operator can forget about exposure and concentrate on shot composition. Professional cameras can adjust exposure automatically, but many operators prefer adjusting exposure manually to achieve a more aesthetic result or to deal with difficult situations in which an automated response could create an undesirable effect. Proper exposure is essential to technically good picture quality. So it is wise to read about your camera's exposure indicators in the operator's manual and experiment with the camera before using it for a critical production.

Operators adjusting exposure manually need a reference point they can use quickly. The human face is frequently the most important feature in a shot, so manufacturers have devised circuits that provide a visual indication in the viewfinder when the exposure is correct for Caucasian flesh tones. One indicator, the "zebra," uses diagonal stripes to signal exposure levels. To use this indicator, the operator frames the talent's face in the view-finder, then adjusts exposure (by opening or closing the iris in the camera lens (see Chapter 2) until faint "zebra stripes" appear on the brightest part of the person's face. Although other parts of the image may be under or overexposed, the face should usually be properly exposed. This is because the face is most often the focus of attention in any shot in which a person appears. Not all shots include a human face and not all human faces are Caucasian. In most cases, however, a reasonable exposure results if the camera is adjusted so faint zebra stripes (or another obvious visual anomaly designed by the manufacturer) begin appearing on the principal focal point within the shot.

From the factory, most zebra circuits come set to produce stripes on any object generating about 78 IRE or more. Technicians can adjust the zebra circuit so the pattern appears at almost any brightness level desired. Many videographers prefer to set the circuit as a peak white (100 IRE) indicator. When set at 100 IRE, anything with zebra stripes is reaching the level where image detail is lost through overexposure (see Figure 1-21). Overexposed video is often referred to as "too hot."

A zebra pattern isn't the only type of viewfinder exposure indicator. Some camera viewfinders use a white bar indicator. Light entering the camera causes a white bar to move vertically up the left side of the viewfinder image. The moving bar acts as a pointer for a scale just to the left of the bar. The scale is marked to indicate peak white level.

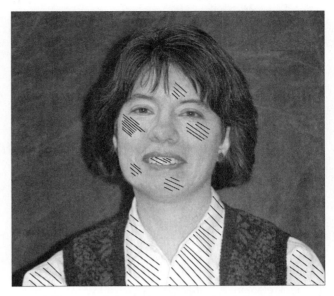

Figure 1-21. *A viewfinder display of a camera with the zebra exposure indicator set for 78 IRE. All portions of the image registering more than 78 IRE are painted with zebra stripes.*

Another type of exposure indicator looks like a waveform display superimposed over the viewfinder image. There's a mark at the top of the viewfinder that represents peak white (100 IRE). If any part of the superimposed waveform extends beyond this reference mark, the exposure must be reduced or white clipping and loss of detail may result (see Figure 1-22).

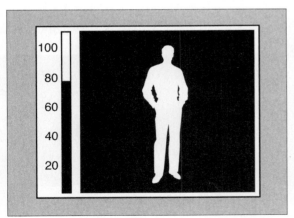

1.

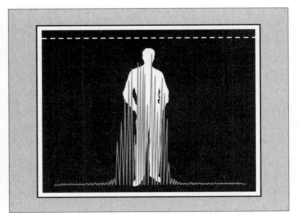

2.

Figure 1-22. *Drawing 1 shows a viewfinder exposure indicator using a moving bar next to a scale showing IRE units. The bar indicates the brightest value in the image. If the bar exceeds 100, this is an indication of overexposure and calls for using a smaller lens aperture, less light on the scene or removal of the excessively reflective object in the shot. In drawing 2, this viewfinder exposure indicator uses a superimposed WFM display over the shot. If any part of the superimposed waveform extends above the dotted line at the top, this indicates overexposure. An advantage of this indicator is that it shows both overexposure and the excessively bright areas in the image causing the overexposure.*

Unlike the zebra pattern, which appears only when a certain level of video is present, these last two indicators must be left on all the time if they're to be useful. Such displays can be a distraction if you're attempting to concentrate on composing the shot, especially if you aren't accustomed to working with them. It's important to remember that exposure indicators are helpful, but they can't think and make creative decisions. Humans must do that.

tech manual 1-4   *Lens Maintenance*

Although we discuss lenses in depth in the next chapter, we have included some lens maintenance tips here. Most TV camera lenses detach from the camera body, and technicians periodically remove them to clean the back element (the small end). This is important because dirt on the back element is sometimes visible in the picture, even when dust on the front surface of the lens isn't. Fortunately, the rear of the lens is enclosed and needs cleaning infrequently, but the front surface takes a constant beating. We suggest cleaning the front lens element before and sometimes during each shoot. If you're shooting outside, check for lens cleanliness frequently, especially when shooting in rain, snow or wind or in a dusty environment. Keeping the lens capped while the camera is in storage or being transported and during extended periods between takes reduces the need for cleaning.

There are three ways to clean your lens safely. The most benign is to use canned air; the second is to use a soft camel's hair brush; the third, and surprisingly the most dangerous to a lens, is the use of Kodak lens cleaning paper (see Figure 1-23). A good camera store stocks all these supplies. Canned air is just that: compressed air in a can. Aiming the can's nozzle at the lens and pressing the button or lever releases a stream of air that safely dislodges and blows away dirt while nothing else touches the surface of the lens. Canned air is handy in dusty environments such as the desert, fairgrounds and rodeos. Be sure you use canned air designed for cleaning delicate equipment, not just any available source of compressed air. Many production facilities use a compressed air system for filling pneumatic camera mounts, powering tools and spraying paint in the scenery shop. These systems operate at high pressures, which may damage a lens or blow air contaminated with dirt or moisture. Since canned air removes only debris that isn't tightly stuck to the lens, a brush may work if the dirt resists air pressure. A clean camel's hair brush won't damage a lens if used carefully, but a dirty brush only compounds the problem. Store your brush where it won't pick up dirt—such as in a Ziploc sandwich bag.

Neither canned air nor a brush will help if a lens is splattered with rain or mud or—heaven forbid—touched by an oily finger tip! Remember, the driest finger tip still imparts oil to hard, smooth surfaces. Kodak makes a lens paper that's relatively safe for cameras, but don't use paper designed to clean eyeglasses. Most are too rough and may scratch the ultra thin coating on your camera's lens. Even lens cleaning papers designed for professional applications may cause scratches if used improperly. Avoid rubbing too hard, and be sure you use only clean lens paper. Lens paper should be left in its protective container until used. Don't try to reuse lens paper: It picks up dirt with use, and the chemicals on the paper evaporate when exposed to air. There are lens cleaning fluids on the market, but we recommend their use only by technicians.

Many ENG and EFP videographers routinely protect their expensive lenses with an *ultraviolet (UV) filter*. Video cameras are more sensitive to ultraviolet light than our eyes, so unfiltered exterior long shots and aerial scenes reproduce more haze than we see with the naked eye. An inexpensive UV filter simultaneously filters haze and protects expensive lens glass. Adding a high-quality UV filter has

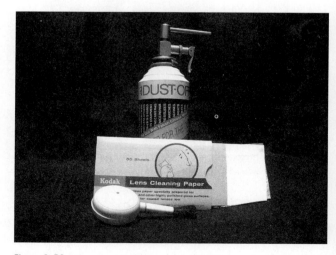

Figure 1-23. *Three products you can use for lens maintenance (from left): camel's hair brush with squeeze bulb, canned air and lens cleaning paper.*

negligible effect on lens performance and may prevent serious damage to the lens surface. The UV filter must, of course, be cleaned on both sides, using the lens cleaning techniques described earlier. Carrying a spare UV filter in a dust-free container on an ENG or EFP allows rapid replacement of one that becomes dirty or damaged.

Important Vocabulary Terms

AC adapter: A device to transform AC power (house current) into DC (battery type) power to operate cameras, portable recorders and lights.

Analog signal: A signal, whether it's carrying audio or video, that is made up of continually varying voltages that imitate, as best it can, the original sound or picture. Analog is an audio or video "analogy" of the original.

Aspect ratio: The width of an image relative to its height. Traditional standard-definition TV and digital, non-high definition video employ a 4:3 aspect ratio, while HDTV uses a 16:9 aspect ratio.

Battery belt: A heavy belt containing several batteries wired in tandem, worn by an ENG camera operator. It is used to provide DC power to cameras and other equipment.

Black balancing: Adjusting a camera to "TV black," 7.5 IRE, the standard broadcast black reference.

Box cursor: An adjustable box superimposed on a point on the screen, used for setting up the camera portion of a newscast's box shot.

Box shot: A term for a composite of two shots, in which a newscaster is typically shown on one side of the screen and a box graphic of some kind is electronically inserted over the picture on the other side of the screen.

Broadcast quality: A term to describe video signal that meets FCC standards for television transmission.

Call button: A studio camera accessory allowing a camera operator to wordlessly signal the technician shading, or adjusting, cameras that his/her camera needs attention.

Camcorder: A camera and videotape recorder in one unit.

Camera control unit (CCU): Rather than mounted on the camera head, CCUs are external controls for making adjustments to studio cameras. In studio productions, the CCU is located in the studio's master control room.

Center screen marker: A small cross in the exact center of the camera viewfinder screen.

Chrominance: The part of a video signal conveying information related to colors in the image.

Code: The analog or digital method used to electronically capture video and audio for storage and eventual playback. See also "decode."

Color bar generator: This circuit provides camera operators with a standard reference signal for use in properly adjusting the viewfinder during shooting, and television monitors and vectorscopes during editing.

Color temperature: A light source's relative position along the spectrum of visible light, measured in degrees on the Kelvin scale. This concept is discussed fully in Chapter 5.

Decode: The ability to electronically convert and play back coded information as video or audio.

Digital cinematography cameras (DCC): High-definition cameras used in some feature film productions in place of traditional 35 mm film cameras.

Digital signal: A signal composed of a series of numbers that define the discrete values of an analog waveform. The numbers used are based on a binary (two-digit) numbering system using only the digits zero and one. If we say that an analog signal attempts to "imitate" the visual and audio input, a digital signal "describes" it; it is also less susceptible to the effects of electrical interference.

Electronic field production (EFP): Television production—including recording, switching and editing—that can take place outside of the studio. Common applications include awards shows, sporting events, concerts, live news remotes, etc.

Electronic news gathering (ENG): A system of news reporting that involves the use of portable TV cameras to record video and sound, and often the transmission of a signal to the TV station for immediate broadcast.

Federal Communications Commission (FCC): A government agency charged with regulating telecommunications and, in the context of this chapter, with setting technical standards for the quality of all radio frequency transmissions in the U.S.

Field: One half of a frame of interlaced video.

Frame: A single video picture. In the 525-line system currently being replaced by digital television, a frame consists of two video fields, one containing all the even-numbered scan lines, and the other containing all the odd-numbered scan lines.

Graphic card: A poster with lettering, a photo or other graphic material.

High-definition television (HDTV): A generic term referring to television images with approximately twice the resolution of "traditional" television.

High resolution: Term used to describe video images, or the devices used to record them, that are characterized by finer detail than standard images.

Hydrogen battery: In this battery, hydrogen cells combine with oxygen to create electricity, representing a new application of the kind of power-storage technology car manufacturers are trying to adapt for automobiles.

Lead acid battery: See "sealed lead acid battery."

Liquid crystal display (LCD): A flat-screen TV monitor that sandwiches liquid crystals between two thin plates of glass. An electric field, applied to these crystal molecules, is patterned to create images.

Lithium ion (Li-Ion) battery: A newer ENG camera battery with a recharge rate faster than lead acid but marginally slower than nicad or NiMH batteries. Good for use in cold conditions.

Luminance: That part of a video signal conveying information related to the brightness levels of the image.

Nickel-cadmium (NiCd, or nicad) battery: Popular camera battery requiring frequent discharge–recharge "exercising."

Nickel metal hydride (NiMH) battery: A relative of the nicad, the NiMH has 40 percent more storage power and doesn't require as much "exercising" as its cousin.

Power select switch: A control to determine whether a camera is run on battery or by some other external power supply.

Prompter: A shortened version of the term "teleprompter." See below.

Quartz light: The variety of artificial light produced by many portable TV and film lighting instruments.

Remote control unit (RCU): Similar in function to a CCU, the RCU contains the controls to make adjustments to the camera but is designed for ENG and EFP cameras. All RCU controls are duplicated on the ENG/EFP camera, but not all studio camera CCU controls can be adjusted on the camera.

Return video: One of the camera's capabilities, this allows the camera operator to view not only the image upon which the camera is focused but also VTR (videotape recorder) playback or other video sources.

Safe title area: A viewfinder indicator that shows how tight a shot of a graphic card can be framed so that none of the card's important information is lost during recording and transmission.

Scene store circuits: These camera memory devices hold camera operating parameters in memory for several particular shooting locations.

Sealed lead acid (SLA) battery: Also called a "gel cell," this battery can be used to power ENG cameras. It requires less "exercising" than either the nicad or the NiMH varieties but recharges only half as many times before exhaustion.

Shading: Adjusting camera controls to attain the best picture possible. This is done with the CCU (for studio cameras) or the RCU (for ENG/EFP cameras).

Split screen: An image containing picture information from more than one video source.

Teleprompter: A device mounted on the front of a camera that allows talent to read copy while giving viewers the impression of looking directly into the camera.

Ultraviolet (UV) filter: A frequently used lens filter that sharpens colors on overcast days and protects the lens from accidental damage.

Videography: Motion picture photography using a video camera.

VTR: An abbreviation for videotape recorder.

Waveform: An electronic representation of a video or an audio signal.

Waveform monitor (WFM): A vertically oriented meter used essentially to measure the luminance, or brightness, of the picture.

White balancing: Adjusting a camera to compensate for the "color" of the light used to illuminate a given scene.

Zoom indicator: This device tells the camera operator how far the lens is zoomed in or out.

Zebra pattern: Diagonal stripes superimposed on a camera viewfinder's image to identify those portions of the scene exceeding a predetermined level of brightness.

chapter **2**

Camera Lenses and Imaging Systems

Chapter 1 introduced you to a variety of television cameras. This chapter discusses the vital components and essential processes performed by the color camera to capture and transmit images (see Figure 2-1). Our discussion focuses on the following elements:

1. the camera lens,
2. the internal optical system,
3. electronic imaging devices,
4. video processing, and
5. signal encoding.

The Camera Lens

A lens captures light reflecting off a scene and transmits it onto a light-sensitive surface (a tube or chip) in the camera. In traditional motion picture and still photography, the light-sensitive surface is photographic film that captures the image chemically. In the television camera, the light-sensitive surface is the face of either a solid-state or older tube-type *imaging device,* which converts light energy into electrical energy. Before discussing lenses as they specifically apply to television cameras, it's important to understand some fundamentals of lenses: 1) focal length, 2) aperture and 3) depth of field.

Focal Length

Focal length is the distance, measured in millimeters, from the optical center of the lens to the face of the camera's imaging device, when the lens is focused on infinity. Unfortunately, this longstanding definition of focal length is also long on technical jargon and short on meaning. For most of us, it's enough to

remember that focal length determines how wide or narrow a field of view the lens provides. The shorter the focal length, the wider the field of view; the longer the focal length, the narrower (or more close-up) the field of view. Television professionals use different focal length lenses to achieve various creative objectives. For example, a director might use a *short focal length lens* (10 mm) to provide a wide-angle view of a news set in a TV studio. In contrast, a *long focal length lens* (120 mm) provides a narrower, close-up view of a plane landing on a distant runway. Falling in between short and long is a *normal lens.* A normal lens approximates the field of view of normal human vision and is the standard to which short and long lenses are compared (see Figure 2-2).

Effects of Lens Focal Length   Focal length has additional effects on the image other than determining field of view. Extremely short focal length lenses, sometimes called *fisheye lenses,* severely distort images around their edges. An example is the view you see when looking through a lens built into a hotel room door—the kind that allows occupants to see who's knocking. This is an extreme example of the kind of distortion very short focal length lenses could add to a television picture. Short focal length lenses also give the picture an unrealistic sense of depth. They distort depth much like the side-view mirrors on automobiles. Remember the warning to drivers on those mirrors that "objects are closer than they appear"?

Long focal length lenses, in contrast, exhibit a "crowding effect," causing widely spaced objects in the shot to appear much closer together (see Figure 2-3).

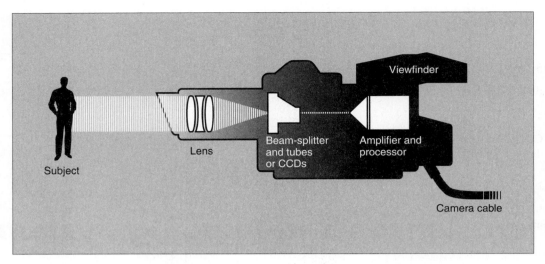

Figure 2-1. *In this basic color camera diagram, light reflecting off the subject is captured by the lens, which focuses and conveys this image to the beam splitter, which separates the red, green and blue elements of the picture and sends them to either the red, green or blue imaging devices (tubes or CCD chips). They, in turn, convert light energy into electronic energy in a form that represents the pictures that the lens sees. These electronic pictures are then conveyed through numerous amplifiers and circuits within the camera. The composite picture (the combination of the red, green and blue pictures) can then be viewed through the viewfinder and conveyed out of this studio camera to the control room.*

Aperture

The second important lens fundamental is *aperture,* the lens opening of variable size through which light enters the camera. Every imaging device functions most efficiently when operating within an ideal range of light intensity. Many camera lenses allow you to manually or automatically vary the light reaching the imaging device, thus accommodating a wide range of lighting conditions on your production. If aperture were not adjustable, a very bright scene could exceed the

1.

2.

3.

Figure 2-2. *In this comparison of shots from the same location, you can see how vast a view an extremely wide-angle lens gives you (shot 1) compared to a normal lens (shot 2) and a long lens (shot 3).*

Figure 2-3. *Compare shot 1, photographed with a wide-angle lens from the same location as shot 2, photographed with a telephoto lens: Shot 1 has the wide view and provides a somewhat distorted view of the line of fence posts. Shot 2 provides the narrower view, and the line of fence posts, while less distorted, exhibits the crowding effect.*

imaging device's capacity, causing *overexposure,* while a very dark scene would not provide enough light for a clear picture, resulting in *underexposure.* Changing the size of the lens aperture governs the amount of light reaching the imaging device, ensuring that it operates within the range needed to provide correct exposure (see Figure 2-4).

Aperture is adjusted by means of an *iris.* Some refer to the iris as the *diaphragm* of the lens. Like the iris of the human eye, the interwoven leaves of a camera lens iris can create a larger or smaller aperture as required by the brightness of the scene. From wide-open to pinhole-sized apertures, iris settings are calibrated in *f-stops* written as the letter "f" followed by a slash and a number, such as "f/8" or "f/4." An important principle to remember: The <u>lower</u> the f-stop number, the <u>larger</u> the aperture and the more light reaching

Figure 2-4. *The amount of light reaching the camera's imaging device varies in these shots, from underexposure in shot 1, to normal exposure in shot 2, to overexposure in shot 3. Normal exposure is the only one of the three that provides good rendition of detail. It also best approximates the actual view of the scene at the time.*

the imaging device. The <u>higher</u> the f-stop number, the <u>smaller</u> the aperture, and the less light reaching the imaging device (see Figure 2-5). Remembering these relationships is easier if you think of f-stops as fractions in which "f" stands for the number one. Think of f/8 as 1/8, and f/4 as 1/4. If you remember

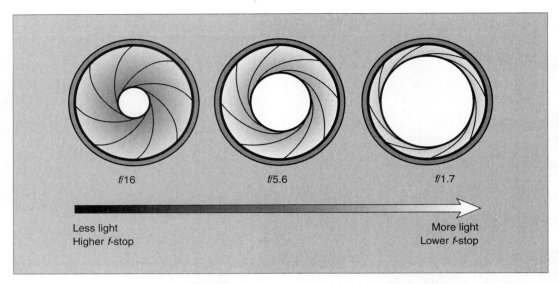

f/16   f/5.6   f/1.7

Less light   More light
Higher *f*-stop   Lower *f*-stop

Figure 2-5. *Three iris settings, showing variable openings ranging from f/16, the narrowest for this particular lens, to f/1.7, the widest.*

that 1/4 of a pie is more than 1/8 of it, you can understand that f/4 passes more light than f/8. This little trick is helpful in determining which of two f-stops lets more light pass, but it would be wrong to assume f/4 allows twice the light of f/8 just because one number is twice as large as the other.

We don't want to belabor the concept of aperture or suggest that you need knowledge of calculus to use most cameras. Given the sophistication of modern cameras, it's possible to turn on the automatic iris and let the microprocessors set the aperture for you. (See the section on lens controls following and Tech Manual 2-2 at the end of this chapter to learn more about the auto iris and how to use it creatively.) But aperture is one factor determining depth of field, a third lens fundamental discussed below. Depth of field is a critical limitation with which camera operators often wrestle when composing a usable shot.

Depth of Field

Try this experiment: Place your index finger six inches from your nose. Close one eye and try to focus the other eye simultaneously on both your finger and an object 10 or more feet behind it. You can't do it, and neither can a camera lens. Because our eyes and brain work together almost unconsciously to focus on the object of our immediate concern, we usually don't notice how fuzzy objects appear that are closer or farther away. But when we view a two-dimensional picture on a television screen, we quickly spot poorly focused areas. So camera

operators must understand the fundamentals of depth of field and learn to manipulate it for their creative purposes.

Depth of field is that area in front of the lens appearing in acceptable focus when you look through the lens. Another way to understand depth of field is to call it "depth of focus." This depth of field area begins with the object closest to the lens that appears in focus and ends with the most distant object in the scene which is in focus. Great depth of field means the distance between these two points is large; shallow depth of field means there is little distance between these two points (see Figure 2-6 and Figure 2-7).

Great depth of field is usually desired in studio productions. If depth of field is too shallow, the camera operator may have great difficulty getting clearly focused shots of more than one subject in the same scene. Physically placing important elements in the scene within the lens's depth of field greatly simplifies a camera operator's task. But there are other ways to manipulate depth of field.

F-Stops and Depth of Field   A low-numbered f-stop (large aperture, more light passing through) yields shallow depth of field. The reverse is also true: A higher-numbered f-stop (smaller aperture, less light passing through) provides greater depth of field. Operating the camera in a dimly lit scene with the lens wide open makes focusing difficult because the large aperture reduces depth of field. Increasing the light level by adding lights or raising a window shade allows you to use a smaller aperture

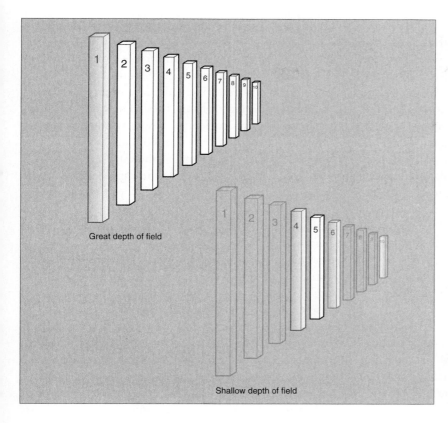

Figure 2-6. *In this drawing, with shallow depth of field, only post 5 and a little of posts 4 and 6 are in critical focus. With great depth of field, all of posts 2 through infinity are in focus.*

(perhaps going from f/2 to f/8). This increases depth of field, and focusing becomes less critical. If adding light to the scene is not possible, you can increase the camera's *gain* setting, which multiplies the amplification of the video signal leaving the image sensor(s). Adding gain allows use of a higher f-stop number, increasing depth of field. However, increasing the gain causes a degradation of picture quality. This degradation usually shows up as a less sharp, snowier picture.

In summary, great depth of field results from using a higher-numbered f-stop (that is, a smaller aperture) with more scene illumination or more electronic gain. But adding light is not always easy, and increasing the gain may compromise picture quality. As the director, you'll have to make both a technical and a creative decision: whether the value of greater depth of field is worth the trouble of adding light or the loss of image quality from adding gain.

1.

2.

Figure 2-7. *In both shots, the camera operator has focused on the chain-link fence. In shot 1, the camera's iris is set for a small lens aperture, yielding great depth of field. In shot 2, with the camera's iris set for a large lens aperture, shallow depth of field is the result.*

Focal Length and Depth of Field   Short focal length, or wide-angle, lenses provide greater depth of field than do long focal length, or telephoto, lenses. The apparent size of an object within a shot depends on both the camera-to-object distance and the focal length of the lens. Moving the camera closer to the object and shortening the focal length increases depth of field while keeping the apparent size of objects constant. There are other reasons for using relatively short focal lengths, as discussed in Tech Manual 2-1. If you move the camera too close, however, focus becomes much more difficult. You may need to try different camera positions and focal lengths to get the composition you want along with your required depth of field. But don't forget our earlier suggestion about repositioning objects in the scene. Sometimes the easiest remedy is just to rearrange items and subjects in your shot so that they'll all be within the depth of field you require.

If you have spent some time doing still photography, a lot of these relationships are clear in your understanding. For those who are new to the photographic arts, keeping these relationships straight in your head is tiresome. For that reason, spend some time with Figure 2-8, "Factors That Influence Depth of Field."

Fixed Focal Length (Prime) Lenses vs. Zoom Lenses

Early TV cameras usually had three, or even four, lenses of different fixed focal lengths mounted on a round plate called a *turret,* which could be rotated in front of the camera's image-sensing tube. The turret typically included a short focal length lens for wide-angle shots, a long focal length lens for telephoto and a normal focal length lens that approximated the human eye's field of view (see Figure 2-9). Unlike the variable focal length *zoom lenses* most often used in TV production today, these early TV lenses were *fixed,* providing only a single, nonadjustable focal length. A lens with a fixed focal length is also called a *prime lens.*

A major disadvantage of the turret lens system was that you could not change lenses while the camera was "on the air." The only way to obtain a "tighter" (close-up) or "looser" (wide-angle) shot while the camera was still on the air was to physically roll the camera forward or back, refocusing as the distance between the camera and the subject changed. TV directors planned lens changes carefully, because even skilled camera operators required a few moments to change lenses, reframe and refocus a shot. When manufacturers perfected zoom lenses, the industry

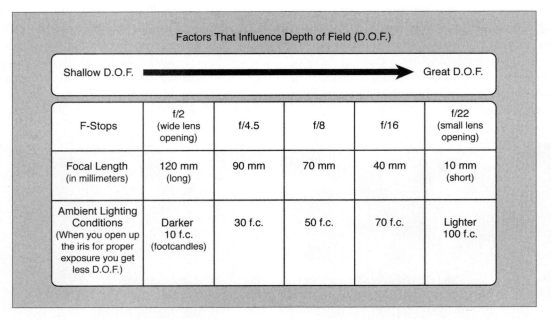

Factors That Influence Depth of Field (D.O.F.)					
Shallow D.O.F. ⟶ Great D.O.F.					
F-Stops	f/2 (wide lens opening)	f/4.5	f/8	f/16	f/22 (small lens opening)
Focal Length (in millimeters)	120 mm (long)	90 mm	70 mm	40 mm	10 mm (short)
Ambient Lighting Conditions (When you open up the iris for proper exposure you get less D.O.F.)	Darker 10 f.c. (footcandles)	30 f.c.	50 f.c.	70 f.c.	Lighter 100 f.c.

Figure 2-8. *When manipulating depth of field for your particular production, you may want to display greater depth of field or less of it. Your needs will vary. But by knowing how to work back and forth with f-stops, focal lengths and the amount of light you shine on the scene, you can control how much of each shot you'll have in focus. Need to use a long lens for this shot because you want the crowding effect, but you also want a little depth of field? OK. Increase the light with which you illuminate the shot so you can use a smaller lens opening, which increases your depth of field. In this manner, you can manipulate depth of field with tradeoffs of these three elements.*

Figure 2-9. *Early TV cameras used multiple fixed focal length lenses on a turret, which the operator rotated into line with the pickup tube. This camera's turret is equipped with four lenses.*

quickly gave up turret systems with their prime lenses. One zoom lens replaces a whole collection of prime lenses.

The Real Purpose of Zoom Lenses

TV production beginners mistakenly assume the zoom control should be used often, and on the air. "The trombone school of zoom lens work" (excessive and mindless use of the zoom) is a distinguishing characteristic of the amateur. The zoom lens was designed to reduce the time a camera had to be taken off the air to change lenses, and to allow changing shot size without physically moving the camera closer to or farther from the subject. Certainly there are many appropriate uses for on-air zooms, especially in news and sports coverage. Restraint is the key to using zoom lenses correctly.

Zoom Ratios and Lens Speed

A zoom lens operates over a range of focal lengths between its zoomed in (longest focal length) and zoomed out (shortest focal length) limits. Typical limits might be 25 mm to 250 mm, or a *zoom ratio* of 10:1 (read as "10 to one"). A 10:1 lens offers more operational flexibility than does a 6:1 lens. The larger the zoom ratio, the more individual focal lengths are available in a single lens.

Unfortunately, lenses with large zoom ratios are more expensive, and most must sacrifice *lens speed* to achieve large ratios. A lens' many glass elements absorb some of the light as it passes through: Light energy coming out of the lens is always less than the light energy entering it (see Figure 2-10). For example, high zoom ratio lenses and long focal length lenses require more glass lens elements, so they are less efficient (referred to as "slower") than lenses with fewer elements. When scene illumination is minimal and adding more light to the scene is not desired, a *fast lens* often produces usable pictures while the same camera fitted with a *slow lens*

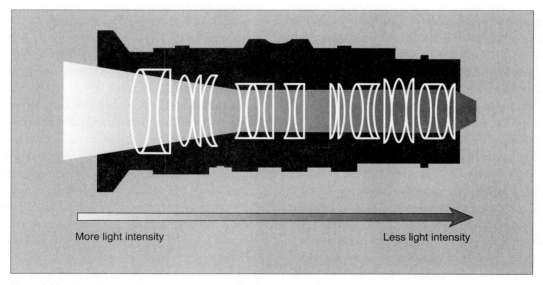

More light intensity   Less light intensity

Figure 2-10. *This illustration shows a cutaway view of the elements of a lens. As light passes through these elements, its intensity decreases.*

could not. So, in this art/science of qualitative trade-offs, the lens capable of delivering the tightest zoom isn't necessarily the most useful to the videographer.

Common Lens Filters

Lenses often need filters to correct problems with lighting or to create an artistic effect. Some frequently used filters are built into the camera body. The most *common filters* are fitted into a filter wheel located behind the lens. The operator rotates the wheel to position the desired filter in the image path as needed.

Color correction filters are the most often used of the common filters. Remarkably, the human brain filters out distortions created by different color light sources so we perceive a white shirt as white whether it's illuminated by sunlight or the orange glow of a bedside lamp. Camera image-sensing devices require color correction filters matched to the type of light falling on the scene. The most common color correction filters are those handling the most typical lighting situations: natural sunlight, television studio lighting and the florescent lights found in many offices and public places.

Among the handiest of the common filters is the *neutral density (ND) filter,* a filter similar to the gray lenses found in sunglasses. However, unlike some colored sunglasses, the gray ND filters do not change the color of light passing through them, only its intensity. Another advantage of the ND filter is that it can reduce the intensity of the light that reaches the imaging device without requiring f-stop adjustments. The ND filter is extremely valuable on bright, sunshiny days, on the water and in snow.

Another common filter is the ultraviolet (UV) filter, which sharpens colors on cloudy or overcast days. The UV filter also improves outdoor shots by making clouds appear more crisp and defined. As noted in Chapter 1, some videographers routinely keep a UV filter attached to the front of the lens to provide additional lens protection rather than use the one on the filter wheel. Expensive cameras sometimes combine ND and UV filters with color correction filters, allowing one filter to perform two or more functions.

Optical color correction filters remain basic camera components, but many newer cameras allow operators to perform color correction electronically using video processing technology. Fluorescent lights in offices, for example, radiate a complex range of colors making "natural looking" video difficult. Some cameras allow the operator to press a button or flip a switch telling microprocessors within the camera that the scene is illuminated by fluorescent fixtures. The microprocessors then electronically "sub-

tract" the effects of the fluorescent lights from the video signal, producing a picture that's mostly free of undesirable color *artifacts*. Microprocessors also can be programmed to compensate for the color effects of other common light sources (intense natural sunlight, incandescent light bulbs, etc.) rather than requiring the operator to manually insert filters into the lens system. The best microprocessors automatically compensate for color problems introduced by the light source and can do so even if the source of illumination changes during a shot. However, not all cameras have these capabilities, and professionals must know how to use optical filters for color correction as needed.

Operators also use a variety of *special effects filters.* These filters typically mount ahead of the lens, not behind the lens in the filter wheel. Among the most often used special effects filters are the *fog filter,* which can add a soft look to the picture; the *polarizing filter,* used to reduce reflected glare off glass, water and so on and to create dramatic sky vistas through enhanced rendition of clouds; and the *star filter,* which makes points of light in the picture sparkle like stars, with shafts of light radiating from the center (see examples of these filters in Figure 2-11, found in the color photo section of this book).

Lens Control

Electronic circuits provide more and more labor-saving help. One of the first controls coming under microprocessor control was the iris. A circuit monitors light entering the camera and automatically opens or closes the iris to provide correct exposure. Electronic news gathering (ENG) and electronic field production (EFP) often require quick shooting under sometimes minimal or rapidly changeable light conditions. An *auto iris* is a great aid to a lone ENG camera operator trying to capture a story as it's happening. Studio productions seldom employ the auto iris, because video technicians provide more precise, subjective iris control than can a "mindless" microprocessor.

Automatic focus first appeared on consumer cameras, but professional cameras, especially those configured for ENG, now sometimes offer this option. *Autofocus* circuits can become "confused" in certain production situations, as can the auto iris. The circuit may cause the camera to focus on the wrong object in the scene, or focus may change constantly (and annoyingly) as the circuit hunts to provide the best focus as defined by the microprocessor's program. That's why many experienced camera operators prefer to disable the autofocus control and focus manually. In the haste imposed by many ENG situations, however, allowing the camera to occasionally perform the task of focusing can be the right decision.

Although lacking the judgment of a human operator, auto iris and autofocus free the shooter to concentrate on following the action with good shot composition and other aesthetics.

Zoom control has been, and largely remains, in the hands of the camera operator. But this control mechanism has evolved with time. Early zoom controls used rotating hand cranks and mechanical linkages, but modern cameras use electric motors called "servos" to change focal length. Servos respond to electrical switches mounted either on the lens assembly itself, or on handles attached to the camera mount, or in both places (see Figure 2-12). The operator can simply apply thumb pressure to a rocker switch to zoom in or out. The zoom speed depends on control settings and how much pressure the operator places on the rocker switch. Some sophisticated servo controls have circuits which automatically bring zooms to a gentle halt at each end

of the range. An expensive studio camera might feature a *shot box,* a device allowing storage of many custom zooms prior to the start of a production. The direction (whether to zoom in or out), the range and the speed of the zoom are all preset.

Camera Automation   Automated operation extends well beyond the iris, focus and zoom controls. In the mid-1980s, NBC became the first major organization to eliminate human camera operators from its nightly newscasts. At NBC and in many other production centers and top 100-market stations, computers control many aspects of the actual operation of studio cameras. Scripts indicate each camera's physical location, zoom setting and focus for each shot in the program. Under the watchful supervision of one camera technician, a computer stores this information and executes these commands as the show is broadcast. These *robotic*

1.

2.

3.

Figure 2-12. *Today's zoom controls mounted on the pan handles of studio and EFP cameras are of two general kinds, crank (shown in shot 1) and servo zoom (shown in shots 2 and 3). Crank controls, which are manual, in that the operator must turn a crank rather than simply push a button, give the operator more complete control of zoom speed. These are mostly used today by live sports camera operators. Servo zoom controls are found more typically in studios. As shown in shot 3, servo zooms are also mounted on the lens barrels of ENG cameras.*

Figure 2-13. *This is the lens shade of a Sony Digital Betacam®, and it is somewhat different than many lens shades, which are round. The reason this lens shade is nearly rectangular is that the digital version of the Sony Betacam can shoot in either 4:3 or 1.85:1 aspect ratios. If it were set for Panavision format (1.85:1) aspect ratio, the edges of a round lens shade might be visible around the outside of the wide-screen shot.*

cameras work best when it's possible to precisely predict shots in advance of production. However, nonbroadcast TV production applications in educational and corporate settings use robotic cameras that lock on a performer and follow along as the talent moves. Increased use of computer-generated *virtual sets* is accelerating development of robotic cameras in broadcast and professional production environments. Virtual sets, in which talent are positioned in front of special effects-generated rather than real backgrounds, require perfectly coordinated and extremely precise camera control to maintain the illusion of reality.

While not a control, the *lens shade* is an additional helper device for lenses. Think of a lens shade as performing the same duty that a sun visor does in your car: It shades the camera's lens when it is necessary to shoot in the general direction of the sun or some other bright light source, such as television lights (see Figure 2-13).

Internal Optical Systems

Prior to the 1960s, most TV cameras produced only black-and-white (*monochrome*) images. The lens focused the image directly onto the front face of a single imaging device, a vacuum tube. This tube converted the picture's pattern of light energy into nearly identical patterns of electrical energy. The first color cameras required three

vacuum tubes, one to process the red elements in the picture, one for the green elements and one for the blue. Red, green and blue (RGB) comprise the *primary additive colors.* Varying combinations of these provide all the visible colors of the color TV system. See Figure 2-14 in the color plates for an illustration of RGB in various combinations. After the red, green and blue tubes separately processed the RGB values of a shot, the camera's electronics recombined red, green and blue into a composite electronic representation of a color television picture. Modern cameras use prism blocks to break a picture into its RGB elements.

The Prism Block

The *prism block* is a single solid device made of high-quality optical glass. It receives the picture from the camera lens and separates this image into its red, green, and blue components (see Figure 2-15). Affixed to the prism block are separate image sensors for red, green and blue. Modern cameras have the chips they use as sensors permanently bonded to the prism, ensuring near-perfect optical alignment and stability. This creates a low-maintenance camera, but failure of any part of the prism block sensor unit, although rare, requires replacement of the whole system. The image-sensing tubes of older cameras attached mechanically to the three (red, green and blue) ports of the prism block but were not integral to it. This allowed individual replacement of a defective tube but resulted in a less rugged prism-sensor interface, which required routine maintenance to ensure a high-quality color picture.

In cameras using prism blocks, the red and blue imaging devices process only those colors found in the picture containing red and blue elements. The image sensor that processes the green chrominance in the picture also processes the luminance, which you will recall is the brightness and contrast information contained in the picture. The luminance information provides the signal needed for the monochrome pictures of black-and-white TV sets.

Electronic Imaging Devices

As we have learned, light energy passes through the camera lens and the *internal optical system* on its way to an image-sensing device, the photosensitive element that will convert light energy to electrical energy. From the first days of television until the 1980s, only one kind of imaging device existed: the photoconductive vacuum tube. The popularity and efficiency of the

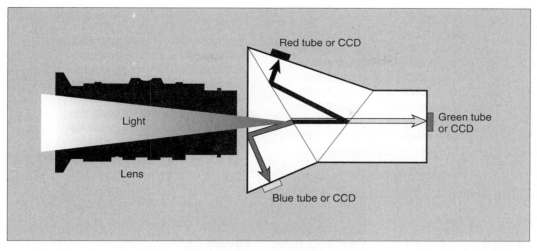

Figure 2-15. *Light passes through the camera's lens and into the body of the camera, where the prism block is located. Prism block design varies, but as this drawing illustrates, the prism splits away all the blue and red elements of the picture captured by the lens and reflects them down to the imaging device designated for blue or up to the imaging device designated to process reds. The prism permits green elements of the picture to pass straight through to the imaging device designated for green.*

modern *charge-coupled device* (CCD), described in this section, has virtually relegated even the highest-quality image-sensing tubes to the broadcasting museum.

How Camera Pickup Tubes Work

Few devices have received as much development and improvement through the years as the photoconductive camera tube. But in the digital age, despite the development away from camera tubes, an explanation of the tube's basic theory is useful in understanding the functioning of the CCD, which operates in an analogous fashion. The camera tube is a slender cylindrical device made largely of glass. The camera lens relays the picture to the internal optical system, which in turn projects the red, green and blue elements of the picture onto the light-sensitive front faces of three tubes. Since the tubes render their colors in an identical manner, and the final phase in which the other image-sensing device, the CCD, renders pictures is analogous to camera tube scanning, we'll follow the path of light through one tube. The light-sensitive front face of a tube is called the *signal plate*. An *electron gun* in the back of the tube scans the picture on the signal plate from top to bottom in 525 horizontal lines. In the same manner that you read this page (scanning across a line to see what the words are and then retracing, or returning, your scanning to the left hand side of the page and beginning another line scan) horizontal scanning begins at the top left of the

picture, goes left to right and ends at the bottom right. Figure 2-16 provides an explanation of how scanning works.

480p, 720p, 1080i and 1080p

At this writing, however, while the *National Television System Committee* (NTSC) video described above is still the main means by which American viewers receive and watch TV, there are four other imaging systems, all digital, being used in production and transmitted by TV stations in anticipation of the eventual changeover to all-digital television mandated by the Federal Communications Commission (FCC).

The first two of these use a scanning method that differs markedly from the interlaced scanning described above. This newer system is called *progressive scanning*. Basically, progressive scanning means that the entire frame of video, both the even <u>and</u> the odd lines, is scanned and presented at once and at the rate of 1/60 of a second. One of these progressive scan methods is called *480p* (the "p" stands for "progressive," and 480 is the number of active lines scanned). It looks better on the screen than NTSC video, but it's not the highest *resolution* of the digital systems. A similar system, *720p,* is a sharper high-definition scanning method, completely compatible with new flat-panel TVs, which adds 240 more lines. This difference results in better resolution than 480p. The third system, *1080i,* uses interlaced scanning like NTSC, but that's where the resemblance

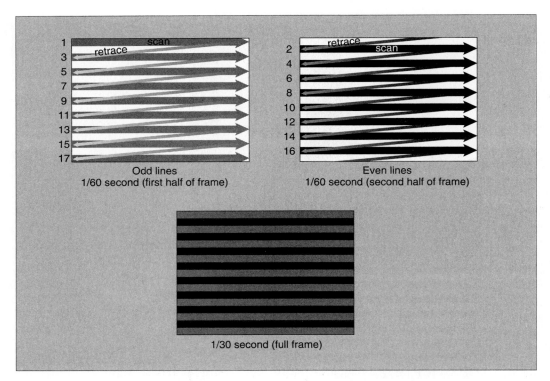

Figure 2-16. *Since the establishment of National Television System Committee (NTSC) standard video in the 1940s, all of the even lines and then all of the odd lines of the 525-line picture are scanned alternately and then shown alternately on a TV screen to viewers. This is referred to as* interlaced *scanning. The alternate combination of even and odd line scans, called video* fields, *within just 1/30 of a second, makes up a complete two-field NTSC video frame. The even and odd fields are being scanned and replaced by the next set of fields so fast that viewers don't notice it, nor do they notice that in any 1/60 of a second they're only seeing one field, just half of the scan lines of a single frame. A complex electromagnetic system conveys 30 of these scanned pictures, or frames, every second from the tube to picture amplifiers within the camera. In the history of television prior to the CCD, four basic families of tubes were most popular. They are, for your information, the* Image Orthicon (I-O), *the* Vidicon, *the* Saticon *and the* Plumbicon. *Finally only the Saticon and Plumbicon were used in new broadcast-quality cameras. Today, no one sells tubed cameras. All new cameras contain CCDs.*

ends. 1080i is a very-high-resolution digital format, delivering truly remarkable high-definition images. At this writing, the fourth system, *1080p,* is the very best available. This progressive scan system produces the most beautiful pictures consumers can currently see on home televisions—if their sets are properly equipped. 1080p capability will undoubtedly play a pivotal role as competing media giants try to market their mutually incompatible versions of the high-definition DVD players.

The Charge-Coupled Device

The Charge-coupled device, or CCD (also called a chip), was first publicly demonstrated in 1967. Early CCDs were low resolution, but by the early 1990s, CCDs had become state-of-the-art for television (see Figure 2-17). One by one, engineering directors for large broadcast corporations have replaced their old

tubed cameras with CCD-equipped cameras, and major manufacturers discontinued design and manufacture of tubed cameras. There are still tubed cameras in use in the industry, but not for much longer.

Theory of CCD Operation   While the pickup tube was long and cylindrical, the CCD looks like a chubby postage stamp (see Figure 2-18). Rather than having a photoconductive layer of chemicals on its face, the CCD features rows of tiny discrete *pixels,* each comprised of a light-sensitive element called a *photodiode,* plus associated storage devices. The photodiodes and storage devices are mounted on microscopically thin layers of material, accounting for the CCD's compact dimensions. Light conducted through the lens and the prism block strikes the CCD's photodiodes, causing each to release photo-

Figure 2-17. *Compared to a quarter, a CCD is tiny.*

electrons. The brightness of the light striking each pixel determines the number of photoelectrons given off. The photoelectrons constitute an electrical charge which is then coupled (moved) to the pixel's storage layer. Then these individual stored charges are "read" at times determined by a high-speed electronic clock (and also, in most CCD cameras, by an electronic shutter) until all the charges in the array of pixels have been sampled. *Sampling* refers to the digital phenomenon in which some, but not all, of these

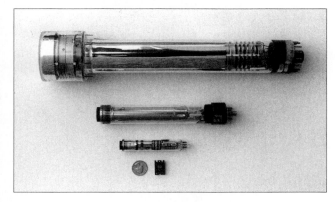

Figure 2-18. *As shown here, a CCD is a tiny thing compared to photoconductive tubes. This permits very small CCD cameras to be designed for conventional TV production. This CCD chip, as might be found in a studio or ENG camera, is smaller across than a quarter. Above it is a 2/3-inch Diode Gun Plumbicon tube as was formerly used in ENG cameras. Above that is a one-inch Plumbicon tube once used in the finest studio cameras. Above the one-inch tube is a comparatively "small" I-O tube, manufactured after the original, much-larger Orthicon tubes first used in TV production had been downsized.*

pixels will be used to represent the complete picture. Sampling reduces both cost and the milliseconds it takes to create frames of digital video or streams of audio. The resultant image, in electronic form, is a mosaic of the original image focused by the lens on the front face of the CCD. So, as you can see, the "reading out" of pixel charges is analogous to the scanning of the signal plate in tubes.

There's more than one kind of CCD design. The earliest CCDs used the *frame transfer* (FT) system. Later, CCDs began using a more complex design called an *interline transfer* (IT) system. By the end of the 1980s a combination *frame interline transfer* (FIT) system emerged as an extremely popular, albeit expensive, CCD design. Although some manufacturers still feature improved, inexpensive versions of the FT chip, advanced versions of the FIT, such as the Sony Hyper-HAD ("HAD" stands for "*hole-accumulated diode*") are, at this writing, preferred designs for broadcast production.

Chip Formats   Chips measuring 1/3 inch, half inch, 2/3 inch and one inch are marketed. Surveillance-quality cameras typically use 1/3-inch chips while most professional cameras use half-inch or larger chips. Although technology makes better performance possible in ever-smaller packages, compact and industrial- and consumer-grade cameras use half-inch chips, while video professionals use cameras employing higher resolution 2/3-inch chips. Chips measuring 2/3 inch are common in many modern cameras, both for standard and high-definition resolution pictures. The top high-definition cameras use CCDs measuring a full inch, featuring millions of pixels.

Video Processing

The "raw" video signal exiting the image-sensing device is weak and requires strengthening before being transmitted outside the camera body. This process is called *amplifying* the signal. If the signal isn't amplified, it is subject to degradation, including the possible addition of snow-like interference called *video noise*. Additionally, the video signal undergoes a variety of electronic modifications to improve image quality (see Figure 2-19). As noted earlier in this chapter, microprocessors can be programmed to perform color correction electronically. *Digital signal processing* (DSP) technology contributes significantly to the outstanding video images provided by modern cameras. A major function of DSP circuits is to compensate for image artifacts created by flaws in the

Figure 2-19. *This photo shows a view of just some of the circuit boards found in a modern digital camera.*

lens, the prism block or the imaging devices. For example, there are circuits in digital cameras to reduce or remove *aliasing,* or the rendering of diagonal lines as stair steps or the appearance of curves with saw-toothed outlines rather than round ones. DSP circuits also modify the video signal to create image effects considered more aesthetically pleasing. Many modern cameras, for example, process flesh tones to eliminate minor facial blemishes and soften wrinkles. Other processors selectively enhance the edges of images, improving definition and sharpening the picture.

Signal Encoding

Following amplification and processing, other circuits *encode* the video signal into a format (or formats) required by other production equipment, such as video recorders and switchers. Some production gear needs *composite video,* in which color and luminance information are combined into a single signal, while other equipment needs separate red, green and blue signals from the imaging devices. In this case, the camera provides *component video.* Encoding circuits also allow some cameras to output the video signal in digital or analog form.

Signal Processing and HDTV

Now that you have learned more about the way a television camera processes video, we again return to the discussion of high-definition television (HDTV) and digital television that began in Chapter 1. Because it's likely that soon all TV will consist of high-definition images (1,080 interlaced or progressive scan lines at a frame rate of 60 Hertz cycles per second, abbreviated as Hz), displayed in a 16:9 wide-screen aspect ratio), during the transition period, camera manufacturers are producing cameras capable of providing pictures meeting multiple production requirements. (See Figure 2-20 for a shot of an HDTV camera configured for Hollywood motion picture production.) Just as some *prosumer* (a professional/consumer hybrid) *cameras* are capable of producing HDTV pictures, some cameras allow producers to output *standard-definition* (SDTV) digital video in either the 4:3 or 16:9 format. Some of these cameras are also capable of producing high resolution digital video in 16:9 (HDTV) format (see Figure 2-21).

Figure 2-20. *A Panasonic AJ-HDC27H VariCam® Variable Frame Rate 16:9 High Definition Cinema Camera. This camera, specially configured for work on a motion picture set, is capable of shooting at the rate of 30 frames per second for television, but also at the 24-frame-per-second rate used in motion pictures.*

Photo courtesy of Panasonic.

Figure 2-21. *The 16:9 format is much wider than the 4:3 format. A 4:3 image on a 16:9 display would fill only the area between the vertical lines in the shot of the Nebraska capitol building above. The areas on each end would be empty (black). Reducing a 16:9 image to fit on a 4:3 display results in empty areas above and below the image, much like the letterbox format sometimes used to show a wide-screen movie on a conventional analog TV set. Also see Figure 4-1 for a comparison of the NTSC and HDTV aspect ratios.*

Image resolution is also adjustable in the sense that it is possible to lower, or *downconvert,* a high-definition digital image, permitting a better camera to accommodate less capable equipment along its signal path.

However, the image resolution leaving the camera <u>cannot</u> later be increased to high definition. And the reverse, *upconverting* SDTV video, can only imitate but not completely match HDTV quality. Achieving the very best picture resolution requires starting with a camera and recording equipment capable of producing the best level of quality.

Just as when TV converted to color from black-and-white, most stations changed from all-analog to all-digital transmission by initially just retransmitting programming provided by networks or major production studios rather than producing many digital programs locally. As digital TV becomes the norm, stations will begin to originate more shows in digital.

Eastman Kodak estimates that the majority of all prime-time, dramatic TV programming still originates on film. Film technology (at least 35 mm and larger formats) provides all the resolution needed by HDTV, and much of it is shot in the Panavision format (1.85:1 aspect ratio), which very closely matches HDTV's 16:9 dimensions.

Now that we've examined both the inside and the outside of the television camera, in Chapter 3 we'll discuss the mounting devices that support cameras. We'll also discuss the first skill set required of most beginning television production students: operating a camera.

tech manual **2-1**   *Focal Length and the ENG Camera Operator*

A working understanding of focal length has practical advantages. A short focal length lens helps when you must hand-hold the camera by increasing a shot's depth of field. If they can do it safely, experienced ENG and documentary camera operators get physically close to their subjects and shoot using a short focal length. The resulting wide field of view and apparent increase in depth minimizes the minor bumps and wobbles inherent in hand-held work. It also makes keeping the shot in focus much easier. While experienced videographers use this technique, novice ENG camera operators typically position the camera far from the subject and zoom in (using the longest focal length). The image jerks with every operator heartbeat, and the subject often moves left or right,

out of the lens's narrow field of view, and in and out of critical focus as minute distance changes occur between operator and subject. If the microphone is camera mounted, audio recorded from a distance is also of poorer quality.

There are occasions, of course, when you must use a long focal length to get the shot—when circumstances, or people with badges, don't allow you to get close to the action. If you must use a long focal length, minimize image instability by abandoning the handheld approach and using either a tripod or another stabilizing object (table, ledge, floor, desk, stool, wall, tree, etc.). Your authors, and many people who employ news and documentary photogs, encourage shooting from tripods in most situations where movement of the subject is either unlikely or can be anticipated. A moving camera shot is effective if it is done well, of course. But remember: The more you zoom in, the more shallow your depth of field becomes. If you're trying to focus on a number of individuals or objects positioned in successively deeper planes of your shot, you're fighting the physics of lenses.

The crowding effect, the narrow field of view and the shallow depth of field make getting the shot much more difficult.

Use focal length to your advantage and shoot like the pros: ABC Sports used to call it "up close and personal": Move in, zoom back to a wide-angle setting and mike close!

tech manual 2-2   *The Auto Iris and You*

The auto iris is a light meter inside your camera which sets the iris of the lens based on the <u>average</u> amount of illumination in the shot. This characteristic makes it possible, and indeed likely, that a key element in your shot will be grossly underexposed if there's some nonessential part of the shot that's excessively bright. The bright exterior window behind a subject's dark desk is the classic example, although any bright area in the shot (reflected metal object, electric light, the sun, etc.) can produce the same problem (see Figure 2-22). In addition to the videographer's solution described in Figure 2-22's caption, there are other ways to fix this shot:

1. turn the auto iris off and adjust the exposure (f-stop) manually while looking at the image in a properly set-up camera viewfinder;

2. leave the auto iris on and change the angle of the shot so the bright area is no longer in the shot; or

3. turn off the auto iris and use an incident light meter or a portable waveform monitor to determine the correct exposure setting.

Any of these remedies will "work," but the first is imprecise; the second may ruin what you want to do with the shot, or be difficult or impossible in some physical situations; and the third assumes you have time and control of the shooting situation so you can use the meter or waveform monitor.

Here's another, better way to "fool" the auto iris into helping, instead of hindering, your shot. Identify the excessively bright portion(s) of the picture. Next, decide on the portion of the shot that you want to expose

1.

2.

Figure 2-22. *As these two shots indicate, compensating for backlight is important. In shot 1, the subject appears too dark, because the auto iris circuit in the camera, in determining an f-stop based on the average between the lightest and darkest elements of the scene, has failed to expose the subject at the desk adequately. The auto iris, in trying to properly expose detail in the background outside, underexposed the subject in the foreground. Before shooting shot 2, the camera operator zoomed in on just the subject and locked the iris setting to properly expose him. Locking down the iris prevents the camera's auto iris from factoring in the bright background in choosing an f-stop. The result is much better exposure for the subject and a background out the window intentionally overexposed.*

properly, such as the person speaking or the object in the foreground. Then, like the photographer of Figure 2-22, zoom into this portion of the shot until you exclude any of the overly bright elements. While you're still zoomed in on the critical subject matter in the shot, switch the iris from "automatic" to "manual." Most ENG cameras will lock the iris on the f-stop setting it was set on when the circuit was switched to "manual." You have thus effectively used the auto iris as a light meter to determine the correct iris setting for the most important part of your shot. When you zoom back to your desired composition and shoot, you'll find the brightest portion(s) of the picture will be overexposed. But the important picture elements will be correctly exposed, and that's what counts. You've made a conscious decision that some areas in your picture can be sacrificed through overexposure and that another area in your shot is vital and must take priority.

If overexposing the background isn't acceptable, there are other ways to solve your backlighting problem. You can simply add more light on the person in the foreground, which will help to balance his/her level of illumination relative to the background. And if they're available, you could place large sheets of ND filter gel over the windows, or simply draw the drapes behind the subject!

Important Vocabulary Terms

480p: The lower resolution of the progressive scan digital video formats, scanning 480 lines and presenting them at once (rather than alternately) in 1/60 of a second.

720p: A higher-resolution progressive scan digital video format, scanning and presenting 720 lines and presenting them at once (rather than alternately) in 1/60 of a second.

1080i: The very-high-resolution digital video format, and the only one that uses interlaced scanning.

1080p: The highest-resolution digital video format available at the time of writing, scanning 1,080 lines and presenting them progressively.

Aliasing: An artifact of chip technology, rendering diagonal lines as "stair steps," and curves as having saw-toothed, rather than round, edges. Antialiasing DSP circuits can remedy this situation.

Amplifying: Strengthening a video or audio signal to allow it to be conveyed to another location and to avoid noise contamination.

Aperture: The opening in the iris through which light passes.

Artifact: Flaw in a video image created by unique weaknesses in the performance of a certain piece of equipment, due to its design characteristics.

Auto iris: A circuit that monitors the light entering the camera and automatically opens or closes the iris to provide correct exposure.

Autofocus: A circuit that automatically focuses the image seen through a lens according to a program stored in a microprocessor.

Charge-coupled device (CCD): Also called a chip. A solid-state image-sensing device replacing tubes in modern color cameras.

Color correction filters: Lens filters permitting cameras to correctly render colors in a scene. Some color correction filters also incorporate neutral density (ND) and ultraviolet (UV) filters.

Common Filters: Frequently used filters typically built into filter wheels located behind the lens of video cameras.

Component video: Video composed of separate red, blue and green signals from the imaging device.

Composite video: Video in which color and luminance information are combined into a single signal.

Depth of field: The area, beginning with the object closest to the lens which appears in focus and ending with the most distant object in the scene which is still in focus.

Diaphragm: A synonym for the iris of a lens.

Digital signal processing (DSP): Electronic modifications to the video signal performed by digital microprocessors in the camera to improve image quality.

Downconvert: The process of converting HDTV video to SDTV video.

Electron Gun: The element of a pickup tube that horizontally scans the signal plate to render picture information.

Encoding: Conversion by the camera of the video signal into format(s) required by other production equipment.

F-stop: A numerical symbol used for calibrating the size of the iris opening through which the light travels. The smaller the f-stop number, the larger the opening. The larger the opening, the more light conveyed to the imaging device.

Fast lens: Due to their design and their relatively smaller number of internal elements, these lenses have the ability to transmit light to an imaging device with only a minimum loss of light intensity. Lenses with smaller zoom ratios and shorter focal lengths tend to be faster.

Field: Not to be confused with "depth of field," a video field is one half, comprised of either the even or the odd scanned lines, of a frame. In NTSC interlaced scanning, two fields comprise one frame of video.

Fisheye lens: A lens with a very short focal length that creates an extremely wide-angle view of a scene. This view appears somewhat distorted around the edges.

Fixed focal length lenses: Also called prime lenses. These are lenses with nonadjustable focal lengths.

Focal length: The distance, measured in millimeters, from the optical center of the lens to the front face of the imaging device, when the lens is focused on infinity. Focal length determines how wide or narrow a field of view the lens provides. The shorter the focal length, the wider the field of view; the longer the focal length, the narrower (or more close-up) the field of view.

Fog filter: A lens filter that provides a soft, gauzy look for the picture.

Frame: A single video picture. In the NTSC 525-line system, a frame consists of two video fields and is a combination of those fields' even- and odd-numbered scan lines. TV video is transmitted at a rate of 30 frames (or 60 fields) per second.

Frame transfer (FT): The earliest and least expensive CCD design.

Frame-interline transfer (FIT): A popular CCD design, the combination of the qualities of the frame transfer and interline transfer technologies.

Gain: The amplification of the video signal at the image sensor. An increase in gain allows an image to be recorded with a higher-numbered f-stop (meaning a greater depth of field), but it also reduces the resolution of the image.

Hole-accumulated diode: A variety of Sony CCD that uses pin holes over each pixel to focus light on the portion of its surface that is light sensitive.

Image Orthicon (I-O): Now obsolete, an early model pickup tube used in NTSC television production.

Imaging device: The device inside the camera that converts light energy into electrical energy. These include vacuum tubes and CCDs.

Interlaced scanning: The alternate scanning pattern of even and odd lines used in NTSC video and 1080i digital video.

Interline transfer (IT): A CCD chip featuring collector sectors that appear in rows on the front face of the device. These collectors permit the chip to operate without the need of an electronic shutter.

Internal optical system: Camera component that receives the light from the camera lens and splits it into its component RGB colors, and conveys these red, green and blue image elements to three separate image-sensing devices.

Iris: A device within a lens consisting of interwoven metallic leaves that adjust to create a larger or smaller aperture, as required to ensure proper exposure. Another term for the iris is "diaphragm."

Lens shade: A rounded or rectangular hood placed over the lens to provide shade when shooting in the direction of a bright light source.

Lens speed: A term used to describe the efficiency of a lens, based on the amount of light energy lost between the actual scene and the recorded image. Lens speed is dependent on, among other things, the number of glass elements through which light passes as it travels through the lens.

Long focal length lens: Any lens with a focal length greater than a normal lens; that is, lenses that make objects appear closer than when viewing with a normal lens. Sometimes called "telephoto" lenses.

Monochrome: Black-and-white.

National Television System Committee (NTSC): The governmental/industry body that in 1940 assisted the Federal Communications Commission in determining standards for American analog television. Basic standards: 525 lines, 30 frames per second, interlaced scanning.

Neutral density (ND) filter: A frequently used lens filter that reduces the intensity of light reaching the camera's image-sensing device(s) without affecting color values.

Normal lens: A lens that approximates the field of view of normal human vision and is the standard to which short and long lenses are compared.

Overexposure: When too much light enters the camera, resulting in an image or part of an image that is washed out or whitened, with loss of detail.

Panavision format: A wide-screen motion picture format, Panavision has an aspect ratio of 1.85:1. This format is the most popular today in theatrical motion pictures. The proposed U.S. digital HDTV standard aspect ratio of 16:9 is a close approximation of Panavision's aspect ratio.

Photodiode: A semiconductor device found on pixels that releases an amount of photoelectrons determined by the intensity of a light.

Pixel: A tiny, discrete light-sensitive element comprised of a photodiode and associated storage devices that convert light energy to electrical energy in a solid-state (CCD) imaging device.

Plumbicon: A high-quality camera pickup tube. The Plumbicon provided the best overall performance of all tubes except a later refinement called the Diode Gun Plumbicon. Before CCD cameras replaced them, these two varieties of tubes provided the best-quality pictures available on television.

Polarizing filter: A frequently used lens filter that reduces reflected glare off glass, water, etc.

Primary additive colors: Red, green and blue (RGB). Combinations of these three colors create all the colors seen on a TV screen.

Prime lens: A lens with a fixed, nonadjustable focal length.

Prism block optics: A prism of fine optical glass separating the picture into its RGB components. It is the currently favored internal optical system.

Progressive scanning: Building an image on a display screen by scanning lines in sequential order (1, 2, 3, 4, etc.) rather than scanning alternate lines (1, 3, 5, 7, etc.) in an interlaced pattern. Three digital TV formats, 480p, 720p and 1080p, use progressive scanning.

Prosumer cameras: Cameras that bridge both the professional and consumer markets.

Resolution: An engineering term used to define and measure the sharpness and clarity of a TV picture. The common unit of measurement of resolution is a line. The more lines, the higher the resolution.

Robotic cameras: Computer-controlled cameras programmed to adjust physical location, zoom setting and focus without benefit of camera operators.

Sampling: The digital phenomenon in which some, but not all, pixels in a frame will be used to represent the complete picture. Sampling reduces both cost and the milliseconds it takes to create frames of digital video or streams of audio.

Saticon: A high-quality pickup tube, second only to the Plumbicon. Because of their comparatively lower cost, Saticon cameras were used in many industrial, educational and broadcast news cameras before the CCD camera made them obsolete.

Short focal length lens: Any lens with a focal length less than that of a normal lens; lenses that make objects appear more distant than when viewing with a normal lens. Sometimes called wide-angle lenses.

Shot box: A device allowing storage of many zoom parameters prior to the start of a production.

Signal plate: The front face of the photoconductive camera tube.

Slow lens: Due to their design and their relatively large number of internal elements, these lenses transmit light to an imaging device with greater loss of light intensity than fast lenses.

Special effects filters: Filters, usually placed in front of rather than behind the lens, that add special effects to the image. The star filter, polarizing filter and fog filter are common examples.

Standard-definition television (SDTV): A digital television signal in either 4:3 or 16:9 aspect ratio providing less image resolution than HDTV.

Star filter: A frequently used lens filter that causes points of light in the picture to sparkle like stars, with shafts of light radiating from the center.

Turret: A round plate, usually containing three fixed focal length lenses, affixed to the front of early television and film cameras.

Underexposure: When not enough light enters the camera, resulting in an image or part of an image that is too dark and lacks detail.

Upconvert: The process used to convert SDTV video to an approximation of HDTV. The quality of these images cannot compare with video that began as HDTV, but the video can be converted so it technically imitates HDTV and may then be intercut with HDTV footage.

Video noise: Undesirable interference introduced by electrical or electronic devices either within or outside of a piece of television equipment. It often appears as "snow" in the displayed image.

Vidicon: The first small camera pickup tube, mostly used in industrial-type productions. Now obsolete, replaced by the CCD.

Virtual sets: Sets in which talent are positioned in front of backgrounds created with electronic special effects rather than with physical objects such as flats and other pieces of scenery.

Zoom control: The manipulation of a camera's zoom by the camera operator, often through the use of cranks or servos.

Zoom lenses: Variable focal length lenses.

Zoom ratio: The mathematical ratio of a lens's longest and shortest focal lengths.

chapter **3**

Camera Mounts, Camera Operation and Floor Managing

Chapter 2 discussed how a color camera functions technically. This chapter covers camera mounts and basic camera operation and outlines the duties performed by a TV studio floor manager.

All camera mounts exist to achieve a single purpose: to make camera movement as smooth and free of bumps and jerks as possible. With some artful exceptions, veteran camera operators avoid handheld shots whenever possible. Fortunately, an amazing array of mounting devices exists to aid in getting any shot needed—and if an imaginative director invents a new kind of shot, some creative individual will design a new gadget to get it.

Perhaps you're familiar with the simple one-piece tripods used in amateur video. In contrast, most professional camera supports feature three separate major components: the mounting plate, the head and the base. As the illustration on this page shows, the *mounting plate* is an interface device that attaches to the bottom of the camera. It provides a means of quickly attaching and releasing the camera from the head. The *head* attaches to the underside of the mounting plate. The head is a mechanism permitting the operator to smoothly swivel the camera horizontally (called "panning") and vertically (called "tilting"). The *base* is that part of the support device in contact with the floor or ground and to which the head is attached (see Figure 3-1). The nature of the shot determines which camera mount you need.

Mounting Plates

Cameras typically screw onto one of several kinds of mounting plates generically called *mounting wedges* or *quick-release shoes*. Both allow removal of the camera from the head quickly, usually by depressing a single lever.

These devices are extremely helpful when camera mobility is essential—as in single-camera documentary work. Quick-release shoes save many minutes of wrestling with cumbersome cameras (see Figures 3-2 and 3-3).

Varieties of Heads

There are five families of heads: the friction head, the fluid head, the cradle head, the cam head and the geared head. Although heads are defined generically by the mechanism they use for tilting, all but one uses either friction or hydraulic counterpressure to control panning. One or two handles attached to the heads control head movement. All heads incorporate controls allowing the operator to adjust the resistance, or *drag,* the head exhibits when an operator moves the handles. Movement is smoother when the operator must overcome just a bit of drag. Let's examine each head family, noting their applications, their cost and how they function.

quick-release mounting plate

tripod head

tripod base

Figure 3-1. *A typical tripod mounting system used for ENG and EFP. The quick-release mounting plate allows for rapid mounting or detachment of a camera.*

1.

2.

3.

Figure 3-2. *Shot 1 shows a close-up view of a quick-release, wedge-type mounting plate that attaches to a cam-type tripod head; shot 2 shows the matching hardware that attaches to the camera and slides into the mounting plate on the cam head. In shot 3, the camera-mounted plate is pushed into its matching wedge-shaped slot on the head. The operator is moving a handle that firmly locks the mounting system into place, securing the camera to the tripod.*

1.

3.

2.

Figure 3-3. *Shot 1 is the type of quick-release mounting plate that might be found attached to a tripod head supporting an ENG/EFT camera. Shot 2 shows this plate attached to the bottom of the camera. Shot 3 displays the camera and plate mounted on the tripod, ready for quick release, if needed.*

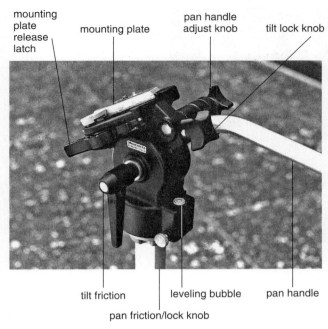

mounting plate release latch

mounting plate

pan handle adjust knob

tilt lock knob

tilt friction

leveling bubble

pan handle

pan friction/lock knob

Figure 3-4. *This is a typical, inexpensive friction head.*

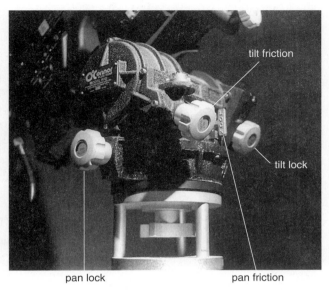

tilt friction

tilt lock

pan lock

pan friction

Figure 3-5. *This is a typical professional fluid head, mounted on a universal tripod riser. Tilt and pan locks prevent the camera mounted on the head from moving unintentionally in any direction. When tilt (up and down) and pan (side to side) controls are unlocked, friction controls on each allow the operator to adjust the amount of drag (counterpressure against one's hand) to his/her needs.*

Friction Heads

The *friction head* often is used with lightweight cameras when the production budget is tiny or when the shots required are not physically or aesthetically demanding. As the name implies, friction heads use internal friction devices to provide simple counterpressure against the force the camera operator exerts on the control handles. Friction heads are used most often in applications varying from surveillance cameras in banks to home video to productions you might shoot while studying TV production (see Figure 3-4).

Fluid Heads

Fluid heads are more expensive than friction heads, but their high performance is worth the investment. Fluid heads can support more camera weight than friction heads. They also control movement more precisely and smoothly by providing hydraulic counterpressure (rather than friction) against the force you exert on the control handles (see Figure 3-5). Some manufacturers offer combination friction/fluid heads (that is, fluid for the tilt function, friction for pans). These models cost more than friction heads but less than fluid heads.

Cradle Heads

The *cradle head* was once the clear choice for heavy studio cameras. A cradle head permits a large, heavy camera assembly to tilt by balancing its weight in the middle of two crescent-shaped runners. These runners

in turn ride on a series of rollers. Simple friction devices control the amount of drag the cradle head provides against the upward and downward (tilt) force applied by the operator. Friction devices also control the cradle head's pan (left and right) resistance (see Figure 3-6).

Cam Heads

Cam heads provide better control than do cradle heads and are now the television industry's state-of-the-art choice for heavy cameras and accessories. This head design uses an oblong shaped cam to provide the most efficient resistance to the weight of the camera when it is at either extreme of tilt. Cam heads are expensive, but they execute the smoothest tilts, even when burdened by heavy cameras, lenses and other weighty production gear, such as teleprompters (see Figure 3-7).

Geared Heads

TV productions rarely use *geared heads,* but they're commonplace in motion picture work. Geared heads handle a heavy camera and accessories while providing more precise camera movement than any other kind of head. Geared heads pan and tilt through a series of interlocking steel cogs, finely machined and lubricated for smoothness and accuracy. One must turn a side-mounted crank forward (counterclockwise) to tilt down (and the reverse to tilt up), while turning a rear-mounted crank clockwise to pan right (and the reverse

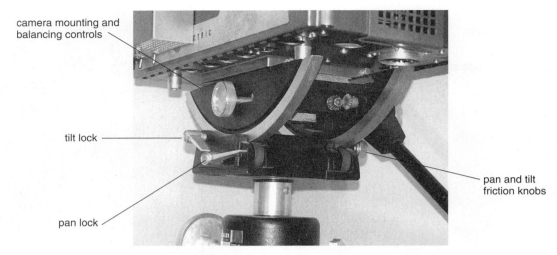

camera mounting and balancing controls

tilt lock

pan and tilt friction knobs

pan lock

Figure 3-6. *A cradle head used for mounting studio cameras.*

1.

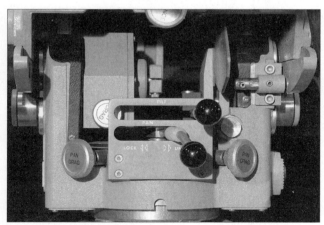

2.

Figure 3-7. *In shot 1, a cam head used for mounting heavy studio cameras is seen from a side view. Note the cam and roller assembly right above the smaller Vinten company label. In shot 2, we see the controls of this cam head: black-tipped tilt lock and pan lock levers in the center, and pan drag knobs on the left and right. The one tilt drag knob visible in this shot is located above the left pan drag knob.*

to pan left), making geared heads by far the hardest of the five types to operate. To pan and tilt simultaneously requires physical coordination, serious concentration and a great deal of practice (see Figure 3-8).

The operator of a camera mounted on a geared head rarely works alone. With both hands required to pan

Figure 3-8. *The ARRI Geared Head, shown here supporting an Arriflex D20 motion picture camera with video assist, provides incredibly precise panning and tilting capabilities for the "coordinated" camera operator. The crank in the lower center of the picture tilts the head and camera up and down; the crank at the right of the picture pans the head and camera left and right.*

Photo courtesy of ARRI Corporation.

and tilt, you always need at least one camera assistant to help with changes of focus, zoom or f-stop performed in midshot.

Choosing the correct head for a particular shot requires the director and the technical director (TD) to consider many variables. Ideally, the quality of the shot is the most important variable, but the production budget and equipment availability often make compromises necessary.

Varieties of Bases

Like heads, bases are designed for diverse production applications. They vary from the stationary to the extremely mobile, from a simple tripod to computerized motion-controlled mounts providing the precise multiple repetitions of the same camera movement needed in some sophisticated special effects applications in film.

Pedestals

The infant television industry borrowed many practices from the more mature motion picture industry, but there were limits. For example, film cameras typically had a support crew consisting of a director of cinematography, a camera operator, a camera assistant, a focus puller and, if the shot required motion, assistants to push the camera around. Budget-minded television station managers soon recognized the advantage of cameras operated by just one person. Accordingly, designers moved all controls (plus the viewing screen) to the rear of the camera so that one operator could manipulate everything. This, in turn, led to development of the heavy *studio pedestal,* a base allowing a single operator to pan, tilt, focus, raise or lower the camera and smoothly push it in any direction on specially designed, smooth TV studio floors. Studio pedestals, with their heavy-duty sets of double wheels, easily handled the large cameras of television's golden era and, later, the additional weight of prompting devices. Because of the pedestal's flexibility, well-equipped TV studios still favor it, although today's lighter cameras no longer require a pedestal's massive support.

There are two main kinds of pedestals, counterweighted and pneumatic. Both refer to the method by which the pedestal raises and lowers its center column which adjusts the height of the camera.

As Figure 3-9 indicates, the *lead-counterweighted pedestal* uses internal lead weights to counterbalance the weight of the camera, lens and accessories. The operator needs to apply only slight hand pressure to raise or lower the camera smoothly.

A *pneumatic pedestal,* such as the model shown in Figure 3-10, uses air pressure to counter the weight of the camera, lens and accessories, providing smoother

1.

2.

Figure 3-9. *Shot 1 shows the inside of a counterweighted pedestal, where one lead weight provides balance for the amount of weight of the camera and head above it, as seen in shot 2. Additional weights can be added to this counterweight for heavier cameras or if a prompter or other equipment are added.*

Figure 3-10. *A Vinten Fulmar, a pneumatic pedestal.*

Photo courtesy of Vinten Corporation.

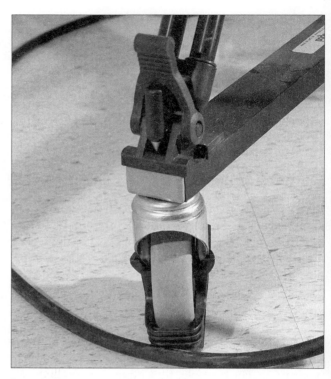

Figure 3-12. Cable guards *surround this studio tripod's wheels to prevent cameras from running over cables, possibly damaging both the cables and cameras.*

movement than a counterweighted model. Some pneumatic models collapse telescopically as low as two feet from the floor. But such increased flexibility and quality comes at a higher cost. Pneumatic pedestals also require more routine maintenance than counterweighted models.

One operator can maneuver a pedestal laterally, on a curved or S-shaped path or even in a circle by steering it with a rotating center wheel (see Figure 3-11). The pedestal is a flexible performer, but its size and weight limit it mostly to in-studio applications.

Tripods

Tripods, sometimes called "sticks," are three-legged bases with adjustable-length legs. Some heavier, less portable models also feature a center post that allows

the camera to be cranked up or down an additional one to three feet. Because pedestals are comparatively quite costly and studio camera weight is decreasing, heavy wheeled tripods increasingly substitute for pedestals in many studios (see Figure 3-12).

ENG and other field applications use tripods extensively. Camera operators often take along an assortment of them. For example, a camera operator may carry as

1.

2.

Figure 3-11. *In shot 1, a camera operator turns the large wheel of the pedestal to point the wheels underneath it in the direction of travel. In shot 2, we see foot-operated buttons that permit the camera operator to switch back and forth between this pedestal's different crabbing (side to side) and dollying (forward and back) options.*

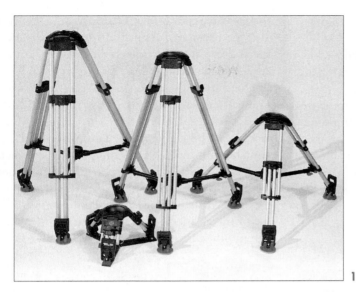

Figure 3-13. *In shot 1 are Sachtler's versions of long legs, medium legs, baby legs and a hi-hat. In this shot, the footing configuration is set up for a hard, flat floor. The tiny hi-hat is attached to a spreader for stability. All these tripods can be quickly configured with spreaders or with pointed feet for use outdoors on grass, dirt, etc. Note the standard O-ring sockets on these tripods, into which the ball (mounting) portion of a head would attach. Shot 2 shows a set of Sachtler long legs with a fluid head mounted on them.*

Photos courtesy of Sachtler Corporation.

many as three sizes of tripod legs that quickly attach to the same fluid head (see Figure 3-13):

- *Long legs:* capable of adjustment from six or seven feet down to about three feet in height
- *Baby legs:* adjustable from four feet down to about one foot in height
- A *hi-hat:* a misnamed short tripod that positions the camera approximately four inches from the ground

Tripod accessories include a device known as either a *triangle, spreader* or a *spider* (although it has three, not eight, legs). By whatever name, this apparatus secures the three tripod legs, preventing them from splaying outward, sliding or otherwise moving during a shot. The tips of some tripod legs slip into slots on the top side of the spider, while others are also tied or clamped down. Weighting the spider's center with a sand bag, water bag, camera bag, battery belt or any other handy weight can provide additional stability. Some tripods have convertible tips, allowing operators to use sharp tips on dirt or grass and then switch to soft tips on harder surfaces, like concrete, asphalt or interior floor surfaces. For tripods with only pointed tips, spiders provide additional stability and help prevent floor damage when used indoors.

Dollies

The *dolly* often allows you to create steadier moving shots than you might be able to achieve with a camera

pedestal. This is because some studio camera pedestals are heavy and relatively cumbersome, especially for long dolly shots, whereas many dollies are lighter and specially designed for movement.

Many professional productions use a device called a *crab dolly,* such as Chapman's *Peewee* shown in Figure 3-14. This type of dolly allows a crab-like movement from which the dolly gets its name (and which also led to the term "crabbing" for side-to-side camera movement).

Figure 3-14. *This small, versatile dolly, the Chapman Super Peewee II, is shown in one of its many configurations. Here the dolly is set up to mount a camera on a riser a few inches off the floor. Steering and crabbing controls are at left.*

Photo by Christine Chapman-Huenergardt, courtesy of Chapman Leonard.

Crab dollies also allow "wagon steering," which means the direction its front wheels point determines the dolly's direction of travel. The crab dolly is extremely adaptable and performs many tasks in both open and cramped spaces. The Peewee also features an arm that, despite its angled appearance, permits a camera mounted on it to rise and descend vertically from a height of five feet nine inches down to only three inches from the floor. The arm works with any professional camera mount and adjusts for various camera mounting heights (see Figure 3-15). On most dollies, camera operators can position their on-board seats in one of four locations, depending on shot requirements. As in film production, the camera operator can sit at the rear of the dolly while an assistant sits beside the lens to adjust focus as needed.

The crab dolly rolls on dual sets of hard rubber tires. These tires work well on the firm, smooth floors of studios and some location sites. Quickly mounted shock-absorbing pneumatic tires help if the surface is just a bit bumpy. There are times, however, when laying track is required. Tubular tracks provide a smooth path for the wheels of some varieties of dolly. It's possible to lay track virtually anywhere the director needs the camera to travel, including sandy beaches or rock-strewn, bumpy stretches of ground (see Figure 3-16).

Cranes

Producers use *cranes* when a production requires the camera to move vertically or diagonally over a greater range than that provided by a camera pedestal or the arm of a crab dolly. Varying greatly in size and application,

1.

Figure 3-15. *Shot 1 shows three different sizes of riser. Most risers use the universal camera O-mount to help fasten the camera head to the tripod, pedestal or dolly or other camera base. In television, there are two items referred to as risers: this mounting device and a platform used in stagecraft to elevate subjects or sets off the floor. You will learn about the stagecraft kind of riser later in this text. Shot 2 shows a close-up of a riser mounted within Chapman's 4-way leveling head.*

Photo by Christine Chapman-Huenergardt, courtesy of Chapman Leonard.

Figure 3-16. *This dolly, a J. L. Fisher Eleven, supporting a Panavision motion picture camera mounted on a geared head, glides on its rubber wheels on a steel track, laid precisely where the path of the shot is to follow.*

Photo courtesy of J. L. Fisher.

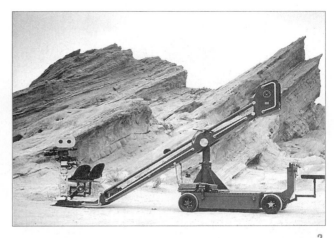

1.

2.

Figure 3-17. *Through the use of lead counterweights, operators can support a camera operator and assistant, or the director, in the air (as in shot 1) on this Chapman Zeus crane. The crane itself can also be trucked and dollied. In shot 2, we see the Zeus craned all the way down to eye level.*

Photo by Christine Chapman-Huenergardt, courtesy of Chapman Leonard.

cranes are basically larger, heavier dollies with counter-weighted boom arms. Typical of a big studio crane is the Chapman *Zeus*. The Zeus sits on a wagon driven and steered from the rear by an assistant called a *dolly grip*. Up front is a huge boom arm capable of moving two seated camera operators (or a director and a camera operator) from below floor level to a height of more than 16 feet (see Figure 3-17). Lead weights added to or removed from the back end of the boom balance the weight of the camera equipment and operators.

Yet another type of crane is actually a heavy-duty flatbed truck with a huge crane mounted on it. The Chapman *Titan/Nova* is designed for shooting on a highway or other road. It can lift the camera up to 27 feet above the road and dolly along with fast car action (see Figure 3-18).

Another model crane, the Chapman *Olympian,* is designed principally for television sports and can lift a four-foot, circular platform with side rails to a maximum height of 22 feet. This crane often serves as a mobile camera platform, capable of running up and down the sidelines during live football coverage. It can travel 18 mph using battery power. Another relatively new addition to sports coverage is the Stealth Aerial Camera. Capable of capturing dramatic overhead shots, this robotic camera support apparatus is suspended over the stadium. Using a computer-controlled cable grid system, the Stealth can cover all the action from above (see Figure 3-19).

Flying Mounts

Although providing great production flexibility, there's a maximum camera height and a maximum speed that crane rigs and even the Stealth Arial Camera can travel. When producers and directors must exceed these limits,

they use airplanes and helicopters. Aircraft often serve as camera bases to provide high and fast-moving shots, shots following vehicles and actors on the move, tracking over difficult terrain or obtaining shots that start on the ground and pull back dramatically into the heavens. Camera operators often use *gyroscopic motionless mounts* (GMMs) to isolate the camera from engine vibration and buffeting by air turbulence. These devices provide audiences with aerial shots that appear to float on air (see Figure 3-20).

Some of these GMMs, which are sometimes called camera pods, can be mounted on track to be rapidly moved back and forth along the front of a stage,

Figure 3-18. *The Chapman Titan/Nova crane counterbalances in the same manner as the Chapman Zeus, but is heavier and features a truck for a base.*

Photo courtesy of Chapman Leonard.

1.

2.

3.

Figure 3-19. *In Shot 1, with a narrow, electrically powered vehicle for a base, this Chapman Olympian crane can move up and down the sidelines, providing shots at many different heights. In shots 2 and 3, the Stealth Aerial Camera is shown in close-up and suspended over a football stadium. The Stealth is a robotic camera mounting system suspended from a matrix of rapidly movable cables that propel it up and down the field.*

Photo courtesy of Chapman Leonard;   Photos courtesy of Stealth Aerial Camera.

1.

2.

3.

Figure 3-20. *Shot 1, above left, shows a full-sized helicopter with a Gyron Systems GMM camera mounted outside. A GMM allows a camera operator to remotely control externally mounted film or ENG cameras from the safety of the inside of airplanes or helicopters. Shot 2, left, shows a miniature remote-controlled helicopter, made by Coptervision Corp., flying inside a stadium getting shots that, for a full-sized helicopter, would be impossible (and probably illegal, according to the FAA). Shot 3, above right, shows an operator remotely controlling the Coptervision. This miniature is only five and a half feet long with a blade spread of only six feet, and either film or video cameras can be mounted on board. It can fly as fast as 75 mph forward, and 45 mph in reverse, at an altitude as high as 14,000 feet. Like normal-sized helicopters, Coptervision is gyrostabilized for smooth shots. But due to its size, Coptervision can safely fly through tunnels and into places too tight for normal-sized helicopters.*

Photo 1 courtesy of Gyron Systems International;   Photos 2 and 3 courtesy of Coptervision.

panning and tilting to follow swiftly moving performers. Videographers shooting performers at rock concerts make use of this mount to obtain dynamic footage of musical artists at work.

As anyone familiar with major national outdoor sporting events knows, hot air balloons and dirigibles (blimps) sometimes carry cameras. The familiar blimps first sponsored by Goodyear and later by other companies have provided panoramic overhead shots at football and baseball games for decades (see Figure 3-21).

A GMM for Handheld Cinema and Videography

There are times when only a handheld camera provides the shot you want. Sometimes you must follow talent up stairs, around or under obstacles or props, through crowds of people or into and out of places where cranes, boom arms, track laying or dollying can't do the job, or would be very expensive to set up. It's in these situations where the *Steadicam*®, Garrett Brown's and Cinema Products' Oscar- and Emmy-winning GMM, does the trick (see Figure 3-22).

Figure 3-21. *Flying high over the stadium at Ohio State University is the Goodyear Blimp. Now many companies sponsor blimps at sporting and other public events.*

Photo by A. Vandersommers, courtesy of Goodyear Tire and Rubber Co.

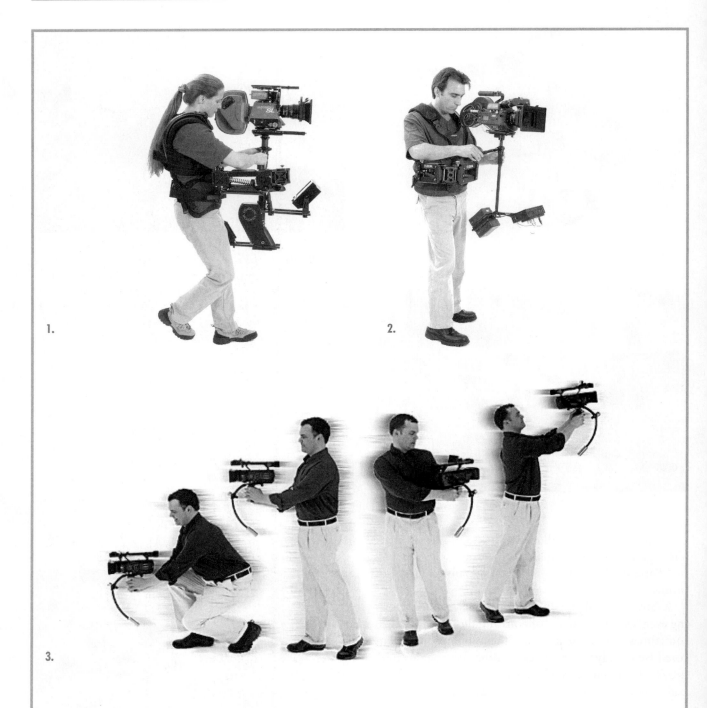

Figure 3-22. *All Steadicams, from the smallest to the most complex, have certain features in common: A camera operator can hand-hold a steady shot while walking in and around objects, or while riding a dolly or any other vehicle. On many Steadicams, remote controls allow the operator to manipulate camera functions such as focus and zoom and to view the picture without pressing his/her eye against the camera viewfinder. Shot 1 is the Steadicam Clipper2, a top-of-the-line system for high-end video and film. It is capable of shooting in high definition and can be used to shoot both video and film. Shot 2 is the Steadicam Flyer 24, a more affordable model. Nonetheless, the Flyer is also capable of standard and high-definition work. Shot 3 demonstrates a Steadicam called the Merlin that could be used with the kind of small digital cameras often used in college and university productions. This model is inexpensive and lightweight, offering students and small-budget producers many of the benefits of the more sophisticated Steadicams.*

Photos courtesy of © The Tiffen Company.

Garrett Brown's Steadicam principle is similar to that of other gyroscopically controlled mounts that came later: Isolate the camera from the source of vibrations, bumps and bounces so it effectively "floats" in the air. All but the smallest Steadicam models utilize a complicated vest—an exoskeletal camera-arm apparatus—worn by the Steadicam operator, isolating the camera from the operator's body motions and bounces. A unique balancing post supporting the camera provides additional isolation. Contact between the operator's head and the camera's viewfinder eyepiece is another source of vibration and movement in most handheld shots. The Steadicam doesn't require pressing the operator's eye against the camera's viewfinder. Instead, the operator views the shot from an externally mounted viewfinder monitor, removing this source of unnecessary motion and vibration. Other camera functions can be remotely controlled, such as powering the camcorder on and off and controlling zoom and focus. The degree of camera isolation provided by the Steadicam system permits the operator to virtually run alongside talent while the camera glides along as if suspended on air. Effective use of the Steadicam requires considerable practice, however, and wearing all the heavy Steadicam apparatus becomes very tiring during a long shooting day.

Camera Mounts for Teleprompters

The choice of mounting device often depends to a degree on whether it must support a prompter device in addition to the camera. "Teleprompter" is the generic term (as well as the brand name of one model) for the family of devices that provide camera-mounted scripts for talent. A prompter was originally a well-lit rolling scroll of paper mounted above the studio camera's lens. Although it required an operator to control the scrolling speed, prompters replaced one or sometimes two cue card holders. This early prompter was more efficient than cue cards because it provided talent better eye–lens alignment and took less preparation time. Prompter typewriters with very large letters permitted extremely quick manual transfers of scripts to scroll paper.

Scrolling paper devices gave way to semi-electronic prompters for studio work during the 1970s. These systems laid the script flat on a moving belt or ramp similar to those found at a supermarket checkout. An overhead black-and-white camera focused on the script as it rolled underneath. Video cable from the black-and-white camera was sent to a TV monitor mounted above or below, and at a right angle to, the lens of the studio camera. The picture from the monitor was reflected by a 45-degree-angled mirror into another mirror placed in

Figure 3-23. *Partially silvered glass permits talent to read the copy displayed on the flat-panel prompter monitor below while the camera lens focuses through the glass on the talent.*

front of the camera lens. Like mirrored sunglasses, this partially silvered glass allowed the camera to shoot the talent through it while the talent read the copy from the mirrored side of the glass (see Figure 3-23).

Modern teleprompters replace the heavy TV monitor with a flat-panel version, drastically reducing the unit's weight. And newsroom computer systems take the story from the reporter's work station where it is originally typed, convey it via the newsroom server to the editor's desk, where the editor makes desired changes, and then insert the story into the newscast's prompter script. Teleprompter copy for other programs is generated using similar computer-based technology. Since the introduction of the flat-panel display in a prompter, ever smaller prompter devices can be used in ENG and EFP work.

In the studio, news anchors use prompters that display complete copies of the script, but many semi-scripted productions require talent to work from simple cue cards. We find that beginning talent too often excessively rely on prompter copy if it's available. A more natural, conversational performance often results when fully scripted prompter copy is not used. Since the live remote is an important part of TV field reporting, learning to work extemporaneously and without a prompter is essential for anyone seeking work as a TV reporter—and good news anchors begin their careers as reporters.

Operating the Prompter How to operate teleprompter computers depends on what brand of software is bundled with your prompter hardware. However, some general statements about prompter computer operation can be made.

Most brands of prompter software allow you to import documents, such as scripts written in Microsoft Word, into the prompter computer. Some, however, require that you first save the script in rich text format (that is, with the extension ".rtf") rather than as a Word document (which carries the ".doc" extension). Other prompter software systems can't handle the importation of your two-column scripts, and you will have to select and copy the right-hand column of the script (where the words are), save it as a separate file and then import it into the prompter computer. Many newsroom computer systems work in tandem with teleprompter computers, so the script can be sent directly to the prompter.

Most prompter software has two basic modes. Generically, the first is called "edit," and the second is "prompt." You can quickly switch back and forth between them. Edit mode is used to import scripts, write or make changes in scripts for the prompter. Edit mode allows you to change the font you will use and its size, margins and spacing and to make other adjustments necessary for your talent's comfort and convenience while reading from the prompter.

When you're finished importing, writing or editing in edit mode, switch to prompt mode. In prompt mode, you will be able to control the speed at which the prompter script scrolls up, by means of a knob on a cylindrically shaped scrolling controller. In prompt mode, the prompter software also lets you control scrolling speed or return the script to its beginning, or any other desired location, by using the computer keyboard or the controller.

Assuming talent doesn't operate the controller him/herself, as is sometimes the case, the success of the talent's prompter-script reading is up to you. Listen carefully to the talent as he/she reads and do everything you can to keep up with them, adjusting the scrolling speed so talent can read ahead in the script a few lines. In the chapter on announcing later in this text, you will learn more about the importance of reading ahead. Just remember this rule of script scrolling: You should try to scroll the script at the rate the talent is reading. Don't make the talent speed up or slow down to follow you. Your job is to follow them.

Camera Operation

We have studied cameras, how they work and what kinds of devices are used to mount them. Now we will discuss how to operate one. There are three distinct phases of camera work in television: *camera setup, camera operation* and the *wrap*. We'll discuss each in turn, as they apply to both studio and ENG productions.

Studio Camera Setup

Among their many duties, video technicians typically perform all setup functions for professional studio productions. Studio camera setup includes white and black balancing and precisely matching the color values of each camera, so that when you cut back and forth between them, these values will appear identical.

We discussed the theory and technique of automatic white and black balancing of ENG cameras in Chapter 1, "The Color Camera." All modern studio cameras provide the same automatic color correction capabilities described for ENG cameras. If staffing or budget restraints don't permit a video technician, it's comforting to know that ENG-type camera setup procedures are available in the studio. But studio cameras typically offer producers and directors more picture control than do ENG/EFP cameras. Also, even if the studio cameras are automatically white balanced, they are usually slightly out of adjustment relative to each other. The studio camera's control unit, the CCU, has fine tuning controls allowing the video engineer to match the cameras' color saturation, hue and contrast precisely. This ensures that color, hue and contrast will not shift when the director cuts from camera to camera, each with a shot of the same talent or object. If a video technician isn't available, producers, directors or TDs of small budget productions must assume the responsibility for matching the color performance of studio cameras.

Studio Camera Procedures

Camera procedure varies widely from studio to studio. Although we provide a logical series of steps below, it's important to consider these procedural steps as illustrative rather than definitive. No two production facilities are likely to have exactly the same cameras, mounts, studio configuration and staffing. We anticipate that your instructor will outline a procedure that differs from this text. We will also remind you, as will your instructor, that the procedures learned in class will not be exactly the same as those required at your first studio production job or internship. It's important to know the procedures of the facility at which you are working, but also understand that each facility will require you to learn new ways of doing things. With this caveat firmly in mind, in Tech Manual 3-1 at the end of this chapter, we offer our list of typical procedures.

ENG Camera Setup

Even beginners need to have sufficient knowledge to handle unsupervised camera setup in field production. This is not a serious problem, however, because modern ENG cameras make setup easy or, with the most modern models, unnecessary. In some ways ENG setup is even easier than in a studio. At least, in single-camera ENG work, you don't have to contend with the problem of precisely matching picture quality among multiple cameras.

It's important to consult your camera operating manual long before you set out to shoot your first ENG project, because every manufacturer's camera systems (and their individual models) differ. If equipment is available, we strongly suggest that you do a test shoot, a "shakedown cruise" for both yourself and your equipment, before shooting your first class project. Many professionals routinely conduct a test shoot with their equipment before their productions, and it's equally or even more important for beginners. As with studio camera setup, we have suggested some generic procedures for ENG setup in Tech Manual 3-2 at the end of this chapter.

Studio and EFP Camera Movements

The second phase of studio and EFP camera operation is the rehearsal or show itself. There are a number of commands that studio, EFP or ENG directors may give their camera operators. We will now discuss them, along with some tips for the camera operator.

Two basic variables are critical to all camera movements: smoothness and speed. Smoothness is an almost universal requirement. Seldom will a director want any camera movement on the air executed with anything less than the maximum smoothness possible under the prevailing conditions. Speed, however, is highly variable, and camera operators must coordinate with the director to determine the proper speed of their movements. Unfortunately, smoothness and speed tend to operate in contradiction, with smoothness suffering as speed increases. Beginning camera operators tend to perform movements much too rapidly with a resulting loss of smoothness. As a general rule, beginning operators would be wise to forget about speed and concentrate more on smoothness.

We introduced two basic camera movements, pan and tilt, earlier in this chapter. Note that directors always give these commands with reference to the <u>camera operator's</u> left or right, not the talent's left or right. The director refers to talent's right or left as "stage right" or "stage left," the reverse of "camera right" and "camera left" because talent is positioned opposite the camera (see Figure 3-24).

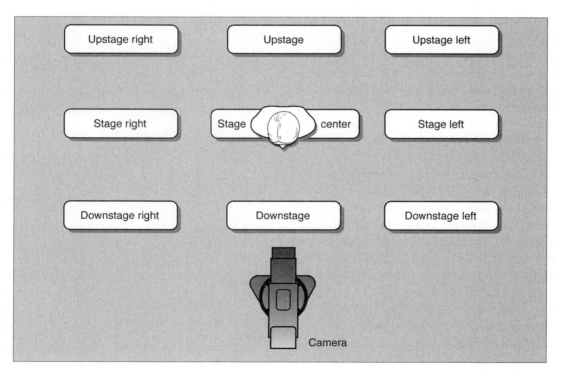

Figure 3-24. *From camera operators' points of view, directions heard in their headsets refer to their left or right. But when addressing actors, directors reverse directions, so that "right" refers to the actor's right, and "left," to the actor's left. So, a standard stage direction to an actor who is standing at center stage might be, "OK, now cross to downstage right," which means to the actor's right but to the camera operator's left.*

When you're operating a camera on a tripod or pedestal, you're panning and tilting by moving a rear-mounted handle left or right, up or down. But like the tiller of a boat, you move the handle to the left to pan right and to the right to pan left; up for down, and down for up. If you're not a sailor, this can be a bit confusing at first. Consider this helpful advice: When the director says, "Pan right," think instead that the director said, "Point the camera lens right." Then your brain will send a signal to your arm to turn the pan handle to the left. The same mental game works for up or down. With practice, this becomes second nature.

Although technically not a camera movement, we include the *zoom* at this point because it is a common command frequently used in combination with many other movements discussed. The director may say, "Zoom in," "Tighten up your shot" or "Go in a little." In each instance the director is asking you to either crank a zoom handle forward (clockwise) or depress the camera's servo zoom control, mounted on the pan handle, to the right. The faster you crank the zoom handle, or the more thumb pressure placed on the servo control, the faster the zoom. Zooming out requires cranking the handle counterclockwise or exerting pressure on the left end of the servo control.

Zooming in live, on the air, is more difficult than zooming out. This is because focus is lost easily when zooming in. However, prefocusing on the spot where the zoom-in will eventually stop <u>while your camera is off the air</u> eliminates this problem. You do this by zooming in to your lens's longest focal length and focusing on the subject. Using the lens's maximum focal length creates shallow depth of field, assuring that the subject is now in the sharpest possible focus. Then zoom out to the shot size the director wants for the beginning of your zoom and wait for the director's command to zoom in.

If the director orders you to zoom when your camera is *not* on the air, speed is the critical factor, not smoothness or maintaining focus. Simply zoom, refocus and compose the requested shot as fast as you can. The speedy, cooperative camera operator who composes and focuses a new shot in a scant few seconds is remembered and requested by directors again and again, especially for live or live-on-tape productions.

We've previously noted that beginners tend to use the zoom excessively. It's good practice to keep your hand away from the zoom handle and on the pan handle whenever possible. This reduces the temptation to overuse the zoom and assists you in smoother pans and tilts. When directors ask rookie camera operators to shape up their shots (for example, when the shot is cutting off part of a talent's head), their first instinct is to zoom

out. But zooming out changes the size of the shot the director needs. Instead, to correct the lack of headroom problem, you should simply tilt the camera up.

A camera movement toward or away from the talent is called a <u>dolly</u>. This movement is shown in Figure 3-25. The director's command would be, "Camera three, dolly in about three feet." The visual effect of a dolly performed on-air is different from that of an on-air zoom. However, dolly commands are rare because smooth on-air dollies are difficult, and a zoom lens provides a closer shot without the time and effort required to move the camera.

More often, directors order camera operators to *truck*. Trucking means moving the entire camera tripod or

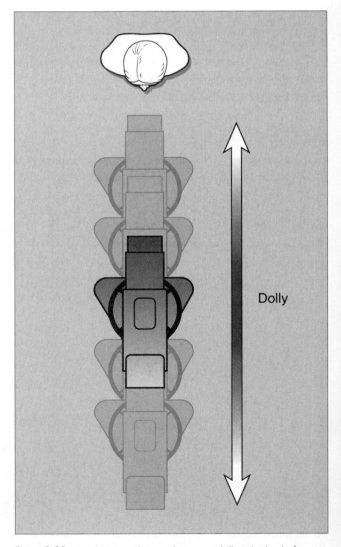

Figure 3-25. *In television, there is the noun "dolly," the kind of mounting device described earlier in this chapter, and there is the movement called the "dolly," which is actually rolling the camera pedestal closer to or farther away from talent (or whatever you're assigned to shoot).*

pedestal sideways to the left or right. The command will be, "truck right" or "truck left." Sometimes this is accomplished live, but such a move is rarely ordered without providing a camera assistant to help. Figure 3-26 demonstrates trucking. When the trucking movement is on a curved path, it's called an *arc* (see Figure 3-27). The command will be to "arc left (or right)."

Again, remember that with arc, dolly or trucking movements performed live, move as smoothly and as unobtrusively as you can, keeping your shot well composed as you go. Unless the action is well rehearsed and there's adequate help to perform them successfully, directors avoid movements requiring the operator to *follow focus* (that is, adjust focus) while also executing a camera movement. You can reduce the need to follow focus if your shot permits you to set your zoom lens on a short focal length to increase depth of field and enhance image stability. When requested to truck, arc or dolly while your camera is off the air, do so as fast as you can, and don't forget to zoom in and refocus any time your movement alters the distance between camera and subject.

The director or assistant director may order you to raise or lower the camera to achieve a better vertical angle relative to your subject. The command is usually to "*pedestal up*" or "*pedestal down*." You can easily comply by lifting or lowering one of the pedestal's circular rings if your camera is mounted on a standard pedestal.

This could conceivably be done even when you're on the air—if you're careful (see Figure 3-28).

Beginners rarely find themselves assigned a camera mounted on a crane. But when you do, depending on the size and design of the crane, you may either ride on it, or you may instead be operating a smaller, lighter mini-crane. Mini-cranes usually feature servo remote control of camera pan, tilt, zoom and picture monitoring. In either case, crane assistants help camera operators respond to the director's commands. Generally, there are three commands for crane camera operators: "Truck (or arc or dolly) the crane left (or right)," "*crane up* (or down)" and "*tongue* right (or left)." In trucking a crane, the director wishes the entire unit moved laterally in some way. The command "crane up (or down)" calls for raising or lowering the boom arm of the crane. This is performed by assistants if the camera operator is on board the crane. Depending on the model, the operator may perform this function when using a mini-crane. With practice, it's possible to execute craning live. The same procedures we discussed earlier for trucking, arcing and pedestalling up and down still apply. The command "tongue left (or right)" instructs your crane's boom operator to pan the boom arm to the left or right (see Figure 3-29).

More often used in film production, a *tracking shot* either requires the crew to lay two portable tubular tracks

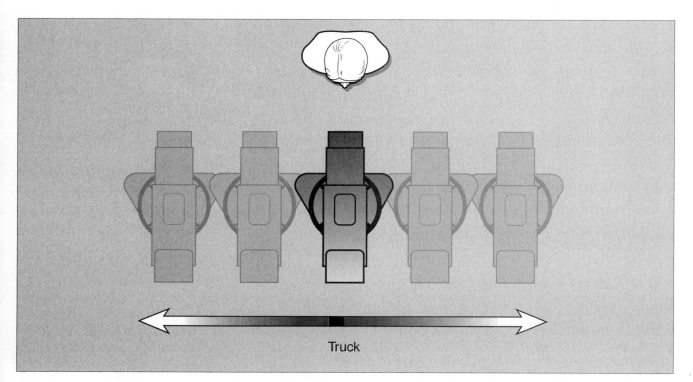

Truck

Figure 3-26. *Like the dolly, "truck" is both a noun and a verb. "To truck" is to move the camera pedestal to the left or right in a relatively straight line of travel.*

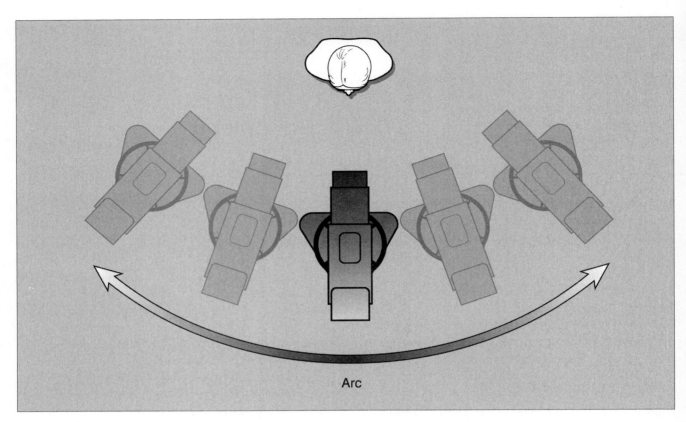

Figure 3-27. *An arc is similar to a trucking movement, except an arc is a curved truck.*

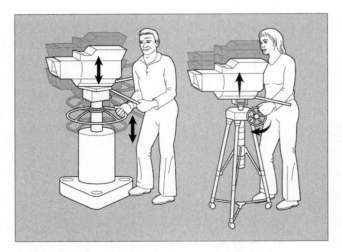

Figure 3-28. *Pedestal-up or pedestal-down movements are relatively easy if you're operating a camera pedestal, as the operator is on the left in this illustration. However, if the camera is mounted on a tripod with an adjustable center post such as the one on the right, the operator must crank a wheel that slowly adjusts height. Since these mechanisms aren't designed for smooth vertical adjustments, this movement is too jerky to be done on the air. You cannot do this particular movement at all if your camera is mounted on simple tripod legs and universal O-mount.*

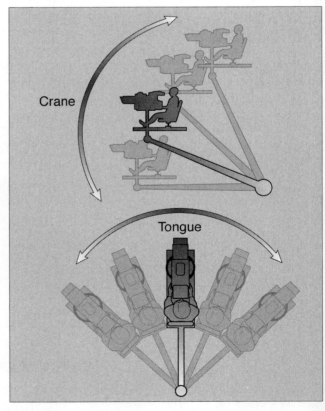

Figure 3-29. *Craning a boom arm tilts it up or down; tonguing pans the boom arm left or right.*

Figure 3-30. *A J. L. Fisher model Ten. Note the two seats for camera operator and assistant (or director). This model features a small boom, which can be raised or lowered to nearly floor level. With the help of assistants, a smooth tracking shot can be accomplished with such a device.*

Photo courtesy of J. L. Fisher Corporation.

along the route the camera must travel, as shown earlier in this chapter, or the camera and head are mounted to a dolly with rubber wheels and pushed around a smooth floor, such as the polished concrete of a television studio. The operator, camera and an assistant can ride on the dolly, pushed along by two assistants (see Figure 3-30).

ENG Camera Movements

Hand-holding lightweight cameras is an alternative, intrinsically bumpier method of providing a base for camera shots. We suggested earlier that the mobility provided by handheld camera operation is often poor compensation for the loss of stability. Even the most dedicated "run-and-gun" TV news organizations try to use tripods when possible. But sometimes a handheld shot is the only option, and inventive videographers often produce satisfactory video by following the few simple guidelines found in the "How to Hand-hold" box on page 78.

Wrapping Up

Children may be forgiven for leaving their toys scattered around when they finish playing, but professional camera operators are not children. Wrap-up procedures vary from studio to studio, and the rule is to follow the guidelines provided by the instructor or, in the workplace, the person responsible for camera operators. Some procedures are fairly common, and we offer them for your consideration with the usual reminder that they are generic and may differ from those of your particular production facility.

Studio Wrap Up   The general goal is to leave everything in the studio much as it was when you entered. You also must store your camera correctly. Here are some common procedures to achieve that goal:

1. Lock the pan control of your camera head.
2. Tilt the camera down just below level and lock it. This was a simple safety precaution for tubed cameras to prevent damage from burn-in. Although not strictly necessary with cameras that use a charge-coupled device (CCD), leaving the lens pointing slightly below eye level is a harmless practice. Besides, it is still technically possible to damage a CCD with long-term exposure to an exceptionally bright object.
3. Cap the lens and rotate the filter wheel behind the lens to its "C" or "cap" position.
4. Hang up your headset in the place appointed, and move your camera to wherever cameras are parked when not in use. Then carefully coil the camera cable. See Figure 3-31.
5. If it is the custom in your studio, turn down the brightness on your camera viewfinder. This helps

Figure 3-31. *Cameras properly positioned after a studio shoot, with cables neatly coiled.*

How to Hand-hold

1. Stabilize your body. Stand on secure footing, with your feet a little farther apart than normal. Place one foot slightly behind the other. Avoid panting, especially if you must shoot with your zoom lens set at a long focal length. Take several slow, deep breaths through your nose. Take another deep breath, let half of it escape, and then begin your shot. ENG shots often last only a few seconds and you may be able to hold your breath long enough to complete the shot. But don't hold your breath too long. If you need to breathe, breathe slowly through your nose, concentrating on keeping your camera shoulder from rising and dipping (see Figure 3-32).

2. Look for ways to anchor yourself. Rather than shooting standing up, sit on something high, like a brick ledge. Better yet, rest the camera on top of the ledge if it's the right height. Pressing your back or shoulder against a wall can help steady a shot. Backing into a corner, with both shoulders supported by walls, is a good technique. Basically the rules that apply to shooting a rifle apply to shooting a camera: You will be more accurate if you use a stabilizing support. Lean on objects; rest your arms and elbows on mailboxes, garbage cans, automobiles, pillows or bean bags . . . whatever is available. In short, be as creative in finding ways to anchor yourself as you are when composing a shot (see Figure 3-33).

3. Be smooth. Pan and tilt by rotating the upper body, not by shuffling your feet. Some people find it helps if they bend their knees slightly. Unless you're following fast action (for example, the flight of a football pass), don't pan or tilt speedily. Overly fast *swish pans* make audiences ill.

4. Avoid unnecessary zooming. The longer the focal length of your lens, the less stable your shot and shallower the depth of field. Instead of zooming unnecessarily, move closer to the subject and use a shorter focal length. This is especially helpful in news and documentary work where the action is unpredictable. ENG camera operators sometimes have enough time to pan but not to zoom and focus.

5. If you must walk while shooting, walk like Groucho Marx: Groucho's famous bent-knee walk made his upper body appear to float across a movie set. It will do the same for a handheld camera. And if you've never heard of Groucho, you owe yourself a treat: Go rent *Duck Soup* or *A Night at the Opera*.

Figure 3-32. *An ENG camera operator standing with one foot slightly behind the other, which can make hand-holding a camera somewhat smoother.*

1.

2.

3.

Figure 3-33. *In shot 1, the ENG camera operator uses a brick ledge to steady his shot. In shot 2, the operator finds that leaning against a wall steadies him more than just standing upright. In shot 3, this same ledge can serve as a base to sit on. In all three instances, an object as simple as a wall serves to make the shots smoother and more professional looking.*

extend the life of viewfinders in studios where cameras are left running most of the time.

If the production you're working on is completed, remove any *shot sheets* (a list of shots for one particular camera, given to the camera operator by the director) and other notes taped to your camera for this production and return them to the director. Never throw away shot sheets without asking. It's always wise for a director to save such things in case some untoward event requires this paperwork to be used again in a reshoot.

Check with the floor manager or director to see if they have additional tasks to assign. When unions permit, it is not unusual in studio production environments for camera operators to assist with prop storage and similar work following a production.

Wrapping an ENG Shoot   Wrapping an ENG shoot requires a different set of skills and more responsibilities, because you must not only wrap your gear but also return it to the studio or rental facility. The procedures below deal mainly with wrapping the ENG camera and associated production gear.

1. Follow the relevant camera shutdown procedures described for studio cameras.
2. Turn the camera power off and disconnect all microphone and other cables.
3. Coil the various cables neatly and put them and their associated peripherals (microphones, VCRs, etc.) into their respective storage areas, latching their cases securely.
4. Carefully remove the camera from the tripod head.
5. Eject your tape and mark the cassette with the date and title of today's shoot and so on.
6. Remove the battery and label it as used, so that later you can identify which of your batteries needs recharging. Pack it away.
7. Carefully pack the camera and any accessories (such as a camera-mounted light) in appropriate carrying cases; close and latch the cases.
8. Fold your tripod and accessories, and store them in their protective carrier.
9. Collect and properly store reflectors, extension cords, gaffer's tape and other gear.

Some video facilities provide lists of items checked out or rented. Often these lists are taped inside the cover of carrying cases. Before you leave the location, check packed items against these lists to be sure you have accounted for all the gear that has been checked out.

Take a good look around the site. Beginners often overlook small but valuable items, such as extension cords, lens caps and filters, light meters, microphone cables, small mikes and so on. A checklist of items helps, but items are frequently brought to the shoot that are not included in the lists, so examining the site carefully before leaving is prudent.

Finally, as if you were on a camping trip, "pack out your trash."

More General Advice to Beginning Camera Operators

We have several suggestions for a beginning camera operator. First, listen to your director! Television is a producer's medium, but for camera operators the director's word is final. Directors may do things that you feel are incorrect, but remember the operator's credo, often thought but wisely left unsaid: "You may be wrong, but it's your show." Of course, you should not blindly follow directions that jeopardize safety. As you gain experience, you'll discover ways to help your director, but we warn beginning operators against exercising too much initiative too soon. The balance between showing initiative and impertinence is delicate.

Also heed instructions from your assistant director and TD. They are also your supervisors; they help relay information of importance from the director, plus provide some of their own.

In addition, it is important to avoid intercom chatter. The best camera operators only speak when spoken to, freeing the intercom line for important communications.

While staying silent, follow the action! Especially in loosely scripted, live or live-on-tape programs, a good camera operator anticipates the movement of talent, keeps good composition while following movement and, when not on line, provides the director with an alternative shot.

But as you follow the action, exercise special care when moving a camera while it's still attached to a tripod. You never know when a mounting pin will break or an improperly set mounting lever will let go, sending your valuable camera hurtling to the ground. Cameras are expensive to replace. Remove the camera from the tripod if you're moving to any new shooting setup more than a few yards away.

As another safety precaution, watch out for all cables! Much ENG camera damage results when operators forget that there are cables of limited length attached to cameras, lighting instruments and so on.

Studio Floor Management

The crewperson physically closest to camera operators during a studio production is the floor manager (the FM, also occasionally called the "floor director"). Floor management is a skill learned early in studio production class labs.

In the physical absence of the director, the floor manager acts as the extension, or agent, of the director. The FM's primary duty is to cue the talent during a show and relay messages from the director to talent who are not privy to the intercom or to an *internal feedback (IFB) earpiece,* which is a one-way intercom allowing the director or producer to communicate to talent. Before a show, the FM also relays messages to talent from other crewmembers in the control room as needed. Good, crisp timing in a TV show is often related directly to good, clear hand signals from the FM. The chart on the following page explains an FM's standard hand signals (see Figure 3-34).

Now we've covered camera-mounting equipment and the basics of camera operation—with one important exception: composing the camera shot. This is so important that we've devoted an entire chapter to it. Stay tuned.

Figure 3-34. *A. Stand by: Arm extended straight up, palm facing talent. B. Cue: From the standby position, drop arm forward 90 degrees and point to talent. Do this all in one distinct motion. C. We're on time: While facing talent, touch the tip of your nose with your finger. D. Speed up your speaking/reading: Rotate your hand, pointing upward, in a vigorous clockwise motion. Make sure your hand is below your head or talent may think you're giving him/her the "wind it up" signal. E. Slow down: Also called the "stretch it" command, pantomime pulling taffy with your hands. F. Wind it up (end the show/segment): With hand in the air high over your head, rotate hand and arm. G. Cut: A throat-slitting motion with your arm. H. Okay (things are going all right): Make an "O" with your thumb and forefinger. I. Speak up: Cup your hand to your ear as if you can't hear very well. J. Speak softer: Put your hands out flat in front of you and push downward. K. Keep talking: Imitate the beak of a bird opening and closing with your hand. L. Three minutes to go: Hold up three fingers, palm away from talent. (The same gesture, with a different number of fingers, works for four minutes, five minutes and so on.) M. One half minute to go: Cross forearms toward talent. N. Fifteen seconds to go: Raise fist above head, pointing fingers toward talent. O. Film/Tape roll (tape is rolling, so end what you're saying quickly): Hold extended right hand in front of you, point a few fingers of the left hand toward right palm and rotate in a cranking motion. P. Ten seconds down to one second: Same as for minutes, but point your palm toward the talent instead of away. In some studios, large countdown cards (marked "5 minutes," "1 minute," "30 seconds," etc.) are shown to talent instead of the FM hand signals for times. Time cues may also be conveyed to talent via the prompter.*

Figure 3-34. *(Continued)*

Dos and Don'ts of Floor Managing

1. Give crisp, clean signals. Your talent is facing harsh studio lights; wimpy hand signals can't be seen.

2. Repeat your signal until you're sure the talent sees it. Talent's recognition must not, of course, be so overt it is noticeable by viewers. Subtle recognition signals will become clearer the longer you work with each performer.

3. Give your signal standing <u>very close to the camera lens</u> the talent is facing. Don't force talent to look away from the lens to see your signal.

4. Since you're close to the lens, make sure your hands (especially during the "stretch it" signal) do not enter the lens's field of view.

5. Pay attention to the director! Inexperienced FMs sometimes get caught up in what's going on in the show, forgetting why they're there. Listen to what the director tells camera operators. Perhaps you can help them execute the director's commands by pulling cable out of the way, etc.

6. Anticipate trouble, and try to help everyone. Remember that you are the eyes and ears of the director on the studio floor. Many times the FM can speak to the director and the TD on behalf of the floor crew. This often saves time by reducing unnecessary intercom traffic.

If camera setup is performed by a video technician, you will probably find the cameras facing the set and focused on a setup chart. If a video technician is not available to perform setup, the cameras may be parked to one side of the studio, safely out of the traffic path, perhaps with a protective cap covering the lens if the camera is not equipped with a prompter. If a lens cap is in place, remove it, being careful to store it where it can be easily found following production. In some cases the lens may be capped by the filter wheel. If the wheel is in the "C" (capped) position, rotate the wheel until the proper color correction filter for studio lighting is in place. Typically the correct filter is the one for 3,200-degrees Kelvin. It is unusual for technicians to replace the lens cap following setup or to cap the camera using the filter wheel. However, some cameras have an "electronic cap," and technicians may engage it following setup. If your camera has an electronic cap, it must be disengaged by pressing the appropriate control on the body of camera.

It is standard practice to leave any unattended camera with the various camera mount controls locked. These must be released before moving the camera or its mount. Attempting to move the camera or mount before releasing all locks is a common error resulting in frustration and, too often, damage to the equipment. Unlocking camera and mount functions is a basic procedure that varies with the brand of camera/mount. Heed the instructions of your instructor or studio technician.

With the camera in position for the first shot of the production, it's time to set the camera viewfinder properly. Position the viewfinder to provide easy viewing. You may need to reposition the viewfinder during production if shot composition requires the camera pedestal be set very high or very low. Also, adjust the brightness and contrast of your viewfinder.

Adjust the head's pan and tilt drags (also called "friction controls") to your personal requirements.

Then, adjust your intercom headset to comfortably fit your head. Set the volume to your requirements, but avoid a volume level so high there will be audio feedback (screeching) when you remove the headset.

Next, prepare the tripod/pedestal wheels and cable for any camera movement your shots require. Review the illustrations earlier in this chapter for tips on the mechanical operation of camera pedestals.

Use the headset to notify your director (or TD) that you are in position and ready for instructions.

If there is time remaining before the production or rehearsal begins and the director does not need you to help with other preproduction duties, practice your assigned shots. It's especially important to practice any movements you will have to perform. Ambitious and industrious camera operators are rarely bored: They can almost always find something to do before production begins that will save time (and perhaps embarrassment) later.

If you need to attend to other duties after checking in with the director or TD, ask for and be sure you get permission before leaving your position. Nothing is more frustrating to a director than discovering a camera operator has disappeared just when needed. And remember, all controls of an unattended camera must be locked!

Many ENG setup procedures are identical to studio cameras, but the differences are also important. Automation has relieved the ENG operator of many tasks, but leveling the camera and white balancing are critical. Once a studio camera is white balanced for a production, it usually holds its balance all day. But the typical ENG camera operator must white balance much more often to cope with changing outdoor light at different times of day and the way light varies in different shooting locations.

1. After unpacking your gear, mount your camera on the tripod, making sure it's level. Some tripods have built-in *spirit levels* (similar to those used by carpenters) to help in leveling the tripod head. Centering a floating bubble in a small

Figure 3-35. *A tripod bubble level.*

circle positions the tripod's head so that the camera is level, at least at the outset (see Figure 3-35). This is one procedure that has not been automated, and shots from a camera not properly leveled look odd.

2. Next, connect your battery (or other power source, such as an AC adapter) and turn on the camera. After setting the camera's filter wheel for the appropriate light source (3,200 degrees Kelvin for portable quartz lights, 5,600 degrees Kelvin for average daylight, etc.; consult your camera manual to choose the right filters), you're ready to uncap the lens. White balance procedures may vary, depending on the camera brand and model. Often, however, you simply zoom in tight on a white object within the scene and press the auto-white-balance switch.

A viewfinder indicator tells you when white balance is achieved. If balance is not achieved, recheck the position of your filter wheel. And be <u>sure</u> that the object in the scene is really white! Where most beginners fail is in forgetting to do another white balance when they move from one location to another, or they turn off the camera and don't rebalance when they resume shooting. Some, but not all, cameras hold the previous balance in memory even when they are turned off. Check the manual to see if your camera retains the balance in memory, or make it a habit to balance each time you turn on the camera.

3. Some cameras allow the camera to store all setup parameters in memory for shooting situations commonly encountered. Sometimes ENG setup involves little more than recalling the proper information from memory. But the operator must remember to pull up the scene from memory: The camera doesn't do it automatically! Some of the newest cameras have microprocessors that handle routine setup functions automatically, requiring no operator involvement. However, operators may need to set function switches if they do not want to use the automated default functions, such as auto iris and autofocus.

ENG setup is neither difficult nor does it require great technical skill, but some judgment and effort is required. Failure to level the camera properly and to perform any required color corrections shows up instantly when reviewing footage.

Important Vocabulary Terms

Arc: A curved truck movement.

Baby legs: Tripod legs adjustable from four feet down to one foot in height.

Base: A general name for the mounting device (such as a tripod, studio pedestal, crane, etc.) on which the camera head is mounted.

Cable guard: Device surrounding a studio tripod's wheels that prevents cameras from running over cables, possibly damaging both cables and cameras.

Cam head: A head using a series of cams and cylinders to control tilts. This is the preferred heavy-camera studio head.

Camera operation: The second phase of the camera operator's job: listening to the director's commands and reacting in a professional, artistic manner.

Camera setup: The first phase of the camera operator's job: preparing the camera physically and electronically for the task at hand.

Crab dolly: A dolly capable of motion directed by the front wheels, wagon-style, or in its alternate mode, sideways like a crab.

Crabbing: Moving a crab dolly sideways.

Cradle head: A head for heavy studio cameras that balances camera weight to perform smooth tilts; it is gradually being replaced in studios by the cam head.

Crane: A base design that allows raising and lowering the camera far beyond the range of studio pedestals. Cranes raise and lower cameras (and sometimes their operators) using a counterweighted boom arm, which can also be panned laterally (tongued).

Crane up/down: A director's command to raise or lower the boom arm of a crane.

Dolly: Either camera movement toward or away from the talent/set, or a camera base designed to perform this and other moves.

Dolly grip: A crewperson assigned to pushing and pulling a dolly around the studio or set.

Drag: The resistance the head exhibits when an operator moves the handles to pan or tilt the camera.

Fluid head: A head that uses hydraulics to provide resistance against operator pressure on the control handles. This is the favorite head for ENG/EFP camera work.

Follow focus: Maintaining focus during a camera or talent move while panning and/or zooming the camera simultaneously.

Friction head: A head for lightweight cameras using simple mechanical friction to provide resistance against operator pressure on the control handles. This is the least-desirable type of head.

Geared head: A head using interlocking steel cogs for panning and tilting. This type of head is the most precise as well as the most difficult to operate; it is most often used in motion picture work.

Gyroscopic motionless mount (GMM): A device used to isolate the camera from vibration or other movement to create a steadier image.

Head: A device that directly attaches to the bottom of the camera, or to a mounting plate, allowing the operator to smoothly pan and tilt the camera.

Hi-hat: A misnamed short tripod that positions the camera approximately four inches from the ground.

Internal feedback (IFB) earpiece: A device providing a separate, one-way intercom that allows the director or producer to communicate with talent, even when the talent is live on the air. Also called interruptible feedback, because it sometimes is used to feed back program audio when not providing instructions from the director or producer.

Lead-counterweighted studio pedestal: A pedestal design that balances camera/lens weight on the center column with lead weights.

Long legs: Tripod legs adjustable from seven feet down to three feet in height.

Mounting plate: Interface device fitting between the camera and head that allows quick and easy attachment and removal of the camera from the base.

Mounting wedge: A type of mounting plate frequently used to interface cameras and heads.

Olympian: An exceptionally mobile, medium-sized Chapman crane designed for television sports applications.

Pedestal up/down: A director's command to raise or lower a studio pedestal's center column.

Peewee: A popular model of Chapman dolly that allows both wagon and crab mode steering.

Pneumatic studio pedestal: A pedestal design that balances camera/lens weight on the center column using air pressure.

Quick-release shoe: A type of mounting plate frequently used to interface cameras and heads.

Riser: In television, there are two items referred to as risers: a device to mount a camera head to a pedestal and a platform used in stagecraft to elevate subjects or sets off the floor.

Shot sheet: A list of shots for the production for one particular camera, given to the camera operator by the director.

Spider: A camera support accessory preventing tripod legs from splaying outward or otherwise moving during a shot. Also called a "spreader" or "triangle."

Spirit level: A device built into some heads that assists the operator in leveling the head. The operator levels the head by adjusting the support until the spirit level's bubble is perfectly centered.

Spreader: See "Spider."

Steadicam®: Brand name for a gyroscopic motionless body mount. Steadicam has also become a generic term for this kind of mount.

Studio pedestal: A base designed to provide maximum support for a heavy studio camera, teleprompter and other accessories. Pedestals are designed so that one person typically performs many camera operation functions (panning, tilting, focusing and even trucking) without assistance.

Swish pan: A too-rapid pan movement that tends to make the audience dizzy.

Titan/Nova: Chapman's combination heavy truck and 27-foot camera crane.

Tongue left/right: A director's command to pan a crane's boom arm.

Tracking shot: A complex shot using a special camera dolly supporting both the camera and operator that rides along parallel tubular tracks. The dolly and its cargo are pushed along the tracks during the shot to follow action. More often used in film than TV production.

Triangle: See "Spider."

Tripod: A three-legged camera base.

Truck: Director's command to push the camera tripod or pedestal to the left or to the right.

Wrap: The third phase of the camera operator's job: securing camera equipment after the production.

Zeus: A large Chapman studio crane capable of elevations from below floor level up to 16 feet.

Zoom: Director's command to change zoom lens focal length.

chapter 4

Fundamentals of Composition

Camera *composition* is the art of creatively framing the elements in a shot to best communicate your meaning to the audience. As noted in Chapter 3, the director has the final say in determining the composition of each shot. The task of the camera operator is to compose the best shot possible within the parameters of shot size and angle established by the director.

This chapter concentrates on basic composition theory and practice. Later in this text, in Chapter 15, "Directing I: Aesthetics," you will learn more advanced concepts.

Technical Restraints on Creative Composition

You, as television producers, exercise control over many facets of composition. But television technology often imposes limitations on our creative freedom and we must be aware of those limitations, such as image resolution and contrast range, in composing our shots. But in this basic chapter we wish you to consider two fundamental limitations that constrain and inform us: aspect ratio and picture cutoff. Later in this text we will deal with others.

Aspect Ratio

As defined in Chapter 1, aspect ratio is how we express the relationship between the horizontal and vertical dimensions of the television screen. In 1941 the Federal Communications Commission (FCC) accepted the recommendation of the *National Television System Committee* (NTSC) by adopting a 4:3 (stated as "four by three") aspect ratio for American telecasting. The four refers to the screen's horizontal dimension and the three to the vertical measurement. This means the image is four units wide for every three units high. The 4:3 aspect ratio was chosen for television because it approximated the aspect ratio of American motion picture screens in the early 1940s. This was prior to the development of widescreen formats.

Faced with declining box office receipts in the early 1950s, Hollywood experimented with ways to offer a different, and more attractive, alternative to its new competitor, television, including wide-screen picture formats such as *Cinemascope,* which featured an aspect ratio of 2.5:1 (a screen two and a half times wider than its height). However, today most feature films are shot in the Panavision format, which has an aspect ratio of 1.85:1 (see Figure 4-1).

As we discussed in Chapter 1, the FCC in 1996 adopted new broadcast standards for digital TV but did not mandate an aspect ratio. At this writing, two ratios are still evolving in the digital television marketplace: the traditional 4:3 ratio and a wide-screen 16:9 ratio. The 16:9 aspect ratio and Panavision's are nearly identical, so this will allow the most popular movies shown in theaters to appear virtually the same—aspect ratio-wise—when watching high-definition television (HDTV) screens at home.

When films shot in Panavision or wider formats, such as Cinemascope, are shown on TV's traditional 4:3 aspect ratio screens without chopping off the left and right sides of the picture, they must be changed into the *letterbox format.* This reduces Cinemascope and Panavision images to fit within the horizontal

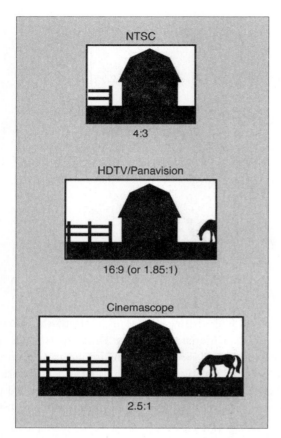

Figure 4-1. *This demonstrates the relative widths of NTSC, high-definition television (HDTV) and Panavision (which are very close to being the same) and film's Cinemascope aspect ratios.*

Figure 4-2. *This 16:9 picture shows the amount of picture cutoff you should allow for when composing. Some camera manufacturers superimpose cutoff lines like this onto the viewfinders of their cameras to remind operators to make allowances for this phenomenon.*

dimension of conventional 4:3 TV screens. Then black bars are placed at the top and bottom to fill the empty space. In the case of foreign-language pictures, subtitles may be placed in the bottom black bar of letterboxed films.

At this writing, even though more and more video is being produced in the 16:9 format, many viewers continue to watch TV on conventional 4:3 sets. The need to accommodate both 4:3 and 16:9 aspect ratios places an additional burden on today's producers, directors and camera operators. This chapter focuses both on composition within the 4:3 and 16:9 aspect ratios, with special attention to the unique requirements of the newer format.

TV Picture Cutoff

Picture cutoff is another technical consideration affecting shot composition. Consumer TV sets display only about 90 percent of any picture you compose in your camera viewfinder. It's as if your TV set takes a set of electronic scissors and trims camera pictures around all four edges, with some TV sets trimming away more from one edge than another.

How can you compose your shot to allow for picture cutoff? Once you've framed the shot at the exact size you desire, zoom out enough to allow for a 10 percent loss around the outside. Eventually, you won't need to use this two-step framing thought process: With experience, you'll remember always to frame shots, especially close-ups, a little "looser" than you want them to appear (see Figure 4-2).

Shot Nomenclature

Shot nomenclature is defined as the set of names used to describe standard shot sizes and the compositional shorthand commands directors use when describing the shots to camera operators. For example, rather than say, "Camera one, zoom in on Sam and compose a shot that starts a little above his waist and extends upward just above his head," the director says, "Camera one, get me a medium close-up of Sam." This efficient command shorthand works only if the director and camera operator share the same definition of "medium close-up." Your acceptance as a professional in the production environment depends upon your knowing and using the proper terminology.

Standard shot sizes, along with their abbreviations as found on television scripts, are listed here (see Figure 4-3):

> *Extreme close-up* (ECU)
> *Close-up* (CU)
> *Medium close-up* (MCU)
> *Medium shot* (MS)

ECU

CU

MCU

MS

MLS

LS

ELS

Figure 4-3.
ECU = Extreme close-up
CU = Close-up
MCU = Medium close-up
MS = Medium shot
MLS = Medium long shot
LS = Long shot
ELS = Extreme long shot

Medium long shot (MLS)
Long shot (LS)
Extreme long shot (ELS)

But there is more traditional shot nomenclature to learn: *Two shot* and *three shot* usually refer to shots containing some arrangement of two people or three people. *Knee shots* frame talent from just above or below the knees. Another common one is the *head-and-shoulders* (H&S) shot, which frames talent from just below the shoulders. The H&S shot is also called a "*bust shot.*" The *over-the-shoulder shot,* often abbreviated in scripts as "OTS," is a shot from behind one shoulder of an actor, providing the audience a view of what the actor sees. As demonstrated below, directors frequently use OTS to emphasize the physical and emotional relationship between two people conversing in a shared scene. The nomenclature for these kinds of shots is useful when people are the focus of the composition. But it's equally important for you to learn to work with shot-size nomenclature (ECU, LS, MS, CU, etc.) when the focus of the composition is not people (see Figure 4-4).

The previous paragraph's discussion of knee shots and head and shoulders shots may make you think that these are natural cutoff points for camera composition, but this is not the case. Beginners frequently violate another compositional principle called *closure* by cutting human subjects off <u>exactly</u> at natural points, such as the ankles, knees, waist, bust and chin. When you frame your shot along one of these natural dividing lines, the phenomenon of closure suggests that the human eye and brain tend to continue the length of that portion of the body or object beyond the boundaries of the frame. Thus, when you cut your talent off right at the waist, viewer perception extends the waist beyond its actual end point. So frame your shots either just above or below these natural dividing lines of the human body so closure is achieved within the frame (see Figure 4-5).

Central Point of Interest and Horizontal Balance

A well-composed camera shot usually has a *central point of interest,* the element of the shot you wish to emphasize most. It may be the actor's face delivering the important line, or the actor's finger applying pressure to a trigger. Attempting to emphasize too many points of interest simultaneously results in a weak shot. Although there may be secondary and tertiary points of interest in a shot, you can usually identify the one most important.

1.

2.

Figure 4-4. *Shot 1 is a two shot on a "homey" studio set; shot 2 is a bust shot.*

Shot 1 courtesy of Nebraska Educational Telecommunications.

Shot composition is not the only way to highlight the central point of interest in a shot. Color, lighting, height and movement (discussed in later chapters) are also effective and may be used independently or in combination with other methods of emphasis.

Once the central point of interest is determined, a basic compositional concern becomes balancing the shot horizontally. We assume the head of the camera mount is properly leveled and aren't concerned at this point with that technical requirement. Rather, what we refer to here is aesthetic balance of elements within the frame. Imagine that your picture rests on the tip of an imaginary triangular fulcrum, as in Figure 4-6.

Balance in a shot responds to our human aesthetic need for order and equilibrium in nature. Teaching composition would be easy if there were a set of absolute rules with no exceptions. But the next section demonstrates other, conflicting, notions about balance.

Figure 4-5. *Shot 1 shows improper closure at the talent's chin, while shot 2 shows that cutting off below the talent's chin provides proper closure. In shot 3, cutting off talent exactly at the waist does not provide proper closure, while cutting slightly below waist level in shot 4 provides proper closure. In shot 5, we see that cutting talent at the knees is incorrect, while shot 6 demonstrates that cutting below the knee allows for closure.*

1.

3.

2.

Figure 4-6. *This shows how pictorial balance might be expressed if pictures had to balance on a fulcrum. Shot 1 is an unbalanced picture, with most of the weight on the right. Audiences viewing this shot may begin to anticipate someone or something entering the shot from the left, as if space was intentionally left in the shot for something to enter the frame—providing balance. Shot 2 is a much more evenly balanced picture, with more weight on one side than the other, but with both sides of the fulcrum possessing pictorial interest and weight. Shot 3 is a balanced picture, with weight on the left and right nearly evenly balanced on the fulcrum. However, sometimes a shot with too much balance can be less interesting than a nearly balanced picture like shot 2.*

Once you're familiar with all of them, you should be better able to judge which to use, and when.

The Rule of Thirds

Composing a medium shot with talent dead-center in the screen would seem the best way to ensure horizontal shot balance—and you would be correct. However, trying to balance our shot by having talent look straight into the camera lens and positioning the actor's eyes in the center of the picture won't work vertically. A good director will have you tilt down a little because there's too much *headroom* (that is, empty space above the actor's head) in the shot. Tilting down leaves the subject

horizontally centered, but now talent's eyes are approximately one-third of the way from the top of the screen. This example is a practical application of the *rule of thirds*. Derived from an ancient Greek mathematical principle called the *"golden mean,"* the rule of thirds suggests that composition is strengthened by dividing a 4:3 picture into three horizontal and three vertical sections and placing points of interest at the intersections of the imaginary dividing lines. The rule of thirds is the theory behind the suggestion, introduced in Figure 4-6, that most compositions gain aesthetic strength if you place the central point of interest at certain slightly off-center points (see Figure 4-7). Although we used a vertical

1.

2.

Figure 4-7. *In shot 1, centering the talent's head in the middle of the screen produces a shot with excess headroom. In shot 2, tilting the camera down to place the talent's eyes on the top line of the "rule of thirds" diagram produces a shot with proper headroom.*

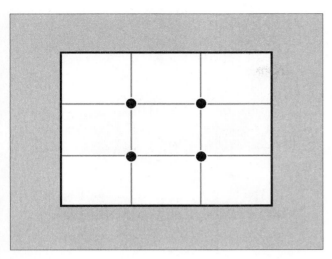

Figure 4-8. *Here we've drawn circles where the lines intersect. These circled areas in the frame are areas of aesthetic strength, and according to the rule of thirds, these are excellent points at which to place one's central point of interest.*

application of the rule, it also assists camera operators with horizontal placement of the central point of interest (see Figure 4-8).

The Principle of Leadroom, or Noseroom

Once a person is properly composed, if he/she turns camera right and assumes a 3/4 profile, you should pan right slightly to provide *leadroom* in the shot. "Leading" the talent in this way creates an aesthetic space just ahead of the talent's face; this leadroom in shots featuring human subjects is sometimes called *noseroom* (see Figure 4-9).

Leadroom is important because viewers become aesthetically uncomfortable when it seems a subject is running out of space within the frame (see Figure 4-10).

As introduced in the caption to Figure 4-6, sometimes audiences are tipped off to the impending entrance of a character (or a monster!) by a shot with *reverse leadroom*.

Figure 4-9. *In this series, shot 1 shows centered composition for a subject looking right at the camera. Some leadroom has been added in shot 2 to allow for the subject's turning to a three-quarter stance. Finally, in shot 3, as the subject turns to profile, the camera operator adds even more leadroom. This principle also applies to other objects such as cars and the like.*

The shot is purposely composed out of balance: There's an empty space left in the shot, often behind the talent's back. The lack of balance creates viewer anxiety, climaxed when someone—or something—enters the space abruptly to interact with—or frighten—the talent and the viewer!

Background Concerns

Although the central point of interest is your primary concern, camera operators must always remember to examine shot backgrounds. Be sure your tripod is level

Figure 4-10. *The lack of leadroom makes viewers feel anxious because it appears the car in shot 1 may run right off the edge of the picture. Adding leadroom in shot 2 provides a look ahead, helping reduce subconscious viewer anxiety.*

1.

2.

Figure 4-11. *As seen in shot 1, a properly leveled camera provides a level background in this OTS ENG shot. In shot 2, failing to level the camera provides a background that appears tilted.*

Figure 4-12. *Check viewfinders carefully to avoid unflattering, poorly composed shots such as this where the talent appears to have a halo of flowers. Trees, telephone poles and traffic signs frequently cause similar composition problems when shooting on location.*

consider the vertical angle of a shot, because an otherwise good shot composed from an unusual angle can send unintended messages to your audience. It's standard practice to place the camera lens at or slightly below the talent's eye level, whether the talent is standing or seated. Placing the lens at talent eye level makes the talent look "normal." Although adjusting camera height may inconvenience exceptionally short or tall operators, the goal is to satisfy artistic/aesthetic requirements, not enhance the comfort of the camera operator. Good operators adjust camera height to achieve good shot composition and then adjust the viewfinder as necessary to provide a clear view of the shot.

Occasionally directors wish to convey visually that an actor is either dominant or powerful. Lowering the camera and shooting talent from below talent eye level effectively makes the actor appear larger, more striking. If the goal is to make the actor into a menacing monster, the camera is lowered still further. Objects, such as buildings, also look larger and more imposing when shot from a vertical angle lower than normal. Conversely, elevating the camera—shooting a person from above—suggests the person is smaller, has a submissive, diminished character or is in a precarious situation (see Figure 4-13).

Sometimes cameras are positioned above or below subject level simply to provide the best view. It's often necessary to pedestal cameras higher than normal height to get the best view of items on tables, especially in cooking shows and other programs in which a straight-on eye-level shot is not effective. Because the angle needed for a good view into pots and pans is so far above normal, directors often use a remote-controlled camera mounted on the light grid above the food preparation area. Yes, the carrots and beans may be "diminished" by being shot

and that horizontal lines in the background also appear level. This does not mean canted angles, discussed below, are inappropriate, but most straight-on shots look odd and tilted when the background horizon appears slanted (see Figure 4-11).

While checking for level horizons, also check for accidentally aligned foreground subjects and background objects that create silly or embarrassing visual effects (see Figure 4-12). As the example on this page illustrates, simply trucking the camera left or right or asking a subject to move slightly is often all that's required to remove undesirable alignments of foreground subjects and background objects.

Shot Angles: High and Low

It's usually possible to place the camera high or low with respect to the central point of interest. It's important to

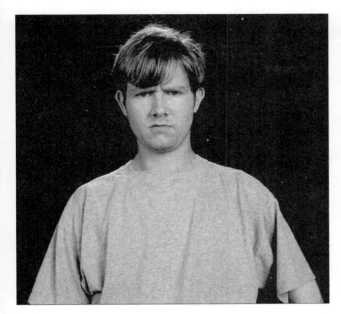

1.

2.

Figure 4-13. *As in shot 1, shooting up at a subject makes him more imposing, as if a child is looking up at a "giant" adult. Shooting down at a subject, as in shot 2, has the reverse effect.*

Figure 4-14. *In shot 1, canting the angle in the direction the subject is running increases the vehemence and the drama of this left to right motion.*

from above, but that's how we usually view them when we cook, so these shots look "normal." Interestingly, however, directors often shoot their products in commercials either straight-on (lens level with the product) or even from a slightly low angle to give the product more "power."

Canted Camera

Although camera mounts (and heads) are usually leveled to provide shots with un-slanted horizons, sometimes the camera is intentionally set off-level to produce a *canted angle* shot. Canted angles convey extremes of motion or mood, as illustrated in Figure 4-14.

Creating Compositional Emphasis

Using various production elements to create visual emphasis, we guide the viewers' eyes to what we want them to concentrate on in a scene. Visual emphasis may be strong or weak, depending on how one uses production elements such as size, mass, color, focus and subject placement on screen. The box on the following page outlines how some elements contribute to compositional emphasis, assuming other variables, such as lighting, shot size and perspective, are held constant.

Composing for Multiple Aspect Ratios

As you have seen in photos in this chapter, both 4:3 and 16:9 aspect ratios work aesthetically well, provided the video is both produced and displayed on equipment using the same format. Problems that need to be overcome happen when video shot in one format is displayed using the other. This can occur when displaying

Production Element	Strong Emphasis	Weak Emphasis
Size	Large object	Small object
Mass	Object with more apparent mass	Object with less apparent mass
Shape	Familiar-shaped objects	Unfamiliar-shaped objects
Complexity	Complex-looking objects	Simple-looking objects
Motion	Objects moving toward camera	Objects moving away from camera
Luminance	Highly reflective objects	Objects that are not very reflective
Color	Brightly colored objects Warmly colored objects	Darkly colored objects Cool-colored objects
Placement	Object in upper half of picture	Object in lower half of picture
	Object isolated from other masses	Object not isolated from other masses
	An isolated object toward the side	An object in the exact middle of the frame
Focus	Objects in sharp focus	Objects in soft focus, or out of focus

widescreen motion pictures on conventional TV sets, as discussed earlier.

In the late 1990s, network executives began telling producers to shoot programs in the 16:9 format, but to keep all the main action within the "safe" 4:3 area of the screen. This is necessary because broadcasters must provide owners of new 16:9 HDTV receivers a full-screen image but simultaneously avoid cutting off important elements in shots viewed on 4:3 TV sets. Broadcasters will, of course, produce programs for exclusive distribution on their digital channels, and these will take full advantage of the 16:9 format. But with more than 150 million conventional sets in consumer hands, broadcasters dependent on a mass audience must still concern themselves more with providing 4:3 images, which guarantee proper viewing to all audiences, than with exploiting the advantages of the 16:9 format.

What this means to you is that the principles introduced in this chapter and elsewhere dealing with composition for NTSC's 4:3 aspect ratio still apply. At least for the moment, many viewers continue watching TV on 4:3 screens, even if the program is shot using the 16:9 format for broadcast on digital channels. For camera operators shooting in the 16:9 ratio, knowing that their work will be displayed on some 4:3 sets, the best practice is to compromise by composing shots "looser" horizontally than they would when shooting with a 4:3 camera. This compromise is based on the assumption that it is preferable to treat viewers watching TV on 16:9 screens to a little "wasted" space rather than anger those watching on 4:3 screens by cutting off vital parts of the image. This doesn't mean that this space has to be uninteresting for the 16:9 viewer. For example, one could employ the compositional tool called *framing*. Framing occurs when you compose shots in which the central point of interest is seen through visual elements placed on the left and right that create an aesthetic border, guiding the audience's eyes to the center like blinders on a horse. For example, you could frame what's going on in the center of the 16:9 shot by including items of visual weight on the far left and right sides of the shot (think of the fulcrum in Figure 4-6). Camera manufacturers will need to help operators deal with the challenge of composing with two aspect ratios in mind by including a viewfinder showing how the shot fits into a 4:3 aspect ratio when the camera is configured for shooting 16:9 video.

How Long Will the Transition Take?

A decade ago, it was predicted that all TV in the new millennium would be shot and displayed in 16:9 aspect ratio and that the image would be high definition as well. That will happen eventually, but at this writing, the 4:3 aspect ratio—even in many digital broadcasts—still vastly outnumbers 16:9. But other technologies, such as large-screen plasma, LCD and LCD/projection hybrids producing 50- and 60-inch pictures are appearing in more American homes. When contemporary widescreen, high-definition sets come down in price and appear in more living rooms, more stations, cable companies and networks will probably abandon the standard-definition, digital 4:3-aspect ratio picture and give consumers what they demand.

Thomas Bohn and Richard Stromgren titled their classic motion-picture history text *Light and Shadows.* They chose that name because much of what a filmmaker or television director manipulates in telling a story involves managing the light reflecting off objects and the darkness an absence of light creates. So far, we've discussed how the camera captures images lit by others. In the next chapter, we'll examine the basics of how to manipulate light to help tell your story.

Important Vocabulary Terms

Bust shot: A shot framed from approximately six inches below the shoulder line to slightly above the head. Also called a head-and-shoulders (H&S) shot.

Canted angles: Angles used to create shots in which camera tilt creates a slanted horizon. Canted angles convey extremes of motion or mood.

Central point of interest: The part of any shot one wishes to emphasize more than all others.

Cinemascope format: A motion picture format, also referred to simply as "'Scope," with an aspect ratio of 2.5:1. 'Scope was the most popular of the wide-screen formats in the 1950s and into the 1960s.

Close-up (CU): When using a human subject, a CU is a tight shot of the face, extending down just below the neckline.

Closure: The idea that the human eye and brain continue the length of a portion of a body or object beyond the boundaries of the frame. This means that subjects in a shot should be cut off slightly above or below natural boundaries, so that closure can take place within the frame.

Composition: The art of creatively framing elements in a shot to best convey the communicator's meaning to the audience.

Extreme close-up (ECU): When using a human subject, an ECU is a very tight shot of the face, typically from the hairline to the chin.

Extreme long shot (ELS): Longer than an LS, a panoramic shot establishing a large interior area or exterior vista.

Framing: Composing shots in which the central point of interest is seen through visual elements on the left and right that create an aesthetic border, guiding the audience's eyes to the center like blinders on a horse.

Golden mean: The mathematical concept on which the rule of thirds is based. In 4:3 composition, the golden mean dictates that dividing a picture into horizontal and vertical thirds will help achieve greater balance.

Head-and-shoulders (H&S) shot: A shot framed from approximately six inches below the shoulder line to slightly above the head. Also called a bust shot.

Headroom: Empty space above an actor's head in the shot.

Knee shot: Director's shorthand for a shot in which talent is framed from just above or below the knee to slightly above the top of the head.

Leadroom: Leadroom is space left in front of a moving object or in front of a subject's face (in which case it is called "noseroom") when composing a shot. This is important because viewers become uncomfortable when subjects move laterally too close to the edge of the frame. The leadroom principle suggests camera operators reduce viewer anxiety by providing space (leadroom) ahead of the subject.

Letterbox format: A way to present a wide-screen format film on television without chopping off the left and right sides of the picture. The wide-screen picture is reduced until it fits horizontally into NTSC's 4:3 aspect ratio. Black bars fill in the empty spaces at the top and bottom.

Long shot (LS): When using a human subject, a shot from the feet up. When there is more than one subject in the scene, a shot showing all subjects roughly from the feet up. Also called an establishing shot.

Medium close-up (MCU): When using a human subject, a shot from approximately six inches above the waist up to slightly above the head.

Medium long shot (MLS): When using a human subject, a shot from below the knee up.

Medium shot (MS): When using a human subject, a shot from just below the waistline up.

The National Television System Committee (NTSC): The organization that recommended analog standards for American television to the FCC. NTSC standards, until 1996, called for a 4:3 aspect ratio for broadcast television productions.

Noseroom: See "Leadroom."

Over-the-shoulder (OTS) shot: A shot taken from behind the shoulder of talent providing a view of what the talent sees.

Picture cutoff: The approximately 10-percent image loss around the edges of any shot during transmission. Operators must compensate for this peripheral image loss when composing shots.

Reverse leadroom: "Empty" space intentionally left in a shot, often behind the talent's back, to unbalance the composition and create viewer anxiety. Typically the space is "filled" abruptly once the shot is established, shocking the viewer.

Rule of thirds: A theory suggesting that composition is strengthened by placing the central point of interest at any point in the frame corresponding to the intersection of lines dividing the frame into thirds horizontally and vertically.

Shot nomenclature: The set of names describing standard shot sizes; the shorthand commands directors use when requesting that camera operators compose shots thus described.

Two shot (or three shot): Director's shorthand for a shot of two people (or three people).

chapter **5**

Lighting Techniques and Equipment

There are both technical and artistic reasons to light a set artificially. The technical reason is easy to explain: Cameras need a minimum light level—called *baselight*—to operate efficiently. Failure to provide baselight illumination can cause portions of the picture, especially the darker areas, to suffer from *video noise,* which appears as graininess or "snow" in the picture. In camera operation manuals, manufacturers usually specify how much light is needed. The artistic reasons for artificial lighting can fill entire textbooks, ranging from highlighting an important area in a shot to making subtle mood and character statements with well-aimed and thoughtfully shaded shafts of light. Some TV sets look like they have been blasted with light for the sole purpose of removing shadows. But remember that good lighting is not necessarily the total absence of shadows, but instead the placement of shadows where you want them. Any light will give off a shadow—the trick is putting it either in a place where it will not be seen at all, or where it will actually enhance the aesthetics of the shot.

In many situations, one's lighting is provided courtesy of Mother Nature. *Available light,* the natural, unaugmented light found at a location, often provides a technically acceptable video image while conveying the artistically correct mood. But we can't depend on Mother Nature alone: There's nearly always a shadow that needs softening or a small spot to highlight. Portable lighting instruments and other tools we'll discuss, such as reflectors, can do this task. Even Hollywood's classic close-up of the cowboy astride his horse overlooking a majestic Western skyline usually contains some element of artificial light and shadow

control. Just out of the camera's field of view, the audience doesn't see the lighting technician with the large foil reflector, filling in the deep shadows under the cowboy's ten-gallon hat.

Compared to the human eye, film and television cameras have some disadvantages: One of them is that normal cameras render only two-dimensional images, displaying length and width, but no depth. Unlike a human's binocular (two-eyed) vision, the camera views the world through a single eye, and thus cannot naturally reproduce a scene in the third dimension. So artists in the visual media have learned to artificially create the illusion of depth in a scene. These efforts peaked in the 1950s, when Hollywood experimented with three-dimensional (*3-D*) images in one of the industry's attempts to bolster sagging box office revenues by offering audiences something they couldn't see on television (see Figure 5-1). Today 3-D movies remain a curiosity, a novelty, used for an occasional horror film, a Disney World attraction, an IMAX movie or even an occasional television special. ABC and NBC offered some prime-time programs in 3-D during 1997, but they used incompatible techniques, viewing glasses were in short supply, and the effort was effective for little more than publicity value. Aside from 3-D, the most effective way to create the illusion of depth in a flat image is to use good lighting techniques.

In this chapter, you'll learn the fundamentals of lighting and lighting technology for television. You'll also learn what's required of a person who must execute someone else's lighting design. There will also be discussion of some artistic designs for mood lighting, such as those used in music videos.

Figure 5-1. *In an attempt to lure audiences back into theaters after the advent of television, Hollywood tried many new ideas, such as 3-D.* Photo courtesy of the Museum of Modern Art.

Figure 5-2. *The typical incident-light meter has a photosphere, shaped like half of a Ping-Pong ball, which collects the light. Place the meter with its back to the talent/subject, and point the photosphere in the direction of the camera to get your reading.*

Lighting Variables: Measuring Light Intensity

Video producers routinely manipulate light intensity, light character and color temperature to create the desired lighting for a particular shot. Lighting directors and other professionals often need to quantify *light intensity,* which is a measure of light's brightness. In normal practice, professionals measure light intensity using a photosensitive device called a *light meter.* Light meters are designed to read either *incident light,* the light falling directly on the subject, or *reflected light,* the light bouncing off the subject. The most commonly used measure of this light intensity is the *footcandle* (fc). A footcandle is defined as the intensity of light falling on a surface placed one foot away from a point source of light of one candlepower. The footcandle is a measure of incident light intensity. Reflected light is measured in *footlamberts* (fl), the product of the incident light falling on a subject and the subject's reflection factor. Most objects reflect only part of the incident light falling on them, absorbing the rest. The average Caucasian face, for example, absorbs about 64 percent of the light falling on it and reflects 36 percent.

Lighting directors use handheld *incident-light meters* to determine if there is sufficient baselight for proper camera operation. Incident-light meters also help in establishing initial intensity ratios in the lighting triangle, discussed later in this chapter. These meters must be placed near the subject, with the instrument's photosensitive element facing the camera. The meter's

180-degree photosphere captures a broad range of light aimed at the subject (see Figure 5-2). Note: This assumes that your set is what might be termed *normally reflective.* If your set is in the snow, on water or full of bright, shiny objects, incident meter readings are often inaccurate. To properly expose subjects in unusually reflective conditions, use a *reflected-light meter* reading. Also note that incident-light meters are designed to properly expose a shade of middle gray that corresponds to average Caucasian skin. If you are metering very light-skinned or dark-skinned people, use a reflected meter reading. This is because very light- or dark-skinned people are not represented in black and white as middle gray. To properly expose a light-skinned person, close down approximately one f-stop more than the light meter reading indicates; to properly expose a dark-skinned person, open up an extra f-stop.

Although digital cameras have a much better contrast ratio than the older tubed cameras, they still are stretched to their limits when trying to properly render dark-skinned people wearing white shirts or photographed against white walls. The best way to solve this problem is in preproduction. Tell your dark-skinned talent not to wear white, and don't shoot them against white backgrounds. If you can't avoid the white shirt, and you have some control over the lighting, such as in the studio, here are a few things to try: Adjust the barn doors of the dark-skinned person's key light (the principal light in the lighting triangle, which will be discussed later), raising the bottom barn door to reduce the illumination of the white shirt. Thus the face is fully lit, but not the shirt. Another option is to adjust the barn door of the subject's fill light (if it has barn doors; flag it if it doesn't). This is not as efficient as adjusting the key light, but it might help a little. Overall, to avoid this

Figure 5-3. *A reflected-light meter, held as close as possible to the subject, pointed from the direction of the camera at the spot/area the videographer wants to properly expose, will provide the most accurate reading in most circumstances.*

kind of situation, nothing beats careful preproduction planning.

Inexperienced people often misuse the incident-light meter by holding it only a few feet from the camera lens rather than placing it near the subject of the shot. In the majority of television cameras made today with light-meter systems, reflected-light metering is used and is installed behind the camera's lens. These systems read the light intensity striking the imaging device and provide the electrical signals necessary for operation of the auto-iris circuit discussed in Chapters 1 and 2. As mentioned above, a handheld reflected-light meter is excellent for measuring light in unusual, highly reflective scenes (see Figure 5-3).

When the central point of interest is either highly reflective (such as someone dressed in white) or highly nonreflective (such as someone dressed in black) compared to the scene as a whole, a *spot meter,* a kind of reflected-light meter measuring the light reflecting only off the central point of interest, such as the subject's face, provides a more accurate exposure of the key elements of your shot. You may achieve the same effect without one of these spot meters if you are able to take your incident meter right into the scene and use it a foot or less away from the subject.

We also use reflected-light meters to avoid exceeding the *contrast ratio* limits of the TV system. Keeping the reflected light within the design limits of the TV cameras is important, because image detail is lost if either too little or too much light strikes the imaging device. Contrast ratio expresses numerically the extreme range of light reflected from objects in a shot. A scene with a 30:1 (read as "thirty to one") contrast ratio means the brightest object in the scene reflects 30 times as much light as the darkest object in the scene. As discussed, advancing technology has increased the capability of

cameras to accommodate bigger contrast ratios. Most lighting directors and set designers hold normal contrast ratios to 40:1 or less, although many cameras can handle somewhat greater extremes and still retain image details. Tech Manual 5-1 at the end of this chapter explains the procedure for determining the contrast ratio of a scene.

Controlling Light Intensity

Light intensity was once an enormous problem. Early TV cameras required so many hot lights that the climate in a television studio was like a scorching afternoon in the Sahara Desert. Today, cameras operate at light intensities barely sufficient for the human eye, so lighting design now focuses more on artistic objectives than satisfying the camera's basic technical requirements.

The simplest ways to control light intensity are familiar to you. For example, if the lamp you're using to read this book isn't providing enough intensity, you can do two simple things: Move the lamp closer to your book, or replace the bulb with one with a higher wattage rating (for example, replace a 40-watt bulb with a 60- or 75-watt bulb). The same kinds of adjustments are often done in TV lighting.

Yet another way to control light intensity involves partially blocking light as it enters the camera. The iris provides primary control over light flowing into the camera, and you can increase or decrease the amount of light that reaches the camera's charge-coupled device (CCD) by opening or closing the iris. However, as you learned in Chapter 2, manipulating the camera's f-stop will change the depth of field. If your current depth of field is satisfactory for your shot's creative requirements, but the scene—especially outdoors—is too bright, neutral density (ND) filters, like sunglass material, can reduce the light intensity reaching the CCD. Lighting technicians also affix ND gel material to the fronts of lighting instruments or insert big sheets of ND material into window panes to achieve similar results, reducing light at its source. ND filter materials come in various grades, numbered one through four. The higher the ND filter number, the more light is blocked.

Television studios and equipment used in many sophisticated remote productions provide additional options for controlling light intensity. Like light dimmers found in many homes, *rheostats* (in this case, in-line slide controls) on studio lighting consoles (discussed later in this chapter) increase or decrease the electrical current reaching your lighting instruments, dimming or brightening any number of instruments. Many professional lighting instruments feature focusing controls that allow technicians to adjust the width of the light beam, providing yet another means of manipulating light intensity.

Light Character

The second characteristic TV professionals control is *light character*, the relative harshness or softness—also called the degree of diffusion—of the light beam. Consider the difference between lighting a person with a flashlight and a portable fluorescent light. The flashlight creates a narrow, "hard" beam of light, which creates heavy shadows, while the fluorescent lamp bathes the subject with a more diffused light, creating fewer and less dark shadows. Theatrical, television and film lighting techniques employ both hard and soft lighting to define the mood of a scene or the "soul" of individuals. The lavish budgets and extended production schedules of feature films allow their producers to devote greater attention to the artistic use of lighting than is common in programs produced exclusively for TV.

While the typical TV show—especially one shot in the studio—doesn't always provide the opportunities for creative lighting you see in feature films, one still must learn to choose the correct lighting instruments and accessories—some created for hard light, others designed to deliver diffused light—that you'll need to achieve the appropriate lighting for particular programs. Later in this chapter, we'll introduce the basic TV lighting instruments and how proper use can help you control light character.

Color Temperature

The third important lighting variable you control is color temperature. In Chapter 1, you learned that various light sources (studio lights, fluorescents, the sun, etc.) provide different-colored versions of nominally "white" light. Within the spectrum of visible light (the wavelengths falling between infrared and ultraviolet), there are many gradations of color. Sources emitting light closer to infrared have, as you would imagine, more of a red/orange tinge, and likewise, those further up toward the ultraviolet end of the spectrum look more bluish.

We've noted in earlier chapters that subtle color differences among light sources are often imperceptible to us. Some newer cameras automatically compensate for the color characteristics of the light source. Usually, however, we must "tell" the camera where the light illuminating the subject is approximately found on the

spectrum, using the process called white balancing (or color balancing) previously described in Tech Manual 1-1. For this and many other purposes, there exists a color temperature scale calibrated in units called "degrees Kelvin." A common color temperature in professional productions is 3,200 degrees on the Kelvin scale (abbreviated 3,200 deg. K). This was chosen because studio quartz *lamps* ("lamp" is another word for high-wattage light bulbs used in production) are designed to emit light at 3,200 deg. K. TV camera manufacturers correspondingly designed their cameras to operate unfiltered at 3,200 deg. K. Quartz lamps are popular incandescent-type light sources with a tungsten filament that glows in an iodide (also known as halogen) gas. The "glass" envelope is made of quartz, from which the quartz lamp gets its name, although they also are often called tungsten-halogen or quartz-iodide lamps (see Figure 5-4). With quartz lamps serving as our reference for "pure white light," sources with a higher Kelvin rating emit white light with a bluish tint, and those with a lower color temperature radiate white light with a reddish tint.

Daylight color temperatures vary greatly depending upon the time of day, weather conditions and other factors, but under the noonday sun, the average is about 5,600 deg. K. A video camera white balanced for 3,200 deg. K quartz light produces a bluish image when used outdoors, unless the higher daylight color temperature is filtered and the camera's electronics rebalanced to compensate for the bluer light. The electronic circuits of the camera can balance for white over a rather broad range without changing the filter, but there are limits. Most

Figure 5-4. *A quartz bulb, the most often-used illumination lamp in television, mounted inside a Fresnel instrument.*

professional cameras provide built-in color filters for the most commonly encountered light sources, such as quartz lights (3,200 deg. K), bright sunlight (5,600 deg. K) and fluorescent lights/cloudy or foggy days (6,500 to 7,000 deg. K). However, some standard room lights vary greatly in color temperature and have long been the bane of ENG camera operators. Rather than worry about color errors, many professionals instead overpower fluorescent lights by *punching in* portable quartz lights balanced for 3,200 deg. K. "Punching in" means adding additional lighting instruments to a scene, either to highlight certain areas (such as a central point of interest) or to overcome a baselight problem; for example, one might use quartz lights to "punch up" the color temperature of a greenish-looking, fluorescent-lit location set.

As with adjusting and manipulating light intensity, it's possible to modify the color temperature of artificial light at the source. Take the *camera light,* for example. Most TV news camera lights (small, battery-powered lighting instruments mounted atop ENG cameras) have an attachment called a *dichroic filter.* This glass filter flips down in front of the quartz camera light, raising its color temperature from 3,200 to 5,600 deg. K. So, if an ENG camera operator needs extra light to shoot a speaker addressing a crowd in an auditorium, the camera light is used unfiltered. But in an outdoor shoot, if there are deep shadows to fill, or inside, if the predominant light source happens to be sunlight streaming in a window, the camera operator uses the camera light's dichroic filter (see Figure 5-5).

As mentioned earlier in our discussion of ND gel material, you can also color-correct the daylight streaming through windows by covering them with large sheets of filter gel. This effectively corrects the 5,600 deg. K daylight streaming in the window to 3,200 deg. K. Then you may set up a camera for 3,200 deg. K., even augmenting the color-corrected daylight with 3,200 deg. K quartz instruments.

Another more expensive and more cumbersome instrument, called a *halogen-metal-iodide (HMI) light,* is yet another option for controlling color temperature. Somewhat similar in design and intent to quartz lights, HMIs have one important difference: They produce a 5,600 deg. K light that mixes, unfiltered, with daylight (see Figure 5-15 for pictures of an HMI).

The Basic Lighting Triangle: Three-Point Lighting

ENG camera operators must often use one light, mounted atop a camera, to illuminate subjects in swiftly moving news events, but the result has the aesthetic appeal of a flashbulb snapshot. Subjects lit with a single, head-on light source appear flat and often cast ugly shadows behind them. Whenever possible, professionals add more lights to illuminate the subject more artistically.

There are the three objectives of what is called the *basic lighting triangle,* so named because of the three lights involved:

1. Properly illuminate the subject from a *motivated light source,*
2. Fill in shadows made by this primary source of light and
3. Separate the subject from the background.

1.

2.

Figure 5-5. *In shot 1, a camera operator shoots with a Panasonic DVCPro ENG camera, a Frezzi Full Spectrum 50-watt "Mini-Arc" camera light with barn doors and swing-down dichroic filter. In shot 2, the dichroic filter swings open and closed like a door.*

Shot 1 courtesy of Frezzi Energy Systems.

Figure 5-6. *The lighting triangle permits us to illuminate both the product and the talent in this shot. The important elements, her face and the package, are well lit in the "crossfire" of key and fill light.*

Figure 5-7. *Silhouette shot of two talents at a studio news anchor desk. Lighting the background set at full intensity while keeping light off the talent in the foreground provides this dramatic effect.*

The main source of illumination in a scene is called the *key light.* The key light is the logical, dominant light source. It's called a motivated light source because the key light strikes the subject from the most logical direction—there's some reason for the light to be coming along that path. For example, if a long shot of an afternoon scene in a living room establishes that the windows are on the west wall, then, when it's time for a close-up, it's logical and "motivated" for the key light to appear to come from the west.

The *fill light* softens and fills in shadows made by the key light. Key lights often create harsh shadows on the opposite sides of people and objects. We brighten and soften these shadows by aiming fill lights directly into the shadowy areas created by the key light (see Figure 5-6).

The third main source of illumination is called the *backlight,* also sometimes referred to as a rim light. The backlight's chief function is to separate the subject from the background. This helps create the illusion of depth and three-dimensionality on our two-dimensional television screen. In a normal lighting design, backlights are placed behind the subject, hence the name backlight. Sometimes backlights are placed behind the subject directly opposite the key light.

Sometimes, at the beginnings and endings of programs, producers go for a silhouette effect, achieved by turning off key and fill lights, using backlights only. Often credits are shown over this darkened set, in which objects and people appear as shadows (see Figure 5-7).

As a very general rule in television, all three lights are set on a 45-degree vertical angle relative to the studio floor (see Figure 5-8). Sometimes the vertical angle is

varied to achieve a more aesthetically pleasing image. And remember: The triangle is often where you start in lighting; sometimes you make adjustments and end up somewhere else. The story you're telling and/or the message you're sending ultimately dictate your strategy for illuminating your subjects.

Ratios in the Lighting Triangle

Lighting designers often disagree about the relative intensities of the key, back and fill lights. However, many recommend starting with a *lighting ratio* of $1:1:\frac{1}{2}$ (key–back–fill). Begin by evenly matching the relative intensity of the key light and backlight—that is, a 1:1 relationship. This means that when your incident-light meter indicates that your key light intensity is 200 fc, make sure that your backlight also is 200 fc. But this is simply a rule of thumb. Some other ratio may work better for a particular shot. For example, you may want a brighter backlight when illuminating a darkly dressed or dark-haired individual set against a dim background. In this case, your key–backlight ratio might be $1:1\frac{1}{2}$. So, where you'd use a 200 fc key light, you set your backlight intensity at 300 fc. The fill light intensity is usually less than the key light, perhaps a ratio of $1:\frac{1}{2}$. So, if the key light is 200 fc, the fill is typically set for about 100 fc.

However, the final test of fill light intensity doesn't come from mathematical ratios. Rather, as with all final judgments on lighting, the ultimate judge is your own eye, as you look at the set and through the camera and decide how the shot looks on a properly adjusted color TV monitor. If your key–back–fill ratio doesn't look

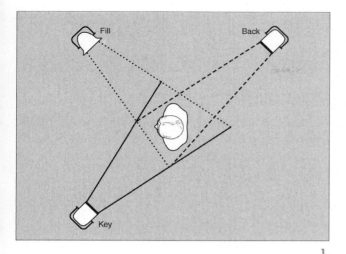

1.

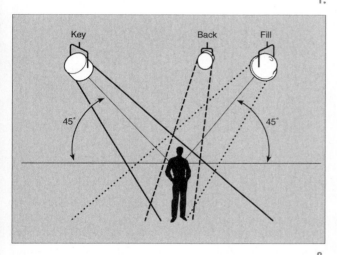

2.

Figure 5-8. *In drawing 1, we see an overhead view of the key light placed at near right angles to the fill light, catching the subject in the "crossfire." The backlight is often placed opposite the key in this situation. In drawing 2, we note that in the standard TV studio lighting triangle, key, back and fill are ideally aimed at 45-degree angles down to the subject.*

right for the mood you want, adjust it until the mixture is more pleasing.

Lighting is very subjective: Some individuals illuminate for the eye first, as if lighting a stage for a theater production, then check the light meter for intensity ratios and consult the waveform monitor (discussed in Tech Manual 1-2) to ensure that the overall light level provides good exposure without hot spots. Others light for technical requirements first, setting lighting triangles and checking meter readings to ensure good, balanced exposure; then they make adjustments to satisfy the eye. This approach is especially helpful if, for example, you wish to maximize the depth of field in a

scene by creating a high overall level of light intensity— so that cameras achieve correct exposure using a small iris aperture. As you learned in Chapter 4, using a small aperture contributes to great depth of field.

Two-Point Lighting With the increased sensitivity of electronic field production (EFP) cameras, producers, videographers and lighting directors have begun using the *two-point lighting* technique for field interviews. This permits the interview subjects to be shot in an aesthetically pleasing manner that provides more shadow, texture and definition. The look that this method generates is nothing new. It is sometimes called Rembrandt lighting, since it results in the same appearance displayed in many of the portraits by the famous painter. This type of lighting can be seen most often on TV newsmagazine shows, like "60 Minutes," "Dateline" and "20-20" (see Figure 5-9).

1.

2.

Figure 5-9. *Shot 1 is an example of a subject illuminated with two-point lighting. Shot 2 shows the placement of lighting instruments for this example.*

There are at least four advantages to the two-point lighting technique: (1) As mentioned, it gives a more artistic look to the interview subject. (2) It also differentiates the studio appearance from the field productions. (3) It's easier in the sense that only two lights have to be lifted and set up. (4) With only minor adjustments, the lights can be used for shooting the interview subject, then used for shooting the interviewer. This is a big help in news style, "run and gun" productions.

The obvious difference between two-point and three-point lighting is that the fill light is omitted. The placement of two lights is a bit trickier than three point lighting. As seen in Figure 5-9, backlight has to be carefully placed, or the subject will have the side of her face "fried" by the light, causing a harsh glare where there is supposed to be shadow. In addition, with the key light coming in on the other side of the face, the two lights would combine to place an ugly shadow right down the middle of the face—most unpleasant. So start by placing the backlight at about a 30-degree angle behind the subject. Eyeball it through the lens until you get the desired, semi-halo look with highlights on one side of the head. Then place the key light at about a 100-degree angle, just off to the same side of the camera as the interviewer (not shown in Figure 5-9). This should cast a shadow on the cheek of the interview subject, displayed toward the camera. If the light placement is perfect, there will be a triangle of light on the person's cheek on the dark side of the face. This will create the third dimension of depth, showing the curvature of the face.

Since the backlight is almost directly behind the subject, it's necessary to frame the subject in a tight shot. The old news videographer saying applies here: "Light tight and shoot tight." As is the case with practically <u>any</u> remote lighting situation, the subject should be 10 to 15 feet away from the background wall. The more space you have to place and move the backlight, the better. Just because the subject is sitting behind a desk in a cramped office doesn't mean you have to do the interview there. Find alternative areas for lighting and staging the interview. Take the subject to a conference room where there is more space to utilize. Bring the subject to the center of the room, even if it means the camera has to be situated out in a hallway. Or even bring the subject out in a hallway and do the interview there.

Think about moving the subject into the middle of whatever they manage. For example, interview the county sheriff in the parking lot of the station, with dozens of police cruisers behind him. This is so much better than sitting in his office, surrounded by awards and pictures on his wall. Interview the president of the school board in front of one of the schools that he/she supervises. And if there are kids milling around, all the better.

Other Lighting Objectives

Aesthetically illuminating main subjects within the scene is the principal objective of triangular lighting. But there are other lighting objectives, and appropriate names that describe their intentions.

Background light: In theater, background lights are called "specials." They're instruments that illuminate, and thus highlight, certain items in the background of the shot. Properly designed background light also greatly aids in simulating three-dimensionality (see Figure 5-10). Be careful not to confuse "backlight" (light falling <u>on the subject</u> from behind) and "background light" (light illuminating objects <u>behind the subject</u>). Sometimes the term "special" is used to describe an instrument used to highlight a particular object placed anywhere in the scene.

Set light: Diffused lights are used to provide sufficient baselight in the scene to avoid video noise and to flatly illuminate all relevant portions of the set.

Kicker light: This is a kind of backlighting. While rim light/backlight illuminates subjects from behind and above, kickers illuminate the subject dramatically from below and behind. Kickers provide an almost saintly "halo effect" surrounding the head, hair and shoulders of the subject. Shampoo commercials featuring fashion models often use this technique (see Figure 5-11).

Sidelight: When lighting any scene in which there is considerable movement or action across the stage (dance, sword fight, chase, etc.), it may be impractical to

Figure 5-10. *"Special" lighting at the table in the foreground and in the background corner of the set draws viewer attention to these areas. These lights may also be called "practicals" because the instruments are typical of those commonly used in "real life," and their appearance in the shot contributes to the overall realism of the set. See Chapter 14 for another example of the use of "specials."*

1.

2.

Figure 5-11. *In shot 1, we see a model photographed with kicker light. Key light here comes from the right, and fill from the left at normal 45-degree angles. In shot 2, we see the placement of the kicker light.*

design individual lighting triangles for each location on the set to which the dancers/actors may go. Instead, from offstage on both sides of the set, sidelights wash the entire area. This rather indiscriminate lighting scheme is sometimes also called *flat lighting* (see Figure 5-12).

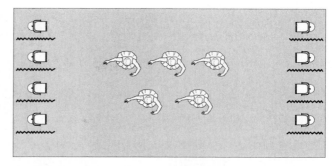

Figure 5-12. *In this illustration, we see sidelights in use, softly illuminating a broad area of the dance floor for these dancers.*

Lighting Instruments and Accessories

So far, we've discussed the basic objectives of TV lighting and strategies to achieve them. This section discusses tactical equipment you can use—instruments and accessories you'll need to accomplish these ends. There are two generic categories of instruments: *spotlights,* simply called "spots," and *fill lights,* referred to as "fills" or "floods" (short for "floodlights").

Spotlights

Versatile spotlights are used for many different functions, among them key, back and kicker lights. Sometimes certain adjustable types are used as specials, and as fill lighting and sidelighting. Spots also can project patterns on the walls and floors of sets. There are three major varieties of spots.

The most common and flexible spot is the *Fresnel* (pronounced "Fren—ELL"; the "s" is silent.) Named after Augustine Fresnel, the inventor of the instrument's concentric-circled lens, this instrument adjusts for use as either key or fill light. See Fresnel lights in Figure 5-13, and later in close-up in Figure 5-18. As Figure 5-13 illustrates, a Fresnel with the lens removed can help project patterns with the aid of a *cucalorus* ("*cookie*" is the more commonly used short name).

A Fresnel can be adjusted to project a "hard," focused, narrow beam of light—this is called *pinning* a Fresnel— or a less intense, "softer," broader beam—referred to as *spreading* or *flooding* a Fresnel (see Figure 5-14).

Most Fresnels use the 3,200 deg. K quartz lamps discussed earlier. However, HMI lights also come with Fresnel lenses, as well as in open-front, non-lensed designs (see Figure 5-15). HMI lights were created primarily for shooting outside on location when reflectors were not (or could not be) used to soften shadows made by the sun. Unfortunately, most HMIs are

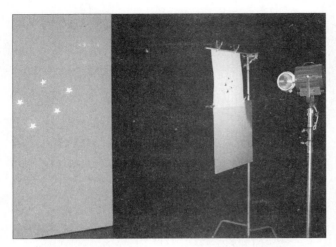

Figure 5-13. *A stand-mounted Fresnel and external cookie produce a light pattern of stars on a flat. Note that the lens of the instrument is opened and pulled aside, so the Fresnel operates in this application as an open-front instrument. This sharpens the image pattern projected on the flat.*

expensive and heavy, and the larger portable ones require a bulky starter ballast/power supply unit. These aren't severe drawbacks to high-budget Hollywood productions, but the weight, bulk and high cost of HMI units are major impediments for lower-budget EFP or ENG productions. However, manufacturers also market smaller, lightweight, battery-powered HMIs. These units combine the ballast and battery power unit in one small package that attaches to the camera operator's belt.

The second kind of lensed spotlight is the *ellipsoidal*, sometimes called a *Leko light*. The ellipsoidal spotlight

Figure 5-14. *To demonstrate the focusing capabilities of a Fresnel-lensed instrument, the Fresnel on the left is spread, while an identical Fresnel is pinned. Adjusting a Fresnel along a range from spread to pin is a matter of using an adjustment lever on the instrument to move its bulb and reflector assembly closer to, or farther away from, the lens.*

1.

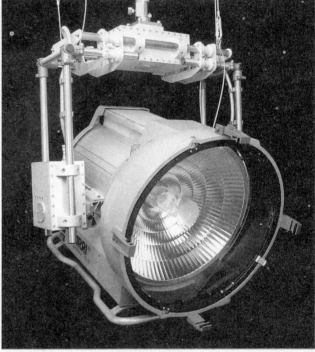

2.

Figure 5-15. *Shot 1 is a stand-mounted Arrisun HMI light. Note that this instrument is equipped with barn doors for controlling the light beam. Shot 2 shows an Arrimax HMI light, mounted aboard an ARRI automated stirrup, called a MaxMover. This yoke offers remote-controlled pan, tilt and focus for large lighting fixtures.*

Shot 2 courtesy of Arriflex ARRI Corporation.

creates a narrower, more precisely shaped beam than the pinned Fresnel. The ellipsoidal's primary advantage is its ability to throw a sharply- defined, intense light beam across a relatively long distance. The ellipsoidal features beam-shaping "leaves" within its inner mecha-

Figure 5-16. *An ellipsoidal. Note the leaves to adjust the shape of the light and the gel frame. Not pictured is a slot into which metal "cookies" can be inserted to project patterns on set walls and other surfaces.*

Figure 5-17. *A typical ENG portable light kit. Kits come with many different assortments of lighting instruments, mounting devices, gels, scrims and other devices to manipulate light.*
Photo courtesy of Lowel Light Manufacturing, Inc.

nism, which can project a great number of shaped beams of light, including sharp or softly edged circles, squares and other geometrics. Ellipsoidal spotlights permit the insertion of cookies into the instrument to project a wide variety of patterns on curtains, floors and walls (see Figure 5-16). Ellipsoidals are employed quite frequently in theater and stage productions but see more limited application in TV production.

Unlike the relatively bulky Fresnels and ellipsoidals, *open-front spots* have no lenses. This reduces their weight and makes them ideal for field productions with small crews. Sometimes called *bashers,* open-front spots, like Fresnels, can serve both as spots and fills, but they don't focus quite as efficiently as Fresnels. Open-front spots are relatively inexpensive. A portable kit containing three open fronts costs less than two Fresnels or one HMI light. And, on location, lightweight open fronts are more easily positioned as needed. Lighting manufacturers market many excellent lighting kits designed around open-front spot and fill instruments, with lightweight, collapsible stands and other ingeniously designed accessories (see Figure 5-17).

Accessories for Spotlights   There are many devices designed to assist in controlling the intensity, character and color temperature of spotlights. Some of these are the same as those used with fill lights. You'll recall that dichroic filters placed over quartz lamps convert them from 3,200 deg. K to 5,600 deg. K for use outside, and ND *gels* attached to lighting instruments reduce light intensity. Other gels can suggest times of day (for example, blue for night, red for sunset). Many Fresnels

provide slots into which *gel frames* (gels are made more rigid by being enclosed in a metal frame) are inserted, making color changes easy (see Figure 5-18).

Scrims are diffusion media, made from either a metal screen material, spun fiberglass or a plastic-like sheet. Scrims disrupt the straight-line path that light beams travel, bathing the scene in softer, more diffused light. Open-front spots typically use metal diffusers. The spunglass variety, the more efficient of the two, is inserted into a frame that mounts on the front of Fresnels or any open-front instrument whose heat will not melt the spun glass.

Figure 5-18. *Two Fresnel lights. On the right a yellow gel has been placed in the instrument's gel-frame holder.*

The metal variety is also used with Fresnels. Another type of scrim is a plastic-like material sometimes called "frost." Any of these materials will soften the glare of lights and give off a softer, more aesthetically pleasing appearance. Especially with field lighting instruments, scrim should be used to avoid harsh glares on people's faces.

There are other accessories with such quaint names as *flags, gobos, barn doors* and *snoots* (also called "top hats" or "stovepipes") that further shape the light these instruments emit. Flags are usually rectangular devices, frequently black in color, used to block light from a certain area on the set (see Figure 5-19).

1.

2.

3.

4.

5.

6.

Figure 5-19. *In shot 1, flags on flexible arms provide lighting control for this open-faced instrument. In shot 2, a snoot, with barn doors and filter holder, allows the beam of this instrument to be narrowly focused. Shot 3 shows how lighting manufacturers provide a wide variety of adjustable external light controls in many shapes to help the gaffer get just the effect desired. Experienced lighting directors, however, often improvise such devices as needed using open frames and black foil. Shot 4 shows barn doors, the most commonly used external light controls. Note that these are adjustable segmented barn doors, rather than the fixed rectangular-shaped flaps of conventional design. This allows the gaffer to adjust the size and shape of each door to better meet the needs of different lighting situations. Shot 5 looks like an entirely different kind of instrument, but actually, a Rifa lite is just a tungsten-halogen lamp fixture that's centered in a collapsible, silvered, high-temperature-resistant tent. The result is a fill light with maximum diffusion, resulting in soft shadows. Shot 6 shows a technician inserting a scrim in front of an open-front Lowell Omni Lite. The scrim serves two important purposes: It helps diffuse the beam from the Omni, and, in case the lamp should explode and shatter, the metal scrim provides protection for talent, crew and products being lit.*

Shots 1–4 and shot 6 courtesy of Lowel Light Manufacturing, Inc.; Shot 5 courtesy of Matthews Studio Equipment, Inc.

Fill Lights

Some fill lights are designed primarily for studio work, some for shooting on location, while others are used for both. Usually tasked with providing fill, baselight, background and sidelighting, fills come in five main varieties:

The *scoop:* A round, half-egg-shaped instrument, the scoop provides diffused light by using its shell as a reflector. Scoops are open-fronted instruments. Most scoops used for TV are about 24 to 30 inches in diameter, but occasionally a miniature version (12 to 18 inches) is used to light small areas (see Figure 5-20).

The *broad* is a modern design improvement on the scoop. Broads come in many sizes, from large to mini, depending on their use. Small, rectangular, light-weight broads are usually better than scoops for location work. Both scoops and broads use 3,200 deg. K quartz lamps (see Figure 5-21).

The *softlight:* Scoops and broads have lamps that directly face the subject. In contrast, the quartz lamp(s) of the softlight faces 180 degrees away from the subject, aimed inward at the softlight's internal reflector (see Figure 5-22). Only the softlight's indirect, highly diffused, reflected beams strike the subject, reducing shadows more than scoops or broads. Like broads, softlights come in various sizes with an array of lamp wattages. Because their design makes them less efficient, virtually all softlights require at least two quartz lamps to deliver

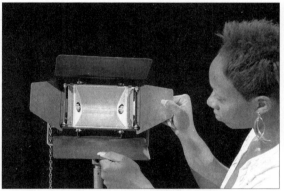

Figure 5-21. *In shot 1, a crewperson carries a medium-sized broad fill light up a studio ladder. In shot 2, a crewperson adjusts the barn doors of a minibroad.*

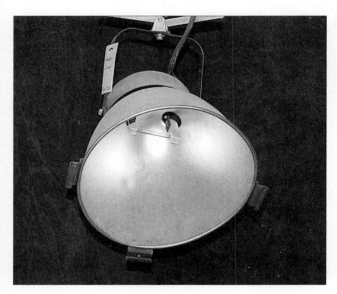

Figure 5-20. *The large bucket-like reflector scatters light over a large area, providing more diffused light than a Fresnel focused in spread/flood mode. The diffusion material often attached to the front of a scoop to further diffuse its light was removed for this photograph to show detail inside.*

the light intensity of a broad or scoop. Delicate, filmy or highly reflective products in commercials often look better when illuminated by softlights.

Cyc Lights and *Strip Lights:* These are used to illuminate, and often to colorize, backgrounds such as a *cyclorama* (cyc), a tightly stretched white curtain that, when properly lit, suggests a limitless background. Cyc lights usually are small-to-medium-sized broads, hung near the rear of the set, pointing toward the cyc. Strip lights ("strips") perform the same general function as cyc lights. Unlike a cyc light, which is a single open-front

1.

Figure 5-22. *Shot 1 is a large softlight on a studio stand. Softlights are also often suspended from the studio's light grid. Shot 2 shows a lightweight softlight used for EFP applications. It's made of materials so it can be folded into a compact size for easy transport. Shot 3 shows how a softlight might be used to light a product. Note that the softlight is suspended over the product with a counterweighted boom.*

Shots 2 and 3 courtesy of Lowel Light Manufacturing, Inc.

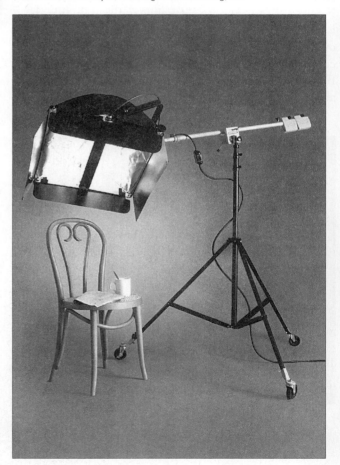

2.

3.

Figure 5-23. *A PAR lamp.*

Figure 5-24. *A fluorescent floodlight. Fluorescent lamps producing light of approximately 3,200 degree Kelvin color temperature allow the mixing of conventional quartz instruments with fluorescent instruments.*

broad, a strip consists of many red, green, blue and white *PAR* (parabolic aluminized reflector) *lamps,* mounted one after another in a long, narrow, rectangular metal housing. PARs are factory-set at one broad focus setting (see Figure 5-23). A lighting technician uses dimmer circuits to separately control the intensity of each PAR to adjust the electrical current fed to the red, green and blue PARs in the strip. Varying the red, green and blue lights allows the lighting technician to project any shade of light desired onto a cyc (or any other surface).

A relatively new kind of fill light is gaining prominence in video production. Resembling the fluorescent tubes used in ceiling fixtures of businesses and institutions but designed to produce light at 3,200 or 5,600 deg. K, these fixtures provide extremely diffused, soft light of sufficient intensity to completely light a set. Using what scientists call "sustained RGB lighting" to softly illuminate their sets, *fluorescent floodlight banks* generate relatively little heat. A studio full of these instruments is much cooler than one lit with conventional incandescent lamps. Many TV stations light their standard news sets with fluorescent floodlight banks because they operate cooler, require less electrical power and provide a soft light that flatters the talent. Fluorescent-type instruments are also finding applications in ENG and EFP work (see Figure 5-24).

Spots, Reflectors and PAR Banks as Fills   In a pinch, both Fresnels and open-front spots sometimes can serve as fill lights. However, the Fresnel is designed principally

for spot lighting, so the broad, scoop or softlight is the usual choice for fill lighting.

Reflectors are passive devices that simply redirect light and also usually diffuse it. They are especially handy for ENG and EFP because they require no electricity and reduce the need for more lighting instruments by simply redirecting sunlight to fill in harsh shadows. Inexpensive homemade reflectors are fashioned easily from plywood and crumpled household aluminum foil. They also are available from manufacturers in portable kits (see Figure 5-25).

A *PAR bank* is an array of PARs mounted together in a large, usually square housing. PAR banks provide intense,

Figure 5-25. *This reflector will be used to fill in the shadow on the left side of the subject's face. The right side is illuminated by diffused light from a large picture window. The reflector, which will not appear in the close-up planned for this lighting setup, bounces soft fill from the window onto the subject's left without the use of a lighting instrument.*

Figure 5-26. *A six-lamp PAR bank on a portable studio stand.*

Figure 5-27. *A Lowel Tota-lite with diffusion umbrella. Also, the gaffer has clipped neutral density gel to the front of this Tota to reduce the intensity of the light reaching the umbrella.*

Photo courtesy of Lowel Light Manufacturing, Inc.

diffused light over a relatively large area. This makes them useful as fill lights for large studio and remote sets. However, they are expensive, bulky and not often used in small-scale field productions (see Figure 5-26).

Fill Light Accessories   Fill lights share many of the accessories used with spotlights to control intensity, character and color temperature: Scrims and gels diffuse and colorize their outputs; flags, gobos and barn doors also shape and confine their beams. Additionally, *lighting umbrellas* diffuse the beams of both flooded open-front spots and fills even more. Indeed, pointing any open-front Fresnel or fill light 180 degrees away from the subject into the reflective inner lining of a lighting umbrella effectively turns the instrument into a softlight. In this mode, you can control the intensity of this soft fill light by either pinning or spreading its focus (see Figure 5-27).

Professionals can substitute a light-colored, reasonably low (8 to 10 foot) ceiling (or even a side wall) for an umbrella. This technique is called *bounce lighting.* Instruments are aimed at the ceiling or wall, rather than directly at subjects. Like a bank shot in billiards, the light beam bounces off the ceiling or wall onto the subject, creating a low-intensity, extremely diffused, pleasing fill light.

Mounts and Connectors for Lighting Equipment

Ideally, studio lights are mounted approximately 12 feet above the studio floor to either a *stationary grid* found in most TV stations or, in larger production studios, on theater-style *counterweight battens,* which, as the illustration demonstrates, can be raised or lowered via sturdy ropes that are lashed to pin rails (see Figure 5-28). Stationary grids are the more common of the two, especially in smaller studios.

Regardless of the studio mounting system used, lights attach to one-and-a-half-inch-diameter pipes that form the stationary grid or hang down from the counterweight

1.

2.

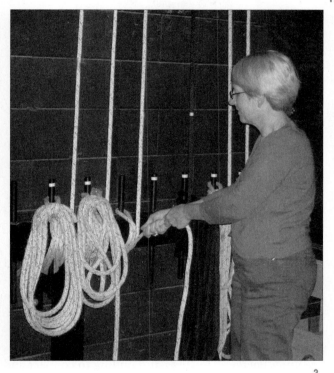

3.

Figure 5-28. *Shot 1 is a stationary lighting grid. In shot 2, a lighting technician hangs a light on a counterweight batten. In shot 3, a lighting technician lashes off a counterweight batten to a pin rail.*

Shot 2 courtesy of Nebraska Educational Telecommunications.

battens. Usually the instrument attaches to the grid/batten with a hefty-looking *C-clamp,* as seen in Figure 5-29.

The C-clamp bolts directly to the *yoke* of the instrument, the U-shaped device seen in Figure 5-29. Suspended in the yoke, the instrument is free to pan and tilt as needed. Sometimes, the C-clamp isn't connected directly to the pipe but instead bolts onto a *hanger,* which in turn is connected to the pipe. Hangers come in many varieties. One of the oldest and most common is the *pantograph.* As the next figure illustrates, a pantograph allows a lighting instrument to be lowered to various distances below the grid/batten. This can also be done with a simpler hanger known as a *sliding rod.* This is normally a half- to three-quarter-inch length of vertical pipe, clamped onto the horizontal pipe of the grid or

counterweight batten. Either square or wing nuts screwed into the pipe secure the sliding rod at various heights, just like the pantograph (see Figure 5-30).

Lights bolted directly by their yokes to heavy *floor stands* provide another approach to obtaining low-angled studio lighting (see Figure 5-31). One of the most useful kinds of floor stands is the *C-stand.* It got its name because it was created by the Century Strand lighting company. Extremely versatile, it can be used to mount a light or to attach an accessory. It has a swivel arm that can be raised or lowered as the need arises. Because they are lightweight and portable yet often used to hold up heavy weights, C-stands frequently need sandbags or weights attached to their base for safety's sake (see Figure 5-32).

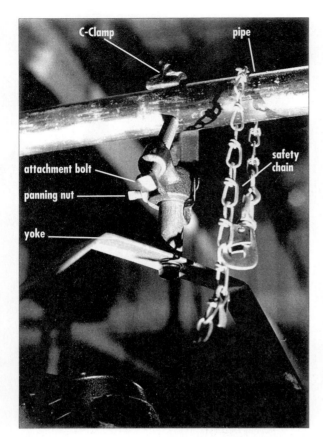

Figure 5-29. *Here a lighting instrument is C-clamped to a pipe. The attachment bolt is tightened to secure the C-clamp. Note the safety chain, which should be attached as soon as the C-clamp is hung on the pipe. The panning nut on the C-clamp permits the yoke on which the light is suspended to be adjusted to help aim the instrument.*

Figure 5-30. *Both the pantograph and the sliding rod allow an instrument attached to the light grid to be raised or lowered easily to the desired height.*

Figure 5-31. *A Fresnel mounted on a floor stand.*
Photo courtesy of ARRI Corporation.

Light, portable floor stands and an array of other gadgets help position instruments in ENG and EFP productions. Some of the most popular gadgets are alligator grips, door mounts, clamps and pole kings (see Figure 5-33).

Professional lighting instruments use three kinds of alternating-current (AC) power plugs. They are the *twist-lock,* the *three-prong* and the *grounded plug.* Except for a heavier cable and plug, the grounded plug variety is identical to those found on many modern home appliances and will fit into any modern 120-volt AC outlet. The three-prong is one of two heavier connectors found in studios. But the three-prong is potentially dangerous, because it sometimes requires energetic pushing and pulling to connect and

Figure 5-32. *A crewperson uses a C-stand to hold a scrim to diffuse a lighting instrument.*

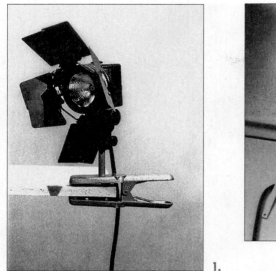

Figure 5-33. *In shot 1, a minibasher is suspended from a plank by a gator grip. In shot 2, a minibroad is used for fill while suspended from a door mount. In shot 3, another minibroad hangs from a clamp. In shot 4, an adjustable extension pole with suction grip, typically called a pole king, extends from floor to ceiling, providing a standard diameter pole for attaching lighting instruments with C-clamps.*

disconnect it. Surprised by the amount of jerking and yanking required, an inexperienced lighting technician could lose balance and fall from the ladder or lighting scaffold. Although this three-prong plug is commonplace, OSHA, the Federal Government's Occupation Safety and Health Administration, recommends against its use.

The twist-lock is the preferred heavy duty studio AC connector. One simply aligns the three prongs, which are set in a circle, and lightly twists. The prongs safely lock in place (see Figure 5-34).

Lighting Control Consoles

Lighting control consoles allow you to adjust the intensity of many lighting instruments at the same time and to program sophisticated changes in your lighting effects to occur on cue. Consoles allow groupings of instruments to be preset, faded up, faded out and/or replaced by an entirely different array of lights for the next scene. The more sophisticated control consoles electronically store hundreds of these lighting configurations.

As shown in Figure 5-35, a typical lighting control console, or board, consists of three main elements:

1. a *patch panel* and/or one or more *preset boards,* allowing adjustment of each instrument in the studio during preproduction to a certain intensity level (in a totally computerized lighting console, this information is programmed into a computer, then stored for future use on a floppy disc, memory chip or some other device);

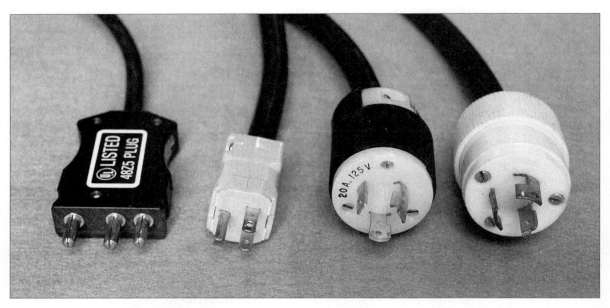

Figure 5-34. *Typical plugs used with TV lighting instruments, from left: Three-prong, grounded plug and twist-lock. The two twist-locks to the right look identical, but they carry different current ratings and are not mechanically compatible. Each type of plug requires a matching type receptacle (female end).*

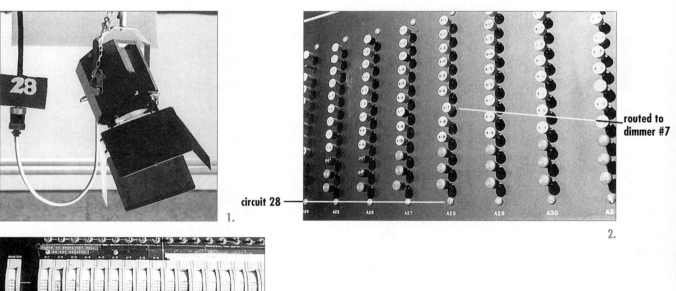

**dimmer #7
turned up**

Figure 5-35. *To demonstrate how a rather common, older light board works, note in shot 1 that the Fresnel is plugged into a pigtail, a kind of lighting connector, labeled "circuit 28" on the lighting grid. In shot 2, we see that circuit number 28 can be routed to one of nine dimmers. Dimmer A-7 is depressed. In shot 3, we see that dimmer A-7 is faded up. To fade dimmer A-7 out, the slider is brought down.*

2. *non-dim* circuits, permitting certain instruments to be turned on and off at full intensity (like the light switch on the wall) with the push of a button;

3. and *submaster* and *master dimmer* controls, permitting certain preselected groups of lighting instruments (or the entire dimmable output of the board) to be faded up or down simultaneously.

Older lighting consoles have patch panels that allow control of individual instruments, or groups of three to four instruments, by a single dimmer circuit. Newer designs eliminate patch panels completely. They use separate preset boards for each light circuit in the studio. Some noncomputerized, manually operated light consoles feature as many as 15 rows of preset boards, each row set with different intensity levels for different scenes. Computerized consoles provide a nearly unlimited number of preset panel rows and use much less hardware (see Figure 5-36).

Many college and small production facilities can't afford light control consoles. Lights are turned off and on using the same kind of circuit breaker panels found in modern homes. Since lights are turned on and off but not dimmed, light intensity control becomes more difficult, but not impossible. Gelling with ND filters, placing higher- or lower-wattage quartz lamps in lighting instruments, moving instruments closer to or farther away from the subject and adjusting beam focus create results similar to many, but not all, of those performed by a lighting control console.

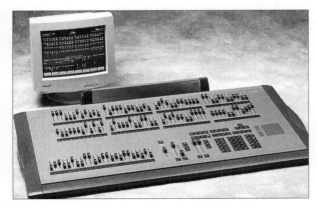

Figure 5-36. *Today's computerized light board is only about four or five times larger than a computer keyboard—about the same size as the average video switcher. This ETC model 4896 studio lighting console is capable of programming a show with hundreds of scenes, or a simple program with a few light cues. Scene memory is stored on a standard 1.4 megabyte micro floppy disc.*

Photo courtesy of Electronic Theatre Controls, Inc.

Safety and Efficiency

Accidents in television productions sometimes happen during activities associated with lighting a set. Safety must always be a prime consideration during a production, and we offer the following list of tips for beginning lighting technicians:

1. Secure lights to the pipe not only with the C-clamp but also with a *safety chain* or cable (see Figure 5-37). Avoid excessively tightening the C-clamp to the pipe or you'll weaken, bend or possibly break the clamp. Simply tighten the clamp until the instrument is secure—and no more.

2. Whether you're on location or on a studio shoot, be sure to secure lights mounted to portable floor stands with some kind of weight. This avoids

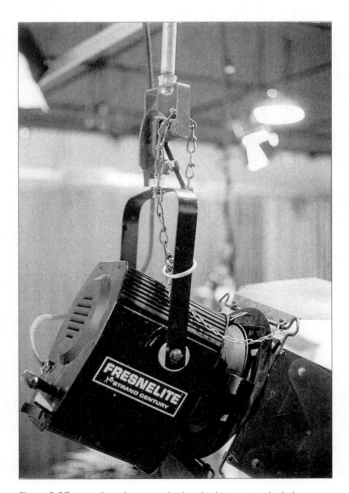

Figure 5-37. *A safety chain attached to the hanger to which the instrument is C-clamped. Another safety chain assures that the Fresnel's barn doors are likewise secured.*

tip-over accidents, since the lighting instruments are usually heavier and larger than the base. Studios often use sandbags for this purpose.

3. Remember ladder safety: One university's studio operations rule book prescribes that no student may climb a ladder unless there's someone else standing on the ladder's bottom rung to steady it.

4. When you're working at or near the top of a ladder or on a studio scaffold, never simply put down the wrench or other tool you're using. Place it in your pocket or securely hook it onto something. Otherwise you may knock it off, and it will fall onto the floor, a camera or your helper's head. Some studios call for attaching one end of a short safety chain to the wrench and the other to the ladder.

5. Lighting instruments become very hot very fast. If you must adjust an instrument after it is lit, use gloves made of heat-insulating material.

6. Don't trust the student lighting control console operator who says, "The power is off," when you're replacing the lamp in a lighting instrument. Always be sure the power is off by physically unplugging the instrument. Otherwise, you may plug a new lamp into a live socket and suffer serious hand or finger burns.

7. Be sure you hang instruments right side up. Failing to do so greatly reduces the lives of very expensive lightbulbs (the average cost is $35 to $65 each). Also, many instruments' gel-frame and barn-door holders are designed so that if you hang the light upside down, these sharp, metal accessories suddenly turn into demented Frisbees, careening down to the floor, damaging themselves, other equipment and occasionally people.

Although not directly related to safety, the following tips will make you more efficient and help get the most out of your time and equipment:

1. Adjust the instruments one at a time with the other instruments turned off. This gives you a "clean" measurement of each light's intensity and allows you to aim, adjust and meter its output more accurately. Also, don't forget to "kill the work lights" in the studio. Work lights are general room lighting fixtures not used during productions. They illuminate the studio while set building, maintenance and other activities are going on. Leaving work lights on while you're setting

instruments can give you incorrect light meter and color temperature readings and make lighting by the eye much more difficult.

2. Never touch a quartz lamp with your bare hands, even when it's cold. Oil from your skin leaves a film on the quartz envelope, reducing the lamp's lifespan. If you're permitted to change bulbs in an instrument, handle the glass end of the bulb with the protective paper it comes in. If the paper's not available, use a clean cloth. Be sure to remove all the protective paper or cloth before firing up the instrument.

Lighting in the uncontrolled environment of a field production requires special attention to detail. Tech Manual 5-2, located at the end of this chapter, discusses some of the things you'll need to consider when you begin lighting for "remotes."

Artistic or Mood Lighting

Often there are situations that call for techniques other than two- or three-point lighting. To provide some examples, here we will cover some of the methods used in lighting music videos, product shots and dramatic scenes. This is by no means an all-encompassing list, but it should give you an array of techniques to cope with unusual circumstances.

Music Videos

Since all or parts of many music videos are shot in the studio, they can be enhanced with more than just ordinary flat lighting. Here are some suggestions for lighting the set and backgrounds for a more picturesque appearance. (1) Crossed spots: Two Fresnels mounted on the grid with the barn doors pinched tight should give off narrow shafts of light that can give a V-shaped highlight that accentuates the performers (see Figure 5-38, shot 1). If you can't get the barn doors tight enough, you can wrap them in aluminum foil to extend and narrow the shafts of light. If they're available, you can also use snoots to narrow the beams of light. (2) Ellipsoidals: These instruments are ideal for artistic applications. Besides substituting for crossed spots, a pattern created by an ellipsoidal, projected onto a wall or curtain, can provide wonderful framing for a performer (see Figure 5-38, shot 2, in the color plate section of this book). (3) Colored gels: These plastic-like sheets of colored materials provide a variety of appearances and techniques. Avoid blasting the performers' faces with harsh glares of

1.

4.

Figure 5-38. *Shot 1. By putting crossed spots on the wall behind the performer, the lighting director can create a dramatic appearance. Shot 4. An example of one-point (semi-limbo) lighting.*

colored lights. For instance, a blue gel can make a performer's face look like a corpse. A green gel can make someone appear like an alien, and a red gel can "nuke" the person's face and make him or her glow in an undistinguishable blob. Instead, try projecting the lights onto the background wall or curtain, utilizing the barn doors to make smaller shafts of light. Gelled lights can be added to the shot one at a time during the performance, giving your lighting an even more artistic look. Another very theatrical method of using colored gels is to hang them down from the light grid on extender poles or pantographs and make them visible in the shot. By carefully presetting the dimmers at about 25 percent

capacity, such lights, used as set pieces, provide a beautiful backdrop (see Figure 5-38, shot 3, found in the color plate section of this book).

The next technique can be done in a studio or in the field, given the right circumstances. (5) Semi-limbo, also known as *one-point lighting:* This is an even more dramatic look, with the face half-obscured by shadow, or with a soft, bounced light barely illuminating the darker side of the face. This can be accomplished by placing the key light at a 90 degree angle to the performer with a foam core board on the opposite side to bounce the light back (see Figure 5-38, shot 4).

Using these techniques individually or in various combinations, you can enhance the look of your music videos beyond the realm of flat lighting. For instance, if you have a band with several musicians, you can light each of them in a different way to create a more picturesque appearance.

Product Shots or Tabletop Lighting

There are instances—particularly in commercial production, home-shopping shows, infomercials and game shows—when objects must be placed on a table and carefully lit for maximum quality. There are many techniques used in such instances. Here we'll deal with some of the fundamentals:

1. Straight-down lighting: As the name implies, this application involves hanging a light—either a Fresnel or broad with scrim will do—almost directly overhead of the object. You can place the light slightly in front of the product and tilt the light back at a slight angle. This gives you a flat, almost shadowless light that gives no competition to the attention placed on the product. This is simple, but effective, with products or items that lend themselves to overhead illumation (see Figure 5-39A, shots 1 and 2).
2. Parallel lighting: Many times the product has a mirrorlike, shiny element to it that will give off a glare if you light it using the conventional lighting triangle. Or perhaps there are several products that make straight-down lighting ineffective. A solution is parallel lighting. Place two lights—either broads or Fresnels—facing each other, at an almost 90 degree angle to both sides of the product. Get them far enough away so there are no hot spots on the edges or where the lights cross. Using softlights, umbrellas or instruments otherwise diffused by being covered with scrim minimizes those hot spots (see Figure 5-39A, shots 3 and 4).

1.

3.

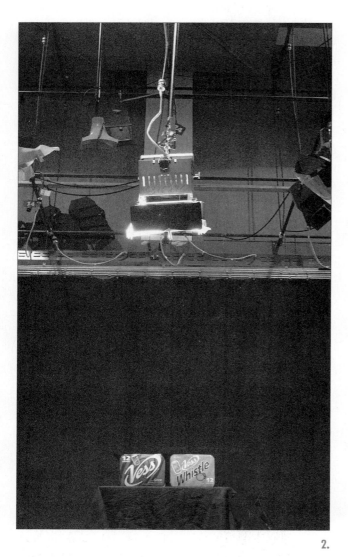

2.

4.

Figure 5-39A. *Shot 1 shows the overhead lighting of a product. Shot 2 shows where the straight-down light instrument was placed. In shot 3, you see the shot of the glass display case. In shot 4, you see how the parallel lights were positioned on opposite sides of the display case. Note that one is aimed high, the other low.*

3. Textured lighting: Frequently you will want to emphasize a certain part of the product — perhaps the name or logo. You can do your basic lighting, such as three-point lighting or, as in the next example, straight-down lights, with a flag to soften the overall illumination. Then, for a specialized, product-only light, you use a textured floor light. Do this either with an instrument with a snoot or, more likely in college productions, jury-rigged with aluminum foil or another handy, home-made device made of black spray paint on alu-

minum foil. The foil is placed on the end of the barn doors and textured to give off a narrow slash of light custom made for the product. It's also possible to use a specially patterned cookie in an ellipsoidal for this purpose. In any case, adjust this light and bring it to a proper level of intensity, either on a dimmer or by moving it closer or farther away from the subject, so the designated area is hit with a "beauty spot" of proper light intensity (see Figure 5-39B, shots 5 through 7, for an example).

These lighting techniques should get you started. Whenever you have the luxury of being around to watch a veteran lighting designer, videographer or producer, make sure you pick their brains to expand your lighting solution repertoire. Good lighting is frequently a process of trial and error, so don't be discouraged if you try some fancy methods and they fail miserably. Rethinking your ideas and placing lights in different positions can frequently save what appears to be a hopeless situation. Remember that good lighting is the difference between mundane, home-movie-looking productions and truly professional, sometimes downright beautiful shots.

This chapter focused on the equipment and the fundamentals of illuminating the subject on televi-

5.

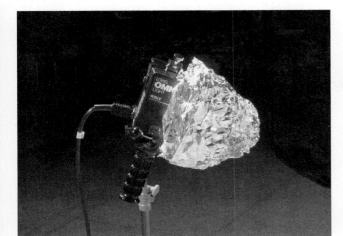

6.

Figure 5-39B. *In shot 5, a product's name has been specially illuminated with a rectangular point of light. In shot 6, aluminum foil is used in front of the instrument to shape that rectangular light point. Shot 7 shows how the entire product shot was lit: Primarily, it was illuminated from overhead, using a scrim mounted on a C-stand to diffuse and reduce the amount of light striking the product. Then, the aluminum-foiled instrument was aimed right at the product's name. This "special" light also makes the product brighter than the coffee cup or the muffin, therefore attracting the viewer's eye to the product.*

7.

sion, with special concern to three main variables you can manipulate: light intensity, light character and color temperature. We also discussed the instruments available to manipulate these variables to achieve both technical and aesthetic objectives.

In these initial chapters, we've been concerned exclusively with the part of this medium that meets the eye. In Chapter 6, we turn our attention to what many say is the neglected "other half" of the medium—the part that we hear.

tech manual 5-1   *Measuring Contrast Ratios*

It is important to understand that contrast ratios depend upon the intensity of reflected light reaching the camera. Simply reading the light falling on various parts of the set with an incident-light meter provides no indication of contrast ratios, because different objects in the scene have differing values of reflectance. It is the <u>combination</u> of incident-light intensity and the reflective quality of the objects that determine the intensity of reflected light and, therefore, the range of contrast in the shot.

To determine the contrast ratio, we "sweep" the lighted set with a reflected-light meter to locate the brightest and darkest spots on the set, noting the light intensity in footlamberts. We then divide the larger number by the smaller number. For example, if you find the darkest spot in the scene

measures 4 fl and brightest spot shows 160 fl, the lighting falls within the 40:1 range (a 160:4 ratio is the same as 40:1). If the contrast ratio is greater than 40:1, the lighting may require adjustment to avoid exceeding the technical limitations of the TV transmission system. Sometimes, however, the problem is caused by a single highly reflective object in the shot that can be replaced with something less reflective. Occasionally a strip of black tape or "dulling spray" on the offending object solves the problem.

It's important that you use the meter properly when measuring reflected light for calculating the contrast ratio. You need readings from the very brightest and darkest areas in the scene, not a general measurement of the scene as a whole, to perform the calculation.

tech manual 5-2   *Lighting and Power Considerations for EFP*

When surveying a location site, check the fuse or breaker box in the house or building to determine how much current (measured in amperes, or amps) you can draw for your portable lights. Most circuit breakers or fuses in modern homes and businesses accommodate between 15 and 20 amps. The power outlets protected by each breaker or fuse should be labeled but aren't always, and even if there are labels present, they aren't always accurate. That's one reason that large budget EFP productions either generate their own power on site or employ licensed electricians to tap into the main power line coming into the house ahead of the breaker/fuse box. Either approach ensures a sufficient, uninterrupted power supply. Unless you're a licensed electrician, do *not* try bypassing the breaker/fuse box yourself: Results could be fatal! You generally won't have such resources, so you

must check the current your portable lighting instruments draw. The label attached to the instrument generally provides this information. If not, dividing the wattage of the instrument's lamp by 100 provides a conservative estimate of the current required. For example, a 400-watt lamp draws about 4 amps (400 divided by 100 = 4). Most open-front, portable lighting instruments used in ENG and EFP draw less than 10 amps each. So, if a particular circuit has a 20-amp breaker or fuse, you can theoretically plug two 10-amp instruments into that circuit. However, other devices may be plugged into the circuit that you don't know about. For example, on one of your authors' shoots in a particularly old home, we had all the current needed for a setup in the living room until the kitchen refrigerator's chiller cycled on! That blew the fuse supplying power for one of our lights, ruining a scene. A production assistant unplugged the refrigerator and shooting continued. But when we wrapped for the day, the PA forgot to plug in the refrigerator again! Replacing all the ruined food stored in that refrigerator significantly increased the cost of that day's shoot.

If the most conveniently located circuits appear inadequate, bring heavy-duty extension cords to the location, so you can "import" power from circuits in other rooms. Here's an important rule of thumb about extension cords: Avoid using extension cords that are narrower in diameter than the cords that come out of your portable lighting instruments: This could create a fire hazard. If a cord is thicker, it is designed to handle more current. Carefully route all of these extension cords at your location to reduce the risk of people tripping over them, knocking down light stands and breaking electrical connections. Use *gaffer's tape* to hold down wires in particularly busy areas. Gaffer's tape is a heavy-duty, two-inch-wide, cloth-backed adhesive tape used for many jobs in TV production. Common duct tape

works if it isn't left in place too long, but duct tape's adhesive is of lesser quality and is often difficult to remove later on. Incidentally, as seen in the overview chapter, the term *gaffer* refers to the head electrician working on a film/video production. The gaffer's crew handles all electrical needs, but his/her principal job is setting up all artificial lighting. The gaffer works under the supervision of the director of photography/videography. Sometimes in television, a gaffer is called the lighting director.

Remember that lighting instruments on location are hot, too. Heat from open-front instruments can scorch wallpaper, ignite curtains and even trigger a building's heat-activated sprinkler system!

Finally, the easiest way to break the filament of an expensive lamp is to move the instrument with the power on, or even when it's still hot from recent operation. When you wrap your location, turn off the lights immediately, but don't move them until they've cooled down. This also reduces the risk of scorched hands.

Important Vocabulary Terms

Available light: Naturally existing light found on location.

Background lights: Called "specials" in theatre, they illuminate certain talent or objects in the background of the shot.

Backlight: The third element of the lighting triangle. Striking the subject from behind, it separates subject from background. Rim and kicker lights are varieties of backlights.

Barn doors: Comprised of either two or four metal flags (flaps), barn doors attach directly to the front of spot lights and are opened or closed to shape the instrument's beam. Although serving a similar function, barn doors, unlike flags and gobos, pan and tilt with the instrument.

Baselight: The minimum light intensity needed for a certain camera to function without video noise.

Basher: See "Open-front spot."

Basic lighting triangle: The correct combination of key light, backlight and fill light to properly and artistically illuminate a subject. Also called triangular and Rembrandt lighting.

Board: See "Lighting control console."

Bounce lighting: A technique in which instruments are aimed at a ceiling or wall, rather than directly at the subject, creating a low-intensity, extremely diffused fill light.

Broad: A rectangular, open-front fill light.

C-clamp: A C-shaped device used to attach the yoke of a lighting instrument or a hanger to lighting grid or batten pipes.

C-stand: A floor stand that provides more flexibility in placing lights since it has a hinged arm that can be raised, lowered or swiveled to a desired location. It can also be used for mounting gels, flags or scrim.

Camera light: A battery-powered quartz light, usually mounted atop an ENG camera. There is also an HMI version.

Contrast ratio: The range of light reflected from objects in a shot expressed as a ratio. Set and light designers typically avoid allowing any object in a shot to reflect more than 40 times the light reflected by the darkest object; this situation is said to have a contrast ratio of 40:1.

Counterweight batten: A long, rectangular conduit for "pig tails" (female plugs connected to light circuits), onto which lighting pipes are also mounted. Counterweight battens hang from the ceiling by a network of ropes and cables and can be raised and lowered at will.

Cucalorus (cookie): A patterned piece of metal, wood or cardboard placed in front of a Fresnel to project a pattern on a wall or other surface; also a patterned metal insert placed inside and behind the lens of an ellipsoidal light used for the same purpose.

Cyc light: A broad used to illuminate, and often to colorize, a cyclorama.

Cyclorama (cyc): A tightly stretched curtain used to suggest a limitless background.

Dichroic filter: A glass filter that raises quartz lamp color temperature from 3,200 deg. K to 5,600 deg. K.

Ellipsoidal (Leko) light: A spotlight creating the narrowest, most clearly shaped and intense beam of light of any instrument used in TV production. Also used with a cookie to project patterns and, using its internal system of metal leaves, to project light in various shapes. Also called a Leko light.

Fill light: This term has two meanings. Fill light may be the light responsible for softening shadows made by the key light in the basic lighting triangle. The term may also refer to lighting instruments, which are also called fills, such as broads and scoops with beams broadly focused and more diffused than spots, used in fill lighting, baselight and some sidelighting applications.

Flag: A flat, rectangular metal device placed in front of a lighting instrument to control the direction the light beam travels.

Flat lighting: Virtually a synonym for sidelighting, this involves setting up a field of view in which all areas are flatly lit. This is especially helpful in scenes in which there is too much action or movement to set up dozens of lighting triangles.

Flooding: Adjusting a lighting instrument such as a Fresnel spotlight to project a broader, more diffused beam of light. Also called spreading.

Floor stand: Light-mounting device with weighted base that supports a single vertical shaft onto which yokes are bolted. Floor stands provide lower-angled lighting than lights suspended from above but take up studio floor space. Floor stands designed for ENG/EFP are lighter than studio stands, and their shafts telescope to a much smaller size for convenient storage in a light kit.

Fluorescent floodlight banks: A variety of fill light instrument containing lamps resembling the fluorescent lights found in office building ceilings. Instead it uses what has been called sustained RGB lighting to softly illuminate sets. Its main advantage is the relatively small amount of heat it generates, compared to other designs, and the soft quality of its light.

Focusing: Either narrowing or widening the beam of light an instrument emits.

Foil: This material can be used to shape the beam of light in a custom-designed fashion. It can be regular aluminum foil, specially designed black-wrap foil or aluminum foil covered with black spray paint.

Footcandle (fc): The intensity of light falling on a surface placed one foot away from a point light source of one candle power. This is the unit of measurement used to measure incident-light intensity.

Footlambert (fl): The measuring unit for reflected light. The Caucasian face with a typical reflectance of .36 reflects 36 fl when illuminated with 100 fc of incident light (100 fc times .36 = 36 fl).

Fresnel: An adjustable-focus spot light with a unique glass lens, consisting of a series of concentric circles.

Gaffer: The head electrician, whose crew handles all electrical needs, but whose principal job is the setting up of all artificial lighting.

Gaffer's tape: A heavy-duty, two-inch wide, cloth-backed adhesive tape used for a variety of jobs, including securing cables and holding items together.

Gel: Thin sheet of colored material to place in front of lighting instruments to give off colored glows of light.

Gel frame: A metal holder for gels placed in front of lighting instruments.

Gobo: In film terminology, a gobo is a round flag.

Grounded plug: One of three kinds of AC power plugs; similar to those found in the home except for its ruggedness.

Halogen-metal-iodide (HMI) light: Similar in design and intent to a Fresnel, HMI lights operate at a color temperature of 5,600 deg. K, compared to a quartz lamp's 3,200 deg. K.

Hanger: A device such as a pantograph that attaches to a lighting pipe by means of a C-clamp. Hangers allow a lighting instrument to be more easily lowered or raised to various heights below the grid or batten.

Incident light: Light that falls directly on the subject rather than light bouncing off the subject. See also "Reflected light."

Incident-light meter: A light meter that measures the amount of light striking the subject, in contrast to a reflected light meter, that measures the amount of light reflected by the subject.

Key light: The main source of illumination in the lighting triangle.

Kicker light: A type of backlight striking the subject from a low angle. Kickers provide subjects with a "halo effect."

Lamp: Another term for the high-wattage lightbulbs found in professional lighting instruments.

Light character: The relative harshness or diffusion of the light beam.

Light intensity: The level of brightness provided by a light source, be it a lighting device or a reflective surface.

Light meter: A photosensitive device that measures light intensity.

Lighting control console: A device used to switch lights on and off and/or control the intensities of one or more lighting instruments in a studio. Also called a board.

Lighting ratios: The relative intensities of the key light, backlight and fill lights in the lighting triangle.

Lighting umbrella: A lighting accessory used to diffuse the harsh quality of spotlights, allowing them to simulate the effect of softlights.

Master dimmer: A control on a light console allowing the entire dimmable output of the console to be increased or decreased.

Motivated light source: The logical direction in the shot from which the key light should come.

Non-dim circuit: A circuit on a lighting console not wired into the dimmer system. Lights assigned to non-dim circuits may only be switched on to full intensity or turned entirely off.

Normally reflective: Used to describe a surface or a set that reflects a normal amount of light, unlike a snow-covered hillside or a bright, shiny surface such as water, so an incident-light-meter reading can be used.

One-point lighting: Also known as semi-limbo lighting, it is a dramatic lighting technique, usually using one instrument. It creates light on only one side of the subject, throwing dramatic shadows on the other side.

Open-front spot: A focusable spot without a Fresnel lens. Lighter and less expensive than Fresnels, and thus often used in ENG/EFP. Sometimes called bashers.

Pantograph: A scissors-like hanger used to adjust the height at which a lighting instrument is hung.

PAR bank: A large, heavy frame containing six or more PARs, used to flood bright light over a relatively large area.

PAR lamp: A lamp with a parabolic aluminized reflector, hence the name, used in strip lights and in PAR banks.

Patch panel: A device resembling an old telephone switchboard allowing one or several instruments to be "patched" (plugged) into and controlled by a single circuit of a lighting console.

Pigtail: A short length of heavy lighting cable featuring a female lighting connector into which instruments attached to a lighting grid/batten are plugged.

Pinning: Focusing an adjustable lighting instrument such as a Fresnel to project a narrow, intense beam of light.

Preset board: A long strip of dimmers, one for each pigtail in the studio light grid/batten system, used to set the relative intensities of each lighting instrument.

Punching in: Adding additional lighting instruments to a scene, either to highlight certain areas (such as a central point of interest) or to overcome a baselight problem (for example, using quartz lights to "punch up" the color temperature of a greenish-looking, fluorescent-lit location).

Reflected light: Light that bounces off the subject rather than light striking the subject directly. See also "Incident light."

Reflected-light meter: A light meter that measures the amount of light reflecting from a subject, in contrast to an incident light meter, which measures the amount of light striking the subject.

Rheostat: In-line slide controls on studio lighting consoles.

Safety chain/cable: Heavy chain or metal cable used to catch a falling lighting instrument should the C-clamp slip or break.

Scoop: A round, half-egg-shaped open-front fill light.

Scrim: Lighting accessory made either of metal mesh or spun fiberglass placed in front of lighting instruments to diffuse their beams.

Set light: A kind of lighting utilizing diffused lights to provide sufficient baselight and to flatly illuminate all relevant portions of the set.

Sidelight: Lights positioned at right angles to the camera providing illumination across the set from left and right rather than front to back; often used to illuminate large areas of stage or set for dance, action, etc.

Sliding rod: A kind of hanger, this half- or three-quarter-inch length of vertical pipe clamps onto the horizontal pipe of the grid or counterweight batten. It is used to raise or lower the height of an instrument from the studio floor. Either square or wing nuts screwed into the pipe secure the sliding rod at various heights in the same manner as a pantograph.

Snoot: Metallic device mounted on lighting instruments to shape the light beam into a narrow circle. These are excellent for use as background lights (specials) and are also called "top hats" or "stovepipes."

Softlight: Open-face instruments featuring lamps facing away from the subject, toward the instrument's internal reflective surface. Softlights provide highly diffused soft light without using scrims.

Spot meter: A kind of reflected-light meter designed to measure light reflected from a small area of the scene rather than the average intensity of light reflected from the scene as a whole.

Spotlight (Spot): Lighting instruments with narrowly focused beams, used especially for key lighting, backlighting and background lighting.

Spreading: See "Flooding."

Stationary grid: One of two methods by which light pipes are mounted. A grid usually consists of a latticework of 1.5-inch pipes, intersecting in four-foot squares. As the name implies, the grid cannot be raised or lowered.

Strip light: A long, rectangular metal housing containing an array of red, green, blue and white PARs or other instruments used to colorize and/or illuminate a cyclorama.

Submaster dimmer: Submasters allow certain groups of instruments to be simultaneously controlled.

3-D: Three-dimensional.

Three-prong plug: An AC power connector sometimes encountered in studio lighting systems. Because technicians may have difficulty plugging and unplugging instruments using this connector and lose their balance in the process, the three-prong plug is considered a safety hazard.

Twist-lock plug: The preferred heavy-duty AC connector for studio lighting. The three electrical contacts (prongs) are inserted into a matching receptacle and then twisted to lock in place.

Two-point lighting: This technique, most often used in field productions, utilizes a key light and backlight, omitting the fill light. It provides a different look than the traditional triangle, or three-point, lighting. The subject should have a semi-halo backlit area on one side of the head, with a key lit area on the opposite side of the face. The other side of the face should have a shadow outlining the curve of the face, adding more depth and texture.

Video noise: Graininess or "snow" visible in the picture, especially in the darker areas. Video noise is a problem when a camera operates with less than baselight levels of illumination.

Yoke: The U-shaped part of a lighting instrument, which allows the light to pan and tilt as needed. C-clamps bolt directly to the yoke.

chapter **6**

Audio

No one wants to watch silent TV. Yet we sometimes become so tightly focused on the "vision" part of television that the audio component becomes an afterthought. This is probably understandable, because effective pictures are critically important in TV, and the speakers found in many TV sets are so poor that producers have had little incentive to provide high-quality sound. But this is changing rapidly. Today's television audience grew up with FM stereo, compact disc players and surround sound in motion picture theaters. Now they're demanding better audio from television. A Consumer Electronics Association survey found almost 30 percent of U.S. homes had an audio/video receiver with a surround sound processor by the end of 2005. Clearly, manufacturers are responding to consumer demands for better audio by building TV sets with higher-fidelity multichannel sound systems, and as viewers move to digital television, even more homes will have sophisticated audio equipment.

As is true of practically every facet of TV production, audio is a subject meriting much greater attention than we can give it. This chapter provides the fundamentals of audio for TV, a foundation on which you can begin building the knowledge and skills you'll need if you pursue a career in TV production.

The Audio Production Process

Let's first examine audio as it relates to the three phases of the television production process presented in the "Overview and Tour" chapter:

1. **Preproduction:** This is when you must answer four basic questions regarding the sound portion of the final program:

First, what sounds will we need in the program? For example, will we need the sound of birds in a scene we have planned? Will the sound of a few birds be adequate, or do we need the sounds of many birds? Will the sound of any kind of bird serve the purpose, or do we need the sounds of crows or doves or some other breed?

Second, how will we acquire these sounds? Must we record them in the wild ourselves, or can we use prerecorded bird sounds from a sound-effects library?

Third, what equipment is needed for acquiring the sounds we must record ourselves? Can we get by using the equipment we have available, or do we need to buy, rent or borrow special microphones or other audio gear?

Finally, what processing and manipulation of these sounds is required before they're integrated effectively into the program? Will we need to add a hollow echo to the voice of someone portraying a ghost returned from "the other side"? Or will we need to make a modern musical recording sound tinny as if it were being reproduced through the huge "horn" speaker of a 1920s-era radio that's visible in the matching video image?

Obviously, we must inventory our audio needs and make appropriate plans during preproduction to ensure we can accomplish our goals in the production and postproduction phases.

2. **Production:** At this stage, the desired sounds are captured or created and converted to electrical signals using the most appropriate equipment and techniques. Then they are either processed immediately for "live" transmission to the audience, or

recorded for processing and manipulation later in the postproduction phase.

3. **Postproduction:** Audio posting involves processing and manipulating sound recorded during the production stage. It also involves adding sounds obtained from sources other than those available during the production phase. For example, it's standard practice to focus on recording only the voices of the principal characters during production and wait until postproduction to add background sounds such as city traffic, wind or the ocean. The process of enhancing a program's audio track during postproduction is called *sweetening.*

Human Perception of Sound

Sound is the interpretation our brains give to a particular physical stimulus received through our ears. This perception of sound involves our individual interpretation, so it's possible for viewers receiving the same physical stimulus to "hear" different sounds. The interpretation is determined by the individual's ability to hear well, the person's previous memory of that particular audio stimulus and by the context in which the stimulus occurs. Context is especially important. For example, viewers might perceive the sound of paper crumpled near a microphone as a roaring forest fire if the screen is filled with smoke and flames and people are heard shouting "Help!"

Physical Aspects of Sound

Although we shouldn't forget that the "meaning" of sound is ultimately an individual psychological function, we must deal with sound's physical aspects, the acoustic and electronic energy created and controlled in the production process. Some basic information about sound's physical characteristics may help us select and use audio devices more wisely.

The physics of sound is a complex subject. We'll focus on just two fundamental physical characteristics of sound: *amplitude* and *frequency.* Sound amplitude is what we often call loudness, or volume. Sound frequency refers to the musical note of a sound, how high or low it is. We often describe this quality as pitch. A baby's cry has a higher frequency (or higher pitch) than a note played on a bass fiddle. The baby's scream may also have greater amplitude (loudness) than the bass fiddle, depending on how long it has been since the last feeding!

Our ears function only within a limited range of amplitudes and frequencies, but the amplitude range is rather amazing. The loudest sound we can tolerate is many times stronger than the weakest sound we can hear. Frequency is measured in cycles per second, which are called *Hertz* (Hz), in honor of Heinrich Hertz, a German physicist who made significant contributions to the study of electromagnetic waves. The frequency range of human hearing begins at approximately 20 Hz and ends around 20,000 Hz (or 20 kHz), but individuals vary greatly in their ability to hear sounds at different frequencies.

Audio Transduction: Sound to Signal

Air is an excellent medium for transmitting sound if the listener is physically close to the source. But we must convert sound to another form of energy to convey it beyond a few yards or to store it for later use. In video production, the desired conversion is from sound energy to electrical energy, and the most common *transducer* (converter) that performs this function is the microphone. There are many ways to classify microphones, but *method of transduction, directivity* and *output impedance* provide guideposts for discussion.

Methods of Transduction

Microphones transduce (that is, convert) sound to electrical signals in a variety of ways, depending on their design. Based on their conversion system, microphones are classified as being *carbon, crystal* (or *ceramic*), dynamic, ribbon or condenser (or electret). Condenser microphones are also sometimes called electrostatic microphones. We use only dynamic, ribbon and condenser microphones in producing video programs. Carbon and crystal/ceramic transducers aren't technically good enough for professional applications.

Ribbon Microphones   The *ribbon microphone,* also called the *velocity* or *pressure-gradient microphone,* features a paper-thin metallic element (the ribbon) positioned between two magnets (see Figure 6-1). Sound waves entering the microphone cause the ribbon to vibrate, duplicating the sound waves' amplitude and frequency. The vibrating ribbon creates a patterned electrical current, which is conveyed out of the microphone to an amplifier, then to either a speaker, a broadcast transmitter or to some kind of audio recording device.

Older "classic" ribbon microphones such as the RCA DX-77 are noted for their mellow sound quality, but they're large and rather distracting on screen. They're

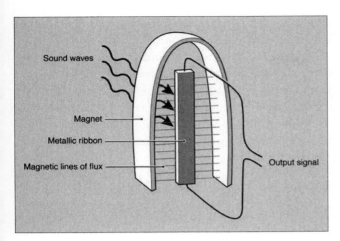

Figure 6-1. *Interior view of a ribbon microphone showing major components. Sound waves cause the metal ribbon to vibrate within the magnetic field, generating electrical signals analogous to the sound waves.*

also easily damaged, making them appropriate only for studio productions. Newer ribbon microphones are both smaller and more rugged, but as a group, ribbon microphones are not popular in modern TV production. Ribbon microphones do not require a battery or external power source for their operation, as do condenser microphones.

Dynamic Microphones   The *dynamic* (or *electrodynamic*) microphone, also known as a *moving coil* or *pressure* microphone, is a workhorse in all kinds of video productions. The dynamic microphone consists of a movable disc (the diaphragm) attached to a coil of wire suspended within a magnetic field. When sound waves

strike the diaphragm, it moves in response to the variations in pressure. This, in turn, causes the coil to move within the magnetic field, creating a patterned electrical current (see Figure 6-2). The amplitude and frequency of this current duplicates the amplitude and frequency of the sound waves striking the diaphragm.

The advantages of the dynamic microphone are its physical ruggedness, its ability to operate without external power and its ability to withstand very loud sounds without either damage to the microphone or much distortion of the sound. On the negative side, most dynamic microphones are relatively large and they don't respond especially well to rapid changes, called *transients,* in sound amplitude or frequency. They lack the "crispness" of some other types.

Condenser Microphones   The transducer of the *condenser* microphone, also known as the *electrostatic* microphone, consists of two very thin electrically charged plates, one of which is fixed in place (see Figure 6-3).

The other vibrates in response to sounds entering the microphone. The movement of this plate creates patterns of electrical currents corresponding to the sounds the microphone picks up. The *electret* microphone is a popular variety of condenser microphone, in which one of the plates of the transducer element is permanently charged. Electret microphones typically do not respond to high frequency sounds as well as a condenser microphone using an external voltage source to charge the plates, but they are inexpensive to produce. Condenser microphones produce a very weak signal and require an amplifier near the transducer. The electrical power source for this

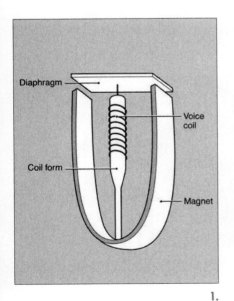

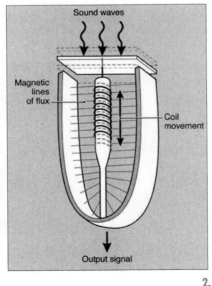

1.   2.

Figure 6-2. *In shot 1, we see the interior view of a dynamic (moving coil) microphone, showing major components. In shot 2, sound waves strike the diaphragm causing the attached coil to move within the magnetic field, generating electrical signals analogous to the sound waves.*

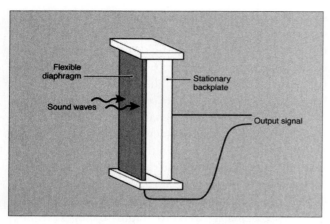

Figure 6-3. *Basic components of a condenser microphone. Sound waves strike the flexible diaphragm, causing it to move and varying the electrical property (known as capacitance) existing between it and the stationary back plate. This change in capacitance alters the flow of electrical current in a pattern analogous to the sound waves causing the diaphragm to move.*

amplifier is either a small battery contained in the microphone's cabling or the audio mixer console to which the microphone is attached. When an audio console supplies the power, the microphone is said to be *phantom powered*.

Condenser microphones are rugged, small and capable of responding rapidly to transients. Their small size

and excellent response characteristics make them popular for television production. But they do have some disadvantages. A condenser microphone's battery can die in the middle of a production. This is an inconvenience during a recording session, but a potential disaster during a live production. This isn't a problem when using phantom power. Also, some condenser microphones have difficulty reproducing very loud sounds without distortion.

Directivity

Microphones differ dramatically in their sensitivity to sound coming from different directions. *Omnidirectional microphones* pick up sound arriving from all directions equally well (see Figure 6-4). Other microphones capture sound best when it comes from opposite directions and are called *bidirectional microphones* (see Figure 6-5). A third category of microphones have heart-shaped pickup patterns and thus are known as *cardioid microphones* (see Figure 6-6). Cardioid microphones are also called unidirectional microphones because they tend to pick up sounds coming from one general direction. Within the cardioid family, there are also microphones with extremely narrow heart-shaped pickup patterns known as *supercardioids* (see Figure 6-7) and *hypercardioids*.

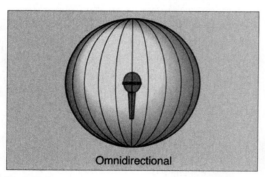

Omnidirectional

Figure 6-4.

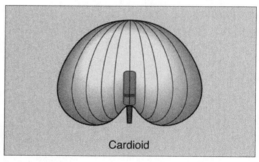

Cardioid

Figure 6-6.

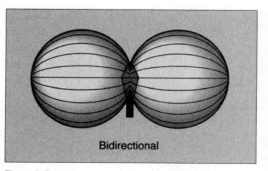

Bidirectional

Figure 6-5.

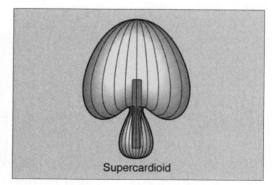

Supercardioid

Figure 6-7.

Figure 6-4 through 6-7. *These graphic representations show the polar patterns of omnidirectional, bidirectional, cardioid and supercardioid microphones.*

Figure 6-8. *Turning the slotted screw changes the pickup pattern of this classic RCA ribbon mike.*

Figure 6-9. *Changing the elements of this modular mike provides different pickup patterns, allowing the same mike body to be used in a variety of applications.*

It's easier to visualize these pickup patterns by using a *polar diagram* (or pattern*)* so named because it resembles a map of the Earth viewed from directly above one of the poles. The microphone is located at the center of the diagram with its "face" pointing toward 12 o'clock along the zero-degree axis. Microphone manufacturers provide a polar diagram, along with other technical information, in a *specification (spec) sheet* with each microphone.

The manufacturer determines the directional characteristics of a microphone, and most can't be changed by the user. But a few microphones have adjustable pickup patterns the user can alter as needed for a particular task (see Figure 6-8).

Several manufacturers of condenser microphones have gone a step further: They provide a microphone system consisting of several different transducer elements (see Figure 6-9) that fit the same microphone body. These *multiple-transducer-system microphones* allow the user to change both the pickup pattern and the frequency response characteristics of the microphone.

Impedance

Impedance (often represented in manufacturers' technical literature by the letter "Z") is a complex electrical phenomenon that exists in every alternating current (AC) electrical circuit. For our purposes, the term simply means the degree to which current flow in a device or between devices is restricted, resisted or "impeded." The unit of impedance is the Ohm, and mikes are typically categorized as being either low impedance ("low Z") or high impedance ("high Z"). A microphone in the low-Z category will have an impedance of 600 Ohms or less,

while a high-Z microphone's impedance may be many thousands of Ohms. Some microphones have provisions for changing their impedance, but the impedance of most microphones is fixed by the manufacturer. One of the major advantages of low-impedance microphones is that they allow the use of a long cable between the microphone and the audio amplifier without losing audio quality. This can be an important consideration when producing outside the studio environment.

In the era of vacuum-tube amplifiers, it was important to match the impedance of the microphone closely to that of the audio amplifier to avoid a loss of performance. Today, most audio amplifiers use transistors or solid-state chips rather than tubes. Fortunately, microphones designed for professional use (those with three-pin XLR connectors) work well with modern solid-state amplifiers. However, connecting a very high-impedance audio device, such as an electric guitar, to a lower-impedance amplifier (even a modern solid-state model) can create problems. Impedance matching transformers and similar audio "problem solvers" such as those seen later in this chapter, in Figure 6-50, make connections between such devices workable.

Typical Applications

Another way of classifying microphones is in terms of how they're commonly used, which of course depends on the microphone's physical and electrical characteristics. But it's customary and helpful to use shorthand for some of these long, technical names. An audio technician is more likely to call for a "desk" or "clip" microphone

Figure 6-10. *Consumer and prosumer model cameras often come with on-board microphones such as the one pictured. Such microphones suffice for capturing ambient sound in some situations but should not be relied on for recording interviews. They lack the necessary directionality to avoid pickup of distracting background sound in noisy locations.*

Figure 6-11. *A camera-mounted directional microphone is useful for picking up interview sound if the mike is relatively close to the speaker.*

rather than request a "bidirectional ribbon" or "electret supercardioid." Let's examine some typical microphone applications you're likely to encounter in television.

Camera-Mounted Microphones

Some consumer- and industrial-quality camcorders come with permanently mounted *external microphones* (see Figure 6-10). These are usually condenser mikes with an omnidirectional pickup pattern that's primarily useful for recording *ambient sound,* which is also called natural, or wild, sound. Most professional electronic news gathering (ENG) and electronic field production (EFP) cameras provide an *accessory shoe,* a clip or bracket that allows the operator to mount an appropriate auxiliary external microphone on the camera. This auxiliary mike is often a supercardioid or hypercardioid dynamic or condenser microphone with a relatively narrow pickup pattern. Like permanently mounted camera mikes, these auxiliary directional mikes are often used by ENG/EFP operators to capture wild sound. But if the operator positions the camera close to the person speaking, these mikes can record satisfactory interview audio that doesn't sound "hollow" (see Figure 6-11). However, there's a limit to any microphone's effective reach, and it's often wise to avoid depending on a mike attached to the camera body to get good audio quality. However, using an off-camera mike may require an additional person, either a reporter or a sound technician, to position the mike unless it's attached to the person(s) speaking. In ENG work, where the "one-man

band" is common, operators often use a clip mike attached to the newsmaker's clothing for "sit down" formal interviews but otherwise depend on a camera-mounted mike, accepting the tradeoff of poorer-quality audio for lower production cost.

Newer portable cameras, even those targeted for the consumer market, often allow recording multiple channels of sound. This allows the operator to use a stereo mike (discussed below) or more than one mike to record stereophonic audio. In TV news, however, some professionals use this multichannel capability to record direct sound from an interviewee using close miking (usually with a directional mike) while simultaneously recording ambient natural sound on another channel (often with an omnidirectional mike). This technique allows the editor to combine the two channels of sound during postproduction to provide the most pleasing mix of clear interview audio with appropriate background sound.

Your authors have some reservations about this technique, however, because it requires that the mike recording ambient sound be well out of the range of the person speaking. If the interviewee's voice is also picked up clearly by the omnidirectional mike, there can be some degree of degradation to the interviewee's audio when the two channels are mixed. This degradation is the result of phase differences between the interviewee's audio contributed by the close mike and the same audio picked up by the distant mike.

It's easy to understand that the amplitude of the interviewee's voice will be greater for the mike positioned close to the interviewee, and the voice will be somewhat less loud by the time the sound reaches the more distant mike being used to record ambient sound. The difference in loudness between the two mikes would not be as much a problem were it not for the phase differences between the audio from the two mikes. *Phase* is another term for time. Clearly, in addition to a difference in loudness, there will be a time, or phase, difference between the instant a given sound reaches mikes placed at unequal distances from the sound source. Mixing the interviewee's voice captured by the near and far mikes will combine two versions of the same sound, but they will be out of phase. The result is that some frequencies will combine to reinforce each other, while other frequencies will be cancelled out either partially or fully. In any case, mixing the interviewee's audio from two mikes that produce waveforms out of phase does not result in the highest-quality sound. The ideal way to avoid this problem, we think, is simply to record the interviewee's audio at one time and the ambient sound at another.

Phase problems are also encountered in studio productions. For example, if Talent A and Talent B are close together, and each performer has his own microphone (we'll call them mikes A and B), both mikes will pick up audio from both performers. Although mike A will be closer to Talent A than mike B, mike B will still pick up some of Talent A's audio because the two performers are close together. When both mike A and mike B are "on" and their audio combined, there will be phase differences introduced. Perhaps you have noticed this when watching a local newscast featuring two reporters seated side by side.

When the show begins, both mikes are on, but when the first news item is announced, only the mike for the speaking talent is left on. You will hear a distinctive difference in the quality of the audio when both mikes are on as opposed to when only one is on.

Audio professionals try to minimize phase problems by following the *three-to-one rule*. The rule states that the distance between two sound sources should be at least three times the distance there is between each sound source and the nearest mike. It is perhaps easier to understand the rule by examining Figure 6-12. By placing the mike close to the source (12 inches in this illustration) and keeping the sources at least three times this distance (36 inches) apart, degradation caused by phase differences will be minimal.

It may be relatively easy to follow the three-to-one rule for radio and general audio recording, but in video production, it may be impractical to separate the performers enough to achieve the minimal spacing required by the rule while still maintaining effective shot composition. Audio technicians working on video productions, however, do what they can. Often they simply put the mikes as close to the sound sources as possible, frequently attaching the mikes directly to the

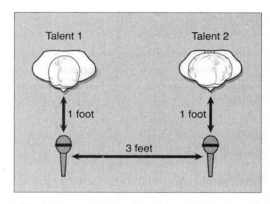

Figure 6-12. *Problems with degraded audio quality can be reduced by following the three-to-one rule when placing mikes and sound sources.*

talent's coat or blouse (as illustrated in Figure 6-19). They may also use ultradirectional microphones (see page 139) to limit audio pickup coming from any direction other than the desired source. And, of course, using a single mike to capture sound from multiple sources, such as a mike suspended on a boom just above a couple of soap opera performers, also avoids phase problems.

Hand Microphones

As you would guess, *hand microphones* are designed to be handheld by the talent. Reporters frequently use hand microphones for interviews or "stand ups" at news events (see Figure 6-13). Talk show hosts also frequently

Figure 6-13. *Reporter uses wireless hand mike while interviewee puts on wireless tie-clip mike. In foreground, battery-powered receivers pick up signals from the two wireless mikes.*

Photo courtesy of Sennheiser Corp.

use hand microphones when interacting with members of the audience. Often hand microphones are either omnidirectional or cardioid dynamic types, although many newer models feature condenser transducers. Hand microphones must be physically rugged and, because they're seen by viewers, they usually have nondistracting, nonreflective finishes. Some hand microphones feature well-insulated transducers that reduce "handling" noises.

Desk Microphones

Hand microphones placed in a holder and mounted on a desk, microphone stand or podium are often referred to as *desk microphones.* Typically the microphone rests in a stand with a heavy base or is attached to the desk or podium via a flexible *gooseneck,* a boom arm (see Figure 6-14) or some other device allowing easy positioning. Typical desk microphone applications include press conferences, panel discussions and meetings where several persons speak or answer questions in random order.

Figure 6-14. *This announcer's microphone in an audio production suite is suspended by an adjustable boom arm to whatever distance and angle the announcer wishes.*

Boom Microphones

It's common practice to refer to any mike supported by a boom as a boom mike. A *boom* is a device with a long "arm" that positions the microphone near the talent but outside the camera's view. The most simple boom is the *fishpole,* a light, hollow, telescoping metal pole with a microphone attached to one end (see Figure 6-15). A fishpole allows a sound technician to move the microphone quickly and easily, but an audio technician can't hold one overhead during extended scenes without a break. As in shot 2, an underhand grip to position the microphone below the talent's head, rather than overhead, eases the strain.

Other booms are more sophisticated, self-supporting wheeled contraptions, often with various pulleys, cables and cranks for positioning the microphone relative to the talent. Studio productions and large-budget EFP most often use such booms. A small, self-supporting studio boom is called a *giraffe* (see Figure 6-16). It's helpful to think of a giraffe as a fishpole on wheels, with a counterweight near the operator's end that makes raising or lowering the microphone easier. On most giraffe booms, there's a control at the operator's end that adjusts the direction the microphone points. A giraffe is larger, more expensive and not as mobile as the fishpole, but it prevents muscle fatigue during long scenes. Larger and more efficient than the giraffe is the studio *perambulator boom,* a large, heavy device requiring two operators, one to push the boom around the studio and another to do the actual positioning of the microphone (see Figure 6-17). A perambulator boom can move the microphone in almost any direction quickly, and with great precision. The trade-offs for these desirable features are expense, size and number of operators required.

Microphones used with booms are often dynamics with some type of cardioid pickup pattern. A principal reason for using a boom is to keep the microphone out of sight, so boom-mounted microphones are some distance from the sound source, depending on shot composition. This requires that the microphone have a highly directional pattern to avoid picking up unwanted sounds. But the narrower the pickup pattern, the more critical it is that the boom operator keep the microphone aimed directly at the sound source (see Figure 6-18). This is a problem if the talent moves quickly or if you need to pick up the voices of several people in separate locations. Talent movements require careful planning, and boom operators must be extremely agile. Wearing a set of headphones or an interrupted-feedback earpiece (discussed below) to monitor the microphone's output

1.

2.

3.

Figure 6-15. *In shots 1 and 2, crewpersons use fishpole booms to suspend shotgun mikes over a scene and just under the bottom edge of a two-shot, respectively, just out of camera range. In shot 3, the mike is in a zeppelin, a device often used outside to deaden wind noise. Using either a zeppelin or a windscreen, as in shot 2, is wise when miking outside.*

Photo 1 courtesy of Sennheiser Corporation.

helps a boom operator keep it properly aimed. Boom operators should also keep a close eye on a video monitor to be sure they are keeping the mike out of the shot.

Students like booms on the set, perhaps because they give the production a "Hollywood" aura. But student boom operators often incorrectly place the microphone and forget to watch for boom shadows falling on the talent's face or the background set. Proper boom placement requires paying attention to both sound and picture quality.

Hanging Microphones

Sometimes inexperienced people avoid complications inherent in using booms by simply hanging one or more microphones from the studio's light grid. Usually this is a poor practice, because people don't emit sound from the top of their skulls, and *hanging microphones* can't move with the talent. Positioned to accommodate the widest shot, a hanging microphone is often a considerable distance from the talent resulting in hollow, "off-mike" sound quality. However, hanging microphones are effective if all that's wanted is ambient, nonspecific background sound, such as audience applause. A hanging microphone also works for large choral groups, orchestras or bands, where it's desirable to pick up a blended acoustical environment. Hanging microphones have their uses, but they aren't always the best solution.

Lavaliere and Clip Microphones

Lavaliere and *clip microphones* are microphones physically attached to the talent. Technically, a "lav" microphone hangs by a cord from the talent's neck, while clip

Figure 6-16. *A giraffe keeps the mike out of the shot and allows some mike movement if necessary, but not the quick movement provided by a fishpole. This shot also illustrates the use of an umbrella reflector and a flag, concepts discussed in Chapter 5.*

Courtesy of Nebraska Educational Telecommunications.

1.

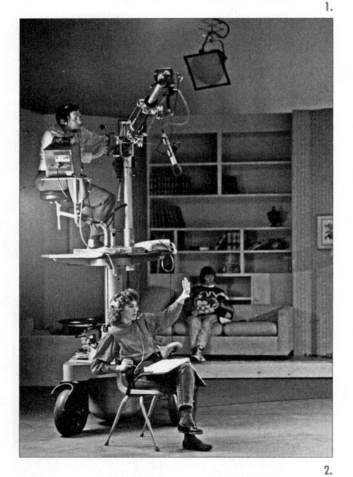

2.

Figure 6-17. *In shot 1, a perambulator boom. In shot 2, the boom is extended, as the operator sits on this boom platform, which can also be raised as needed. The boom arm can be retracted or extended many feet into a scene. The mikes shown mounted in these two shots can be remotely controlled from the operator's station.*

Shot 1 courtesy of J. L. Fisher Corporation; shot 2 courtesy of Nebraska Educational Telecommunications.

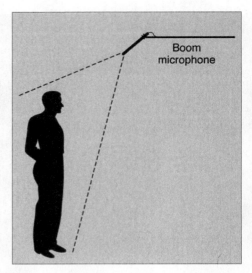

Figure 6-18. *The main thing to remember is to point the boom mike, often a very sensitive directional mike, at the mouths of the talent (or the "business end" of other sound sources). Also remember to keep the mike in front of the subject. A very common beginner's error is to forget that sound waves, once expelled, travel forward. So don't overshoot when aiming and point the mike over the heads of your talent.*

microphones attach to the talent's clothing with a small pin or tie-clip device (see Figure 6-19). However, some people use the term "lav" to identify any small microphone worn by talent. Most older lavs are dynamic microphones with an omnidirectional or cardioid pickup pattern. Smaller, lighter clip microphones have mostly replaced these larger, less efficient lavs, and you're unlikely to encounter a true lav mike in modern production situations. Clip microphones often use condenser-type transducers and have an omnidirectional or cardioid pickup pattern. Condenser-type clip microphones are usually in two sections: a small pickup head containing the transducer, and a large interface housing, or amplifier pod, about two feet down the line holding the battery, power switch, amplifiers and often a cable connector attaching to a cable leading to an audio console or recorder (see Figure 6-20). However, wireless clip mikes are popular for ENG/EFP and studio productions because they eliminate problems caused by an audio cable. We discuss wireless mikes later in this chapter.

Microphones worn close to the chest would excessively emphasize lower frequencies in the talent's voice were they not designed to compensate for this effect. That's why using a lav or clip microphone as a hand or desk microphone may result in a tinny sound. Modern

1.

2.

Figure 6-19. *In shot 1, a performer with a dynamic lav mike. Such mikes were once common, but small clip mikes have largely replaced them. In shot 2, a performer with a small condenser clip mike. Ideally, you should run the wire to the mike under talent's clothing, but the mike itself should never be covered.*

clip microphones are so small that many professional performers wear two of them mounted together (see Figure 6-21). Only one microphone is "hot" (on the air); the other is a backup that's switched on instantly if a problem develops with the primary microphone. This is sometimes called *dual redundancy,* a term which itself sounds a bit redundant.

Special Purpose Microphones

The microphones already discussed satisfy the audio demands of most productions, but occasionally there are unique situations requiring special equipment.

In the following discussion, the microphones used are not unique: They're simply specially adapted versions of designs previously described.

Ultradirectional Microphones

It's sometimes necessary to capture sound from a great distance, or with highly discreet separation of sound sources. This requires either a *shotgun* or a *parabolic* microphone. The shotgun microphone (actually a misnomer, since shotguns spray pellets in a wide pattern and a shotgun mike picks up sound in a narrow area) is typically a dynamic super- or hypercardioid

Figure 6-20. *A typical condenser tie-clip microphone. The mike also comes with an amplifier, called by this manufacturer, Audio-Technica, a power module, which is usually hidden among the talent's clothing.*

Figure 6-21. *A dual redundancy mike clip with mikes.*

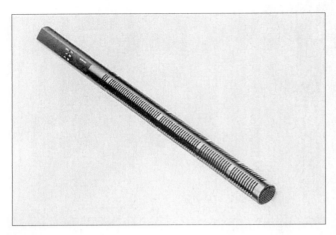

Figure 6-22. *A Sennheiser MKH-70 shotgun mike.*

Photo courtesy of Sennheiser Corporation.

mounted in a specially designed housing comprised of one or more tubes of different lengths, which narrow the pickup pattern dramatically (see Figure 6-22). Figure 6-23 shows a camera-mounted shotgun microphone capturing the sounds of celebration at the end of a marathon.

The parabolic microphone typically consists of a dynamic omnidirectional mike mounted in a dish-shaped reflector several feet in diameter. The dish collects sounds approaching from its curved side and concentrates them at the acoustical focal point where the microphone is located (see Figure 6-24). These ultradirectional microphones are physically large and,

Figure 6-23. *A Sennheiser MKH 70-P48 shotgun microphone.*

Photo courtesy of Sennheiser Corporation.

Figure 6-24. *A Crystal Partners "Big Ears" parabolic mike picks up the sounds of the action from the sidelines at a football game.*

Photo courtesy of Crystal Partners, Inc.

because they have an extremely narrow pickup pattern, require careful aiming by an operator monitoring their output.

Boundary Microphones

These microphones use a condenser-type pickup element mounted extremely close to a carefully designed hard surface, or boundary, that reflects sound and forms part of the microphone's structure. Actually, most microphones placed on a hard reflective surface will exhibit, to a degree, the characteristics of specially designed boundary microphones. That's why simply laying a hand or clip microphone on a desk or lectern can sometimes provide amazingly good audio, although microphones designed specifically for such use work much better. *Boundary microphones* often have a hemispherical pickup pattern, responding equally well to sounds coming from all directions within the hemisphere. They are, in effect, half of an omnidirectional microphone, with response limited to the hemisphere located above the boundary surface. Crown International Inc. calls its model featuring hemispherical pickup characteristics a pressure-zone microphone, or *PZM*. But boundary microphones can have other pickup patterns, including stereophonic (see Figure 6-25). Shure Brothers Inc. offers the MX391, a boundary microphone with changeable cartridges that allows you to modify the pickup pattern to accommodate different production situations (see Figure 6-35). A boundary microphone with a hemispherical pickup pattern can be both a blessing and a curse; a blessing in that the microphone effectively captures sound over a

wide area without echo problems, a curse in that it treats all sounds within the hemisphere indiscriminately, including unwanted noises. The boundary microphone is a useful replacement for a battery of desk microphones in situations where several people seated around a table are speaking. It also can replace hanging microphones in stage productions involving musical groups and instruments.

Wireless Microphones

Wireless microphones, also called *RF mikes,* use a radio frequency transmitter and receiver rather than an audio cable to deliver the microphone's output to the recorder or console. They are modifications of traditional hand, lav and clip microphones worn or carried by the talent. The part of the system attached to the talent includes a low-powered transmitter which broadcasts the microphone's output to a receiver located somewhere off-camera (see Figures 6-13 and 6-26). The obvious advantage of wireless microphones, both in the studio and on location, is the elimination of an audio cable in the shot. This means the talent is freed from the cord, and cameras and equipment won't run over it, either.

But there are also disadvantages. The good ones are expensive; often the transmitter-antenna-battery unit is somewhat bulky, and hiding everything on the talent's body sometimes is difficult; the system is subject to both interference and unexpected battery failure, both of which can be problems in a live production. As well, because the microphone often is "hot" even when the talent is off camera, technicians must take care to avoid recording or airing something embarrassing. Despite these limitations, the freedom of movement provided is so advantageous that, budget permitting, wireless microphones are desirable for the majority of ENG/EFP and studio TV productions, as well as a necessity these days in live musical theater.

Headset Microphones

Microphones attached to single- or double-ear-muff headsets are useful when the talent must work in a very noisy location, such as a political convention or a sports event (see Figure 6-27). Modern *headset microphones* use either condenser or dynamic transducers designed to minimize noise pickup while ensuring the talent is clearly heard. Because these microphones are positioned close to the talent's mouth, their frequency response is tailored accordingly. Their design also minimizes overload if the announcer shouts and compensates for plosive consonants of speech, such as "popped p's."

Figure 6-25. *A stereophonic boundary microphone.*
Photo courtesy of Crown International Inc.

 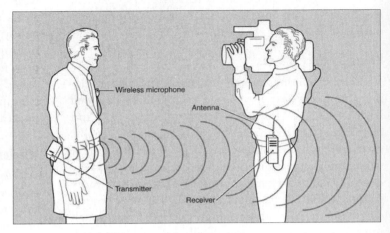

Figure 6-26. *In the photo, we see a small clip mike and its associated transmitter. Together they form a mini radio station that broadcasts the output of the mike to nearby receivers. In the drawing, the wireless mike attached to the lapel of the reporter's overcoat is feeding a signal to the amplifier/transmitter clipped to his belt. The transmitter then broadcasts this signal to the receiver clipped to the belt of the ENG camera operator. This signal then is conveyed via mike cable to the camera. Some systems do this step wirelessly, too, and yet other receivers are already mounted on the back of the camera, as seen in Figure 6-13.*

A two-ear-muff (double-muff) headset arrangement allows feeding program audio to one ear while instructions from the director are relayed into the other. However, a single-muff headset is preferable if the talent needs to hear ambient sound clearly.

Multichannel Sound

Entire books can be, and have been, devoted to the history of multichannel sound. We will note only that the topic has a long history, dating back to experiments in the late 1800s, and today is an extremely complex subject we can touch on but lightly in this introductory text. We must note, however, that TV producers must pay more attention to multichannel sound because

Figure 6-27. *Single-muff and double-muff headsets with boom mikes.*

increasing numbers of consumers will have the technology needed to enjoy it.

Television sound has traditionally been *monophonic,* also called *monaural.* This means all the sound elements in any program—from the singular "talking head" reporter to a 100-piece symphony orchestra broadcast—were all mixed together in one audio channel and dumped into the living room through a single speaker built into the TV set. Sound in the "real world" reaches us from all directions but, in the TV world, sound has emanated from wherever the TV set happened to be located in the room.

To understand multichannel sound, we must begin with human anatomy and the way the brain works. We have ears on each side of our head, so a sound coming from the left reaches our left ear slightly before it reaches our right ear. The sound has slightly farther to travel, so in our right ear the sound is also slightly weaker than when it reaches our left. The same applies to sound coming from any direction. Our brain uses these minute differences in time (or phase) and strength (or amplitude) and provides cues regarding the directionality of sounds, allowing us to determine whether they are coming from left or right, high or low, front or back. It's important to understand that the original sound does not necessarily have to originate in a given location for us to perceive it as doing so. It is only necessary that the phase and intensity of the sounds reaching our ears be such that the brain "places" the sound in space where the creator of the sounds wants them to appear. It's this *psychoacoustic* effect that allows modern recording engineers to produce a rather realistic illusion of 360-degree *surround sound* using a single speaker enclosure along one wall of a room. It's also worth noting that the most commonly practiced microphone techniques depend only on differences in the intensity of sound coming from different directions, not differences in phase, to create directional cues for listeners.

Surround sound began its development in movie theaters starting in the 1940s and became more sophisticated in the following decades. Consumers appreciated the new theater sound experience and, starting in the 1950s, began buying stereophonic phonographs allowing them to enjoy some elements of that experience at home. *Stereophonic sound* adds an additional audio channel and an additional speaker to the monophonic sound system. Recording sound coming from left and right separately and reproducing it with two widely spaced speakers placed to the listener's front-left and front-right creates a "soundstage" with left and right dimensions. If, for example, more of the piano sounds come from the left speaker than from the right speaker (and the phase relationship is correct), the listener perceives the piano to be at the left end of the stage. If the sound of the violin section comes mostly out of the right speaker, the listener perceives the violins to be on the other end of the stage. And, if the voice of the soloist comes through each speaker equally loud, the listener "sees" that performer

at center stage. It's not surround sound by any means, but it beats monophonic audio. Indeed, the Federal Communications Commission's approval of FM stereophonic broadcasting in 1961 often is credited with saving FM radio from oblivion and accounts in large measure for FM's dominance over standard AM broadcasting today.

Several techniques have developed for recording stereophonic sound. The most obvious technique, of course, is to simply place mikes where our ears are found: Mount two omnidirectional mikes on the side of someone's head and record each mike's output on a separate audio channel. However, the presence of a human head with its variable hard (bone) and soft (flesh and hair) surfaces so close to the mikes was found to affect the characteristics of the recorded sound in undesirable and unpredictable ways. And, of course, the recorded sound experience changes with even the slightest head/mike movement. Engineers have solved some of these problems by mounting mikes on a standardized and fixed dummy head, and the stereophonic effect is good, but only when listening to the recorded audio on headphones. When played back through speakers, many audiophiles find that stereophonic sound recorded using the dummy-head technique has a rather narrow soundstage.

Another technique, dating from the early days of stereophonic recording, involved placing two omnidirectional or cardioid mikes several yards apart (see Figure 6-28.) This technique provides strong separation between sounds at each end of the soundstage, but

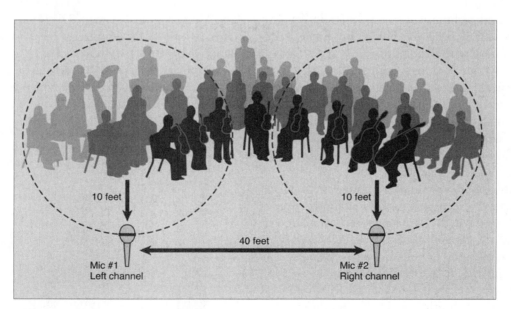

Figure 6-28. *Placing the microphones far apart creates a dramatic stereophonic effect, but this can sometimes leave a "hole" in the middle of the soundstage.*

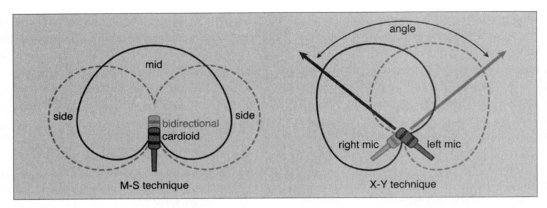

Figure 6-29. *The diagrams illustrate the placement and pickup patterns of microphones using the popular X-Y and M-S stereo techniques.*

sounds from center stage sound distant, leaving a "hole in the middle" effect. In many cases, a third mike is placed in the center and its output is fed equally to the left and right signals to help fill the hole. The technique also makes achieving a compatible monophonic signal difficult. This is a significant disadvantage, because the ability to broadcast a stereophonic signal that still sounds good when reproduced on a single-speaker monophonic TV set is a vital requirement.

This experimentation led to three techniques often used today. These techniques use two mikes, or at least two mike elements, close to each other and are often called *coincident-microphone* techniques because of their proximity. Coincident techniques are favored by broadcasters because they provide uncomplicated monophonic compatibility.

One coincident technique was pioneered by British engineer Alan Blumlein in the 1930s. Blumlein used two microphones with bidirectional (figure-eight) pickup patterns placed close together but with their pickup patterns at right angles. This technique, often called a *Blumlein pair,* provides a good left–right stereophonic image but picks up sound coming from the back side equally well. This can be a problem for stereo reproduction using only two speakers in front of the listener.

Another coincident technique, known as the *X-Y technique,* uses two directional (usually cardioid) mikes (or mike elements) at the same spot but pointing at opposite ends of the soundstage (see Figure 6-29). Often the two mikes are mounted one above the other, or the mike consists of two cardioid elements in the same mike enclosure angled at around 90 to about 130 degrees from each other, as in the Beyerdynamic MCE 82 (see Figure 6-30). A possible problem with the X-Y technique is that sound coming from the center

of the soundstage may sound a bit strange, because it is not being picked up along the main axis of either microphone.

A third coincident microphone technique, called the *M-S* or *mid-side technique* (see Figure 6-29), also uses two mikes, or two mike elements in a single housing. One mike has a cardioid or supercardiod pickup pattern, and this mike is aimed directly at the sound source, providing a signal from the middle of the soundstage (hence the "mid" in the name "mid-side"). A second mike with a bidirectional pattern is positioned at a 90-degree angle from the directional mike and picks up sound coming from the side. Electronic circuitry allows the middle and side audio signals to be blended to reproduce a strong left and right stereophonic separation as well as a solid center, without a "hole" in the middle. The Shure VP88 (see Figure 6-35) is a popular M-S stereo mike combining both a cardioid and a bidirectional element in the same housing.

A number of expensive stereo mikes have multiple mike elements in the same housing and provide user-adjustable

Figure 6-30. *A Beyerdynamic MCE 82 stereophonic microphone featuring two cardioid elements in the same housing for stereo pickup using the X-Y technique.*

Photo courtesy of Beyerdynamic GmbH & Co. KG.

Figure 6-31. *The AKG C426B, with a retail price of more than $6,000, is an example of a microphone that can be adjusted to use either the X-Y or M-S miking technique.*

Photo courtesy AKG Acoustics.

pickup pattern configurations. This allows the operator to switch easily between X-Y and M-S techniques to best accommodate a variety of recording environments. The AKG C426B is an example of such mikes (see Figure 6-31).

Stereophonic mikes with multiple elements in the same housing make life easier for the producer and are clearly the obvious choice for camera-mounted stereo mikes and run-and-gun news videographers. Some experts, however, believe using separate mikes offers greater flexibility and superior audio performance. We will only note that using separate mikes does require more effort and, ideally, special mike mounting devices. It's also true that separate mikes used for stereo recording should have closely matched technical specifications to achieve optimum results. Mounting two cardioid mikes from different manufacturers in X-Y configuration can lead to poor stereophonic audio. Using a stereo mike with all the mike elements in a single housing built by one manufacturer provides some assurance that the individual elements are well matched.

There are other techniques used to capture stereophonic sound, including the ORTF (Office de Radiodiffusion Télévision Française) technique favored in France, the NOS (Nederlandse Omroep Stichting-Holland Radio) technique, techniques using baffles and one that uses a special mike-mounting device called a "Decca Tree." All the techniques introduced in this discussion have been the basis for endless experimentation by serious (and not-so-serious) audiophiles, and information about them is widely available.

As noted, surround sound began in motion picture theaters in the 1940s, but only in the 1970s did surround sound (sound apparently arriving from a direction other than a soundstage stretching from the front left to the front right of the listener) begin showing up

in homes. *Quadraphonic* sound added two speakers behind the listener to the typical stereophonic setup. It was an analog world at that time, however, and providing four discrete audio channels required doubling the number of bulky, expensive amplifiers compared to stereo. Quad never did catch on.

The digital revolution and chip technology has changed that. So has our knowledge about how humans perceive sound. It was learned that a great deal of information in the original sound, if selected carefully, could be eliminated without its loss being noticed. Digital technology instantly determines what sound information "doesn't matter" and leaves it out, while simultaneously giving more emphasis to the information that "does matter." Digital technology also allows the different discrete channels of information to be mixed into a single data stream when being recorded or broadcast but then separated again into discrete channels and fed to individual speakers. This is, obviously, a simplified explanation of an extremely complex process. However, the ability of digital technology to reduce the amount of data stored or transmitted, to mix it together for storage or transmission and then to separate it again into discrete audio channels for our use is at the heart of modern digital TV sound. When the Advanced Television Systems Committee (ATSC) adopted U.S. standards for digital TV broadcasting in 1996, it established *Dolby Lab's AC-3* audio-encoding system, often called simply *Dolby Digital,* for the audio portion of the DTV signal.

Dolby Digital allows transmission of *5.1 surround sound.* The 5.1 comes from the fact that there are five main channels of sound and one subchannel. The five main channels are front left, center, front right, left surround (or back left) and right surround (or back right). The subchannel carries only extremely low-frequency audio, often called the bass (see Figure 6-32).

During production, audio information needed to create the six channels of 5.1 surround sound is digitally encoded into a complex mix-matrix and then decoded at the receiving end. A variety of microphone types and techniques are used to capture the original sound during production, and experimentation continues among recording engineers seeking the best methods for different production situations. Ultimately, the reproduced surround sound at the listening point is dependent on both the digital processing applied by the producer/recording engineer and the playback equipment and settings selected by the listener.

A thorough treatment of production techniques for 5.1 surround sound is far beyond the level of this

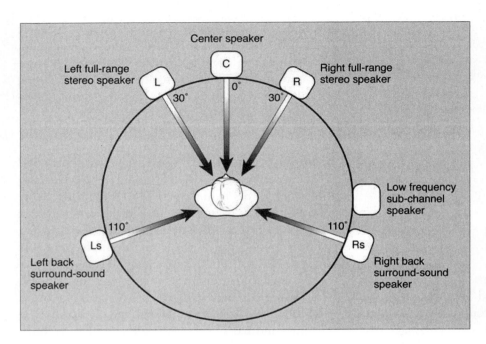

Figure 6-32. *This diagram illustrates the typical placement of the five main-channel speakers and the low-frequency subchannel speaker for 5.1 surround sound reproduction. The placement of the low-frequency subchannel speaker is not particularly critical.*

introductory text. However, it is helpful to note that 5.1 surround sound begins with two-channel stereo and then adds four additional channels. The left and right channels of 5.1 surround sound comprise conventional stereophonic sound. The center channel of 5.1 surround may be created through selectively mixing the left and right channels of the X-Y stereo microphone technique or by using the middle microphone signal

when using the M-S stereo technique. Some producers then add one or a pair of rear-facing cardioid microphones to produce the left surround and right surround channels (see Figure 6-33).

Matrix encoding is used to take sound captured by all five main channels to create the very low-frequency subchannel audio. The SoundField microphone (SoundField Ltd.) uses four separate microphone

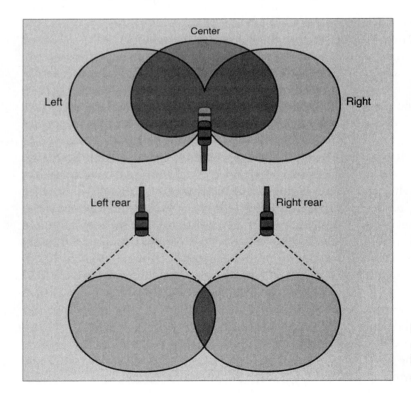

Figure 6-33. *One method of capturing 5.1 surround sound employs conventional X-Y or M-S techniques plus a pair of rear-facing cardioid microphones for the left and right surround channels.*

Figure 6-34. *The SoundField microphone can capture 5.1 surround sound but can also be used for recording surround sound involving more than six channels.*

Photo courtesy of SoundField Ltd.

elements to capture sound coming from front/back, left/right and up/down directions (see Figure 6-34). SoundField Technology then converts this information into the 5.1 surround channel using proprietary software and hardware. Indeed, SoundField says its microphone and encoding system allows it to adapt to "any conceivable future surround format" without modification, including seven-channel (6.1) and eight-channel (7.1) surround formats.

In closing this discussion of multichannel sound, it's important to remember that adding more channels during production means listeners must add more equipment to get the maximum benefit. A listener needs six speakers arrayed as displayed in Figure 6-32 to fully appreciate "true" 5.1 surround sound, according to most audiophiles. However, as suggested at the beginning of this discussion, manufacturers such as Samsung and Yamaha have used computer technology, digital signal processing and elaborate algorithms to help create a semblance of the surround sound experience using fewer components. These technologies use phasing, sound intensity and a sophisticated understanding of how humans perceive

sound to create a "pseudo" surround sound experience that many listeners find entirely satisfactory.

Selecting the Proper Microphone

The best microphone for a given situation depends on many, sometimes conflicting, factors. Let's examine some of them:

- **Microphone visibility:** Is it permissible to show the microphone in the shot, such as in most news and music productions, or must it be hidden, as in a soap opera or sitcom?
- **Mobility of the talent:** Will the talent remain stationary during the shot or will the talent move? Are the talent's hands free so the talent can hold a microphone?
- **Number of sources to be miked in the shot:** Will one microphone do the job or will you need multiple microphones?
- **Danger to the equipment:** Will the microphone be used indoors under controlled conditions or outside in high winds, rain or snow? What are the chances that talent will handle the microphone roughly or even drop it?
- **Pickup pattern required:** Will the microphone be close to the sound source or at a distance? Will there be distracting ambient noise you wish the microphone to reject, or will your source be the only sound in the area?
- **Frequency response:** Will the microphone need an especially *flat response* (responding to all sound frequencies relatively equally over a wide frequency range), such as for miking music, or can a microphone with a less demanding response curve be used, such as when recording ENG interviews? Will the microphone need extremely good response at either high or low frequencies?
- **Sensitivity:** Will the microphone need to put out a strong electrical signal when low-amplitude sounds are present or must the microphone be able to tolerate very loud sounds without distortion?

There are dozens of microphones made by almost as many manufacturers. Audio technicians develop favorites based on their personal research and experiences, the recommendations of respected practitioners and, sometimes, blind prejudice. We won't try to tell you, or your technicians, which is the best microphone for any particular situation. Instead, we've provided a chart in Figure 6-35 to outline the most important characteristics of some popular microphones, so that you can decide.

Figure 6-35. *This table illustrates microphones often used in television production. Some models are older than others, but all were in production at the time this book went to press. This exhibit is not a complete listing of all microphones used in television, and we do not wish to imply that the models illustrated are superior to those not shown. While we indicate one or more common applications for each model, some may be used for other purposes.*

Name	Type of Transducer	Application	
AKG C-451E	Condenser cardioid	Instruments, especially piano.	
Bruel & Kjaer DPA-4060	Condenser omnidirectional	Extremely small clip mike for spoken voice. Small size makes it useful where a concealed microphone is needed.	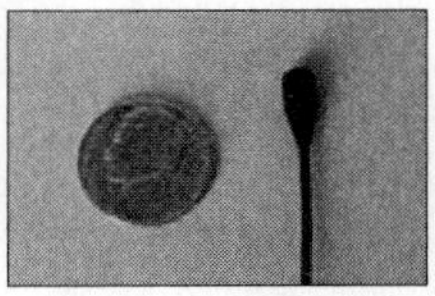
Electro-Voice RE-11	Dynamic supercardioid	Boom and stand mike. Provides extended reach. Reduced wind noise for ENG/EFP.	
Electro-Voice DS-35	Dynamic cardioid	Spoken voice; vocals and some instruments, such as bass drum. Pronounced proximity effect when placed close to sound source. Helpful for thin voices.	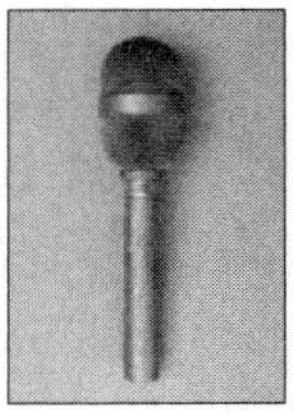
Electro-Voice RE-45N/D	Dynamic supercardioid	High sensitivity, low weight for handheld or fishpole use. Provides long reach for distant miking	
Electro-Voice RE-50	Dynamic omnidirectional	Extremely rugged mike. Electrically similar to Electro-Voice 635A, but with a better shock mount. Very popular ENG mike.	
Electro-Voice RE-55	Dynamic omnidirectional	Boom and stand mike. Also good for handheld interviews and instruments.	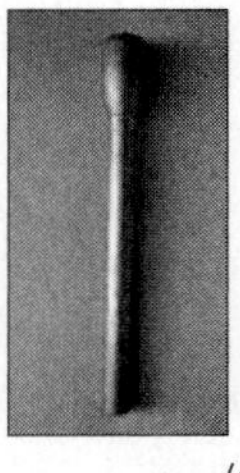

(Continued)

(Continued)

Electro-Voice 635A	Dynamic omnidirectional	Rugged and economical. Good for ENG and other physically demanding applications. Used in TV news for generations.
Neumann U-87A	Condenser, variable pattern (omnidirectional/ bidirectional/cardioid)	Studio voice-overs and vocals; instruments. A large mike.
Sennheiser MKE-2	Condenser omnidirectional	Clip mike for spoken voice
Sennheiser MHK-70	Condenser hypercardioid	Boom and fishpole microphone.
Sennheiser MD-421	Dynamic cardioid	Group vocals, instruments such as guitars and drums.
Shure SM 7	Dynamic cardioid	Studio voice-over; provides four selectable response curves.
Shure SM 57	Dynamic cardioid	Vocals; instruments, especially drums, percussion, and instrument amplifiers.
Shure SM 58S	Dynamic cardioid	Vocals; features mid-frequency boost to provide "presence."

(Continued)

(Continued)

Shure SM 63L	Dynamic omnidirectional	Used for voice, ENG/EFP.	
Shure SM 87	Condenser supercardioid	Vocals; lead singers.	
Shure VP 88	Condenser stereo	Single-point stereo microphone with monaural compatibility.	
Shure MX 391	Condenser boundary	Pickup of multiple spoken voices, microphone using changeable cartridges for omnidirectional, cardioid and supercardioid patterns.	
Sony ECM-55B	Condenser omnidirectional	Subminiature clip mike for voice in studio	

Photos courtesy of AKG, Bruel & Kjaer, Electro-Voice, Neumann, Sennheiser, Shure Brothers and Sony.

Note: More information about a microphone's specifications and recommended uses is often available online from the manufacturers.

Microphone Accessories and Special Features

Microphones used outdoors may need a windscreen, which is an attachment, typically made of foam rubber, that slips over the entrance to the microphone's transducer element to minimize the sound of air rushing past (see Figure 6-36).

Another type of windscreen, sometimes called a *studio "pop" filter,* or voice screen, does not cover the mike but is attached to it and prevents the performer from getting too close (see Figure 6-37). The makers of such devices also claim the material used helps block "pops" from reaching the mike.

Often a microphone comes with a *stand mount adapter,* a plastic fitting with standard threads for connecting the microphone to a stand (see Figure 6-38). *Shock mounts* help isolate microphones from their supports and prevent the pickup of noises when the mount is bumped (see Figure 6-39). Headset microphones and others "worked

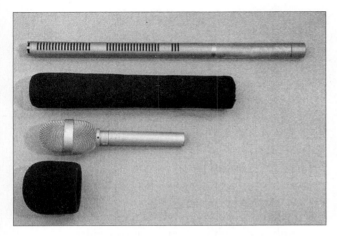

Figure 6-36. *Microphones and their associated windscreens come in many shapes and sizes.*

Figure 6-38. *A plastic holder screwed on a stand allows easy attachment and removal of the microphone.*

close" to the mouth often have built-in *pop filters* to reduce popped plosive sounds, such as the consonants "b," "d," "t," and "p." Directional microphones tend to excessively emphasize low frequencies when the source of the sound is close to the transducer element. This *proximity effect* may be desirable if a talent has a "thin" or high-pitched voice. In most cases the proximity effect is undesirable, and some microphones have *low-end roll-off filters* that reduce a mike's tendency to emphasize low

frequencies when worked close. Microphones typically are worked at a greater distance from the talent in TV than in radio, so proximity effect is not often pronounced in any case.

Microphone manufacturers constantly modify old models and create new ones. You can check the features and accessories currently available by getting the manufacturer's most recent product catalog or specifications literature.

Line-Level Audio Sources

Microphones capture all TV audio originally, except for electronically *synthesized* music and sound effects. However, audio often is recorded for later use, and the

Figure 6-37. *This type of windscreen is both physically and acoustically transparent and, by keeping the performer's mouth at a distance from the mike, reduces the likelihood of vocal "pops" on hard plosive sounds.*

Photo courtesy of Popless Voice Screens™.

Figure 6-39. *A Neumann stereo mike and shock mount. The elastic bands supporting the mike mechanically isolate it from vibrations transmitted through the stand.*

machines used to reproduce this audio are known as *line-level* sources. The term refers to the fact their output signals are preamplified and much stronger than the weaker output of microphones. This is an important technical distinction because much production gear is engineered to accept one of the two signal levels, but not both. Some gear handles both but requires you to use the proper input/output terminal or flip a switch. In any case, you must take care to match output and input levels when connecting audio gear. Plugging a *microphone-level* signal into a line-level input results in little audio getting through. Plugging a line-level signal into a microphone-level input results in severe audio distortion, and possible damage to the equipment. Fortunately, equipment manufacturers clearly label inputs as "microphone" (or "mic") or "line-in" to help you avoid making an incorrect connection (see Figure 6-40).

1.

2.

Figure 6-40. *In shot 1, we see XLR audio inputs on an ENG camera. In shot 2, controls on the camera head allow the inputs to handle either mike-level or line-level signals.*

Line-level sources are undergoing two major technology transitions as this book goes to press. One is the shift from analog to digital; the other is from tape to disk. These transitions will take several years and you're likely to encounter old and new technologies operating side by side. You will encounter line-level sources most often during live studio and EFP work where it's common practice to add prerecorded audio, such as music and sound effects, as the program is broadcast. All audio sources used during postproduction editing are line-level devices. Microphones are the source of most ENG audio so you're less likely to use line-level sources on an ENG shoot. Some line-level sources record and reproduce only audio while others also store video.

Turntables are disk-based analog audio playback machines (see Figure 6-41). Your grandparents called them "phonographs," and your parents called them "hi-fis." You probably call them "antiques." Little new audio is released on long-play (LP) 33-RPM discs, but a great deal of useful audio is archived on LPs. If you need audio from an LP disc during a live production, it's best to *dub* (transfer) it to another storage medium, such as tape or digital disk, to aid you in cueing your sound sources. LPs are hard to keep cued during a production. The slightest bump on the turntable base can cause the needle to jump.

The analog *reel-to-reel ATR* (*audio tape recorder*) was the workhorse of audio production for decades. Because magnetic tape is easily erasable and reusable, it provides both record and playback capability. In addition, reel-to-reel tapes can be edited as needed using either physical (cut and splice) or electronic editing techniques. Professional analog ATRs use tapes in standard widths of $\frac{1}{4}$, $\frac{1}{2}$, 1, and 2 inches with the wider tapes accommodating a greater number of individual audio tracks (see Figure 6-42). Analog audio quality improves as tape speed increases. A standard speed for analog ATRs is 7.5 *ips* (inches per second), but 15 or even 30 ips is common when the ultimate audio quality is desired using an analog ATR. However, like the LP, the analog ATR has largely been replaced by digital equipment.

Often called cart machines, *cartridge tape recorders* are analog tape recorder/playback devices using an "endless" loop of $\frac{1}{4}$-inch audio tape wound around a single rotating hub in a plastic box (cartridge). Unlike reel-to-reel ATRs, carts don't require manual threading and automatically recue themselves, a feature that made them popular for inserting sound effects, jingles and theme music during studio productions and postproduction editing. However, relatively slow tape speed and the cart's physical construction limits its audio quality. Digital devices, such as CDs and Sony's Mini-Disc, have largely replaced

Figure 6-41. *Turntables and LP records are rarely used in live productions or postproduction editing today, but you may still encounter them occasionally.*

Figure 6-42. *An Ampex 16-track analog reel-to-reel audio tape recorder.*

Figure 6-43. *Audio cart machines (top in this rack mounting), workhorses used in audio production for decades, have lost ground to digital media. Like the turntable, one may occasionally see a cart machine in the audio studios of a television facility, but they are increasingly rare. Next in this rack is a CD player, and on the bottom is a cassette recorder.*

Figure 6-44. *A portable VCR used for ENG and EFP.*

analog carts in most TV production applications. Analog *audio cassette recorders* combine features of both the reel-to-reel format and the cart. Cassettes use tape about 1/6-inch wide, wound on two reels contained in a plastic case. Cassettes provide the cart's ease of handling and tape protection with the reel-to-reel machine's ability to rewind and fast-forward. But cassettes are hard to use in editing and don't recue themselves like carts. Their narrow tape also limits the number of tracks they can record. Figure 6-43 shows an analog audio tape cartridge machine and a cassette recorder, with a more modern digital-audio CD player sandwiched in between.

Video tape recorders (VTR) often are sources of prerecorded video-with-audio footage and "packages" (edited audio-video segments) inserted in live broadcasts. VTRs also serve as sources of prerecorded footage during postproduction editing. The VTR in playback mode, therefore, is a critical line-level audio source. A VTR is any video recorder using video tape, but often the term VTR denotes a recorder employing open-reel tape. A *video cassette recorder* (VCR) is a VTR that uses tape in a protective and easily removable cassette. Older VTRs record audio (and video) in analog format, but all-digital VTRs are gaining popularity rapidly. Figure 6-44 shows a portable videocassette recorder (VCR) for ENG/EFP applications that can record four tracks of audio. VTRs are discussed further in Chapter 9.

Digital audio tape (DAT) is a cassette-based storage device resembling the analog cassette, but the two are incompatible (see Figure 6-45). The sound quality provided by DAT is better than that recorded using

analog tape formats. DAT and digital VTRs share the stage with disc-based devices.

The best example of a disc-based device is the familiar *compact audio disc* (CD). The CD is an optical digital storage device that uses a laser to both record and playback audio on the disc. Although you'll see the terms used interchangeably, "disc" with a "c" is often used when referring to media and devices that employ optical laser technology. "Disk" with a "k" is commonly used when magnetic principles are involved, such as with floppy disks and computer hard drives. The CD provides excellent audio quality, and that quality isn't degraded with repeated use as is true when using LPs. Many CD players use sophisticated microprocessors to control playback, so repeated cueing at a particular section of a track is easy. Initially CDs were playback-only devices, like the LPs they replaced. However, recordable CDs and the

Figure 6-45. *Cassettes used by analog cassette recorders (top) and DAT.*

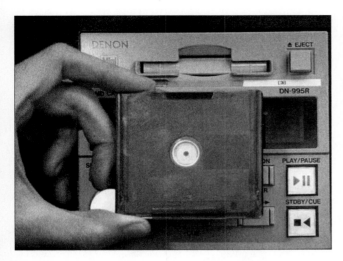

Figure 6-46. *Rack-mounted Sony Mini-Disc recorder/player and a Mini-Disc.*

equipment needed to record, or *burn,* the audio on a blank disc is widely available today at low cost. Using appropriate software and hardware, some CD media (CD-R) allow you to record only once, but play back many times. A CD-RW disc allows you to record new audio on the disc many times and play back many times, the same as with magnetic media. The *digital video disc* (DVD) looks and functions much like a CD, but has much greater storage capacity, making it popular for the recording and playback of both audio and video. Sony's *Mini-Disc* (MD) is smaller than a CD or DVD and, when introduced in 1992, was capable of recording about 70 minutes of stereo audio (see Figure 6-46). The MD provides quick access to any information on the disc and it became a popular replacement for analog cartridge tapes in TV production facilities during the 1990s. A higher capacity version of the Mini-Disc (called Hi-MD) introduced in 2004 allows the recording of up to 94 minutes of CD-quality audio.

A family of technologies, developed originally by the computer industry but now used widely in video production, also provide record and playback capability. Included in this category are the more or less stationary *hard drives* and a variety of floppy and semi-floppy removable-disk formats. Cameras and portable recorders using disks to record audio and video are available, but disk technology finds its most common application in digital postproduction editing. Multiple disks and disk drives combine to form audio and video servers that store edited program material for insertion in live programs or serve as replacements for tape-based playback machines. Disk-based digital storage devices are replacing other types of equipment because of their ability to handle both audio and video and, unlike tape-

based digital technologies, to allow practically instantaneous random access to recorded materials.

Cables, Connectors and Adapters

Audio cable conveys microphone output and provides connections among line-level devices, serving as a vital link in the audio chain. Damaged or improperly used audio cables, connectors or adapters cause many audio problems.

Analog audio cable designed for professional applications consists of three wires wrapped in metal foil within a protective plastic outer covering (see Figure 6-47). The two insulated wires carry the audio signal, while the metal foil and third (bare) wire provide a shield against external electrical interference. A three-wire audio cable is often called a *balanced line.* Two of the wires also carry a direct current if the cable provides phantom power for condenser microphones. Balanced-line audio cable uses *XLR Cannon connectors*™ (simply called XLR connectors), although they're now made by firms other than the Cannon Electric Company. The XLR's metallic body continues the shielding of the balanced line, and XLR plugs and receptacles lock together mechanically when connected. You must press a lock-release button to separate an XLR plug from its receptacle without damaging the cable (see Figures 6-40 and 6-48). Sometimes you may encounter *unbalanced lines* and their associated connectors, especially during ENG and EFP work. Unbalanced lines have only two wires, both of which

Figure 6-47. *Three-conductor audio cable. From left, the ground shield and two live signal-conducting wires.*

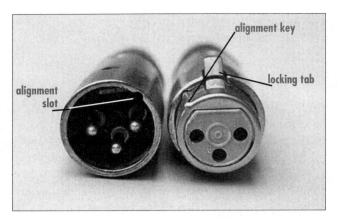

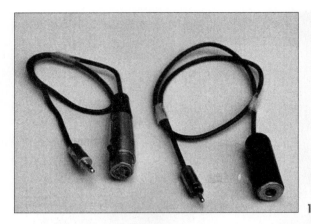

Figure 6-48. *Male and female XLR audio connectors. Note the key and slot that ensure proper pin alignment, and the locking tab on top of the female connector on the right. This tab must be depressed to separate the connectors when they are locked together.*

carry the audio signal and one of which is electrically connected to the ground. They lack the shielding of balanced lines and are more susceptible to interference. Most audio equipment designed for the consumer or industrial market uses unbalanced lines. Figure 6-49 shows XLR balanced-line connectors and three types of unbalanced-line connectors you may encounter.

Various adapters are available for joining equipment and cables using different style connectors. Adapters physically lengthen the connection, making it weaker and easier to damage. The major problem with adapters, however, is that they often connect balanced lines to unbalanced lines. Connecting unbalanced elements to a balanced audio system may create hum or allow other forms of interference to enter the system. Figure 6-50 shows both homemade and professional-quality adapters

Figure 6-50. *In shot 1, "homemade" audio adapter cables are used to link audio devices with different style connectors. At left is a balanced female XLR connector attached to an unbalanced male miniplug, a combination conducive to picking up hum. At right is an RCA photo plug attached to a quarter-inch phone jack. In shot 2 are a number of commercially manufactured audio "problem solvers." These devices are preferable to the homemade variety because their transformers handle - balanced/unbalanced line connections and perform impedance matching.*

Shot 2 courtesy of Shure Brothers Inc.

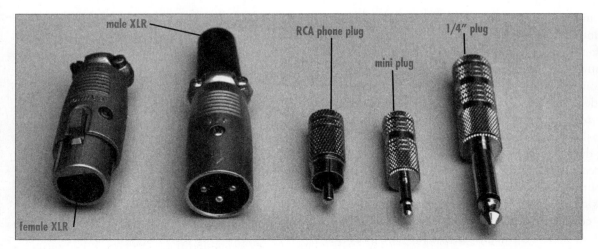

Figure 6-49. *Two XLRs and three other common audio connectors encountered during many TV productions. All but the XLR connectors on the left are used with unbalanced audio lines often associated with consumer-quality audio gear.*

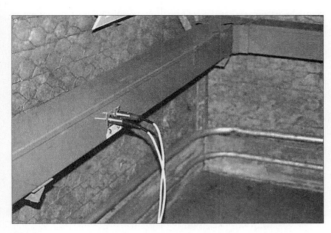

Figure 6-51. *A cable tray with XLR audio receptacles, with mike cables inserted. The tray runs around the perimeter of the studio with paired receptacles every four or five feet.*

Figure 6-52. *A mike cable snake. Multiple mike lines connect to a single connector box, and one large audio cable then attaches to the routing switcher or patch bay. This reduces the number of wires crossing the studio floor, aiding easy camera movement.*

that may help you overcome problems associated with using equipment with incompatible audio connectors.

Cable Trays and Snakes

The microphone cable often plugs directly into a recorder if the production is simple and requires only one mike. But if the production needs several mikes, or you're working in a studio, the microphone cords probably plug into a *cable tray* or *connector box.* A cable tray is a metal enclosure around the perimeter of the studio with female XLR connectors (sometimes called jacks) every few feet along its surface (see Figure 6-51). Mike cables plug into the closest jack, reducing problems caused by cables running in all directions on the studio floor. Sometimes technicians provide an audio *snake* as an alternative or an addition to the cable tray. A snake is a bundle of bound cables running from the audio console (or patch panel) to a movable metal connector box containing multiple audio jacks (see Figure 6-52). The snake's "head" (the box containing the jacks) is positioned as needed to route microphone cables out of the way of sets and the view of cameras. Snakes are especially handy for multi-microphone productions in the field where loose cables invite problems.

Patch Panels and Routing Switchers

At one time, near most audio consoles was a device called a *patch panel* consisting of labeled jacks, some of which were the outputs of microphone and line-level sources, while other jacks led to the input circuits of the audio mixing console. As in an old-fashioned telephone

switchboard, short *patch cords* connected any audio source to any console input channel, provided the output and input levels were compatible (see Figure 6-53). This provided maximum flexibility during production. Often certain patch panel jacks were *normaled,* that is, they connected audio sources to the console without inserting patch cords. This was a common practice in studios used frequently for a particular program such as local news requiring the same audio configuration each time. Inserting a patch cord into a normaled jack broke the connection, allowing easy reconfiguration of the audio inputs and outputs for other programs.

The modern replacement for the patch bay is the *audio routing switcher.* Routing switchers make connections using electronic switches rather than patch cords (see Figure 6-54). Electronic switches aren't subject to the mechanical wear, or the contact corrosion, associated with patch panels—and they're faster. Some routing switchers are computerized, allowing storage and

Figure 6-53. *A balanced-line patch bay, permitting mikes and other input devices to be routed to various input channels on an audio console.*

Figure 6-54. *An audio and video routing switcher. Electronic switches replace the patch cords and patch panel of a traditional patch bay.*

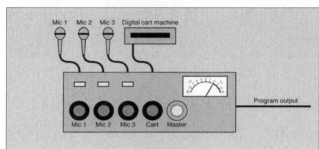

Figure 6-55. *The photo shows the Shure Model M367 portable audio mixer, an example of those kinds of mixers typically used for small-scale EFP and ENG work. Note that switches allow the input of either mike- or line-level signals. The output is also switchable between mike and line level. Although the M367 features six inputs, the diagram shows a simple four-channel mixer with three mikes (low- or mike-level sources) and a digital cart machine (high- or line-level source) connected. The operator controls the loudness of each mike and the cart machine individually using the rotary pots on the mixer. The combined output of all sources is adjusted using the master pot. The operator monitors the program level by watching the VU meter (a visual indicator of the program's amplitude discussed later in this chapter) and the quality of the mix by listening to the program output with earphones plugged into the mixer's phone jack.*

Photo courtesy of Shure Brothers Inc.

instant reestablishment of frequently used configurations. Routing switchers are also made that perform these functions for both audio and video signals.

The Audio Mixing Console

Much ENG work requires only one microphone, whose output feeds the recorder directly. The operator chooses which channel (track) will store the audio and sets the volume level for proper recording. During the stress of ENG work, operators sometimes simply let the recorder's *automatic gain control* (AGC) circuit adjust the volume level. A well-designed AGC does an adequate job of "*riding gain*" (controlling volume) but, like auto-iris circuits, the AGC sometimes introduces undesirable artifacts such as excessive background noise during long pauses in an interview. Professionals monitor the audio while shooting and set volume levels manually if they notice problems caused by AGC action. Most studio and EFP audio equipment has AGC available, but manual control using an audio mixing console is preferred.

In their most sophisticated forms, *audio mixing consoles* allow complex changes in the frequency and phase relationships of the original signal. But even the most elaborate audio mixing console, or *board,* performs the same basic functions as a simple portable mixer, such as the Shure Model M367 (see Figure 6-55).

Audio consoles provide an individual input circuit (sometimes called a channel) for each sound source in the production. They also have a means of controlling the amplitude (volume, or gain) of that source as well as a means of controlling the amplitude of the combined sound sources "mixed" together. Consoles have circuits for monitoring the amplitude of the console's output visually and for listening to the mix. Let's look at each of these items in a bit more detail. Referring to Figure 6-56, which provides a simplified view of how signals are handled by a basic audio mixing console, may help as you read the following explanation of mixer functions.

The output of each audio source feeds an individual numbered input circuit in the audio console. Small portable mixers, such as the Shure Model M367, have only a few input circuits, limiting the number of sources the operator can mix together. Large studio consoles may have dozens of input circuits. Some of these input circuits may accept only microphone-level signals, while others may require line-level signals. Often some or all of the inputs are switchable, accepting either microphone- or line-level signals.

The volume of each input circuit is adjusted with its own *fader,* also called a *potentiometer,* or pot. Having the volume of each audio source individually controlled allows the operator to creatively mix two or more sound sources. For example, it's often better to fade out one musical selection while fading in

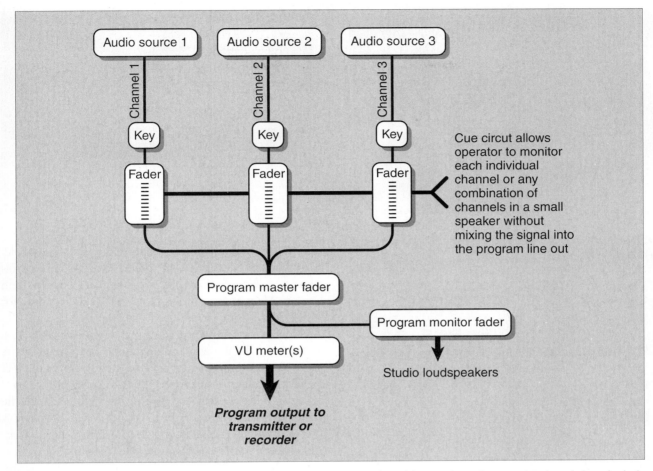

Figure 6-56. *This diagram shows the audio signal flow from three audio sources through keys on the audio mixer, then through the individual channel fader controls. The audio sources are then combined to produce the program audio. This audio passes through the program master fader, where the level of the entire program is controlled. A sample of the program audio goes to the program monitor fader, where the operator sets a comfortable listening level for the studio loudspeakers. The operator can listen to the mix or an individual audio source independent of the program level by adjusting a cue circuit control. The operator monitors the final program audio mix by watching the VU meter(s) before the audio passes to a transmitter for broadcast or to a recording device where the audio is stored for later use.*

another (called a *cross-fade* or segue [pronounced "segway"]) rather than abruptly ending and starting each selection.

Pots in older studio consoles and many small portable mixers use rotary knob controls, while modern studio consoles usually have linear (sliding) faders (see Figure 6-57). Faders have a pointer or mark on the movable knob or slider and a fixed numerical scale on the body of the console allowing the operator to see the degree to which each pot is "open" or "closed." Studio consoles and some mixers also have a switch called a *key,* or *knife,* on each input which turns the source audio on or off without changing the fader's volume setting. Older consoles use lever-type switches, but modern consoles increasingly use push-button switches to key audio sources on and off.

All audio consoles provide *master level* controls, faders that simultaneously increase or decrease the volume of a group of audio channels equally. A monaural audio console would have one master level control affecting all the board's audio channels, but a stereo console would have two, one for the left channel and another for the right. The master control doesn't change the loudness of one source compared to another, but does increase or decrease the volume of all sources in the group. Sometimes an audio console appears "dead" because someone turned one or more master level controls all the way off. Always check the master level controls to be sure they are properly set before you begin looking for more serious problems.

Many audio consoles have various controls that selectively boost or *attenuate* (reduce) the volume of certain

Figure 6-58. *Traditional analog VU meters showing "normal" audio peaks.*

Figure 6-57. *In shot 1, rotary pots on a studio audio console. The trend for many years has been away from rotary pots, and such controls are seldom seen on modern studio audio gear. In shot 2, slide pots are used.*

frequencies relative to all others, allowing the operator to "shape" the acoustic characteristics of sound sources. Most often these *equalization* (EQ) controls help compensate for a perceived flaw in the audio, such as an interviewee whose voice sounds excessively tinny, or an old LP recording with too much low-frequency rumble. Sometimes producers may use the console's EQ functions to create a special effect, but more often special audio effects are added during postproduction. For the sake of simplicity, equalization functions were not included in Figure 6-56.

VU Metering

The traditional device used for visually monitoring the console's combined audio output is an analog meter with scales calibrated in both volume units (VU) and percent of modulation (this meter is often simply called a *VU meter;* see Figure 6-58). The VU meter eliminates the subjective judgments of sound intensity which occur when loudness is determined by ear alone. There's a VU

meter for each output channel of the mixing console. A monaural console has one VU meter, since it controls just one channel of output; a stereo board has two, and so on. Most audio consoles provide VU meters only for the console's output, but elaborate consoles also use VU meters for monitoring each input circuit as well. As a very general rule, good analog audio levels require the signals leaving your audio console to show up on the VU meter as audio peaks between 80 to 100 percent of modulation (–2 to 0 decibels [dB] on the VU's scale). In the analog world, signals failing to peak at the 80-percent level at least occasionally may be too weak, causing background noise to become noticeable. This is what technicians define as a poor *signal-to-noise ratio.* Consistently allowing signals to peak far above 100 percent (0 dB on the VU scale) usually leads to audio distortion when working with analog audio, and certainly creates distortion in the digital domain. Digital recording devices are especially sensitive to excessively strong signals and, unfortunately, traditional analog meters often can't respond rapidly to short bursts of high-level audio. The VU meter needle may never deflect into the red zone of the scale, yet the recorded audio may be distorted. Sophisticated consoles may use meters to indicate average levels, plus one or more flashing light-emitting diodes (LEDs) to show instantaneous peak audio levels. Some consoles use a series of LEDs or a liquid crystal display (LCD) rather than conventional meters to indicate either peak or average levels (see Figure 6-59). An LED-type meter, or a traditional VU meter with an LED to indicate audio peaks, is much preferred when monitoring levels being recorded digitally. When recording in the digital domain, a slightly low level is preferable to one which is too strong, because it later can be increased to normal levels without bringing up excessive noise in the signal, as would be true for an analog recording. But a digital recording with distortion created by recording too "hot" <u>cannot</u> be corrected.

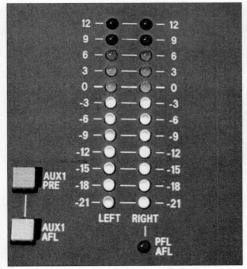

1.

2.

Figure 6-59. *Shot 1 is an LED-type VU meter. The lighted LEDs indicate an instantaneous signal strength just below zero VU. In shot 2, LED peak indicators above analog VU meters flash when signals peak above zero VU. LED indicators react much faster to high level signals than do analog meters, often flashing on brief but excessively strong audio signals not indicated by the analog meters.*

As one would assume, watching levels becomes increasingly complex as you add sources. Riding gain on the audio from a mike on a single news reporter is not too daunting, but keeping levels in hand when many sound sources are involved is more difficult. Difficulty increases again when we move to multiple channels of discrete audio. Monaural recording with all sources mixed to a single channel is sometimes hard enough. With two-channel stereo, the job becomes a bit trickier. When we get to surround sound with six discrete channels of audio, the task becomes even more challenging. The monitoring equipment for such work is also more complex, as you can see by looking at RTW's Model 10800X surround sound monitor in Figure 6-60. In addition to monitoring the VU meters (visible on the right side of the 10800X), we must also be concerned about the phase relationships among the different channels, as displayed visually on the left side of the 10800X.

We introduce these issues not to discourage you, but because we want you to understand that production, both audio and video, is becoming increasingly sophisticated. You must continue to incorporate new information and develop new skills throughout your career.

Monitoring the Mix

Although VU indicators show if the audio level is technically too high or low, they can't tell you if the sound mix is aesthetically correct. A meter may show a perfectly normal level when the background music is so loud the talent's words can't be understood. The only way to properly adjust the mix is to listen to it critically using headphones or loudspeakers. The headphone and loudspeaker monitoring system is a separate circuit with its own independent volume controls. It's important to remember that adjusting the volume of the monitor speakers or your headset has no effect on the output level reaching the transmitter or a recording device. Only VU indicators show the strength of audio signals leaving the console that eventually reach viewers.

Cue Circuits

It's often helpful to check audio sources before they go on live during a show. It's especially helpful to preposition tape-recorded materials so they start instantly when needed. Most consoles provide special *cue circuits* allowing you to hear an individual sound source before it's mixed into the program audio. You typically activate

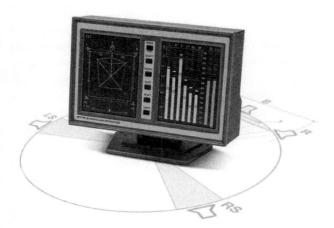

Figure 6-60. *The complexity of monitoring multichannel audio is suggested by the displays of the RTW Model 10800X 5.1 surround sound monitor.*

Photo courtesy of RTW RADIO-TECHNISCHE WERKSTAETTEN GmbH & Co.KG™.

these cue circuits by turning the rotary fader associated with that source completely counterclockwise or pulling the slider-type fader all the way to the bottom of its travel. The audio source is then heard over a cue speaker. There's a volume control for the cue speaker you can adjust as needed to help you cue the source material. Some consoles also offer a *pre-fade listen,* or *pre-fade level,* (PFL) circuit. The PFL is also sometimes called a *solo* circuit. PFL works differently on different consoles, but basically pressing the PFL/solo button for a given input signal allows you to monitor (hear) the incoming audio on only that channel, regardless of where you have the channel fader positioned. If you are working with a console with PFL, check the console's operator's manual for its operation, because PFL has many user advantages not available with simple cue circuits.

Automatic Muting Circuits

We've all heard public address systems squeal when the microphone picks up audio from loudspeakers in the area and feeds it back into itself. This squeal is the result of *acoustical feedback* from the speakers to the microphone to the speakers, round and round. To avoid this, audio consoles have *automatic muting circuits,* which turn off the studio's monitoring speakers when a microphone is turned on in the same studio. Studio talent sometimes find the sudden muting of studio speakers disconcerting, causing them to think something is wrong. Actually, the muting of studio speakers serves as a warning that a studio microphone is activated and talent should be silent and alert until given their cue by the floor director.

IFB and Private Line Communication

Often the talent needs to hear program audio while using a live microphone. This is accomplished without creating acoustical feedback by having talent wear an inconspicuous earplug to hear program audio. In addition, producers and directors can interrupt the program audio fed to the earplug to instruct talent to ask a question, or transition to another topic. We have learned earlier that this is called an *IFB* (interrupted feedback, also called interruptible fold back) line and is used by news anchors and other talent hosting live programs. Camera operators and other crew members usually don't need to hear the program audio. Instead, they listen to an intercom circuit called the *private line* (PL) using a combination mike-headphone set (see Figure 6-61). The PL allows them to hear the director's commands

Figure 6-61. *A camera operator wearing an intercom headset.*

and respond vocally, if necessary. Studio crew members should not respond orally via the PL more than necessary during productions, because the talent's live microphone may pick up their voices. The person operating the audio console may wear a PL headset, but he/she usually monitors the PL through a cue speaker on the console. In some systems the PL and IFB are combined, and the director uses push buttons to determine if the intercom audio goes to the talent or crew, or both. The IFB and PL audio is usually carried by cable in a studio production. On a remote production where talent and crew members may be located at considerable distances from the control room or when crew members must move a great deal during production, wireless devices may convey the IFB and PL signals, as well as the talent's audio.

In concluding our discussion of audio consoles, we should note that some modern consoles offer computer-assisted automated functions and that computer-based *"virtual consoles"* are becoming popular for certain situations. Virtual consoles perform the same functions as traditional physical consoles, but the keys, faders, VU meters and other controls are images on a display screen rather than physical objects. The operator manipulates these controls using a computer keyboard, a mouse, or by touching the display screen. The major advantages of virtual consoles are lower initial cost plus the ability to upgrade and reconfigure the system's functions by simple software changes. Many professionals, however, still prefer working with conventional consoles that give them the tactile "feel" they desire for making precise adjustments, especially during fast-paced live productions.

This introductory chapter touched on many fundamentals of audio production for television. Now we'll leave audio to explore another area of the control room, where we'll find that most imposing piece of control room equipment, the video switcher.

Important Vocabulary Terms

5.1 Surround sound: A form of surround sound (see separate vocabulary entry) featuring six discrete audio channels. There are five directional channels (front left, front middle, front right, left surround [or back left], right surround [or back right], plus a sixth nondirectional low-frequency channel. Dolby Digital (see separate vocabulary entry) is most often associated with 5.1 surround sound.

Accessory shoe: A clip or bracket that allows mounting an auxiliary external microphone of the operator's choice on the camera.

Acoustical feedback: A loud screeching sound created when a microphone picks up its own output over a nearby speaker and reconveys it though the system.

Ambient sound: Naturally occurring sounds intrinsic to a particular location which contribute to the mood of the scene. Also called natural or wild sound.

Amplitude: The strength or power of a sound wave, known colloquially as loudness or volume. Amplitude also refers to the strength or magnitude of a varying electrical signal.

Attenuate: To reduce the amplitude of a sound or electrical signal.

Audio cassette recorder: A recorder/playback machine which uses two reels of $^1/_6$-inch tape contained in a plastic container (cassette), thus combining features of the open-reel and cartridge tape recording systems. Most cassette recorders use analog techniques, but some cassette machines record audio in digital format.

Audio mixing console: A device which allows the operator to control the selection and mixing of various audio signals to form the sound portion of a television production. Also called an "audio board," "board" or "mixing desk."

Audio routing switcher: A form of patch panel using electrical switches rather than patch cords to connect audio sources to the audio mixing console.

Audio tape recorder (ATR): Although technically applicable to any audio tape recorder, the term usually refers to open-reel analog devices using tape from a quarter-inch to two-inches in width.

Automatic gain control (AGC): An electrical circuit which automatically adjusts the volume of audio signals.

Automatic muting circuit: A device in an audio mixing console that automatically mutes (silences) all speakers in the vicinity of a microphone when the microphone is keyed on, thus preventing acoustical feedback.

Balanced line: A three-wire cable in which analog audio signals are conveyed over two insulated wires, shielded from outside interference by a bare wire and metallic foil. Professional-quality audio equipment is designed to operate with balanced lines.

Bidirectional microphone: A microphone which is sensitive predominantly to sounds arriving from only two directions.

Blumlein pair: A coincident-microphone technique used for stereophonic recording. The technique uses two bidirectional microphones. Named after British stereophonic recording pioneer Alan Blumlein.

Board: Another term for an audio mixing console. See "Audio mixing console."

Boom: A device with a long arm that positions the microphone near the talent but outside the camera's view.

Boundary microphone: Also known as a PZM microphone. A specially designed microphone using a close-mounted reflective surface to achieve a desired audio pickup quality.

Burn: A term referring to the recording of audio on a CD using heat created by a laser.

Cable tray: A metal enclosure surrounding a production studio with female XLR connectors into which microphones are plugged.

Capacitance: The ability of a nonconductor to store energy because of voltages on conductive surfaces on either side of the nonconductor. This phenomenon is important in the functioning of a condenser microphone.

Carbon microphone: A microphone that uses a capsule containing carbon granules pressed between two metal plates as the transducer. Sound waves striking one of the metal plates change the pressure on the carbon granules, thus changing the resistance to a current flowing through the transducer. Carbon mikes provide poor audio and are likely to be used only for special audio effects.

Cardioid microphone: Also known as a unidirectional microphone, the cardioid is sensitive predominantly to sounds arriving from only one direction. The area of greatest sensitivity has the general shape of a heart.

Cartridge tape recorder: An analog recorder/playback machine which uses an "endless" loop of $1/4$-inch audio tape wound around a single rotating hub in a plastic container, or cartridge. Valued for its self-cueing feature. Often called cart machines in the industry. Some cart machines are playback-only devices.

Ceramic microphone: A microphone using a ceramic element with the same physical and electrical characteristics as a crystal in a crystal microphone. See "Crystal microphone."

Clip microphone: A very small microphone that attaches to the talent's clothing at chest level.

Coincident-microphone technique: Any stereophonic recording technique in which the microphones are in close proximity to each other. Variations include the X-Y and M-S techniques.

Compact audio disc (CD): A line-level audio source which uses a clear vinyl-coated metal disc as a digital storage medium. Initially available as playback-only devices, CDs are now popular for audio recording. CDs provide higher fidelity audio than LPs and suffer no degradation in performance with repeated use.

Condenser microphone: A microphone using a pair of electrically charged metallic plates separated by an insulator as the transduction element. Condenser microphones require a power source for operating the microphone's associated amplifier and sometimes for charging the metallic plates of the transducer. Condenser microphones are also called electrostatic microphones.

Connector box: A metal box with many female XLR connectors providing a central point into which microphones used during a production are plugged. The entirety of the connector box and its multi-wire cable leading to the audio mixing console is often called a snake.

Cross-fading: An aesthetically pleasing audio mixing technique in which the sound from one source fades out as a second source fades in. The two sounds blend briefly during the transition between sources.

Crystal microphone: A microphone that uses a natural mineral (crystal) that has the peculiar ability to generate an electrical voltage when placed under pressure. In a crystal mike, the sound waves place varying pressures on the crystal element, producing a voltage that is the electrical analog of the original sound. Crystal mikes do not produce high-quality sound and are seldom encountered in a professional production environment.

Cue circuit: A special amplifier in an audio mixing console allowing the operator to hear an audio source without mixing that source into the program.

Desk microphone: Often a hand microphone supported by a stand with a heavy base or by a flexible gooseneck mount attached to a desk or podium. Also called a stand or podium microphone.

Digital audio tape (DAT) recorder: A type of cassette audio tape recorder which records and reproduces audio using digital techniques. DAT provides higher quality audio reproduction than analog recorders. DAT and analog audio cassettes are not physically or electrically compatible.

Digital video disc (DVD): An extremely high-capacity optical disc. The DVD's large capacity makes it ideal for feature films or interactive games and instructional programs.

Directivity: A microphone characteristic referring to a microphone's increased sensitivity to sounds arriving from a particular direction or particular directions.

Dolby Digital: A trademarked marketing term for Dolby Laboratories' AC-3 audio encoding technology. Dolby Digital and Dolby AC-3 are terms frequently used interchangeably.

Dolby Lab's AC-3: The audio standard developed by Dolby Laboratories and approved by the Advanced Television Systems Committee for digital television broadcasting in the United States.

Dual redundancy: The mounting of two clip microphones in a single holder worn by the talent. Only one microphone is used; the second serves as a backup should the first malfunction during production.

Dub: To make a duplicate copy of recorded audio, such as recording music from an LP to tape. Dubs made using analog recording techniques invariably lose audio quality; the copy never sounds as "clean" as the original.

Dynamic microphone: A rugged and widely used microphone employing a disc (diaphragm) attached to a moving coil within a magnetic field as the transduction element. Also known as an electrodynamic, moving coil or pressure microphone.

Electret condenser microphone: A special type of condenser microphone in which the metallic plates of the transducer are permanently charged.

Electrodynamic microphone: Another, more technically correct, term for a dynamic microphone. See "Dynamic microphone."

Electrostatic microphone: Another term for a condenser microphone. See "Condenser microphone."

Equalization (EQ): Altering the electrical characteristics of an audio signal to correct perceived flaws in the original sound. EQ is also used to produce special acoustical effects.

External Microphone: A microphone physically attached to a camera, but not built into the body of the camera.

Fader: Also known as a "potentiometer" or "pot." A control on an audio mixing console which adjusts the volume of an audio signal.

Fishpole boom: A lightweight telescoping rod supported by a crew member that allows an attached microphone to be located near the talent but outside the camera's view.

Flat response: A reference to a mike that responds to sounds of all frequencies equally. A mike that faithfully reproduces the original sound without emphasizing or de-emphasizing high or low frequencies.

Frequency: The rate at which an object vibrates or a wave (sound or electrical) completes a full cycle in both magnitude and polarity. Frequency, when applied to audible sound, is commonly known as pitch and is measured in Hertz (Hz).

Giraffe: A small, self-supporting microphone boom mount on wheels. Basically a fishpole boom held aloft by a metal stand rather than by a crew member.

Gooseneck: Flexible metal tubing used as a microphone support attached to a desk or podium allowing easy repositioning of the microphone to fit the needs of different talent.

Hand microphone: A microphone designed to be held vertically in front of the talent's chest.

Hanging microphone: A microphone suspended immobile by its audio cable above the talent from the studio's light grid or any improvised overhead support.

Hard drives: High-capacity digital storage devices providing almost instantaneous random access. Originally designed for the computer industry, various forms of magnetic and optical digital disks are used in TV production, especially for editing.

Headset microphone: A small microphone on a (usually) flexible rod along with one or two earmuff speakers attached to a clamp mount worn on the talent's head. The microphone's close proximity to the mouth helps ensure the talent is heard clearly above the ambient noise level.

Hertz (Hz): The unit of measurement associated with frequency, named after scientist Heinrich Hertz. Hertz represent cycles per second.

Hypercardioid microphone: A microphone that accepts sound only from one direction along a very narrow axis. The most highly directional cardioid pickup pattern.

IFB: Interrupted feedback. Also sometimes called interruptible fold back. An audio circuit providing program audio to a small earplug worn by talent. The producer or director may interrupt the program audio to provide cues to the talent during production.

Impedance: The degree of opposition to AC flow exhibited by an electrical circuit. Impedance is measured in Ohms.

ips: inches per second. The speed at which a tape moves during recording and playback. In analog recording, higher speeds produce higher quality recordings. Typical speeds are 7.5, 15, and 30 ips.

Key: A switch on an audio mixing console which instantaneously turns an audio source's signal on or off. Also known as a "knife."

Knife: Another term for the audio console term "key." See above.

Lavaliere microphone: A relatively small microphone designed to hang by a cord around the talent's neck, resting on the talent's upper chest.

Line level: Refers to the relatively strong electrical signals reaching an audio mixing console from audio storage devices, such as compact discs and tape recorders, that significantly amplify their own output.

Low-end roll-off filter: A built-in device that reduces the tendency of a microphone to excessively emphasize the low frequencies in sound originating in close proximity.

Master level control: A special fader on an audio mixing console which simultaneously increases or decreases the signal strength (volume) of all audio sources.

Method of transduction: The particular way in which a device, such as a mike, converts mechanical sound energy into electrical energy. Different kinds of mikes use different methods of transduction.

Microphone (mike) level: Refers to the relatively weak electrical signals reaching an audio mixing console from microphones and other sources that do not significantly amplify their own output. Mike-level sources require somewhat more amplification by the audio mixing console than do line-level sources.

Mid-side (M-S) technique: A coincident-microphone technique used for stereophonic recording. This technique uses a unidirectional (often a supercardioid or cardioid) mike pointing at the middle of the sound stage and a bidirectional mike at right angles to the unidirectional mike to pick up sound coming from the sides.

Mini-Disc (MD): A digital disc-based audio recording device using small (approximately two inches in diameter) removable discs as the storage medium. Some stations use the MD as a replacement for analog cartridge tape machines and ATRs.

Monaural: Description of an audio device which processes only one audio channel.

Monophonic: Sometimes shortened to "mono." See "Monaural."

Moving coil microphone: Another term for a dynamic microphone. See "Dynamic microphone."

Multiple-transducer-system microphone: A microphone body with an assortment of matching transducers, thus allowing the user to modify the microphone's characteristics to suit the production situation.

Normaled: Referring to outputs and inputs on a patch panel that are connected without patch cords; commonly used in studio productions where certain output–input connections were used repeatedly. This patch-panel wiring technique reduces the number of patch cord connections required in routine productions.

Omnidirectional microphone: A microphone that accepts sound arriving from all directions in a nondiscriminatory manner.

Output impedance: A term equipment makers typically use with reference to the load impedance a device, such as a mike, should encounter when properly matched to the next electrical device, such as an amplifier, in a circuit. See also "Impedance."

Parabolic microphone: A dish-shaped concave reflector with a directional microphone at its acoustic focal point facing inward, toward the dish. The parabolic reflector

and its associated microphone provide good pickup of distant sounds.

Patch cord: A short length of cable with male plugs used to connect outputs and inputs on a patch panel.

Patch panel: An array of female connectors (jacks), some of which are outputs of microphones and other audio sources while others are input circuits to the audio mixing console, thus providing a flexible means of connecting audio sources to the audio mixing console.

Perambulator boom: A large, heavy boom allowing microphone movement in any direction quickly and with precision during a production. Two operators are required to achieve maximum efficiency during production.

Phantom power: Electrical energy provided by an audio mixing console to operate condenser microphones.

Phase: Another term for time. When sound waveforms with different phase relationships are combined, the resultant sound is degraded by undesirable reinforcement and cancellation of frequencies in the original waveforms.

Polar diagram: The graphical depiction of a microphone's pickup pattern.

Pop filter: A device built into a microphone to reduce the popping of plosive consonant sounds such as "b" and "p." See also "Studio 'pop' filter."

Potentiometer: A technical term for a fader. Often shortened to "pot." See "Fader."

Pre-fade listen, or pre-fade level (PFL): A feature of some audio consoles that allows monitoring the audio input of any channel, regardless of the position of the channel's fader control. Sometimes called a solo circuit.

Pressure-gradient microphone: Technically, a microphone in which both sides of the diaphragm are exposed to the sound wave striking the mike. Often used as another term for a ribbon microphone, although some ribbon mikes provide pickup patterns other than bidirectional. See "Ribbon microphone."

Pressure microphone: Technically, a microphone in which only one side of the diaphragm is exposed to the sound wave striking the mike. Often used as another term for a nondirectional (omnidirectional) dynamic microphone, although other types of mike satisfying the technical definition may be considered pressure mikes. See "dynamic microphone."

Private line (PL): An intercom system allowing the producer or director to give instructions to camera operators and other crew members during a production. Sometimes the PL also carries the program audio, which is interrupted as necessary for instructions from the control room.

Proximity effect: The tendency of a directional microphone to excessively emphasize the low frequencies in a sound source placed close to the transducer element.

Psychoacoustic: Psychoacoustics is the study of how humans subjectively perceive sound. A reference to the psychological perception of sound rather than the sound's physical characteristics.

PZM microphone: A boundary microphone often referred to as a pressure-zone microphone by its creator, Crown International Co.

Quadraphonic sound: Basically, a sound system with four separate audio channels of audio delivered through four speakers located at four corners of the sound space. An early form of surround sound. Also known as quad sound.

Radio frequency (RF) microphone: A wireless microphone.

Reel-to-reel ATR: A tape-based audio recording system featuring two open reels of audio tape. See also "Audio tape recorder."

RF Microphone: A wireless microphone.

Ribbon microphone: A relatively large microphone using a thin metallic ribbon moving within a magnetic field as its transducing element. Also called a velocity microphone.

Riding gain: The process of monitoring a VU meter and adjusting the amplification to ensure a technically good recording. This is usually performed by an audio board operator but can be performed by an AGC circuit. See "Automatic gain control."

Shock mount: A flexible microphone mount that isolates a microphone from its support, reducing the amount of mechanical vibration reaching the transducer element.

Shotgun microphone: A large, extremely directional microphone which uses a collection of tubes of different lengths to provide directivity.

Signal-to-noise ratio: Sometimes identified as S/N, it's a comparison of the desired audio (music, voice) to the undesired noise (such as tape hiss). Audio with little inherent system noise compared to the desirable voice and/or music is always preferred.

Snake: A bundle of bound cables running from the audio console (or patch panel) to a movable metal connector box containing multiple audio jacks.

Solo: A circuit on an audio board, similar to a cue circuit, except more versatile. It allows you to listen to an audio channel, or, on some boards, a mix of audio channels, without affecting the sound going out on the main or auxiliary outputs of the board. Another name for a PFL circuit.

Sound: The interpretation the brain gives to a particular physical stimulus sensed with our ears.

Specification (spec) sheet: Technical data about a microphone's performance characteristics provided by the manufacturer. A specification sheet is provided with each new microphone designed and marketed for professional applications.

Stand mount adapter: A threaded plastic fitting which attaches to a microphone and can be screwed onto the matching threads of a microphone stand or flexible gooseneck support.

Stereophonic sound: Stereophonic sound reproduction, also called stereo sound, provides an "image" in the listener's mind of the relative location, left to right, of each sound source in the mix. Stereo reproduction requires capturing the original sound with two transducers and keeping the signals separated until they are converted back into sound by speakers or earphones.

Studio "pop" filter: A microphone attachment made from an acoustically transparent material within a hoop and positioned between the mike and the performer's mouth. Designed to minimize "pops" from harsh plosive sounds. See also "Pop filter."

Supercardioid microphone: A unidirectional microphone with a narrower heart-shaped pickup pattern than a standard cardioid but that is less directional than a hypercardioid microphone.

Surround sound: A generic term for a sound system that features sound coming toward the listener from all directions, including the sides and back, not just from the front. The goal of surround sound is to place the listener in the middle of the sound environment.

Sweetening: The process of enhancing a program's audio during postproduction.

Synthesized audio: Audio signals generated by electronic oscillators and amplifiers rather than by vibrating physical bodies in contact with the air.

Three-to-one rule: A microphone placement technique employed to minimize problems caused by phase differences when multiple microphones are being used. The rule specifies that the distance between two sources should be a minimum of three times the distance between a source and the nearest microphone.

Transducer: A device that converts energy from one form to another; in an audio context, the converter that changes sound into an electrical form.

Transduction: The process of converting energy in one form (such as sound) into energy in another form (such as electricity).

Transient: Extremely brief burst of high-amplitude, high-frequency sound. The mass of some transducer elements prevent them from responding to sound bursts of such short duration causing the reproduced sound to be less crisp.

Turntable: A line-level audio source using vinyl discs as an analog storage medium Colloquially known as a phonograph or hi-fi.

Unbalanced lines: Two-wire audio cables. Both wires carry the audio signal and one is electrically connected to the ground. Most audio equipment designed for the consumer or industrial market uses unbalanced lines.

Velocity microphone: Another term for a ribbon microphone. See "Ribbon microphone."

Video cassette recorder (VCR): A video tape recorder (VTR) using tape contained in a cassette.

Virtual console: A computer-based audio console that uses images of keys, faders, VU meters and other controls on a display screen. The controls are manipulated using a keyboard, mouse or by touching the display screen.

VU meter: A monitoring device which provides a visual indication of the volume (amplitude) of audio passing through an audio recorder or mixing console. Named for the volume units used to measure the amplitude of the sound.

Windscreen: A smooth-surfaced (usually foam rubber) microphone attachment which slips over the entrance to the microphone's transducer element to minimize the pickup of wind noise.

Wireless microphone: A microphone used with a small radio transmitter, usually hidden on the talent, and an off-camera receiver rather than a cable to convey the audio signal. Also called an RF (radio frequency) microphone.

XLR Cannon connector™: The self-locking metal connectors attached to the ends of balanced lines or similar connectors into which balanced lines are plugged. These devices are now manufactured by firms other than Cannon Electric Company and are sometimes called simply XLR connectors.

X-Y Technique: A coincident-microphone technique used for stereophonic recording that uses two directional (usually cardioid) mikes (or mike elements) pointing at opposite ends of the soundstage.

Zeppelin: A device used on a shotgun mike to deaden wind noise.

chapter 7

Production Switchers and Special Effects

The most exotic-looking piece of space-age technology that visitors see during a television studio tour is the video production switcher. With its rows of colorfully lit buttons, knobs and fader handles, the switcher is a television icon, a symbol of the daunting breed of complex technology associated with this medium. When film director George Lucas wanted something technologically sophisticated to portray the main weapons control panel of the Death Star space station in *Star Wars,* he cast an especially complex-looking video production switcher for the part.

Despite its formidable appearance, the production switcher is basically just what its name implies: a device allowing production personnel to easily and seamlessly "switch" from one video source to another. Admittedly, even the simplest video switchers do more than change which camera or other video source is currently on the air. This chapter introduces the fundamental capabilities of the video switcher, explains the logic behind switcher design and discusses a variety of transitions and effects.

However, before we begin, one comment: This chapter tells you a great deal about switchers and special effects, but that's as far as any textbook like this can take you in the learning process. We'll provide the basics, but you won't develop the skills you need until you've spent considerable time actually using the switcher in your studio. To help you, later in this chapter we've included a page of illustrations that shows some of the features and abilities of a re-entry logic switcher and a cascading logic switcher. There are many switchers in use today, each with slightly different user interfaces. We can't provide a totally complete, how-to discussion for even one of these switchers. But after practicing with the brand of switcher in your studio, it won't take you long to master the basic features of others. Switchers are like cars or personal computers: Their basic functions are the same; only the interfaces and controls that you use to perform them differ.

Our study of switching basics begins with learning how video switching fits into the process of television production.

The Three Purposes of Switching

There are three basic, generic tasks switchers perform. First, they change which picture you're showing on the screen. At the most basic level, switchers take many video sources (cameras, video playback devices, graphics storage devices, video servers) and instantaneously "switch" them from a standby status onto the air. We refer to this as switching a video source *on line,* sending the signal to either a TV broadcast transmitter or to some variety of video recording device.

Second, switchers *mix* pictures together, transitioning from one shot to another so that for a moment they both appear on the screen at the same time (see Figure 7-1).

Third, switchers produce a wide variety of special effects and visual transitions that have the ability to creatively move, merge and otherwise manipulate video from several sources simultaneously.

Regardless of their complexity, switchers perform five basic kinds of effects and transitions: cuts, fades, dissolves, wipes and keys.

1.   2.   3.

Figure 7-1. *In shot 1, we see a picture of a can of instant coffee. In shot 2, we see the visual effect at the halfway point of the dissolve as the video switcher gradually dissolves to shot 3, a picture of a stopwatch.*

The Cut, the Bus and the Bank

The simplest transition is the *cut,* an instantaneous change from one video source to another. The cut gets its name from film editing where one shot is snipped out of a longer reel of film and fastened to the end of another shot. A cut is often called a take in television to prevent a director's command to "cut to" a video source being misinterpreted as a command to "cut" (stop) the program. However, switcher manufacturers use the term "cut" to describe an instantaneous change of video source, so we will also.

Switchers perform cuts during the *vertical blanking interval* (VBI), a tiny fraction of a second that separates one frame of video from the next. All video sources manipulated by the switcher require perfectly timed blanking, or the images will "tear" or "break up" during transitions or special effects. A device called a *synchronization (sync) generator* provides the required uniform blanking signals. These blanking signals are called *house sync* because they provide coordinated timing pulses to all video sources in the production facility (the "house"). And video sources using the same sync signals are said to be *gen-locked* together.

Each video source is assigned its own individual push button on a switcher. Push buttons have identifying labels, such as CAM-3, VTR-2 and CG-1, which are abbreviations for "camera number three," "videotape recorder number two" and "character generator number one," respectively. College TV studios usually identify the kind of video source, but some professional studios don't. Instead, every video source has a number. For example, in one TV station's production studio, their three studio cameras might be numbered 1, 2, and 3 on the switcher; 4, 5, 6 and 7 might be the studio's four video record and playback machines; sources 8 and 9 might be the feeds from the studio's two remote trucks;

10 and 11 might be the newsroom's and the rest of the studio's video servers, and so forth.

A *bus* is a horizontal row of push buttons like these, one for each of the video sources. Figure 7-2 displays a bus on a small video switcher.

A pair of busses (sometimes busses come in threes in switchers that feature a separate bus for keying—more on this later) is called a *bank.* In the smallest switchers, there may only be one bank. In the largest switchers, there may be four banks, allowing you to create complex effects four layers deep.

Needless to say, if all you ever wanted to do was cut back and forth between picture sources, you could just punch buttons on the program bus and use no other portions of the switcher. Cuts are appropriate when action in the two shots is occurring at the same time and place, as most action does. This is why cuts appear so frequently in

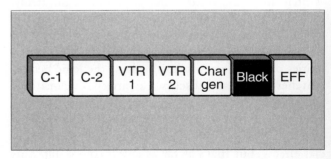

Figure 7-2. *This might be a typical bus on a small, probably portable video switcher. Many switchers have numerous sources per bus, and some have many busses, including a preview bus, used by the technical director (TD), director and other control room personnel to view the shot or effect that will be switched on line next. In this illustration, if CAM-1 were on line, its button would be lit. If you wished to perform a simple cut to the picture on CAM-2, you simply punch the CAM-2 button. Instantly CAM-1's video disappears, CAM-1's button light goes out, CAM-2's video appears in its place on the line (program) monitor and CAM-2's button lights up. You can tell which video source is on line by checking to see which push button is lit on a program bus such as this.*

TV programs. But using only cuts might produce a choppy and potentially boring television show.

The Fade

The next most basic transition is the *fade,* a gradual transition (usually of an approximately 1.5-second duration) between black and any other selected video source. A *fadeup* is a transition from black to picture. A *fadeout* is a transition from a picture to black. Because a fade is a gradual transition between black and another video source, you can't do fades by just punching a button on a single bus. The way fades and other transitions are performed depends on the logical *architecture* of the switcher. Some switchers use *re-entry logic,* also known as *Central Dynamics logic* (named after the switcher manufacturer that had much to do with its popularity). In contrast, switchers currently manufactured by Grass Valley Group and others now use a logic referred to as *cascading,* because after any transition, the switcher automatically prepares for a potential next transition without requiring you to preset a new video source.

The Dissolve: A Fade by Another Name

Dissolves are closely related to fades. Electronically, a fade is just a dissolve between a black video signal and a picture, so dissolves are accomplished the same way as fades. A *dissolve* is defined as a gradual transition between one video source and any other video source, but not black. If your transition was to be between a video source and black, it would be a fade. Likewise, it's inappropriate to refer to a dissolve as a fade. A fade means going from black to an image, or vice versa. In a dissolve, when the transition is halfway between these two picture sources, both briefly appear as ghost images superimposed over each other. Although seldom used, this halfway-point-effect is also called a *super,* short for "superimposition." Continuing the dissolve, one video source dissipates, while the other gradually forms in its place.

Dissolves are the second most common transition in TV production. Dissolves are appropriate when the action in the two shots is not occurring in the same location or the same time. The dissolve takes the viewer to another time or another place in the story. Dissolves are also appropriate transitions in musical and dramatic programs where a smooth flow of images melding together is desirable for artistic effect.

Wipes

A *wipe* is also a transition effect between one picture and another. Simple analog wipes create the impression that a shape or pattern forms either within or on the edge of the picture that's on line. As the wipe transition continues, the shape or pattern enlarges or moves across the picture until it has, so to speak, wiped the old picture away. As the wipe replaces the old picture, a new picture is revealed over the top of the old one. Professionals use wipe transitions less often than cuts, fades or dissolves, because wipes are showy and often draw attention to themselves. Wipes often appear as bridges between instant replay and live action during sports shows and in many music programs, in which more showy transitions would not disrupt the storyline. Wipe transitions are seldom seen in dramas, but sophisticated combinations of digital wipes and animation appear in some situation comedies. For example, highly creative, animated digital wipes were a signature scene transition device in the classic situation comedy *Home Improvement* (see Figure 7-3).

1.   2.   3.

Figure 7-3. *These three photos document a simple wipe transition between images from two different video sources. In this instance, the wipe is moving from left to right. In shot 1, the wipe transition is shown about one-third of the way across the shot of the monument. In shot 2, the wipe transition is about three-quarters completed, and in shot 3, the wipe is complete. For this illustration, a white border was used at the wipe point to emphasize the division between the two video images. However, the border is optional.*

Not all wipes are complete picture transitions: Sometimes we use them to create a space within one video source where we display video from another source (a picture within a picture). A good example is the rectangular, box-shaped wipe (simply called a *box wipe*) placed over the anchorperson's shoulder during newscasts. As you saw earlier in Figure 1-14 on page 28, a box wipe doesn't result in a complete transition from the anchor to the boxed information, but rather appears as two pictures sharing the screen at the same time: one inside the box wipe, one outside. However, as we're about to discover below, with other analog and digital video effects, something that looks like a box wipe is often keyed, rather than wiped in.

Keying

A *key* is similar to a wipe because, in both effects, a portion of a foreground video source appears to be "cut into" a background picture. Keys are used extensively in television production, especially in newscasts, commercials, show credits and live sports events. When lettering, logos, some boxes over newscasters' shoulders and even people appear to be cut into another picture, you're probably viewing a key.

The most common kind of key in television is one in which lettering appears over a background picture. In early television production, this lettering came from *key cards* (also called graphic cards), made of black poster board with white lettering placed on a *graphic stand* and shot with a studio camera (see Figure 7-4).

The switcher's keying circuits caused the white portions of the key card (the lettering) to become a "cutout pattern" replacing the corresponding locations on the background picture. The black elements of the key card became invisible. Modern electronic graphic devices such as the character generator and paint box have replaced actual key cards. It's no longer necessary to dedicate a camera and operator just to shoot such cards, except in an emergency. The electronic equivalent of the key card is now a digital file called a *key page* on a graphics storage device (see Figure 7-5).

On some switchers you'll find an effects function called *wipe key*. This allows you to select a wipe pattern, and then, as though it were a wipe transition, wipe the key in rather than dissolve or cut to it. A cut to a key is an abrupt transition. A dissolve to a key gradually reveals all the keyed information. Using the wipe key progressively reveals only the portions of the keyed information that you choose. You control this by your choice of wipe pattern (see Figure 7-6).

Before we finish with keying, we should mention two other kinds of basic keys, the *matte key* and the *chroma key.*

1.   2.

Figure 7-4. *In shot 1, we see a studio video camera shooting a key card, a graphic with a black background and white numerals. In shot 2, the black background from the key card in shot 1 has been electronically removed, leaving only the white numerals etched into the image of a person who is pictured on another studio camera.*

1.   2.

Figure 7-5. *In shot 1, we see a Chyron Duet character generator operator creating a key page for a news show and, in shot 2, an artist using a paint box palette to create a video graphic.*

Shot 1 courtesy of Bill Brinson; shot 2 courtesy of Nebraska Educational Telecommunications.

Figure 7-6. *In these three shots, we see a hard-edged, diagonal wipe-key transition in progress. In this case, the team logo is in the process of being wiped on, over the shot of the bookshelf. A wipe key progressively reveals or removes portions of the keyed material as the transition is performed. Note: Using the video switcher, graphics other than lettering can be keyed over other video.*

Matte Keys

The matte key function works much like a normal key. What we refer to as a normal key is often an *internal key*. This means the source video that will be etched into the hole in the background video appears in the final keyed shot exactly as it looks on the key page seen on the character generator's monitor. In contrast, a matte key, sometimes called an *external key*, allows us to fill in those keyed-in white letters or light-colored artwork with video from a different, external source. This might be a shade of color or a colored pattern generated by the switcher, or from any other video source you may choose. In other words, a matte key uses three video sources: the background video, the key video and a third "filler" video. See Figure 7-7 in the color photo section of this book for examples of matte keying.

Chroma Keys

Weathercasters use chroma keys regularly to create the illusion that they're standing in front of an animated weather map. Actually, the reporter is standing in front of a solid green (or blue) screen in the studio. Just like the black backgrounds on the key cards and character generator key sources mentioned earlier, in a chroma key the green (or blue) background disappears in the final, composite picture. As Figure 7-8, found among this book's color photos, indicates, whatever appears in front of the blue screen (in this case, an announcer) becomes the key cutout and is electronically pasted into the video of an animated weather map (in this case) or any other video source that is designated as the chroma key background. See the discussion in Chapter 8 regarding the evolution of weather graphics. Although you typically see stations use chroma key every night during the weather segments of their newscasts, there are many other applications for chroma keying. Whenever you wish to put people or objects into places where it would be difficult to stage action, chroma keying is a viable, often inexpensive option.

Larger Production Switchers

Typically, the larger the production switcher, the greater its ability to perform complicated effects and transitions and to mix many sources together. Although many modern production switchers employ some form of cascading architecture, many large switchers using re-entry logic remain in service. Many are at colleges and public television stations where equipment budgets rarely keep pace with technology. This somewhat older style of architecture produces effects and creative transitions by adding more *effects banks* (see Figures 7-9 and 7-10). As mentioned earlier, some models have up to four effects banks, permitting *quadruple re-entry*. This allows you, for example, to key over a wipe over another key over yet another wipe. As well, switchers built today feature *downstream keyers* (DSKs). DSKs permit a technical director to key a selected source, such as a character generator, over the final output of a switcher, effectively adding yet another level of effects. It is called "downstream" because, in a river metaphor, it is added after all the other "upstream" effects have been accomplished. Figures 7-9 and 7-10 feature two typical larger production switchers, one that uses a triple re-entry design, and one that uses a cascading logic system designed for either live or postproduction work.

Digital Video Effects

Digital video is the future. As we've noted earlier in this book, the television industry is galloping toward conversion to an entirely digital television system, from image creation to consumers' home TVs. As studios and stations make the big switch, video will remain in the

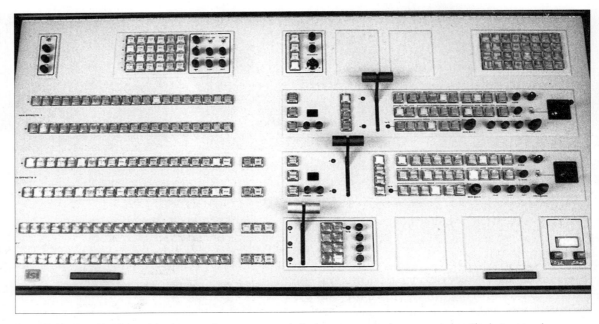

Figure 7-9. *This older ISI Model 1206 switcher is very typical of a large re-entry architecture switcher. The bottom two busses (bottom left), usually called the program bank, and the downstream keyers in the lower right might be all you would need for simple shows. The switcher also features two sets of mix/effects (M/E) busses (the two pair of busses directly above the program bank) and chroma key capability. One could set an effect in M/E 1 (the top two busses) and set up another effect on M/E 2 (the second set of busses), and then dissolve or wipe to the combination of these two effects from a camera or digital video effect (see below) on the program busses. Because this particular model switcher cannot perform digital effects, an external digital video effect was added as one of its inputs.*

digital domain throughout the entire production and distribution process. As analog video completely gives way to digital, there will only be one kind of video effects.

When *digital video effects* (DVE) were introduced, they were built into a few upscale analog switchers or sold as separate add-on digital image processor units. They received analog video, changed it to digital, manipulated it to create the desired effects, then converted the digital effects back to analog video and returned them to the analog switcher. In an all-digital production studio, the signal remains digitally encoded from start to finish. Figures 7-11 through 7-22, provided by Tektronix/Grass Valley, are found in the color plates section of this book on Plate 3 and Plate 4. Figure 7-11 pictures a high-end digital production switcher, the GVG Kalyposo. Figures 7-12 through 7-22 illustrate and provide names for many of the hundreds of DVEs used in video production.

Manipulation performed by DVEs often involves "image stretching," effectively altering a picture's aspect ratio. A variant of stretching is *warping*, in which a

Figure 7-10. *This Ross Synergy Digital Switcher is typical of a switcher featuring cascading architecture and digital effects on board. Although it's a sophisticated cascading switcher, the TD still can use the bottom two busses to set up a routine fade, dissolve or cut. The difference is that although you can cut back and forth on one bus (all switchers' program busses let you do that), cascading architecture lets you preset the next take on whichever of the two bottom busses is not currently on the air and then go over to the buttons beside the fader and hit the "cut" button. This switches from the bus previously on the air to the other one, where you've already preset which camera you wish to cut to next. This also causes the previous camera or other video source to cascade down to the off-air bus, standing by to cut back to it. So if you're cutting between two cameras, you can just rest your finger near the "cut" button and punch, punch, punch back and forth between two cameras.*

Ross Synergy 3 Switcher photo courtesy of Bill Brinson.

PLATE 1

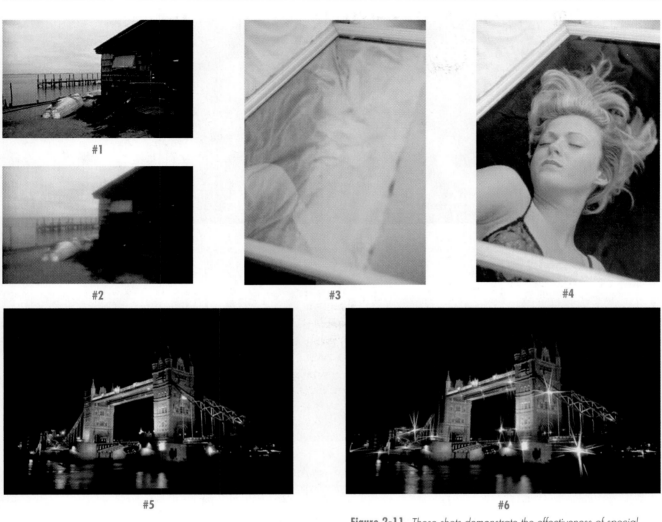

#1

#2

#3

#4

#5

#6

Figure 2-11. *These shots demonstrate the effectiveness of special effects filters: shots 1 and 2 show a picturesque seaside house, with and without fog filter; shots 3 and 4 dramatically demonstrate the Tiffen polarizing filter's ability to reduce reflected glare; and shots 5 and 6 show how a star filter adds glitter to a shot of the London Bridge. All photos courtesy of The Tiffen Company ©.*

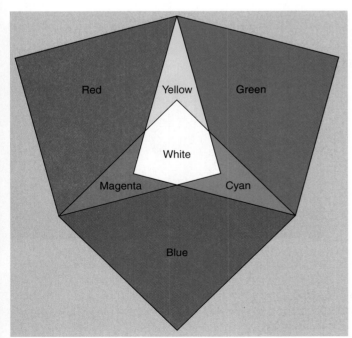

Red   Yellow   Green

White

Magenta   Cyan

Blue

Figure 2-14. *As these combinations illustrate, red, green and blue in various combinations render all shades of color. RGB in equal amounts comprise the color white.*

PLATE 2

#2   #3

Figure 5-38. *The use of an ellipsoidal to project a pattern in the background of a shot of a performer. Using gelled lights as set pieces can be very creative! Shots 1 and 4 located on page 121.*

#1   #2   #3

Figure 7-7. *Shot 1 shows the letters "SIUE" keyed over a shot of a paneled wall. In this first shot, the "SIUE" is a simple, unadorned key of the original white letters. In shot 2, the "SIUE" is filled in with a pattern created by matte keying video from the switcher's color bar generator. Of course, you could use a switcher's color generator to matte the "SIUE" with any color you want, adjusting the hue (the shade of color), the luminance (the brightness of the color) and the saturation (the amount of color you want, from a very light pastel to very rich and full). You make these adjustments using the switcher's hue, luminance, and saturation knobs, located among the controls used for keying. Shot 3 shows the letters "SIUE" matted with video from a shot of a red and white checkered tablecloth.*

#1   #2

Figure 7-8. *In shot 1 we see an announcer working in front of a blue chroma-key wall. In shot 2, we see the announcer as he appears to the audience. The blue chroma-key wall is replaced by a shot of downtown St. Louis and its arch, which is provided by an electronic still picture that is stored in the station's video server. These form the composite shot of the announcer, who appears to be standing in some high place, overlooking the St. Louis skyline.) Although you typically see stations use chroma key every night during the weather segments of their newscasts, there are many other applications for chroma keying. Whenever you wish to put people or objects into places where it would be difficult to stage action, chroma keying is a viable, often inexpensive option.*

PLATE 3

Figure 7-11. *This is the Grass Valley Kalypso, typical of a high-end digital production switcher. Photo courtesy of Tektronix/Grass Valley.*

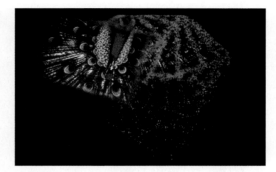

Figure 7-12. *Borders and trail.*

Figure 7-13. *"Wind."*

Figure 7-14. *Z-axis depth intersect of planes.*

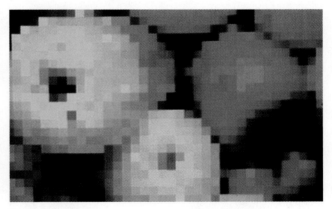

Figure 7-15. *Mosaic.*

Figure 7-16. *Embossing.*

Figure 7-17. *Corner pinning.*

PLATE 4

Figure 7-18. *Page turn*

Figure 7-19. *Kurl with ripple.*

Figure 7-20. *Cylinder.*

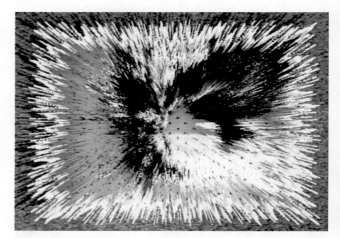

Figure 7-21. *Splash.*

Figure 7-22. *Intersect planes with dissolve. DVE Photos courtesy of Tektronix/Grass Valley.*

PLATE 5

Figure 8-4. Poor color selection. The lettering color and that of the foliage lack the contrast needed to make readng the graphic easy.

Figure 8-5#2. In shot 2, a Fox box, as it is sometimes called, also helps to separate lettering from the background. In this case, a partially transparent background helps identify the news organization as well as separate the talent's name from the background.

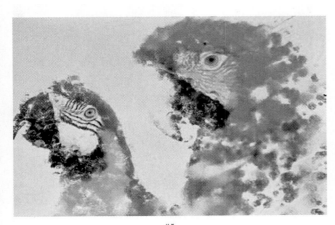

#1

#2

#3

#4

Figure 8-15. In shot 1, parrots are created entirely on Quantel Paintbox F.A.T. Shot 2 shows another composite Paintbox effect. Paintbox F.A.T. offers as many as 99 layers of effects at the artist's disposal. In shot 3, you see a video frame of a cathedral; in shot 4, you see the result after importing the shot into Paintbox and adding effects. All Paintbox photos courtesy of Quantel.

PLATE 6

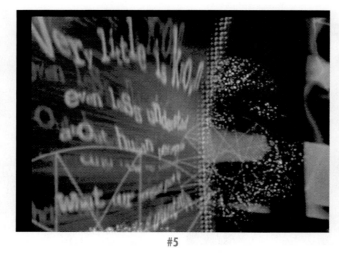

#5

Figure 8-15. *"Ghosts" Paintbox artwork manipulated using Quantel Transform FX. All Paintbox shots courtesy of Quantel.*

#1

#2

#3

Figure 8-16. *These are just a few examples of the many ways that Photoshop can alter normal shots in your video productions*

PLATE 7

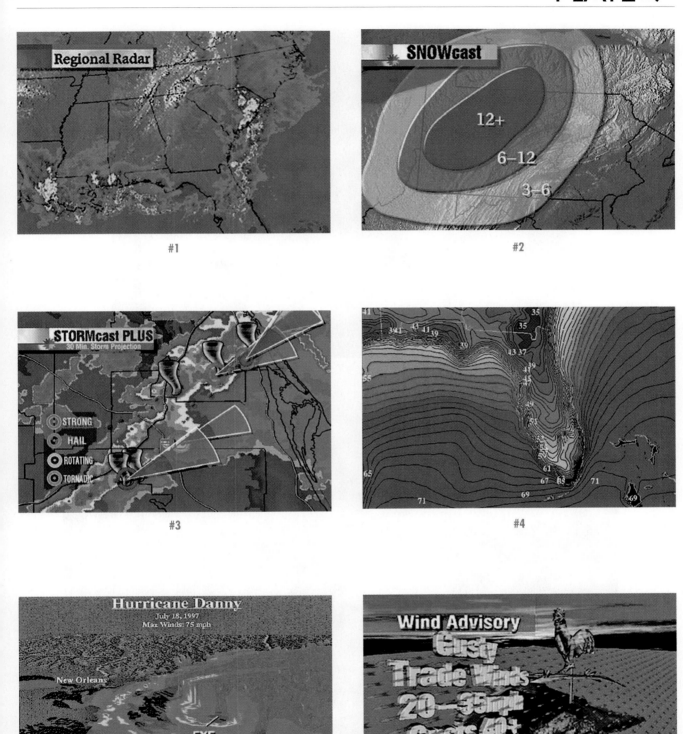

Figure 8-18. These six photos show the range and sophistication of weather graphics available for the nightly news. Photos courtesy of WSI

PLATE 8

#1

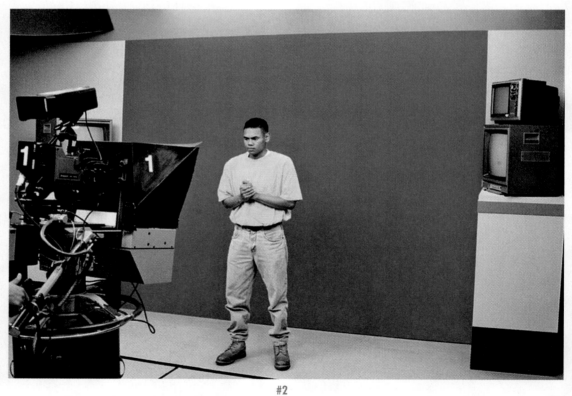

#2

Figure 14-15. *As you recall from our earlier discussion of chroma key, the chroma-key drop in shot 1 provides a soon-to-be invisible background. The difference here is that this drop is hung from a batten in the studio, and can be raised out of sight when necessary. Shot 2 is a permanent chroma-key wall for shooting local weather and sports reports. This wall is blue rather than green. Blue and green are used for chroma keying. Performers must remember not to wear anything that is the same shade of blue or green as the chroma-key wall, or else that part of their clothing will disappear and become part of the chroma keyed background.*

picture is intentionally misshapen, like an image in a fun house mirror. Such effects used to be the sole purview of DVE machines, but now many digital editing systems, such as those made by Avid Corp., can perform many of these effects (see Figure 7-23). One of the most popular digital effects—first seen in movies such as *Terminator II* and the TV series *Star Trek: Deep Space Nine*—is *morphing,* essentially a digital dissolve. As we learned earlier in this chapter, an analog dissolve cross-fades between two video sources with one picture displacing another. But morphing appears to turn one object into another object (see Figure 7-24).

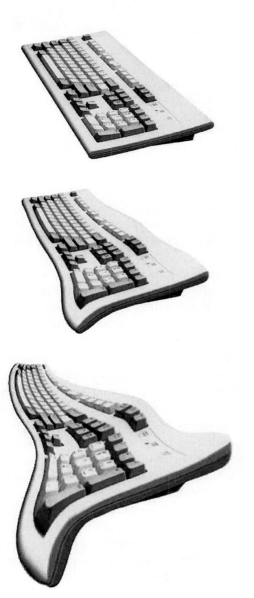

Figure 7-23. *This three-shot sequence shows how a shot of a computer keyboard can be distorted, using the warp effect.*

Courtesy of Avid® Technology Inc.

Figure 7-24. *Essentially a digital dissolve, a morph effect integrates the elements of the dissolve more completely than an analog dissolve, as we see in this morphing of President George Washington into President Ulysses S. Grant.*

Courtesy of Avid Technology Inc.

DVEs as Problem Solvers

Either as separate units, as a part of digital editing software or built into digital switchers, DVEs can be helpful in postproduction to correct problems. If the top edge of a shot accidentally shows the tip of a boom mike, a DVE can digitally expand the shot or simply erase the mike. DVEs can center a shot recorded slightly off center and even level shots recorded on a slightly canted angle. DVEs can paint a few frames of video or color-correct entire programs. Indeed, there's little in the way of image manipulation one can't do once the image is digitized. The possibilities are limited more by the imagination of the producer than by the hardware and software.

Desktop Switching

Along with the uproar in video production circles caused by the changeover from analog to digital production comes a strong trend referred to popularly as desktop, or nonlinear, video. The increasingly popular computer platforms performing DVE, switching and editing, along with the ascendance of "digital studios in a PC" continue to fascinate current and would-be video professionals. The digital effects these units perform, the increasingly high quality of the video they produce and reproduce and their highly competitive price (compared to traditional large, stand-alone switchers and DVEs) make them attractive to small-budget producers. Plus, the *open architecture* of these systems makes software upgrades to an existing computer platform easy and relatively inexpensive. Thanks to open architecture, defined as the ability to upgrade your unit with updated software when a more efficient tool comes along (and these days, that's about every three months), you're not stuck with expensive, extinct hardware, such as a $60,000-plus switcher (see Figure 7-25). In response to such innovations, switcher manufacturers now provide their own proprietary, but open, architecture, offering inexpensive upgrades of their software.

Most studios in a PC are best in postproduction rather than in live, real-time work at a TV station or in an EFP van. The traditional stand-alone analog or digital switcher still has a place in the modern TV studio and for EFP—at least for now.

Mechanical Effects

Mechanical effects are special effects made by means other than electronic—and most of them are borrowed from effects experts in the motion picture

Figure 7-25. *This is the video switcher interface of the Play Inc. Trinity®. Other interfaces accessible from the Trinity include an array of special digital effects, a nonlinear editing interface, a character generator and a paint, animation and image compositing screen.*

industry. Mechanical effects appeared in films made by Thomas Edison and in those of French magician/filmmaker Georges Melies as early as the 1880s. By starting and stopping the camera and cutting together before-and-after shots, Melies often made people and things in his films disappear and reappear in a puff of smoke.

Many stage production effects also made their way into television shows, especially studio productions. Styrofoam flakes sprinkled onto a set create the illusion that it's snowing. Large fans blowing across the set provide the illusion of a windy exterior location.

Today's producers increasingly avoid the problem of creating illusions artificially by simply shooting the real thing. For example, a crew may go out and shoot in a downpour instead of going to the expense of faking a studio rainstorm. Modern portable equipment encourages shooting on location. Contemporary audiences are less forgiving of clumsily contrived mechanical effects, and often a location shoot is easier and cheaper than creating the necessary images with mechanical or even digital electronic trickery.

Using chroma key effects, TV and motion picture producers can shoot their actors in a scene and then add exterior footage or computer-generated scenery and effects to the background.

However, older techniques can still play a role. Carefully shaking the camera while simultaneously cueing actors to react can, with the addition of appropriate sound effects, create the illusion of an earthquake. Breakaway props, such as chairs and bottles, rubber knives and guns loaded with blank cartridges contribute to the illusion of reality in a barroom fight—or something worse. As you read in Chapter 2, many visual effects can be accomplished with camera filters, such as fog, polarizing and star filters. Even more basic, if used as a point-of-view shot that follows a close-up of an actor who appears to be fainting, simply defocusing the camera and tilting it wildly up to the ceiling can communicate to viewers that a character lost consciousness and fell. Although dating from earlier days in the history of motion pictures, these techniques communicate meaning to audiences as well today as they did almost a century ago.

In this chapter we've introduced you to video switchers that create transitions between shots or blend together more than one shot during live production and postproduction editing. We've also discussed a few mechanical means for creating or enhancing the illusion of reality. We'll introduce more mechanical means to create and maintain these illusions in Chapter 14, "Production Design." The next chapter, "TV Graphics," introduces more devices and electronically created images that add visual interest to modern video productions.

Important Vocabulary Terms

Architecture: The term used to describe the logic switchers use to create their transitions and effects. Re-entry architecture and cascading architecture are the most common forms, along with open architecture. (See "Re-entry logic," "Cascading logic" and "Open architecture.")

Bank: A pair (or on some switchers, a trio) of busses.

Box wipe: A wipe effect in which two video sources share the screen at the same time, one inside a box and one outside.

Bus: A horizontal row of switcher input buttons, one for each of the video sources available.

Cascading logic: A modern switcher architecture that allows operators to preset transitions and effects in a preset background bus and then switch to these effects instantaneously; the switcher then "flip flops" the selected video input between the preset bus and the program bus, so that an operator can easily switch back and forth with ease.

Central dynamics logic: See "Re-entry logic."

Chroma key: A special effect in which color (usually blue or green) in an image serves as the keying element. The blue or green areas of the foreground image are filled in with video from another source.

Cut: The most simple video transition, in which one shot is instantaneously replaced by another.

Digital video effect (DVE): Any of the limitless special effects created by digital manipulation of the image.

Dissolve: A gradual transition between a video source and any other source, except black, during which images from both sources are superimposed briefly.

Downstream keyer (DSK): A keying mechanism separate from and after (thus downstream) all other effects performed on a switcher, allowing an operator to add a key over the output of the switcher, effectively adding another layer of effects.

Effects bank: A set of busses used to preset video inputs for special effects.

Effects Bus: One of a set of busses used to preset video inputs for special effects. Two effects busses constitute an effects bank.

External key: See "Matte key."

Fade: A gradual dissolve between any selected video source and black. See also "Fadeout" and "Fadeup."

Fadeout: A dissolve transition from any video source to black; the opposite of a fadeup.

Fadeup: A dissolve transition from black to any video source; the opposite of a fadeout.

Gen-locked: All video sources in a studio that use house sync are said to be gen-locked, or locked to the synchronization generator. Only gen-locked video sources can be used in combination with each other in a switcher.

Graphic stand: An either horizontal or vertical easel for supporting key cards, photographs or other graphic materials shot by video cameras during production.

House sync: Blanking, or VBI, signals produced, usually, by a sync generator, to which all video sources are gen-locked (see "Gen-locked").

Hue: A video term for color shade.

Internal key: A key in which the source video that will be etched into the hole in the background video appears in the final keyed shot exactly as it looks on the key page seen on the character generator's monitor.

Key: A special effect that electronically "cuts and pastes" brighter elements of a foreground key source into a background picture.

Key card: A black card with white lettering on it, used extensively before the advent of character generators to provide key signals.

Key page: The electronic equivalent of a key card. A key page is a digital file on a graphics storage device.

Matte key: A special effect in which white lettering (or the brightest elements in the key source picture) is filled in with video from a second source and cut into another picture. Also called an external key.

Mechanical effects: Special effects that don't involve electronic image manipulation. There are generally two kinds of mechanical effects: those accomplished by interposing something in front of the television camera, such as a filter, and those effects created through traditional stagecraft.

Mix: Switcher manufacturer's term to describe a fade or dissolve.

Morphing: This is a digital dissolve that does more than a visual cross fade from one source to another. A morph effect actually causes one image to appear to slowly become the other, as if by magic.

On line: A reference to the video output of a switcher. When a video source is placed "on line," its output is routed through the switcher to a transmitter or recording device.

Open architecture: An attribute of computer-based switching and effects systems allowing updating by replacement of relatively inexpensive software and/or hardware rather than the entire computer platform.

Preview bus: A bus used to view video sources or effects prior to switching them on line.

Program bus: The main (on-line) bus on a switcher.

Quadruple (or triple, or double) re-entry switcher: A switcher with quadruple re-entry capability has the equivalent of four mix/effect (M/E) busses with which to create complex layered effects. Double (or triple) re-entry switchers have the equivalent of two (or three) of these M/E busses.

Re-entry logic: The video switcher architecture that preceded cascading effects. Also called Central Dynamics logic.

Saturation: The amount of color in a shot, from a very light pastel to very rich and full.

Super: The visual effect created by halting a dissolve at its midpoint, with both pictures sharing the screen as ghost images. Short for "superimposition."

Synchronization (sync) generator: A device used in a studio to provide video devices with uniform blanking, or VBI, signals to lock onto.

Vertical blanking interval (VBI): That tiny fraction of a second between one frame of video and the next.

Warping: A digital video effect in which a picture is intentionally misshapen, like an image in a fun house mirror.

Wipe: Transition that replaces the original picture by introducing a new image that appears to move across the original, to form within the original and then expand to full screen or to "swallow" the original starting at the outer borders.

Wipe key: A special effect in which a key is placed on line via a wipe pattern, rather than by a cut or dissolve.

chapter **8**

TV Graphics

Anyone who's watched TV knows that graphic materials, both still and animated, play a major role in video production. Graphics are the lettering and artwork that provide alphanumeric symbols and representational pictures in television programs.

At one time, nearly all graphic materials (except filmed animation) were made with traditional graphic arts techniques and subsequently broadcast live or recorded in analog format onto magnetic tape. Today most TV graphics are created and stored electronically in digital format on an optical or magnetic disk. We will refer to graphics made the traditional way as *organic graphics* and to those done with digital computers as *synthetic graphics.*

Organic graphics are usually made to be shot by a camera. They can be artistically created or found already available. Using a street sign is one example of an organic graphic, or as it is sometimes called, "graphics without graphics." It can also be as simple as a sheet of paper with words printed from a word processor. Created with paints, press-on lettering or other artists' supplies, mechanical organic graphics were a mainstay of television production for the first three decades of the medium's existence. But in the 1980s, artists began switching to computer-based technologies—for many good reasons. Synthetic graphics are more powerful visually; they're easier to create and change; they allow animation. Plus, the price of computer technology continues to drop even as its capability escalates. Craig Birkmaier, editor of *Videography* magazine, has three words of advice for people who want careers in video but don't like computers: "Find another job!" That's good advice.

With the current broadcasting dichotomy—stations operating in both the analog and digital domains—our graphics chapter will cover techniques for both. Because the aesthetic and proportional principles of graphic creation apply equally to both organic mechanical and synthetic graphics, they provide a preamble to our discussion of production methods later on.

Aspect Ratio

In Chapter 4 you learned that the National Television System Committee (NTSC) television screen has an aspect ratio of 4:3, and so that full-screen graphics created for NTSC presentation must fit within a 4×3 rectangle. You'll also recall that NTSC's 4:3 format will share the spotlight with the 16:9 aspect ratio as we transition to digital television, but that we must "protect" the 4:3 format during the transition, until most viewers own sets with 16:9 screens. Figure 8-1 contrasts the two aspect ratios.

The Essential Area

In Chapter 4 we also noted that by the time an analog TV signal travels from the studio camera to the control room monitor, as much as ten percent of what's seen in the viewfinder is cut off around the edges. Indeed, each

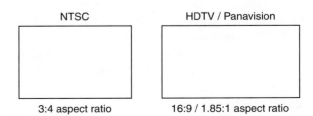

Figure 8-1.

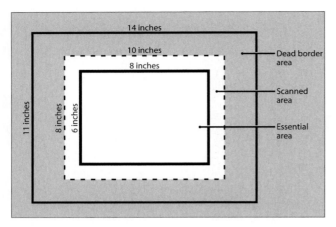

Figure 8-2.

1.

2.

Figure 8-3. *In shot 1, we see a title graphic that has left room around the edges for TV cutoff. Shot 2 shows the same title graphics that were not set with TV cutoff in mind.*

time an analog television signal travels down a cable, some picture information is lost around the outside edges. We must consider picture cutoff not only when operating a video camera but also when creating mechanical or electronic graphics. Sponsors get upset when part of the phone number is cut off on the viewer's screen because someone designed a poor graphic. We can avoid problems with picture cutoff when designing graphics by working within the *essential area* (sometimes called the critical area, or *safe title area*). Artwork or lettering positioned outside the essential area may not survive picture cutoff. On a standard 11 × 14-inch studio *graphic card* or *art card* (a graphic card has alphanumeric symbols; an art card has representational drawings or paintings, or a combination of both) as shown in Figure 8-2, you can see three areas: the essential area, the *scanned area* and the *dead border area*. The dead border area is the outside perimeter of the card. It cannot contain any artwork, and it's outside the area seen on the camera viewfinder. Inside the dead border area is the scanned area, which on our 11 × 14 card is roughly 10 × 8 inches (80 square inches). This is the portion of the art card visible in your camera's viewfinder. But only the 8 × 6-inch essential area (48 square inches) inside this scanned area is sure to survive picture cutoff. As you can see, the essential area fills the central 60 percent of the scanning area, with 10 percent on each of the four sides left for potential cutoff. This same proportional relationship exists for graphics produced electronically. Be aware of picture cutoff when creating any kind of graphic and make sure you place the essential information safely within the essential area (see Figure 8-3).

A common TV rule was to place name keys so that they appeared in "the lower third" of the picture, but

within the essential area, to ensure proper graphics composition; placing them any lower than that would risk picture cutoff. But with digital TV receivers, the scanning area is much more uniform. Since all screens have the same essential areas, graphics can be closer to the top or bottom of the screens. The lower third rule has become more like the lower sixth. It is common to see sports graphics put at the very top or bottom of the screen so as to eliminate interference with the live action. Financial networks also make use of the lower sixth to put one or more lines of stock information on a crawl across the screen. When designing graphics for digital reception, you can allow for more control of the essential area.

Contrast Ratio

Another concern in creating graphics is luminance contrast ratio, the approximate 40:1 relationship between the brightest and darkest portions of a picture as seen on analog home TV sets. Like aspect ratio, this is another technical limitation of conventional TV that applies to graphic images, with one exception: the key card or key page, a mechanical or electronic graphic supplying the video switcher with alphanumeric symbols or artwork to key over another picture. As you saw in Figure 7-4, the background for a key page can be as dark as you wish, even if it's more than 40 times darker than the lettering. This is because only the letters will appear in the composite shot. The switcher's keying circuits cut out only the lettering and/or artwork to place into some other video image. Therefore, our key page's failure to adhere to the limits of television's contrast ratio is not harmful.

But contrast ratios in television apply to more than just the picture's luminance (brightness) values. One also has to be concerned with color (chrominance) contrast, and it's important to consider what colors provide clearly readable information on TV graphics. For example, wearing a pastel yellow blouse and a light tan sweater is fine for a late-spring wardrobe, but pale yellow lettering over a dusty brown background lacks the *color contrast* needed for easy reading on home TV sets. See Figure 8-4 on Plate 5 of the color plate section. Another color difficulty in analog television is overuse of the color red. For instance, a full screen background of red has a tendency to have dark, snow-like interference, or "noise," running through it, causing an irritating distraction. The reproduction capabilities vary from one TV screen to another, with a frequent propensity for red colors to glow, or "bleed." Because of these difficulties, red is used judiciously in graphics. It is better to have a small logo or a splash of red rather than extensive application of this color.

To insure adequate color contrast, trust luminance values more than differences in chrominance. Use colors that show up far apart on the gray scale, such as dark shades for the background and much brighter shades for the foreground. For example, television news routinely requires keyed graphics over all sorts of video, so one sees a lot of white, yellow or orange lettering. Electronically created graphics often use letters edged or drop-shadowed in black, or some other dramatically contrasting color, to help viewers distinguish lettering from backgrounds (see Figure 8-5). Regardless of their video backgrounds, it has become common practice to put graphics in an opaque box to ensure good legibility.

Putting the Message First

Now that we've reviewed a few technical limitations on graphic production, we'll discuss content issues. In creating any kind of graphic message for an audience, you must keep your primary goal constantly in mind: to simply and clearly communicate ideas. Anything that conflicts with this objective, including excessive

1.

Figure 8-5. *In shot 1, adding an edge to lettering keyed over a picture helps it stand out from the background. In shot 2, found in the color photo section of this book, a Fox box, as it is sometimes called, also helps to separate lettering from the background. In this case, a partially transparent background helps identify the news organization as well as separate the talent's name from the background. The term "Fox box" comes from the innovation of the Fox TV network to use a series of panels, or boxes, at the top or bottom of the screen to convey information, such as during sports events. For instance, a football game may include a series of boxes with the team names, score, down, yardage, time and the Fox logo.*

"creativity," is counterproductive and should be reduced or removed. Especially avoid "upstaging" the vital information. Beginning students, wanting to do something "different," often key letters over moving or detailed video images, failing to realize the distracting effects of these backgrounds. This same misdirected desire sometimes produces psychedelic color combinations that focus viewer attention more on the unique quality of the letters themselves than the ideas the letters are intended to convey.

Paradoxically, too much information is worse than no information at all. Always check both the number of letters and words on screen at any time, as well as the size of the letters. It's easy to compose wonderfully legible graphics using a monitor only a few feet away, forgetting viewers seldom sit that close to their sets. Expert opinion varies, but most say the maximum number of words on screen at any time should be between 12 and 25. We favor the lower number, allowing you to increase the letter size so even viewers some distance from their sets can easily read your words. One formula for spacing graphics is the "5 × 5 rule." This edict says that graphics should have no more than five words on a line nor more than five lines on the page (see Figure 8-6). If you have more information than 12 to 15 words, you can still get your message across. Either break your message up into two or more graphics, or consider rolling your

Figure 8-6. *Keys over these identical backgrounds show the problem with crowding too much information onto one screen. Which communicates better?*

message. A *roll,* or *scroll,* begins below the bottom of the screen, continues up and exits at the top. You may also use a *crawl* to increase the number of letters in a message without overloading the screen. A crawl is a horizontal row of electronically generated characters parading from right to left across a location on the bottom third of the screen. Stations often use crawls to warn viewers about potentially dangerous weather conditions without unnecessarily interrupting programs (see Figure 8-7).

For keys, use large, thick, simple lettering rather than ornate or thinly lined letters. Simple block lettering is more readable on the screen and keys much more cleanly. Thin, wispy letters or Baroque-styled lettering keyed over anything but the blandest backgrounds often get lost in background detail. The message has been upstaged again (see Figure 8-8).

Another technique for displaying large amounts of graphics information is to control the flow and the color of the information. Let's say you have five lines of data you wish to show. Rather than put all five lines on the screen at once, you can reveal one line at a time and cue it to the audio. The first line is yellow in color. After the second line appears, the first line can change color to gray and the second line is yellow. When the third line is revealed, the first two change to gray. This pattern prevents the audience from reading ahead of the narrator.

Ultimately, the way to judge a graphic is to try to put yourself in the position of someone seeing it for the first time. Is it clear, readable and understandable? Is the message simple and clean? Will it show up clearly on any kind of TV set a viewer might use? And don't be ashamed to ask others for their opinions. It's easy to become so involved with our creations that we lose perspective.

Finally, how long should your graphics be visible on the screen? The answer might depend on what kind of message you're trying to deliver to your audience. As a rule of thumb, leave it on the screen long enough for you, the person who wrote the words, to read it twice.

1.

2.

Figure 8-8. *Shot 1 has a clear, bold font that makes reading the graphic easy. Shot 2 has a "fancy" font that can make a graphic hard to read—even if the graphic contrasts well with the background.*

Figure 8-7. *A crawl in progress as the lettering marches across the screen from right to left.*

Why twice? Because you already know what the graphic says. By the time you've read it twice at a normal reading speed, the average viewer will have time to read it once and understand it.

Creating Graphics Organically

Whether organic or synthetic, graphic production occurs in four phases: creation, capture, storage and retrieval. We'll begin by discussing these phases with respect to organically created graphics. Organic graphics begin as artwork on cards, and are then photographed with a video camera and aired live or stored using various media, including:

- motion picture film and 35 mm slides (although this practice is now practically obsolete);
- videotape or videodisc;
- computer-based magnetic/optical drives or discs; or
- solid-state memory microchips.

Graphic cards begin as blank card stock (poster board) available in various colors, textures and finishes. On these cards the artist fashions the message/artwork using the full range of traditional art materials and techniques, from paints and colored ink pens to decoupage. Once prepared, the next step often is converting the card to a more easily used form. Traditionally, frequently used graphics, such as a television station ID, were made into 35 mm slides. These slides were given a file number and then loaded into a carousel slide projection unit called a *slide chain.* The slide chain projected the slide into a *multiplexer,* a box containing movable mirrors, which in turn directed the image into the lens of a dedicated video camera. Many slide chains shared the same camera with 16 mm motion picture film projectors. Depending on the orientation of the multiplexer's mirrors, either slide or film images were projected into the camera lens. This system—slide projector, film projector(s), multiplexer and video camera—is called a *film chain,* or *telecine island* (see Figure 8-9).

Graphics cards used in live productions were placed on a graphics stand and shot with a studio camera. Key cards often were placed on a copy stand and shot with a dedicated black-and-white video camera (see Figure 8-10). We've used the past tense in discussing graphic cards and the film chain, because electronic methods have nearly completely replaced them in TV production. About the only service telecines perform

Figure 8-9. *Prior to videotape, television studios and stations had two or three of these units. Now you seldom find one. Two 16 mm film projectors could alternately project their pictures into a multiplexer unit, essentially a mirrored box, which reflected their pictures into a film chain camera (mostly hidden in this picture behind the projector labeled "5"). The multiplexer would remove the mirrors from the path to allow the dual slide projector to project its images straight through the multiplexer to the camera.*

in modern facilities is the occasional transfer of 16 mm movie film to videotape.

In 1976, Ampex developed the ESS-1, the first electronic/magnetic device designed for storing individual video images. "ESS" stands for *electronic still store.* The ESS makes capturing and retrieving a graphic quick and easy, thanks in large measure to the fact the ESS provides *random access* to all stored materials (see Figure 8-11).

A newer method of organic graphics is the usage of a cucalorus (or cookie, discussed in Chapter 5) to project printed materials or symbols onto a studio wall or floor. Newer pyrex cookies are becoming more commonplace to project show titles, particularly on game shows and network newscasts. By inserting the cucalorus into an ellipsoidal light, a graphics designer can give his work a unique look that is difficult to create with a computer (see Figure 8-12).

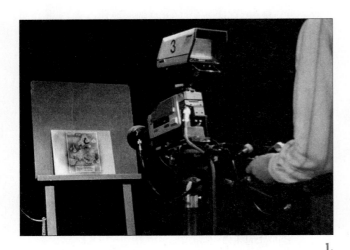

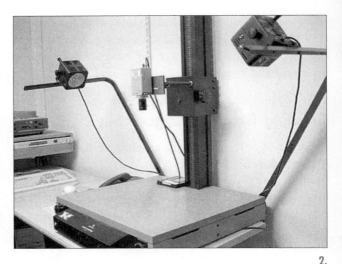

1.

2.

Figure 8-10. *Shot 1 is a studio camera shooting a graphic card on a graphic stand; shot 2 is a copy stand used to shoot graphic cards. Sometimes graphic cards were videotaped for future insertion into a program, but this was not a popular, speedy, efficient or economical way to store and retrieve graphics.*

Creating Graphics Synthetically

Virtually everything once done with card stock, paint, press-on lettering and scissors is now accomplished synthetically. Even artists relatively unfamiliar with computer languages and operating systems find that user-friendly computers and software allow them to create and alter graphics more easily, more quickly and at increasingly lower cost each year.

There are two kinds of application-specific devices designed for electronic graphics production: the *character generator* (CG) and the *paint box.* Some manufacturers also make hardware and software combining both CG and paint box functions. Many desktop computers feature software/hardware packages that perform these same tasks, using sophisticated, frequently upgraded artist software that maximize the advantages of the computer's open architecture. To better understand the capabilities of these devices, we'll examine their functions separately, beginning with the CG.

Character Generators

In 1967 the A. B. Dick Videograph 900 was one of the first machines allowing producers to set type directly onto a television screen. In the 1970s, Chyron (pronounced "KAI-ron") Vidifont and Quantel refined the CG into an amazing tool for those who could afford their astronomically high prices. These manufacturers and others soon began producing smaller, less capable machines for producers on a budget, and today character generators range

Figure 8-11. *A welcome replacement for the 35 mm slide and film chain is the still-store device, a computerized way to store single frames of video for rapid retrieval. Shown here is the Quantel Picturebox.*

Photo courtesy of Quantel.

Figure 8-12. *Another way to incorporate graphic material into your show is to create a cookie that, with the help of an ellipsoidal light, projects words onto the wall or floor of a set.*

from simple CG chips in consumer cameras to workstations costing $100,000 and more (see Figure 8-13).

Dedicated stand-alone CGs designed for professional video applications perform at least six basic functions:

1. They set type and create lines and some geometric shapes on a television screen.
2. They offer a selection of character *fonts,* which are easily sized and put in different styles (regular, bold, italics, etc.).
3. They can change the colors of the lettering and fashion outlines and drop-shadows around letters.
4. They can change the colors of the backgrounds and produce multicolored backgrounds, or gradually lightened or darkened versions of the same background color.
5. They can create varying speed rolls (vertical movement) and crawls (horizontal movement) of foreground information over selected backgrounds.
6. Unlike most computer-based models, stand-alone CGs can operate in real time.

Real time operation means they possess the ability to change graphics files, roll, crawl and render new images

Figure 8-13. *A top-of-the-line CG: a two-channel-output Chyron Duet. The Duet has dozens of fonts, along with capabilities for animation, special effects and image processing. With the right software configurations, graphics can be imported from the Chyron to a nonlinear editor or vice versa. Consult with your software or equipment vendors.*

nearly as fast as the CG operator can enter the data. Many computers provide the first four functions described, but few computers can also do items five and six at all, let alone as well as character generators.

The Paint Box

Like the legendary trouble in the Garden of Eden, the paint box came into being because of the Apple. At the end of the 1980s, Steve Wozniak and Steve Jobs' amazing new personal computer, the Apple Macintosh, showed what could be accomplished with a user-friendly interface combined with programs permitting individuals to "paint" on a TV screen. Jobs and his collaborators also inspired other hardware and software designers. The CG already existed, but it operated more like a prodigious, scrolling typewriter than an artist's palette, brushes and easel. And, befitting to its design, most early CG operators were not artists or even production personnel. In that precomputer world, many were just clerk-typists who were retrained as CG specialists—because they could type.

Graphic artists still labored over their easels and spilled paint on their hands. Inspired by Apple's Macintosh, TV equipment manufacturers created machines to lure artists away from their studios. They designed equipment capable of producing the same graphic artwork traditionally created with conventional techniques but with user-friendly interfaces like the Apple. Instead of making artists learn computer languages and programming skills, they designed computers responsive to artists' needs. As shown in Figure 8-14, they created electronic, pressure-sensitive tablets and pens to apply the pressure. By touching simple menu boxes with the pen, the artist can access any color imaginable and can size and shape the pen from a thin, sharp line to a wide, wispy brush stroke (or air brush), producing the video equivalent of illustrator-quality images. Plus, paint box artists can bring any still video image into this environment, cut, size and paste it into other artwork, modify it through a function called stenciling, color or paint over it and more (see Figure 8-15 on plate 5 of the color plate section).

Figure 8-14. *A paint box artist uses a digital paintbrush on a Quantel Paintbox F.A.T. (The initials stand for "full animation toolset.")*
Photo courtesy of Quantel.

Video Still Storage and Retrieval

Completed graphics can be stored and retrieved in five different ways. They can be:

1. stored temporarily within the CG or paint box's memory;
2. recorded as a frame or "page" on hard or removable disks (note: These storage options can either be component parts of CG/paint box hardware or separate peripheral devices);
3. recorded on a separate, nondedicated ESS storage device or a disk-based archival system or station server used as a common file storage device for the many sources found in a studio;
4. directly recorded onto videotape and then integrated into a live TV show or edited into a videotape at a later postproduction session; or
5. temporarily stored on a *frame-store synchronizer,* a device that corrects errors in videotape playbacks and live video feeds via microwave or satellite.

Retrieval of images using any of these devices usually takes just a push of a button or two and a waiting time of a second or less.

Style Pointers: Organic and Synthetic Backgrounds

Entire college courses and textbooks are devoted to graphic arts, but there are a few basic techniques that are widespread enough to give beginners a starting point in composing graphics. Backgrounds for graphics have evolved a great deal due to the evolution of computer-based equipment. Editors and animation specialists are no longer content to use black backgrounds with white letters. Even plain, one-color foundations are increasingly rare for building professional-looking graphics. Now backgrounds can have a plethora of colors, textures and movements. There is a trend toward combining organic and synthetic elements. For example, an organic background can contain video footage of natural elements— trees, water, grass or smoke. This can permit the background to move or change texture. It provides an interesting, but not overwhelming, backdrop for building a composition with synthetic letters and symbols. Another approach is to use layering for backgrounds. This method can also mix organic with synthetic elements. For example, a background for a message about the federal government can layer together pictures of the bald eagle, the Washington Monument and a portrait of Abraham Lincoln. Any or all of the elements can move across the screen, and there is even more artistic freedom.

Computer-Based Graphics and Animation

In the 1990s, many computer companies and software designers dedicated themselves to erasing the distinctions between video graphic production and computer graphic production. This was a natural path of development, because it is easier to create graphics for both computers and video applications in the digital domain. The only problem is converting the completed work back to analog format for use by analog equipment. And in a digital turn of the worm, some computer programs can now remotely operate standard analog video production equipment, making use of this equipment easier and increasing the graphic artist's productivity.

Software companies also continue to challenge high-priced video paint boxes with sophisticated drawing and picture editing software such as Adobe Illustrator, After Effects, Macromedia's Freehand and Adobe Photoshop. These extremely powerful production tools can create graphics, incorporate photos and video into graphics and output their products to either analog or digital video. Some of the more popular three-dimensional animation software packages include Maya and Light Wave. Due to bankruptcies, mergers, name changes, updates and new companies springing up frequently, all this software information is due to change over the life of this textbook. See Figure 8-16, shots 1 through 3, in the color plate section of this book. As you'll discover in Chapter 10, "Video Editing," computer-based systems have almost complete domination of the video editing market.

Ethical and Legal Concerns

Novel technologies often force new issues to the surface. As our ability to effortlessly capture, create and modify graphic materials increases, so do opportunities for abuse. Consider how often a celebrity's head is pasted onto another body on the front pages of lurid supermarket tabloids. Few people really believe there's much truth behind the pictures when the publications themselves generally have questionable credibility. Abuse is not limited to grocery store tabloids, however. A prestigious national news magazine was criticized for manipulating a cover photo of O. J. Simpson to make the former sports star accused of murder appear darker and more menacing. Because video offers motion and sound not possible in print media, making television a potentially more believable medium and escalating the possibilities for abuse to levels limited only by the imagination, video producers face an even greater ethical challenge.

The Evolution of TV Weather Graphics

From TV's earliest days, and continuing at some stations into the late 1960s, weather graphics often consisted of drawings and temperature notations on butcher paper draped over an easel, or equally crude chalk images on a blackboard. In those days, the more "advanced" weathercasters stood with grease pencil or magic marker in hand, drawing on a colored plastic backdrop. To the horror of the American Meteorology Society, most weathercasters were better cartoonists than meteorologists. Many weathercasters were women selected more for their physical attributes than anything else, since weather sadly was the only part of local TV news' "holy trinity" (news, sports and weather) that was open to women during the early years of the medium.

Eventually clever set designers developed the technique of painting weather maps on a wall or flat and mixing metal filings in with the paint (or painting over a metal surface). This allowed the weather reporter to stick magnetic lettering and cutouts of clouds, weather fronts, rain and smiling suns (some wearing sunglasses!) on the metallic map prior to the weathercast. Another breakthrough occurred when designers learned how to treat the magnetic cutouts so the smiling suns appeared to give off pulsating energy rays and water droplets seemed to fall from the clouds.

Weathercasting and the Chroma Key Wall

Standard procedure for today's weathercasters is to work in front of a green or blue chroma key wall, while sophisticated, animated weather graphics are electronically keyed behind them. Weathercasters point to the proper graphic elements by coordinating their movements with the chroma keyed background. As demonstrated in the last chapter, they do this by watching the composite chroma key shot on color monitors placed just off-camera. Watch a weather cast carefully, and you may spot the small handheld remote control device that many weathercasters use to change the graphic images keyed behind them.

Thorough preproduction preparation is necessary so that the weathercast's assortment of data and graphics shows up effortlessly and in the proper sequence during the report. Prior to the show, weathercasters must put their portion of the program together at a computer workstation. Weather information is delivered via an integrated weather information and computer graphic system such as WSI's Weather Spectrum 9000. This combines the weather predictions of WSI's meteorologists, graphics created by the group's staff of artists and weather photos and animations that WSI obtains from satellites (see Figure 8-17). All are transmitted to the station by satellite. The local station's weathercaster combines this proprietary data with local weather information from other sources, such as the AP or UPI regional wires and the National Weather Service, and then decides what predictions to make. Finally, the weathercaster uses the computer workstation to create the weather graphics actually used in the program. In addition to maps, weathercasters produce character-generated graphics, listing highs, lows and expected precipitation for the local forecast. These are keyed over locally produced "weather shots" taped on location or electronically generated maps and backgrounds. See Figure 8-18 on plate 7 of the color plate section for examples of weather graphics. Weather reporting has come a long, long way from the chalkboard and butcher paper, thanks to satellites and computer-generated graphics.

Figure 8-17. *WSI's Weather Spectrum 9000 hardware.*
Photo courtesy of WSI Corporation.

There also are legal issues to ponder, such as copyright. The technology makes it easy to bring any image—from still photos, film or video—into your video-graphic environment. Will you always stop to ask permission and agree to provide the copyright holder with a royalty for its use? That's what the law requires, but the issue is also an ethical consideration, because copyright enforcement is not uniform. These and other legal and ethical questions confront producers daily. Often the answers depend on your personal ethical code and the very practical need to maintain credibility with your audience and retain the respect of your professional colleagues.

In the next three chapters, we'll continue our examination of fundamental television production principles and skills. Next up is a discussion of the recording of video. Since the late 1950s, an increasing proportion of TV programming has been recorded rather than aired live. A basic knowledge of the technology and techniques of video recording is essential to your success in video production.

Important Vocabulary Terms

Art card: A physical, as opposed to electronic, graphic card, usually 11 × 14 inches, featuring drawn or painted representations and symbols, with or without alphanumeric lettering. A card with only alphanumeric lettering is called a graphic card.

Character generator (CG): A device permitting video typesetting for use in electronic graphics production.

Color contrast: The difference in chrominance between foreground and background elements in an image. A production goal is to maintain adequate color contrast to provide a clear distinction between objects on screen.

Crawl: Presentation of alphanumeric information using a row of electronically generated characters parading horizontally across the screen from right to left.

Dead border area: That area of a TV graphic lying outside of the scanned area. The dead border area is not seen in the camera viewfinder.

Electronic still store (ESS): Ampex's name—which has since become the generic phrase—used to describe a device designed for storage and swift, random-access retrieval of individual frames of video.

Essential area: That portion of a graphic close enough to the center to survive picture cutoff. All the information in the essential area appears on the home viewer's screen. Synonymous with the terms "safe title area" and "critical area." Digital TV sets have expanded the area now deemed safe for inserting graphics.

Film chain: The system used to transfer 16 mm film (or 35 mm slides) to video for on-air use or for recording onto an electronic storage medium, such as ESS, videotape, etc. Also called a telecine island. A film chain typically included slide projectors, film projector, a multiplexer and a video camera.

Fonts: Different styles of type. Block fonts, as opposed to thin-lined and decorative fonts, are typically easier to read in on-screen graphics.

Fox box: A graphics innovation pioneered by the Fox TV network that includes text information in a series of boxes at the top or bottom of the screen. These techniques are most often seen in sports or news programming.

Frame-store synchronizer: A device that corrects time-based errors in videotape playbacks and live video feeds via either microwave or satellite transmission. Frame-store synchronizers can also temporarily store and retrieve several video frames.

Graphic card: A physical, as opposed to electronic graphic card, usually 11 × 14 inches, featuring only alphanumeric lettering.

Multiplexer: A box containing movable mirrors that, as part of a film chain, selectively directs either images on 35 mm slides or film into the lens of a video camera.

Organic graphics: Graphics created through traditional (non-computer-based) graphic arts techniques and usually shot with a camera.

Paint box: The generic phrase, derived from Quantel's Paintbox, for a device that electronically emulates an artist's traditional tools, permitting equivalent results.

Random access: With reference to graphics, the ability to directly retrieve a frame of video without the necessity of cycling through other frames to arrive at its point of storage.

Roll: A method of displaying CG output with information entering from the screen's bottom, continuing up and exiting the top of the TV screen. Also called a scroll.

Safe title area: See "Essential area."

Scanned area: That portion of the TV graphic visible on the camera's viewfinder. The entire scanned area does not necessarily appear on the home viewer's screen due to picture cutoff.

Scroll: A method of displaying CG output with information entering from the screen's bottom, continuing up and exiting the top of the screen. Also called a roll.

Slide chain: A carousel slide projection unit that was used as part of a film chain to transfer 35 mm slides to video.

Synthetic graphics: Television graphics created via computer-based techniques.

Telecine island: See "Film chain."

chapter **9**

Video Recording

The years 1947 to 1957, television's first decade, featured many hours of live programming, although a considerable percentage consisted of old movies. But from the start, industry leaders looked for ways to preserve their expensive live productions for archival and repeat broadcast uses. Performers, too, wanted to record several versions of their performances and then edit them to show only their best work, a practice common first in motion pictures and later when recording became an acceptable radio network practice. Recording is a vital part of all phases of modern video production, and there's a bewildering array of methods available. This chapter provides an introduction to the most common technologies, some historical perspective and a look at contemporary trends.

Magnetic Recording Basics

We'll begin by discussing how analog magnetic tape records audio and video signals. Whether we speak about recording audio or video on tape, the method is essentially the same. In previous chapters we explained how microphones and cameras convert sound and light energy into electrical patterns that are analogous to their sound and light counterparts. Traditionally, these analog electrical patterns were recorded in their "natural" analog state. However, many modern recording techniques involve converting these analog patterns into digitally encoded data. Although magnetic tape remains the most popular medium for storage and retrieval of both analog signals and digitally encoded data, tapeless recording technologies are gaining popularity and are likely to replace tape in the future.

But how does magnetic tape record either analog signals or digital data? Perhaps a greatly simplified analogy helps: Let's take a long, rectangular box of iron filings and pass a magnet over them from one end of the box to the other. Attracted to the magnet as it passes over, the iron filings in the box rearrange themselves into a new pattern, approximating the path the magnet traveled. Now imagine that instead of a box of iron filings, something more sophisticated is used: Mylar plastic tape with an *emulsion* (coating) of extremely tiny oxide (or metal) particles. And instead of passing a magnet over the tape, the tape passes across the face of a stationary magnet. In tape recorders, this stationary device is an electromagnet called a *head*. When magnetic tape comes near a head, the particles on the tape magnetically realign themselves at the subatomic level into new patterns determined by the electrical current fed to the head. When it's time to play back the audio or videotape, another head or (set of heads) "reads" these patterns in a manner that reverses the process. Digital audio and video are recorded on magnetic tape in the same way, the difference being that the audio and video information is first converted to a series of digital, binary codes rather than into a varying analog waveform.

An analog *videotape recorder* (VTR) has both audio and video heads. The analog VTR's audio heads record sound in unison with the video. Video is much more complex than audio, and the video signal potentially requires more than 200 times the tape space of a simple audio signal. So running analog tape past stationary audio-type heads to record a video signal is impractical. A 1/4-inch analog tape would have to roar past a stationary head at a speed of hundreds of *ips* (inches per second), a daunting challenge to tape transport designers. Compare this to the standard reel-to-reel audio recording/playback speed of just 7.5 ips. Engineers tried many approaches to the problem, eventually learning that an assembly of rotating video heads permitted them to use a slow tape speed while increasing the head-to-tape "writing" speed dramatically. This discovery and its application led to the first commercially successful videotape recorder, and the dramatic development of video recording technology began.

Videotape History and Development

The history of videotape is a history of formats introduced to fill a specific role in some phase of television production, followed by a fight for survival as manufacturers of competing videotape formats vied for critical market shares. Compared to *kinescoping,* a somewhat crude method of recording programs directly from a TV screen with a 16 mm film camera, videotape was a boon to the industry. Videotape renders better-quality recordings than kinescopes, and unlike film, videotape is easily erased and re-used. The first of many videotape formats was the *quadruplex* (or simply *quad*) method, developed by Ampex and other manufacturers in 1956. The quad format features four rotating video heads, from which it gets its name (see Figure 9-1). The quad format was a milestone development, but it was a *segmented format* (a videotape format in which an entire video frame is not contained in one 360-degree head pass across the tape), so it could not support freeze frames or slow- and fast-motion playback.

U-Matic

In 1971 Sony introduced the *U-matic* format, featuring a 3/4-inch tape housed in an easy-to-use cassette. Recorders using tape in such cassettes are usually called *VCRs* (videocassette recorders) rather than VTRs. The smaller format made portable recorders possible. U-matic machines were less expensive and easier to maintain and operate than quad machines. U-matic's compact proportions and tape economy were made possible by partially wrapping the tape around a rotating cylindrical chamber containing the video heads, a recording process called *helical-scan* (also called slant-track) recording. U-matic's relatively small size, light weight and economy made electronic news gathering (ENG) possible. However, the U-matic format did not allow combining the camera and recorder into a single unit: The U-matic recorder was attached to the camera

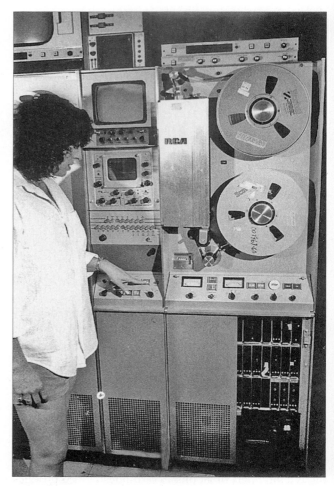

Figure 9-1. *Quad machines were hardly portable. This quad machine is taller (and weighs much, much more) than this videotape operator. But if you think this quad is big, one of RCA's first videotape machines, the all-vacuum-tube, no-transistor TVT-1B was so huge that its components were housed in seven, eight-foot-high electronic relay racks, each 21 inches wide.*

by a cable (see Figure 9-2). U-matic tape was an *unsegmented format,* recording an entire video frame in a single head pass. This unsegmented design enabled later-model U-matic VCRs to play back still frames and slow and fast motion—a big creative assist in editing.

Videotape machines exhibit flaws in playback that are referred to as *time base errors,* deviations in the timing of the video signal's *synchronization (sync) pulses,* which ensure that all the video equipment is performing in perfect simultaneity, caused by mechanical tape speed and tension variations during recording and playback of all these lines of video information. U-matic video, with its more visible time base errors, was not technically acceptable for broadcast until the digital *time base corrector* (TBC) appeared in 1973. Early TBCs were expensive

Figure 9-2. *The old and the new: It was an athletic feat to carry around a heavy camera on one shoulder and a U-matic recorder on a strap over the other. Camcorders changed all that, and they've continued to get smaller and smaller ever since.*

One-Inch Type C Helical

Manufacturers working on a replacement for the bulky, two-inch quad format eventually invented three successively better reel-to-reel, helical-scan videotape formats called *one-inch types A, B* and *C*. Type C, the best, rendered a better picture than quad and used cheaper reel-to-reel tape, and its recorder was smaller and lighter. Type C replaced quad as the premium TV broadcast format in the American market and remained a top choice through the early 1990s (see Figure 9-4).

Half-Inch Helical Scan for Consumers

In the mid-1970s, Sony and Panasonic created a new consumer video market with their relatively inexpensive *Betamax* and *VHS* (Video Home System) 1/2-inch cassette formats for use with much smaller machines, popularly called VCRs. Sony initially refused to license their Betamax patents to other manufacturers, but Matsushita, Panasonic's parent company, did, and VHS recorders flooded the country. Sony's Betamax languished, eventually disappearing from the market.

Neither Betamax nor VHS were ever considered acceptable for broadcast or multiple-generation (making a copy of a copy) editing by professionals.

A more expensive enhanced version of VHS called *S-VHS* (super VHS) appeared in 1987. S-VHS provided better video than VHS, but consumers were satisfied with the performance of VHS and showed little interest in paying more for higher resolution pictures. S-VHS enjoyed

($20,000 or more) but they permitted U-matic machines to meet Federal Communications Commission (FCC) standards. Early TBCs stored and corrected only a few lines of video at a time. Later TBCs stored and corrected a full frame or more of incoming video at a time. Such TBCs are sometimes called frame synchronizers. Recorders that require TBCs now have them built in (see Figure 9-3). As introduced briefly in Chapter 5, a *vectorscope* is used to measure your picture's color, relative to a color bar standard. See Tech Manual 9-2 for more information on the operation of vectorscopes.

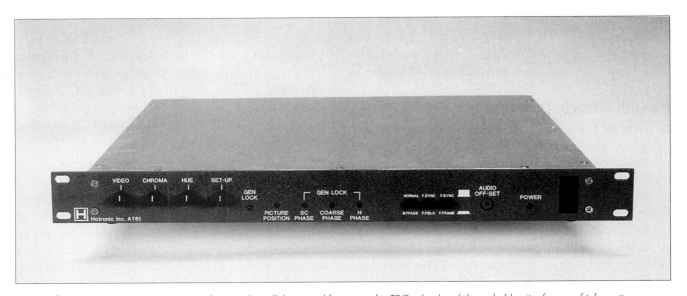

Figure 9-3. *This Hotronic AT61 Frame Synchronizer has all the typical functions of a TBC, plus the ability to hold entire frames of information. It can freeze either a field or a frame, plus adjust video level, color (chroma), tint (hue) and contrast (setup).*

Photo courtesy of Hotronic Corporation.

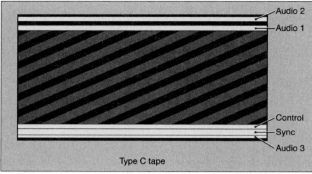

1.

2.

Figure 9-4. *In shot 1, we see that type C offers three audio tracks, plus an optional fourth, and a data-quality audio track, used to record the time code needed for precise videotape editing. Time code is explained in detail a little later, in Chapter 10. Running at a tape speed of only 9.6 ips compared to quad's 15 ips and providing more recording time on a tape half as wide, type C, as seen in its production studio configuration in shot 2, was a great advancement. But even smaller, less expensive and easier-to-use formats became available, and the heavy, bulky, expensive, battery-powered type C portable recorder was never a popular ENG/EFP machine. Modern production often takes place outside the studio, and a format small enough for use in both studio and EFP/ENG applications has great appeal.*

some success in the industrial and educational video market, but it was not widely accepted by professionals.

8mm Helical Scan for Consumers

In the mid-1980s Sony introduced *Video8,* a format using tape 8mm wide with video performance roughly equivalent to VHS. The 8mm format allowed manufacturers to build camcorders somewhat smaller than those using the 1/2-inch (approximately 12mm) VHS format. This made Video8 a popular consumer camcorder format although it never threatened VHS for home recording of TV programs off the air or cable. An enhanced version of the format called *HI8* provided performance roughly the same as S-VHS. Although both these 8mm analog formats remain in use, their popularity declined dramatically with the arrival of 1/4-inch digital formats.

Sony introduced a digital version of the format, called *Digital8,* in 1999. Although still using 8mm tape, Digital8 is similar to the 1/4-inch DV format (discussed below) in terms of technical performance. As of this writing, the future of Digital8 is uncertain because of DV's greater popularity.

Half-Inch Helical Scan for Professionals

In 1981, Sony announced a 1/2-inch format superior to U-matic and practically equal in quality to one-inch type C for acquiring original footage, if not for editing. Professionals initially scoffed, but Sony's *Betacam* format was revolutionary in its use of *component video recording.* Instead of combining luminance and chrominance information into a single signal as with *composite video recording,* component video processes and records them separately. Separating the video into components and processing them independently increased the quality of the end product.

Betacam's 1/2-inch tape made it possible to combine camera and recorder into a single unit, or *camcorder*. Betacam became the preferred technology for ENG/EFP, and the significant savings for both hardware and tape (compared to one-inch type C) also made Betacam attractive for studio productions. An improved version of Betacam called *Betacam-SP* ("Superior Performance") came along in 1987 and was used in the majority of broadcast stations in the mid-1990s (see Figure 9-5).

Panasonic's *M format* (1982) and an improved *M-II format* (1986) competed unsuccessfully with Sony's Betacam. Panasonic's product was incompatible with Betacam but less expensive. Because of Sony's headstart in

1.

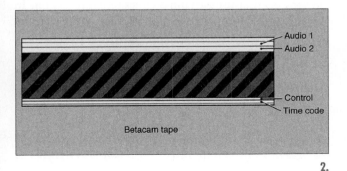

2.

Figure 9-5. *In shot 1, a Betacam recorder. Shot 2 shows the audio, video, control and time code tracks found on a Betacam tape.*

Shot 1 courtesy of Sony Corp.

the market, M-II never seriously threatened Betacam's dominance in professional circles.

Digital Video Recording

The methods of recording discussed to this point have all been analog formats. All analog recordings are stored electrical patterns approximating those of the sound or light energy's original form. The electrical patterns are analogous to the originals. As analog signals are processed, amplified and edited through multiple *generations* (a generation occurs each time an audio or video copy is made), errors multiply, causing a gradual mutation in the original sound or picture. But *digital recording* techniques convert sound and pictures to easy-to-reproduce data consisting of only two discrete energy levels represented numerically by either a one or a zero. Combinations of ones and zeros make up digital "words" representing, but not analogous to, the original sound or picture.

Digital video recording involves the process of digitization of analog information, and often the process of *compression*. A thorough explanation of these two processes would require many pages of highly detailed technical information written by a staff of engineers. Instead, we offer a general explanation of these concepts in Tech Manual 9-1 for those who wish to explore these topics a bit more deeply.

Professional Digital Videotape Formats

A number of digital tape formats have competed, and many still compete, in the professional marketplace. Even seasoned video professionals have trouble keeping track of their claims and counterclaims. In this introductory text, we'll provide only a fundamental review of a few digital videotape formats.

We should note as we begin this discussion that the technical parameters of some formats have been accepted as industry standards by the Society of Motion Picture and Television Engineers (SMPTE). Some digital formats (such as D-1 and D-2) are referred to simply by their SMPTE designation. Other formats (such as DVCPRO), although designated as standardized formats by SMPTE, are better known by the name given them by their developers.

D-1 Component

Sony introduced the component digital video recording format known as *D-1* in 1987. D-1 digitized video is uncompressed, eliminating compression errors. The result was a format with high quality video that does not degrade rapidly with each new generation, but it carried a hefty price tag because the machines were expensive, and converting to D-1 also required changing many other pieces of production equipment as well.

D-2 Digital Composite

Ampex's *D-2* (1988), the composite digital cassette answer to analog one-inch type C, used 3/4-inch tape in a cassette package and no compression in the recording process. D-2 was easily integrated into a production facility's existing structure and sold at half the price of D-1 (and about the same as some type C analog machines), thus providing at the time an attractive lower cost digital alternative. However, composite formats such as D-2 and D-3 (discussed below) are considered inferior to more modern component formats, so D-2 is seldom encountered today.

D-3, D-5 and D-6 (and Why There's No D-4)

Panasonic introduced *D-3* (1991), an uncompressed composite digital format using 1/2-inch tape and offering virtually all the features of D-2. D-3's smaller packaging made its use in camcorders possible, whereas D-2's larger cassettes restricted that format to the studio (see Figure 9-6). Being a composite format, D-3's popularity faded with the introduction of later component formats such as D-5.

D-5 (1994) is a Panasonic component format using the same size cassettes as D-3 (1/2-inch tape). D-5 is an uncompressed format using 10-bit digitizing, compared to 8 bits for D-1, D-2 and D-3. Panasonic marketed it

Figure 9-7. *A D-5 digital format videotape recorder.*
Photo Courtesy of Panasonic Corporation.

in the United States to assist high-end producers in sophisticated graphics production and to transfer motion picture film to tape (see Figure 9-7).

Since it's next in line after D-3, why isn't D-5 numbered D-4? Panasonic did not choose the next logical number designation, D-4, for their 1/2-inch component product because the Japanese consider any reference to the number four as unlucky.

D-6 (1995), introduced by Toshiba/BTS (Philips and later Thomson), is a digital format for recording up to 64 minutes of high-definition (HD) video on cassettes the size of the large D-1 cassettes. D-6 has been a popular choice for recording HD programming in Europe and Japan, but has been less successful than D-5 HD (discussed below) in the United States.

Formats for Compressed Digital Video

In addition to the D-formats that record uncompressed digital video, there are a number of other digital formats that use varying degrees of compression. In general, the compressed digital formats are not quite as good for editing as the uncompressed formats just discussed.

By the mid-1990s, most professional production facilities were using some version of the analog Betacam format. Responding to Panasonic's competitive digital formats and to pacify those with a large investment in analog Betacam equipment, Sony introduced *Digital Betacam* (1993), sometimes shortened to DigiBeta, a format with one foot in the analog camp and the other in the digital domain. Properly set up with optional equipment, Digital Betacam recorders and camcorders

Figure 9-6. *Panasonic's D-3 format comes equipped to accept three different sizes of 1/2-inch tape, capable of recording video from 50 minutes to four hours in length.*

Photo courtesy of Panasonic Corporation.

provide interformat compatibility between Sony Betacam SP analog component tapes and Sony digital component video. Sony markets a family of Digital Betacam products, and *Betacam SX* targets the professional ENG market. Betacam SX uses 1/2-inch cassettes, but uses MPEG-2 compression with a *compression ratio* of about 10:1. That's a lot compared to other formats, and a factor that concerns some professionals who need a format capable of multigenerational editing. However, Betacam SX equipment sells for about the same price as analog Betacam SP, and its tape costs are lower. Sony also offers a dockable Betacam SX recorder, the DNV-5, that can be attached to some camcorders originally equipped with analog recorders, making Betacam SX attractive to broadcasters wanting to "go digital." As an added incentive, Sony offered the "hybrid" DNW-A100 Betacam SX recorder containing both a tape recorder and hard disk drive (for random-access digital editing) in the same box (see Figure 9-8). In 2001 Sony announced yet another 1/2-inch digital format, *MPEG IMX.* Like Betacam SX, this format uses MPEG-2 compression but provides video quality superior to Betacam SX, but inferior to DigiBeta. MPEG IMX's popularity is helped by the fact that an IMX machine can play back not only IMX tapes, but also DigiBeta, Betacam SX and analog Betacam SP. Sony initially promoted MPEG IMX as a studio-only format, but the company soon introduced a camcorder using the new format. SMPTE designated MPEG IMX as D-10, adding it to the growing list of standardized digital formats.

JVC also introduced a 1/2-inch component digital format initially called *Digital-S.* In 1999 SMPTE designated

Figure 9-9. *A JVC D-9/Digital-S camcorder.*
Photo courtesy of JVC Corporation.

the format as D-9 and JVC now uses this designation rather than Digital-S when referring to the format. D-9 uses a rather mild 3.3:1 compression ratio. JVC claims, and some professionals agree, that D-9 provides DigiBeta performance at an economy price (see Figure 9-9).

Quarter-Inch Digital Formats

In 1995 a consortium of Japanese companies including Sony, Panasonic, JVC and Sharp introduced a consumer-oriented digital format called *DV,* for "digital video," using tape only 1/4-inch wide, the same size as conventional reel-to-reel analog audio tape. The new format generated great interest among educational and industrial producers as well as broadcasters seeking a high-quality, low-cost ENG format. Responding to this interest, Panasonic and Sony in 1996 unveiled improved versions of DV called *DVCPRO* and *DVCAM* targeted to the business and professional markets. Although they use different tape speeds and tape emulsions, both employ 5:1 compression and produce video rivaling analog Betacam SP. SMPTE has designated DVCPRO as *D-7* but the format is best known as DVCPRO.

Panasonic later introduced an enhanced version, the *DVCPRO-50,* featuring a digitizing process equaling Digital Betacam. The enhanced format required adding two more heads to the recorders and doubling the tape speed, but tapes recorded using the "basic" DVCPRO format will still play on the "improved" machines (see Figure 9-10, shot 2).

These 1/4-inch systems allow editing the "old-fashioned way"—in a linear mode (machine to machine)—or you can transfer their digital signals (like virtually any

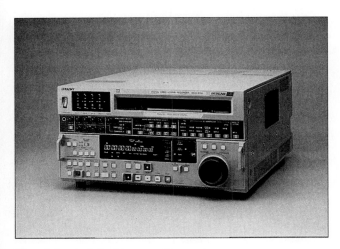

Figure 9-8. *The hybrid Betacam SX recorder.*
Photo courtesy of Sony Corporation.

1.

2.

Figure 9-10. *In shot 1, the Panasonic DVCPRO camcorder, and in shot 2, a DVCPRO-50 video recorder. The DVCPRO and, especially, the DVCPRO-50 gained wide acceptance for business and ENG applications during the late 1990s.*

Photos courtesy of Panasonic Corporation.

standard digital video format's output) directly to computers, often using an input-output connection based on the industry-standard *IEEE 1394* serial bus interface or a version of it, such as Apple's Firewire or Sony's I.LINK. Once in the editing system, the digital video is edited in a nonlinear fashion using whichever software the producer prefers. Linear and nonlinear editing are explained in detail in Chapter 10.

Sony Strikes Back

In 2003, Sony introduced its *XDCAM* technology for digital recording. Sony's XDCAM was unique in that XDCAM camcorders allowed the operator to record using several different digital formats, including the company's DVCAM format discussed later. In addition, XDCAM camcorders use blue-violet laser technology (often referred to as "Blu-ray") to record the data on an optical disc. Other "tapeless" recording systems are also discussed below.

MiniDV

We have not mentioned *MiniDV* to this point, yet college students may be most familiar with this format. Where does MiniDV fit into this story? MiniDV is simply DV tape in a physically smaller cassette. MiniDV reduces the recording time available (assuming similar tape speeds) compared to the larger "standard" DV cassettes, but makes extremely small and inexpensive digital camcorders possible. A comparison of a MiniDV cassette with the first recording format (2-inch quad), or even a 1-inch type C reel, visually demonstrates how advancing technology has put ever more information into ever-smaller packages (see Figure 9-11).

MiniDV recorders will not play standard DV, because DV cassettes are too large, but DV VTRs will play MiniDV tapes, although on some VTRs an adaptor may be needed. In addition, DVCAM and DVCPRO VTRs will play DV and MiniDV tapes. There is also some compatibility regarding playback between DVCAM and DVCPRO, depending on the make and model of the VTR. DVCPRO and DVCPRO-50 machines seem to be the most flexible when it comes to playing tapes recorded using other DV-based formats.

We should also mention that the machine used for recording most often determines the format used, not the tape being used. For example, a Panasonic DVCPRO tape can be used in a Sony DVCAM recorder to record in DVCAM format. In general, however, we would recommend using a tape designed for the format being recorded for consistent results and peace of mind.

Figure 9-11. *Professional quality videotapes have certainly gotten smaller through the years. From right, a type C reel-to-reel tape, a small quad reel and a MiniDV cassette.*

High-Definition Formats

As mentioned in Chapter 4, Hollywood movie producers in the 1950s experimented with a variety of wide-screen formats in their quest to lure consumers away from the "small screen" images provided by television. It was not until the FCC adopted rules in 1996 for digital television (DTV) transmission that broadcasters could offer pictures rivaling movie theaters in terms of both aspect ratio and resolution. Although wide-screen images can be, and often are, presented in standard definition (SD), the larger format images scream for higher resolution if they are to be truly impressive. As viewers increasingly purchased wide-screen displays capable of handling high-definition images, equipment makers brought forward a variety of recording formats for capturing high-def video.

The larger aspect ratio (16:9) and vastly improved image resolution of HD places a greater burden on almost every piece of video production hardware and software. In the case of video recording, HD translates into the need to store more digital information than for SD images in either traditional small-screen (4:3 aspect ratio) or wide-screen (16:9 aspect ratio) format.

As was true of standard definition, there are a number of competing HD formats. Unlike SD formats, however, all HD formats are digital, and most employ some degree of compression to deal with the enormous amount of data required. And, as always, there is a compromise between image quality and required storage capacity.

One popular high-end professional HD format is *D-5 HD.* Panasonic's D-5 HD is an extension of the company's standard-definition D-5 format that uses 1/2-inch tape as the storage medium. D-5 HD is targeted to mastering (and editing) very high-quality HD images in a studio or sophisticated remote production environment. Another high-end professional format using 1/2-inch tape is Sony's *HDCAM* and a higher performance version, *HDCAM SR.*

Stepping down a bit in terms of technical superiority, if not necessarily in price, Panasonic offers *DVCPRO HD* (also known as DVCPRO 100), an extension of its DVCPRO format, for professional HD acquisition and editing. A major advantage of DVCPRO HD is that the format uses the same 1/4-inch tape as earlier versions of the DVCPRO format. DVCPRO HD equipment is also backward compatible, which means it can play back tapes recorded using any DVCPRO format and even

consumer level DV tapes. DVCPRO HD is, therefore, especially attractive to professionals wanting to move up to HD who already have standard-definition DVCPRO equipment and, perhaps, lots of video archived on DVCPRO tapes.

Sony has *XDCAM HD,* an extension of the company's standard-definition digital format XDCAM. Like the SD format, the XDCAM HD uses optical Blu-ray discs as the storage medium.

JVC also offers a competing HD format for professionals, *Digital-S HD,* more commonly called *D-9 HD.* Just as DVCPRO HD is an extension of DVCPRO-50, Digital-S HD is based on the Digital-S format. Digital-S HD uses the same cassettes as standard-definition Digital-S, and Digital-S HD machines can play Digital-S recordings.

The HD formats introduced to this point are all considered "professional grade," because of both their performance and the expense of their associated hardware.

In 2003 a consortium of manufacturers (again including Sony, JVC and Sharp, this time along with Canon) introduced *HDV,* a high-definition format developed primarily for the consumer market. HDV is yet another formulation based on the original DV format from which DVCAM and the various flavors of DVRPRO evolved. Unlike the professional DVCPRO HD format, however, HDV retains the same bit rate as conventional DV and uses a rather severe form of MPEG-2 compression to do so. Even the audio associated with HDV is compressed using a lossy algorithm (see Tech Manual 9-1 for a discussion of lossy compression). Accordingly, there are some trade-offs in terms of image quality and durability in postproduction editing. Even so, the HDV format brings the cost of shooting HD down to levels affordable by prosumers and consumers.

It is also important to remember that, when discussing all the digital formats, the distinction between "professional grade" and "consumer grade" video becomes seriously blurred. "Consumer" digital formats in the 21st century easily exceed the video standards of many "professional" analog formats popular two decades ago.

Video on Disk

In typical Hollywood fashion, films such as 1993's *Rising Sun* projected viewers into the future by showing tiny discs used for high-resolution video recording and editing. In this instance, Hollywood's futuristic fantasy was only slightly premature, as we will explain later.

Magnetic Disk and Optical Disc Recording

As you recall from Chapter 6 (Audio), the term "disc," with a "c," often refers to optical media while magnetic media (like floppy disks or computer drives) are associated with the term "disk," with a "k," but you'll frequently see these two terms used interchangeably. Many disk-based systems use the same magnetic principles discussed regarding videotape recording, but some employ optical-scanning techniques. As we noted in Chapter 6, the common audio compact disc *(CD)* or digital video disc *(DVD)* uses a laser to read the encoded information. Optical disc recordings are noted for their durability because, unlike tape, the "head" reading the information on the disc never contacts the disc's surface. Magnetic disk systems use heads that "float" just above the disc's surface and, in theory, never touch it (see Figure 9-12).

The optical disc provides excellent playback capabilities, but recording was initially somewhat more difficult, and disc recording was restricted to high-tech manufacturing facilities. However, the computer industry developed technology that first made one-time

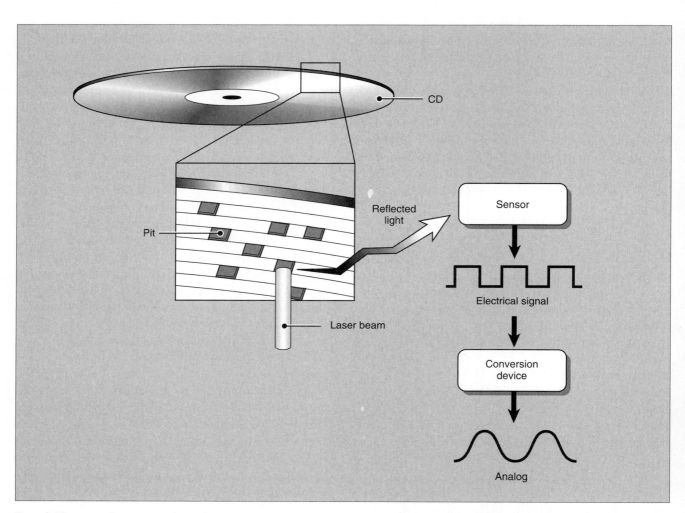

Figure 9-12. *During the commercial manufacture of an optical disc such as a CD or DVD, the digital information is impressed in the form of small pits in a metallic substrate that forms the heart of the disc. The varying shape of the pits is what corresponds to the ones and zeros constituting the digital information stored on the disc. The pits form tracks spiraling from the edge of the disc inward. A small beam of laser-generated light shines on these microscopic pits as the disc rotates during replay, and the pits modulate the beam, causing the reflected light to vary according to the physical configuration of the pits. A sensor detects these variations in the reflected light and converts them back into electrical signals which are amplified, processed and eventually passed on to another device or converted to analog output for presentation as sounds or images understandable to humans. When digital information is written to a recordable CD or DVD by a consumer using a disc drive, the pits are formed using heat produced by a laser beam that is more intense than when playing the disc. This is why a newly recorded disc is warm to the touch and why recording to a CD or DVD using this approach is called "burning" a disc.*

"burning" (recording) to disc possible and later developed discs for consumers that can be recorded, erased and rerecorded many times.

Hard Disk Drive Digital Video Storage

Another method of digital recording and storage has found great favor among both professional and not-so-professional video producers: *hard disk drive* (HDD) storage (see Figure 9-13). These devices use magnetic recording technology. Once analog video and its accompanying audio are digitized, they can be stored on speedy, high-capacity computer hard drives. Compared to full-motion video, still images require relatively modest HDD technology. It was logical that one of the first uses for HDDs in video production was in *electronic still store* (ESS) devices, discussed in Chapter 8. The ESS quickly replaced the traditional trays of 35 mm film slides in modern production facilities. These ESS devices provide almost instant random access to any image stored on the disk. Unlike still images, full-motion video and audio files require a huge amount of space even when compressed. Manufacturers responded to this need for greater capacity in the 1990s by developing HDD storage solutions for larger and larger files. One popular solution is the *hard disk array,* a single device containing a number of hard disks and multiple actuators (disk-reading devices) sandwiched together. This *RAID* (redundant array of independent drives) technology allows fast microprocessors to read data stored on

several disks simultaneously, reducing the problem of inadequate data access speeds associated with conventional disk drives that hampered real-time playback of video from disks. This technology originally found applications only in postproduction, where still images or brief segments of moving video were needed. Thanks to advances in HDD technology, broadcasters and cable-system operators now use disk-based *video servers* to provide random-access storage for commercials, promos and even longer segments. Typically, programming is transferred from tape to the server and cached (temporally stored) until playback from the disk. Sometimes newly created programming is recorded directly to the server and, if there is a need to store the programming indefinitely, "dumped back to tape" until needed again. As the capacity of disk and solid-state technology continues to increase even as prices fall, tape is likely to be chosen less often as a medium for archiving audio and video.

Many stations and production houses electronically network digital storage devices, allowing instantaneous transfer of image files throughout their facilities. Some storage devices have removable, easily portable disks, which allow the movement of stored images from place to place using "shoe leather technology" rather than employing hard-wired or wireless networks. Networking all the hardware in a production facility, however, is increasingly popular.

Tapeless Camcorders

Although tape remained the predominant video storage medium throughout the 1990s and the first part of the new century, as evidenced by the many tape-based recording formats previously mentioned, it was clear that tapeless video recording offered many advantages. With the video already on a random-access digital disk or solid-state memory device (any transistorized, semiconductor or film memory that contains no mechanical parts), no time is lost digitizing and transferring it for use in a compatible computer-based editing system. Additionally, tapeless technology provides basic editing capability within the camera. For example, using the camera to do an opening stand-up and then switching to the digital disk or solid-state memory for an edited insert, all while reporting "live" from the field, is entirely practical.

Tapeless consumer-level camcorders using micro hard disk drives, recordable DVDs and solid-state memory devices have enjoyed growing popularity in recent years. Hard-nosed professionals, however, have

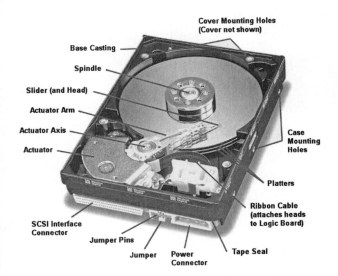

Figure 9-13. *This cutaway view of a hard disk drive reveals the complex architecture of this modern magnetic storage technology.*

Photo courtesy of Western Digital Corporation.

been slower to abandon tape. Many simply considered disk-based equipment too fragile for use in the rough and tumble EFP/ENG environment. Plus, solid-state memory devices have lacked the storage capacity (at an acceptable price) needed to make them practical in a professional environment. Tapeless cameras designed for use by professionals have been on the market for more than a decade, however.

In 1995 Avid and Ikegami jointly introduced a camera targeted for the professional market that used a dockable magnetic hard disk drive as the recording mechanism. The original Avid *CamCutter* recording module recorded component video to a disk capable of storing 20 minutes of compressed video. The limited recording time, the bulkiness of the dockable recorder/camera package, its relatively high power consumption and the cost of the system were barriers to widespread adoption. Development continued, however, and by 1999 a number of Ikegami EditCams (the brand name of Ikegami's tapeless camcorder, as seen in Figure 9-14), were in service, perhaps most notably by the U.S. Army Broadcasting Service.

In addition to the disk-based FieldPak, Ikegami later introduced an interchangeable RAMPak, a solid-state memory module. Although Avid and Ikegami pioneered tapeless video acquisition, they soon were joined by the other major video equipment manufacturers. At this

Figure 9-14. *Ikegami has been a pioneer in the development of professional tapeless camcorders since the middle 1990s, and the EditCam is an example.*

Photo courtesy of Ikegami Electronics.

writing, Sony is offering its XDCAM Professional Disc System using Blu-ray optical discs. Also, Hitachi was using a dockable magnetic hard disk recorder with its cameras, while Panasonic's P2 was using solid-state memory cards. Like Ikegami, Grass Valley's Infinity Series digital camcorders could employ either Iomega REV PRO removable hard disks or CompactFlash solid-state memory cards (see Figure 9-15).

Figure 9-15. *The Grass Valley Infinity Series consists of the Grass Valley Infinity Digital Media Camcorder, the Digital Media Recorder, and the Grass Valley REV PRO drives and removable media.*

Photo courtesy of Grass Valley.

In addition, Focus Enhancements was offering HDD recorders that would dock to certain model JVC, Canon, Ikegami, Panasonic and Sony cameras as well as HDD recorders designed for studio use.

Whether disc/disk systems or solid-state memory technology will dominate tapeless video acquisition in the professional arena is at this writing unknown. Solid-state technology's lack of moving parts is a factor strongly in its favor for the rough and tumble world of field production. However, disc/disk based systems have proven themselves reliable in other professional video applications, and at least initially, such systems offer longer recording times at somewhat lower cost than solid-state solutions. As increasing emphasis is placed on wide-screen high-definition production, recording time (storage capacity) is a significant consideration.

We bring this chapter to a close as we so often do: noting that video production technology is advancing rapidly. Nowhere is this happening faster than in video recording, so predicting the future is risky. However, we will conclude by noting two trends that we think will continue into the future.

First, future recording gear will allow the operator to select the desired recording parameters and not be limited to a single format "native" to a particular brand name or model. Operators will be able to select the number of horizontal and vertical lines of video recorded, the number of pixels per line and the number of video frames per second, all depending on the needs of the particular production. This increased flexibility is already evident in the marketplace, and we believe we've only seen the tip of the iceberg. Increased options are desirable in many ways, but they will require that producers make more choices. That, in turn, means future producers must know more than their predecessors if they are to make wise choices.

A second trend is the transition from tape to other storage media. This trend is presently most apparent at the consumer level, but we expect professionals to migrate to tapeless technologies as their dependability in harsh production environments becomes better proven and prices decline. The potential advantages of tapeless storage media are just too great to do otherwise.

Next, in Chapter 10, we'll discuss how analog and digital video is edited, in both machine-to-machine (linear) format and using computerized (non-linear) methods.

tech manual 9-1 *Analog to Digital Conversion and Compression*

Humans can see and hear sound and pictures only when they are presented as information in analog form. Unfortunately, information in analog form degrades when copied from one machine to another, as commonly happens in the process of TV production. The information holds up much better during production and transmission if it is converted to a series of numbers (digits, hence the term "digital") first, then converted back into analog form just before it's presented to a viewer as a TV program.

How closely digital information represents the original video depends on how the image is converted to digital data. The analog waveform, whether it be audio or video, is constantly and continuously changing, as represented by the dark wavy line in Figure 9-16. One of the first things that must be decided is how often to sample the analog wave, that is, measure the value of the wave and convert that value to a discrete number. If, for example, we sample and measure the value once every second, as illustrated in Figure 9-16, we will miss whatever value(s) the analog wave may have between measurements. The

wave's value may be 2 volts at second number one (T-1) and 3 volts at second number two (T-2), but in between second one and second two the value may have various values between 2 and 3 volts, as in Figure 9-16. However, it could also have zoomed up to 10 volts or fallen to 1 volt. If we sample only once each second,

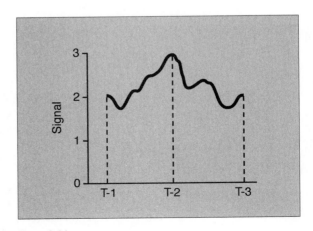

Figure 9-16.

we've missed all the many values the wave may have had <u>between</u> samples. If we convert these two sample values back to analog form, we will have something that looks nothing like the original analog waveform!

If we sample twice as often and convert the values to a number every half second, we get a better representation. If we step up the sample rate to every tenth of a second, we get an even better representation of what the wave is doing and can come closer to duplicating it when we convert back to analog. Obviously, the higher the *sampling* rate, the better the digital data will represent the original analog waveform. Unfortunately, the more often we take a sample, the more numbers we generate. The more numbers, the more storage space we need for the numbers. Clearly, there has to be a compromise when it comes to deciding how often to sample the analog waveform.

In our simple illustration, we've decided to sample only once every second and show the values of the analog waveform at only three times. Those values are seen at T-1, T-2 and T-3 in Figure 9-17. When we connect these three values, as we do in Figure 9-18, to reconstruct the analog waveform seen in Figure 9-16, we get an analog waveform that doesn't look much like the original. Indeed, it doesn't look much like anything we'd recognize as a "wave."

We also must compromise when deciding how precisely we will measure the value of the waveform each time we take a sample. A continuously changing analog waveform has, in theory, an infinite number of values. Just as we cannot take an infinite number of samples, we can't have an infinite number of values. We need to decide how many different discrete values we are interested in having.

If we know our waveform will always have a value somewhere between 0 and 3 volts (as we have done in the diagrams associated with this discussion), we could decide we want four numbers (0, 1, 2 and 3) to represent any particular sample value. If at T-1 the waveform has a value of exactly 2 volts (as it does in our example), we simply assign

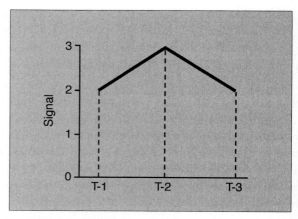

Figure 9-18.

it the number 2. If at T-2 the voltage has jumped to 3 volts, we can assign it the number 3. But what would we do if at T-2 the waveform had a value of 2.6 volts? That's not one of the four discrete values we're using! We can call it a 3 because that's the closest discrete number we've agreed to use, but that means we aren't precisely representing the actual value of the waveform at this particular sample time.

If we doubled the number of discrete values we are willing to use, we would have values of 0, .5, 1, 1.5, 2, 2.5 and 3. Now we could round the 2.6-volt value to 2.5 (rather than 3) and our error would be much less. Our ability to faithfully reproduce the wave when we convert back from digital to analog would be better. Without getting into a discussion of the binary number system and similar arcane matters, let it suffice to say that engineers talk about the number of discrete values recorded during the digitization process in terms of the number of bits used. You may see or hear references to 8-bit sampling, or 16-bit sampling, for example.

So, what does this mean? It means, for example, that a sample rate of 48 kHz (48,000 samples per second) using 16-bit sampling will produce a more accurate representation of an analog audio waveform than will a sample rate of 32 kHz (32,000 samples per second) using 12-bit sampling. We are not only taking more samples each second, we are also making more precise measurements of the value of the analog waveform each time. The higher sample frequency and greater precision of measurement combined will help us more accurately recreate the analog wave. But it will also create a lot more digital information that has to be stored or transmitted. Engineers and technicians often juggle different sample rates and number of bits per sample in trying to establish the "best" combination for a particular application.

Just as early analog recorders employed composite video recording techniques but later changed to recording component video, the trend has been toward digital

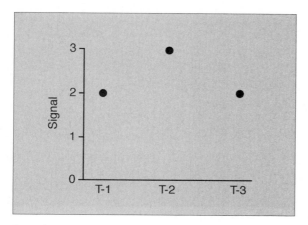

Figure 9-17.

component video recording. Again, without getting too technical, the "best" digital video recording formats use component 4:2:2 sampling, other factors being equal. The first number (4) indicates the sampling rate of the luminance (brightness) information compared to the sampling rate for the red and blue chrominance (color) information, 2:2. With 4:2:2 sampling, the luminance sampling rate is twice that of the color components. Since luminance is more important to the quality of the image reproduced, using a lower sampling rate for the color information is acceptable and saves space. Some "weaker" formats use what is sometimes called "downsampling," such as 4:1:1 sampling, where the color information is sampled once for every four samples of the luminance information. Using 4:2:2 preserves the resolution of the video better; 4:1:1 reduces the amount of digital data produced. Even 4:2:2 is a compromise, but experts agree it's "plenty good enough" even for superlative high-definition video that will be subjected to extensive postproduction editing.

As we've noted, converting information from analog form to digital form creates a lot of data. Were it not for compression, dealing with this glut of numbers would be almost impossible. Compression involves reducing the amount of digital information actually stored (recorded) or transmitted while retaining the ability to reconstruct the original visual image with acceptable resolution. The amount of compression is usually expressed numerically as a compression ratio, such as 10:1 (read as "ten to one"). What that means is that the compressed video signal is only a tenth as large as the original. What is "acceptable" resolution, and therefore how much compression is employed, depends on how the final video product will be distributed and "consumed" by the end user.

Engineers talk about two categories of compression: *Lossless* compression preserves all the original digital information created. *Lossy* compression preserves only part of the original information. Fortunately, video can survive a lot of compression (even lossy compression) and still look very good.

There are many ways to achieve digital compression of video, but one basic idea is to use only those samples that have a different strength value from the sample before and after it. If, for example, five samples in a row all have a strength value very close to 3, we can store the first and last sample and tell the equipment to "fill in" the three middle ones because they are almost identical. There's no need to store all five samples, because the middle three don't tell us much new about the analog information. You can begin to see how a compressed digital signal takes a lot less space than one that is not compressed. In our original example illustrated in Figure 9-16, two of our three samples (T-1 and T-3) did have the exact same value: 2 volts. Although our reconstructed analog signal (seen in Figure 9-17), based on the original three sample values, is a poor representation of the original waveform (as seen in Figure 9-16), it would be even worse if we threw out the value at T-2. Our reconstructed analog waveform would not be a wave at all but simply a flat line indicating <u>no change</u> in the video signal between T-1 and T-3.

It should be clear from this extremely simplified discussion that engineers must make complex decisions about sampling and compression processes, always trying to find an acceptable balance between the quality required of the reconstructed audio and video and the need to keep the demands on data storage devices and transmission systems as low as possible.

tech manual 9-2 *The Vectorscope and Videotape Machines*

As we learned in Chapter 5, the *waveform monitor* (WFM) measures the luminance (brightness) information in a video signal, and the vectorscope measures the other important element of a video signal, its chrominance (color). The vectorscope is useful when checking and/or correcting the color variables of the video when recording during the production stage and when manipulating it during postproduction editing.

Hue and saturation are the two most important chrominance variables the vectorscope measures. *Hue* is the term used to describe a specific color: red, yellow, green, blue

and so forth. *Saturation* refers to the intensity of a color—how much white light is mixed with the color. For example, pink is really red that's been desaturated with white; pastels are "softer" versions of their more color-saturated relatives.

Waveform monitors are valuable tools for setting up cameras prior to production. The WFM is also helpful during a production because it allows the operator to observe the amplitude of the luminance signal during a production and make adjustments to ensure the picture's luminance remains within an acceptable range, neither excessively bright nor dark, all times. Vectorscopes, in contrast, are usually less valuable during the recording process. The display becomes a whirling blur impossible to interpret if there's much movement in the scene, making precise color adjustments difficult. Shooting a static shot of the scene, or a close up of a color test chart, before production begins provides a stable display that can be used for adjusting the color.

WFMs and vectorscopes are used for both analog and digital production. Video quality in the digital domain tends to be more robust than in the analog environment, however, and some techniques evolved to deal with color variations among analog VTRs.

It became customary when making video recordings to begin with color bars fed from either a color bar generator in a production studio, or from an EFP/ENG camera switched so that it feeds color bars to the video recorder. These test bars provide the color standard needed to ensure that tapes recorded at one place on a particular machine will play back with proper color fidelity in other places on other machines. Ideally, images reproduced by Machine A in Hawaii appear exactly as they were recorded on Machine B in Maine. But slight differences in machine setup cause changes in the reproduced image unless Machine A's playback is adjusted to match the unique characteristics of the recorder originally recording the program. Once the playback machine in Hawaii is adjusted (while observing hue and saturation as indicated on the vectorscope) to reproduce the test bars as originally recorded at the head of the tape by the machine in Maine, the color values of scenes in the program itself will also appear as they were intended by the producer.

The vectorscope display is circular and shows color relationships on a 360-degree scale. Before you can use a vectorscope to measure anything, you must be sure the scope itself is properly calibrated. You do this by feeding test color bars into your vectorscope. It's important that the source of these test color bars be reliable and correctly set up, because these parameters then become your standard for comparing signals from all other sources. In most studio and EFP shoots using multiple cameras and other video sources feeding a video switcher, a color bar test signal, fed usually from a test signal generator, comes up on the video switcher, so all you must do is punch up the house's test bars. The vectorscope is connected to the switcher, so the bars appear on the scope. Next, you use the "phase" knob on the scope to rotate the display until the <u>color burst,</u> the shortest-length vector normally shown, is located at 9 o'clock (see Figure 9-19). Color burst is a reference signal that home TV sets use to lock onto and correctly interpret chrominance information in an analog broadcast signal. Next, put the scope's chrominance gain control in the "calibrate" position and adjust the vectorscope's

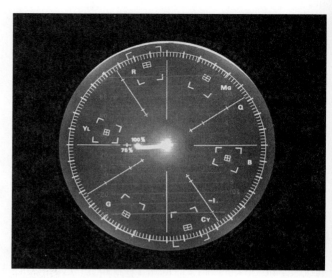

Figure 9-19. *A vectorscope showing the color burst as it should appear when the video system is functioning properly.*

controls until all the color vectors (magenta, blue, cyan, green and yellow) fill their respective boxes etched on the scope's face. Now that the vectorscope is calibrated, you can feed the color bar signal recorded on the tape you want to play to the vectorscope and compare its pattern to that of the reference signal. If its pattern is somewhat different than that of the reference signal, you need to adjust the playback machine's color controls or otherwise adjust the color signal, perhaps using special color-correction amplifiers called processing (proc) amps, before using the video for broadcast or editing (see Figure 9-20).

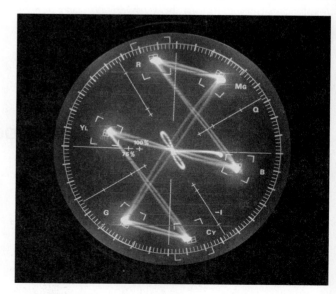

Figure 9-20. *This vectorscope shows a properly functioning video system when color bars are used as the test signal. Deviation from this display when passing the standard color bar signal is an indication that adjustments are needed.*

WFMs and vectorscopes are available as separate pieces of test equipment, but often these days they are combined in a single device. The trend in video monitoring equipment is to make gear that can not only perform as a WFM/vectorscope for both analog and digital video, but also monitor the bit stream of digital video for a variety of additional parameters. Computer-based video editing systems also typically provide built-in vectorscope and WFM functions. These tools provide a convenient means of comparing the color characteristics and luminance of video from various sources and bring all video into conformity. They also make it easier for a creative producer to modify the color and brightness of the entire program or selected parts of it to create a distinctive "look."

Important Vocabulary Terms

Betacam: Sony's successful 1/2-inch analog component videotape format. Betacam and improved Betacam SP provide video quality similar to one-inch type C and have been the top ENG format for those who can afford it.

Betacam SP: Sony's second generation Betacam format, with improved quality in nearly all categories. The "SP" stands for "superior performance."

Betacam SX: Betacam SP's all-digital successor, designed for high-sample-rate, high-quality digital production.

Betamax: Sony's now-defunct analog format for consumer VCRs, beaten out in the marketplace by Panasonic's VHS format.

Camcorder: A combination camera/videocassette recorder. Camcorders use cassettes containing 1/2-inch or smaller tape.

CamCutter: A video camcorder developed jointly by Avid and Ikegami that uses a digital disk rather than tape as the recording medium.

CD: A CD (compact disc) is an optical disc-based playback-only digital storage medium. A CD operates on the same principle and looks much like a DVD but has much less storage capacity.

Component video recording: Recording technology that processes and records luminance and chrominance information separately rather than combining them as in composite recording. Separating the components provides video with fewer unwanted artifacts.

Composite video recording: Recording technology that processes luminance and chrominance together, rather than separately, as in component video recording. See above.

Compression: The process of eliminating nonessential information in a digitized audio or video signal. Compression allows the transmission of a digital signal through a smaller channel or storage of more information in a given space. See also "Compression ratio."

Compression ratio: The amount of compression performed on a digital signal. A compression ratio of 10:1 (read as "ten to one") means the compressed video signal is only a tenth as large as the original.

D-1, D-2, D-3 and D-5: Four uncompressed cassette formats for digital video recording. D-1 and D-5 record component video, and D-2 and D-3 are composite digital formats. D-2 and D-3 are considered obsolete formats. D-1 and D-5 remain viable, with D-5 being more widely used.

D-5 HD: An enhanced version of Panasonic's D-5 format targeted for top-quality, high-definition applications.

D-6: Toshiba's digital format for recording high-definition video on cassettes the size of large D-1 cassettes.

D-7: See "DVCPRO."

D-9/Digital-S and D-9/Digital-S HD: Originally called Digital-S, D-9 is a component digital format developed by JVC using a 1/2-inch tape cassette and a 3.3 to 1 (3.3:1) compression ratio. D-9 compares favorably to Sony's more popular Digital Beta format. D-9 HD/Digital-S HD is an enhanced version for high-definition recording.

Digital8: A digital format developed by Sony that uses 8mm tape and provides video performance equal to DV. The greater popularity of DV makes the future of Digital8 uncertain. See also "DV."

Digital Betacam: Sometimes called simply DigiBeta, Digital Betacam is a digital component recording format providing a degree of interformat compatibility between Sony Betacam SP analog component tapes and Sony digital component video. Some Digital Betacam machines play back tapes recorded on analog Betacam machines. Digital Betacam SX is a variant of Digital Beta that uses a more severe form of compression.

Digital recording: A technically robust method of electronic recording in which analog waveforms are converted into numerical codes. Digital recording eliminates many of the undesirable artifacts inherent in analog recording technology.

Digital-S: See "D-9."

DV: Digital video, a consumer-oriented digital format using 1/4-inch tape and a great deal of compression. Enhanced versions of the DV format have evolved, including DVCPRO and DVCAM, which have attracted the interest of business, educational and professional users.

DVCAM: Sony's small 1/4-inch component digital video cassette format using 5:1 compression. See also "DVCPRO."

DVCPRO: One of Panasonic's small 1/4-inch component digital video cassette formats. Both DVCPRO and DVCAM (see above) use 5:1 compression to fit the digital information on the small tapes. Of the two, DVCPRO is the format favored by more broadcasters for ENG. DVCPRO is also known as D-7.

DVCPRO-50: An advanced version of Panasonic's DVCPRO 1/4-inch component digital video cassette format featuring a milder 3.3:1 compression ratio and a tape speed twice that of DVCPRO, improving the format's ability to handle the signal manipulation involved in editing.

DVCPRO HD: Panasonic's enhanced high-definition version of its popular DVCPRO and DVCPRO 50 formats. DVCPRO HD is also known as DVCPRO 100.

DVD: Digital video disc, sometimes also called Digital Versatile Disc. An extremely high-capacity optical disc. The DVD's large capacity makes it ideal for feature films or interactive games and instructional programs.

Electronic still store (ESS): A device that records still images on disk allowing almost instant access to any image. The ESS replaced 35 mm film slides for storage of still images used in video production.

Emulsion: A coating on film or tape. On film, this layer contains light-sensitive silver compounds and other chemicals. On tape, this coating is composed of tiny oxide or metal particles.

Generation: A generation of audio or video occurs each time a copy is made. Thus, a copy of an original tape is the second generation, a copy of the second generation is the third generation, and so on.

Hard disk array: A digital storage device containing a number of hard disks and disk-reading heads sandwiched together, permitting the array to play back video and audio efficiently in real time. Sometimes called RAID (redundant array of inexpensive drives) technology.

Hard disk drive (HDD): A data storage device that records information on a rapidly rotating magnetic disk. Unlike magnetic tape, the HDD makes random access to any data on the disk available almost instantly. HDD and optical-disc-based technology are challenging magnetic tape in all phases of video production.

HDCAM and HDCAM SR: Sony formats targeted for top-quality, high-cost, high-definition recording. HDCAM SR is an improved version of the HDCAM format.

HDV: An enhanced version of the DV format providing inexpensive high-definition to consumers but with significant tradeoffs compared to professional high-def formats.

Head: An electromagnetic transducer used to impress electrical signals onto magnetic recording media in the form of magnetic patterns. During playback the head reverses the process, converting magnetic patterns into electrical signals.

Helical scan: A videotape threading configuration, so-called because video is recorded in slanted, helix-shaped tracks. All analog and digital videotape formats except quad use this configuration. Also sometimes called slant track.

HI8: An enhanced version of Sony's 8mm analog Video8 format. HI8 provided video performance similar to S-VHS.

Hue: The term used to describe a specific color: red, yellow, green, blue and so forth.

IEEE 1394: A standard interface protocol for the serial distribution of digital data between and among digital devices. In other words, the technical specifications for a cable used to move digital information from one machine to another. Versions of the protocol, such as Firewire and I.LINK, are widely used in video production to transfer video and audio from digital recorders to nonlinear editing systems and other devices. The "IEEE" stands for "Institute of Electrical and Electronics Engineers Inc."

ips: inches per second. The speed at which a tape moves during recording and playback.

Kinescoping: The pre-videotape process of recording television programs using a 16 mm film camera running at 30 frames per second to photograph images directly from a TV screen.

Lossless compression: Compression of the digital video signal that results in no loss of the original data but does reduce the amount of data stored. Compare to "Lossy compression."

Lossy compression: Compression of the digital video signal that reduces the amount of data stored but results in some loss of original data.

M format and M-II format: Panasonic's 1/2-inch analog component formats positioned to compete with Sony's Betacam format. M-II was an improved version of the original M format. Because of Betacam's headstart in the market, these formats never seriously threatened Betacam's dominance.

MiniDV: A packaging of the popular consumer-oriented DV format in small cassettes that make possible light and highly portable camcorders at low prices. See also "DV."

MPEG IMX: A 1/2-inch digital format using MPEG compression developed by Sony and offering video performance better than the company's Betacam SX format, but inferior to DigiBeta.

One-inch types A, B, and C: Three types of one-inch reel-to-reel videotape. Type A is now an obsolete format, the segmented type B was only really used in Europe, and the unsegmented type C was the American broadcast standard. All three types were used for analog recording.

Quadruplex (quad): The first videotape format, developed by Ampex in the mid-1950s. Also called the transverse method because its video tracks are laid transversely (at right angles) to the tape's path through the machine. Quad machines featured four rotating heads.

RAID: See "Hard disk array."

S-VHS (super VHS): An enhanced version of VHS providing superior picture resolution. S-VHS was not widely accepted either by consumers or professionals. Also see "VHS."

Sampling: Refers to the periodic measurement of an analog waveform for its conversion to digital data. The sampling rate is the number of times per second that the waveform is measured. The higher the rate, the better the digital data represents the original analog waveform.

Saturation: The intensity of a color—how much white light is mixed with the color.

Segmented format: An analog videotape format with a head-tracking configuration in which less than a complete video frame is recorded on the tape during a single head pass, making freeze frames and slow- and fast-motion playback impossible.

Synchronization (sync) pulses: Electronic signals that ensure all studio equipment is operating in exact simultaneity.

Time base corrector (TBC): A device used to correct time base errors on helical-scan videotape. Development of a digital TBC in the early 1970s allowed helical-scan recorders to meet FCC broadcast requirements. Also called frame synchronizers.

Time base errors: Mechanical errors (specifically, deviations in the timing of the video's sync pulses) caused by variations in tape speed and tension that occur during recording and playing back of helical-scan videotape.

U-matic: Sony's 3/4-inch, unsegmented, hetrodyne color video cassette format. The U-matic format made possible small, lightweight portable video recorders that replaced film for TV news and inspired a new field of video production: ENG.

Unsegmented format: An analog videotape format with a head-tracking configuration in which a complete video frame is recorded on the tape during a single head pass. See also "Segmented format."

Vectorscope: Traditionally, a type of testing device to measure the chrominance (color) values in a video signal. Typically, modern computer-based editing systems now include a "virtual" vectorscope for monitoring and adjusting chrominance values.

VHS (Video Home System): Panasonic's highly successful consumer VCR format, dominant in America and many foreign countries.

Video8: An analog format introduced by Sony that uses tape 8mm wide and offers video performance roughly equivalent to VHS. Video8 and enhanced HI8 were popular formats for consumer camcorders. See also "HI8."

Video server: A disk-based recording device providing random access to video files and employing RAID technology allowing playback in real time.

Video cassette recorder (VCR): A video recorder using a cassette rather than an open reel-to-reel method of tape transport; also a popular name for the home video playback machine using the small cassettes.

Video tape recorder (VTR): Technically, any device that records video (and audio) using magnetic tape as the storage medium. Often the term is used with reference to video recorders using open reels of tape as contrasted with recorders using cassette tapes. Also see "video cassette recorder."

Waveform monitor (WFM): Traditionally, a type of testing device to monitor the luminance (brightness) values in a video signal. Typically, modern computer-based editing systems now include a "virtual" waveform monitor for checking and setting brightness values.

XDCAM and XDCAM HD: A digital recording technology introduced by Sony that allows the operator to record data on an optical Blu-ray disc using several different standard-definition digital formats, including DVCAM. XDCAM HD, an enhanced version, records in digital high definition.

## chapter 10

Editing: Technology and Techniques

Little broadcast television is live. Even local and network news and sports consist of a combination of prerecorded, edited segments and live anchor lead-ins. Live sports programming contains many pre-produced features and background pieces, plus the instant replay.

Given editing's ubiquitous nature, perhaps it's wise to begin by examining the three principal reasons TV producers edit.

The first purpose is to take footage shot in the field or the studio and give it *story continuity*. Story continuity means correctly arranging your shots in an order that best tells your story. Often in single-camera, film-style production, events are recorded out of order, perhaps at different times and at different places. This jumble of events must then be rearranged, and then the final version copied/recorded onto a new tape.

The second general purpose of editing is to trim this newly combined footage to the correct length. Once the shots are selected and placed in a logical order, how long should each run? Where is the best place to start and end each shot? Ultimately, experience, further study of editing aesthetics and your own creative instincts will help you answer these questions.

The third general purpose is to combine your footage with additional elements, both pictures and sounds. Since this can require the use of video switchers, audio mixers, computers, paint boxes or character generators and combining more than one source at a time, sophisticated and expensive editing systems may be needed.

On- and Off-Line Editing

Traditional videotape editing is divided into *on-line editing* and *off-line editing*. In on-line editing, you edit your original footage tapes, shot by shot, compiling the final version of your program as you go. Speed and economy were this strategy's main advantages. In contrast, off-line editing occurs at a more leisurely pace. Using copies of the original footage, the goal of this method is for editors to rehearse edits until satisfied and then create a computerized list of electronic instructions called an *edit decision list* (EDL). In the past, such an EDL was used to control edits made using a bank of VTRs, a switcher and an audio board arrayed in a sophisticated editing suite that could pass as a complete production control room. Now, more often, in the age of the computerized editing era, the EDL performs the same service but in a digital editing suite. Such EDLs can also be used as a shot-by-shot editing guide for a traditional film editor.

Initially, a major advantage of working off line was the ability to easily revise an EDL. Making changes in an off-line edited program requires only the alteration of the show's EDL, a process known as *laundering an EDL*. This is as easy as making a change in a word-processing document on your personal computer and then saving the changes. The laundered EDL is then fed into the computerized system controlling the edit suite, and a new version of the show is created in what amounts to real time. In contrast, to alter a show that's been edited on line without the benefit of an EDL, you must literally redo every edit in the show that occurs

When Video Editing Began . . .

When videotape was introduced to the television industry, it couldn't be edited. Only film could. And editing 16 mm television news film was hardly a sophisticated process. Editing film stocks designed for television news and documentary production began with the light-sensitive material: A sturdy variety of Kodak film, called *VNF*, for *video news film*, was a reversal film stock. That meant that like slide film for a 35 mm camera, you developed and projected the original film. To edit VNF, you sat down with a couple of rewinders and a film splicer, physically cut the film and fused shots together, end to end, with glue in the order desired (see Figure 10-1).

When the lightweight video camera, the portable U-matic videocassette recorder and swift, inexpensive, electronic videotape editing came along, VNF quickly left the TV production scene. Electronic news gathering and electronic field production equipment and techniques replaced 16 mm film for many forms of television production—especially those with limited budgets.

Rather crude early methods of videotape editing predated the introduction of the U-matic. Soon after the introduction of two-inch-wide quad tape in 1956, Ampex devised an editing technique analogous to film in which technicians physically cut and spliced the tape. Video frames are invisible, so technicians had to identify ("develop") these frames with a fluid called Edivue, which was painted directly on the tape. This solution permitted them to see the video and audio tracks with

Figure 10-1. *A film editor sitting at a table with film, rewinders and a splicer.*

the aid of a microscope. Having marked the approximate spot on the tape where an edit should be made, editors could then cut and splice the tape between the video frames, thus avoiding a "glitch" (momentary loss of picture stability) at the edit point. This method of editing took considerable time, often had to be repeated to get it right, and was limited only to cuts. After all that, this frustrating method still often yielded video glitches during playback.

Engineers later developed a method of editing that didn't require physically cutting the tape. Instead, selected shots were rerecorded from original footage tapes onto a new tape, arranged in the desired order.

Early electronic editing produced results almost as crude as the "cut and splice" method. Slow videotape recorder (VTR) start-up speeds required editors to use a manually cued, manually operated method called *punch and crunch* editing. To obtain a smooth edit, two skilled technicians operating separate machines used a complicated manual timing routine to start the record and playback VTRs approximately five to ten seconds before their respective editing points and, at precisely the right moment, one of them would punch the "record" button on the VTR used for recording. After a few bad takes (accompanied by loud cursing), and a great deal of luck, edits were accomplished. "Punch and crunch" did not allow editors to preview edits. They performed the edit and then prayed as they played back the result.

Much to the happiness of these harassed technicians, computer control later replaced "punch and crunch," providing producers much more precise control of rollback and record functions. Later, computer control of all editing functions, plus the ability to preview edits and make clean edits inside another shot (previously impossible for technical reasons), revolutionized editing. The nearly simultaneous development of microprocessor-controlled editing systems and the U-matic format were largely responsible for the ENG revolution.

after the change. This takes considerably more time, and in television, time is money (see Figure 10-2).

Straight-Cut Edits

For a quarter century, relatively simple on-line editing systems, called either *straight-cut editors* or *control-track editors,* were (and in many cases, still <u>are</u>) the workhorses of

the broadcast industry. Especially for news, many straight-cut systems are still in use in television stations that have not yet acquired digital editing systems. Usually these systems consist of one playback machine and one record machine, governed by some form of edit controller. This edit controller may be a separate unit or built into the recording edit machine. As the name "straight cut" implies, this equipment performs only cuts—nothing fancier. It's

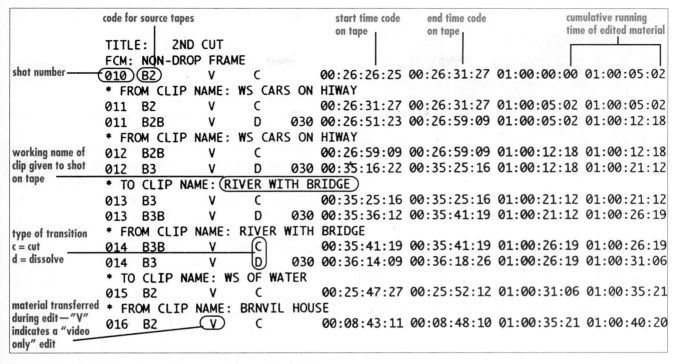

Figure 10-2. *An edit decision list (EDL) provided by a nonlinear editing system.*

also called "control track" because this kind of editing equipment uses electrical pulses recorded on the videotapes' control tracks to perform the cuts. Dissolves, wipes and other more complex transitions usually require the simultaneous presence on the screen of pictures from more than one playback machine. Complex transitions using multiple decks also require either a separate video switcher or a more sophisticated editing controller with built-in video special effects circuitry. The configuration of a straight-cuts editing system and a discussion of its operation appears later in this chapter. But let's first look at the kinds of edits performed by these systems (see Figure 10-3).

Assemble and Insert Edits

Making the important distinction between assemble and insert editing requires an understanding of the way audio, video and control-track signals on videotape are manipulated. Different formats place these signals in different locations on the tape, but the editing process is basically the same. The video track occupies the center of the tape, with the linear audio tracks along one edge and the control track along the other, as depicted in Figure 10-4. Other video formats that embed their audio digitally in the video track pose a different editing challenge, but in the following discussion we'll restrict

ourselves to formats using separate linear audio tracks recorded by stationary heads.

Straight-cut and more complex editing systems perform both assemble and insert edits depending on the wishes of the operator. The *assemble edit* is easiest to describe (see Figure 10-5). An assemble edit does the

Figure 10-3. *This is a typical cuts-only linear (not digital) editing bay. The playback machine and its monitor are to the left, the edit controller is in the center, and the editing recorder and its monitor are on the right. Editing bays used for ENG sometimes also include a simple audio mixer and microphone allowing the operator to record voice-over audio while editing to speed production.*

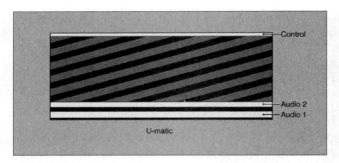

Figure 10-4. *Video and audio tracks on a common format of analog videotape.*

following to a tape as it simultaneously records all video and audio tracks:

- A stationary bulk erase head contacts the tape first, and as the tape passes by, erases everything on it: video, audio and control-track pulses.
- As the tape moves along, three more recordings are made onto the tape: The stationary control-track head records new control-track pulses, and the stationary audio heads record any new audio signals. At the same time, the rotating video heads record new pictures onto the video track.

In short, in assemble editing, all the information originally on the tape is erased and replaced with new information. The process is essentially the same as when you use a VCR at home to record a new program. In an editing studio, the major difference is that the source of your new audio and video isn't an incoming TV or cable TV signal; it's the output of some source of video source in your editing suite, or from somewhere else in the studio.

Assemble editing performs simple duplications of entire tapes, as you would at home if you set up two VCRs and dubbed a copy of your favorite program. However we also use assemble editing to prepare tapes for insert editing in a manner analogous to formatting computer disks. In assemble editing, there is no way to

selectively erase only the video, or only the audio. That's what insert editing does. And because a VTR's bulk erase head precedes all other recording heads, an assemble edit leaves behind a half second of "salt and pepper video," the snowy-looking picture you see if you play back an unused blank tape. If you were to use assemble editing to place a shot inside of another shot, among other problems, your inserted video will have a second or so of "salt and pepper" at the end of the edit.

Although the term "assemble" suggests the possibility of adding new shots (audio and video combined) one after another to build a program, remember that assemble editing erases the control track starting with each new edit, forcing the playback machine to "resynchronize" at each edit point. While it's possible that a program developed by adding one assemble edit after the other will play perfectly, there's a chance it won't. The odds improve if you carefully overlap the end of each edit several seconds to cover the "salt and pepper." But even if all you plan to do is to compile a program consisting of individual audio/video segments recorded sequentially, you'll create a more electronically stable series of edits if you build the program using insert editing.

Insert editing provides much greater versatility than assemble editing. Insert editing allows you to record new audio and video in the middle of existing material without breaking the continuity of the original control track. And because during insert editing the VTR's bulk erase head is disabled, there's no "salt and pepper video" at the end of your edits.

Let's examine a common use of insert editing. Suppose you have a head-and-shoulders shot of the local mayor making a 20-second statement about the need to clean up roadside rubbish. That's a long time for a talking head and, while the mayor's words may be worth 20 seconds, you want to give viewers something more interesting to watch. Insert editing allows us to plug a 10-second shot of a trashy roadside into the middle of the mayor's statement

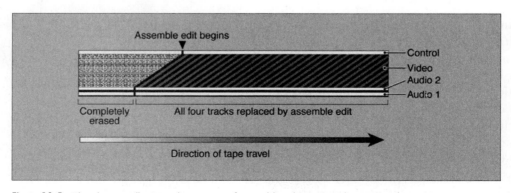

Figure 10-5. *This drawing illustrates the process of assemble editing. See description above.*

while the audience listens to the mayor's words. This is called a video-only insert.

We could as easily choose to edit only one audio track on the tape, or two audio tracks and no video, or video only, or any combination. For example, if the roadside shot inserted into the mayor's shot has the sound of cars rushing past, we can put the car sound on an audio track as we insert new video. The result is a shot of the rubbish with the sound of cars below the mayor's voice.

Blacking a Tape

You can't perform inserts on blank videotape. Cuts-only edit controllers perform insert edits by counting the video frames on both the *record* and *playback tapes* (playback tapes contain the raw, unedited footage; the record tape, also called the edit master, is the tape on which footage is compiled during editing). This frame-counting requires a smooth, uninterrupted control track. You can't use a tape for insert editing until it is prepared for this. Mentioned earlier as analogous to formatting a computer disk, you also must format a blank videotape by assemble editing control track onto the tape. This signal is usually recorded along with color black (black with color burst) video or color bars from either your studio's video switcher or a test signal generator. This formatting process is called "*blacking* a tape," "laying track" or "striping a tape." Once these essential control-track pulses are laid down, you can perform insert edits. In TV news operations that still do analog tape editing, an intern's first task is often blacking the day's edit tapes.

A Cuts-Only Editing System

A simple control-track editing system usually consists of five major components:

- a videotape machine (called a source deck) for playing back original footage (this may be a less expensive playback-only machine without the ability to record);
- a videotape machine capable of recording;
- a video monitor and speaker for viewing/hearing the output of the playback machine;
- a video monitor and speaker for viewing/hearing both the input and output of the record machine; and
- an edit controller to switch the flow of audio and video and to provide the controlling signals needed to synchronize the two machines while performing edits.

We assume the various components of the system are properly wired and adjusted, but it is important that you check the videotape machines' controls to be sure they are configured for editing. Sometimes you find the previous user has flipped a switch, preventing the machines from performing the function you desire. Machines differ so greatly we can't provide a definitive list of items to check. This is something your technical support people or your instructor will provide.

Exploring the Edit Controller

Figure 10-6 shows a generic controller with important controls labeled. Frequently refer to Figure 10-6 as you read our description below.

Most of these edit controllers have three main sections. The first is the remote control section, with buttons and knobs duplicating the tape transport controls on both videotape machines. This includes the ability to play, pause, fast-forward and reverse tapes, as well as a large, round *search knob* that permits *shuttling* (fast-forward/rewind while you watch the video flash by) and *jogging* (manually controlling frame speed by rotating the search knob 360 degrees). Typically you switch from shuttle to jog and back by pushing down on the search knob until it clicks.

The second section of the edit controller is the display area, consisting of two windows at the top of the controller, one for the playback machine and the other for the record machine. Reading the pulses on the control track of the two tapes, the displays provide editors with what appears to be time code. But there's a difference between actual time-code editing and control-track editing. First, let's see how control-track editing works: If you press the reset button opposite the tape's counter, then begin playing a fully rewound tape, a code appears on the display starting at zero and consisting of hours, minutes, seconds and frames (0:00:00:00).

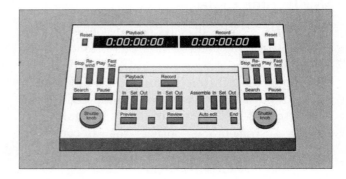

Figure 10-6. *A generic edit controller.*

As the editing control equipment counts control-track pulses, the counter increases this code every time a frame appears. Thus, 0:00:00:00 is followed by 0:00:00:01, and then by 0:00:00:02, etc. If your tape is completely rewound, this is a helpful feature as you begin editing for three reasons:

* You know (relatively) where you are on each tape.
* You can time a complete program or program segment precisely, down to 1/30th of a second.
* When you want to insert a shot onto the record tape, you can time the shot you want to insert and the hole you want to put it in to see if it will fit.

The difference between control-track pulse code and *SMPTE (Society of Motion Picture and Television Engineers) time code* described below is this: Control-track code allows you to zero the counter any time you like: You can fast-forward to any place you wish on the tape and press "reset," and the counter returns to zero. With SMPTE time code, the frames of video are on the tape itself and can't be changed. They're precisely coded, so that each frame is different from all other frames on that tape. Because the time displayed is "locked" to a specific frame of video on the tape, SMPTE time code provides an <u>absolute</u> reference to other frames of video on the same tape, not a <u>relative</u> reference as is the case with control-track pulses.

The third section of the edit controller is the area usually found between the two remote controls: It's where you preselect and initiate each edit. Here you'll find buttons to select the kind of edit you want— either assemble or insert, and if it's an insert edit, whether you will need to insert video, channel 1 audio, channel 2 audio, all of these tracks or any combination. There are also buttons permitting you to "mark" the locations on your playback and record tapes where the edit occurs.

SMPTE Time Code

Control-track editor displays provide only a display capable of reading control-track pulses to arbitrarily time shots, scenes or programs. SMPTE (the acronym is pronounced "SIM-tee") time code is different. It still reads out in hours, minutes, seconds and frames, but these readings are not arbitrary. In addition to showing the time in the display on the edit controller, SMPTE time code allows display of the information in a "window" on the tape machine monitors where you view the video images. As shown in Figure 10-7,

Figure 10-7. *Although time code is visible on monitors during an editing session, it does not appear in the final version.*

time code information is seen over the pictures only in the editing suite, never in the final edited version. SMPTE time code's most important feature, however, remains its ability to provide *frame accuracy* in your edits (edits that occur at <u>exactly</u> the frame you select). Complicated fades, dissolves and other work require this frame-accurate precision, so it's good to know that when you enter an "in-point" of 0:24:36:07, you can depend on your edit beginning precisely at 0:24:36:07. If there is some mechanical or other error and the VTRs can't synchronize to make the edit at precisely the point you select, most SMPTE time code controllers will abort the edit.

EDLs (see Figure 10-2) consist basically of SMPTE time code and computer instructions.

A-B Roll Editing

When editing motion picture film, effects are created through the use of an optical printer by sending first an "A-roll" and then a "B-roll" of film through the printer (see Figure 10-8). By overlapping images from the two rolls of film at certain points, the printer creates effects such as fades and dissolves. Thus, *A-B roll editing* has become both a film and television industry shorthand for edits requiring more than a single playback source. An A-B roll editing system is more expensive and requires SMPTE time code, but it offers enhanced effects capabilities. A-B roll edit controllers and their related video effects equipment are used for both on-line and off-line editing. In nonlinear, computerized editing, the same A-B roll metaphor is used, as you are about to discover.

1.　　2.

Figure 10-8. *In shot 1, editors work in an A-B editing suite that doubles for a production control room. In shot 2, the production suite is connected to a number of VTRs that provide multiple simultaneous playbacks for A-B roll editing.*
Shots courtesy of Nebraska Educational Telecommunications.

Nonlinear Editing

The evolution of editing technology from linear to nonlinear continues, as the use of linear editing systems decreases. However, we included a discussion of linear editing in this edition because at this writing, interns and entry-level production employees at many studios and even major market stations are still expected to understand, if not be proficient at, this technology.

But *nonlinear editing* continues to replace linear tape editing suites in TV stations, production houses and colleges and universities around the country. In a nutshell, the differences between linear and nonlinear are whether you gain access to your shots in a serial or random manner and the video environment (analog vs. digital) in which edits are made. If you've operated an audio CD player and an audio cassette machine, you already understand the difference between random and serial access. The CD allows you to select any cut on the album in an instant, without fast-forwarding through other songs on the disc. This is random access. The cassette provides linear access, requiring you to play or fast-forward through songs at the "head" of the tape to reach the songs located at the "tail." Likewise, in linear videotape editing, if the next shot you need is at the far end of the cassette, you must wait while the playback machine fast-forwards or rewinds to find the spot. Sophisticated VTRs and editing systems automatically shuttle to the desired time code, but shuttling forward or backward in a linear (straight-line) manner to reach your next shot is still a time-consuming process. Nonlinear editing doesn't use VTRs to store the footage you'll use for edit playback.

Early nonlinear on-line editing required shipping taped footage to a lab for transfer to expensive laser discs. These discs provided almost instantaneous random access to all shots, which were then recorded onto a master edit tape in proper sequence to form the edited program. The same procedure was used for off-line edit sessions, but the product was an EDL, which was then taken to a standard on-line linear edit suite and used to automatically compile the final edit master from master footage tapes. Sending the footage tapes to a lab for transfer to disc negated virtually all the time savings provided by random access.

Everything changed with the development of sophisticated video compression techniques and the declining cost of large-capacity computer hard drives and hard drive arrays capable of storing hundreds and thousands of *gigabytes* (GB; a gigabyte is a billion bytes of digitized information) and even *terabytes* (TB; a trillion bytes) of digitally encoded audio and video. Nonlinear editing systems use computers as a control platform and (usually) hard disks for file storage.

Pros and Cons of Nonlinear Editing

In most applications and conditions, nonlinear editing beats linear editing. Among the most important advantages is price. A single VTR plus a computer loaded with special purpose hardware and a powerful software program can do the work of a traditionally equipped videotape editing suite at a small fraction of the price. A second important advantage is that a random-access system provides the ability to make editing revisions in a much shorter, less labor-intensive time. Typically, editing suites are billed by the hour, so an efficient nonlinear editing system saves you money. Nonlinear systems also provide reduced maintenance cost. Nonlinear storage systems have fewer electromechanical parts compared to higher-maintenance videotape machines. These financial advantages alone make nonlinear systems appealing, but there are also creative advantages.

Since nonlinear editing involves either the digitizing of analog footage or the transfer of digital video onto the hard drive of the computer system used for editing, all the editing and special effects occur in a digital environment. This means that a great number of digital video effects (DVE) are available, depending on the nonlinear edit system's sophistication. The audio, too, is digital, making digital signal processing possible through the use of either the video editing program or other, even more sophisticated, audio and video editing software and special effects packages. Once the desired original footage is transferred to the editing system, the image degradation associated with signal processing during analog editing is no longer a concern. This means that the traditional distinction between high-quality on-line editing and lower-quality off-line editing is blurred. Eliminating the need for separate on- and off-line editing of a program reduces costs and postproduction time significantly. Another advantage is the ability to network nonlinear systems, so portions of the same show can be handed back and forth between editors, allowing many to work on different parts of the same production simultaneously.

Nonlinear editing systems have many compelling advantages, but they also have a scant few limitations that must be addressed. One problem is the need to take the time to transfer tape footage—often in real time—to the editing system's hard drives before editing can begin. However, some sophisticated tape-based editing machines speed up this process. The newer digital formats discussed earlier (the ones capable of transferring data at four times normal playback speed) shorten the time needed to transfer data. Now that new, tapeless cameras are entering the marketplace, the last big advantage of nonlinear editing—speed in starting an edit session—may be gone altogether. Tapeless cameras use different kinds of recording media, such as flash

memory cards and removable hard drives, giving them one big advantage over tape: They don't require a real-time, serial transfer of footage from tape to the computer before beginning an edit session.

Producers still face the problem of obtaining adequate disk storage capacity at a reasonable cost, although that price is dropping dramatically. Lacking enough disk space to digitize all the raw footage, sometimes a producer must first log all the source tapes and perform a "mental pre-edit," deciding which segments to transfer to editing system or studio server hard drives. If an editing system is used by others, such as in a university editing lab, even more limited disk space can create traffic problems.

Hard drives can, however, store a much greater volume of lower resolution, highly compressed, video. This provides all the speed advantages of nonlinear random access during the time-consuming off-line phase of editing in which you create your EDL. However, there's no speed advantage or much of a networking advantage when the EDL is later used to transfer the original footage from analog playback VTRs to a final edit master videotape. But where there is an off-line advantage is this scenario: A production company or a TV station provides all its producers with laptops loaded with editing software. The footage for the producer's latest show is loaded into the laptop, but in a low-resolution, highly compressed form. The producer is now enabled to work on this editing project at home or in his/her office at the station, all without tying up an expensive on-line editing suite. Then, when his/her edit is complete, the producer provides a technician with his/her EDL, which is fed into the computer in one of the station's on-line editing suites. This computer has access to the server where all the original high-resolution footage for the show is stored. With a few mouse clicks, the technician then creates and records a final, high-resolution, uncompressed, edited version of the show.

Advances in video compression technology occur almost weekly, and new, more efficient compression algorithms will increase the amount of high-quality video a storage unit can hold.

A "Typical" Nonlinear Editing System

There are many excellent NLEs—some relatively low cost, such as the extremely popular models manufactured by Avid and Apple. Also, Adobe Premiere can be found in use in some lower-budget professional applications, as well as in cable production and in colleges and universities. Such systems need just one VTR to serve as both the video source for playback of original footage into the computer system and to record the finished product when the edit session is completed. If you've shot analog footage, your editing software must be capable of *digitizing* it, that is, of converting the analog footage to digital during the process of capturing it for editing. Other varieties of editing software work only with digital video.

Let's run through a brief edit session using a generic NLE to give you an idea of its operation and capabilities.

The first step is to transfer footage from your VTR to either your computer's hard drive or to the server your studio uses for editing. Although we're using tapes and a VTR as our source for most of our footage, if you chose to, you can also capture other sources, such as CD music and sound-effects audio, DVD-recorded video footage, JPEGs created by any number of software programs and so on, creating additional digital video and audio files to enhance your final edited piece.

Some like to "clean up" the video or audio (correct color or luminance, equalize audio or increase volume, etc.) before beginning an editing session. It's possible to do this while feeding the footage from our sources into the computer, or afterward, using either software included in the editing system or other software packages (see Figure 10-9). It's probably best to wait until after you've completed the rough cut of your edit to do your cleanup. (Note that although much can be done on an NLE to clean up your video and audio, your footage will rarely look or sound as good as if you recorded it right in the first place! So don't rely on software to fix your shots: Take the time to carefully white balance and light your scenes, and remember to place your mikes correctly and maintain good audio levels.)

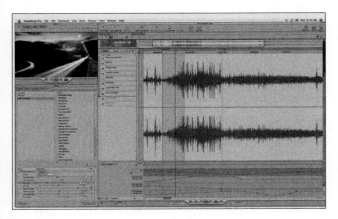

Figure 10-9. *This is an interface screen from Apple's Final Cut Pro 5 editing software. This screen is used when the editor wants to work on improving a scene's audio. The main display shows an audio waveform.*

Picture courtesy of Apple Computer Inc.

Figure 10-10. *A main display interface from Apple's Final Cut Pro 5 nonlinear editing system, showing, from top left clockwise, four shots that will be edited into this scene, a window showing the edited final result, sliders to adjust audio levels, a left-to-right timeline display (at the bottom) of video and audio edits and a window displaying a number of shots, listed by file name.*

Picture courtesy of Apple Computer Inc.

Once the computer has stored the scenes we wish to edit, they appear in a box, often called a *bin,* on the system's screen display. The program can provide us with either a list of scenes in text form, as shown in Figure 10-10 (you assigned a file name for each scene as it was being transferred to disk), or as a series of tiny pictures showing the first frame of each scene, also tagged with a file name.

Figure 10-10 illustrates an NLE's main windows: one which includes one or more shots that you're currently working on, windows to view a list of other video clips soon to be used in the edit session, a handy horizontal timeline display and other windows you can choose to display.

As the principal editing interface tool, the timeline display offers you the choice of viewing many helpful and attractive features, including a strip of tiny thumbnail pictures representing the first frames of each edit we've made. The display also shows the audio tracks, identifying them and showing at what points the audio and video tracks are set to change and perform transitions.

Unless we designate otherwise, the audio in each scene will follow its corresponding video. This means that it will abruptly change in a cut, or match the overlap and duration in any A/B (two source) transition. For example, in a video dissolve, the audio that accompanies both scenes will cross-fade in an identical manner, so that for a moment we will hear both audio tracks playing on top of each other. But we have control of these elements and can adjust audio in- and out-points or vary the volume of each audio source on the four audio channels on our edit timeline—all with simple drag and drop mouse clicks. Plus, on extra audio tracks the software provides, you can add sound effects and music to add meaning and production values to the audio mix.

Full-function NLE's have a built-in character generator (CG) that can use any number of scalable type fonts installed in the computer. The best NLEs also allow you to use other software systems to import graphics. The use of *scalable type fonts* in these character generators allows the type you use to be made as large or as small as necessary. Text can be positioned and repositioned within a shot, colorized, drop-shadowed or edged with various selectable colors. Since CG pages are saved as files, we can use any available digital transition (wipe, push-off, etc.) provided by the NLE to bring in the CG text.

Finally, when our edit is complete, the easiest step in the process begins. We load a new tape or disc into the same VTR/disc-recording machine used earlier to transfer original footage into the computer. Then we press "record" on the VTR/disc recorder and "play" on our NLE. The entire edited program is transferred from the domain of the NLE and back to the videotape or other video-recording device. Or the edited video can remain as a digital file, stored in the computer or on the studio's server, to be used later as a part of a multimedia production incorporated into a web page or a CD-ROM.

And if you later wish to make changes in the edit master, it's a simple process to re-edit, and then dub it onto videotape or videodisc. This is a huge help when dealing with picky clients who insist on changes and want them done <u>immediately</u>.

Sooner or later you must package your final, edited tapes to send to your client, a station, an ad agency or, in the case of a resume tape, to a potential employer. Tech Manual 10-1, found at the end of the chapter, is entitled "Setting Up Leader on Your Tapes." It has some helpful instructions on how to prepare your tape for that world out there.

A Glimpse Into the Future

As sophisticated as it sounds, the generic system we've used for discussing nonlinear editing would still be classed as comparatively low-end. However, as we have seen in Figures 10-9 and 10-10, Apple's Final Cut Pro, Avid's various nonlinear editing products and other NLE systems used by professionals are adding new and exciting features all the time, and the cost remains relatively low. There are other systems using closed-architecture software made by manufacturers such as Sony and Panasonic and more expensive, upscale systems available from companies including Avid and Quantel. The most sophisticated nonlinear editing/production systems can cost a quarter of a million dollars. These high-end systems provide considerably more storage for uncompressed (and therefore higher-quality) video, require little to no time be wasted waiting for effects to be rendered and offer new and marvelous special effects and other creative options. Most feature films in Hollywood are no longer edited ("cut") the old-fashioned way on film, even though the feature may have been shot on film. Film scenes are transferred to digital video and edited on an NLE.

We've noted that nonlinear editing systems make the traditional distinction between on-line and off-line editing increasingly fuzzy. One day these two terms may no longer have meaning, and all linear video recording, storage and retrieval systems will be obsolete. Videotape will remain an important archival medium for many years, but its role in the editing suite seems destined to diminish as computer-based systems evolve to take its place.

The Art of Editing

Editing video requires equipment and some technical expertise, and until now we've only focused on the array of technology one uses. But the most adept technicians may be painfully inept editors unless they possess some background in the art and conventions of editing. Humans have edited motion pictures for more than 100 years, on film and then on video, and viewers accept many important aesthetic principles as standard practice today. We've selected some of these fundamental concepts to guide you as you learn to edit video.

Students typically shoot the footage they edit, but in larger production organizations, shooting and editing frequently are functions performed by different people. Experienced videographers always shoot with editing in mind. A skilled editor can, given enough of the right kind of raw footage, perform miracles. But every editor appreciates video shot with an eye toward how the material will subsequently fit together. Later in this chapter we suggest some shooting techniques intended to make an editor's work easier.

The first step is determining what footage is available for editing. If the amount of footage is minimal, as is often true for ENG work, and the videographer is also the editor, a mental note of shots recorded may be adequate. When there is an extensive amount of footage, or when someone other than the shooter will edit the program, the need for detailed shot logging increases. Videographers often maintain a written record of shots as they shoot, attaching the log sheet to the tape when it's removed from the recorder. Especially when covering live events, frequently the shooter is too busy looking for and composing shots to maintain a footage log, so logging may occur later. Postproduction logging usually is required in any case, because logging involves determining the "usability" of each shot, something often very difficult to judge during the hustle and bustle of production.

Modern database programs allow producers to log shots on a computer using a variety of descriptive qualities: tape number, shot number, scene location, date, shot length, subject matter, overall video quality, composition (CU, MLS, etc.), filters used, lighting and so on. Once entered, the database allows the editor to randomly search all the footage using any of the descriptive qualities. The search provides the location of a particular shot needed, or allows the editor to determine if a needed shot doesn't exist and more footage is required. Nonlinear editing systems require the operator to identify each segment of video as it is digitized and/or transferred to disk, so some degree of logging is unavoidable, although it's possible to digitize or transfer to disk a long sequence of shots and store them under one heading. This "batch processing" approach is quick but provides little useful information about individual shots once editing begins.

Logging sometimes consists of just remembering a dozen or so shots; other times logging becomes a complex process requiring days of work. In all cases, however, before making much progress in the editing suite, the editor must know what video is available. Note, however, that logging need not tie up valuable edit suite time. Students often spend hours in the edit suites checking footage tapes, never making a single edit. They quickly break the habit when they enter the profession and begin paying for editing time by the hour!

There are some standard items often placed at the head of an edited tape that help identify it, assist in setting up a playback machine for proper reproduction and provide an easy method of cueing the program for playback. Tech Manual 10-1, located at the end of this chapter, discusses these in detail.

An Overall Editing Strategy

Usually, the best edit is the unobtrusive one. This means the audience is not consciously distracted because you, the director or editor, changed from one shot to the next. Your purpose in using television or film to communicate meaning is usually to explain something or to tell a story—not to show off what you learned in editing class. Flashy cuts, transitions that radically change image size, or those that suddenly switch from a static shot to an in-motion shot shift attention away from the message, prematurely releasing viewers from their state of blissfully suspended reality. There _are_ times when "breaking the rules" of editing is permissible, even desirable—just as a novelist sometimes breaks the rules of grammar or spelling for artistic purposes. But would-be professionals should first learn the rules; then when they <u>choose</u> to break them, it's for a purpose consistent with an overall strategy.

Avoiding the Jump Cut

One way to keep routine edits unobtrusive and keep the audience's attention focused on the story you're trying to tell is to avoid the _jump cut._ A jump cut is often simply an incorrectly chosen edit, usually from one shot of a person or thing to another shot of that person or thing—about the same size and angle—that is somewhat similar, but different enough when edited together to cause the illusion of a "jump" on the screen. Cutting the two shots together gives the impression that during the cut, the subject suddenly "jumps" into a new pose. For example, in shot 1, a man holds a drink in his hand. In shot 2, photographed from the same angle and about the same size, the man has his hands at his side. When shot 1 and 2 are cut together, this magical "jump" appears, and audiences see the drink and the hand "disappear." In the old TV series, _Bewitched,_ a jump cut was quite useful when the director needed to make Samanthia's long-suffering husband, Darren, turn into a frog. He would shoot a long shot of Darren standing in the living room, and then, without moving the camera, replace Darren in the shot with a frog. Then he'd make an edit starting with the shot of Darren and then cutting to the shot of the frog, add a "twang" sound effect and voilà! Poor Darren turned into a frog again!

So the jump cut has some value in special effects, but in normal editing, it's the last thing you want. As Figure 10-11 demonstrates, one easy way to avoid the jump cut is to insert some other shot between the two similar shots, taking away the illusion of the jump cut.

1.   2.   3.

Figure 10-11. *Remember our mayor's 20-second H&S shot as she talks about rubbish along the city's streets? This time let's suppose the mayor makes a 90-second comment and you need to cut it to 20 seconds, perhaps using only the first and last 10 seconds. If you take out the middle 70 seconds and splice the beginning and end sentences together, the two shots won't match: The mayor is bound to have moved at least slightly, and at the edit point audiences will see the major appear to jump. To avoid showing this jump cut in the edited version of the story, you can insert B-roll footage. Earlier we said that we would insert a shot of the roadside trash that the mayor was describing. This same shot can be inserted to "cover" the jump cut. This is good B-roll, also called cutaway or coverage (see below), because it clearly illustrates what the story is about. It's critical that you or your videographer record a number of B-roll shots showing what a news source is discussing. Then you can insert them to cover jump cuts and for the reporter to talk about in voice-over later in the story. Always make sure your inserted B-roll video makes sense. If the mayor is talking about littered roads and you cover the jump cut with a shot of an aardvark, you'll cause more damage to your story than had you stayed with the jump cut. The more closely the inserted video relates to what the person is saying, the better—and less obtrusive—the edit.*

Cutaways, Cut-ins and Cover Shots

In the preceding example, we used what's called a *cutaway shot* to cover our jump cut. A cutaway is a shot we cut to that is not visible in the first shot. The opposite of a cutaway is called a *cut-in* (see Figure 10-12). A cut-in close-up, for example, reveals much more detail than is easily seen in a medium shot. A cut-in requires more preparation and care than a cutaway to preserve *pictorial continuity,* the logical progression of action shot to shot in such a way as to avoid jump cuts. The cut-in shot is subject to jump cutting errors in the editing room, because detail in the close-up cut-in shot is visible in the medium shot. For example, if it's obvious that the subject in your long shot is holding an orange in his hand, he shouldn't

be eating an already peeled orange when you cut to a close-up of his face. But if you first insert a cutaway shot of someone or something else (such as a close-up of orange peel piling up around the talent's shoes), and then cut back to the talent again, he doesn't necessarily have to be in the same posture or doing the same thing as he was before. Without thinking about it, audiences assume that the person changed stances during the time you cut away.

The Griffith Formula

American pioneer filmmaker D. W. Griffith was responsible for creating or improving upon much of the visual grammar used in motion pictures and television today. Griffith devised a formulaic method for introducing

1.   2.   3.

Figure 10-12. *In shot 1, the establishing shot, the model is pictured with her hand to her mouth. In shot 2, the cut-in, her hand is gone. This is a continuity error between shots 1 and 2. Shot 3 is the correct way to do a cut-in, matching the hand to the mouth as it is in the establishing shot.*

1.

2.

3.

Figure 10-13. *In this series, in shot 1, the long shot, we first establish the relative positions of the two persons in the scene. In shot 2, the medium shot, we get more detail in their facial expressions as dialog takes place. In shot 3, the closeup, we see the man's reaction.*

a new scene that merits your imitation (see Figure 10.13). You shouldn't edit all scenes using Griffith's formula—or any formula—but when you're learning, it helps to begin by copying the masters. Griffith's formula is easy to remember: LS, MS, CU. This means that you begin, and often shoot the entire action of the sequence, with a long shot. This is also called a *cover shot,* or *establishing shot.* If the shot records all the action you'll show later in the edited scene, it's called a *master shot.* This shot sets the scene, shows the audience where people and things are on the set—a visual orientation device. Then, as action begins, you can cut in from the long shot to a tighter shot, a medium shot. Eventually, as the script either calls for more detail or heightened drama, you cut even tighter to close-ups. Then the editor works the shots back and forth between medium shots and close-ups. If the action requires a wider view to follow the action (or sometimes just for visual variation), you cut back to the long shot from time to time. The long shot is also handy to cut back to when you just can't edit two tighter shots together without creating a jump cut. Cutting back to longer shots (or to medium long shots or even medium shots) also allows viewers the opportunity to reestablish a sense of space orientation in the scene. This is especially important in television, where viewers often tune into a program late. If they tune in late and all you ever show is close-ups, they have little idea of the setting in which the action is occurring.

A word of warning about shooting the shots needed to execute Griffith's LS-MS-CU formula is in order. Each time you change the focal length of your lens or move the camera forward to record the MS and CU, be sure you change the camera's position laterally as well. Transitioning from an LS to an MS or CU by simply zooming in with the camera in a fixed location can produce shots that are "jumpy" in and of themselves: The camera appears to take giant, jarring "leaps" toward

the focus of action. Figure 10-14 illustrates how, even in a one-shot (a shot featuring one person, as discussed in Chapter 4), you can position the camera to provide shots that will cut together smoothly.

It's important to remember, too, that Griffith's formula involves the use of cut-in shots, so the same precautions apply about matching the position of the talent shot to shot. Film and television directors often solve this problem by shooting the same action repeated three or four times from different angles and with different focal length lenses. Of course, to simplify match-cuts in the editing room, one can also shoot one take of the scene with three cameras feeding three VTRs.

Crossing the Line

While framing your shots and changing camera angles, there's another way of inadvertently calling attention to yourself and your edits and away from the story. This

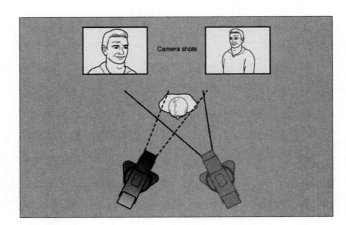

Figure 10-14. *In cutting from a one-shot to a one-shot, be sure to vary at least the size and, if you can, the camera angle. This will avoid the jump cut.*

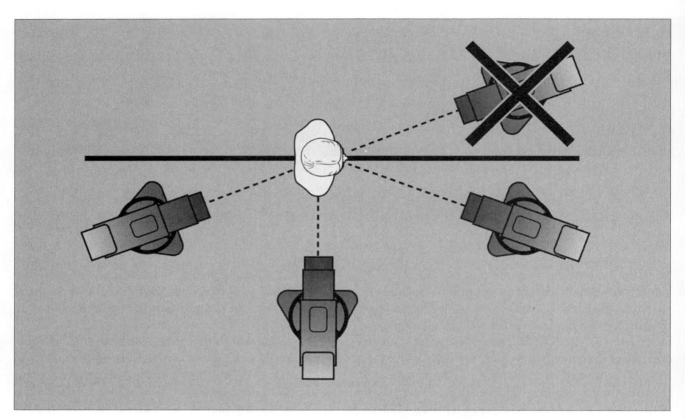

Figure 10-15. *Consider the following: You're shooting someone walking down the lane. Assume that there's an imaginary line and that he's walking down it. On one side of the line are three different camera setups, as shown in this drawing. All three are fine, because they will result in shots of our walker walking from left to right. But if you make a mistake and cross this line (the X-ed out camera position), the shot of the walker will appear to be going from right to left. Your audience will be disoriented. Especially in action scenes with many participants, mistakes regarding the action axis can be confusing to the audience. One of the authors fondly remembers a student who placed cameras on both sides of a basketball court. The audience, and director, immediately became so confused trying to follow the action, the producer quickly corrected the error by moving all cameras to one side of the action axis.*

occurs when you accidentally cross *the line* and violate the *180-degree rule* (see Figure 10-15). Sometimes called the *action axis*, the line may be imaginary, but it can cause an unwary director or editor some embarrassment.

Neutral Screen Direction

Once an action axis is established, it doesn't mean the line cannot be crossed: You simply must prepare your audience for the change so it isn't distracting. This is where *neutral screen direction* is helpful (see Figure 10-16). Neutral screen direction is created when we shoot the subject, such as our runner, running toward or away from the camera. In these cases, the subject is going neither left nor right—screen direction is neutral. As the three shots in Figure 10-16 demonstrate, it's possible to

cut from one side of the line to the other by preparing the audience with a neutral screen direction shot.

Too Much to Process

Another sure way to distract the audience is to provide too much information for them to process visually. Audiences have grown accustomed to gradual changes in shot size because most filmmakers and television directors routinely use variations of Griffith's LS-MS-CU formula. Viewers sometimes lose concentration when shown more radical shot changes. This is especially likely if you cut from a long shot or extreme long shot to a tight close-up, or vice versa. The visual "shock" resulting from the sudden change from processing close-up detail to dealing with a long shot (and the reverse) will detract

1.   2.   3.

Figure 10-16. *In this sequence, the walkers are shot from one side of the line in shot 1, then from neutral screen direction (in this case, head on) in shot 2, and then in shot 3 from the other side of the line without disorienting the audience's sense of direction.*

from your story and needlessly call attention to the editing process. As a general rule, to get smoothly from an LS to a CU, first cut to something in-between, such as an MS. Like all general rules, this one is sometimes broken for good reason, especially in commercials and music videos. Often a director wants to communicate an emotional state (excitement, confusion) more than relay a logical chain of events. A series of brief images without regard to image size can suggest such moods.

When to Cut

Besides knowing what to cut and how to cut it, it's also important to know <u>when</u> to cut. Take a simple problem: You begin with a medium close-up of a person sitting in a chair, then plan to cut to a medium long shot of the person as she gets up and exits the room. But when do you make the cut? Here are your choices:

a. <u>Before</u> she gets up
b. <u>As</u> she gets up
c. <u>After</u> she has gotten up, while she is walking toward the door

The answer is (b), <u>as she gets up</u>. Remember: The idea is to make the least obtrusive cut. In answer (b), as the seated person rises, the audience unconsciously anticipates action, movement of some sort. Some may even feel anxiety at the tightness of the shot. But as she

rises, we release that tension by cutting to the medium long shot, enlarging the frame and continuing to serve the visual needs of the audience by following the action. If we cut to the wide shot before she moves, the audience wonders why—we distract our viewers with what looks like an unnecessary cut. If we wait to cut from the medium close-up until after she rises, we would once again cause audience anxiety by not following the action. So the basic rule is this: <u>Cut on action</u>. Cutting on action has another important benefit: Sometimes we make small continuity errors when shooting shots that should match in detail, costume and body position. Perhaps they weren't even shot on the same day. Regardless, cutting on the action rather than before the action often draws attention away from small continuity errors. If you cut too early, the audience doesn't know why and has nothing better to do than to search the frame for inconsistencies. If you cut on action, the audience is busy reorienting itself to a new shot, from a new angle and with a different shot size, and may not notice small continuity errors.

Cut for a Reason

The final fundamental editing rule—cut for a reason— also conforms to our overall strategy of unobtrusiveness in editing. This may seem too obvious to mention, but many beginning directors and editors become enamored with their ability to manipulate and change shots. They forget their prime directive: The story is everything—everything you do either explains or advances the story line or detracts from it. And needless cutting detracts from the story. The urge to add distracting transitions increases as technology makes doing so easier. The wide array of transitions provided by nonlinear editing systems is a temptation you must learn to resist.

If a shot plays well as is, then why cut? Great performances sometimes mean just letting the camera record what's going on without an editor's interruption. If a shot doesn't play well, if detail is needed, if a cutaway or a cut-in helps make a point more clearly or dramatically, then cut. If you can't articulate a reason for cutting, don't cut. Go back to the beginning of the chapter and reconsider why we edit in the first place.

We've now come full circle in this introduction to the fundamentals of editing. In the next chapter, we'll discuss the technology, techniques and aesthetics of field production. We'll cover both multiple camera remotes, in which the director must make editing decisions in real time, and single camera remotes, in which video is shot film-style, with a single camera, to be edited later.

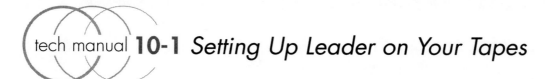

tech manual 10-1 *Setting Up Leader on Your Tapes*

In the TV production business, it's common practice to provide certain information in a *leader* ahead of an edited program. The leader provides a visual and aural test signal for setting up a playback recorder, a graphic identifying the program and its producer along with any other relevant information and a countdown helpful for cueing the program for playback on air.

There is no absolute standard formula for the leader, but the following list is typical.

1. Approximately 30 seconds to a minute of black. The head of a tape takes a beating because it is the part "leading the way" when the machine goes through the threading process. It's therefore subject to damage, so leaving some "safe" area well ahead of the program material is a good idea.

2. One minute of color bars and audio tone (usually 400 Hz to 1 kHz) at zero decibels (100) on the volume-unit meter. These are standard test signals that a playback machine operator can use to adjust video and audio levels before the program begins. Many studios and editing suites use test signal generators to create these signals. It's important that the editor laying these signals onto the record tape adjusts the machine properly. Students often make two errors when editing these test signals: They turn down the audio input level on the record machine, and they fail to record more than a few seconds of what is called "bars and tone." Both errors result from the annoying nature of the audio tone. Yes, it is loud, and a full 60 seconds of it seems like an eternity. But the proper procedure is to turn down the audio <u>monitor</u> level, not the input level to the recording VTR. Then, actually time the edit to ensure there's approximately a minute of it on the tape. Bothersome as laying these signals to tape may be, they are extremely helpful in ensuring a properly adjusted machine prior to playback.

3. About 5 seconds of black. This separates the bars and tone from the next leader item.

4. A *slate* containing important information identifying the program to follow. The slate (a graphic) should remain on screen long enough for someone with average reading ability to read it twice without having to pause the tape or replay it. The information on a slate varies from place to place. Typically the slate contains at least this information: The program's title, the producer's (or producing agency's) name and contact information, the date the program was produced and the running time of the program (program length).

   Additional information is added, depending on the nature of the program, the needs of the end user or just the whim of the producer. The most frequent error students make regarding the slate is failing to record enough of it so a playback operator can read what's on it!

5. Another five seconds of black (optional).

6. A countdown sequence, starting with the number 10 and counting down each second to the number 2. There should be an audio beep for each second. The countdown sequence is a cueing device, and some production facilities have produced proprietary countdown leaders that rival Hollywood productions. Those found in educational institutions are typically mundane but

adequate for the purpose. Sometimes countdown leader is found on a tape that's left in the editing suite and used by everyone. Some facilities have it on a video server. NLEs like the Avid bundle their own countdown leader on their software discs. Of course, you can store your own on one of the NLE's hard drives.

7. Precisely two seconds of black following the "2" on the countdown sequence, followed by the program itself. The countdown's numeral "2" indicates that the show should begin in exactly two seconds. Directors often cue a tape and pause it showing a "4" or "3" to give the playback machine time to get up to speed. When the "2" flashes past, the director then cuts (or dissolves) to the playback VTR to complete the transition to the program. Beginners often err in making the delay after the "2" either too long or too short. Either, of course, defeats the whole purpose of the countdown and is a great frustration to anyone using it for cueing. The exact nature of the leader may vary from facility to facility, so learn what's expected wherever you do your editing!

In some TV station news departments we find a common variant of those last two seconds of leader. Some editors of video news packages replace the black in those last seconds before program audio and video begin with what they may refer to as *slop video* or *pad video*. This is usually the two seconds of footage preceding the frame of video where the news package begins. Using slop video in place of black footage ensures that a picture of something relevant, instead of black, will appear on the screen if the news package is rolled-in live and the director of the news show accidentally takes the video on the air a second or so early. Oftentimes slop video is also inserted at the end of a piece, in case the video is still on the air after the report is complete. That way, there are still a few seconds of video—rather than black—on the screen to cover the late switch back to the anchor.

A final comment about leaders: Students looking for employment need résumé tapes called demo reels showing their work to potential employers. Employers differ regarding whether they want to see a leader on a demo reel or not. Some feel it's basic and may wonder why it's missing if they don't see it. However, it is our experience that employers often have dozens of demo reels to review when an opening comes along, and most don't want to wade through a leader to see what the applicant has to offer. As a general rule, deleting the leader on a demo reel will win more points than not. Since demo reels generally aren't adjusted on a time

base corrector but are simply played back on a machine in someone's office, consultants advise job hunters to skip the color bars, too. Begin with your slate, and then immediately transition—using whatever creative means you desire—to your short assemblage of carefully selected, impeccably edited, most creative demo reel footage.

And don't forget to *tail slate* your demo reel, using the same slate information you put on the front. After your tail slate, insert 10 seconds of black. Then don't forget to rewind the tape and cue it up to your slate on the head end. Finally, when you're finished, make sure that the tape and the tape box are neatly and professionally labeled. Labeling seems like a minor point, but it's the first impression you have a chance to make.

Résumé Tape Setup

A few words on the setup of résumé tapes: For TV production graduates looking for work in the business, begin as noted above with a slate, followed immediately by program audio and video. The entire tape should never be longer than 10 minutes.

Never show entire productions, other than very good commercials or promos. The best résumé tape displays the finest pieces of all your productions, edited together in an attractive, entertaining, alluring way. You should "tease" viewers, giving them only a taste of what you can produce. Be very stingy with the amount you show: Give viewers just enough to display what you can do, and then move on to something else. Don't include two pieces that are basically the same. Show the breadth of your production abilities. If you only have one or two long pieces to show for your entire time in college, you're probably not ready for a full-time, professional TV production job. Employers expect to see many pieces. If you don't have enough, start writing and shooting! Then use your best pieces to get your foot in the door at stations and production companies as a part-time production assistant or intern, and collect more tape on yourself. Then, after graduation, choose the very best to edit into a tape to show to potential full-time employers.

Remember that employers have seen hundreds of resume tapes, especially from beginners. Edit yours so it will be professional, stylish and memorable! Remember also to analyze your target audience. Employers are usually older than you and perhaps are not that fond of your kind of music. Fashion your résumé tape production for their sensibilities.

Résumé tapes for TV news graduates are much more regimented. News directors expect a certain format and usually brand as amateurish those that do not adhere to those standards. So carefully note the following instructions, courtesy of www.newsblues.com:

1. Unless otherwise noted, use VHS tape. Most news directors have a VHS recorder in their office, and some take tapes home to review.

2. Attach a rundown to the tape box—not to the tape itself. (The news director can't read your rundown when the tape is in the machine.) Besides the rundown, include your name, address, home and work telephone numbers and e-mail or Web address.

3. Label the tape with your name and the kind of position you're applying for: "Mary Smith, reporter."

4. Begin (and end) the tape with a slate, showing your name and address. Don't use black, color bars or countdowns. Leave the slate on long enough for you to read it twice, then begin with your program audio and video. Then the first thing the news director should see is you.

5. Start with a 30- to 45-second montage of great studio work, brilliant stand-ups, compelling live shots . . . whatever you have to grab the news director's attention. Keep the montage short and punchy. If you don't hook the viewer immediately, he'll eject the tape.

6. Follow with short segments of your very best work. Some say to include a few complete packages, but if you do, they'd better hold the news director's attention through to the end. No pieces longer than 1:30.

7. Limit the total run time of your tape to less than 10 minutes. If a news director is interested, he or she may request an additional tape of your most current work. But the initial tape should be a compilation highlighting only your best work.

Important Vocabulary Terms

180-degree rule: A reminder to camera operators to not cross the action axis line but rather to shoot all footage with the camera located on one side of the line to avoid an undesirable change in screen direction.

A-B roll editing: A film and videotape editing technique in which at least two playback sources are employed.

Action axis: An imaginary line along which a subject of interest travels or along which eye contact between two subjects is maintained during a sequence of shots. If shots of the subject recorded with the camera on each side of the action axis are edited together, the direction of travel will appear to reverse or subjects facing each other will appear to be looking in the same direction. Also called the line. See "180-degree rule."

Assemble editing: An edit in which all existing signals on the tape are erased, followed immediately by the recording of new signals on all tracks: audio, video and control.

B-roll: Footage illustrative of what your story is about, used to cover jump cuts and provide visual variation. Also called coverage.

Bin: A window in your NLE's display that lists the shots you have recorded into digital storage for this production.

Blacking: The formatting process during which control track and a video signal (usually black or color bars) are recorded onto a videotape prior to editing. Blacking is required before a tape can be insert edited.

Control-track editor: Editing equipment that counts pulses to synchronize the playback and record functions of two tape machines and makes edits at tape locations preprogrammed by the operator. Also called straight-cut editors, because the equipment is limited to performing only cuts.

Cover shot: Another term for a long shot, or a shot taken from far enough away to give the viewer an idea of where people and things are in the scene. Also called an establishing shot.

Coverage: See "B-roll."

Cut-in shot: A shot of subject matter visible in the previous shot.

Cutaway shot: A shot of subject matter not visible in the previous shot.

Digitize: To digitize footage means to convert analog video to digital video.

Edit decision list (EDL): A digitized list of instructions enabling equipment in a computerized edit suite to perform a series of edits.

Edit master tape: See "Record tape."

Establishing shot: See "Cover shot."

Frame accuracy: A term describing an editing system accurate to the exact frame, in contrast to other (control-track) systems allowing editing errors as large as plus/minus seven frames.

Gigabyte (GB): A billion bytes of computer information.

Insert editing: An edit in which one records over existing audio or video, replacing it. Unlike assemble edits, the inserted material can be video only, audio only or a combination.

Jog: Manually playing back a videotape at very slow speeds, all the way down to one frame at a time.

Jump cut: An edit joining two shots of the same subject in different locations or poses, causing the subject to appear to "jump" on screen during playback.

Laundering an EDL: Revising the editing instructions you've previously recorded on your edit decision list.

Leader: Information recorded on a program tape ahead of the program itself that provides information about the program along with test signals and a cueing aid.

Line, the: See "Action axis."

Linear editing: A traditional form of videotape editing. The absence of random access means the editor has to scroll past footage (in a linear manner) in order to reach the desired point in the video.

Master shot: A wide shot recording all the action you'll show in an edited sequence composed of cut-in shots.

Neutral screen direction: Describes a shot framed with the camera aligned with, rather than located on either side of, the action axis. These shots can prepare audiences for a change in screen direction.

Nonlinear editing: A form of editing in which all source video is randomly rather than serially accessible. Such editing requires a disk-based storage device.

Nonlinear editor (NLE): A nonlinear (random-access) editing machine.

Off-line editing: Editing using a lesser-quality copy of original footage for purposes of developing an edit decision list (EDL) rather than a final program tape.

On-line editing: Editing using original footage to produce a final program tape rather than an edit decision list (EDL).

Pad video: See "Slop video."

Pictorial continuity: Maintaining the logical progression of action shot to shot in such a way as to avoid jump cuts.

Playback tape: A tape containing footage or a copy of footage to be recorded onto an edit tape during linear editing.

"Punch and crunch" editing: A manually cued, manually controlled editing procedure involving a playback VTR and a record VTR. This method was used to electronically edit videotape before the invention of computer edit controllers.

Record tape: The final program tape on which footage from the playback tape is compiled during editing. Also called the "edit master tape."

Scalable type font: A feature of computer-based typesetting that allows letters of any size to appear on screen.

Search knob: A tape-transport control on edit controllers permitting the user to access jog or shuttle scanning of a record or playback tape.

Shuttle: Playing back a videotape at fast-forward or rewind speed, while retaining the ability to view the video.

Slate: Information on the leader of a video production containing important identification information.

Slop video: Also known as pad video, it's the two seconds of footage inserted immediately preceding the frame of video where a news package actually begins. This may be used to replace the two seconds of black at the end of a leader.

SMPTE time code: Information recorded along with video permitting editors to identify each video frame separately to provide frame-accurate editing; time code is permanently associated with each frame, providing an absolute rather than relative means of identifying location on the tape. Off-line editing requires SMPTE time code. "SMPTE" stands for "Society of Motion Picture and Television Engineers."

Story continuity: The first of three main purposes of editing: correctly arranging your shots in a manner that best tells your story.

Straight-cut editor: See "Control-track editor."

Tail slate: Usually a repetition of the slate that begins your tape, added to the end.

Terabyte (TB): A trillion bytes of computer information.

VNF (video news film (VNF): A 16 mm reversal film stock made by Kodak for television news. It came in both silent (double-perforation) and in magnetic stripe (single-perforation) formats.

chapter 11

Field Production

This chapter discusses various kinds of nonstudio (EFP and ENG) productions. Many multiple-camera EFP productions require little or no formal editing, because they are either broadcast live or recorded "live on tape" for delayed airing. We'll discuss these first and then those requiring subsequent editing.

Multiple-Camera Remotes

Many types of field productions use multiple cameras. Among them are sports, parades, news coverage of meetings and conventions, theatrical shows, concerts and specials such as the Oscars and Emmys. Remote versions of programs usually anchored and shot in the studio are also shot in this fashion. Local and network newscasts and morning programs such as *The Today Show* are typical examples.

Most multiple-camera productions are shot in the controlled atmosphere of the studio, but the advantage of remote field production is obvious: Audiences can see things in real locations, not in a "make-believe" environment, adding to the program's credibility and excitement. The disadvantages include higher costs, larger production crews and more logistical headaches. Advancing technology, however, makes field production an increasingly attractive option as the size, weight and power consumption of equipment declines while its reliability and ease of use increase.

The Remote Van or Truck

"Headache Central" for multiple-camera field productions is the *remote van* or *truck,* a vehicle that serves as the field equivalent of the production control room and master control facility of a television studio. Some remote vans are the size of small delivery trucks; others, the size of recreational vehicles; while others are as large as two oversized truck trailers. Smaller vehicles typically serve the multiple-camera EFP needs of local TV stations and production companies. Large truck trailers capable of handling major sporting events are usually owned or rented by networks or by the major production companies that market their services to networks or syndicators (see Figure 11-1).

All field production vehicles contain essentially the same types of equipment: video switcher, character generator (CG), audio control console, audio recorders, videotape machines, camera control units and transmission gear for feeding the program to a TV station or network. The quality and quantity of equipment needed depends largely on the demands of the job at hand (see Figure 11-2).

ISOs

Complex productions, such as major sports remotes, usually require some equipment duplication to support an *ISO unit.* An ISO ("isolated") unit's job is to tape certain shots and activities other than those currently on the air. For example, an ISO unit for a network's football coverage typically requires a separate video switcher and audio console, CGs, several videotape recorders (VTRs) and an ISO director and crew. An ISO unit serves as "another set of eyes and ears" for the director of a program being taped live to be aired later. Using ISOs for concerts or entertainment specials allows the director to concentrate on getting shots of the overall performance, while the ISO unit records close-up shots of

1.

2.

Figure 11-1. *Shot 1 shows a typical ENG/EFP production van. Shot 2 is of a large production trailer.*
Shot 1, courtesy of KMTV, Omaha, Nebraska; shot 2, courtesy of Nebraska Educational Telecommunications.

individual performers, the audience's reactions and interesting video opportunities not occurring on stage. During postproduction editing, the producer selects the best video from the tapes recorded by the ISO unit and combines them with video of the performance recorded by the first unit.

The most frequent use of an ISO unit, however, is to provide instant replays of sporting events covered on the air by the first unit. Sometimes the ISO unit's shots chosen for replay by the producer and director simply duplicate the main unit's shots that just aired, but ISO shots also provide alternative views of the action. Before a play begins, the producer chooses camera shots likely to yield good views of the action in the

next play. The ISO director's job is to get these shots recorded on separate VTRs as the play unfolds, while the "on-air" director follows the main action. Depending on which ISO cameras and VTRs recorded the best views of the action, the ISO director prepares some or all of the ISO VTRs for playback at the director's command. Getting great ISO shots in a production such as football requires great sports expertise and technical skill acquired through years of experience. Most viewers are unaware of the coordinated

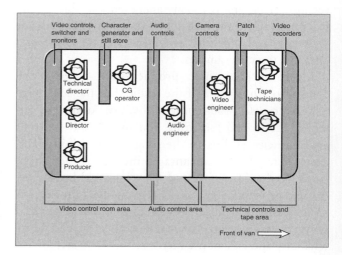

1.

2.

Figure 11-2. *Drawing 1 is an interior layout of a typical ENG van. Note that often such vans are operated by only two people, a reporter and an ENG photographer. Ideally, a video engineer would serve as operator during a live shot. In drawing 2, you see a typical layout for a large remote broadcast van. The video control room is at the rear, where one finds the producer, director and technical director (TD), or switcher, along with the CG operator. The audio engineer works in the audio control area. A video engineer and tape technicians work at the front of the van, adjusting the cameras as necessary, handling signal routing and performing any tape recording and playbacks. The doors on the side of the trailer provide direct access to the video control room, the audio control area and the video/routing/tape area.*

efforts necessary for an announcer to say, "Let's take another look at that play!"

Remote Cameras

Remote vans and truck trailers also carry cameras, tripods, cables, audio equipment and support gear, items as important on location as they are in the studio. Smaller vans required for less sophisticated productions usually carry convertible cameras configured for ENG/EFP. These versatile cameras work well for either multiple- or single-camera productions. Larger trailers associated with complex EFP work usually contain studio-quality cameras fitted with extremely long focal length zoom lenses.

EFP cameras usually need longer focal length lenses than studio cameras, because the cameras must often stay out of the way, far from the action. For example, in baseball, the center field camera that provides views from behind the pitcher is located in the center field bleachers, perhaps 400 to 440 feet from home plate, and must use an extremely long focal length zoom lens to get the shot. Staying out of the way isn't a requirement just for sports, but for any production where the event (concert, parade or convention) is conducted by someone other than the producers. Many field productions usually require the production crew to assume the role of "distant observer," unlike in the studio, where the director has nearly total control of the action. The director of a baseball broadcast, for example, can't place cameras down on the field and certainly can't order a play repeated because the shots didn't look good.

Remote Audio Gear

Field productions often require the specialty mikes discussed in Chapter 6. Although it's possible to capture crowd noise, applause and cheers with a simple dynamic omnidirectional mike, a multiple-camera remote production often uses more exotic apparatus. For example, basketball game announcers seated on the gym floor at half-court can't use a simple hand mike on a table stand. Turning their heads first one way and then the other, as sports announcers must do, would make their voices "off mike" most of the time. Instead, most sports announcers, parade commentators and convention reporters favor a headset-mounted mike permitting them the freedom to turn their heads in any direction and still transmit good audio (see Figure 11-3).

Concerts and conventions often allow audio technicians to place their mikes next to those used for public address or to patch directly into the PA system. Sometimes concert or

Figure 11-3. *A sports announcer using a double-muff headset microphone during a live remote broadcast.*
Photo courtesy of Nebraska Educational Telecommunications.

stage show talent use wireless mikes, which transmit sound to the PA system, the TV audio engineer or to both simultaneously. But often, getting acceptable audio isn't this easy. When a football quarterback barks his signals, the audio technician can't stand next to him with a hand mike. Instead, a crewperson runs up and down the sidelines pointing a parabolic or shotgun mike at the quarterback throughout the game, while the audio engineer in the EFP van or truck receives these mike signals and combines them into the final audio mix (see Figure 11-4).

Figure 11-4. *A remote audio engineer at work.*
Photo courtesy of Nebraska Educational Telecommunications.

Transmission

Productions that are not taped for airing or editing later—truly live productions—must be sent somewhere. Sending the video and audio signals to a nearby TV station or to a satellite link is called *transmission*. Before the invention of the microwave transmitter, the only way to send programs from a field production site was to use a special hookup provided by the local "telco" (the telephone company). This was one of the many tasks performed by remote production engineers during the days of preparation preceding an event. A special, high-quality telephone-line hookup was installed at the site and, after testing, the composite audio-video signal was sent over this line to the network's master control room in New York, or whichever city the network was based in. The network leased additional telco lines to distribute the signal to affiliates across the nation. This method is obsolete today, both as a transmission medium and for network interconnection. Radio-frequency uplinks transmit modern field-produced programs from the remote truck to either a land station to relay to a satellite or direct to satellite, then to network control, which retransmits the signal—again by satellite—to its broadcast or cable network affiliates, who broadcast them to the homes in their broadcast market and to the head ends of local cable TV companies (see Figure 11-5).

Although some stations and production companies use satellite links, most local news and sports remotes transmit live programs from the van to the station by terrestrial *microwave* (see Figure 11-6). A "narrowcast" format for point-to-point wireless communication, microwave requires the EFP van to establish a line-of-sight path between the van and a microwave receiver at the station. When direct line-of-sight isn't possible, stations often install microwave repeaters on tall buildings or hilltops around the city to relay signals. In unusual situations, a station may use a microwave repeater mounted aboard a helicopter or other aircraft hovering somewhere between the remote site and the station as part of a temporary relay system.

The Site Survey

The key to successful multiple-camera field production, or any production for that matter, is good preparation. And good preparation begins with a site survey. Weeks before the event (or sometimes years before, as in the case of network coverage of the Olympic Games), the production company's field staff visits the site. If this is a regular stop (an annual professional golf tour site or

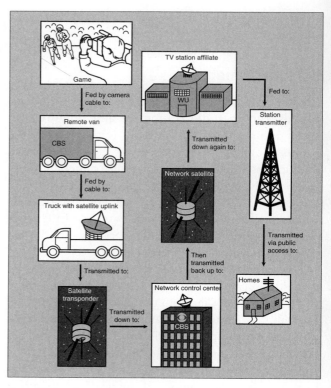

Figure 11-5. *The signal path of a camera shot from a remote location to your home.*

a football stadium the crew uses every year), the production staff makes sure that all electrical hookups, communications apparatus, stadium lighting, camera cable runs and platforms, locations for parking trucks and security areas for storing gear haven't changed since the last visit. If it's an unfamiliar location, all these considerations and others are checked, arranged for and tested the first time.

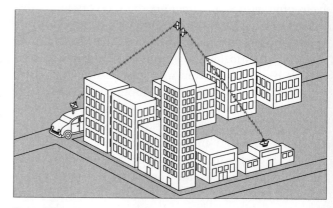

Figure 11-6. *This is a sketch of a microwave signal sent from a van to the top of a building and then relayed on to the station. Microwaves can't pass through solid objects and require "line-of-sight" to pass on the signal.*

A Handy Checklist

To the greatest degree possible, try to plan so that the conditions during your survey will duplicate as closely as possible the conditions during the broadcast. If possible, visit the site on the same day of the week and the same time of day that the broadcast is scheduled.

Establish an on-site contact who knows the location well. If you're working at a state park, a fairground or an auditorium, find the person in charge (or their designated representative) and arrange for that person to go with you on your survey. If your remote takes place where other broadcasts have been produced, this contact person probably has worked with other TV producers and can provide valuable information about what worked and what didn't. Often the remote-location contact person has access to building diagrams that show power connections, telephone hookups and equipment storage areas. Some sites even provide locally produced books designed to help TV crews set up. Don't forget to ask if such a publication is available, and then study it before you undertake your survey. The contact person can also help you resolve problems and establish relationships with police or security personnel, the fire marshal, trade unions and other important locals.

Consider where you'll park the remote truck. It must be close enough to the event for cable runs to the cameras at the various locations around the site. It must also be close to the transmission link to your station or network. Whether the link is a satellite *uplink* (a transmitter from the ground to a communications satellite) or a terrestrial microwave transmitter, you must set up close to it. You must also be close to the truck's source of electrical power. This must be a safe place, too, one that provides security for your crew and equipment.

Consider camera placement. Obviously you want to place cameras where they provide the best shots. Views of sports action and almost all other kinds of remote coverage are enhanced with shots from high angles. This often requires building or renting platforms and scaffolding of sturdy construction. You'll also need equally sturdy crewmembers to brave the heights and sometimes severe weather encountered during outdoor field production (see Figure 11-7).

Don't forget security and protection for the cameras. What happens if it rains or snows? Often you set up your cameras hours, or even days, before the event. This means taking security precautions to avoid damage and theft. The placement, anchoring and security requirements of equipment contribute to the high cost of remotes.

You must also allow for conduit for *cable runs* (bundled audio, video, intercom and power cables stretching from the cameras and microphone positions back to the van). Newer stadiums and public complexes incorporate provisions in their design and construction for cable runs, but in older facilities, thick bundles of cables must be "snaked" out to the camera locations following routes infrequently taken by participants and audiences. Small-diameter modern cables make the task less burdensome, and wireless camera and audio interconnection systems are now available, but "pulling cable" remains a dirty and difficult part of many field productions (see Figure 11-8 on page 234).

Consider lighting. Is there enough natural light for good video? Modern cameras operate under relatively low light conditions, but all cameras make better pictures and provide greater depth of field if they have more than the minimum required light. Where can you position your lights to avoid bothering the audience? Do you have the electrical power necessary? At 500 or 1,000 watts or more per lighting instrument, just a few instruments can overload the electrical systems of many

Figure 11-7. *Erecting sturdy camera platforms is a common job required for many remote productions.*

(Continued)

remote locations. One of the most important members of your remote crew is your gaffer, the chief electrician and lighting boss, because without electrical power your production won't happen.

Consider audio. How noisy will the site be on the day of the event? How many mikes will you need, and what kinds of mikes? Will you need to tie into the PA system? And don't forget intercom and IFB lines (that is, interrupted feedback lines, so your director, crew and talent can communicate with each other). Like camera cabling, you must route these wires so the crowds attending the event aren't likely to damage them. Besides the audio equipment necessary to record the program, there are other nonprogram audio logistics. A remote often requires much more sophisticated intercom capabilities than a typical studio private-line (intercom) system provides. A multiple-camera remote often involves many more individuals scattered over a larger area than a studio production. And often the communication needs are unique to the type of production. Here are just a few examples of the unique wireless communication needs a producer may face in a field production:

Figure 11-8. *Preparing cable connections for bad weather is a standard practice for outdoor remote productions. In this photo, the point at which two video cables are connected is carefully wrapped with plastic and taped for waterproofing.*

- The pilot of the blimp and the blimp's camera operator must keep in touch with the director.
- Spotters up the slope in ski-racing coverage, or following groups of professional golfers around the golf course or just out of sight around the corner of a parade help keep the director and producer aware of situations developing outside their field of view.
- The stage manager of a football bowl game's half-time extravaganza needs to relay cues to the television crew.
- Correspondents on the floor of a national political convention must coordinate interviews of various political figures with the producer, director and the anchor announcer.

Consider your remote crew. How will they get to and from the remote? Will you arrange transportation, or is this the responsibility of each individual? How about food and lodging? Work schedules? You may be hiring union labor, who work under contracts specifying hours, breaks and other important employment conditions. Even in the uproar and chaos of field productions, labor contract regulations still apply.

Consider the unexpected. What disasters could happen, and what contingency plans should you make to react to them? If you're shooting outside, what about the weather? What about equipment problems, such as a vital camera that suddenly fails during a live production? The audio for a major network presidential debate program once went dead at the beginning of the remote telecast. Nobody could find a simple replacement part to repair a critical amplifier—and there was no backup amplifier available!

Permits

Because television is so pervasive in our lives, some think that TV crews just barge into any location they wish, quickly set up their equipment and start shooting. This is not how it goes. In the case of major sports and similar events, television networks pay huge sums for permission to cover games with their remote crews. When TV coverage of a parade or convention is planned, you may need permits from the city, permission to place cameras on convenient rooftops or clearance from the Federal Aviation Administration for lower-than-normal helicopter or blimp flying. Sometimes permission to shoot on private property involves a *site fee,* a stipend paid to a property owner before the crew can set foot on the location. Even if no site fee is required, it's a good practice to get at least oral (and preferably written) permission before shooting on private property.

Single-Camera Remotes

We now turn our attention to the single-camera remote. Common sense suggests that many production concerns listed for the multiple-camera shoot are still important in single-camera work. A major difference is that single-camera field production places all production burdens on one or, at most, a few persons.

Single-camera EFP remotes differ from ENG both in objectives and in the ability to control picture quality. Although news stories may use an ENG/EFP camera connected to a mobile van, usually the part of the live remote that is shot in EFP style is limited to the reporter's live stand-up or a well-prepared, staged interview. Lighting for single-camera EFP is often more carefully crafted than for many ENG setups, and, if the shoot is outside, added reflectors can fill in shadows that might be ignored in an ENG shot. Also, EFP camera shots are sometimes more carefully composed and adjusted than in ENG. In ENG, the photog often must capture whatever video possible under transitory and unrepeatable circumstances. In contrast, when the network news anchor says, "Now we go live to our correspondent at the White House," a carefully prepared and orchestrated remote feed usually follows. Often, during or after this live feed, an ENG package prepared earlier is inserted, with the EFP correspondent acting as a kind of secondary anchor.

Electronic News Gathering

News and documentaries employ ENG shooting techniques and equipment, using either a small crew or just one combination reporter/camera operator. Use of two cameras usually is reserved for important, higher-budget ENG interviews. For example, when a high-profile news reporter, such as one of the *Sixty Minutes* correspondents, interviews a subject, they often use two cameras crossed on the participants with separate tapes rolling. During editing, the two tapes are cut together (see Figure 11-9). The ENG photog working alone may have little control over the circumstances of the coverage, and thus must be experienced, resourceful and quick-witted to get all the shots needed to tell the story. Many events, great and small, happen only once in a split second, and ENG photogs often must earn their pay in a hurry (see Figure 11-10).

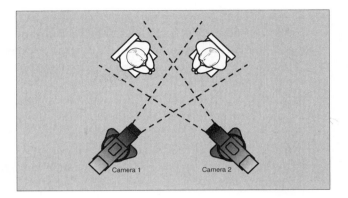

Figure 11-9. *This is a very typical camera setup for a two-person interview.*

Helpful Hints for Single-Camera and ENG Production

Much of the same preproduction preparation as in multiple-camera remotes must be done—usually with much less lead time. Unlike multiple-camera remotes, no truck or van filled with engineers, spare parts and extra equipment goes along on an ENG shoot. Single-camera productions often use a van, but its primary function is to provide signal transmission rather than carry production engineers and spare gear. Only the richest stations now send an engineer on a single-camera EFP shoot. Those performing single-camera EFP as well as ENG work must learn to be self-contained, self-reliant and safety conscious. For example, there have been a number of cases involving electrocutions and other injuries to EFP van operators

Figure 11-10. *The "one-man band" is increasingly common in ENG work around the country.*

whose extended microwave dishes have come in contact with high-power electrical lines. The bottom line is simple: Be careful, and always check to make sure that your microwave transmission boom is lowered before you move the van!

Begin with an inventory of basic equipment and accessories. Not every item mentioned below is required on every shoot; experience will help you decide what to carry with you, what you can leave in the car and what you can leave at the studio for each kind of field production:

The List

- The camera, along with camera case or carry bag.
- Any filters and other lens accessories.
- More tape than you think you could possibly use.
- Batteries. It's possible to get power for your camera and recorder from an AC adapter, but you should never count on an AC power source being available. Bring enough batteries to power your equipment for the amount of tape you brought—plus one extra battery. Rechargeable batteries don't always get recharged or recharged fully. Consult your equipment manual to determine how long each battery will last with your particular gear. And remember, the colder the location is, the shorter your battery time. Count on each battery underperforming on a cold day.
- A 9 × 12-inch clip board, with a white card (for white balancing), field footage log sheets, pens, etc (see Figure 11-11).
- A slate (rarely used in ENG, but important for visually as well as orally logging takes in EFP work). Because of the small crew and haste of ENG work, takes are slated orally, if at all.
- A small tool kit with screwdrivers (both a Phillips head and a slender regular head), regular and needle-nose pliers, and other small items you may need, including three-prong-to-two-prong AC adapters and other small items. Your kit should always include gaffer's tape and a few dozen nylon cable ties (see Figure 11-12).
- A tripod with tripod accessories (and sometimes a carrying case for all of this).
- A lighting kit with extra lamps and extra AC extension cords. You should also take along a battery-powered camera light (the small open-front light mounted atop the camera). Take some additional gator clamps and light hangers for those places where floor stands won't fit. Also, many lighting kits are augmented with colored filter gels to aid in

CAMERA SHOT LOG

DATE __7/10__   PRODUCTION __Herald Motors__
TAPE CODE __6__   PHOTOGRAPHER __Smith__
FORMAT __Beta__   TAPE LENGTH _____   PAGE __1__ OF __4__

SHOT NO.	DESCRIPTION	START	STOP	COMMENTS
3	Car moves toward cam	0	0:00:20	NGC
3	" " "	0:00:20	0:00:42	NGA
3	" " "	0:00:42	0:01:00	OK
8	ELS, aerial shot of car	0:01:00	0:03:16	NGC
8	" " " "	0:03:16	0:06:26	NGC
8	" " " "	0:06:26	0:09:56	OK

Figure 11-11. *Field footage logs are used by production teams to keep accurate records of what is shot and for how long, which take is good and which videotape (of all the ones you shot) contains which shots. In this example, we see the notations made by a production assistant for a few shots from a commercial that you will study in our chapter on writing. For shot 3, "Car moves toward cam," three takes were necessary to satisfy the director. The "comments" column indicates that the first take was "NGC" ("No Good—Camera"), either because the camera operator or the director didn't like the way the shot turned out. This is typical in motion shots, especially shots of fast-moving vehicles. The second take was "NGA" ("No Good—Actor"), because the stunt driver of the car missed his mark. The "OK" on the third take indicates that this is the one the director will use in the editing room. Likewise, the first two takes of the aerial shot, shot 8, were unsatisfactory due to camera work. Finally, on the third take, the coordination of the helicopter, camera operator and stunt driver resulted in a good take.*

the color temperature conversion of ambient light and neutral density gels to reduce bright light levels.

- An assortment of mikes and mike cables (along with one extra mike cable—just in case one fails). Usually this assortment will include one or two rugged, omnidirectional hand mikes and at least two electret condenser clip mikes, with extra mike batteries. Also, a line level–mike level transformer is very handy.
- Wind screens ("socks") fitting all mikes you're taking with you, for use in windy outdoor locations. Most news organizations require attaching mike flags (small signs showing the company logo, and/or channel number).
- A set of headphones to monitor the audio you're recording. These plug into the recorder's audio headphone jack. However, many ENG and single-camera EFP photogs prefer a simple earplug for monitoring. Also handy are audio accessories such as connector adapters and/or extra clip holders for lav mikes.

1.

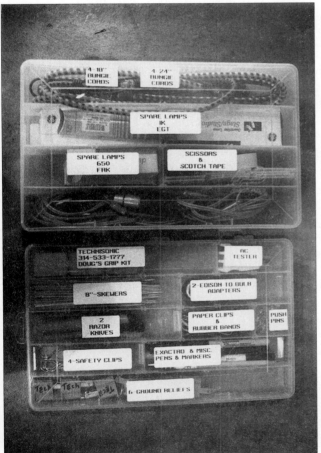

2.

Figure 11-12. *Shot 1 shows the typical contents of a small tool kit; shot 2 is the "ditty bag" (two plastic, see-through boxes) of a lighting gaffer.*

- A color television monitor, its battery (or AC adapter) and cables to connect it to your particular camera. Few ENG units regularly carry such a bulky piece of equipment. Single-camera EFP shoots often use a color monitor for on-site test-

ing of camera equipment and as a second camera viewfinder, so both the director and camera operator can watch the scene as it's being shot.

As you become more experienced, you'll add other items that have proven helpful on prior shoots. Although not technically a component of ENG production gear, the cell phone is "standard issue" for ENG work. ENG units need some means of keeping in touch with the assignment editor or home base—both to get updates on breaking stories, or to report progress or difficulties. Regardless of the method, a well-established "com-link" to home base is vital to successful ENG production.

Six Tips for Shooting a News Package

Most news directors prefer the remote package, as we described in the "An Overview and Tour" chapter. Using a self-contained, pretaped and edited story, which will later be inserted into the live news broadcast, makes it easier to keep track of time in the newscast production, and while a package is playing, the show's director has time to talk to talent and keep track of all production elements. In shooting a package, reporters and field producers should keep the following six aspects in mind:

1. Shoot the interview first, if possible. Even liberal arts graduates can't be authorities on every possible subject. One of the main reasons for doing interviews is to get an expert's perspective on the news topic. Many times the expert will not only give you a good quote, but his or her quotes will give you an idea of how to produce the package. Think about moving the subject into the middle of whatever he/she manages. This is so much better than sitting in his/her office, surrounded by awards and pictures on his wall. Interview the president of the school board in front of one of the schools that he/she supervises. And if there are kids milling around, all the better.

2. Shoot plenty of cutaways and B-roll (see page 238 on five shots you should get with every interview). Cutaways are the reverse angle shots of the interview subject and reporter. B-roll shots, as discussed in the last chapter, are footage of the actual subject matter discussed in the package, be it urban renewal, feature shots of beekeepers or sports action. It's nearly impossible to overshoot this footage, but it's a frequent error—committed especially by students—to undershoot it.

3. A good ratio of shots in the edited package is 20 per minute. Unless you have reason to linger on something, you can use three-second shots on average to keep the package moving at a good pace.

4. Avoid superfluous zooming and panning. Because it takes time to complete these moves, they limit flexibility in editing. Locked (static) shots can be shortened or lengthened according to time constraints. Cutting into or out of a moving shot is aesthetically displeasing as well as disorienting to the viewer. Therefore, "30 seconds becomes 3 seconds": Hold the locked shot for 30 seconds, and then take the best 3 seconds of that shot for the final edit.

5. Edit in the camera. This means plan your shot before you hit the record button. Compose the shot, then turn on the camera. This saves precious time in the editing room. You won't have to wade through tons of useless, meandering shots while you look for the good stuff.

6. Shoot a stand-up. This takes forethought and planning. Many professionals start thinking about their stand-ups as soon as the interview portion is completed. You want to say something insightful, informative or illuminating. Just repeating your name is useless. Some reporters resort to the "time will tell" cliché or something equally meaningless. You can ask practically any question and answer, "Time will tell." Expect plenty of razzing from your colleagues if you use this tactic.

Five Shots to Get With Every Interview

Shooting an adequate amount of cutaways can become a habit instead of a guessing game. With these methods, every reporter can ensure a sufficient quantity and quality of shots for ease in editing.

(Shot 1) First, the interviewee: Some news directors prefer a medium shot from the waist up while others like a medium close-up. Find out. Either way there is space allowed for adding the name key graphics during the newscast. Shoot the entire interview with this shot. You'll get the other shots afterward.

(Shot 2) The easiest shot to get involves zooming out for an over-the-shoulder (OTS) two shot. This is over the <u>reporter's</u> shoulder. Have the reporter re-ask a question or even just count to 10. Either way we can see a little of the reporter's jaw flapping and the microphone being passed toward the subject. Questions can be added later to fit the sound bite chosen, if necessary.

(Shot 3) You can frequently move the camera around so it's shooting over the interviewee's shoulder for a reverse-angle OTS two shot. This time, have the interview subject's jaw flapping.

(Shot 4) Next, get a tight shot of the reporter, matching the shot size you used for the interviewee. Some news directors like to see a "noddie," also called a "nodder," while others do not. This is the shot of the reporter nodding and looking astute while presumably listening to the interviewee speaking. Other reaction shots can be tested—a raising of the eyebrow, a smile, a furrowing of the brow. Then match the proper reaction to the quote.

(Shot 5) The fifth shot is a medium long shot of both the reporter and subject with alternate jaw flapping. This is a good cutaway to use for either person talking, or for adding a question in the editing room to match an edited sound bite. If the interview is conducted in an office with both subjects seated, you might add a sixth shot (not shown). If the reporter has a notepad, frame an OTS medium close-up of this notepad. Don't zoom in so close the viewer can read the writing—just enough to see the reporter taking notes.

1.

2.

(Continued)

(Continued)

3.

5.

4.

As always, the reporter, field producer or videographer can look around an office for the *anytime cutaway*—a shot that can be used at any time in the final edit. This can be a nameplate, a picture or some artifact in the room that adds to the story. In a time pinch, these cutaway shots can be fashioned into a 20- to 30-second story with the sound bite. It may not be the most artistic treatment, but it can help meet a deadline.

Figure 11-13.

There's another standard shot that those of us who teach TV production see all too often. It's the <u>wrong shot</u> (see Figure 11-14). This shot is taken 90 degrees to the action axis and draws attention away from the intended focus of the shot, the interviewee. It also is aesthetically less pleasing than the OTS shot, because there is all that wasted space in the center of the picture. It also shows both people in unflattering profile shots. As a general rule, in any ENG two shot, keep <u>both eyes</u> of at least one person visible at all times. And when shooting toward the interviewee, keep in mind that the <u>newsmaker</u> is the focal point of the story, <u>not</u> the reporter. Viewers want to see the newsmaker straight on and look into his/her face.

When You Arrive . . .

Provided you have the time, taking a few minutes to check out your equipment pays large dividends. Begin by getting a white balance and, if time permits, do a test recording. Then review the footage through your camera viewfinder and listen to the sound on your headset. One good way to ruin your day is to shoot what you think is an excellent story, only to discover later that a video record head was clogged and you have no picture, or an audio cable was faulty, and all you have are great-looking silent pictures. Switch your camera's output to "bars" and record a minute or so of color bars at the head of each tape you use. This allows you to do color and luminance setup with ease during editing.

Figure 11-14. *A poorly composed two shot such as this detracts attention from the interviewee and doesn't effectively use the space in the picture.*

It's a good practice to use a handheld omnidirectional mike for quickly arranged, on-the-spot interviews, or for any audio requiring camera mobility. Two clip mikes, one for the newsmaker and the other for the reporter, are more effective when you have the luxury of preparing sit-down (or "stand-still") interviews with newsmakers. If you're equipped with wireless mikes, all the better. The fewer encumbering wires and the more comfortable your subject, the better the responses.

Audio from a shotgun or unidirectional cardioid mike mounted atop a camera is inferior to audio from mikes placed closer to the subject. However, when a photog must act as a "one-person band" and can't hook up the subject with a clip mike, the camera-mounted mike may be the only option. The resultant loss of clarity and the echolike quality of the sound are unavoidable. If you must use a camera-mounted mike to interview a newsmaker, zoom out all the way and move the camera closer to the newsmaker. Remember the general rule of thumb from Chapter 6: The closer the mike is to the speaker, the better the audio quality.

It's wise to roll five to 10 seconds of video footage before and after every shot. You need this "slop video" to provide stable control track for analog editing. And, if this is the first shot in a news story, two seconds of video can be inserted in place of two seconds of black between the leader and the first shot. Many professional news photogs roll tape while still walking (or running) to where the action will occur to ensure they have enough "slop" and are ready to focus and shoot as soon as the important action starts. Tape is the cheapest thing you're working with: "Waste not, want not" usually doesn't apply to tape. Conserve on "slop video" only when you're extremely low on battery power. Generally, the cheaper your camcorder, the longer it takes for it to get up to speed mechanically and the earlier you need to roll tape to avoid missing critical action.

You may think that "slop video" is irrelevant if you're editing video on a nonlinear editing system, because the computer requires no preroll to make a cut. Not true, for three reasons: First, there's nothing worse than missing the beginning of candid action while the camera you're holding is turned off; second, camcorders need a few seconds from the time you start the tape until recording is completely "locked up," and the first few seconds of recorded video are often unstable and unusable; third, you need extra frames if you later decide to do a dissolve or some other effect. So the move into the age of digital editing doesn't mean you can forget about slop video.

Don't just shoot the interview or the speech or the main action and then pack up and go home. Before or after taping the main action, shoot plenty of that B-roll footage: cutaways, cut-ins and cover shots. Having shots related to the main action is important because, as your interviewee or voice-over audio describes the story, you can insert these related shots, with or without sound, that help illustrate the story and make it more visually compelling. Experienced photogs can shoot just enough B-roll to do the job without shooting excess footage, but beginners almost always find they lack either enough B-roll or the B-roll shots they need most.

There are many occasions when it's important to roll tape without regard to the video, such as when you are recording the sound of a crowd, the seashore or whatever sounds characterize the location. As you may recall from the "An Overview and a Tour" chapter, this is called "taking tone," film jargon for recording room tone, the ambient sound found at any location. During postproduction editing, this ambient sound can help cover an abrupt or awkward change in audio, or "patch up" a damaged or partially erased section of videotape.

Other Important Interview Techniques

When planning a news interview, think and research. What is the purpose of the interview? What would you want the person to say? What would be the perfect quote? Can you shape a question to elicit that perfect sound bite? What are your first three questions? You may glance at your notes, but you should memorize your first three questions.

Call to schedule the interview. Try an ideal time for you first, but be willing and able to accommodate your subject. After all, this person is doing you a favor. During this process, this person becomes the most important person on the planet for you. You don't necessarily have any expertise in the subject matter. You should become an expert in finding out what your audience needs to know about the interviewee's subject matter, and then shaping the package to communicate this information.

Remember you're in charge, but don't be a prima donna about it. Charm your way through the entire experience. Be a pleasure to work with, and you're more likely to get repeat interviews. If possible, set up the lights and camera and then bring the subject to this area. Don't make the person wait while you take 20 minutes to set up the equipment. This causes the subject to become bored, go stale and lose focus of the topic.

This sounds simple, but it's frequently forgotten. While you're doing the interview, listen! The best questions often come from context, not from the list you've prepared on your clipboard. Try to shape your next question from the quote you've just gotten. Lock eyes with your subject. Let him or her know (nonverbally) that you're hanging on every word. Know when you've gotten your perfect sound bite. Immediately begin producing the package in your head.

Editing the News Package

A common formula for the news package is "*voicer-bite-voicer-tag.*" This is news lingo for a voice-over, sound bite, another voice-over followed by a standup tag. Additional sound bites (opposing viewpoints?) can be added as your judgment dictates. The first voice-over works in conjunction with the video to set the context of the story, establish the location and set up the first sound bite. This is usually done in about 10 to 15 seconds. Naturally, being concise is a must. To set up the quote, tease the bite, but don't steal the thunder. This means you give the viewer an idea of what the quote is going to be, but don't give it away verbatim. If you say, "The mayor says college students shouldn't drink too much," and then you show the mayor saying, "College students shouldn't drink too much this weekend," the audience will wonder why you bothered to include the sound bite. Instead, use something more like this: "The mayor issued a warning about public consumption of alcohol." And avoid using those awful, vague banalities, like, "He had this to say." Bridge out of the bite the same way—by taking a word or two from the tail end of the quote—and then ease into the next voice over and/or bite. Finally, do a standup tag. It doesn't always have to come at the end.

You can do it between two sound bites. This is called an *interior bridge.* Whatever you do, don't just say your name; you can do that with a voice over. And don't just say, "I'm standing here in front of City Hall"; we can see that. Why are you standing there? Show us you know something about this subject, this interview, this topic. Find a good backdrop that also adds perspective to the story—perhaps the exterior of the building where you conducted the interview. Sometimes tags are done outside the station after the package has been shaped. You can find a nondescript background, such as a brick wall or a tree. It isn't art, but it can still give us valuable information.

This chapter and others in this section have concentrated on introductory discussions of production equipment, basic operations and techniques, and fundamental terms and concepts. In the next section we'll explore in greater detail how to use this equipment and basic information to build and shape the pictures and sounds that comprise television productions.

Important Vocabulary Terms

Anytime cutaway: A shot, usually in an office setting, that can be used at any time in the edited piece. It can be a picture, a nameplate or an artifact that adds to the overall feel of the production.

Cable run: A collection of bundled cables (audio, video, AC power, intercom, etc.) stretching from camera sites on a field production to the van.

Interior bridge: In a news package, a stand-up placed between two sound bites or footage from two different scenes or locations.

ISOA unit: Short for "isolated," the description of a production unit that tapes shots other than those currently on air.

Microwave: A type of point-to-point wireless transmission. An EFP van equipped with a microwave link can transmit audio and video from remote production locations to a TV station or other destination.

Nodder, or noddie: A reporter's reaction shot, often showing the reporter listening attentively and perhaps nodding.

Remote van (or truck): A vehicle, with all the necessary equipment, that serves as the field-production equivalent of a TV studio control room and engineering center.

Site fee: A stipend paid to a property owner before a production crew can set foot on his/her property.

Transmission: Occasionally called the "backhaul," this is the process of conveying programs from the remote site to a station or common carrier such as the phone company or a satellite link.

Uplink: A transmitter from the ground to a communications satellite.

Voicer-bite-voicer-tag: A formula for editing news packages where the reporter begins with a voice-over, follows with a sound bite, adds another voice-over for additional information and concludes with a standup tag.

chapter **12**

TV Performance

Few areas of human endeavor are more fraught with misconceptions than television performance. Many viewers pay undue attention to facial features. Some anchorpersons dwell upon cosmetic frills such as hairstyles and clothing accessories. Teachers find it difficult to offer general guidelines while correcting individual shortcomings. Beginners often cannot get constructive criticism from anyone. Meaningful, intelligent help is hard to come by, while cheap shots abound.

Two Categories of Students

Students usually fall into two categories: those who are scared that they're going to be on camera, and those who are scared they're <u>not</u> going to be on camera. Armed with a little knowledge and practice, both groups can approach the concept in more reasonable terms. For the first group, just because you don't plan on being on-air talent doesn't mean you shouldn't learn the details involved. If you stay in the communications business long enough, you're going to have to coach a better performance out of someone, whether he/she's an accomplished veteran or a rank beginner. It's especially important to know how to handle beginners or "civilians," the nonprofessionals you often must patiently, skillfully direct in some commercials, documentaries and especially in corporate videos. This can be a tense situation if the coach has no idea what he or she is talking about. Experience, no matter how anxious you are about it, is a good teacher. Learn to use the right terminology for specific pointers rather than vague phrases such as, "I can't put my finger on it, but there's something missing." By familiarizing

yourself with the terms and techniques of voice and on-camera delivery, you can be very clear about what you, as a director or a producer, need from your talent. The performers who are being evaluated will be most appreciative.

For the second group, those who yearn to perform, being an on-camera professional requires a huge commitment to improving all aspects of your talent delivery. You should be versatile in your approach, resilient in your response to criticism and dedicated to self-improvement by endless hours of practice.

This chapter is designed to give everyone a more thorough understanding of the elements needed for a successful performance, both on and off camera. After all, you can't direct what you don't understand.

The PEER CAPE Formula

The following three-step method is not only a good starting point for developing performance abilities, but it is also helpful for self-evaluation. The first part of the formula is called PEER CAPE, or more precisely, the acronym. "PEER" stands for "poise, eye contact, energy and rhythm." "CAPE" refers to "correcting mistakes, animation, pacing and emphasis."

The first "P" represents something almost intangible: poise. It can take years to acquire, but it is an excellent starting point for everything to follow. At a minimum, performers should maintain a serious, dignified demeanor. It is a must for newscasters; some commercials require zaniness occasionally, but talent must maintain their composure and stay in character at all times. If you make a mistake, don't drop your head, roll your eyes or make some remark to others on the set. Hold your pose, and hold your poise. In acting, it's called "keeping in character," and it is fundamental. Try putting yourself in the proper frame of mind before you go on the set. Then when the red light comes on, you're poised and ready.

The first "E," eye contact, is somewhat self-explanatory. You want to extend your visual connection with the viewer, especially in newscasts. There are two situations to consider here: reading from scripts, or reading from teleprompters.

If you are reading from a handheld script, try these suggestions: First, study the script. Read it out loud ten times before going on the set. Then, sweep in several lines of copy, look up and recite it to the camera (you can practice by reading into a mirror and noticing how long you can maintain eye contact). Glimpse down, sweep in more lines of copy and look up again immediately. Recite these lines of copy and repeat the process. Do this by glimpsing down and up—don't bob your head and show the crown of your scalp. Using a pencil or your finger to keep your place on the copy is helpful. Acquiring expertise in this fashion is also a big help in reading cold copy. It is not uncommon for professionals to have a script shoved before them to read on camera, even live, with no practice or forewarning. This reading technique is comparable to learning how to drive on a manual transmission. Making the adjustment to an automatic transmission, or teleprompter, is much easier than vice-versa.

The teleprompter does not automatically make one poised and competent. It simply places the copy in front of the camera lens. If you have no script-reading skills, you will not instantly become credible when the copy zings upward on the prompter screen. The biggest hazard for most prompter-reading beginners is prompter lock, or the "deer in the headlights" look. Neophytes sometimes make the mistake of never looking away from the camera. It often seems as if they aren't even blinking. One technique for newscasters is to look down between stories, check the script, confirm that it's the same story on the prompter and then proceed. Develop the habit of looking away for short periods to avoid the panic-stricken appearance. If you know your copy, you can be more confident in this regard.

The next "E," energy, is a difficult concept for novices to grasp. The overwhelming majority of rookies sound dull, dull, dull. Again, experience and practice will help. A performer's every word and gesture must convey the importance of the script content. Amateurs must strive for energy in their voices, eyes, faces and demeanors.

Figure 12-1. *Energy is an essential element to make field reports and studio anchor/announcing performances come alive. A big difference between droning on and communicating with your audience is looking like you're excited to be there and interested in the story you're reading.*

Command the viewers' attention by your presence. Many beginners will be afraid of overdoing it, but this is extremely rare. Furthermore, it is easier to tone down an overly exuberant delivery than it is to pep up a boring one. This is something that executives and talent agents look for—the ability to make copy seem important without over dramatizing it (see Figure 12-1).

The "R" is for rhythm, or the basic speed at which you read. News and commercial copy must be read a bit faster than normal speaking rhythm. This is another way to get energy into the delivery: You will occasionally slow down for a word or two, but you must speed up your rhythm while making it seem natural.

"C" is for correcting mistakes. This is one aspect that's almost always misdirected. Too many amateurs obsess over trying not to make mistakes. Then, when they make the inevitable error, they go to pieces. The simple truth is, everyone, from the beginner to the most experienced performer, is going to make mistakes. The question becomes, how do you handle it when you make a mistake? The answer is, it depends on the error. The ability to decide instantaneously how to handle mistakes comes with practice and experience. Simple, rather meaningless mistakes can be more or less ignored. Important facts or figures must be clarified for the viewers. A good rule of thumb is, "Make it make sense." When reading a long of list of numbers, such as on election night, correct your error. When a newscaster flubs a number, he can say something to the effect, "Pardon me, make that total for Congressman Smith 346-thousand-nine-hundred-eighteen." Just correcting one part of the number, such as the 900 in 918, would only add to the confusion. The same holds true for dollar amounts in commercial copy or other precise facts in live announcing. Don't be afraid to back up to the beginning of the sentence, or even the beginning of the ad, if necessary. On the other hand, if it is only one word in a relatively simple phrase, use the words "rather," or "make that" (for example, "Make that 'three for a dollar'"), correct the mistake and go on with the copy.

Instead of placing a lot of importance on insignificant miscues, emphasize an overall approach. Performers, like sports teams, must play to win instead of playing not to lose. Think of the best way to handle stories and other copy rather than being scared to make a mistake. The blunders will decrease.

The "A" is for animation. This is another aspect that beginners often overlook or ignore. Announcers can't look like a statue whose lips are moving. They must master the use of their eyes, their lips, their faces, their heads and their hands. To illustrate the point, students should watch newscasts and commercials with the sound turned down. Watch how anchors and experienced on-camera commercial announcers tilt their heads forward for emphasis. Perhaps they'll lift their eyebrows or cock their heads. They don't just sit or stand motionless. They employ movement, albeit limited movement, within the range of the camera shot. The gesture or animation must fit the tone of the copy. Assassination reports must not be handled with desk thumping, but rather with a more somber tone. Offbeat commercials should be handled with the amusement necessary to convey the feel of the ad. Though few amateurs know the importance of animation, they seem to learn it quickly. Then it looks—here's the magic word again—natural.

The final two letters, "P" and "E," stand for the most important parts of announcing delivery. They go hand in hand and must work together for effective announcing. They are pacing and emphasis. Pacing is setting it up, and emphasis is driving it home. There are several ways to do both, and you must vary the techniques. For pacing, the usual way is to read up to the key word or phrase, pause slightly and then punch that word or phrase with emphasis. Other pacing methods include reading slightly faster and then pausing before emphasizing. You can also read a bit slower, pause and then accentuate the important elements. Emphasis can be accomplished one of three ways. One is by raising the inflection of the voice. Most beginners tend to shout. This is not only wrong, it also drives audio technicians crazy. Use an upward lilt of the voice, but don't scream.

Conversely, the second tactic for emphasis is by lowering your tone. Here, there is no substitute for a strong, deep voice, or as announcers describe it, "a good set of pipes." The final technique for getting emphasis is one we all use from time to time but are largely unaware of. That is, s-t-r-e-t-c-h the word. Haven't you said something like, "It's f-r-e-e-z-i-n-g in here!" Now learn to use this technique to your advantage. It works best with one- or two-syllable words. Don't try saying "everybody" this way: It sounds like the tape is being played at the wrong speed.

Since proper pacing and emphasis are the most effective tactics for professionalizing an announcing delivery, they should be mastered as quickly as possible. Vary the pacing methods and definitely alter the emphasis procedures.

All of the aforementioned eight aspects are essential; none are optional. Students shouldn't pick and choose the steps in which they wish to excel and ignore other areas. Indeed, by practicing diligently for just three hours, beginners can see great improvement in their delivery. While this would be a giant step in anyone's development, it alone won't be enough to make that person a professional. That comes only after painstaking work on those elements that are not yet perfected, which vary from person to person. The performer should grade himself or herself on the PEER CAPE items. Score the items with a number from one to 10, 10 being the highest. Be brutally honest. You should be your own worst critic. Then no one else can hurt your feelings. Once you've evaluated each skill, you'll be ready to start work on the areas that need it.

Twenty Additional Concerns

Now that we've covered eight essential points, we have 20—yes, 20—additional concerns and potential problem areas for you to keep in mind, so you can avoid some of the most common problems that face beginning performers.

1. On-the-set adjustments are to correct some of the most fundamental aspects in a professional performer's repertoire. Flexibility is a key concern for producers, clients and bosses. If you have to speed it up, omit a few words, change your rhythm—whatever it takes, you can do it. One of my favorite orders came from a producer who said, "Soften it a bit, but put an edge on it." Got you: Make it softer, but also make it harder. No problem.

2. Clarity of speech, both while reading and simply talking, is fundamental for any performer. We all have idiosyncrasies in our speech patterns, but to be paid for speaking and performing, we must learn the proper way to present—and communicate—the words in our scripts.

3. Breath control is another trick of the trade. You must be able to take in air quickly and imperceptibly. Otherwise you'll run out of breath in the middle of a sentence and start gulping while no words come out of your mouth. You only have to embarrass yourself once or twice before you start paying attention to it.

4. Knowledge of phonetics is the mark of a true professional. At the very least, you should know how to break down difficult words for yourself or for other announcers. Imagine yourself trying to cope with this river in Pennsylvania, the Youghiogheny. Few outside the region would know the proper way to pronounce it: "Yock-ug-GAIN-ee." Such tough words and phrases must be brought to the announcer's attention beforehand.

5. Chopping off "-ing" from the ends of words and saying "-in'" instead is common to many of us. One should not over-enunciate, but don't lapse into a street slang.

6. Phrasing means being able to put words together so they make sense to the viewers. Being able to say things like "run-of-the-mill" so they are meaningful can help with the understanding of the overall sentence. Basically, correct phrasing is the interpretation of the words to impart the most meaning.

7. Being nervous can be a positive thing if you use it the right way. Instead of being negative and anticipating failure, use your nervous energy to pay attention to detail: "I am going to punch the first sentence and then lighten up for the remainder of the first story."

8. Punctuation is there for a reason—it signals the construction of a sentence. Ignoring punctuation is a risky way to read copy: You can find yourself running out of breath at awkward times. Even worse, galloping through periods and commas can confuse the viewers. Try to read the copy in the way it's constructed rather than morphing it into something else on the fly.

9. Articulate clearly. Turning "th" into "f" or "v" sounds is a bad habit that some of us have picked up on the way. Making "both" sound like "bohf" or "either" sound like "ee-ver" does

Figure 12-2. *Experience as a radio announcer is great preparation for a career in voice-over work in television. Many successful TV announcers started in radio, and then made the transition. If you listen closely to voice-overs of network television promos, commercials and continuity copy such as IDs, scheduling announcements and program intros and outros, you'll begin to recognize many of the same seasoned, professional-sounding voices.*

not make you sound like an educated, articulate announcer.

10. Avoid unnecessary repetition and stammering, even when trying to buy time while thinking of other words to say. Sometimes it's best to just pause until the right thought comes.

11. To make your copy come alive, savor the words. Phrases like "smooth and creamy" should be presented in a smooth and creamy manner. Commercial copy must be thoroughly studied and stylized to make the words come alive. As the old saying goes, "We make dog food sound so good you wish you were a dog." See Figure 12-2.

12. Tonal range (bass and treble) should be exploited. Work both ends of your inflection. One or the other gets tiresome quickly. Mix it up appropriately to the nature of the copy.

13. Comfortable posture is a way to make you look both alert and energetic. If you're reading while standing up, don't slouch. If you're at a table, try putting your wrists on the edge of the table rather than your elbows.

14. Projection control is a technique you'll have to learn. It takes practice to raise the tone of your voice without shouting. Also, know how to drop your voice without mumbling. Work with the audio technician on the proper level for you.

15. Tension while reading is perfectly normal, given the pressure put on a performer. But this tense condition must not come through in your vocal

delivery. Anxiety usually results in a quaky, high-pitched voice. The audience can smell your fear when you do this. Repeated practice is the best way to eliminate it.

16. Insertions and omissions are mistakes that drive producers crazy. Stick to the copy, especially commercial copy.

17. When there are multiple performers on set, reading too loudly or too softly can be a problem. A loud performer can be picked up on another actor's mike, and if an actor speaks too softly, his mike must be cranked up so high that it picks up the delivery of someone else. Be conscious of speaking at appropriate volume levels.

18. A strained voice is irksome to listen to and is difficult for a performer to maintain. It can result in an announcer losing his or her voice midway through the taping session. Experimentation and practice can help a performer find a natural, effective voice. Listen to playbacks of yourself until you find a comfortable range.

19. A performer who loses his place quickly falls into disfavor with everyone on the set. If you have trouble with a particular section of the script, practice saying it out loud 10 times until you can gallop through the copy.

20. Flubs are inevitable in any performing venue. However, repeated foul-ups are a strain on everyone involved. Don't be the person who keeps making the same mistake again and again. A thorough rehearsal regimen is the best cure for this.

Just as with the PEER CAPE section, you should grade yourself from 1 to 10 in all 20 of these areas. No one is strong in all of them. You should have a much better feel for strengths and weaknesses after evaluating yourself.

Seventeen Pointers

Now that we've outlined the eight fundamental aspects of delivery and pointed out 20 potential problem areas to look out for, here are 17—yes, 17—specific pointers to boost the quality of your delivery.

1. Down at the end, up at the beginning. This rule about voice inflection is particularly true in news copy. Every story should end in a downward inflection of the voice, usually on the last three words. Imagine how your favorite newscaster might drop his or her voice and say, "This . . . is the end." After

Figure 12-3. *Knowing the first sentence is very important to a field reporter. Memorize it, and don't look down to your notes until the end of the first sentence. Not looking down at the beginning creates great eye contact, and gives the audience the impression that you're on top of the story. Later, looking down shows that you're a careful, trustworthy reporter who makes sure to get the facts right. This establishes your credibility.*

you've marked the end of the story this way, pause, get a breath, sync your copy to the teleprompter and slightly raise the tone of your voice. "This . . . is the beginning." Then lapse into your natural tone. This keeps the newscast from sounding like one continuous story.

2. Know the first sentence. Just getting into the newscast, commercial or narration is a big hurdle, and it's very embarrassing to mess up in the first second after the cue. Say to yourself, "I'm going to nail the first sentence no matter what." See Figure 12-3.

3. Smile in and smile out. Nothing makes you look better than a relaxed, confident smile. Start and end with an effective smile and people will forgive a few sins in the middle. This is good advice not just for the taping but for the audition, too. Of course, there's a time to smile, and a time to appear serious. The copy will determine your mood.

4. Hold your pose, and hold your poise. We covered this before, but it bears repeating. Don't foul up the whole production in the last half-second. Stay in character—usually with a smile—and hold it until the director tells you it's okay to relax.

5. Tag your script with little marks to help in your delivery. Underline key words or phrases, Underline them two or three times or with red ink if it's the most important part of the script. Use

diagonal lines to tip you off to tricky sections of the copy, and circle difficult words to let you know they're coming.

6. Bring your acoustics with you. If you have to project, as is generally the case in outdoor filming, project. If you have to back off a bit in volume, such as in an announce booth, you can do that, too. Be flexible and be able to give them what they want, regardless of the setting.

7. Read into a mirror after you've gotten your voice work down pat. It helps you with your animation and your gestures.

8. It's better to look good than to feel good. This comedy line is actually true in on-camera performance. Just because you're uncomfortable with the setting or your chair or your copy doesn't mean you have to let it show. Learn to fake the smile and the gestures, and you'll get through the uncomfortable aspects. It's part of being a professional.

9. Record one reading, turn off the tape recorder and read the copy ten more times. Then turn on the recorder and read again. Listen to the two recordings. Are they different? How? Can you read it another way? Is there something you can add to the performance? Take away? Remember that on the set, adjustments are frequently called for, so you should rehearse more than one style of reading, just in case.

10. Dress the part, whatever the part. When in doubt, a man should bring a coat and tie and a woman should bring a business suit. It's not that unusual for a performer to bring ten different outfits to a shoot. This prevents the odd feeling of looking like a homeless person while everyone else is dressed to the nines. Don't ruin everyone's chance for a good take by being underdressed. Try to find out ahead of time what the producer wants. If it's coveralls, bring coveralls—even if you have to buy them (see Figure 12-4).

11. For news and sports announcers: Sit on the tails of your coat. Also, "belly up to the bar"and pull the seat to your back. Then you can't slouch, and your coat won't ride up in the back. This prevents the look of a turtle sticking its neck out of a shell-like suit collar. You may not feel comfortable, but you'll look marvelous.

12. Criticism is the road map to success. Asking for advice from an accomplished pro is sure to result in some negative remarks. Just remember that this person is taking time from a busy schedule to

Figure 12-4. *Talent must frequently bring several costumes to a shoot to provide a producer with visual options.*

offer you some suggestions. Even if you don't agree, take the remarks to heart and assume they're 100 percent correct. Then ask yourself, "What can I do to make sure no one can ever say this again about my delivery?" Answering this question and putting the techniques into action is almost certain to improve your delivery. If nothing else, it will give you flexibility and the ability to do material in more than one way.

13. A = "uh," the = "thuh," news = "nyews" and w = "double you." Some words are deliberately mispronounced. When Americans talk, we don't overpronounce like schoolchildren and read, "A man went to thee store." We say, "Uh man went to the thuh store." Sometimes you punch words like "a" and "the," but not often. And nothing sounds more uneducated than a person pronouncing news as NOOZ. Trying adding a "y" and saying, "Nyews." Then drop the "y" and notice how different it sounds. Using the "y" is better than the NOOZ option. The same goes for the letter "w." Regardless of popular presidential nicknames, "dub-yuh" is not a viable option. Say the letter as if you're pronouncing, "Double you." Then drop the "l" to say, "Dubba-you." It is embarrassing to pronounce your call letters as "Dub-yuh-S-I-E." This is also worth remembering if you have to read out a Web address.

14. Make your ego work for you, not against you. No matter how unpleasant things may be on the set, you should be remembered by every member of

the crew as "a pleasure to work with." No matter how many takes you have to do to get it right, give your very best performance on the next take—after all, you've had so many opportunities to rehearse. Drive yourself to rise to the occasion. You're probably letting your ego get in the way if you find yourself saying or thinking, "Who does he think he is to say that to me?" Don't make a bad situation worse. Producers, clients and bosses remember which performers are the best to work with. You'll end up getting future work on this basis alone.

15. Learn the "no" head shake. This is a technique used by nearly every on camera performer: When you encounter a negative word in your copy— "no," "nothing," "never," and so on—shake your head from side to side in a subtle fashion. The method most often used is one big shake followed by two small, quick ones. Practice this until it becomes automatic, and it will greatly help your animation.

16. Lip smacking and deep breaths can affect the audio levels, especially when there is automatic gain control involved. This is most often heard at the very beginning of a taping session. The technician will cue the talent, who will then part his or her lips and gasp for breath. The AGC will pick up this low level noise and amplify it. Rather than starting the recording with these unpleasant sounds, performers should get a good, deep breath on the "stand by" cue and slightly part their lips. The recording can then start in a clean fashion.

17. Finally, there are two techniques to make lists actually sound like lists when you read them. The more familiar method is to take the tone of the voice up at the end of each item (and then start the next item at a normal tone) until the end of the list is reached. At that point, the performer can lower and stretch the final word or words involved to signal that the list is finished. Another, more interesting technique is to give each word on the list its own sound and meaning. This tactic is more involved, but it's also more fun. Try to make each word on the list unique. Like everything else in announcing, it takes practice. It <u>will</u> be worth the effort.

Practice, Practice, Practice

The operative word for improvement early in your career is practice. It takes years of concentrated effort to become a competent announcer, and you can't wait for a camera to be in front of you before you practice. Much learning is trial and error, and should be done in the privacy of your own home or practice area. You'll try and discard some techniques as inappropriate to your particular style, just as you'll find others that fit you like a glove.

It's only after this extended, even painful learning process that you can lay claim to the title of professional announcer. Most performers will testify that there's one magic moment when it all comes together. That instant may come several years into a career. There is one term used to describe the feeling: confidence. This is not the false confidence of an egomaniacal dilettante, but the calm, quiet assurance of an accomplished television performer. It shows on camera and in the voice. It's well worth the effort.

But before there was an announcer, there was a writer who put the words in his/her mouth. Scriptwriting is what we'll turn to next in Chapter 13.

Important Vocabulary Term

Continuity Copy: IDs, scheduling announcements and program intros/outros.

Scriptwriting

The script may be the least visible component of any television program. Unless audiences read the credits carefully, they might believe that the talent or actors simply dreamed up the story and the accompanying dialog. Actually, performers and directors occasionally do improvise some dialog in scenes. For example, talk show hosts and their staffs prepare for what they and their guests may discuss, but what these individuals actually say is largely spontaneous.

But most words that TV talent speak begin as scripts.

This chapter is an introduction to the fundamental aesthetics and practical techniques for writing dramatic fiction, news, documentary, commercial and promotional scripts for television.

We'll begin our treatment of scriptwriting with an observation: Although you can see the structural similarities between television drama and comedy and their counterparts in motion pictures, you have to look below the surface of other program forms to see that all successful television products, from newscasts to commercials, are constructed using the principles of dramatic/comedic fiction. Audiences don't realize that the values that make a dramatic script exciting can also make a mundane news story dynamic, gripping and memorable. An understanding of the principles of drama, articulated as early as 320 B.C. in Aristotle's *Poetics,* is as valuable to the commercial copywriter as knowledge of TV script formats and terminology. But before we can discuss any principles, let's put television scriptwriting into its own, unique frame of reference regarding time.

Units of Time

Print and film media producers are concerned with time, but time factors often overshadow all other considerations in television scriptwriting. Feature films often run from 70 to 150 minutes, stage plays last from two and a half to three hours, and books often vary from 120 to 700 pages. But dramatic (narrative) scripts for commercial television routinely conform to relatively inflexible half-hour, one-hour or two-hour time blocks. Within these rigid time constraints, scripts are carefully fashioned into *acts* (dramatic units) to accommodate the periodic insertion of commercials and station and network identification and promos. Most of these conventions also apply to documentary, news, commercial and promotional scripts. Short documentaries such as those on CBS's *Sixty Minutes* vary from about 10 to as long as 18 minutes, but all the combined segments of the show, as the name implies, must add up to exactly 60 minutes. Other documentary shows can be longer, but they still are slaves to the clock. Similarly, newscast scriptwriting often means finding ways to communicate complex stories in either 20 seconds of copy read by an anchor or in a minute-and-a-half taped *package* (a complete, edited, self-contained report).

Nowhere does time pose a greater challenge than in commercial and promotion writing, during which complete dramatic stories or complex persuasive messages must be boiled down into compact propaganda messages of just 30 seconds. So, the strict timing dictated by TV scriptwriting places a premium on structural cohesiveness, conciseness and clarity.

A-, B- and C-Plots

A screenplay is a complex creation, yet it is basically just a story told with pictures and sound. The screenplay, like a narrative in any medium, begins with a pretty simple story idea. For example, in one classic *Seinfeld* episode entitled "The Barber," there are three story ideas, often referred to in scriptwriting jargon as the *A-plot,* the *B-plot* and the *C-plot.* In the A-plot, Jerry tries to find a way to change barbers without offending the cheery but growingly incompetent scissor-man who's cut his hair for many years. In the B-plot, George is pretty sure he's landed a new job, but the boss who hired him is out of town, so he decides to just show up for work and find out. In this sitcom and in other dramatic series, there sometimes is a third plot, the C-plot. In this *Seinfeld* episode, there was a tiny C-plot inserted into the screenplay during last-minute revisions to give Elaine and especially Kramer more air time in the episode.

There is no rule, but most TV scriptwriters, especially sitcom writers, content themselves with developing just two—or at the most three—story threads in each half-hour episode. This practice is also evident in hour-long dramatic shows, despite their longer length. For example, in most episodes in the multiseries franchise *CSI,* script formula has the crime scene investigators working on solving two different crimes—the A-plot and the B-plot—during the hour-long show. There may be a C-plot churning in the background of CSI involving problems at work or the protagonists' interpersonal relationships, but these C-plots are usually minor compared to the A and B-plots.

Screenplay Nomenclature

Once the screenplay writer has developed the story idea, the next step is to flesh out the idea into a considerably more detailed *plot outline.* In a plot outline, sometimes written on a series of 3 × 5 cards, the story is divided into major *sequences,* which themselves are a collection of *scenes.* Later, in deciding how to visualize the script, the director divides these scenes into *shots,* the basic building blocks of a production. In book literature, the shot, the scene and the sequence are analogous to the sentence, the paragraph and the chapter.

Because of the need to cut away at relatively regular intervals for commercials, sequences work like—and are regularly called—acts, often specifically written with suspenseful endings to keep viewers from channel-flipping during the commercial breaks. Commercial breaks occur at approximately seven-minute intervals, so acts are often written to run about that long.

Each act begins with the primary goal of resolving the story crisis created by the preceding act and then continues building to its own dramatic crisis.

Depending on its length, a dramatic TV script can have many acts, but most screenplays follow the same basic structure as a three-act stage play: Act 1 establishes the situation and introduces the *protagonist's* (the hero's) problem. Act 2 dramatizes the protagonist's efforts to overcome the problem and expands upon most of the people (called *antagonists*), places and things that work against the protagonist achieving success in overcoming the problem. Act 3 includes the positive or negative resolution of the main problem and of any other minor problems that occur along the way, followed by a brief epilogue that ties up any dramatic loose ends.

The Treatment

Once sequences and their component scenes are outlined, you're ready to write a *treatment,* a two-to-three-page prose version of your plot outline. Think of the treatment as an "executive summary" of your more detailed and lengthy plot outline. If it is a script for a network TV show, the treatment is what you and your agent would use to "pitch" the story to a producer or program executive. If you're successful, you would be commissioned to write a script. But treatments are used by many different kinds of people who work in television and video production. For example, you may be a producer working with a client to create a promotional video for a product the client manufactures. After researching the product and listening to the client's marketing goals, you create a story idea, an outline and finally a treatment for this promotional video. This is presented to your client. It's better for the client to read your treatment over and suggest changes at this stage than later on, when you've gone to all the work of developing a complete script.

Once your treatment is approved, you'll go back to your plot outline and begin the process of fleshing out—actually writing—your script. This is also the first time that you'll use a script format designed for film and television. Until now, your story idea, outline and treatment could be used for virtually any mass medium. (See Tech Manual 13-1 at the end of this chapter for a discussion of how many script pages the Writers Guild says are required for the various lengths of screenplays and teleplays.)

Plot

In television, whether you're writing a safety video for a manufacturer, a 30-second commercial for toothpaste, a nightly news report or a network sitcom, you're engaged in storytelling. And storytelling begins with developing a plot.

Everyone has problems. Some say that life consists of two elements: our problems and our efforts to overcome them. Regardless, there's one thing all writers know: If you don't have a problem, you don't have drama. If you write a script in which everything is wonderful and no one has any problems, you'll have one dull show.

Writers and theorists generally agree that plots are characterized by protagonists' conflicts with four kinds of antagonists: (1) other people; (2) the physical environment; (3) the nonphysical (the supernatural); and (4) the protagonists themselves. In resolving these conflicts, there are many potential plot patterns a writer may follow. In his book, *A Practical Manual for Theater and Television Films,* Louis Herman groups plot patterns into nine prototypes:

1. Love: Boy meets girl, boy loses girl, boy gets girl back again.
2. Success: The protagonist sets out to achieve a positive goal.
3. Cinderella: In various forms, an ugly duckling becomes a beautiful swan.
4. Triangle: A love story or other relationship with one too many participants.
5. The Return: Someone absent from the locale where the story occurs returns—and precipitates story conflict.
6. Vengeance: Revenge motivates either the protagonist or the antagonist.
7. Conversion: The protagonist undergoes a profound change in attitudes and motivations because of his/her experiences in the story.
8. Sacrifice: The protagonist is motivated by noble ideals, giving up something valuable to aid another.
9. Family: This pattern is a mixture of many interplays between characters related either by blood or because they were thrown together by circumstance.

Note especially that few of these patterns exist independently. Most stories combine more than one.

Character

When you create plots, your patterns are carried out by people. What kinds of people these people are and how they behave make your plots interesting, entertaining and capable of selling products, services or ideas. In his book, *Screenplay,* Syd Field outlines six ways to reveal character in a plot: point of view, attitude, personality, behavior, revelation and identification. Most writers use variations of these six to create the people who will then move forward the action of the story. Let's investigate:

A point of view: The way the character sees the world ranges from Pollyanna-like optimism to deep cynicism. In the film *The Two Jakes* (1990), the sequel to the classic *Chinatown* (1974), private detective Jake Geddes tersely describes how he views Los Angeles in the 1940s and his place in it: "I'm the guy in the leper colony with the most fingers."

An attitude: Whatever a protagonist's point of view, a character's method of dealing with his/her environment can vary greatly. For example, Karen, Grace's nasal-voiced, socialite assistant in the sitcom *Will and Grace,* faces each day as though its sole purpose were to provide her with nothing but hedonistic pleasure. Anything else in her environment or, heaven help us, anything in her way, is summarily brushed aside as irrelevant.

Personality: Various quirks and habits help make a character unique, memorable and/or fascinating. Consider Indiana Jones's disdain for snakes, bugs and Nazis, his signature leather jacket, fedora hat and bullwhip. Or ponder James Bond's incessant womanizing, drinking his vodka martinis only when they're "shaken, not stirred," his flippant attitude toward superiors, his flirtatious but platonic relationship with Miss Moneypenny and his encyclopedic command of the most trivial facts from science to diamonds to foreign languages. These idiosyncrasies make the character seem real, like he has a life and mind of his own, and allow us to forget that he is a writer's creation.

Behavior: Regardless of beliefs, behavior supports the other elements. A person ultimately <u>is</u> what he/she does, or does not do. When characters' convictions conflict with circumstances, dramatic decisions cause characters to act. Those actions can make great drama. A great example is found in the film classic *Casablanca* (1943), when Humphrey Bogart's character, Rick, risks death and gives up the love of his life so she and her husband can escape to continue the fight against the Nazis. This occurs despite the fact that Rick's stated credo of life is "I stick my neck out for nobody."

Revelation: This element allows us to learn the truth about characters. In the climax to *Star Wars: The Empire Strikes Back* (1980), we discover that Luke Skywalker's fearsome nemesis, Darth Vader, is actually Luke's father.

Identification: Finally, the best way to make a character come to life is to allow the audience to identify with him or her. This is a vital element: if you create characters that no one in the audience cares about, no one will care enough to watch your show. In television especially, many antagonists are given some quirky, interesting or sometimes attractive qualities to add balance and identification. For example, in the *Law and Order* series of police/prosecutor dramas, defense attorneys are the antagonists. Most of these attorneys have attractive features or interesting character quirks and are highly intelligent. From time to time, former prosecuting attorney cast members from the original *Law and Order* series, with whom the audience has great affinity, return to the program as defense attorneys and antagonists. Although many of the evil villains in James Bond films are sinister looking or unattractive (e.g., Auric Goldfinger, Dr. No,

Rosa Klebb, "Jaws," "May Day," Hugo Drax), others are handsome, suave, talented and beautiful (e.g., Kamal Khan, Max Zorin, Gustav Graves, Alec Trevelyan, Fiona Volpe, Pola Ivanova, Xenia Onatopp and Elektra King).

Script Form

Dramatic script form begins with a *master scene script*. This is a complete description of the surroundings, dialog, character attitudes and actions that take place in the story. As you'll learn in Chapter 15, the director takes this master scene script and adds shots, shot sizes and angles and decides how to make transitions between them. Then it's called a *shooting script* and is ready for use by the director in the production phase (see Figure 13-1).

If the master scene script is shot multiple-camera style, the director often uses a two-column shooting script, with the director's shots, camera numbers and talent movements in the left column, while the audio and dialog are in the right column (see Figure 13-2).

```
AARDVARK ADVERTISING

HERALD MOTORS OF AMERICA

PRODUCT/TITLE:  HX-3SP

LENGTH:  30

_____


FADE IN:

A road raceway that winds around and through a forest
setting. A car approaches and speeds by camera.  Lower third
key appears: "Sears Point Raceway."

                    ANNCR.
              This is the new Herald HX3-SP.

ANGLE ON CAR

Car as it rushes by a tree.

                    ANNCR.
              Rest assured, this SP does not stand for
              "slowpoke."

ANGLE ON TREE

Tree, buffeted by the wind in the wake of the car, loses all
its leaves. It sounds more like a hurricane than a car
passing by. A hot jazz score begins and continues to the end
of the commercial.


ANGLE ON FRONT OF CAR

Car rushes toward camera and exits right.

                    ANNCR.
              It's got an air dam up front ... a
              remarkable, improved rotary engine.


ANGLE ON WATER JUG

As car rushes by water jug on the side of the road, the wake
of the car and the "whoosh" of SFX smashes the jug.
```

```
CLOSE ON WATER JUG

Water jug explodes in slow motion with a great crash.


LONG SHOT OF CAR AS IT CAREENS BY CAMERA

                    ANNCR.
              Independent suspension system ...

ANGLE ON SHED BY SIDE OF ROAD

                    ANNCR.
              ... semi-monocoque construction ...

Shed collapses as if a hurricane had hit it.


LONG AERIAL SHOT OF CAR.

  Car goes through its paces around corners in hilly terrain.


                    ANNCR.
              ... and the breeding of over one hundred
              racing victories in international
              competitions.

CLOSE ON DRIVER

Driver smiles and gives the "thumbs up."


                    ANNCR.
              The Herald HX3-SP ...It'll make a
              believer out of you -- FAST!


DISSOLVE TO

Herald Logo, with music score up.


FADEOUT.
```

Figure 13-1. *A master scene script for a television commercial.*

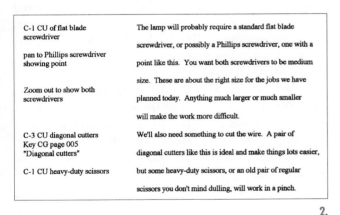

```
Aardvark Advertising          CLIENT: Herald Motors of America
201 W. Sixth Street           PRODUCT: HX-3 -- Rotary Engine
Los Angeles, California       TITLE: "HX-3 SP-30"
BROADCAST DEPT.               WRITER: John Jones
                              LENGTH: 30

        VIDEO                           AUDIO

1. Fadeup on: LS of car driving    1. ANNCR. V/O OVER NAT. SOUND:
   by camera, with lower third        This is the new Herald HX3-SP.
   key: "Sears Point Raceway"
                           (:03)
   CUT TO:
2. MLS of car driving by tree      2. Rest assured, the SP does not stand for
                           (:03)     "slowpoke."

2A. (Tree loses all its leaves)    2A. SFX: (wind blowing and leaves rustling)
                           (:02)
                                   MUSIC: (jazz score under)

3. MLS of car moving toward camera 3. It's got an air dam up front . . .
                           (:02)      a remarkable, improved rotary engine.

4. MLS of water jug as car goes by. 4. SFX: (Whoosh) as car zooms by
                           (:01)
5. CU of water jug breaking        5. SFX: (Water jug breaking)
                           (:02)
6. LS of car driving by camera     6. Independent suspension system . . .
                           (:03)
7. LS of car driving by shed       7. semi-monocoque construction . . .
                           (:03)
7A. (Shed collapses)   (:03.5)     7A. SFX: (Shed collapsing)

8. ELS, aerial shot of car going   8. . . . and the breeding of over one hundred
   through corners in hilly area      racing victories in international
                           (:03)      competitions.

9. CU of driver giving thumbs-up   9. The Herald HX3-SP . . . It'll make
   sign.                   (:01.5)    a believer out of you -- FAST!

   DISSOLVE TO:
10. Herald logo        (:02)       10. MUSIC: (jazz score up)

11. FADEOUT           (:0.5)       11. MUSIC: (jazz score fadeout)
```
                                                              1.

```
C-1 CU of flat blade          The lamp will probably require a standard flat blade
screwdriver
                              screwdriver, or possibly a Phillips screwdriver, one with a
pan to Phillips screwdriver
showing point                 point like this.  You want both screwdrivers to be medium

                              size.  These are about the right size for the jobs we have
Zoom out to show both
screwdrivers                  planned today.  Anything much larger or much smaller

                              will make the work more difficult.

C-3 CU diagonal cutters       We'll also need something to cut the wire.  A pair of
Key CG page 005
"Diagonal cutters"            diagonal cutters like this is ideal and make things lots easier,

C-1 CU heavy-duty scissors    but some heavy-duty scissors, or an old pair of regular

                              scissors you don't mind dulling, will work in a pinch.
```
                                                              2.

Figure 13-2. *The first is the two-column version of the commercial's master scene script, seen in Figure 13-1. The second, for a simple studio-demonstration show, is an excerpt from a two-column script rendered in slightly different format (no shot numbers or elapsed times in seconds for each shot).*

Writing Scripts for Television News

Writing news for television is considerably different than creating fiction on the screen. For one thing, news writing and reporting is about the factual information. A reporter who can't be counted on to report factual information accurately doesn't last very long.

Television news writing shares many goals with newspaper writing but differs in important ways. As we discuss the basics of broadcast news writing, we'll point out these differences.

Most news stories aren't complete unless they contain the *"five Ws and How,"* the "Who, What, Where, When, Why and How" of any story. A story skipping one of these elements often leaves the viewer with unanswered questions. A newspaper story without an accompanying news photo must have answers to all five Ws written out. A television story has the advantage of being able to answer some of these W questions visually. For example, if the story takes place in front of the White House, the television reporter can show it instead of just talk about it. As well, most newspaper stories follow a style called the *inverted pyramid.* This means that the most important facts in the story, the foundational facts, come first and are on top (see Figure 13-3). The inverted pyramid is popular with newspaper editors, because it allows them to cut a news story from the bottom to fit it into a smaller space without leaving out the most vital details. The inverted pyramid's lead sentences tend to be quite long (often compound-complex sentences), while broadcast writing stresses short, punchy sentences. TV news stories' two top priorities are a) telling the story in as few words as possible and b) making the written copy correspond closely to the visuals.

Newspaper stories allow mental absorption of the copy at the individual reader's pace. If a newspaper reader doesn't fully understand a sentence, it's easy to reread difficult passages. Television copy is heard only once. TV news copy must complement, rather than

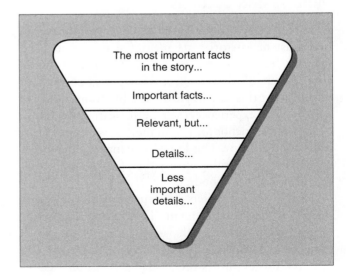

Figure 13-3. *The inverted pyramid.*

redundantly describe, the video on the screen. TV news copy also must be written for easy and clear oral presentation by a newscaster, because audiences may not always concentrate fully on what's being said. This means that you should avoid writing copy containing tongue-twisters or build sentences that run on too long without a pause for breath. Consider how the following lead sentences for a newspaper and a TV story differ:

<u>Newspaper:</u> When the U.S. Senate's holiday vacation is over and the Congress returns to Washington next Monday, legislators in both houses will face a chief executive who says that he is ready to engage in battle over the proposed new tax cut, the president's press secretary said today.

<u>Television:</u> The president says he's eager to fight over tax cuts when Congress reconvenes Monday.

Although newspapers like *USA Today* are leading the trend away from long sentences, many other editors still allow them.

As there are stylebooks for writing term papers, there are handy style guides for radio and television news writing. Among the many fine textbooks that can assist you in learning to write in broadcast style are *Broadcast News Writing and Reporting,* by Peter Mayeux; *Broadcast News,* by Mitchell Stephens; *Broadcast News and Writing Stylebook,* by Robert Papper and *The Associated Press Stylebook.* These texts and many others explain the numerous conventions of broadcast style, including when to spell out numbers and when not to, when to abbreviate and how to punctuate. These rules are designed for one purpose: to help the announcer read the copy and the audience to understand it.

Minutes and Seconds

Newspaper copy is measured in column inches, but broadcast news stories are measured in minutes and seconds. The average time required to read a line of copy on an $8\frac{1}{2} \times 11$ sheet of paper is about four seconds, but this can vary considerably from person to person. With experience, the reporter learns how fast he or she (or the anchor for whom they are writing) usually reads a line of copy. This knowledge makes a big difference in properly timing a story that, for example, needs to run exactly 45 seconds.

Television news writers also must deal with the dominance of the visual element. This means that before writing copy for use with visuals, the reporter must examine and time the footage shot on location. The reporter also examines the available *sound bites* (short

comments by news sources or those witnessing news events). These, too, are timed and edited into the final visual story. The reporter writes copy to use with these visuals and records the narration for use in the edited news package. Some reporters record their narration on audio tape or a disk-based digital audio recorder, while others record directly to a sound track of an ENG videotape. In either case, the narration is later insert-edited to the master edit tape.

Script Form

Written in two-column format, television news scripts have almost completely evolved from a typewriter-and-paper product to an electronic display system (see Figure 13-4).

If written on a personal computer tied into a newsroom network, the PC can directly feed teleprompter monitor displays in the studio, thus avoiding many disasters common to old, obsolete paper-fed prompter equipment. Printed script copies are still needed for some production personnel and as backup for talent in case the electronic prompting system fails on-air. But in a totally electronic newsroom, fewer hard copies are needed these days (see Figure 13-5).

The newscast director works from an abbreviated version of the newscast script, called a *rundown* sheet. The rundown usually lists all the visual elements in the script, the running time of each element and the last few words of copy preceding each visual change. These last words are called *outcues.* The director can call the shots for an entire newscast from the rundown sheet, but directors and producers usually also keep a copy of the script handy in case of trouble, malfunctions, updates and other changes that often occur during the newscast (see Figure 13-6).

Writing Documentaries

In his history of the documentary film, Paul Rotha simply and broadly defines the documentary as "fact film," completely distinct from fictional movies, which he calls "the story film." Today, there are three kinds of film and television documentaries:

a. productions intended to serve some journalistic purpose;
b. those intended for promotional, entertainment, marketing or training purposes; and
c. those written and produced for the educational market.

Fig. 12-6   SAMPLE NEWSCAST SCRIPT

VIDEO   **AUDIO**

DISS VTR-1/OPENING   (SOT)

DISS C-1 TWO-SHOT JOHN &   JOHN: GOOD EVENING, I'M
  LORETTA W/ESS-54 KEY   _____.
  "ACTION NEWS"
                             LORETTA: AND I'M _____.

  LOSE KEY

C-2 (H&S LORETTA)   ONLY MINUTES AGO FIRE

                             FIGHTERS ARRIVED AT

                             KING'S RESTAURANT ON

                             SOUTH 52ND STREET IN

                             RESPONSE TO MULTIPLE

                             ALARMS. ACTION NEWS

REMOTE 4   REPORTER SUE PETERSON
  (PETERSON W/ESS-34 "LIVE")
                             IS ALSO ON THE SCENE.

                             SUE, WHAT'S GOING ON?

                                 SUE: (ad-lib..... :25)

KEY ESS-43 "SUE PETERSON"

LOSE KEY ESS-43   out:" all we know now.")

C-2 (H&S LORETTA)   LORETTA: SUE, DO OFFICIALS

                             ON THE SCENE THINK THIS

                             FIRE IS POSSIBLY RELATED

TO OTHER RECENT FIRES IN

THIS PART OF TOWN?

REMOTE 4 (PETERSON)   SUE: (ad-lib.......:15)

C-2 (H&S LORETTA)   LORETTA: SUE PETERSON REPORTING

                             LIVE FROM KING'S

                             RESTAURANT. WE'LL CHECK

                             BACK FOR AN UPDATE LATER

                             IN TONIGHT'S NEWSCAST.

C-3 (H&S JOHN W/ESS-14   JOHN: THIS FIRE AT KING'S
  "JOHN FREEMAN")
                             IS THE THIRD BLAZE IN

                             THE BUSINESS DISTRICT

LOSE KEY ESS-14   SINCE LAST SUNDAY.

                             EARLIER THIS WEEK

                             OFFICIALS SAID ARSON

                             MAY BE INVOLVED

                             IN THE FIRST TWO FIRES..

                             REPORTER ROBIN BLOCK

                             IS ON THE STORY AND FILED

                             THIS   REPORT.

VTR-4 PACKAGE 1   (SOT)

  ARSON TRT :94

  KEYS:

  ESS-80 "ROBERT EDDINS"

  ESS-81 "WILMA WRIGHT"

Figure 13-4. *The first two pages of a sample TV news program script.*

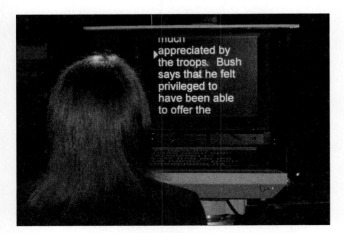

Figure 13-5. *This shot taken over the shoulder of a TV news anchor shows the script on the teleprompter.*

Promotional, entertainment, marketing and educational documentaries are less objective productions, commissioned by organizations to serve some entertainment, propaganda, commercial or instructional goal. These include corporate-sponsored videos produced by or for the public relations, marketing or training departments of a company, videos produced by political or social action organizations to promote an ideology or a politician's campaign, pseudo-journalistic documentaries that use a journalistic style to investigate fluffy topics for their entertainment value and tapes produced to introduce the public to the nature of a service agency, charity or other organization. Many videos are designed for education and/or training inside and outside organizations. A company may make a safety video designed to reduce accidents in the workplace, or a video intended to instruct new workers in the techniques required for their

B. Kelly	Thur July 2	01:55	Page 1				
SLUG	TAL	WTR	FORM	READ	TAPE	TRT	BKTIME
5 PM CAST••••••••••••••••••••••••••••						30:00	30:00
OPEN			PRE-PRO			:20	29:40
ELEVATOR FIRE	JC/HH	BK	PACKAGE	:15	1.30	1:45	27:55
FOREST FIRES	HH	BK	VOSOC	:30		:30	27:25
DROUGHT UPDATE	JC	BK	READER	:15		:15	27:10
EL NINO	HH	LW	PACKAGE	:10	1:20	1:30	25:40
TEASER ONE	JC/HH	BK	VOSOC	:15		:15	25:25
COMM POD ONE			PRE-PRO		3:30	3:30	21:55
MICROSOFT	HH	LW	PACKAGE	:10	1:00	1:10	20:45
SCHOOL BOARD	HH	BK	VOSOC	:35		:35	20:10
SUMMER GRADS	JC	BK	PACKAGE	:15	1:30	1:45	18:25
PERSONAL DEBT	HH	LW	PACKAGE	:10	1:05	1:15	17:10
FEDERAL DEFICIT	JC	LW	READER	:20		:20	16:50
TEASER TWO/SPORTS	JC/HH	BK	READER	:15		:15	16:35
COMM POD TWO			PRE-PRO		2:25	2:45	13:50
SPORTS LEAD	JC/HH	BS	READER	:15		:15	13:35
CUBS VICTORY	BS	BS	VOSOC	:20	1:10	1:30	12:05
HS COACH RESIGN	BS	BS	PACKAGE	:15	:45	1:00	11:05
SPORTS MEDICINE	BS	BS	PACKAGE	:10	:55	1:05	10:00
POOL SAFETY	BS	BS	VOSOC	:45		:45	9:15
TONIGHT'S GAMES	BS	BS	READER	:30		:30	8:45
WEATHER TEASE	JC/HH	BK	READER	:15		:15	8:30
COMM POD THREE			PRE-PRO		3:00	3:00	5:30
WEATHER LEAD	JC/HH		READER	:15		:15	5:15
WEATHER MAPS	JR	JR	READER	3:30		3:30	2:15

Figure 13-6. *A sample rundown sheet for a TV newscast.*

jobs; a manufacturer may package a marketing videotape to mail to prospective customers. Other commercial videos range from how to build a gazebo in your back yard to improving your study habits or your golf game.

Promotional and educational videos fall under the general category of the documentary, because these productions photograph, discuss and display facts rather than fiction. But the way facts are interpreted can cause the message to conflict with the truth. Journalistic documentaries seek to present the facts as truthfully as possible, while other documentary forms may use facts to achieve goals unique to the producer.

News-style documentaries produced for TV are structured in a manner similar to news stories—but they cover the topic much more thoroughly than the short, minute-and-a-half packages on the nightly news. Writers don't script news-style documentaries tightly, as one would for a dramatic show or even a commercial. This is because they don't always know what documentary footage they're going to get until it happens. The exact content of the interview footage can't be planned in advance either. So many news-style documentaries are shot from an outline rather than a complete script. Later, after much or all of the location video is shot, you write, record and edit your narration into the documentary.

Many nonjournalistic (we'll call them *sponsored*) documentaries are shot from very carefully prepared scripts. Because their goals are informational, instructional or propagandistic, most sponsored documentaries' visuals are well-planned and often staged. Typically, narration or other lines spoken by talent aren't recorded randomly: They're carefully scripted and shot on location or on studio sets. In some sponsored documentaries, dramatic scenes are interwoven into the script. For example, while scripting a documentary on industrial safety, you may create a dramatic scene in which an unsafe practice causes an accident.

Writers use both the master scene script form and the two-column format in creating scripts for sponsored documentaries. This choice depends on whether the footage is shot single-camera (master scene script format is often used) or multiple-camera style in the studio (two-column format is more common).

Avant-garde documentaries often follow the barest of written outlines, whether they are journalistic, political, social, designed to entertain or shot just for art's sake. Their outcome depends mostly on the artistic or narrative instincts of their creators. For example, writer-producer-director-narrator Michael Moore has had phenomenal success (and even Oscar recognition) for politically charged, quirky documentaries on automobile manufacturers and their relationships with their employees, the American gun culture and the Bush presidency's actions in response to Sept. 11, 2001, and Iraq.

Scripting Commercials

First understand what commercials do:

- If there is not already a need for the product or service, commercials create one.
- They persuade viewers that the product or service being advertised is good (or better than others), and worthy of purchase.
- They encourage viewers to buy or order the product or service and provide the means (a shot of the product to help identify it at the store, the address and/or phone number of the company) to get it soon. Remember that successful commercial broadcasting relies on these well-researched, well-designed persuasive messages.

Commercial scriptwriters at advertising agencies and TV stations are simply called *copywriters*. Besides being extremely creative individuals, they possess an understanding of human nature and psychology and are able to apply this knowledge by creating copy and visuals that appeal to basic human needs and wants.

Commercial Formats

In their textbook, *Advertising in the Broadcast and Cable Media*, Elizabeth Heighton and Don Cunningham provided an excellent summary of the combined wisdom of the many theories and practices considered gospel throughout the ad business. They list eight fundamental formats copywriters use in their commercials:

> dramatic
> problem–solution
> demonstration
> interview
> testimonial
> spokesperson
> symbolism
> comparative advertising

The *dramatic format* is a much more compact version of the dramatic scripts we discussed earlier. However, in dramatic format commercials, the product or service becomes the hero, and in the end, the hero is always victorious.

Similar to the dramatic format is the *problem–solution design*. In problem–solution, a more melodramatic and sometimes highly exaggerated version of the drama, the product or service comes to the aid of the helpless consumer. So the detergent in the red bottle rescues the hapless victim suffering the disgrace of "ring around the collar."

The *demonstration* format is next. Unlike print ads, television can do more than make claims for a product or service: It can show evidence. One can demonstrate how many more dishes a detergent cleans with just one squirt, how much whiter your towels are when you use a certain brand of bleach in the wash and how easy it is to clean the tarnish from your silverware when you use the featured brand.

In the *interview* format, advertisers videotape individuals on the street, asking them questions designed to generate positive responses about a product. One typical interview-format commercial shot outside a market asked people who had just purchased the sponsor's product if they would trade it for another manufacturer's product. Loyal to and satisfied with their chosen brand, the consumers whose interviews were used on the air refused the offer. The commercial production unit shot many of these encounters, allowing them to compile enough consumer endorsements for their commercial campaign. Other interview commercials make no journalistic pretense and use actors and carefully worded scripts, yet at first glance, they appear to be real interviews. Some identify themselves as dramatizations; others are not as ethical.

The *testimonial* format exploits consumer loyalty beyond person-on-the-street comments. Few statements add more to the credibility of an advertiser's claims than when apparently ordinary consumers personally confirm their validity. For example, when owners of a certain model truck say that their vehicles operated trouble-free for more than 300,000 miles, the advertiser needs to say little more.

Many communication researchers find that audiences sometimes imitate attractive media models. Celebrity spokespersons often are effective persuaders for consumers who admire them, hence the *spokesperson format*. Although former test pilot Chuck Yeager, the pilot who broke the sound barrier, may not necessarily have been an expert on automobile batteries, many consumers followed his lead and purchased the battery he endorsed. Music or basketball stars' soft drink preferences may be motivated solely by their endorsement fees, but advertisers still buy millions of dollars of commercial time every year on the premise that they sell cola.

The *symbolism* format is a creative way to make a point that could be made in other ways. Sometimes the symbols become media icons themselves, and greatly aid in product recognition. A series of bogus commercials interrupted by a bunny banging a drum was enormously successful for Energizer batteries, and the bunny ads have continued for over a decade; showing how a suitcase can withstand a gorilla's mistreatment was an effective and visual way to communicate the indignities one's luggage suffers in the clutches of baggage handlers, and how well a Samsonite suitcase survived this treatment. Joe Camel became a powerful symbol of the pleasurable, laid-back lifestyle that Camel cigarettes wanted associated with its product. The campaign was so successful that parents and government officials focused on this advertising as a major factor encouraging underage smoking, forcing R. J. Reynolds Tobacco Co. to kill the campaign. This is a rare example of an advertising campaign that perhaps was <u>too</u> successful.

The *comparative* commercial format causes many "wars" between competing brands. In subtle and sometimes boldly overt ways, bashing the competition is an effective persuader. When one major truck manufacturer creates a jingle out of a popular country-western song exhorting mothers not to let their babies grow up to drive the competitor's brand, the stage is set for television combat. And, when the visuals augmenting this message show the competitor's brand as unreliable and weak, the comparison is reinforced and the damage to the competition is done. Despite the popularity of ads aired during the Coke vs. Pepsi wars, some academic research indicates that consumers remember <u>both</u> brands mentioned in the ad and sometimes forget which was shown more favorably. But advertising agencies continue using this commercial format, so it must be assumed that their private, unpublished research shows that the comparative format produces satisfactory results.

We can add an additional format to Heighton and Cunningham's list: the *special effects* format. The sole purpose of the special effects format is to create enough visual magic to charm curious, amazed audiences into paying sharp attention to the commercial. By capturing audiences with visual magic, the message is entertainingly packaged and delivered. When a man in an art gallery admiring an imported automobile hanging on the wall suddenly gets in and drives it away, audiences sit in awe. Some simply marvel at the magic, while others try to guess how the producers pulled off this magic trick. Regardless, these viewers don't flip channels or go to the bathroom or the refrigerator when these ads are playing. When viewers stay tuned to the commercial, half the advertiser's battle—holding the viewer's attention—is won.

Steps in Creating a Commercial

After an ad agency decides what message the client wants communicated, copywriters create the ideas, words, actions and visuals for their scripts. As you learned in "An Overview and Tour" chapter, once the agency's account executives approve these scripts, the art department creates *storyboards*. With these in hand to serve as visual aids, the account executive tries to sell the client on the copywriters' work. If the client agrees, TV producers create these *spots* (commercials) with the storyboards as a guide.

Commercial copywriters use either the master scene or two-column format, depending on how the spots will be shot—single camera or multiple camera.

PSAs, Promos and IDs

Public service announcements (PSAs) and *promos* (promotional announcements for programming, personalities

and other station attributes) are written much like commercials, because that's basically what they are: either commercials for nonprofit organizations or messages persuading viewers to watch the station's shows. Most PSAs have one other characteristic: They use the soft-sell approach. Love, sentimentality and hero-worship are common persuasive appeals. The Federal Communications Commission (FCC) once required all licensed broadcast stations to run PSAs, but it's no longer mandatory. Most stations continue to do so voluntarily, although the number of PSAs actually run has declined since the requirement was eliminated.

The typical promo is like a motion picture *trailer,* a "preview of a coming attraction." Promos interest viewers by teasing them with particularly dramatic or funny moments from upcoming programs. If they like what they see, audiences may decide to tune in.

Station IDs are often short and may consist simply of the legal FCC-required information: the station's call letters and location. However, most IDs are combined with a few lines of promo material (see Figure 13-7).

Like the commercials they resemble, PSAs and promos are scripted in either the master scene or two-column format. IDs generally are scripted in two columns. Many PSAs are written and produced by nonprofit agencies and run for free by stations. Some are written and produced by TV stations as a service to local nonprofit groups.

The station's promotion department frequently writes and produces its promos and IDs. If a station

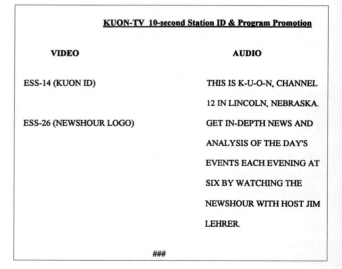

Figure 13-7. *Two-column script for a combined TV station ID and program promo.*

is a network affiliate, the network provides many preproduced promos, IDs and other marketing services.

Copyright Issues

The Copyright Act of 1976 provides authors ownership protection of their work and covers a variety of creative products including literary works, musical compositions and lyrics, dramatic works (including scripts) and music, pantomimes and choreographic works, pictorial, graphic, and sculptural works, motion pictures and other audiovisual works, and sound recordings.

The law protects these works from being reproduced and used without the author's consent and/or compensation. For scriptwriters, this works both ways: If you register your script for copyright, your "product" is legally protected, but this also prevents you from reproducing works of others.

You can protect your completed scripts easily: Just write to the Registrar of Copyrights at the Library of Congress in Washington, D.C., and request a copyright application form. Fill out the form, provide copies of the script, enclose a small fee, and you're protected. The Registrar also has a Web site with additional information and instructions on how to obtain application forms: www.copyright.gov/.

You can also assure yourself that no one will steal any of your undeveloped story ideas. The *Writers Guild of America* (WGA) provides a service that registers stories, treatments and outlines as well as scripts. Later, when you develop your story or treatment or outline a script, you can apply for a copyright. If you live east of the Mississippi, you may phone or write

the WGA-East, headquartered in New York City (https://www.wgaeast.org/script_registration/). If you live west of the Mississippi, call or write the WGA-West office in Los Angeles (www.wga.org/). If you wish to use the works of another copyright holder in any substantive form, you must obtain the rights to do so. Sometimes this is as easy as asking. Many photos in this text are the property of others, but we asked for and received the owners' permissions for their reproduction. However, you must expect that many copyright holders will demand royalties (payment) for use of their work. Be especially careful in dealing with the two major U.S. music licensing organizations, the *American Society of Composers, Authors, and Publishers* (ASCAP) and *Broadcast Music, Incorporated* (BMI). These organizations collect royalties from persons using the creations of their members. Both ASCAP and BMI routinely prosecute copyright violators, especially in the area of musical recordings.

This chapter is only an introduction to the theory, practices and styles of script writing. There are many books devoted to each of these program genres, and we recommend consulting them for a more thorough discussion of scriptwriting. A combination of study, classroom instruction and many hours of writing, rewriting and re-rewriting are necessary to become a television writer. But it should be obvious to anyone reading this chapter that there are many exciting opportunities for the verbally adept person. If you choose television as a career, you inevitably will address the difficult task of looking for that first job. Perhaps it will be in front of a computer screen instead of on air or behind a camera.

Consider the possibilities.

 **tech manual 13-1** *Number of Pages of Script vs. Screen Time*

According to the Writers Guild of America's publication *Professional Writer's Teleplay/Screenplay Format,* your script for a half hour of teleplay will run 30 pages. Double the amount of pages (60) for a one-hour teleplay, and triple it (90 pages) for a 90-minute teleplay. However, the WGA says that there should be only

110 pages for a two-hour teleplay. This difference is probably due to extra station/network break time. For a two-hour feature film screenplay, the WGA says that you would prepare between 125 to 150 pages. The actual number of pages will depend on the amount of dialog and the amount of action in the movie.

Important Vocabulary Terms

A-plot: The first, and sometimes the weightier, of two main story lines developed in a screenplay.

Act: A dramatic unit similar in TV and film to a sequence.

The American Society of Composers, Authors, and Publishers (ASCAP):, A major music licensing company, which collects royalties for the use of its members' creations.

Antagonist: A character in a story who opposes and attempts to thwart the protagonist in achieving his/her goals.

Broadcast Music, Inc. (BMI): A major music licensing company, which collects royalties for the use of its members' creations.

B-plot: The second, and sometimes less weighty, of two main story lines developed in a screenplay.

C-plot: The third, and usually the least in terms of screen time, of three story lines that may be developed in a screenplay.

Comparative (commercial) format: Commercials that by demonstration, inference or direct claim maintain that their product is superior to their competitor's.

Copywriters: The ad agency term for commercial script writers.

Demonstration (commercial) format: A format designed to reveal the superiority of a product or service through an on-screen demonstration of its strengths, often comparing it favorably against its competition.

Dramatic (commercial) format: Fashioned like a dramatic script, the product/service becomes the hero and wins in the end.

"The five Ws and How": The basic questions a news reporter should answer in a story: who, what, where, when, and why. "How" is often added to complete the list.

Interview (commercial) format: Commercials in which people on the street are asked questions designed to generate positive responses about the sponsor's product.

Inverted pyramid: The style in which most newspaper stories are written: The most important facts come first, followed by the less essential details in the story.

Master scene script: A script form that includes a relatively complete description of the surroundings, dialog, character, attitudes and actions that take place in the story.

Outcue: The last words spoken before a visual-element change in a broadcast news story. Only outcue copy appears on a director's rundown.

Package: A short self-contained TV news report, complete with sound bites, reporter narration and associated video footage.

Plot outline: The development of a basic story idea into a series of dramatic units. Later the outline is fleshed out with additional information and becomes a script.

Problem–solution (commercial) format: A commercial format in which the product/service is shown to solve the problem facing a consumer.

Promo: A promotional announcement used by a station to advertise its own programs, personalities or other attributes.

Protagonist: The hero, or lead character, in a drama or comedy.

Public service announcement (PSA): Announcements that promote nonprofit organizations or attempt to raise awareness about particular social/health issues.

Rundown: An abbreviated TV news script, designed to aid the director in calling shots.

Scene: A series of shots at one locale and usually edited together to create a complete dramatic "sentence."

Sequence: A series of scenes joined to create a complete dramatic unit within the story. Similar to an act.

Shooting script: A master scene script that also includes the director's shots, shot sizes and angles.

Shot: The basic visual unit in film and television: the action seen by the camera in one continuous view of the subject without interruption.

Sound bites: Audio or videotape obtained from interviewing news sources or witnesses to news events.

Special effects (commercial) format: Commercials that aim to charm curious, amazed audiences into paying attention to their message by using elaborate or unusual image manipulation techniques ("visual magic").

Spokesperson (commercial) format: Commercials using celebrity spokespersons to endorse the product or service.

Sponsored documentaries: Nonjournalistic documentaries commissioned by commercial, educational, governmental or other organizations and individuals for public relations, instructional, marketing or propaganda purposes.

Spot: A synonym for a commercial.

Storyboard: Cartoon illustrations of a television commercial script, used to explain a proposed commercial to a client. Storyboards are used to obtain bids to produce the spot and as an illustrated script during production.

Symbolism (commercial) format: A format that uses a character, an object or creature as an ongoing representative of the product/service (for example, the Energizer Bunny). Following repeated exposure, a viewer's momentary glance at this symbol instantly reinforces the advertiser's commercial message.

Testimonial (commercial) format: Similar to the interview format, the testimonial format uses everyday people or celebrities to endorse the product/service. The difference is that these individuals are portrayed as extremely happy, longtime users of the product, who exhibit extreme product loyalty.

Trailer: A film term for a preview of a coming attraction.

Treatment: A short (two- or three-page) prose rendition of a story, used to sell the concept and plot to a producer or TV program executive.

Writers Guild of America (WGA): The official union of screen and television writers, with principal offices in New York (WGA-East) and Los Angeles (WGA-West).

chapter **14**

Production Design

Mise-en-scene (from French, and pronounced "meez-on-sen") is the creative arrangement of people and objects, all the visual elements, within a unified space. Many viewers mistakenly assume that mise-en-scene is the exclusive responsibility of the director. In a large-budget show, it's actually the joint responsibility of many individuals, including the director, the lighting director and the *art director*, who may also be called the *set designer, scene designer* or *production designer*. These titles are nearly synonymous in television, with one notable exception. Advertising agency art directors have greater responsibility for the "look" of the TV commercials they design—sometimes even more responsibility than the director.

Defining Production Design

Design's primary function is simply put: to visually support the goals of the script. Good set design complements the script, augmenting whatever you're attempting to communicate.

One way to divide responsibilities for creating mise-en-scene is to say that the director works primarily in the foreground of the scene, while the designer assumes major responsibility for the background. This is by no means any rigid division of labor, as both work back and forth within each scene to create mood and meaning. The smaller the production's budget, the more the producer or director assumes mise-en-scene responsibility. Many low-budget productions have no designer/art director at all, requiring the director/producer to personally take charge of all design elements.

The Five Functions of Production Design

Production design

1. depicts locale,
2. introduces the time of day/era in which the story takes place,
3. demonstrates character personality and quirks,
4. sets the mood of the story and
5. introduces or reinforces themes found in the script.

The moment you see sterile-looking, two-tone-painted hallways, gurneys and people dressed in white medical uniforms, you suspect the scene is in a hospital. If the hallways are dark and shadowy, with few people walking about, you may further assume that it's the hospital's night shift. If the halls are dimly lit by gaslight, and decorated with antique medical equipment, wall hangings and props, you may assume that the era is the late 1800s.

Design aids the director in explaining character personality and quirks. For example, a den set with leather chairs, dark wood paneling decorated with gun racks, a collection of other weapons and trophy heads mounted on the walls suggests that the character residing here is probably an adventurer and big-game hunter.

It doesn't take long to sense danger when we see the interior of an old Victorian house, bathed in cobwebs and dark shadows, brightened only by an occasional flash of lightning. When audio effects such as creaks, groans, pipe organ music, thunder crashing and the relentless beat of rain outside are added, the scene is set for Gothic horror.

Design elements could tell a story that might save a director quite a few pages of script. Cut to an apartment scene in early morning, the camera focused on a pair of high heel shoes strewn on the floor. The camera trucks along to reveal a couch and coffee table, where more articles of male and female outer clothing are strewn helter-skelter over the furniture. Two empty wine glasses on the coffee table and an ice bucket with an upturned bottle indicate that drinking was a part of last night's festivities. As the camera continues to truck down the hallway toward the bedroom, more intimate clothing articles lead the way. In 20 seconds, an entire love scene is played out in the imaginations of the audience, with no words spoken or actor business shown. The designer, in cooperation with the *property master* (the person in charge of props on a show), has painted this picture for the camera to shoot.

Also, design elements introduce or reinforce themes found in the script. In the classic sitcom *M*A*S*H,* the well-known opening helicopter shots of the camp and subsequent shots of doctors wearing Hawaiian shirts and funny hats performing triage on wounded solders establish the situation, the occupation of the protagonists, their tent city locale and hints to their characters—all before a single word of dialog is spoken.

Design's Three Strategies

Three strategic approaches to design are (1) the *realistic,* or *representational,* (2) the *abstract,* or *stylized,* and (3) the *neutral.* The examples from *M*A*S*H* are realistic, intended to represent a mobile army surgical hospital, circa the 1950s. A realistic example of a news set can be an actual newsroom. The living room set of a homey daytime talk show or the totally functional kitchen set of a cooking program are further examples (see Figure 14-1).

A set designed in the abstract imaginatively suggests the theme or style of the production and doesn't attempt to be realistic or representational. An abstract set for a documentary on the history of television may feature two walls decorated with large photos from classic TV shows. A more realistic set for the same documentary would be an exact re-creation of a 1948 TV studio, with a set of black-and-white turret-lens cameras, a perambulator boom equipped with an old-fashioned RCA ribbon mike and other vintage equipment borrowed from the broadcasting museum.

A neutral approach often provides financial and/or visual economy. A bland, unremarkable, solid-color background encourages viewers to concentrate attention exclusively on the person or object in the foreground. One technique features a shape or form in the background purposely left out of focus. Another neutral design strategy uses a simple black backdrop and *cameo lighting*—a lighting technique in which only directional lights illuminate the subject, leaving the background dark (see Figure 14-2). *Silhouette lighting,* discussed and illustrated on page 104 in Chapter 5, provides yet another strategy.

Before we move on to examine how designers apply the technical elements of stagecraft, let's take a moment to consider the aesthetic tools that designers use to create their portion of the mise-en-scene.

1.

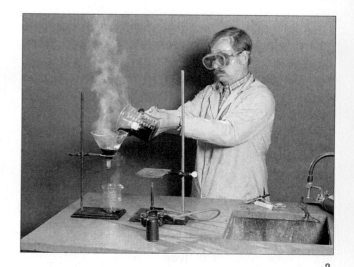

2.

Figure 14-1. *Shot 1 is a homey living room set used for informal talk and interview programs. Shot 2 is a simple but functional set for an instruction program on basic chemistry.*

Figure 14-2. *An example of cameo lighting.*

The Designer's Toolbox

Line

The basic creative tool of design is line. Line creates the form, or shape, of things. Lines may be horizontal, vertical or diagonal and can be drawn straight, curved, broken or in some combination of these. Whether straight or curved, horizontal lines tend to create a sense of calm; vertical lines express height, grandeur or dominance; diagonal lines communicate a sense of the unreal or artificial, or an unbalanced state; broken lines can suggest informality, disorder or mystery (see Figure 14-3). Straight lines suggest strength, structure, rigidity, calm and order. Making those straight lines patterned or symmetrical suggests organization, coherence and structure. And finally, curved lines are more restful, natural, graceful and flexible than straight lines.

Line also creates what visual theorists like Herb Zettl call *vectors*. As shown in Figure 14-4, vectors can draw the viewer's eye toward one direction or another by arranging a line or a series of lines or objects in a pattern.

Dimension refers to the size relationships in the forms you create. Size communicates many comparisons, such as importance/irrelevance or dominance/submission (see Figure 14-5).

1.

2.

3.

4.

Figure 14-3. *In shot 1, the movie theater's width creates horizontal line, despite being peaked in the middle. In shot 2, the silo's vertical dimension, perpendicular to the horizon, dominates. In shot 3, the railings of the stadium suggest diagonal lines. In shot 4, the bales of hay at intervals in the field create broken lines.*

Figure 14-4. *This A-7 aircraft, pointing to the right, and the shape and sweep of its wings forming a dart pointing to the right, and even the right-leaning pedestal on which the aircraft is mounted all lead the viewer's eye toward the right. These are examples of line and shapes creating vectors.*

Because the closer an object is to the camera, the larger its apparent size, *depth* can create the illusion of greater or lesser magnitude (see Figure 14-6).

Also, space and depth between actors or objects communicates meaning. *Forced perspective,* the narrowing of lines into the distance in a frame, can artificially suggest great depth when there is little (see Figure 14-7).

Using Color

Line creates form, but in most modern productions, form gets an assist from color. An unused children's coloring book is simply a dull, flat arrangement of lines on white pages until color is added. Similarly, color helps designers communicate meaning and mood. As we have introduced in earlier chapters, color consists of millions of combinations of three basic variables: hue

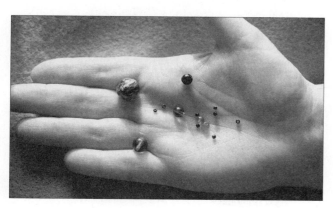

Figure 14-5. *The human hand in this shot provides dimension that allows viewers to understand the size of the beads.*

Figure 14-6. *Depth makes the foreground sculpture appear much larger than it is. The tower in the background is many times larger, but the sculpture's proximity to the camera makes it look larger. The front of the sculpture, nearest the camera, is no taller than the rear of the sculpture, just a few feet back. But again, proximity to the camera makes it appear taller.*

(the specific shade of color in the spectrum of visible light), saturation (the strength of the color from a deep, rich color to a soft pastel) and brightness (how much light the color reflects). Because of technical limitations in the analog system, television properly renders only a small, middle range of hues, saturations and brightnesses that we're capable of seeing with the naked eye.

We emotionally perceive color in a range from warm (reddish) to cold (bluish). The degree of saturation can enhance the effect, so that an extremely saturated red conveys a warmer, more enthusiastic mood than a washed-out, desaturated red. And conversely, a desaturated blue conveys a cooler, more relaxed mood than does a heavily saturated blue.

Figure 14-7. *The bricks are the same size, but placing the camera close to the wall and shooting with a wide-angle lens forces the lines of mortar to appear to converge rapidly, giving the illusion of great depth to a wall only a few yards long.*

Surrounding colors, or lack of them, also contribute to a color's ability to communicate. Although shot in color, some commercials completely desaturate the entire scene to black-and-white, leaving only the product carefully recolorized. This guides the viewer's eyes to exactly what the director wants audiences to see in each shot (the product), places increased emphasis on the product and couples the product with the particular mood associated with the color. Similarly, dressing one person in bright red among others in gray also draws viewer attention.

Finally, *texture* is another important implement in the designer's toolbox. The surface of set materials can be polished to a glassy shine, rough hewn or stippled like stucco. The texture of a surface, and how light illuminates that surface, can suggest a number of different moods (see Figure 14-8).

With a fundamental understanding of the designer's aesthetic tools, we can now move on to applying them, using the various physical and electronic elements at the modern designer's disposal.

Scenery

Selecting scenery for a production depends on your design strategy.

1.

2.

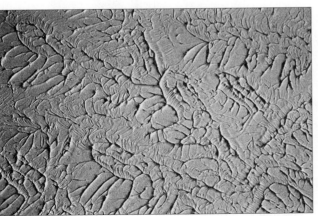

3.

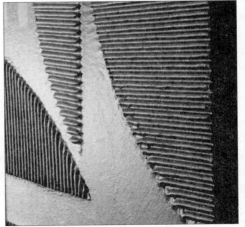

4.

Figure 14-8. *Set designers often use rough textures such as stucco, shapes and geometrics, odd finishes and mixtures of smooth and corrugated surfaces to provide an illusion of depth for a two-dimensional TV image.*

- You can use a natural location, carefully redecorated for effect. Note: When using natural locations, much time is spent replacing or modifying natural items so they look good on camera, for example, removing highly reflective items (or reducing their reflectivity with dulling spray), replacing distracting pictures on the wall and adding props or furniture that communicate a certain mood.
- Your scenery can be part natural and part fabricated.
- It can be part natural or fabricated, and part electronically blended with some other visual element.
- Or, your scenery can be a completely electronic fabrication.

The simplest kinds of scenery are curtains, *scrims,* cycloramas (cycs), regular walls or *seamless paper.* Curtains are either pleated or flat, but some pleated curtains stretch to give a flat, smooth appearance. Cycloramas come in two varieties: soft- and hard-wall. Soft cycs are made of slightly off-white, semireflective canvas or muslin. Cycs give the appearance of a smooth, opaque background when stretched around one or two corners of the set. Colored lights and projectors can illuminate the cyc's surface. Scrims are made of semi-translucent screening material (similar to the scrim material discussed in Chapter 7). Among many uses, stage productions use scrims to create backlit shadow scenes and silhouettes. Scrims are sometimes are used in the backgrounds of TV network variety shows and specials. (see Figure 14-9).

A hard cyc looks like a soft cyc, but the hard variety is a permanent studio fixture, made of masonite, sheet rock or some other rigid material. A hard cyc extends its integral *ground row* to the floor.

Seamless paper is a wide (9 feet or more) roll of heavy paper, either of a solid color or with a design, which is rolled down like a weighted window shade or taped to a wall and used as a neutral background (see Figure 14-10).

Flats

A *flat* is a more complex scenery device. Both hard- and soft-wall flats are painted and/or textured scenery. For television, most flats are built in 4 × 8- or 4 × 10-foot sizes on a frame, or skeleton, made of 1 × 4-inch pine boards. You construct a soft-wall flat by attaching muslin to the frame, then stretching and starching it to create stiffness and opacity. A hard-wall flat is made using materials such as plywood, paneling or composition board which can be painted, textured or covered with

1.

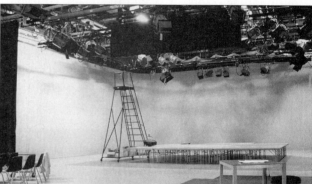

2.

3.

Figure 14-9. *Shot 1 is a studio cyclorama with a ground row. The ground row is slightly curved and helps blend the cyc with the studio floor. Shot 2 is a soft cyclorama, tightly stretched around the corner of a studio floor. Shot 3 is a backlit couple behind a scrim.*

wallpaper. You can use corner or edge moldings with hard-wall flats to cover joints, as well as all the common wooden or plastic trim used in normal construction and interior finishing work (see Figures 14-11 and 14-12).

Figure 14-10. *This is an example of the use of seamless paper to create a neutral background. The roll of paper is hung on two C-stands— all-purpose floor stands made by the Century Company—a staple in any well-equipped studio.*

Flats usually are painted with what appears to the naked eye to be rather dull, flat or semigloss pastel-colored latex paint. This is necessary because the eye sees things differently than the TV camera. What looks dull to your eye often appears more saturated when reproduced on a television screen.

Flats joined together create longer wall lengths. Provided the set is left standing in place until the production is completed, a space between two flats can be masked with a Dutchman, or some other variety of thin, paintable material pasted along the joint. After a few coats of paint or texture, and with correct lighting, the joint becomes invisible to the cameras. A Dutchman is also handy when you plan to cover your flats with wallpaper. The wallpaper covers the crack separating the two flats better with either a Dutchman or sheet rock tape underneath.

1.

2.

3.

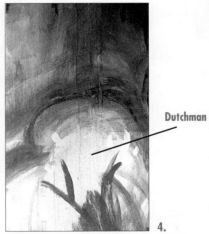

Dutchman

4.

Figure 14-11. *In shots 1 and 2, student workers fasten 1 × 3s together and cut out the curved plywood shape of the flat shown in shot 3. In shot 4, a barely visible strip of muslin called a Dutchman masks the crack between two flats. Painting over "Dutchmaned" flats can successfully erase these joining points—providing audiences don't look too closely. Also, thankfully, NTSC television's lower resolution—compared to human eyesight—is another factor contributing to invisibility. Set builders will have to become much more precise in the world of high-definition television.*

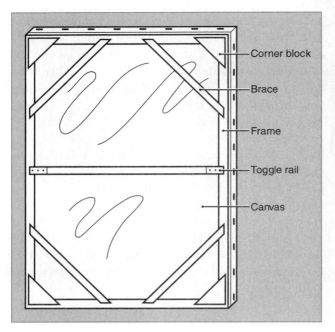

Figure 14-12. *A diagram showing the construction of a simple 4 × 8 canvas flat, complete with corner blocks, toggle rail and corner bracings. A corner block is a triangular piece of wood or metal used in flat construction to make the flat more stable. Corner bracing is usually a 1 × 4-inch diagonal support used in flat construction to create stability. A toggle rail is a diagonal brace used in flat building. Unlike home construction grade materials, set builders often use the lightest grade materials available, since only the look, not the long-term wear characteristics, are important to the camera.*

Flats must stand upright. The most popular way to keep flats vertical is to use a picture-frame-like brace called a *jack.* Jacks are weighted at the bottom with a sandbag, a *pig* of lead (a lead weight) or some other weight (see Figure 14-13).

Flats should be tightly connected when joined to simulate a long stretch of wall. Two or three flats permanently attached with hinges make a *twofold* or a *threefold.* Twofolds and threefolds store easily and compactly and stand upright with minimum bracing. One method used to join flats temporarily is to fasten them with C-clamps, and another is to lash them together with a combination of rope and *lash cleats* (see Figure 14-14).

You can suspend flats from the lighting grid or a studio batten and lower them into place on the studio floor, a technique called *flying* (raising or lowering) a *drop* (a flat, a scrim or any piece of scenery that is hung instead of attached to the floor). A popular drop in television is the solid blue or green *chroma-key drop.* But in many television stations and facilities, a chroma-key surface is more of a permanent fixture and is made of hard-wall construction. This is called a *chroma-key wall* (see Figure 14-15 in the color plate section of the book).

Other flats have special purposes in production design. There are rigid *door flats* or *window flats,* which incorporate working versions of doors and windows. Door flats that lead the talent outside swing open onto the set. When it's assumed a door leads to another part

Figure 14-13. *In shot 1, we see a canvas flat propped up with a jack, which is attached to the flat via screws. If the flat is taken down and occasionally stored, a hinge can be attached to the jack, permitting it to fold up like the back of a picture frame for storage. Shot 2 shows a very temporary way to attach a jack to a flat: a C-clamp. In shot 3, a sand bag is used to weigh down the jack, providing the flat with stability.*

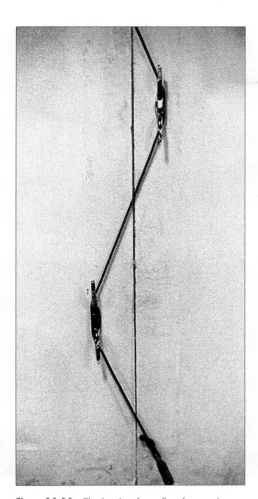

Figure 14-14. *The backs of two flats fastened together with rope and lash cleats.*

of the house, it swings outward. *Masking flats* are used with door and window flats, so that when the camera shoots through a window or open door, viewers will see a painted background, not the back wall of the studio (see Figure 14-16).

Figure 14-16. *The trees that appear in the background are on a masking flat behind the foreground set arches on this stage.*

Platforms, Floors and Furniture

Most television camera pedestals or studio tripods can't lower the camera down to a height that's best for talk shows, newscasts and other programs in which talent is usually seated. Placing chairs directly on the studio floor often forces the cameras to shoot down on the talent, creating unflattering down-angles. Rather than purchase expensive pedestals that lower cameras to talent's eye level (which also is uncomfortable for camera operators), it's easier to elevate the talent with *platforms* and/or *wagons.* It's possible to construct platforms of any size, but most studios build a few standard-sized models on a 2 × 6-inch pine lumber frame. Dimensions vary from large, 8 × 8-foot units to 4 × 8-foot modules that one person can easily move and store upright. Of course, they can be bolted or lashed together to make larger platforms. A wagon is just a platform on casters, permitting it to be easily pushed in and out of the area in the studio used for shooting (see Figure 14-17).

Figure 14-17. *These are 4 × 8 platforms stored horizontally. In some studios, they're stored vertically alongside flats.*

The Floor (and What Sits on It)

Most television studio floors are polished concrete or concrete covered with smooth, 1 × 1-foot squares of asphalt tile. These surfaces don't permit great latitude in floor treatment, although washable paints can temporarily change the floor color. Other options include self-stick tiles, carpets and rugs, colored strips of tape or wallpaper squares fastened to the floor, and similar temporary floor treatments.

Most production facilities use the same pieces of furniture in many different program applications. A small collection of chairs, couches, desks, prop bookshelves and several nondescript flats can be assembled in many configurations, depending on need.

Some companies sell modular platforms and set pieces that can be assembled in different ways (see Figure 14-18). Most production studios also have a small selection of artificial plants, shrubs and other set dressings. Lower-budget studios, or studios with little storage space, may stock only a few pieces of standard furniture, borrowing or renting items as needed.

Props

Properties, or *props,* are divided into two categories, *set props* and *hand props.* The distinction between the two is that hand props usually are functional and are often used and/or picked up by talent during the production. A set prop might be a painting or a drapery, while a hand prop could be a wine glass or a revolver.

Prop persons work for the art director, obtaining or making set dressings and functional items that support the script. The best property master is someone talented at shopping for odd items. Huge prop and costume rental houses in production centers like Los Angeles and New York make these searches both easy and fascinating.

At the appropriate point in preproduction, the property master takes the script, analyzes it page by page and draws up a list of props to be used in each scene. This process assures that on the day of the shoot on *Will and Grace,* the director won't need to halt production while someone locates Karen's pack of cigarettes and gold lighter.

Electronic Design

Production design no longer is limited to simply creating sets to serve as backgrounds. Using a chroma-key wall or drop, the only real object in a set design may be the talent standing in it—and one day, computer-generated

1.

2.

3.

Figure 14-18. *Shot 1 shows modular platforms placed together to provide an open interview set. Shot 2 is a commercially manufactured interlocking modular set. Shot 3 shows one side of the set in shot 2, in which the shiny "buckle" fastener holding the two sections of the set together is highlighted in the lower left of the frame.*

Shot 1 courtesy of Nebraska Educational Telecommunications.

animation quality may become efficient enough to replace live talent. The rest may be a combination of graphic art, such as a matte painting, electronic (computer-generated) art or a real location keyed into the frame.

Paperwork

Production design begins with paperwork. After consulting with the director, the producer and others concerning the script, the designer begins researching the proper visual look for the show. If the production is a period piece, taking place, perhaps, in the era of the French Revolution, the designer reviews paintings, sketches, films and TV programs that portray the same time and place. Then the sketching begins. The designer either "sells" the director and producer on these design sketches, or goes back to the drawing board. Eventually the design is approved, and if time and budget permit, the designer and assistants build table-top set models. These are quite helpful to all creative personnel because they allow everyone to visualize the sets prior to their construction (see Figure 14-19).

On graph paper, the designer also draws an overhead view of the design's floor plan. These overhead views usually include all set pieces, walls and potential camera positions. Floor plans are important to nearly all departments of a production. For example, floor plans are needed to properly design the show's lighting and to create an efficient *light plot*. Also drawn on graph paper, a light plot superimposes the planned placement of lighting instruments over the designer's overhead view of the floor plan. Floor plans are also important to the director when planning camera placement, blocking talent and placing microphones.

A final note on the job of the designer: Don't look for a resident designer at most local TV stations. Most stations need only a few sets because they produce little in-studio programming other than news. When the station needs another news set, the common practice is to

1.

2.

Figure 14-19. *Shot 1 shows one of the designer's set models for* The Music Man. *Shot 2 is the set built from that model. Model and set design by Otis Sweezey.*

hire outside consultants to design and build it. Often the same consultant firm redesigns the lighting for their new set. Most full-time TV designers work for consulting firms, large production houses and network production centers in major cities. Some individuals who regularly design for the theatre also create sets for television.

In the next two chapters, we'll discuss the director, the other key creative participant in mise-en-scene. We'll discuss both the aesthetics and techniques of directing.

Important Vocabulary Terms

Abstract, or stylized, design: A design intended to imaginatively suggest the theme or style of the production but that does not attempt to appear realistic or representational.

Art director: Variously called set designer, scene designer or production designer, this person's creative responsibility is to create the director's concept in the area of production design. In an ad agency's production of a commercial, the art director's and the director's roles may be reversed. In this manner, the director's function would be to produce, on film or videotape, the storyboards created by the ad agency art director.

C-stand: An all-purpose floor stand made by the Century Company, hence the name. A staple in any well-equipped production studio.

Cameo lighting: A style of illumination in which only directional light is used to illuminate the subject, displaying the subject starkly against a dark background.

Chroma-key drop: Rather than a solid Masonite wall, a chroma-key drop is a solid blue or green drop used to provide a background for chroma keying.

Chroma-key wall: Like a chroma-key drop, it's used to provide a background for chroma keying. The chroma key wall is a permanent studio fixture.

Corner block: A triangular piece of wood or metal used in flat construction to make the flat more stable.

Corner bracing: Usually a 1 × 4-inch diagonal support used in flat construction to create stability.

Depth: A design tool in which the background space between actors and objects is used for aesthetic and communicative purposes.

Dimension: The size relationships of forms in a design.

Door flat: A flat featuring a functional door.

Drop: A flat or other piece of scenery that's hung, rather than fastened to the floor, and flown in and out of the set as needed.

Dutchman: A strip of muslin or other thin, paintable material used to obscure the joints between flats.

Flat: Composed of either hard or soft walls, it's a basic scenery device used mostly to create painted backgrounds. Usually built in handy 4 × 8- or 4 × 10-foot sizes, flats are joined to create larger set walls.

Flying: A theatre term referring to raising or lowering drops or curtains from or to the set.

Forced perspective: The narrowing of lines into the distance to create the illusion of increased depth within the scene.

Ground row: A wedge-like device used to mask the point where the bottom of a cyclorama or scrim meets the studio floor.

Hand props: Properties that must be functional, because they are handled by talent.

Jack: A picture-frame-like brace used to vertically support a flat.

Lash cleat: A post used to tie flats together.

Light plot: Drawn on graph paper, a light plot superimposes the planned placement of lighting instruments over the designer's overhead view of the floor plan.

Masking flat: A flat positioned behind a door or window flat to provide a background for the camera shot when the door or window is opened.

Mise-en-scene: Pronounced "meez-on-sen," it is the creative arrangement of all the visual elements within a unified space.

Neutral design: Production design intended as unobtrusive, unnoticed background, forcing the audience to focus attention on foreground elements.

Pig: A production term for a weight used to balance a stand or a jack.

Platform: A set piece on which talent, furniture and/or flats are positioned.

Production design: That portion of mise-en-scene for which the art director, under whichever specific job title he or she is operating, is responsible.

Production designer: See "Art director."

Properties (props): Items for set decoration and/or use by talent, often divided into two categories, hand props and set props.

Property (prop) master: The person in charge of props on a TV show.

Realistic, or representational, design: A design intended to re-create a setting accurately, giving the audience the impression/illusion that it is real.

Scene designer: See "Art director."

Scrim: A smooth, stretched curtain similar to a cyclorama, but more transparent. This material is similar to scrims used to diffuse lighting instruments.

Seamless paper: A neutral paper background on a roll.

Set designer: See "Art director."

Set props: Properties other than furniture used in the production design for their decorative value.

Silhouette lighting: The opposite of cameo lighting, in which the background is lit but the subject in the foreground is dark.

Texture: A design tool referring to how the surface of an element responds to light. Texture may range from glossy to rough and stippled, creating shadows.

Toggle rail: A diagonal brace used in flat building.

Twofold (or threefold): Two or three flats hinged together to form a convenient set piece.

Vectors: An aesthetic term for visual emphasis created when any line or series of lines or masses are arranged in an order that draws the viewer's eye in one direction or another within the frame.

Wagon: A platform on casters, permitting it to be easily pushed in and out of the area in the studio used for shooting.

Window flat: A flat featuring a functional window.

## chapter 15

Directing I: Aesthetics

A director is many things to many people, so, not surprisingly, there are different definitions for what a director is, and descriptions of what a director does. Broadcasting textbook authors Herbert Zettl and Alan Armer describe a director as an artist, parent, priest, psychologist/psychiatrist, friend, writer, actor, photographer, costumer, electronics wizard, musician, graphics artist, technical advisor and coordinator. If you think that being good at all these things simultaneously is a tall task, you're right. As the guiding intelligence and chief interpreters of the message communicated by a production, directors must have a working (if not expert) knowledge of all the skill areas under their control. Author/TV commercial director Ben Gradus summed up a director's job description even more succinctly: "He [or she] answers questions." Everyone in the production looks to the director for speedy, wise, creative, cost-effective answers to everything from minutiae to major controversies.

Many students mistakenly believe that once they've mastered all the studio equipment and know TV vocabulary and procedures, they're ready to try the director's chair. Technical skills are important, and we've spent a large part of this book discussing them. But if that were all there is to directing, any experienced crewperson could be a director. But a director must possess a number of artistic and interpersonal skills that have little to do with button pushing. Students who want to direct television for a living are well advised to enroll in art drawing and art history courses, English literature and creative writing courses, theatre courses in playwriting, acting, directing, stagecraft and makeup. Courses in social sciences such as history, psychology and sociology

can also help develop an understanding of human perception and behavior. Basically, the more liberal-arts-oriented a director becomes, the more he/she can bring to a television production.

Another shock to many students is the discovery that directors spend more time in preproduction preparation than calling shots or editing video. The great motion picture director Alfred Hitchcock was convinced that his creative work as a director was <u>over</u> the moment he stepped onto the set to shoot the first scene of one of his pictures. By then, Hitchcock reasoned, all that remained was capturing on film what he had carefully, meticulously planned at his desk.

Script Analysis

The first thing directors must do is become as familiar with the script as its writer. You do this by reading and analyzing the script repeatedly, eventually developing a creative strategy for how you'll visualize this script for your audience. Sometimes you'll discover that the script needs more work, and you'll provide notes or meet with the writer to discuss a rewrite.

Writers often complain, rightly or wrongly, that some directors interpret their scripts in ways different than they intended. But interpreting scripts—for better or for worse—is one of the main prerogatives of the director. And one of the first questions you must answer about a dramatic script (and, to a certain extent, about a script for any program genre) is "What is this program's *major dramatic value*?" A major dramatic value is the one element of dramatic structure your script favors over all others. As discussed and theorized about through the centuries, from Aristotle's time to the present, one can point to five major dramatic values: *plot, character, language, spectacle/music* and *ideas.*

When directing a show in which plot is the major dramatic value, you must emphasize the script elements that drive and develop the story line, subjugating all other values to it. *Murder, She Wrote* or *Law and Order* are examples of program series that emphasize plot as the major dramatic value.

Character, the second major dramatic value, concentrates on the personal development and interaction of the characters and on the changes they undergo by story's end. The series *ER* often spins interesting plot developments. But week-in and week-out, it's the unique, fascinating collection of guest character actors and the interplay, adventures and development of the regular characters that are the central concern of the series' writers and directors.

Language is the third major dramatic value. The director's efforts favor the portrayal of the language over other factors when the words in the script and the delivery of those words are paramount. For example, whenever a film or television director directs Shakespeare's plays, the language's the thing. And can you imagine directing a talk show and not being primarily concerned with the conversations going on?

In a script featuring the fourth major dramatic value, spectacle/music, one or both of these elements takes center stage. Television budgets don't allow spectacle very often. The film series *Star Wars* and *The Lord of the Rings* trilogy are examples of movie scripts using spectacle as the major dramatic value. An occasional miniseries such as *Gettysburg* displays the huge vistas, the cast of thousands and the epic grandeur that typify this major dramatic value.

Plot, character and other values take a back seat to the spectacle and musical performances when the melodies are the dominant element in films such as *My Fair Lady, The Sound of Music* or *Phantom of the Opera.* But because musicals and productions of spectacle are typically more expensive to produce than shows with other dramatic values, they are made less often than the rest. However, in nondramatic fare, public TV shows such as *An Evening at the Pops,* the wonderful musical event *Celtic Woman* and numerous musical performance specials such as *Garth Brooks in Central Park* utilize this value in all their production decisions.

A script featuring the fifth major dramatic value, ideas, must be directed so that social, political or philosophical concepts become the central focus. Although the acclaimed TV series *Touched by an Angel* features

character development and good plotting, its major dramatic value is ideas. The same can be said of the TV series, *The West Wing.* These programs' scripts explore many important issues, including social justice, God and personal and moral responsibility.

As the person in charge of creative elements throughout the production, the one to whom everyone directs their questions, the director is the only member of the crew who can coordinate the work of everyone effectively to achieve the script's major dramatic value. But not all scripts have one clear-cut major dramatic value. Many scripts have secondary, and even tertiary, values, which also must be interpreted and balanced against the major value. For example, the Academy Award-winning film *Dances With Wolves* is a film of spectacle, but it's also one of character and ideas. *Hamlet* has arguably the greatest use of the English language in dramatic literature, but it also features extraordinary character development and rather bizarre plot twists. Ask Polonius. Productions that combine complex dramatic values challenge the talents of even the most experienced directors.

Directing Tools

Alexander Dean's classic 1941 text, *Fundamentals of Play Directing,* suggests five aesthetics to consider when directing stage plays. They are (1) composition, (2) *picturization,* (3) movement, (4) rhythm and (5) *pantomimic dramatization.* Aspiring television directors should learn to adapt these theatre concepts to the electronic stage, because there's much in this ancient art form that applies to effective TV directing.

Composition

Pictorial composition is a major directorial contribution. Chapter 4 discussed the fundamentals of shot composition, but taking these principles a step further, let's see how directors might use emphasis and balance in composition.

Emphasis　Emphasis is about inducing the audience to focus on what you want them to look at within the shot. Theatre, film and television directors manipulate emphasis through these tools: body position, area, plane, level, contrast, space, focus and repetition.

The talent's body position can establish compositional emphasis. Full front, facing the camera directly, is the strongest. Turning one quarter in either direction creates slightly weaker emphasis. The profile is next weakest, followed in descending order by the full-back position and the three-quarter-back position (see Figure 15-1). Of

Figure 15-1. *In shot 1, full-front composition provides the strongest emphasis. In shot 2, talent turned 45 degrees to the side provides strong emphasis, but is weaker than a full-front shot. In shot 3, talent in profile, 90 degrees to the camera, is weaker still. Many people do not look their best when shot in profile. In shot 4, talent three-quarters away from the camera is the weakest of all positions, because it shows little of the talent's face yet lacks the dramatic impact sometimes provided by a full-back composition. In shot 5, talent with back to the camera is weak in terms of emphasis, but may be extremely useful in certain dramatic scenes, as when a talent is experiencing great emotion and wishes to hide her face from view.*

course, body position is only one variable involved in emphasis: The size of the shot, a change in lighting or some other variable also can affect emphasis.

Area is also a factor in compositional emphasis. Area involves placement of the talent on screen. Positioning talent in the foreground has a stronger impact than if talent is placed in the background, and because American audiences read from left to right, talent positioned on the left side of the screen (stage right for the actor) has stronger compositional emphasis than talent on the right. However, the strongest areas in an <u>establishing shot</u> are the center foreground, followed by foreground left and then foreground right. It's especially important to think through these screen areas in long shots, but you can use area to create emphasis even in closer shots (see Figure 15-2).

The distance of the talent or object from the camera helps determine the strength or weakness of compositional

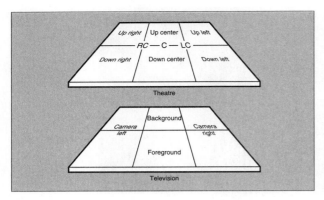

Figure 15-2. *All other variables notwithstanding, for an actor, downstage center is the strongest area, followed by downstage right and downstage left. In television, camera operator directions refer to downstage as the foreground. But most of the same principles of emphasis for the stage prevail in the shot.*

Figure 15-4. *The standing talent in this scene clearly is the focus of the shot. He is facing the camera (strong body position), occupies the camera-left foreground of the set (dominant area), stands above other talent in the scene (higher level) and has other talent focusing their attention on him. Although the seated talent form a larger visual mass, the other factors combine to place the emphasis of this shot on this actor.*

emphasis. Placing talent closer to the camera and in focus is always stronger, and the tighter the shot, the more dramatic the emphasis.

Level, defined as the height of the talent or object within the shot, also affects emphasis. The higher the level, the stronger the emphasis. Level is especially helpful in establishing shots, where it can guide the viewer's eye to a certain location within the frame (see Figure 15-3).

If emphasis is properly manipulated in the long shot, viewers are better prepared, and thus less disoriented, when you cut to a medium shot or medium close-up.

Contrast with other pictorial elements also provides emphasis. Placing talent on the left side of the screen, separate from a group of actors on the right, gives this person more emphasis, even though he occupies less space on the screen than the group. Contrast in body position, plane and level also increases emphasis (see Figure 15-4).

Figure 15-3. *The woman standing in this scene clearly is the focus of the shot. She occupies center stage and has height. As well, the girl playing the piano is at the weakest position, three-quarters, turned upstage. The seated woman is focusing on the woman who is stand-*

The previous photo demonstrates how focus creates emphasis. When a single talent, or a group of people, turns and looks toward another person, the viewer's attention also focuses on that person. Focus also can be indirect. If Talent A focuses on Talent B, who is in turn focusing on Talent C, one can say that in this composition, Talent A is indirectly focusing on Talent C (see Figure 15-5).

Repetition creates emphasis when a director applies the old maxim "the more the merrier." If you draw the viewer's attention to a person in the shot by having three followers focus on him, you can enhance this person's stature and importance by adding more followers. If you wish to show that someone at a restaurant table has done something shocking or unmannerly, you can cue two persons at the next table to react in a scandalized or irritated manner. Directing everyone in the restaurant to react is an example of achieving emphasis through repetition. Having the two news anchors and the sports reporter chit-chat with the weather reporter before she moves to the chroma-key wall for the weather report shifts emphasis to the weathercaster and her segment of the program.

Balance The need for *compositional balance* is one of the aesthetic values many psychologists say humans have collectively inherited through the ages. It's also part of the English language: When something isn't right, it's out of balance. Alexander Dean defined balance as "weight against weight," obtained either through *symmetrical* or *asymmetrical* composition. As Figure 15-6 shows, we attain symmetrical balance by composing the

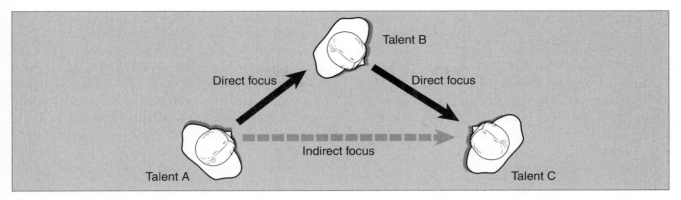

Figure 15-5. *Indirect focus: Because Talent A is focusing on Talent B, who is directly focusing on Talent C, Talent A's focus is indirectly on Talent C.*

shot so that, were it centered on an imaginary fulcrum, identical weights on either side would prevent the frame from leaning left or right. Any compositional element, not just people or objects, can create "weight."

Asymmetrical balance throws away the fulcrum and the laws of physics, allowing people or objects of unequal weights to balance each other. This is accomplished by using light, area, camera angle (and thus plane) and other factors to offset the weight (see Figure 15-7).

Picturization

One of the director's many jobs is picturization, the process of visually interpreting the script for the audience. Ideally, picturization allows a viewer who doesn't speak English to understand what's going on without the aid of a translator.

Arguably, the best picturization in motion picture history occurred when movies communicated plot and character without dialog. The greatest silent films required few or no dialog graphics. Today, directors use

picturization to assist audiences in scenes of *incidental action, background, main action* and *dramatized emotional relationships.* Scenes of incidental action create atmosphere, present characters or assist in character exposition. These non-vital scenes visually set up the action to come, clarifying what follows. For example, early in the film *Star Wars* (1977), we see what appears to be a scene of incidental action in which Luke Skywalker is practicing the skills of a Jedi knight—including hitting a small, rapidly moving target while blindfolded. Later, in another seemingly incidental scene during a pre-flight briefing, we hear Luke tell a fellow fighter pilot that their task—to fly down a trench at high speed and hit a tiny exhaust port on the Death Star with torpedoes—is as easy as Luke's shooting "womp rats" back on his home planet. These scenes prepare viewers during the climax for Luke's "one in a million" shot that destroys the Death Star and saves the day for the rebels.

Figure 15-6. *A two shot of a news anchor team provides a symmetrically balanced shot.*

Shot courtesy of Nebraska Educational Telecommunications.

Figure 15-7. *The talent in the left foreground asymmetrically balances the two talent in the center and right background. This shot also illustrates the use of "specials" to highlight textured curtains and an object (painting) in the background as discussed in Chapter 5.*

Shot courtesy of Nebraska Educational Telecommunications.

Background scenes can help the viewer set the place or time. Instead of a keyed title, such as "Tombstone, Arizona, 1849," it's visually stronger to open with a sequence starting with a shot of a street with horses, wagons and people dressed in mid-19th-century Western costumes. Then cut to cowboys brushing dust from their chaps as they enter the saloon, where we see a man seated at a table, red-eye in hand, reading the town's newspaper, the *Tombstone Epitaph.*

Picturization enhances scenes of main action in many ways. Story emphasis is already working for the director, because action important to main problems in the plot is currently unfolding. Directors take more time with these scenes. Often they edit down the length of shots, raise the volume of the music and sound effects and even (especially in action programs) escalate the level of violence. Scenes of dramatized emotional relationships, designed to develop characters and character interaction, often portray talent in tighter shots, and actors exhibit greater emotional intensity as the plot approaches its climax.

Movement

Like composition, movement has both a technical and an aesthetic value. To advance the plot, it's technically necessary to move your talent and/or objects from place to place on the set, or to accomplish other changes in position. Creatively, movement adds a kinetic element to picturization. Talent sitting motionlessly while speaking their lines miss the chance to use elements of picturization and movement to augment their line recitations. There are six varieties of movement: *story, background, character, technical, compositional* and *transitional.*

Story movement is *business* that directly moves the plot toward its climax. Business is defined as movement, with or without props, intended to communicate meaning in the scene. An example of communicating meaning without props might be as simple as a character stating, "Don't worry, you'll do fine," while only the audience sees that behind his back the character has his fingers crossed.

Background movement helps establish locale and circumstances. An opening shot of people drinking, dancing, flirting and merry-making in a cabaret becomes the perfect setup for the introduction of the opera *Carmen.* Likewise, starting a newscast with a wide shot of a TV newsroom showing busy reporters in the background and an anchor desk in the foreground establishes the news anchors as "working reporters" intimately involved in the gathering of news, not merely attractive people with good reading skills.

Characters are more interesting, understandable and unique when they're assigned certain traits and habits.

Character movement helps illustrate these traits. To establish that a character is tense and worried, direct him to dart his eyes around or wring his hands and appear jumpy. In the sitcom *Seinfeld,* virtually every episode has a moment when Jerry's bizarre neighbor, Kramer, bursts in the front door and makes some outrageous gesture, pratfall or facial contortion.

Technical movements are actions that transport talent and objects from one place to another. Compositional movement is similar in that its purpose is to convey talent and objects into new pictorial compositions. Consider the following sequence, for example: A long shot shows a biker in a bar getting up from his table and crossing (moving across the set) to the protagonist. The next shot shows the protagonist at his table as the biker walks into frame and seeks out the protagonist. When the protagonist stands, we see that the biker is a foot taller than the protagonist, and acting increasingly hostile—causing the protagonist to become increasingly nervous. This blend of composition, picturization and movement works to advance the story line.

Transitional movement is defined as entrances and exits. Transitional movement, a form of technical movement, conveys characters from one place to another to begin and end scenes. For example, when the hero rises, crosses to the door and opens it to leave the room, saying, "I'll get him if it's the last thing I do," the viewer understands that this scene is about to end. It also suggests that in the next scene we're likely to see our hero in pursuit of the villain. However, transitional movement has other uses. In a comedy, the bumbling detective wishes to exit: He grabs the doorknob, only to find that it won't turn. Embarrassed, he pulls hard, the doorknob comes off in his hand, and he loses his balance. He falls backward, knocking over an aquarium, causing a large, wiggling carp to land in the lap of a very dignified-looking woman in a nearby armchair.

These movement principles can be directly applied to program forms other than drama or comedy. For example, on some network morning shows, the weather reporter often walks into the shot with the news update reporter and talks to the reporter for a moment before moving to the chroma-key wall to report the nation's weather, thus providing a smooth transition between the news anchor shot and the weather set. Jay Leno sometimes walks, on camera, from his desk to the orchestra area and says a few words, providing a smooth transition to a musical selection by the band. And sometimes, one of Leno's guests enters or exits the stage via the curtain.

Strong and Weak Movement   Strong movement provides additional emphasis and is created by stepping or leaning toward the camera, standing or straightening up or raising one's arm or one's head. Moving from a lower to a higher level is usually stronger movement than the reverse. Weak movements include stepping or leaning back, sitting, turning away or retreating. The relative strengths and weaknesses of movements enhance picturization. For example, if the talent must make a forceful speech, have her rise, not sit down; if a person must back down from his stated position, direct him to say the line as he bows his head. Documentary directors often have the on-screen narrator walk toward the camera when making a major point. Even news directors sometimes encourage reporters to move toward the camera to add vital emphasis rather than deliver their copy in a static stand-up. In other words, good directors use movement as motivated by, and helpful to, the script as much as possible.

The distance between two characters is usually proportional to the emotional intensity between them. As you move characters closer together, intensity rises. The classic comedic takeoff on this is the famous confrontation scene between Sam and Diane in the sitcom *Cheers.* As Sam and Diane become increasingly angry, they approach each other, closer and closer, finally nose to nose, both shouting passionately hateful insults. Finally Sam, frustrated, exclaims, "Are you as turned on as I am?" She growls, "Yes," and they embrace in an equally passionate kiss as the audience roars with laughter.

Rhythm

Rhythm is a succession of compositions, movements, sounds or any combination of these elements that occur at relatively regular intervals. Rhythm's purpose is both to stimulate good timing and manipulate the audience into reactions you desire. The tools to develop rhythm are found in the script, and in the creative attitude of the director. Although helpful in all genres, rhythm is especially useful in comedy, where viewers expect laugh lines to follow each other within a certain time period. *Cheers, Frazier* and *Seinfeld* were among TV's best sitcoms in establishing laugh line rhythms. Clock a typical episode with a stopwatch and you'll see a consistent laugh line rhythm. Many kinds of rhythms are possible, from dialog rhythms to audio and sound effects rhythms. Each contributes an important sense of structure to the show and creates unconscious audience expectation, sympathy and coordination.

Tempo is the rate at which this rhythm occurs. Tempo can speed up and slow down the pace and the level of excitement. Early motion picture pioneer D. W. Griffith used editing tempo to increase the excitement level at the climaxes of his silent pictures. As he edited, Griffith shortened the length of the shots as a climactic scene drew to a conclusion. Finally, as the cutting tempo increased to a frantic pace, the hero defeated the villain. Because, like good editing, tempo is not meant to be noticed, the effect of tempo is often not apparent to viewers. But all well-directed TV programs of many different genres change tempo to maintain audience interest. Newscasts and talk show directors use segments of different lengths and intensity to vary the tempo. Even the most pedantic educational program consisting only of a classroom lecture is more effective if the director occasionally cuts to a cover shot or a reaction shot of people in the live audience, rather than remaining tightly focused on the instructor. Directors enhance live musical shows via the tempo of their editing, cutting speedily between shots when the music is fast and furious, and cutting less often, even using slow dissolves, when the music is soft and slowly paced.

Pantomimic Dramatization

The last of the five major directing aesthetics is pantomimic dramatization, defined simply as "actions without words." Pantomimic dramatization (pantomime for short) includes both movement and business, plus aspects too small to be called either movement or business. Facial expressions, turns of the head, a raised eyebrow, simple body language—all are pantomimic elements. For example, to communicate consumer satisfaction, commercials often end with the talent admiring (or chewing, drinking, wearing, driving, stroking) the product with a big smile of satisfaction, but without additional dialog.

Pantomimic dramatization is used on many occasions to create the meaning the director and/or actor may intend for the words in the script. Consider the vast difference in meaning communicated by the line, "What are you doing?" when delivered by:

- a smiling young woman as her boyfriend nuzzles the nape of her neck;
- a tired mother with an irritated frown on her tired-looking face as she discovers her children have made a huge mess;
- a tense, worried policeman, as he discovers what appears to be a burglary in progress; or
- a cool, expressionless young man greeting a friend.

Also consider a basic difference between the stage and the camera: Communicating pantomime across the footlights requires larger movements than delivering the same message to a camera in a tight close-up. The tiniest nuance—pantomime likely missed by a theater audience—is blown up to a screen-sized action when captured in a TV close-up.

Cinematic Tools

Television directors have many tools at their disposal that stage directors don't. They include the ability to change shots, to manipulate shots with lenses and camera movement, to change scene (location, for example) in $^1/_{30}$ of a second and to create transitional devices between shots. These advantages are described as *cinematic,* that is, unique to the media of film and television.

The ability to change shots is an important tool: But it's also one of the director's most important creative responsibilities: deciding which shots to take, from what angle, when and for how long. Any given series of events can be covered with a camera in any number of ways, and events can be manipulated and interpreted differently, depending on the skill of the director. Consider this supposedly true story: In the early 1930s, a young director was at a Hollywood party attended by the great Charlie Chaplin. As usual, Chaplin attracted a crowd (which delighted him), and he began holding forth on the subject of directing. The young director, who was shooting a comedy at the time, asked for advice: "Mr. Chaplin, the scene I'm shooting tomorrow calls for a rich, rotund lady to take a big pratfall—to slip on a banana peel. How should I shoot it? Should I begin with a long shot of the lady approaching the banana, cut to a close-up of the banana, and then back to a long shot as she slips and falls?"

"No, no, my good man," Chaplin replied. "Comedy demands much more than that. Begin with the long shot of the lady approaching the banana. Then cut to the close-up of the banana, and then to a medium shot of the lady as she spies the banana. Then cut back to the long shot as she carefully avoids stepping on the banana, and in doing so, falls into an open manhole."

Making such decisions about what to shoot and how to shoot it is arguably the most important thing directors do.

Directing With Lenses

As we discovered in Chapter 2, lenses create many cinematic effects, including manipulating depth of field, zooming and filtering. Directors can isolate foreground or background talent or elements as effectively using the lens

Figure 15-8. *The director has used control over depth of field to isolate the talent in the foreground from distracting background objects, thus placing emphasis on the talent.*

to control depth of field as they can through scene design (see Figure 15-8). Depth of field also allows the director to fill a long shot with action, prompting audience interest throughout the entire depth of a shot (see Figure 15-9).

Zooming permits directors on a budget to use one lens to replace many. If used with skill, great restraint and care, a zoom can replace an expensive and difficult dolly shot. Excessive zooming is an unfortunate artifact of certain arty films of the 1960s and 1970s and occurs much less in modern productions, because "the trombone school of zoom lens work" draws attention to the director's technique and away from the story.

Directing With Filters

Lens filtering creates many cinematic effects, including the softening of shots. Humphrey Bogart's close-up

Figure 15-9. *This shot draws the viewer's eye deeper into the scene by providing many planes of interest for exploration.*

Courtesy of Nebraska Educational Telecommunications.

shots in the great classic *Casablanca* were shot with no lens filtration at all, emphasizing Bogie's face in all its lined, craggy ruggedness. In contrast, director Michael Curtiz shot Ingrid Bergman's close-ups with a filter so viewers saw her as through a gossamer veil. This "veil" effect was close to the truth, because in those days, before glass lens filters (called fog filters) became commonplace, *Casablanca*'s cinematographer Arthur Edeson achieved the softening effect by stretching a silk stocking over the lens. Today, many aging TV stars (who shall remain nameless) require high-numbered fog filters to be used in their close-ups. And diffusion filters are sometimes used in videotaped dramatic programs to give the footage a "film look." In rock concerts, variety programs and football halftime extravaganzas, star filters are often used to highlight reflections from items on the set and from lighting instruments.

Colored filters permit the director to have the overall color in a scene tinted to support the message. For example, shots tinted red help picturize some hellish conflict. A light blue filter adds mystery and cool suspense to a midnight tryst.

Camera Movement

Camera movement within the shot creatively provides continuous change in perspective for your viewers. Film and television productions often include scenes in which two lovers kiss, and, as the music swells, the camera dizzyingly glides 180 to 360 degrees around them. Other movements include long pans and trucks, often used in opening credits to set the location or the mood.

Transitions and Meanings

The basic cinematic transition is the cut, but even this instantaneous change of shot conveys meaning. Within the context of a scene, the cut tells the viewer that the next shot may be happening in real time. Although cuts can transition from scene to scene, they usually indicate that there's been no change of time or location since the last shot.

A dissolve virtually always indicates a change of time, if not a change of place. A fade indicates an even longer duration of time, and often place. For example, if you wish to show a person waiting for a long time, begin with a medium shot of the person sitting. Then dissolve to a long shot of the person pacing up and down, irritated. Then dissolve to the person, now very annoyed, sitting again, checking the time on his watch.

Now that we have discussed some of the fundamental aesthetics of directing, we're ready for the next chapter, which will turn our attention to the more pragmatic techniques of the director's art.

Important Vocabulary Terms

Asymmetrical balance: Balance achieved through manipulation of variables such as light, area, camera angle, etc., rather than simply dividing "weight" evenly on each side of the picture.

Background movement: Business that helps establish locale and circumstances.

Background scenes: Used to set the location and era of a story.

Business: Movement, with or without props, intended to communicate meaning in the scene.

Character: A major dramatic value that focuses directorial efforts on the development of characters in the script.

Character movement: Business that helps establish unique character traits.

Cinematic techniques: Directorial techniques and tools not available to the stage director—those unique to film and television.

Compositional balance: "Weight against weight" in a picture; the sense that visual elements in a shot are evenly distributed, whether through symmetrical or asymmetrical composition.

Compositional movement: Business that conveys characters and objects into new visual combinations to aid in picturization.

Dramatized emotional relationship scenes: Used to develop the interaction between characters in a script.

Ideas: A major dramatic value that focuses directorial efforts on the development of political/social concepts in the script.

Incidental action scenes: Action not vital to the plot but that can be used for character exposition and other purposes.

Language: A major dramatic value that focuses directorial efforts on the delivery of the lines (the words) in the script.

Main action scenes: Used to resolve the main plot problems in the story.

Major dramatic value: The one element of dramatic structure that the director favors over all others in the script. Five major dramatic values include plot, character, language, spectacle/music and ideas.

Pantomimic dramatization: "Actions without words" used to convey story information.

Picturization: Visually interpreting the script for the audience.

Plot: A major dramatic value that focuses directorial efforts on development of the story line elements of the script.

Spectacle/music: A major dramatic value that focuses directorial efforts on the development of visual grandeur or the musical performances in the script.

Story movement: Business that directly moves the plot along.

Symmetrical balance: Balance achieved by equally dividing pictorial weight on each side of the frame.

Technical movement: Business that transports talent and objects from one place to another.

Tempo: The rate at which a scene's (or a program's) rhythm occurs.

Transitional movement: Business mostly used for entrances and exits.

chapter **16**

Directing II: Techniques

This chapter continues our discussion of directing, moving from the last chapter's emphasis on aesthetic principles (the ideas that govern our directing strategy) on to the techniques (the tactics) that successful television directors use to achieve their ends. We'll begin this discussion with the art and craft of directing television talent.

Directing Talent

It's helpful to have done some on-camera performance yourself before you direct others on television. When you find yourself facing a group of performers, you'll realize that your mastery of the technology of television directing does you very little good. Performers, whether they are actors in Hollywood, newscasters in Duluth or talent for a commercial in Memphis, will expect you to be their expert guide through the production, to help them do their jobs well and to make them look good in the final result. To provide this guidance, you must possess the experience necessary to have formed a clear understanding of the performer's craft. Then you can commiserate with talents' problems and their need for reassurance that they're doing a good job. Directing talent also requires you to behave consistently in a mature, reassuring, confident manner, especially if some of your cast or crew do not.

Directors are expected to converse with talent and crew in their own "languages." No one else is expected to learn new lingo just to be able to understand your commands, so you must be artistically "bilingual." You can't give all performers directions the same way you give them to your camera operators. Instead you must

be artistically "bilingual." If your performers are trained in theatre, for example, you must speak to them in theatrical terms, requesting, for example, that they "do a curved cross downstage right," or "focus on her while she's talking." But you'll also be required to speak to your camera operators and crew in TV language. That's why, as Chevy Chase might say, you're the director—and they're not.

Creative Tips for Tryouts and Casting

As we discussed in detail in the "Overview and Tour" chapter, there are certain steps that must be taken before auditions. Whether you're preparing to cast and direct a Hollywood sitcom, a new public affairs program on your PBS affiliate, a commercial campaign or a series of promos on a commercial station, before you announce tryouts for your TV show, you should:

- Know your script(s) backwards and forwards, and do all the creative preparation work outlined in Chapter 15.
- In concert with your production team, develop a production schedule with a timetable for each phase of production. There's nothing worse than selecting talent, only to discover that they are unavailable when you're ready to shoot.

If you're working on a show subject to union rules—and in larger market stations, this is often a consideration—you will probably select actors from casting books provided by talent agents (see Figure 16-1). In contrast, in a college production, you may recruit talent by posting notices of

1.

RATES COLORS TALENT AGENCY, INC. WILL QUOTE ALL MODEL AND ACTOR RATES SEPARATELY. THERE IS A TWO HOUR MINIMUM ON ALL BOOKINGS. IN THE EVENT THE BOOKING EXCEEDS THE HOUR, TIME IS BILLED ON QUARTER HOURS. LENGTH OF BOOKING MUST BE SPECIFIED AT THE TIME OF BOOKING. MODEL OR ACTOR WILL BE PAID FOR TIME SPECIFIED, USED OR NOT. DAY RATES ARE FOR EIGHT CONSECUTIVE HOURS BETWEEN 7:00 AM AND 6:00 PM.

TIME AND A HALF IS CHARGED BEFORE 7:00 AM AND AFTER 6:00 PM AND ON SATURDAY, SUNDAY AND HOLIDAYS.

FITTINGS ARE AT FULL RATE WITH A MINIMUM OF ONE-HALF HOUR CHARGED.

USAGE AND USAGE FEES MUST BE STATED AND NEGOTIATED PRIOR TO THE TIME OF ACTUAL BOOKING. USAGE RIGHTS ARE LIMITED TO THE SPECIFIC RIGHTS GRANTED AND MAY NOT BE EXTENDED WITHOUT NEGOTIATION.

PREPARATION TIME MAKEUP, HAIR, DRESSING AND REHEARSAL TIME WILL BE CHARGED AT FULL FEE.

TRAVEL TIME ARRANGED PRIOR TO BOOKING.

TENTATIVE BOOKINGS MAY BE CANCELED AT ANY TIME BY EITHER TALENT OR CLIENT AT NO CHARGE. IF THE CLIENT DOES NOT RELEASE OR CONFIRM TENTATIVE BOOKINGS, THE AGENCY RESERVES THE RIGHT TO CANCEL.

DEFINITE BOOKINGS SINGLE OR MULTIPLE BOOKINGS, HAIR, MAKEUP, NAIL REQUIREMENTS, BILLING INFORMATION OR ANY OTHER SPECIAL REQUIREMENTS MUST BE SPECIFIED BY THE CLIENT WHEN PLACING DEFINITE BOOKINGS.

LINGERIE-BRAS, PANTIES, SLIPS, PANTYHOSE AND ALL TRANSPARENT LOUNGEWEAR, SLEEPWEAR OR UNDERWEAR IS TIME AND A HALF.

CLIENT MUST SPECIFY TYPE OF LINGERIE AT TIME OF BOOKINGS. AGENCY MUST CLEAR WITH MODEL BEFORE ACCEPTING ANY LINGERIE BOOKINGS. A CLOSED SET MUST BE PROVIDED.

PRODUCT BOOKINGS PLEASE CHECK ALL CONSUMER PRODUCT BOOKINGS WITH US FOR CONFLICTS AND RATES. NO BOOKINGS FOR CONSUMER PRODUCT, PACKAGES, RISER CARDS, POSTERS, USE OF MODEL NAMES, HANG TAGS OR ANY DISPLAY MATERIAL, PACKAGE INSERTS, ETC....MAY BE MADE WITHOUT SPECIFIC CLEARANCE.

EXCLUSIVITY/ENDORSEMENT REQUIRES SEPARATE, NEGOTIATED CONTRACT.

FILM/VIDEO ALL BOOKINGS INVOLVING MOTION PICTURE, FILM, OR VIDEO RECORDINGS MUST BE NEGOTIATED IN ADVANCE.

CANCELLATIONS CONFIRMED BOOKING CANCELLED WITHIN TWO (2) WORKING DAYS: NO FEE. CONFIRMED BOOKING CANCELLED WITHIN ONE (1) DAY: HALF FEE. CONFIRMED BOOKING CANCELLED WITHIN EIGHTEEN (18) HOURS: FULL FEE.

CLIENT RESPONSIBILITIES INCLUDE ADVISING AGENCY OF EXTRAORDINARY CONDITIONS OR REQUIREMENTS; ADVISING OF ALL POSSIBLE USAGE PRIOR TO BOOKING; AND PROVIDING COMPLETE BILLING INFORMATION AT TIME OF BOOKING.

AGENCY SERVICE FEE OF 15% WILL BE ADDED TO ALL BOOKINGS.

FINANCE CHARGE OF 2% PER MONTH (24% ANNUALLY) WILL BE ADDED TO ALL INVOICES NOT PAID IN FULL WITHIN THIRTY DAYS FROM BILLING DATE.

2.

Figure 16-1. *In shot 1, these photographs are Memphis actors then represented by the Colors Agency. This is a photo page from their casting book of a few years ago. Shot 2 is a page in which Colors set out its notes regarding rates and conditions.*

your auditions in prominent places, such as your theatre department's casting board.

Never promise a job to anyone—not even your best friends—before holding open auditions. You may later find someone who auditions much better. Then you must either break your word to your friend or not use the actor who's best for the role.

When performers audition, ask that they bring a bio or résumé and a picture. This goes for beginners as well as pros. This procedure helps you to identify people later on and to ensure that the person has enough experience for the job. Select your most crucial scenes for them to read, scenes that will demonstrate their ability to handle the most troublesome and broadest aspects of the production. Also ask that talent present a short performance—perhaps a monologue—that they've prepared. Some talent may deliver a poor audition performance during a cold reading of new material, but may surprise you if given time to prepare something. Allowing talent to present prepared material of their own selection shows you something about their personality, demonstrates what they can do when well rehearsed, gives you an insight into their experience and abilities, and may indicate that they are better suited for on-camera work other than the role or job for which they are auditioning.

Keeping the required performance clearly in mind, don't forget to consider the following qualities and characteristics of each performer:

- Age and general physical appearance.
- Voice quality and diction.
- Sense of movement and rhythm. If the performance requires movement, and the talent doesn't move during the audition, ask them to do so. This shows you two things: how well they can move and how well they can take direction.
- Sense of drama and background, as evidenced by the ability to add a little interpretation, or a bit of accent, if needed, to the script reading.
- Audience appeal and personality.
- Special abilities needed. For example, if the script requires that the talent ride a horse, find out if the talent has ever ridden before.

After you've cast the talent, there are some things to consider before beginning rehearsal. Blocking rehearsals usually shouldn't occur until:

- you've received significant creative input from your technical people, including the art director, lighting director and (if you need one) your costumer;

- you've completed set design and/or selected locations and made any major alterations in the script and the production schedule that may result from these technical considerations; and
- you've had a sit-down with the production team for a complete read-through and thorough discussion of the script (this ensures the key people understand your creative objectives and strategy in directing the show).

Rehearsals

Francois Truffaut once asked Alfred Hitchcock if he had actually said, "Actors are cattle." Hitch, the dry humorist, responded that he never said anything of the kind: "Actually, I said that actors should be treated like cattle." But few directors can get away with Hitchcock's legendary, autocratic control of all aspects of rehearsal and performance. As a matter of fact, until you become as great a director as Hitchcock, you should listen and learn from your actors as much as you give them orders. This attitude should begin during casting call and as rehearsals begin. And you must be even kinder and more considerate and helpful to less experienced talent.

When you're directing amateurs, rehearse in short, concentrated periods. The more professional your talent and crew, the longer your rehearsals can be. But just because you are a dynamo, don't assume that everyone is. Allow for breaks, stick as much as is practical to the production schedule you have published in advance for everyone, and begin and end rehearsals on time. Remember that breaks are mandatory for union members, and overtime costs extra.

Your goal is not to elicit great performances during the initial rehearsals. The objective in early rehearsals is to familiarize talent with the script, each other and how the show will be put together. In dramatic shows, early blocking rehearsals help the talent to know how they're supposed to move on the set and what business to do. When you tell your talent where to go and what pantomime is appropriate when they get there, allow them time to write down these directions on their scripts. As they study their lines later on, they will use these notes to memorize and perfect these actions. Once they have more time with both elements, better creative performances will begin to emerge.

During camera technical rehearsals, you'll again have to sacrifice creativity for mundane concerns. This is because camera technical rehearsals, like blocking, serve to finalize your camera operators' moves and shots and give them time to practice them. At this point, camera operators, the technical director, talent and others may suggest alternative camera shots or other possibilities for your consideration. Both camera technical rehearsals and blocking rehearsals are mechanical in nature and move slowly. Unlike the actors in rehearsal, you do not rely on camera operators to write down each camera movement and shot in a multiple-camera production. The director provides each camera operator a "shot sheet." Shot sheets include the shot numbers in the master script that correspond to each camera and notations explaining camera movements, such as pans, tilts, zooms, trucks, dollies and crane movements. Then, if directors want to back up and repeat something during a rehearsal, they refer to their master scripts and say, "OK, everyone, let's go back to shot 44 and run that scene again"—and everyone knows where they are in the script.

During final run-through rehearsals (sometimes called "dress rehearsals") in multiple-camera shows, practice scenes at normal performance speed as much as possible, stopping only when insurmountable trouble (a "train wreck") occurs. Maintaining the flow of the show gives cast and crew confidence at this stage of production. You can give the performers and crew *director's notes* (minor corrections and adjustments) during the break between the final rehearsal and the show's taping.

At this point in single-camera remote productions, you're ready for the shoot. More informal rehearsal may occur between takes during the shooting process, but the rest occurs with cameras rolling. Eventually you'll judge one of these takes satisfactory, and that's the one you later edit into the final version of the show or commercial.

A few tips for directors for all phases of rehearsals and shooting:

- When you're trying to explain to an actor how you want a line delivered, avoid *line reading*. This occurs when the director, frustrated with an unsatisfactory performance, takes over and says in effect, "Just imitate me." Don't do this. Many performers view line reading either as a director's ego-trip moment or, worse yet, as an insult, as if the director were saying, "You can't provide the performance I require. So let's try 'monkey see, monkey do.'" Instead of line reading, patiently talk the talent through it. This improves your own oral and interpersonal communication skills and gives your performers an increased sense of dignity and accomplishment.

- Don't automatically fire difficult persons and replace them with more compliant ones. There certainly are good reasons to dismiss performers, but try to be patient. You're often dealing with high-

strung, extremely creative individuals who need to feel they're making artistic contributions to your production. Many actors, especially those trained exclusively for the stage, expect more autonomy than is usually allowed in television and film production. Listen to what your performers say. Sometimes they really do have a better idea. Ask yourself which approach best supports your major dramatic value. Which enhances the theme, mood or rhythm that you've established for the show? Finally, if time and budget allow, you may decide to shoot it both ways and choose which is better later on during editing. Always remember that you must find ways to remain creatively in charge without turning into either a petty dictator or a floor mat. Compromise is acceptable, but you're ultimately responsible. You have the responsibility to keep the vision, that "big picture" for your production, in mind. Don't let the narrow view of a single member of your company, no matter how strongly expressed, cloud your creative judgments.

- Never lose your cool. If you're really angry about something, call a break. Once things cool down, saner behavior usually prevails. There are rare occasions when you just can't work with an individual—you realize that you've made a mistake in casting or crew selection, and that this person is ruining the show. Difficult as it is, you occasionally must fire someone. But do it calmly, dispassionately, quietly and alone with this person, away from the rest of the company. Don't do it during or right after a heated or upsetting episode. Wait a bit—otherwise you may regret your actions later. It is said that a famous director's prayer goes, "Lord, help my words to be gracious and tender today, for tomorrow I may have to eat them."

- Don't be an elitist: Take breaks, eat meals and associate with everyone in your company. Don't discriminate between above- and below-the-line people; be civil and kindhearted to all. One disgruntled or unmotivated crew member can ruin an otherwise fine production, and one loyal crew member performing beyond the call of duty can sometimes save it. You need all your crew members as much as they need you: Everyone's important. No member of your company should be thought of as "one of the little people."

- Insist on promptness from everyone; demand that people show up on time, prepared and ready to work. Of course, you must set the example for the company by doing all these things yourself.

Technical Crew Job Descriptions

A director must be able to work with everyone on the crew. Knowing their job duties can help directors make reasonable requests. The following descriptions aren't universal, but they are a good starting point for defining individual and team responsibilities. Many of these duties are listed as questions for the crew members to answer before, during and after the production. Some of the questions and concerns are duplicated so that various elements can be double-checked. Teamwork and cooperation are essential. These positions and responsibilities are typical of many productions performed by students in academic settings. Check with your professor, producer and director regarding individual projects.

Producer: This person's responsibilities will be addressed in Chapter 17, "Producing."

Director: As you learned in the overview chapter, once the production process begins, the director is in charge of making sure the project is completed. He or she works closely with the producer to accomplish all objectives successfully.

1. Is everyone in place and everything ready at taping time?
2. Are rundown sheets properly prepared, checked by your producer, professor and engineers and distributed to the producer, technical director and floor manager?
3. Is the set ready and lit properly?
4. Is the audio operator set up and ready?
5. Are the cameras in position and the operators on headset and ready?
6. Are the crew and talent informed of everything before taping begins?
7. Was the clock that times the show started on time?
8. Were the preparatory and execution commands properly executed?
9. Were the time cues given properly to the technical director, floor manager and crew?
10. Were the producer's (or professor's, or client's) wants, needs and desires properly fulfilled?
11. Were there any rough spots? How can these be eliminated and/or corrected?
12. Are there any personnel problems, and how can they be corrected and/or eliminated?

Technical Director: This person is in charge of operating the video console and ensuring all the visual elements of the production are blended smoothly. He or she may coach the camera operators from time to time, or point out some video problem that may have escaped the director's attention. He or she may also assist in timing the production.

1. Is the video switcher properly prepared (and programmed, if appropriate for your model) and ready for production time?
2. Are the camera operators properly framed on their first shots, and are they informed when the production is ready to begin?
3. Was the clock started on time?
4. Were the shots punched up when called for in a timely and efficient manner?
5. Were all the special effects ready and available on cue?
6. Did you wait for the tape roll-ins to stabilize (tape machines up and running at speed) before you punched them up?
7. Did you watch the source monitors for early detection of problems? (For example, if the director calls a stand-by to take a camera, is that camera properly composed and focused for the shot?)
8. Did you fade up and out on time?
9. Was the switcher properly struck (cleared of programming and source video) after the production ended so that it is ready for the next production?

Floor Manager: This crewperson is in charge in the studio, and his/her job description is somewhat similar to that of the theatrical stage manager. Floor managers often are the link between the control room and the talent. A good floor manager is aware of the present situation on all fronts—technical and human—and can frequently head off problems before they happen. On occasion, they can also serve as a personal buffer between the director and the cast/crew.

1. Are the monitors placed in spots where everyone can see them?
2. Is the lighting ready before production begins?
3. Are microphones ready and in place? If you are responsible for relaying mike check and level calls from the audio engineer to the talent, have you done so?
4. Is everyone in the studio aware when the production or rehearsal begins?
5. Are you ready and able to keep time cues accurately and independently if necessary?
6. Were all the props ready when needed and then properly disposed of after the production?
7. Were the studio guests escorted in and out of the studio in a professional, courteous manner?

8. Were time cues given promptly and visibly?
9. Were the talent and guests informed verbally or by written cues about any and all situations?
10. Did you maintain a quiet and professional atmosphere during the production?

Audio Console Operator: This person is in charge of the aural components of the production and runs the audio console. He or she is often in charge of preproduction elements of audio, such as setting up the microphones.

1. Is the console set up in a logical, professional, easy-to-understand manner (so that everyone can run the console in the same way)?
2. Did you set up the microphones on the set, dress the cables properly and call for mike checks prior to production?
3. Were the *intros* and *"outros"* (audio and video introductions to the show and the converse, the end audio and video) professionally produced and played back at the appropriate times?
4. Were the microphone and equipment cues ready and on time?
5. Were the levels consistent (no extreme highs or lows)?
6. Were the levels constantly monitored throughout the production?
7. Was there cover music ready and available?
8. Were the microphones and cables put away after the show?

Lighting Designer/Board Operator: This person has heavy responsibilities in preproduction. He or she works closely with the director to design the "look" of the production and then implement this plan. This may involve hanging lights, running cables, changing bulbs, adding scrim and many other manual labor tasks. Usually, most of the lighting designer/board operator's responsibilities may be over when the actual production starts.

1. Are all the sets, positions and talent lit properly at the correct footcandle levels?
2. Do you have a lighting diagram? Has it been approved and designed with the help and consent of the producer, professor and engineers?
3. Can you save and label the settings on the lighting console?
4. Does the lighting look right to you?
5. Did you get the lighting done in plenty of time so that the producer, director, professor and/or engineers could see it beforehand?

6. Are there problems with any fixtures, cables, scrims, gels or supplies?
7. Can you make midshow corrections and changes if necessary?
8. Were the lights turned off, cables and supplies put away and the lighting console turned off after the production?

Graphics Designer/Operator: This person designs the graphic arts visuals for the production. This can involve name keys, visual intros, "outros," bumpers, boxes and factual information inserted into the production. The graphics operator ensures that all these elements are ready in the proper order to be used by the director and technical director.

1. Are all the visuals prepared in accordance with professional standards?
2. Are all the visuals prepared in coordination with the producer and director?
3. Are all the visuals and keys prepared in advance and ready to go before production time?
4. Are all the words spelled correctly and checked by someone else (to give it another set of eyes)?
5. Are all the graphics easy to read and positioned within the essential area?
6. Do the graphics have the borders, drop shadows and/or background boxes required for this production?
7. Do the images and symbols make good visual sense?
8. Were the visuals and keys correctly displayed within the production?

Teleprompter Operator: This person is in charge of loading and running the teleprompter properly before and during production. Although most of his or her work occurs in the preproduction phase, he/she plays a vital role during the production process.

1. Was all the copy turned in to you in a timely fashion?
2. Are all the intros, "outros," bridges, transitions and copy ready to go at production time?
3. Is the prompter properly coordinated with the script?
4. In news, is each story individually labeled to allow for cutting and pasting?
5. Is the copy saved on a separate disk?
6. Was all the copy centered and the roll speed adjusted for each reader?
7. Were there any complaints regarding your spelling, grammar, punctuation? How can you correct them before production time?

8. Were there any complaints regarding your operation of the prompter during production? How can you correct them before the next production?

Tape Operator: Nothing gets recorded unless this very important—and sometimes underappreciated—crewperson rolls tape in record mode on time and with proper levels.

1. Were all the tapes submitted to you in a timely fashion?
2. Who was late, and how can this be corrected by the next program?
3. Are the tapes dubbed (from the nonlinear editors), stacked and cued at production time?
4. Are all the audio and video levels consistent? If not, why not and what can be done before production time (or for next time)?
5. Did you note any discrepancies (both technical and organizational), and inform the producer, director, audio operator, technical director, professor and engineers?
6. Were the tapes cued and rolled properly during the production?
7. Was the final production recorded in a consistent, professional fashion?
8. Were all required dubs made in a timely fashion and distributed properly?

Camera Operator: Camera operators are the most fundamental element in good production. If they cannot do their jobs properly, your show will look horrible. Good visualization is vital. They must be able to perform their duties quickly, competently and aesthetically.

1. Were all shots composed properly (headroom, framing, balance, lead space, LS-MS-CU)?
2. Did you know in advance what your shots were and what other cameras' shots you might have to cover?
3. Did you have your camera balanced and adjusted and your cables properly prepared before the production?
4. Were your shots adjusted and framed in a timely manner as required by the production and/or called by the director?
5. Were any "hot" moves (on line) done smoothly and efficiently?
6. Were any cover shots ready when necessary?
7. Did you know the relationship of your shots and camera to the other cameras and shots?
8. Were the cameras and headsets properly put away after the production (headsets placed underneath the camera monitor, cameras rolled to their storage positions and cables coiled or placed in figure eights)?

Talent: Talent is responsible for the human on-air elements of the production. He or she must connect with audience, convey the information and know the technical aspects of the process.

1. Were you properly attired and groomed?
2. Do you know the script, requirements and procedures for the production?
3. Did you conduct yourself in a professional manner?
4. Were you properly prepared through rehearsals, off-set practice and/or read-throughs?
5. For interviews, were you properly prepared with appropriate questions, intros/outros, cues, transitions, props, etc.?
6. Were mistakes and errors covered and corrected in a professional manner?
7. Did you consult with the producer, prompter operator and floor manager to ensure smooth operations before and after each production?

All Crew Members

1. Did you attend and take notes through preproduction and rehearsal sessions?
2. Were you aware of any potential problems, and did you inform the producer, director, professor and/or engineers?
3. Were you at the production site (for example, the studio) early and did you have your position set up and ready to go at production time?
4. Did you keep headset conversations restricted to the production efforts?
5. Did you treat all guests and peers in a courteous, friendly, professional manner?
6. Were all your activities conducted solely for the prompt, efficient completion of the production?
7. Did you leave any complaints, whines, gripes, smart aleck remarks, internal bickering, roughhousing, silly game playing, flirting and other unprofessional behavior at the studio door?
8. Did you turn in all tapes, scripts, props and related materials in a timely manner?
9. Were you aware of problems and solutions at every position, and what you could do personally to ensure a smooth production?
10. Did you know at all times what was coming up next, and what you would do if there was a problem?

11. Did you know everything required of you going into the production, or did you act like a helpless person who said, "Nobody told me," or "I didn't do it"?

12. Did you make sure you know what is expected of you in future productions?

13. How can we make future productions better?

Technical Tips for Directors

One thing a director may wish to do is draw a floor plan for each scene (or single-camera location) in the script. This is a helpful visual aid when discussing directorial needs with crew members, and also invaluable when planning your shots. This scaled-down, "bird's eye" view of the set allows you to more easily decide where to place cameras and how to best orchestrate them (see Figure 16-2). Fortunately you don't need a sketch artist to draw floor plans, because we view them from overhead. Modest skill with pencil and ruler, or a computer drawing program, is adequate.

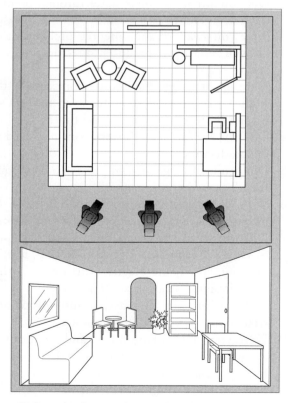

Figure 16-2. *In this drawing, the set at the bottom is shown above in an overhead sketch, including camera placement.*

Storyboarding

Many great directors, such as Alfred Hitchcock, George Lucas and Steven Spielberg, who have directed in both film and television, storyboard/ed every shot. Others never work from 'boards, preferring to direct from the script. So, other than when you're working on a TV commercial, when is it most helpful to storyboard scenes? Personal preference prevails. However, for shows that are more logistically difficult, involve more creative personal, require more. . . . storyboards are especially useful, perhaps even essential. Obviously, the better you draw, the more likely you are to storyboard your productions. But even directors who can draw only rough outlines and stick figures can communicate to crew members and actors with 'boards. The drawing or storyboarding personal computer applications available at modest cost make storyboarding even easier for those of us who can't draw.

Shot-Calling Vocabulary and Technique

It's essential that all crew members speak and understand the same production language. Without such understanding, we build a miniature Tower of Babel with each production. There are no absolute vocabulary standards in television production. Differences exist from station to station and studio to studio, but the vocabulary discussed below can be understood at most production facilities.

As you learned in the "Overview and Tour" chapter, there are two kinds of directorial commands, preparatory commands and commands of execution. Preparatory commands give crew members time to prepare a move, effect, transition or change in status. Execution commands follow preparatory commands and signal that it's now time to perform these changes. You should give preparatory commands whenever humanly possible. The more often you give the crew time to prepare, the more often you'll get what you want when you call for it. There are instances when events move so fast that you don't have time for preparatory commands, and when that happens, you must depend on the crew to respond as fast as they're able.

The following terms and procedures are widely recognized and understood. Some of these terms have appeared earlier in this text, but we want to summarize the basic directing vocabulary and procedures here, in one place.

a. *Ready,* or *Stand by:* Whether you prefer "Stand by to fadeup on Camera 1," or "Ready to bring intro music under," these preparatory commands allow video, audio and other technicians time to set up the next effect or transition.

b. *Fadeup:* An execution command calling for a gradual transition from black to a picture. Duration time for a fade is usually around a second and a half. A *fadeout* is a transition from a picture to black. Although heard occasionally in a studio, the phrase "fade to black" is redundant, because all fades go either to or from black.

c. *Dissolve:* This command results in one picture slowly fading out, while another picture simultaneously fades up to take its place. If you will, a video dissolve is like an audio cross-fade. If you wish to dissolve from Camera 2 to Camera 3, you don't say, "Ready to dissolve from Camera 2 to Camera 3." It's understood that Camera 2 is on line, so you just say, "Ready to dissolve to Camera 3."

d. *Take:* This execution command causes the instantaneous replacement of one video source with another. "Cut" is the analogous term used by switcher manufacturers and motion picture editors. Television directors avoid using "cut" as a transition command, because someone may misinterpret the command and halt a live show in progress, because in a studio "cut" also means "stop the show."

e. *Split-screen:* As you learned in Chapter 7, there are hundreds of split-screen patterns (switcher manufacturers call them wipe patterns) which you may choose. Split-screens allow more than one picture to share the screen with another picture. The wipe pattern chosen for this split creates the shape of the boundary that separates these two pictures.

f. *Wipe:* This is a split-screen pattern in motion that either fully or partially replaces one picture with another.

g. Key commands: In many small studios, when a director wishes to key a graphic on the character generator over a shot of a newscaster on Camera 4, the director says, "Stand by to take a CG-over-Camera-4 key." This command is preparatory to inserting lettering from the character generator over a newscaster on Camera 4. In many larger studios, each video source has an identifying number which appears on all special effects and routing switchers in the facility. Let's assume, for example, that sources 1, 2, 3 and 4 are the station's four cameras; source numbers 5, 6, 7 and 8 are the station's four videotape recorders; sources 9 and 10 are the two outputs from channels A and B of the studio's character generator; 11 and 12 are two network satellite feeds, and 13 is the feed from the remote truck. So in this situation, if the CG information you need is on the character generator with input number 9, and the newscaster appears on Camera 4, the director says, "Stand by to take a 9–4 key," rather than say "Stand by to take a CG-over-Camera-4 key." This could be simply written on the script as a fraction, a "9/4 key." This economy of words is standard procedure in many studios and used in many ways. For example, if the director says, "Ready to roll 8—roll 8," the videotape technician hits the play button on videotape machine number eight. The visual countdown begins (five, four, three, two, one), and at what would be "zero," the director says, "Take 8," placing video from VTR 8 on line.

Lose key is the opposite of the command to take, dissolve or wipe in a key. You can transition to a key by any kind of transition the switcher provides. The series of commands might go like this: "Stand by to dissolve in a 9/4 key—dissolve to key. (A pause of a few seconds occurs, usually long enough for the director to read the keyed information twice.) Lose key." In this situation, the CG key dissolves in, and out. If a simple "lose key" command follows a key command, the technical director (TD) actually performing the transitions at the video switcher uses the same kind of transition going out as going in: Dissolve in, dissolve out. If the TD takes/cuts the key in, it's taken/cut out. But if a director wants to dissolve the key in and take it out, the proper command sequence is "Stand by to dissolve in a 9/4 key—dissolve to key. Stand by to lose the key by taking it out—lose key."

h. *Roll:* This is the command to engage the "start" button on either a VTR, film projector or audio tape—any audio or video source that must be set in motion prior to taking it on the air.

Audio Commands

i. *Roll silent:* This means the same as a roll, except that whatever video source you roll goes on line without sound.

j *Audio fade* and *cross-fade:* As the name implies, an audio fade is a slow reduction in volume to silence. An audio cross-fade is the same as a dissolve in video: One source fades out while another audio source fades up.

k. *Sound up:* This is a generic audio cue to bring the next-scheduled sound device up to its predesignated audio level. This could be a CD, cassette, hard drive playback, audio cart or the playback of an audio track of a videotape/disc.

l. *Sound under:* This is a cue to lower the level of background audio until it is secondary to a foreground audio source. This command would, for example, cause the audio director to fade down a CD playing theme music to *bed level* (a lower audio level) under the narrator's voice.

m. *Mike and cue talent:* This command calls for the audio director to open the talent's mike and for the floor director to simultaneously give the talent the cue to begin speaking. Often the director will specify the talent by name, such as "Mike and cue Bonnie," especially if there are multiple talent on the set and the director wants only one miked and cued at that moment.

Ending the Show

A director must be careful not to convey the impression that a show or segment is finished until it is really over. For this reason directors often say *"thank you"* when they wish to indicate that a show or segment is completed and the crew can stand down. A "cut" command means a segment or a program is finished. However, "cut" isn't the signal to relax. When talent and crew hear "cut," everyone should hold position in a "stand-by" mode until the all-clear command, the thank-you is given. This is the signal that the show is off the air.

An even more definitive ending command is *"Wrap it,"* or "That's a wrap." This means that not only is work finished on a show or show segment, but that work in the studio for this day is over, so crew members can stand down, secure their equipment and lights and, perhaps, prepare to strike a set.

A Director's Shorthand Commands

After you announce the preparatory command, you can use *execution command shorthand* for many commands of execution. A shorthand command orders a number of crew members to execute multiple preparatory commands simultaneously. The preparatory commands "Stand by to fadeup on Camera 1, stand by to mike Sam and stand by to cue Sam" don't necessarily require that you follow with the execution commands "Fadeup on Camera 1, mike Sam, cue Sam." Instead, after announcing these preparatory commands, just say, "Fade, mike, cue." Your preparatory commands tell the technical director to get ready to fadeup on Camera 1; the audio engineer to stand by to mike Sam; and the floor manager to prepare to give the hand signal to cue Sam. So when the time comes to make it all happen at

once, the three words, "Fade, mike, cue" are all that's required. Shorthand is especially helpful if you give a long string of preparatory commands, such as, "Ready to fadeup on Camera 4, ready to dissolve in a 9/4 key, ready to roll Audio Cart 3 under, ready to mike Dan, ready to cue Dan." Without shorthand, the drawn-out (and probably mistimed) execution command would be, "Fadeup on 4, dissolve in the 9/4 key, roll Audio Cart 3 under, mike Dan, cue Dan." The shorthand version would simply be, "Fade, key, cart, mike and cue Dan!" It's possible to shorten these execution commands to a single word, such as "Go!" if everyone on the crew is experienced and understands its meaning. One of your authors recalls a network director whose favorite execution command was not a word at all, but a sharp snap of his fingers. Another used a "cricket" toy to make a snapping sound. Command shorthand is helpful, but it requires extremely clear preparatory commands and an attentive, experienced crew.

Remedial Commands

Inexperienced camera operators often forget to properly compose their shots. A director must know the orders required to "shape up" shots quickly because shot composition is ultimately the responsibility of the director.

A common problem with inexperienced camera operators is "zoom-itis." The director may request a medium shot of talent and get it, but during the show the camera operator may "drift" to a shot with insufficient headroom. When asked for "more headroom," instead of simply tilting the camera up, the operator zooms out, changing the size of the shot. If you're working with inexperienced camera operators, it's wise to remind them before the show begins that once you establish the correct shot size, don't change it. Encourage the habit of holding cameras by their pan handles, not the zoom control. This, along with patient, but firm, direction discourages rookie "zoom-itis."

Rundowns

A spreadsheet known as a *rundown script* is a briefer, columned version of a complete, multiple-camera shooting script, listing the roll-ins, keys and character generator pages in the order they appear in the show. Only the essential information (for example, the title of the videotape roll-in, whether or not it has sound, how long it is, when it begins, when it ends) appears on the rundown, just enough to get the job done. Some directors prefer to mark roll-ins and other rundown information on their master shooting scripts, using the same shorthand information. Some directors also highlight rundown information on the script with felt markers. Directors mark their scripts in idiosyncratic ways. What good directors do <u>not</u> do is mark their scripts excessively. Beginning directors sometimes write every preparatory and execution command they must give on their scripts. Once the show is underway, they read off their list of commands, calling shots with their noses buried in the script, failing to watch the monitors to see if what they order is happening, much less being done well. Reading their commands instead of directing, they don't see problems and errors occurring. These directors would be equally effective if they phoned in their commands from home. Like many symphony conductors, experienced television directors <u>memorize</u> (an unpopular word in some academic settings) standard commands such as those discussed, learning them so well that an occasional glance at the script is all that's needed. They direct by watching the camera, preview and on-line monitors while listening closely to the audio. Because they're directing "heads up," they recognize and correct problems before putting them on line.

Tips for Beginning Directors

Most beginning directors of multiple-camera shows won't begin by calling shots on *Frazier,* the Oscars, the Super Bowl or any such network program. When a television station finally gives a young production assistant the chance to direct in the studio, it may be calling the shots for local newscasts, interview shows or telethon-type programs. Most who work for stations or production companies can get single-camera directing and editing experience by shooting and editing local news, commercials and/or nonbroadcast productions, such as corporate, instructional, public relations or marketing (including those for multimedia and Web sites) videos. Here we'll concentrate on the fundamentals of directing these kinds of programs.

Newscasts

Because they're live and quick paced, newscasts are among the most difficult multiple-camera programs to learn to direct. Directing a newscast becomes much easier after a few weeks, because it is essentially the same program every night: The words and pictures change, but the structure remains the same. Producers plug current news into a well-thought-out, carefully designed format which doesn't vary greatly in style or segment duration day to day. The typical half-hour local newscast allocates a relatively fixed amount of time to local (and sometimes national) "hard" news, commercial breaks, sports, weather and perhaps a feature story.

A television newscast's major dramatic values include language (the words), ideas, character (in the form of "personable" anchors) and spectacle. Ideally ideas would always predominate, but there is a constant battle between journalistic purity and media economics. Even the most dedicated broadcast journalist knows that if audiences wanted only words and ideas, they would choose a newspaper or a radio newscast. A local TV newscast must provide attractive, likable anchors and *visual jiggle* (pictures in motion) to compete with the entertainment programming it precedes and follows. The TV newscast director's goal is to ensure that the carefully planned VTR roll-ins, graphics, full-screen character generator pages and chroma-key effects arrive and depart on time and match the stories read by anchors and reporters.

Shot composition for newscasts is as standard as their formats. *Box shots* featuring a picture or electronically generated material in a rectangular box over the anchor's shoulder liven up single, straight-on medium shots and medium close-ups. Directors cut to two and three shots when anchors talk to each other. Long shots from the floor or a camera mounted overhead showing the news set provide *bumper shots* (visual buffers) to begin and end portions of the program, serving as transitions from the news to commercials. To put a variation on the bumper, or to precede the bumper, newscast directors order a *teaser,* a shot of an anchor (or anchor VO of some dramatic video footage, with CG keys over that), giving viewers tantalizing hints of stories to come.

Local Interview Shows

Interview programs usually involve a station's news or public affairs personnel in a *talking heads* format with newsmakers. Talking heads are visually dull, so the challenge for a director is to find ways to make them interesting. A host such as Oprah Winfrey, surrounded by a live audience, makes it easier to maintain visual interest by swiftly changing which "talking heads" TV viewers see and intercutting them with shots of the audience. Most local programs, except those with studio audiences, challenge you to keep the viewers' attention. Later we'll discuss visuals that can add complexity and interest to such shows.

Camera placement for an interview show is important. As the floor plan in Figure 16-3 illustrates, the

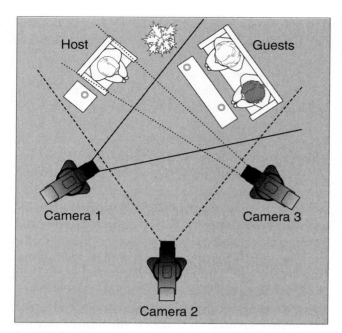

Figure 16-3. *This illustrates an overhead floor plan of an interview set with three cameras: one long-shot camera in the center, and the remaining two crossed on host and guests (Camera 1 on guests, Camera 3 on host, Camera 2 with an LS).*

simplest way to handle such programs in a three-camera studio is to cross two cameras and use the third for wide shots. Camera 3 provides a head-and-shoulders shot of the host (see Figure 16-4). Camera 2 is for the long (cover or establishing) shot (see Figure 16-5). Capable of freely trucking or dollying across a wide area in the center of the studio, Camera 2 provides three or four different extreme-long-shot (ELS) views for bumper shots before and after commercials and for intro and outro long shots over which you can key title and credits. By zooming in from an ELS to an LS or MLS, Camera 2

Figure 16-4. *This is the close-up view from Camera 3.*

Figure 16-5. *Camera 2 provides establishing and "safety" shots.*

becomes a "safety" shot to use when the other cameras are tied up. Unfortunately, beginning directors often "park" for long periods of time on this long shot. Use the LS occasionally, and for only a few seconds to reestablish set orientation, then go back to medium shots and close-ups on the other cameras. Camera 1 can provide either a two shot of the guests, or zoom in to get head-and-shoulder shots of either of the guests (see Figure 16-6).

Sometimes the temptation to use Camera 2 for close-ups is almost irresistible, but wise directors resist it. They know that if everyone begins talking simultaneously, they will have the Camera 2 long shot or medium long shot to capture all speakers until someone regains control of the conversation.

There is no rule saying the guests must be on camera left, and the host on camera right, although this placement is favored on *The Tonight Show, The Late Show with David Letterman* and many other talk-based programs. This suggests that the producers have chosen to place the guests in the most prominent screen position. A case can be made for placing the host on the left, however, and some shows, such as *Larry King Live* do so. Still other programs, such as Bill Maher's cable talk show, place the host in the center, between guests seated to the left and right. In our floor plan, Camera 1 shoots close-ups of the guests. This camera often serves as a "floater," getting medium shots or medium close-ups of the guest who is talking at a given moment. Ideally these shots are composed while another camera is on line. When Camera 3 is on line as the host asks a question, Camera 1 is free to pan swiftly to whichever guest is likely to talk next.

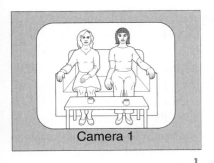

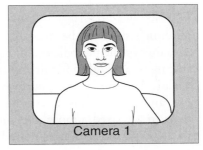

1.   **2.**   **3.**

Figure 16-6. *Camera 1's operator must be very good. This crewperson must be able to follow the conversation, get one shots of both guests and occasionally zoom out to a two shot.*

The most important rules of thumb to remember about interview show directing are as follows:

- Keep the speaking talent on line nearly all the time. If a guest launches a long monolog, create visual variation by cutting to the host for about four *beats* (about the same duration of time as a normal heartbeat) as the host reacts to what's being said, and then cut back to the person talking. You also can key the guest's name/title for visual relief.

- Anticipate who'll speak next by carefully listening to the host's questions and guests' answers. Keep the floater camera free to take the next guest shot when the host's question ends. An ending often is signaled when voice pitch and volume trails off. Anticipating correctly allows you to cut to the person speaking next in sufficient time for him to begin. Nothing is more irritating to viewers than to always be visually behind the rhythm of the conversation. If you cut to the anticipated speaker too soon, use it as a reaction shot. Count four beats (so it appears the shot was planned), then return to the long-winded speaker, and begin your anticipation again.

- Obtain items for use as visual relief during preproduction. This includes videotape, film, brochures, packages, letters, virtually anything that may relieve the visual boredom of talking heads. Request these items 24 hours or more in advance. You need time to consider all these materials for appropriateness, quality and length and decide how to fit them into the show. You may also need the time to dub some odd format of consumer videotape to a format convenient for you to roll in during the program. During preproduction, mount pamphlets, photos, letters or similar items on 14 × 17-inch graphic or key cards and shoot them with a studio camera, preserving the images in an electronic still store or on videotape. This frees an extra studio camera during the production itself. Sometimes the guest or host will want to hold or demonstrate an object during the show. Be sure to rehearse this. Instruct the talent how to manipulate the prop correctly and consistently so your camera operators can get good shots.

Demonstration Shows

Another kind of program beginning directors frequently encounter is the *demonstration program*. This often is a cooking show, a home improvement show or similar "show and tell" video, such as those you see marketing exercise equipment or household or kitchen gadgets. A demonstration program with host and guest resembles an interview or variety show in some ways, but demonstration shows require more preproduction and rehearsal. Less rehearsal is necessary when the host is also the demonstrator, such as in a cooking program, because everyone has experience working together and knows how to handle the usual problems that arise.

A cooking show's kitchen set usually allows for only a 180-degree range of visuals on the horizontal plane. You could assign one long- or medium-long-shot camera and two close-up cameras to follow the action. Often a cooking show features an extra point of view from a small stationary camera mounted on the lighting grid overhead, focused on what's inside the pots and bowls. This frees the talent from having to tip kettles toward the cameras to permit the audience to see inside. Some of these overhead cameras are remote controlled, allowing them to pan and zoom in on certain areas of the table top. If your chef isn't too temperamental about his/her cookware, using transparent containers (glass pots and plastic or glass bowls) also makes shot composition easier, especially if an overhead camera isn't available.

Telethons

Telethons, such as the annual Muscular Dystrophy fundraiser or the periodic public television fund-raising campaigns, are both difficult and easy to direct. They're difficult, because it's uncertain what's going to happen next, and easy, because these shows typically are produced in a relaxed atmosphere. Small gaffes and goof-ups are expected—even exploited. Like the interview show, most directors shoot telethons with a safe long shot and two shots, or two medium shots that follow the talking talent. You often can use character-generated keys or entire CG pages with slogans, the latest fund-raising totals and phone numbers for viewers to call. You can also cut to close-ups of the cheerful volunteers taking phone calls (see Figure 16-7).

You usually encounter the most difficulty in telethons when it's time for volunteer entertainers. They can be awful or wonderful: either hams on an ego trip, painful to watch and hear or old pros slick as a Las Vegas lounge act. You usually have little or no time to rehearse with these acts, so you often must direct "by the seat of your pants." If you're limited to three cameras, use the same camera positions as the interview show, always keeping a wide safety shot you can cut to, and follow the action as best you can with the other cameras.

Commercials

Many local station/cable TV commercials are characterized by their informality, ineffective copywriting, short production schedules and microscopic production budgets. Most small-market businesses, where you're likely to

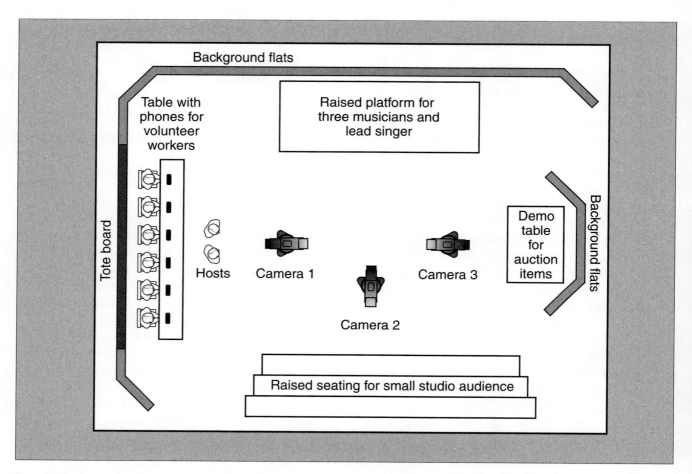

Figure 16-7. *This is a floor plan for a small public station fundraising show. The hosts work in front of a table staffed with volunteers who answer phone callers bidding on items. A tote board (a scoreboard of sorts that shows the amount of money raised) behind the volunteers shows a running total of money collected. A raised platform provides a place for entertainers to perform. A demo table and background flats at the other end of the studio provide an area for showing items being auctioned. A few rows of seats allow a small audience to participate, adding "life" to the program. Camera 2 can swing and truck left to support Camera 1 when the hosts are speaking; both Camera 1 and 3 can truck to provide a variety of shots when entertainers are performing on the raised platform. At the director's command, any of the cameras can truck and pan to take reaction shots of the audience.*

find your first production jobs, can't afford ad agencies, so stations sell spots directly to the local merchant. Larger market stations employ professional copywriters, but smaller stations often assign the production staff to write the copy. Sometimes ad sales personnel write copy, or provide rough fact sheets from which the producer or director creates the copy. Sometimes the clients write their own copy and design their own campaigns, often with disastrous, embarrassing results. One of your authors recalls a male client in his late 50s who enjoyed dressing up in women's clothes to portray a mythical "Aunt Sadie" who hawked furniture. Quirky local car dealers want you to produce commercials in which they smash windshields or offer free elephant rides for the kids. But in this some-times circus-like atmosphere, it's important for you as the director to remember that the client—the person ulti-mately paying your salary—is always right, and your job depends on getting the spots in the can without laughing (or weeping) too noticeably. Directors who now produce spots for Proctor and Gamble, Coca-Cola and General Motors started like this, too. If you're wise, you'll try to be as creative as possible along the way, building a demo reel of the good shots, good writing and well-directed spots. You may never direct a nationally aired McDonald's spot, but a good reel can lead you to better local clients and free you from Aunt Sadie's clutches. Here are more tips that can help:

- Regardless of the amount or quality of informa-tion provided (from professional scripts and sto-ryboards to ad fact sheets to "Oh, don't worry! 'Old Stan' will tell you what he wants when you get there"), try to visualize how the commercial will look when it's finished.

- Choose a good camera operator, or shoot it your-self: Most small-market clients tolerate a lot of waiting while you're there shooting, but reshoots are irritating and waste time and money. And don't forget that audio quality is vitally important.

- Shoot extra coverage, just in case. Unless you're shooting from a tight storyboard (and sometimes even if you are), take extra footage, concentrating on the product or service. As we've noted before, videotape, relative to other supplies, and certainly compared to reshoots, is cheap.

- Take extra care shooting the client's store or the merchant's sign. Make these look especially good. Get distracting cars, trucks, telephone poles and wires out of the shot. Hollywood commercial pro-ducers put enormous effort into the *product shot,* that all-important shot that helps audiences find

the product on retailers' shelves. Put the same effort into your client's product shot, especially the placement, decoration and lighting of a product.

- Listen to the client. No matter how wonderful your new, revolutionary ideas are, if the client wants the same old thing he's always done, do it. That's what you're paid for. Perhaps the next day's client will be more flexible, and you'll have the chance to shoot something terrific that will lead off your personal demo reel. If the client's half-convinced, and if it doesn't cost the client or your station any extra money, shoot it both ways, and allow the client to choose later. This flatters the client, and you're satisfied, too, because regardless of what finally airs in the commercial, you can always re-edit the footage your way for your per-sonal demo reel. Usually, it doesn't cost extra to shoot more footage, because a station's commer-cial production fees are often thrown in for free or for a nominal fee in exchange for the purchase of a large number of airings of the spot, or for an annual contract. Other commercial productions are just billed by the shoot, not the hour.

- Oddly enough, when you finally get to shoot high-budget commercials for ad agencies, you may have much less creative freedom than when you were doing those local spots for Aunt Sadie. National ad agencies usually provide carefully written, detailed storyboards, so all they may want you to do is create the mise-en-scene they've drawn and then "shoot the boards." Even if you have an obviously better idea, don't make ad agency folk look bad the day of the shoot by criti-cizing their boards or proposing radical changes in front of clients. If there are changes you'd like to suggest, make them during preproduction meetings away from clients. Then, if the agency likes your ideas, it can propose them to their client as if they were their ideas. The end result: The client is happy, the agency is happy with you, and you're happy because you get to shoot the spot your way. You also score big points with the agency and you'll get more (and perhaps better) assignments in the future.

"Videos"

Instructional tapes and public relations and marketing videos comprise much of what is referred to as "corporate" or "industrial" video production. You may not always shoot for a corporation, but you'll be working for a client with some sort of business message to communicate.

The video may recruit students for a trade school, explain to factory workers how to assemble a new product, demonstrate a product or service to passers-by in a department store or mall or be used as a downloadable video clip on a firm's web site.

Usually, these videos have three things in common: They're well planned during preproduction, they're heavily scripted and/or storyboarded, and they're designed either to inform or persuade, or both.

They're shot much like commercials, except production schedules and program lengths are usually longer, the atmosphere is more relaxed and creative suggestions during shooting often are more acceptable. However, even in this atmosphere there are pitfalls. You frequently encounter a client's representative who doesn't know much about visual communication but whose boss has nonetheless put him/her in creative charge of the program. This person may insist on doing things you think are awful, such as adding tedious lines of face-saving, official-sounding jargon to the script. Or, as a means of job protection and flattery, he'll insist on including the faces and names of all his supervisors. To save both your professional reputation and the contract, your job is to find tactful ways to convince the client that you're the visual communication expert and that the things he/she wishes to include are counterproductive. Convincing, inoffensive persuasive lines that sometimes work include, "This is an interesting sentence, but let's see if we can find a way of saying the same thing in a simpler manner for TV," or, "People who view your video still expect to see and hear the kind of TV they watch at home. We should try to work within this 'comfort zone' of understanding if we really want to communicate your message," or, "Let's try shooting this both ways. Later, you can see them both and choose which works better."

Timing Productions

Timing is a major concern in television directing. Feature film productions vary considerably above and below the two-hour mark, but television directors must time programs to the second. Television programs most often air in segments of 30 minutes or longer. The sitcom developed into a half-hour format, and the drama, which takes more time to develop characters and action, is usually 60 minutes long. When you write for commercial television, you design segments to ebb and flow around your commercial breaks. As a director of single-camera productions, you must shoot and edit segments with these breaks in mind. The commercials themselves are timed very closely. A 30-second spot must be exactly 29.5 seconds, allowing a half second

for fadeout/transition to the next commercial or program element. Each shot in the commercial is timed precisely. Commercial storyboards often include the estimated *running time* of each shot, so that at the completion of a shot you know how far into the commercial you should be. Directors must concern themselves not only with the aesthetic and technical quality of the shot but also with the amount of time it takes.

No program is more difficult to time properly than a newscast. News happens "out there" and doesn't concern itself with time. It's the arduous task of the news producer to make news events fit the demands of the clock. Much that airs during newscasts occurs live. Experience helps newscasters and news producers estimate story length, but they can still only estimate. During the newscast, directors must keep track of the difference between these segment time estimates and the actual time. The news producer preparing a nightly newscast begins this process knowing the newscast's *running time,* which is the total time, including commercial breaks, the newscast must be. Usually this is either 30 or 60 minutes. Subtracting the program's intro and outro plus the commercial breaks, what remains is called the *news hole,* the portion of the newscast, no more and no less, the news department is assigned to fill. Producers format the news hole into various segments, into which the news of the day is cut to fit. Each page of a newscast script usually features both the *segment time* and the amount of the show's total running time that should have elapsed by the end of the segment. In a story about a controversy at city hall, for example, the script page shows the length of the anchor's lead in, the length of the edited ENG package, the length of the anchor's closing tag and the estimated running time of the show at the story's conclusion. When this page of newscast script is over, the director glances at the clock and compares. Quickly the director (or, in larger-market newscasts, an assistant director) notes the difference between estimated and actual running time, and reports to the producer and/or the anchor during the next break. Another piece of copy may be added at the end, or the anchors may be instructed to adlib a designated amount of seconds if the show is running short. If the show is running long, the news producer or the anchor must cut something.

For less structured programs, a system called *back-timing* often suffices. For example, assume the host of a half-hour interview program receives a cue to introduce a commercial break. During that break, the director uses the private line, interrupted feedback or a relay from the floor manager to tell the host the current back-timing status, that is, the amount of time left in the show. The easiest way for a director to back-time is to use a digital timer that counts backward. The alternative requires some quick calculation and a stopwatch. To calculate the time remaining requires subtracting the elapsed time from the total running time of the show. Sounds simple, but performing calculations under the pressure of a production is not as easy as it seems. It's easier if you write the running time with the last minute always expressed in seconds (29:60 instead of 30:00), so that you don't have to remind yourself to subtract from 60 and not from 100. Calculators that add and subtract time are a great aid in figuring changes in your show's running time. Regardless of how you keep time, as the program progresses toward its conclusion, you give the host either IFB cues, or instruct the floor manager to give hand or card signals.

For a half-hour show, the cues may come at 15 minutes, 10 minutes, 5 minutes, 2 minutes, 1 minute, 30 seconds, 15 seconds and then a countdown from 10 seconds to zero. Timing becomes more critical as the show approaches its conclusion, but some talent and directors like frequent time cues throughout the show.

There are many other forms of video programming you may be called on to direct. We can't anticipate them all, but we've described some of the more common ones. In the next chapter, we'll describe the role of the producer in television, explain how this function both differs from and complements the director's and describe how that person goes about the job of "getting things done."

tech manual 16-1   *Directing a Commercial Project*

The following 20-second commercial is for a soft drink. It is designed to be a simple, yet fast-paced, ad that involves the efforts of 15 people—a typical size for a television production course. Duties can be collapsed for fewer people (for example, the director can also serve as the technical director) or expanded for additional personnel (there can be a person devoted entirely to props and set cleanup). The commercial can be done as a live-on-tape production with three cameras, two cameras or shot film style. There are no graphics, special effects or music in the original design, although these elements can also be added if time and circumstances permit. The graphics, effects and music can also be done in post-production.

A typical crew would be producer, director, technical director, audio technician, video tape operator, graphics person (to change the slate and/or keep time), three camera operators, three on-camera talent, one hand model, a floor manager and a props person.

The product is a low-cost soda produced in the St. Louis area. You can substitute any soda from your area, but it is wise to avoid high-profile brands like Pepsi or Coke. With their multimillion dollar ad budgets, they can only make you look worse by comparison. Producing this commercial effectively is an excellent way to beef up your portfolio of student-produced pieces.

Here is a bare-bones script (as written for three cameras):

VIDEO	AUDIO
FADE UP TO CAM 1 MCU	TALENT 1: "I have good taste."
CAM 2 MCU	TALENT 2: "I have good taste."
CAM 3 MCU	TALENT 3: "I have good taste."
CAM 1 MCU TABLETOP PLACE SETTING HAND PICKS UP SODA & POURS INTO GLASS	VO: "Good tasting soda from Vess puts you in an elite group: people who enjoy the delicious flavor of Vess cola, Vess root beer and Vess orange soda.
CAM 2 SODA DISPLAY MS	No matter what your position in life is, you can still have good taste with Vess. If you want the best, you want Vess.
FADE OUT	(FADE AUDIO)

Below, we show this live onto tape, multiple camera script with a third column added, showing the director's headset commands for various crew members. You wouldn't actually write a script like this, because director's commands must be understood, not written down. But commands are shown here for your information. The capital letters denote the director's commands and the proper responses are listed in parentheses. Of course, if a particular position is not ready, that person should answer something like, "No, I'm not ready. Let me get my first shot set up" (or the proper correction to whatever problem is holding up the production. Don't just say, "No," without an explanation).

COMMANDS	VIDEO	
AUDIO READY ON THE FLOOR?		
(Floor Mgr: "Ready.")		
READY AUDIO?		
(Audio: "Ready.")		
READY VIDEO?		
(TD: "Ready.")		
READY TO ROLL & RECORD?		
(Tape Op: "Ready.")		
[Wait 10 seconds for second response.]		
(Tape Op: "Recording and locked.")		
BARS AND TONE IN (for 30 seconds)		
BARS AND TONE OUT		
SLATE IN 10 SECONDS		
[Name of production, director, talent, date]		
SLATE OUT		
STANDBY TO OPEN MIC		
STANDBY TO CUE ANNOUNCER		
READY TO FADEUP ON CAM 1		
OPEN THE MIC, CUE 'EM, FADEUP ON 1		
READY CAM 2	CAM 1 MCU	TAL 1: "I have good taste."
TAKE CAM 2	CAM 2 MCU	TAL 2: "I have good taste."
READY CAM 3		
TAKE CAM 3	CAM 3 MCU	TAL 3: "I have good taste."
READY CAM 1		
TAKE CAM 1	CAM 1 MS	VO: "Good tasting soda from
CUE HAND TALENT	PLACE SETTING	Vess puts you in an elite group—people who enjoy the delicious flavor of Vess cola, Vess root beer, and Vess orange soda.
READY CAM 2		
TAKE CAM 2	CAM 2 MS SODA DISPLAY	No matter what your position in life is, you can still have good taste with Vess. If you want the best, you want Vess.
READY TO FADE VIDEO AND AUDIO		
FADE TO BLACK, STOP TAPE	FADEOUT	(FADE AUDIO)

It's obvious at a glance that there is a flurry of activity behind the scenes. Coordinating all these elements is a daunting task. The secret to completing this project successfully is to rehearse early and often. The sooner you can get to the rehearsal stage, the sooner you can see exactly where your problems lie. Every group is different, so there is no reliable way to predict all difficulties in advance. Get warm bodies in the studio and start rehearsing. If you cannot get all the personnel together at one time, improvise. Let one person read all the talent parts, or even prerecord the audio. Use chairs or brooms or wig heads to frame the talent shots. Let one person run both audio and tape. But get the timing down. It is virtually impossible to produce this simple ad in a two hour lab, start to finish. There must be ample rehearsal time. Believe it or not, 10 hours rehearsal is not uncommon for beginners to get it perfect. A good editing exercise would be to add graphics and music in postproduction.

The following questions will help you prepare and flesh out ideas before you begin rehearsing or producing the soda commercial.

1. What "types" are the three on-camera talents?

2. What differentiates their deliveries? Their "looks?"

3. Who does the VO? Do we do it live with one of the talents, or do we prerecord it?

4. What types of backgrounds do we need for the talents?

5. What types of settings do we need for the VO shots?

6. How should the hand talent look?

7. Where do we put the place settings in relation to the talent? (Set design)

8. How do we light the various positions? (Lighting diagram)

9. Where are the cameras located? (Camera blocking plan)

10. What props will we need? Who will supply them?

The following form can be used to evaluate the soda commercial, or any group project. Every crew member should fill out the form and write an essay-style analysis of the production.

EVALUATION SHEET—VIDEO PROJECT

Project Title _____   Producer _____   Director _____

In the spaces provided enter the score you think is applicable from 1 to 10 (1 being completely unacceptable, 10 being exceptional). Use the back of the page or additional sheets for explanations and crew evaluations.

Preproduction

_____ Basic concept & purpose	_____ Script	_____ Assignment of duties
_____ Rehearsal(s)	_____ Props	_____ Setup descriptions
_____ Lighting plan	_____ Staging	_____ Set(s)
_____ Teleprompter loading	_____ Script coordination	_____ Graphics

Production

_____ Handling of studio time	_____ Attendance	_____ Promptness
_____ Air worthiness (quality)	_____ Cooperation	_____ Communication
_____ Shot quality	_____ Composition	_____ Shot variety
_____ Familiarity with script	_____ Budgeting (was project completed?)	_____ Graphics timing
_____ Teleprompter operation	_____ Graphics quality	_____ Timing cues
_____ Tape operation	_____ Floor managing	

Direction

_____ Crew handling	_____ Crew commands ("readies" and "takes")	
_____ Pacing and rhythm	_____ Shot timing	_____ Technical directing
_____ Monitor awareness	_____ Rapport	_____ Overall control
_____ Audio set up	_____ Vocal segments	_____ Music segments
_____ Mic timing (on/off cues)	_____ Audio mixing	_____ Lighting quality
_____ Special effects		

(Continued)

EVALUATION SHEET—VIDEO PROJECT *(Continued)*

Postproduction Checklist

____ Studio cleanup   ____ Video console strike   ____ Audio console strike

____ Light board strike   ____ Cams put away   ____ Props removed

____ Video tapes removed   ____ Lights turned off   ____ Audio materials removed

____ Lighting materials cleaned up   ____ Scripts and papers cleaned up

Editing

____ Video levels   ____ Audio levels   ____ Audio mix

____ No jump cuts   ____ Graphics   ____ Flow

____ Transitions   ____ Special effects   ____ Backgrounds

____ Project approval obtained   ____ Quality control   ____ Duplication

Project Report

Write an essay, using complete sentences, that addresses the following questions:

For a commercial: Was it appealing? Will it sell the product? What were the strong points? How good were the production values?

For a newscast: Was it newsworthy, informative, authoritative, well-paced, well-visualized, coordinated? Were there any discrepancies?

For a musical production: Was the approach appropriate to the tone of the music? Were there special effects? Were the takes well timed? Were the shots varied and synchronized? Was there a good flow?

For all productions: Evaluate each crew member's contribution to preproduction, production and postproduction. Use the crew descriptions outlined earlier in the chapter and answer the appropriate questions. Was the copy turned in on time with sufficient copies for all the concerned parties? Did the crew member do his/her assigned tasks efficiently and promptly? What was his/her demeanor during the production? Was he/she part of the problem or part of the solution?

Important Vocabulary Terms

Audio fade: As the name implies, an audio fade is a slow reduction in volume to silence.

Back-timing: Calculating the time remaining in a program.

Beat: A theatrical unit of time, roughly equivalent to a normal heartbeat.

Bed level: An audio level "underneath" (lower than) another audio source (for example, the level of music underneath a narrator's voice).

Box shot: The typical shot of a news anchor on the left side of the frame and a horizontal box on the right side, over the anchor's left shoulder.

Bumper shot: A shot, often a long shot, used as a buffer between program segments and commercial breaks.

Cross-fade: The audio equivalent of a dissolve, simultaneously fading one audio source up and another down.

Demonstration program: A cooking, home improvement or similar show in which the host and/or guests show the audience how to do something.

Director's notes: A list of minor corrections and adjustments given to cast and crew prior to a final show taping.

Dissolve: This command results in one picture slowly fading out, while another picture simultaneously fades up to take its place.

Execution command shorthand: A method of eliminating words in a director's execution commands that allows him/her to communicate his/her meaning in a more terse fashion.

Fadeup: An execution command calling for a gradual transition from black to a picture.

Fadeout: An execution command calling for a gradual transition from a picture to black.

Intro: The beginning audio and video segment of a program.

Line reading: An unsound directing practice in which a director doesn't direct actors, but instead acts the part out and instructs the actors to imitate him/her.

Lose key: A directorial command used to remove a key from the screen, leaving the background picture as it was prior to keying. It is the opposite of the command to take, dissolve or wipe in a key.

Mike and cue talent: This command calls for the audio director to open the talent's mike and for the floor director to simultaneously give the talent the cue to begin speaking.

News hole: The amount of time in a newscast available to a TV news producer to fill, after subtracting the intro, outro and commercial breaks.

Outro: The ending audio and video segment of a program. The opposite of "intro," above.

Product shot: Usually the most important shot in a commercial, the product shot attractively displays the product or service advertised to increase audience recognition.

Ready (or Stand by): A term used as part of a preparatory command to differentiate it from an execution command.

Roll: A directorial command to engage the "start" button of any audio or video device that must be set in motion in order to use it on the air.

Roll silent: The same command as a roll, except that the film or video source rolled goes on line without sound.

Rundown script: An abbreviated multiple-camera TV script listing the roll-ins, keys and CG pages in the order in which they appear in the script.

Running time: The total amount of time a program is allotted; for example, a sitcom's running time is usually 30 minutes.

Segment time: The time an individual program element takes, from start to finish.

Sound under: A general audio cue to lower audio volume to a bed level.

Sound up: A general audio cue to bring a sound device up to its predesignated audio level.

Split-screen: Split-screens allow more than one picture to share the screen with another picture. The wipe pattern chosen for this split creates the shape of the boundary that separates these two pictures.

Stand by: See "Ready."

Take: This execution command causes the instantaneous replacement of one video source with another.

Talking heads: An interview format in which most of the visual elements are medium shots and medium close-ups of persons sitting and talking with each other.

Teaser: A shot of an anchor or other video giving audiences hints of what stories are to come in a newscast so that they will stay tuned.

Thank you: The director's cue to the cast and crew that the program or program segment is finished.

Visual jiggle: Pictures in motion used to make an otherwise static show more visually interesting.

Wipe: This is a split-screen pattern in motion that either fully or partially replaces one picture with another.

Wrap it: This directorial command means that work in the studio or on location is finished for the day, so each crewmember can now secure their equipment. Sometimes directors may say, "That's a wrap."

chapter **17**

Producing

It's often said that television is a producer's medium. This is due to several factors, especially the producer's creative control of the final product. On the other hand, author Joseph Gelmis once described some Hollywood film directors as "superstars" because creative responsibility for the final motion picture product largely rests with directors.

Often the television director's role is that of an employee hired by the real creative force, the producer. It doesn't always happen this way, but the director may be hired long after the writing, casting of principals and other preproduction tasks are well underway. This is especially true during ongoing production of a television series. Until the point when the director is hired, the producer is in charge. Consider local and network newscasts, or such shows as CBS' *Sixty Minutes*. The producers, writers and anchors determine the content, dictate most of the visual style, edit the individual segments and prepare the shooting script. In effect, the director's job is to tie preproduced segments together with anchor continuity and canned intros/outros, bumpers and closing credits.

There's also the matter of ownership. Networks and other distributors usually pay television producers for just the temporary license rights to their productions. When a major broadcast network acquires the broadcast rights for a typical program series, they usually pay the program's producer for at least two airings of each episode. Since the late 1990s, additional airings later on may also be part of such a deal. After these airings, all rights revert to the producer, who can "rent" the series in syndication to individual stations, cable networks, overseas broad- or cablecasters, videocassette and DVD distributors and Internet/iPod and other digital distribution entities. Many early TV series, such as *I Love Lucy,* are still earning money in syndication.

So both creatively and financially, television is essentially a producer's medium.

However, it's incorrect to say that <u>all</u> television producers operate as kings and queens of their domains. Depending on the organization and the situation, the producer's control and financial participation varies greatly. The series producer we've just described is typically associated with big-budget Hollywood productions. Jerry Bruckheimer, Stephen Cannell, Aaron Spelling and Don Bellisario typify this kind of producer.

Below these *executive,* or *supervising producers,* there are *line producers.* To meet the demands of production deadlines, two or more episodes of a series often are underway simultaneously, with a line producer responsible for one or more episodes. It's rare when a line producer earns financial participation in a series. A line producer typically is a production company, station or network employee—albeit an employee with far-ranging creative responsibilities. Regardless of the actual title, the producers of news, documentary and public affairs programs at local stations and the major networks neither share in the station's or network's profits nor enjoy rights of ownership in these productions.

Of course, not all producers work for stations, networks or the Hollywood studios. Many produce video products for industrial, public relations and corporate communications firms. One producer may work at an elaborate facility while another may be a one-man band, operating with a portable video camera and editing on his/her home PC. Some production companies hire outside producers to complete projects on an as-needed basis. In addition to the myriad roles fulfilled by video producers (artist, businessperson, technical expert and psychologist), corporations frequently add two more responsibilities—diplomat and educator. Unlike television station producers, corporate producers frequently deal with people who know everything about making widgets but absolutely nothing about making videos. It is not uncommon for corporate executives to misuse technical terms, thus adding to the difficulties of producing complex productions. The producer must tactfully keep the conversation going until the real meaning of the involved terms becomes clear, and then discreetly slip the proper expression into a sentence. A few such statements may then teach the client the proper wording without being preachy or condescending. This is all in a day's work for the corporate video producer. Such persons may be *independent producers* or producer employees of a larger organization, such as an advertising agency.

Independent producers are well named. These people frequently identify or write a project, secure financial backing for it and then get the most talented people to the proper location at the correct time with the right equipment and the best supporting services (for example, wardrobes, props, catering, makeup, generator trucks, etc). After the shooting is complete, producers usually supervise the final edit, arrange for mass duplications and even market the product. These productions vary from documentaries such as Ken Burns' *The Civil War,* initially an independent production funded by many sources for airing on public television, to narrowly target-marketed videocassettes such as *Gardening Made Easy.* There are producers who specialize in music videos. We will also discuss some of those techniques later in this chapter.

Producers live on the telephone and computer. They have an array of people they can call to perform various tasks, and thus have some combination of a good Rolodex, a convenient personal planner/calendar, a well-loaded Palm Pilot or a lengthy list of phone numbers on their hard drives. Producers know who is dependable, who can work on short notice, who can endure tough conditions without complaining and who can do a quick turnaround—all at reasonable prices.

Producers working for public relations (PR) and advertising agencies or video production departments within companies and corporations are more limited creatively by the policies and aims of their clients and publics. But whether they're preparing *video news releases* (VNRs) for a client at a PR agency, bidding on a contract to shoot a commercial for an advertising agency or sitting down with company engineers to gather notes for a manufacturing safety video, these producers' primary objective is the same: Please the client.

In college classroom productions and, indeed, in many small-budget professional videos, the producer may do it all: writing, shooting, directing, editing and marketing the production. Regardless of where or at what level you find such an individual, anyone who does more than one job is called a *hyphenate*—so named because the person's many job titles are separated by hyphens (such as director-producer-actor, or writer-producer-director).

So, ultimately, can we fashion a definition for the term "producer" that works in all instances to differentiate him/her from a director? Probably not. But consider the following box, which at least helps differentiate the personality traits and job skills of a producer from that of a director.

Producer vs Director

Producer:

- Very good at long-range planning
- Organized and methodical
- Capable of visualizing the whole production process
- Often (but not always) less technically oriented than directors
- Has more knowledge of business/ legal matters than directors
- May or may not have good interpersonal skills

Director:

- Highly familiar with the technical aspects of production
- Capable of reacting quickly with tactical solutions to production problems
- Often prefers to focus intensely on a specific and narrowly defined issue, resolve it and then move on to another narrowly defined issue, rather than deal more with many issues at the same time
- Must have excellent interpersonal skills to deal with a variety of individuals in stressful situations

In some ways, a television producer is like a college football coach: The coach chooses the players, assigns them playing positions, decides the team's practice schedule and supervises the creation of the offensive and defensive game plans. But during the game, the coach stands on the sidelines. While the coach ultimately calls some plays and substitutes players as needed, he permits the quarterback (somewhat analogous to the director) to run the plays, boost morale among the players, adjust to last-second problems on the field and make instinctive, creative adjustments in the head coach's game plan.

Just as a particular coach may be better at leading the defense than the offense, or vice-versa, producers often have individual strengths and weaknesses. If we may be pardoned for excessive simplification, we can divide the producer's role into three broad functions:

1. the creative function,
2. the managerial function and
3. the financial/legal/sales function.

Sometimes you find extremely creative producers who can conceptualize program ideas and often write or coauthor the scripts for their productions. Other producers may lack creative brilliance but are financial and marketing wizards. Still other producers excel neither in artistic creativity nor financial acumen, yet have the managerial talent to identify and lead persons who do. However, we don't want to put too fine a point on these distinctions. Anyone lacking at least some ability in all three categories is unlikely to be a highly successful producer.

Many successful producers recognize their individual deficiencies and hire *assistant* or *associate producers* who complement, rather than duplicate, their intellectual and personal strengths. A creative writer-producer seeks assistant or associate producers strong in management, finance and sales. Conversely, the assistant producer to a financially adept producer is often a creative individual who acts as an effective liaison (or a buffer) between the producer and the director.

Although lacking the term "producer" in their job titles, there are other key people in larger production organizations who work closely with producers. One such key person is the *unit production manager* (UPM). The UPM may work for either the production facility or for individual producer(s). In either case, the UPM has one primary duty: monitoring the production budget. The UPM is the official "bean counter" for the production. The UPM makes certain that bills are paid, payrolls met, and an ongoing record of production expenditures accurately maintained. A strong background in accounting is usually required. The UPM keeps both the director(s) and the producer(s) informed regarding the budget.

A studio or production facility UPM ensures that a producer renting the facility receives the contracted services but doesn't get anything for which the producer hasn't paid. Otherwise the production facility eventually would go broke. A UPM working for an individual producer performs a slightly different function, keeping the producer from inadvertently exceeding the original production budget. If the budget goes overboard, so does the company's profit.

Producer Responsibilities

We turn now from an examination of the various types of producers, their general characteristics and the many producer subspecies to their duties. This is difficult, because many interdependent factors determine the responsibilities of a producer. These include, but are not limited to

1. the goal(s) of the production,
2. the nature of the target audience(s),
3. the size of the production budget,
4. the source(s) of financing and the investors' expectations,
5. time constraints,
6. talent availability and cooperation,
7. equipment requirements and
8. the avenue(s) available for distribution.

Each factor is almost infinitely variable, and changes in one usually impact others. Space prohibits our dealing with every possible situation and permutation, so we'll examine some of the most important duties of the producer during each of our three phases: preproduction, production and postproduction.

Preproduction

The producer has the heaviest workload during preproduction. If preproduction planning is well done and unusual misfortunes don't occur, most of what a producer does during the production and postproduction phases is simply to execute the plans made during preproduction. Despite the fact that the preproduction phase differs a bit with each production situation, some steps are almost universal.

Conceptualization

If you're assuming control of an ongoing series, then your primary task is to supervise the concept and scriptwriting for the episode(s) you produce. This means taking a careful look at episodes preceding yours to ensure series continuity. A writer for an ongoing entertainment series usually receives a *series concordance,* a document that outlines the major characters, their known histories, attributes and attitudes. It also contains a description of the plots of every episode of the series to date. Nonentertainment series often lack such helpful documentation, so the producer must take even greater care to review previous episodes in the series to ensure content and aesthetic continuity.

If you're not continuing an existing series, you must conceive the idea for the show or buy an idea from someone else. This is true whether the program is a game show, a news documentary, a commercial or a training video. Buying an idea is an honorable practice, and many entertainment programs and films are adapted from other media, such as popular novels, movies, plays, comic books and even video games.

Determining Viability

Regardless of the idea's source, part of the preproduction process involves evaluating the viability of the idea. Before moving ahead, the producer must determine both the potential appeal of the idea to the audience and the likelihood of being able to execute the idea given available resources. This evaluation process can be almost entirely intuitive or exactly scientific, or something in between. Students in television production courses sometimes propose program ideas because they personally like the topic but give little thought to audience interests or the problems of production. They can do this because classroom production projects don't always have external audiences and, if the show turns out to be impossible to produce, all that's lost is a project grade. In the "real world," the stakes are much higher, so the evaluation prior to production is much more rigorous before the "green light" is given to pay for the production. Securing funding for production usually involves convincing someone other than yourself that the idea is viable. Researching the viability of a program idea can be as simple as consulting Nielsen rating books and faithfully reading major television and entertainment trade magazines, such as *Broadcasting & Cable* and *Daily Variety.* This level of research helps you determine if similar programs are popular currently and whether there's a likely audience and/or market for the program. Often you'll need more formalized research, including hiring research organizations to do original surveys, discussing the idea with focus groups or testing pilot programs. It's important to remember that no idea is viable if it fails to meet existing legal standards for decency. No American medium can legally produce and

distribute what the U.S. Supreme Court defines as obscene (Miller v. California, 1973). However, some media, such as books, magazines and videocassettes containing content defined by law as pornographic still can be produced and distributed, although laws in every state in the union carefully control who may purchase it and under what conditions.

Programs distributed over stations licensed by the Federal Communications Commission (FCC) must meet a higher standard. What roughly corresponds to the "R" movie rating standards for sex and language is what the FCC currently defines as "indecent" and is considered inappropriate for broadcast without careful trimming. You probably know that R-rated movies are "edited for television" when broadcast over the air. Pornographic or indecent content is a subject of constant debate, and the FCC rules and regulations regarding its production and distribution change frequently.

In 1997, the broadcast and cable industries adopted (under great political pressure) "voluntary" program ratings for sex, violence and strong language. The same year, the FCC established content standards for children's programs. The content of commercials also is subject to legal restrictions. The Federal Trade Commission will move against producers of "deceptive" ads, and Congress banned commercials for tobacco products from broadcast stations and cable. Producers must be constantly alert for such evolving standards and requirements. If you have doubts about the legality of the content of your program, it's wise to consult an attorney specializing in entertainment and mass media law.

There also are a variety of professional codes of ethics, dealing mostly with news and commercial content. Violation of these codes may not get the producer into trouble with the government, but failure to meet industry standards of ethical practice may limit marketing/distribution options and negatively affect the professional careers of those involved.

Developing a Marketing Plan

Once the idea is deemed viable, the producer explores how to best distribute and market the program. This information is vital, because it greatly assists in projecting profit potential and in obtaining financing for the project. Oftentimes market analysis reveals that there's no immediate broadcast or cable distribution deal available for a particular program idea. However, the idea may still have a market: It may become a specialty program or series, distributed via DVD, iPod, Internet or other digital media that makes money for producers and investors through direct sales to specific consumers.

Scripting the Show

Assuming you've successfully pitched your program idea and marketing plan to the financial "powers that be" (a bank, film/TV financing consortium, network, station news director, advertising agency or independent client/foundation), the next step is writing or adapting the story idea(s) and preparing a script. Depending on the scope and size of your production, this may involve hiring a writer, writing it yourself or collaborating with someone. Refer to Chapter 13, "Scriptwriting," to review treatment and script preparation guidelines.

Obtaining Rights

While preparing the script(s), the producer also must secure legal access to music, video, film, photos, and performance rights and releases for noncontract talent ("civilians" you may shoot during your production), as necessary (see Figure 17-1).

Although a thorough discussion of copyright and related laws is beyond the scope of this chapter, it's important that you work within the laws and regulations that govern and limit productions for broadcast, cable and other methods of video distribution. Here, we've offered some clarification on this complex subject. The basic rule is that any time you use someone else's words, lyrics, music, images or WGA-registered story ideas (again refer to Chapter 13), you must obtain the owner's permission. This often involves paying fees called *royalties*. You learned about two of the three major licensing organizations in Chapter 13. ASCAP (the American Society of Composers, Authors and Publishers), BMI (Broadcast Music Inc.) and a third, international, group, the *Society of European Stage Authors and Composers* (SESAC), collect royalties for most of the copyrighted music you may need. Many production facilities purchase music and sound effects "libraries," which also convey certain production rights. Sometimes these rights include unlimited use of the "cuts" in the music library, but others charge an additional fee. Producers also can purchase the rights to use "stock" footage and photos. If you wish to use an author's words, books or scripts, contact the writer's agent and cut a deal.

Copyright

We suggest you study media law to learn how deal with the intricacies of copyright issues, but we can clear up some fallacies and establish a few facts.

One myth that is often bandied about is that a producer can use 90 seconds of anything for free. This is very wrong. The fallacy arises from the fact that TV news stations can use short snippets of events—even music concerts—as a legitimate part of that day's coverage. No one else has this right.

A good basic rule of thumb is that if <u>anyone</u> involved in the project is making money, then money must be paid to the originator of the borrowed content—be it video, audio, script, artwork or anything else.

Another fallacy concerns the use of stock footage. Many beginners write the term "use stock footage" into their scripts as if this is the easiest thing in the world to do. One would think there is an infinite supply of perfect material just waiting to be delivered to anyone who wants it. This is not the case. There are several problems with using stock footage. (1) No one hands it out for free. Even governmental agencies that distribute certain footage for "free" (like NASA, for example) usually require a duplication fee and shipping costs to be borne by the person making the request. (2) Other, more specific video—such as decades-old historical footage—can be quite expensive. Many stock footage companies will send you sample footage of video you've requested. This sample footage will have a "time-code burn" superimposed over the screen. It lists the time available of such video. The person requesting the footage then calls or writes the facility requesting x amount of material—say, 30 seconds worth. This material may cost hundreds of dollars per second, making it cost prohibitive for many low-budget productions. (3) Other, cheaper stock footage is available, but it is frequently extremely generic in nature—backgrounds, scenic footage, bland shots of cityscapes and the like. (4) Another difficulty in using stock footage is that it was shot without your specific needs in mind. Therefore, it's seldom the exact look you want. It may be black and white and your project is color. It may emphasize the wrong aspects of the event you're producing. It may be all long shots when you need close-ups. You end up with a whole lot of expensive nothing.

Similar problems arise with the use of recorded music. Students usually have highly developed—and highly expensive—taste in contemporary music. They are prone to use specific artists and particular songs in their productions even though such practices are costly and unnecessary. Just buying the latest Britney Spears CD or downloading it does not give you the right to use that music in any production. Using it <u>does</u> open you up for an expensive lawsuit. Securing the rights to such songs is often frustrating, expensive, confusing and, worst of all to a producer, time consuming. If you must use a particular song, you would be well served to look in an industry publication or online to find a legal firm that specializes in the acquisition of rights. It will be quicker and frequently cheaper than dealing with record companies yourself.

Program Participant/Material Release

PROGRAM
TITLE:_____ DATE:_____
PRODUCER:_____ PARTICIPANT:_____

I hereby authorize you to use and to record on film, tape or otherwise, my name, voice, likeness, performance and/or the materials described below, in the program or series currently entitled as indicated above, and to authorize others to use this recording or film for television broadcasting or audio-visual purposes, including distribution on disc, through the World Wide Web, or any other technology, and for any other use in perpetuity throughout the world with no claim to rights to such material to be made by me or my representative. You may likewise use my name, likeness and biography for publicizing this program. I also warrant that all material furnished by me for use on this program is my original material or materials that I have authority to use for these purposes. I agree, if by reason of my statements and actions on the program or materials furnished by me for the program, there is any claim or litigation involving any charge by third persons of violation in infringement of their rights, to hold you and your licensees harmless from liability, loss or expense arising from such claim or litigation. I further agree that I shall assert no claim against you or your licensees with respect to injury of any kind that I may charge has been sustained by me in connection with my participation on the program or your exercise of any rights granted to you hereunder.

Signed:_____
Address:_____
_____

Witness:_____
Address:_____
_____

Signature of Parent or Guardian if Participant is less than 18 years old:

Signed:_____
Relationship:_____
Address:_____
_____

List materials supplied, if any:

_____   _____

_____   _____

_____   _____

_____   _____

Figure 17-1. *A noncontract talent release form.*

This brings up an important professional fact of life. Instead of hunting around for footage or music to use, you should develop your own senses of production, music, visualization, writing, shooting and editing. This is all part of being a professional. For instance, by scanning the industry publications or searching on the internet you can usually find very reasonable music libraries with production music CDs priced well below $100 each. More importantly, you can use these CDs again and again with no additional fees—not true of popular music. Instead of thinking in terms of Toby Keith, Diddy or Wynton Marsalis, learn to think in terms of style (country, hip-hop or jazz), tempo (fast, slow or medium) and beat (strong—nearly always strong, for editing purposes). One axiom is "If you don't have a good script and good production value, Willie Nelson can't save you. If you do have a good script and good production value, you don't need Willie Nelson." Let Willie make his own money (which he does quite well) and you learn how to make yours. Also, consider hiring a local musician to compose music just for your production. Most musicians make very little money and often must piece together an existence, going from gig to gig to pay the rent. Right there in your community, or on your campus, are many talented composer-performers (think "Have synthesizer, will make house calls") who can help you, and would do so for a reasonable price.

Just as you can choose to produce your own music, think in terms of producing your own shots as an alternative to stock footage. Often you can do this more cheaply. For instance, if you need 30 seconds of Niagara Falls footage, you can probably fly to Buffalo, rent a car and shoot your own shots cheaper than you can buy it—and probably quicker. Or can you rethink it? Do you need Niagara Falls, specifically? With the magic of close-ups, you can make a small stream look like a raging torrent. You can make a small lake look like an ocean. You can rewrite the script to accommodate such changes. Usually, no one will know—or care—that you made such alterations. But if you miss your deadline or blow your budget, your boss and your clients will know about that—and they will care a great deal. Remember: Much of TV production is the making of illusions. Be creative!

For the best copyright information, contact the copyright office in Washington, D.C. They have an outstanding website: www.copyright.gov. It is loaded with facts and phone numbers where you can get the knowledge you need for various aspects of this important component of your repertoire. For instance, under the heading of "law," you can get a good working definition of "fair use." If you want to copyright your own work, you can get all the forms online. Copyrighting is relatively inexpensive but time consuming—usually months, not days.

By learning to be more self-reliant and resourceful, you can become someone who is paid for his or her productions rather than someone who pays for such material. It is a part of the learning and growing processes involved in becoming a professional producer.

The Production Book

Once the preliminaries and legalities are completed, the producer begins to organize the production. Paperwork is the key to an orderly approach to production organization, and it begins with some form of *production book*. Throughout many larger-scale entertainment productions, a producer or assistant producer keeps a book containing a number of items:

1. A master production schedule, from preproduction through distribution
2. A cast and crew list, including everything from the clothes measurements and medical abnormalities of your cast, to the home phone and cell phone numbers of your lowliest production assistant
3. A rehearsal and production *call schedule,* which documents what time, and where, each actor and crewperson must report to work on any given day of the production
4. A section listing facilities and equipment and supplies that are supposed to be available at certain times
5. A postproduction schedule, including approximate dates, times and places
6. A distribution plan for the show and approximate target dates
7. A copy of the shooting script, and a schedule to indicate what pages of the shooting script are to be shot when and where
8. An appendix containing many or all of the following documents:
   a. Release forms, insurance forms and other contracts, site fee agreements and agreements with trade unions
   b. Caterers' menus and car, limo, truck and bus rental charts and rates
   c. A list of the entities who will "trade out" products or services with you or pay you a fee in exchange for some kind of promotional plug in your show (the use of footage of the hero traveling on American Airlines, drinking Pepsi, etc.)

Today, many production books are not physical books: They are entries on databases or word-processing files on personal computers and laptops, and some of this information is also transferred to Blackberry organizers and other digital aids.

Hiring Others

Next is the process of hiring others to assist you, including the director and videographer. Depending on the size and complexity of your production, these key employees will help you select—or will select for you—the below-the-line specialists such as the gaffer (lighting director), audio director, designer and others we've discussed in earlier chapters. If you employ union members, it's important that you be on good terms with, and understand the requirements of, all the trade unions.

Major Unions in Television

National Association of Broadcast Employees and Technicians–Communications Workers of America (NABET-CWA)

This union is "open to any person employed or qualified for employment in the broadcasting, telecasting, recording, cable or allied industries," but most of its members work in technical areas such as engineering and video camera operation. In 1998, NABET-CWA represented more than 9,000 employees working in broadcasting and broadcast-related fields. Initiation fees are established by each local chapter and vary from market to market. Back in 1993, NABET began a one-year affiliation with the much larger Communications Workers of America, a union representing technically oriented communications workers in a wide variety of nonbroadcast fields. In 1994 the two unions merged.

National office: 501 3rd Street, 8th floor
Washington, DC 20001
(202) 434-1254

American Federation of Musicians of the United States and Canada (AFM)

This organization represents about 130,000 professional musicians. Television producers most often deal with its members when the production involves live music. However, the AFM's Electronic Media Services Division (EMDS) specializes in representing the interests of musicians who record music for use in broadcast productions, including TV variety programs, radio and TV commercials, as well as nonbroadcast industrial films and videos. Music recorded for use in network programs and syndicated programs, for example, is covered under AFM agreements. Member qualifications are established locally. The national initiation fee in 1998 was $65.

National office: 1501 Broadway, Suite 600
New York, NY 10016
(212) 869-1330

American Federation of Television & Radio Artists (AFTRA)

This is an AFL-CIO affiliated union that had about 70,000 members in 2006. Any person who has performed or intends to perform in AFTRA's jurisdiction is eligible for membership. AFTRA represents its members in four major areas: news and broadcasting, entertainment programming, the recording business and commercials and nonbroadcast industrial/educational media. Many local news reporters belong to AFTRA.

National office: 260 Madison Avenue
New York, NY 10016
(212) 532-0800

Screen Actors Guild (SAG)

This AFL-CIO affiliated union has traditionally represented persons with principal or speaking roles in films, videotapes, television programs and commercials. Such performers may join SAG upon proof of employment or prospective employment by a company that has signed an agreement pledging to use SAG members. SAG also allows extra players ("extras") with nonspeaking roles to join. Extras, now officially called "background performers," must show proof they worked for a minimum of three workdays in a production covered by SAG agreements. Background performers were formerly represented by the Screen Extras Guild. SAG also allows members of affiliated performers' unions, such as AFTRA, to join if they meet certain requirements. Many performers belong to both SAG and AFTRA, and in some

(Continued)

(Continued)

markets, such as Dallas/Ft. Worth, the two unions are combined in one office. In 1998, SAG membership totaled about 90,000.

National office: 5757 Wilshire Blvd.
Los Angeles, CA 90036
(213) 954-1600

Directors Guild of America (DGA)

This organization represents film and TV directors, film unit production managers, first assistant directors, technical coordinators, second assistant directors, tape associate directors, stage managers and production associates. The DGA represents more than 14,000 members. Membership requirements vary depending on whether one works in film or tape, with qualifications somewhat more demanding for film. Initiation fees also vary widely. In 1998 initiation fees varied from $6,500 for film directors to about $2,300 for the lowest category of DGA membership.

National office: 7020 Sunset Blvd.
Los Angeles, CA 90046
(310) 289-2000

Writers Guild of America (WGA)

The WGA represents writers of radio and television programs and theatrical motion picture scripts. Members living west of the Mississippi River are represented by WGA-West with headquarters in Los Angeles, while those east of the Mississippi belong to WGA-East, headquartered in New York. Writers seeking WGA-West membership must accumulate within a three-year period a minimum of 24 Units of Credit as set forth on a Schedule of Units of Credit. Units of Credit vary according to the medium (radio, TV, film), the type of script and the length of the script. Varying credit is also awarded for rewrites and "polishes" of existing scripts. The work must, of course, be completed while employed by a company that is a signatory to a WGA Collective Bargaining Agreement. WGA-East requires only that members be employed to write literary material for, or sell literary material to, a company that is a signatory to a guild agreement. About a third of its members write TV news for the major broadcast and cable networks or large-market TV stations. WGA-East is affiliated with the AFL-CIO, while WGA-West is not.

WGA-West
7000 W. Third Street
Los Angeles, CA 90048
(213) 951-4000

WGA-East
555 W. 57th Street
New York, NY 10019
(212) 582-1909

International Brotherhood of Electrical Workers (IBEW)

This is AFL-CIO-affiliated union has about 14,000 members, but only a small percentage work in broadcasting. IBEW members working in broadcasting and television production serve as technicians in support areas. IBEW members working in television are often video, tape and maintenance engineers, as well as studio floor personnel. Some ENG/EFP camera operators may also be represented by the IBEW. IBEW membership is open to persons working for a company covered by an IBEW contract.

National office: 1125 15th Street N.W.
Washington, DC 20005
(202) 833-7000

International Alliance of Theatrical Stage Employees and Moving Picture Technicians, Artists and Allied Crafts of the United States and Canada (IATSE)

IATSE is an AFL-CIO affiliated union representing workers in theater, motion pictures and broadcasting. IATSE members represent a very broad range of crafts. Most IATSE members working in broadcasting perform technical and support jobs such as studio lighting and floor management. They may also work as electronic, sound and computer service technicians, make-up and hair stylists, costumers, sound effects technicians, set designers, model makers and carpenters.

National office: 1515 Broadway, Suite 601
New York, NY 10036
(212) 921-7699

Whether you, as a producer, employ union members or not you must manage labor relations carefully, or the small details that make a production successful will suffer.

One of the difficult concepts to put down in this text is a simple answer to the question, "Who, the director or the producer, hires whom in a production?" As a matter of fact, a simple answer is not possible. The best possible answer is that it depends on the circumstances of the production, the kind of production and the size and complexity of the production.

In some cases, as suggested above, the producer hires individuals who in turn hire their assistants. For example, the technical director may be tasked with hiring all crewpersons who work for him/her, the lighting gaffer and the production designer will hire their assistants, and so on. Often, these individuals have worked together before and are called back to work again. Much time and confusion is saved by working with the same individuals on successive jobs.

If the producer does not also plan to direct the show, this person selects the director, who may or may not hire everyone else, from his/her assistant directors on down. If the producer has, for example, already "packaged" a writer and two or three stars to obtain financing for the production, the director inherits these individuals. Sometimes the director is also part of such a package. On other occasions, especially when the producer plans to use actors/talent other than big-name stars, one of the director's first tasks may be to audition and hire the entire cast. As you have read in the "Overview and Tour" chapter, in the case of the commercial production, the advertising agency producer sits in on the auditions and consults with the director on casting. This consultation and joint decision making is also quite common for productions for which the director does the casting.

Finding Places to Shoot

Simultaneous with identifying and hiring production employees is the task of arranging where you plan to shoot your show. Obtaining access to some shooting locations requires *site fees,* stipends paid to a property owner for permission to shoot there. You should get written permissions even from those who say that they don't require payment. Otherwise you risk setting up a huge remote shoot, only to be chased off by someone supposedly speaking on behalf of the owner. And don't assume you won't need permission to shoot in areas usually considered "open to the public," such as government-owned parks and forests. Access to certain difficult locations, filming dangerous action stunts and

other considerations may require you to purchase more casualty insurance than you would normally. Other kinds of insurance include purchasing a *completion bond,* insurance for your financial backers that you'll deliver a final product by an agreed-upon date, and a bond that protects you against damage claims on someone else's property, plus insurance for the expensive production equipment you've rented. You may even need *negative insurance,* which protects you in the unlikely event that you lose or damage videotape master footage.

Studio shooting doesn't require as much location survey work because the studio's owner usually provides floor and lighting grid plans, but studio shooting still requires a major survey of equipment, facilities and technicians available to you—and their prices. As Figure 17-2 indicates, production rate schedules can include everything from the cost of a four-hour block of studio time, to camera rental, to the required coffee break schedule for studio personnel. With one of these rate schedules as a guide, your key people, the director, technical director, designer, unit production manager and you work together to determine an accurate, detailed production budget and plan for using such a facility.

Arranging for Production Equipment

When you rent studio space, you often rent the necessary equipment as part of the deal. And the same holds true for the rental of time (by the hour or the day) in an editing or sound-recording-dubbing facility. But if you're shooting on location, you must either buy or rent equipment for that shoot. More producers rent rather than own production equipment, because rental is cheaper than buying big-ticket equipment, especially seldom-used gear. Also, since TV equipment becomes obsolete rapidly, producers can stay on the leading edge of video technology by renting rather than buying. Larger equipment rental firms advertise in trade magazines and have toll-free numbers. Most provide a catalog listing equipment available, conditions of rental and costs.

Details, Details!

There are a thousand details to consider when you're the person in charge. Someone must arrange for transportation, security, food and housing for your entire production cast and crew on location. Often you'll need specialists to assist you: from animal *wranglers* to care for, train and control horses, dogs, cats, snakes and insects to perform on cue for the director, to "food designers" who make the food in commercials look appetizing. All these details are ultimately the responsibility of the producer. On a major big-budget production, you'll have assistant directors, second assistant directors, production assistants, assistants to the UPM and other individuals to whom you delegate these details. But when you're doing a one- or two-student production, or working in TV news, doing the reporting and shooting your own video, you're it. If you don't remember it, it doesn't get done.

How well you and your staff handle these preproduction details becomes quickly apparent during production

and postproduction, and also will be evident in your program's quality and financial rewards.

Production

After all the preparation and decision making of preproduction, you're finally ready to move to the production phase. At this point, if you're not a hyphenate, your director takes center stage, and you begin the difficult process of watching others shoot your production. If you've hired a talented pro to direct, you can

---

Sample Top 20 Major Market Station Production Rate Card
As of May, 2006

Production Facilities
(All personnel at an extra charge)

Audio recording studio	$50/hour
Multitrack audio recording studio	$150/ hour
Non-linear off-line editing suite	$150/ hour
Linear on-line editing suite	$300/hour
High definition post-production suite	$450/hour
EFP package (camera [Digi-Beta] and one videographer])	$1,200/day
Studio A Production (3 standard/high def. digital cameras)	$610/hour
Studio B Production (3 standard def. digital cameras)	$325/hour

Personnel

Senior producer	$1,100/day
Assoc. producer/director	$900/day
Producer/Director	$900/day
Unit production manager	$500/day
Scenic designer	$55/hour
Interactive media designer	$50/hour
Production graphics specialist	$35/hour
Videographer/senior videographer	$50/75/hour
Lighting designer/director	$45/hour
CCTV engineer	$55/hour
Engineering supervisor (remote)	$55/hour
Video, remote or EFP engineer	$45/hour
Audio engineer	$35/hour
Dubbing engineer	$35/hour
Still photographer	$45/hour
Closed captionist	$35/hour
Camera operators	$35/hour
Grip/Temporary/On-call	$12/hour

1.

Figure 17-2. *Production facilities have established rates for various services. Shot 1 illustrates the cost for specific services provided by a top-20 Public Television Station. Shots 2 and 3 are forms used by producers to reserve equipment and personnel for productions at the Nebraska ETV network. Similar forms are used elsewhere, paperwork being a necessary evil faced by producers in any production environment.*

BUDGET NUMBER _____

NEBRASKA ETV NETWORK FIELD/REMOTE PRODUCTION FACILITIES REQUEST

AGENCY_____ PRODUCER _____ DIRECTOR _____

PROGRAM TITLE _____ SEGMENT _____

LOCATION _____ DATE _____ TIME _____

VIDEO FACILITIES (Indicate #)

Hard Cameras _____
Portable Cameras _____
Character Generator _____
Teleprompter _____
Generator _____
Video Monitors _____

VIDEOTAPE MACHINES
(Indicate #)

Record only VTRs _____
Record/Playback VTRs _____
Slo-Mo _____

SATELLITE FACILITIES

Flyaway Dish _____
Engineer _____

OPERATIONS PERSONNEL (Indicate #)
(If you are providing, <u>do not</u> fill in)

Videographer _____
Audio Engineer _____
Tape Engineer _____
Video Engineer _____
Extra Engineer _____
Camera Operators _____
Floor Manager _____
Prompter Operator _____
Video Switcher _____
Char. Gen. Operator _____
Boom Operator _____
Grip _____
Make-up (Schedule with Operations)
Lighting Director (Schedule direct)
Other (Explain Below)

EFP UNITS AS SEPERATE UNITS
(Indicate #)

EFP Unit with 1/2" Recorder _____
EFP Unit with 3/4" Recorder _____
EFP Unit with 1" Recorder _____
EFP Unit with Camcorder _____

AUDIO FACILITIES (Indicate #)

# of Talent _____
# of IFBs _____
Call-In (On-Air) _____
Call-In (Card) _____

TRANSMISSION INFORMATION (Indicate #)

# of B-1s _____
# of P-Ls _____
V and A _____
Microwave _____
Simulcast _____

MOTELS:
Name: _____
Address: _____
City & State: _____
Phone #: _____
# of Rooms: _____
Cost per Room: _____
# of Nights: _____
Dates: _____

MOTELS:
Name: _____
Address: _____
City & State: _____
Phone #: _____
# of Rooms: _____
Cost per Room: _____
# of Nights: _____
Dates: _____

MOTELS:
Name: _____
Address: _____
City & State: _____
Phone #: _____
# of Rooms: _____
Cost per Room: _____
# of Nights: _____
Dates: _____

ADDITIONAL INFORMATION: (Brief description of program and/or anticipated block schedule.)

Request submitted by: Date:

Operations Use Only
Approved by: Date:

Production Completed By:_____ Date_____ Hours_____

Production Completed By:_____ Date_____ Hours_____

Production Completed By:_____ Date_____ Hours_____

Production Completed By:_____ Date_____ Hours_____

2.

Figure 17-2. *(Continued)*

Budget number_____

NEBRASKA ETV NETWORK STUDIO/POST PRODUCTION FACILITIES REQUEST

AGENCY_____PRODUCER_____DIRECTOR_____

PROGRAM TITLE_____SERIES TITLE_____

DATE OF BLOCK_____BLOCK TIME_____PROGRAM LENGTH_____

Studio____ Live____ Tape_____ Post Production_____ Operations use only:
Studio#___Control Room #_____

VIDEO FACILITIES(Indicate #)	STUDIO FACILITIES(Indicate # Circle Type)	OPERATIONS PERSONNEL (Indicate # unless you are providing)
Studio Cameras _____	Teleprompter on Camera# 1 2 3 4	Audio Engineer _____
Integrated Portable Cameras_____	Floor Prompter Monitor _____	Editor/Tape Engineer _____
ChromaKey _____	Studio Video Monitor _____	Video/Tape Engineer _____
Character Generator _____	Flip Stands _____	Camera Operators _____
DVE _____	Other (Explain below)	Floor Manager _____
Color Corrector _____		Prompter Operator _____
Still Store _____	AUDIO FACILITIES (Indicate #)	Lighting Director _____
	Reel to Reel _____	Video Switcher _____
VIDEOTAPE MACHINES	P.A. _____	Char. Gen Operator _____
(Indicate #)	IFB _____	Boom Operator _____
SUITE "A"	Number of Talent _____	Grip _____
Record VTR __1"__3/4"__1/2"	Call-In (On-Air) _____	Other _____
Playback VTR__1"__3/4"__1/2"	Call-In (Card) _____	(Explain below)
SUITE "B"		
Record VTR __1"__3/4"__1/2"		
Playback VTR__1"__3/4"__1/2"		

ADDITIONAL INFORMATION: (Brief description of program and/or anticipated block schedule.)

Operations Use Only:

Request submitted by: Date: Approved by: Date:

Studio Production By:_____Date_____Time Required_____Crew #_____

Eng. Production By:_____Date_____Time Required_____Crew #_____

EXTRA FACILITIES USED: VTRs used: #4_____Hrs. #5_____Hrs. #6_____Hrs. #7_____Hrs.
Please define any additional charges not covered above and the hour usage (EFP units, 4th camera, etc.)

_____

_____

_____

EXTRA PERSONNEL USED: (If additional personnel used please list names and define any exceptions to the requested resources.)

_____

_____

3.

Figure 17-2. *(Continued)*

relax as the show comes together smoothly. In most cases, if you're smart, you won't micromanage the director, getting in the way, usurping the director's authority. During relatively slow, single-camera productions, there's more time for the producer to consult with the director. This is when the temptation to micromanage is greatest. But good producers influence productions most effectively during preproduction. Unless the director truly goes "bonkers," the producer usually is wise to stay in the background. When the cast and crew leave for the day, the director and producer may then review the day's footage and discuss possible problems and solutions. During production, the cast and crew should be able to look in only one direction and to one person for leadership: the director.

The "Hands-On" Producer

Having just insisted that a good producer often is wise to sit back and serve as a good director's consultant, we should also add that there are certain kinds of productions in which the producer keeps his/her "hands on" throughout the production. These situations most often occur in

live news and sports productions. While the director is busy calling shots live, the news producer makes changes in the newscast script throughout the telecast, adding or deleting stories to correct running time, and updating stories as new information arrives (see Figure 17-3). Newscast producers often communicate with reporters or news sources outside the studio who will do live reports during the newscast. When they're ready, the producer instructs the director to cue the anchor to introduce such a live segment. Sports and live special productions also require hands-on producers. Especially in coverage of events like the Olympics, football and golf, producers help their directors select what Olympic venue, replay shot or golf hole the director should go to next.

Postproduction

Unless a program is broadcast "live," there's much work for the producer following a shoot. Regardless of their level of participation during shooting, producers begin to take charge again during postproduction. Indeed, with the exception of news, creative producers become exceedingly hands-on, making most postproduction decisions.

1.

2.

Figure 17-3. *In shot 1, a producer-director (in striped shirt) is seen between the technical director (at left) and the character generator operator (at right) during a live broadcast. In shot 2, the producer-director is "calling the shots," instructing the technical director to switch to a live report.*

Shot courtesy of Nebraska Educational Telecommunications.

Editing the Footage

Most postproduction activity centers on the editing function, deciding which pieces of produced video and audio to use, how much and in what order. Poor editing can demolish great production work, and great editing can improve mediocre productions. The manipulative power of electronic editing equipment makes the creation of minor miracles possible, given enough raw footage, time, talent and money. So powerful are the editing tools available for "correcting" errors that during the production phase there is a regrettable tendency to say, "Don't sweat it now, we can clean it up during post." Maybe, but there is a limit to what is possible in the editing room. Often it's more expensive to correct an error in post than to prevent it or reshoot it during the production phase. Experienced directors and producers should know the difference.

We should also note that the power to edit carries with it the power to mislead and distort. If the program is for entertainment purposes, the freedom to edit "for effect" is broad. But when the program proposes to present "reality" or "truth"—such as news and documentaries and, ideally, commercials—there are ethical considerations which may suggest restrictions not imposed by your technological limitations.

Publicity

From the beginning of preproduction, experienced producers of entertainment programming find ways to create free media exposure. News releases to trade and fan publications, newspaper articles and arranged interviews with stars and directors all generate audience interest in entertainment productions. Properly orchestrated, these bits of publicity boost a program's ratings and/or sales. Promotion efforts go into high gear as the release date approaches. If the show is going onto a station or network's schedule, the producer's staff publicist or hired PR firm works with station/network promotion people to provide scenes for TV reviewers, stars for talk show hosts to interview and plenty of copy for newspapers and magazines. Paid advertising simultaneously promotes the show in all appropriate media. Like deodorant or dog food, any TV show requires promotion: Without promotion, viewers will see your show only by accident.

Publicity is almost equally important to mass-distributed, information-based programs. Many of the same promotional techniques associated with entertainment shows work for network and local news programs. Networks and local station managers know that their news anchors and reporters are sometimes as popular with the public, and have the same "star value," as the actors or actresses on a hit TV series. The "anchor team" and, in some weather-sensitive areas of the country, the "storm team" and its associated reporting technologies ("Doppler" or "Fly-through" weather radar, "live" truck and so on) are often the most heavily promoted assets of a local TV station. This is because commercial revenue generated by the news accounts for a large percentage of a station's annual profits.

Nine Lives—and More

Initial release and distribution of a program often is only the start of a long process. "First run" network entertainment programs usually fail to recoup the cost of production during their network run. The producer/owner and those who invested in the production may see no profits until the program is sold again (and again and again!) in syndication, both domestically and abroad. It's the producer's continuing job to give the production or series new life in the different venues available in the marketplace. And then, of course, there's the possibility of a *sequel,* a production that supposedly takes place after the initial drama ends. There's also the *spin-off,* such as the two subsequent programs based on the original show, *CSI: Crime Scene Investigation,* or the three spin-offs of the original *Law and Order* show. These create new situations for one or some of the characters from the original series, or, in the case of *CSI* and *Law and Order,* use the same basic format and new casts of characters to create new programs. The late producer Gene Roddenberry turned one idea, *Star Trek,* into a successful first-run TV series, a phenomenally lucrative series in worldwide syndication, home videocassette sales, dozens of paperback books, toys, lunch boxes, calendars, costumes, a string of hugely successful big-budget feature films and three more TV series: *Star Trek: The Next Generation, Star Trek: Deep Space Nine* and *Star Trek: Voyager.* A talented producer can get a lot of mileage out of one good idea for a program.

Producing the Corporate Video

Many corporate video projects, if not most, bear the look of a long broadcast news package or an extended feature piece. For this reason, you can refer to the previous chapter on field production for techniques to shoot news packages. From the outline you'll find in Tech Manual 17-2, a producer could arrange the interviews, get the answers and shape the project from there. Write the script around the interview questions and talking points of the outline. Remember that a corporate video project differs from the news process in that producers are not always

1.

2.

Figure 17-4. *In shot 1, talent for a corporate safety video conducts a carefully scripted interview with a worker. In shot 2, a close-up of how to safely operate an electric saw.*

striving for objectivity, but rather to put the company's best foot forward, that is, to make the company—the client—look its best. This can mean submitting interview questions well in advance of the interviews, something a broadcast journalist would not do. Some of the questions may even be reshaped to get more favorable or more informative responses (see Figure 17-4).

There are other aspects of corporate video production that warrant discussion, such as the use of amateur talent and how one goes about massaging corporate egos. You should make every effort to hire professional talent and/or narrators. Some corporate officials may want you to use company personnel to give the project more authenticity and familiarity, but try to avoid this if you can. You can't make a foreman into an actor any more than you can make an actor into a foreman. Instead, use company personnel in roles—generally

nonspeaking, "wallpaper" kinds of roles (extras)—in which they can just play themselves. Let them do what they do every day while a professional narrator does the voice over. If there's no way around using company people, let them do simple tasks like answer the phone or point to a sign. Try to reserve the more involved speaking roles for professionals.

As for massaging egos, the producer must be aware that there's a different climate in the corporate world. Most professionals would agree that the number one problem in producing corporate videos is coping with multiple layers of approval. The PR director may love the project, but when it's examined by the vice president, he/she may order changes. You make those changes and the video gets passed along to the CEO, who wants more changes, sometimes countermanding changes made by subordinates.

When managers are asked to look at a video, they often feel obligated to find fault. If they can't find "mistakes," they think that their bosses may believe that they haven't done their jobs. If it isn't difficult enough to get your project past all these experts, you may have to weather the criticisms of spouses and significant others who view rough cuts of video at home—after the project has supposedly met with the approval of all the decision makers in the company. The best techniques for battling this syndrome involve getting everyone involved on the front end of the project. Make sure everyone who has ultimate veto power has seen the questionnaire. Make sure they've seen the outline and signed off on the script.

Later, when you get to the final edit stage, use the "three-by-three-by-three method" to cast the all-important voice-over narrator/s. First, audition three narrators and have them cut a couple of paragraphs of narration. Get three different types—for example, a deep-voiced man, a soft-voiced woman and a newsy sounding person of either gender.

Then pick three different graphics styles and backgrounds. Finally, choose three different cuts of music from a production CD. Put all these on tape (about 30 seconds worth of each set of graphics and music selections) and give them to the appropriate executives. Let <u>them</u> choose the narrator, the music they like best and the look of the graphics. Bear in mind that you have selected three viable options in the first place, so the choice they make is still something you can live with. Then the clients feel more engaged and take ownership of some decisions, and you keep control of important, creative decisions. This greatly reduces the amount of problems that could develop later on. You can now proceed with the important task of editing the final video with creative latitude.

For pointers on editing the video, review the chapters on field producing and editing. Remember to stick to your message, build on the sound bites and make more extensive use of graphics and music than you would in a typical news package. Research has shown that viewers tend to remember the most recent information they've seen on the screen, so if there is anything you want to hammer home, put it last. This doesn't mean you should wait until the very last to make your points. This backloading of message can just be a recapitulation of any of the important information you communicated earlier.

Evaluating the Corporate Video

You don't necessarily have to rely on the subjective whims of clients to get an assessment of the effectiveness of a corporate video. There are more objective standards. The following evaluations can be used in any combination to get feedback on a video project. Some of the evaluation forms require more technical expertise than others and could serve as grading tools in an academic setting.

You can use the first 10 questions in the preproduction phase as well. Building all these elements into a corporate or feature project can ensure greater production value and diversity. Students should see these forms before beginning their projects, so they can understand how they'll be evaluated later.

For grading purposes, the professor could assign a number from 1 to 5 to each category.

Form

1. Camera shot selection _____
2. Shot quality _____
3. Lighting _____
4. Audio _____
5. Backgrounds (both for interviews and graphics) _____
6. Graphics (fonts and images) _____
7. Special effects _____
8. Editing _____
9. Transitions (both written and visual) _____
10. Music (did it fit and/or enhance the mood?) _____

Content

1. Did the production have a clear purpose? _____
2. Was there a good intro? _____
3. Did the whole thing make sense? _____
4. Did it have stylistic touches? _____
5. Did it have an effective ending? _____
6. Was the narration well written and stylish? _____
7. Was the narration professionally delivered and appropriate to the production? _____
8. Was it informative? _____
9. Did it flow? _____
10. Did the client approve of it? _____

Finally, there is an evaluation letter which a "client" (professor) can fill out, which gives you a better impression of how you conducted yourself during the entire process. The questions are in laymen's terms and give the client an easier means of assessing student interaction. Again, students can examine this form before they begin producing their projects so they can have a better understanding of how to conduct themselves in their day-to-day relations with the client.

Client Evaluation for Corporate Project

Please rate the student(s) who produced your corporate video in the following areas (1–10, 10 being the highest).

_____ Professional demeanor
_____ Courtesy
_____ Timeliness and punctuality in dealing with you
_____ Written communication skills (letters, memos, e-mails, etc.)
_____ In-person communication skills
_____ Telephone communication skills
_____ Explanation of video requirements
_____ Written video components (outlines, treatments, interview questions, scripts)
_____ Video production skills (setting up equipment, lighting, efficiency)
_____ Working with people for video (courtesy, professionalism, punctuality)

Final Video

_____ Met expectations (did it accomplish its purpose?)
_____ Technical quality (can you see and hear everything clearly?)
_____ Overall quality

Other Questions

Will you use the video as you planned?
What would you advise the students to do differently next time?

The Corporate Media Environment

Corporate communications has been rapidly expanding in the U.S. since the 1980s. It requires different skills and mindsets from the broadcast environment. To give a better understanding of the working conditions involved in this field, the following lists have been compiled. The two columns are not necessarily paired to discuss the pro and con of each category but rather to give a better overall impression of the lifestyle both in and out of the workplace. Of course, not every single aspect is true in every single company.

Producing Music Videos

Another field of video production that has grown significantly since the 1980s is the music video. Some cable networks play these productions 24 hours a day. Not only have they become a staple of television, they are practically a requirement for every new release by major artists. Even small town bands want to produce videos to advance their careers. The following techniques are meant to be used as a launching point for creative production of this art form. Once you get more established in the field, you can fit your aesthetics to the particular music selections.

One method for producing a music video is the three-stage approach. This involves producing the project with three different looks. The first can be a studio performance of the song; the second, a field production of the music; and the third, an artistic recreation appropriate to the message of the song.

First, it's easier to shoot and edit the video to an existing soundtrack. So get a CD copy of the song and dub it to videotape. Then use this to pantomime the song in the two performance venues. In a TV studio, arrange for monitor playback in the studio. The instruments need not be plugged into the audio console, or they can just be turned off. Perform the song several times utilizing different camera angles and close-ups. If you're a producer who has no musical knowledge, try to time the solos and close-ups with the production clock, so you'll know when to call for the shots and punch them up on the switcher. You can also put in a few visual special effects through the switcher, although it's possible to add these later in postproduction—provided you have the use of a nonlinear editor. A few effects go a long way—don't overdo it. A few lighting changes can also add visual enhancement. Consult the previous chapter on lighting for different ideas.

For the field production, you can find an aesthetically pleasing setting—perhaps a nightclub, nature setting or even a warehouse. Make sure you have access to electrical power and a means of audio playback (for example, a boom box). Ideally the band or singer is cooperating fully and agrees to devote long hours to multiple takes with the one-camera style of production. It is tough enough to pull this off without dealing with divas. Hopefully your group will be helpful and patient. A

Advantages and Disadvantages of Working in Corporate Media

Advantages	Disadvantages
• Normal lifestyle, more stable (nine to five, weekends off, more family friendly)	• Multiple layers of approval
• Higher starting wages	• Lack of understanding in the company
• Clear, coherent messages	• Lack of understanding in the company as to what it is that you do
• Opportunity for setting up a work environment to your standards (physical and psychological)	• Frequent lack of facilities (studios, edit suites, etc.)
• Travel (with the right company)	• Lack of proper equipment or lack of up-to-date equipment
• Positive, meaningful work (e.g., hospital, charity, etc.)	• Lack of peer support
• Still growing as an industry (more jobs, continued expansion)	• Low budget priority
• Contractual jobs that pay more for independents	• More uninformed criticism
• Independent producers get new and different projects	• Difficulty in obtaining insurance for health, family, liability
• Feast	• Taxes are <u>overwhelming</u>
	• Famine

less-than-perfect setting is to tape a live performance of the band or singer. If this turns out to be the case, you must again require full cooperation. For instance, if the band plays four sets during the performance, you should request they play the particular song you're working on as the first number in each of the four sets. This gives you the opportunity to move your camera angles around each time to get a different perspective with each set. Trying to move camera, lights, audio and the like during one two-minute song is an impossibility. During other songs, you can get the anytime cutaways—crowd shots, close-ups of band members' faces, shots from behind the performers into the lights and so on.

The third production look will change with each song. If it is a love ballad, you may want to get a couple of attractive actors to play the parts. Take them to an appropriate setting—a restaurant, an attractive home, a waterfront locale. It is an industry cliché that the female should have a pouty look, but you can use your own judgment. Have them look sullen, romantic, seductive, angry, sad—whatever the mood of the song demands. Get a lot of close-ups, shots of embracing, handheld pans across faces, shots through windows—make them as artistic as possible. Make sure you get everything you want in each location. Storyboarding would not be a bad idea. You want plenty of footage to take into editing.

Take the videotaped version of the CD and put it into the editor. Now mix and match the shots from the three locations. You can work with the band to determine the right ratio of shots from each setting. If you're using a nonlinear editor, you should have an easier time of maintaining lip synch. You can also add special effects in this stage, if you desire.

This is by no means the only method of producing music videos, but these are the fundamentals. You can watch the various forms on TV to get more ideas and/or talk to veterans of this genre. This is one of the most creative uses of video existing today. Have fun with it.

The Life of the Video Producer

There are many different creative fields for a video producer to enter. Some people elect to choose one form (e.g., news) and stick with for a lifetime. Others hop from commercials to corporate to sports as the opportunities arise. Suffice it to say that it takes a few years to master all the elements of successful producing, so be prepared to commit to a learning process measured in years. Once you have achieved professional success as a producer, you'll have a chance to live a very creative and satisfying life. Few endeavors in the artistic world offer as much satisfaction— and as many headaches—as those of the video producer.

 tech manual **17-1**   *Student Producer Checklist*

Producer Responsibilities

For the neophyte or student producer, here is a list of questions to be answered and evaluated before, during and after production projects. This is similar to the crew responsibilities which were listed in the previous "Directing Techniques" chapter. Since television is, by and large, a team sport, these questions must be put into that context. Once again, there is some duplication with questions for other positions, but since the producer is the person with ultimate responsibility, he or she must know these answers.

1. Did the proper people attend the preproduction sessions?

2. Did the proper people attend the rehearsals and run-throughs?

3. Is the script written, corrected and distributed?

4. Is everyone aware of the production time?

5. Are there any problems with the set, crew, scripts, tapes, guests, equipment? How can these problems be corrected before the production?

6. Has the script been coordinated with the teleprompter operator, talent, director, technical director, audio operator, professor, engineer?

7. Is the rundown sheet ready for the director, technical director, audio operator, professor, engineer?

8. Are the graphics ready?

9. Do the camera operators have their shot sheets?

10. Are all the tapes ready?

11. Is the lighting ready and properly done?

12. Do you have backup plans ready for any potential problems with equipment and/or personnel?

13. Was the clock started on time?

14. Were there any discrepancies (errors or changes in the script) during production? Have they been properly noted for later evaluation reports?

15. How can any problems be corrected before the next production?

16. Are there problems which can be corrected by reshooting or editing?

17. When will the evaluation report be ready and whose input do you need?

tech manual 17-2 *Corporate Video Producer's Checklist*

The Corporate Project Questionnaire

Because communication with the client is such a frequent problem, this questionnaire has been devised to get everyone on the same page—literally. If possible, it is a good idea to send this form to all the involved parties before the first meeting so that discussions can begin on a higher plane. Specific problems can be addressed rather than spending time on more conceptual issues. These questions are written in laymen's language to facilitate the process.

1. What is the purpose of your project? State this in a sentence or two if possible.

2. What is (are) your target audience(s)?

3. Do you have a script format in mind?

4. What's the first thing you want to see on the screen? What's the first thing you want to hear?

5. What's the last thing you want to see on the screen? Hear?

6. Do you have any particular type of music in mind?

7. Do you have a narrator or talent in mind?

8. Do you want credits and, if so, whose names do you want and in what order?

9. How long do you think the project should be?

10. How many remote shoots will there be? How many different locations will there be at each shooting site?

11. How many people will be interviewed?

12. Can we do any of the interviews (or cutaways, demonstration shots, etc.) in the studio?

13. What's your deadline?

14. What sort of a budget do you have for the project?

Once this questionnaire is discussed, and everyone is in basic agreement as to how to proceed, the corporate video producer should devise an outline of the project. Initially, this does not have to be anything elaborate. It should be flexible enough to accommodate future changes. Once the client agrees to the beginning structure of the video project, the producer can start fleshing out the outline with more specific details. The following example is for a safety video for the Widget Manufacturing Company.

Project Outline

PURPOSE: This video will describe the company's new safety procedures to employees. A more complete, written safety manual will accompany the video.

I. Intro
   A. Audio: Upbeat, fast-paced synthesizer music
   B. Video: A visual montage of scenes from the plant interspersed with safety signs and equipment.

II. Body
   A. Quick statements from workers on their perspectives on safety (10 seconds or less)
   B. Graphics and narration listing safety performance from most previous measuring period
   C. Interview with CEO John Smith
     1. Why is the company implementing this plan now?
     2. What results are expected and when?
   D. Graphics and narration outlining new procedures
   E. Interview with Superintendent Mary Jones
     1. What will employees be expected to do?
     2. Who will be responsible for enforcing the plan?
   F. Quick graphic recap
     1. Dos and Don'ts

III. Outro
   A. Audio: Same music from throughout the piece
   B. Video montage from the plant with the narrator emphasizing the good effects for the employees as a result of the new plan

There is nothing fancy about this outline. The outline and the project itself look like a typical corporate project. Many producers call this "nuts and bolts video"—nothing fancy, just good, basic production. Other producers may describe it as a "bread and butter" project, meaning the resulting fee will buy the groceries. This is one of the good things about corporate video production—there is always a message. One does not have to get lost in obtuse symbolism or meandering dialogue. Stick to the point, and there's always a point. As more information becomes available, the outline can accommodate more details or possible changes to the intro and outro.

Important Vocabulary Terms

Assistant (or associate) producer: Subordinate producers who perform certain production assignments under the executive producer's supervision.

Call schedule: This documents what time, and where, each actor and crewperson must report to work on any given day of the production.

Completion bond: An insurance policy to protect investors should a producer fail to deliver a finished production.

Executive (or supervising) producer: The individual who holds the ultimate responsibility for all aspects of production.

Hyphenate: A production person who "wears more than one hat," such as director-producer, or writer-producer-director.

Independent producer: A producer not employed by a station, studio or other production company.

Line producer: A TV series episode producer who is in turn supervised by a senior (executive) producer.

Negative insurance: An insurance policy protecting the producer financially if original footage is lost, damaged or destroyed.

Production book: A binder, folder or computer that contains the records of the production.

Royalty: A fee paid to a copyright owner for permission to use his/her work.

Sequel: A TV program or motion picture whose story takes place sometime after the end of the original production (e.g., *Terminator II*).

Series concordance: A book prepared by the executive producer of the series, containing detailed information on the series' plots and characters.

Site fee: A stipend paid to a landowner for the use of an area of land or a building for a location shoot.

Society of European Stage Authors and Composers (SESAC): A rights licensing organization.

Spin-off: A TV series based on characters created in an earlier TV series.

Unit production manager (UPM): Producer's assistant responsible for budgets and bill paying. Sometimes a production facility will designate a studio UPM who monitors the costs of services offered to producers using the facility.

Video news releases (VNRs): PR agency news releases shot and edited like TV news stories and fed to stations in the hope that they will use them in their newscasts.

Wrangler: A production term for an individual whose job it is to care for, train and help to manage the behavior of various kinds of animals and other creatures during a shoot.

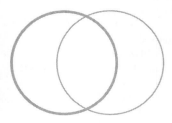

Index

Bold page numbers indicate illustrations or photographs.